MEET THE

BIBLE

Resources by Philip Yancey

The Jesus I Never Knew
What's So Amazing About Grace?
The Bible Jesus Read
Reaching for the Invisible God
Where Is God When It Hurts?
Disappointment with God
The Student Bible, General Edition (with Tim Stafford)
Meet the Bible (with Brenda Quinn)
Church: Why Bother?
Finding God in Unexpected Places
I Was Just Wondering
Soul Survivor

Books by Philip Yancey and Dr. Paul Brand

Fearfully and Wonderfully Made
In His Image
The Gift of Pain

MEET THE

BIBLE

A Panorama of God's Word in
366 Daily Readings and Reflections

PHILIP YANCEY
BRENDA QUINN

ZONDERVAN™

GRAND RAPIDS, MICHIGAN 49530

ZONDERVAN™

Meet the Bible
Copyright © 2000 by Philip D. Yancey and Brenda Quinn

Requests for information should be addressed to:

Zondervan, *Grand Rapids, Michigan 49530*

Library of Congress Cataloging-in-Publication Data

Yancey, Philip.

    Meet the Bible : a panorama of God's Word in 366 daily readings
and reflections / Philip Yancey and Brenda Quinn.
               p.   cm.

    Includes bibliographical references and index.
    ISBN: 0-310-24303-3 (softcover)
    I. Bible Devotional literature. 2. Devotional calendars.
I. Quinn, Brenda. II. Title.
BS491.5.Y37 1999
242' .2--dc21   99-33589
                                                          CIP

Interior design by Korina Kelley

Printed in the United States of America

07 08 09 10 11 • 19 18 17 16 15 14 13 12 11

CONTENTS

PART 2

PART 3   *The Northern Kingdom—Israel*

PART 4   *The Southern Kingdom—Judah*

PART 5   *Starting Over—In Exile and Returning from Exile*

PART 6   *Cries of Pain*

PART 7   *A Surprising Messiah*

PART 8

PART 9

PART 10 *The Word Spreads*

PART 11   *Paul's Legacy*

PART 12   *Vital Letters*

EDITOR'S NOTE

Meet the Bible will help you read and understand the Bible, from Genesis to Revelation.

Why Do I Need Help Understanding the Bible?

Reading the Bible can be discouraging. It is about a thousand pages long, composed of sixty-six different books, and has several dozen authors, whose writing styles vary widely. Written several thousand years ago, the Bible presents a wide chasm between its culture and today's. Outdated customs and unpronounceable names confront the reader on page after page. Add in theology and philosophy that many initially find hard to understand, and the Bible becomes known as a challenging book that many choose to leave unopened. Unless they have a little help.

Who Is *Meet the Bible* For?

You may hardly know the Bible. Maybe you are familiar with many of the Bible's events but haven't read it for years. Or maybe you're a regular reader but would like to read the Bible in a fresh way.

What Is *Meet the Bible* About?

The promise of *Meet the Bible* is a panoramic view of the Bible's key passages, an explanation of personalities and events and ideas as the Old Testament sweeps into the New Testament. The resulting picture is of a mighty nation, searching for a new kingdom, which is finally offered in God's kingdom. It is the same kingdom offered to all of us—because the picture also includes declarations about a Revolutionary Figure whose life and death, foretold and proclaimed from Genesis to Revelation, make that offer of the kingdom real.

How Is *Meet the Bible* Put Together?

There are 366 readings in *Meet the Bible,* one for each day of the year. Each reading consists of either (1) a Bible passage and a commentary or explanation of the passage, or (2) a devotional, called a reflection, which appears less often.

The daily readings present an overview of the Bible through some 300 selected passages, including at least one chapter from each of the Bible's sixty-six books. Such a plan is no substitute for mastering the entire Bible, of course, but it may help lower barriers and point the way down a path for further study. Think of it like an introductory tour through a great art museum. You won't get to see every painting in the museum, but you will learn the basic layout, and may also acquire a taste for art that will entice you to return again and again.

With a few exceptions, we have arranged the biblical material in rough chronological order. You will read the psalms attributed to David as you read about David's life, and the Prophets as you read about their background history. Portions from the

Gospels, too, are interspersed, giving a composite picture of Jesus' life on earth; and Paul's letters are scattered throughout the record of his life. This arrangement should help convey the Bible's "plot."

How does a reader use the Bible passages and their commentaries? Key Bible passages were selected from the Old and New Testaments, passages about the story of God's relationship with his people starting in Genesis and stretching to his promise of eternal life in Revelation. The commentaries explain the passages—examining, for instance, the twists and turns of the Bible's many narratives, the high points and the low points, the good characters and the bad, as well as the eternal thoughts and descriptions of God and his Son found in the Bible's texts. These combinations of Bible passages and commentaries appear on most of the days' entries.

What about the reflections? On some days a reflection, or devotional, will take the place of the Bible reading. The reflections look back at the previous days' readings and consider the truths for daily living.

How Do I Read *Meet the Bible?*

It is possible to start *Meet the Bible* on any day of the year and complete the book in one year. Occasionally a Bible passage is longer than the typical day's reading, and two days may be needed. But the reading schedule doesn't have to be rigid, and a reader should take the time needed.

Who Contributed to *Meet the Bible?*

The material in this book is the result of the contributions of two writers with two different styles. Philip Yancey, with his grasp of biblical truths, his experience as author of *The Student Bible*, his candid and straightforward powers of observation, and his writing skills recognized by numerous awards, contributes key insights and commentaries from his previously published book *Discovering God*, as well as some essays from his recent best-sellers.

From her background with Serendipity House, Brenda Quinn brings to this project organizational and writing skills in Bible study and small group materials as she pens devotional insights and reflections and connects the material. The initials of each writer mark their contributions. Their collective material is a combination of insight, commentary, and devotional that puts biblical plots and subplots together in an understandable chronology (since the Bible does not) and helps explain the vaunted ideas of God that often seem only for theologians.

A Final Note

As the Old Testament unfolds into the New, one plan replaces another. A plan of a mighty nation, God's nation, becomes the plan of a new kingdom, the kingdom of God, which will be led not by Jewish generals and kings but rather by disciples who believe in the One who announced the new kingdom. The Bible is about understanding these two plans. And so is *Meet the Bible*.

This is just a beginning. Continue reading the Bible. God has given believers his Word in full for "teaching, rebuking, correcting and training in righteousness." Keep reading!

PART 1

BEGINNINGS

DAY 1   Genesis 1:1–2:3

CREATION

In the beginning God created the heavens and the earth. Now the earth was formless and empty, darkness was over the surface of the deep, and the Spirit of God was hovering over the waters.

And God said, "Let there be light," and there was light. God saw that the light was good, and he separated the light from the darkness. God called the light "day," and the darkness he called "night." And there was evening, and there was morning—the first day.

And God said, "Let there be an expanse between the waters to separate water from water." So God made the expanse and separated the water under the expanse from the water above it. And it was so. God called the expanse "sky." And there was evening, and there was morning—the second day.

And God said, "Let the water under the sky be gathered to one place, and let dry ground appear." And it was so. God called the dry ground "land," and the gathered waters he called "seas." And God saw that it was good.

Then God said, "Let the land produce vegetation: seed-bearing plants and trees on the land that bear fruit with seed in it, according to their various kinds." And it was so. The land produced vegetation: plants bearing seed according to their kinds and trees bearing fruit with seed in it according to their kinds. And God saw that it was good. And there was evening, and there was morning—the third day.

And God said, "Let there be lights in the expanse of the sky to separate the day from the night, and let them serve as signs to mark seasons and days and years, and let them be lights in the expanse of the sky to give light on the earth." And it was so. God made two great lights—the greater light to govern the day and the lesser light to govern the night. He also made the stars. God set them in the expanse of the sky to give light on the earth, to govern the day and the night, and to separate light from darkness. And God saw that it was good. And there was evening, and there was morning—the fourth day.

And God said, "Let the water teem with living creatures, and let birds fly above the earth across the expanse of the sky." So God created the great creatures of the sea and every living and moving thing with which the water teems, according to their kinds, and every winged bird according to its kind. And God saw that it was good. God blessed them and said, "Be fruitful and increase in number and fill the water in the seas, and let the birds increase on the earth." And there was evening, and there was morning—the fifth day.

And God said, "Let the land produce living creatures according to their kinds: livestock, creatures that move along the ground, and wild animals, each according to its kind." And it was so. God made the wild animals according to their kinds, the livestock according to their kinds, and all the creatures that move along the ground according to their kinds. And God saw that it was good.

Then God said, "Let us make man in our image, in our likeness, and let them rule over the fish of the sea and the birds of the air, over the livestock, over all the earth, and over all the creatures that move along the ground."

So God created man in his own image,
 in the image of God he created him;
 male and female he created them.

God blessed them and said to them, "Be fruitful and increase in number; fill the earth and subdue it. Rule over the fish of the sea and the birds of the air and over every living creature that moves on the ground."

Then God said, "I give you every seed-bearing plant on the face of the whole earth and every tree that has fruit with seed in it. They will be yours for food. And to all the beasts of the earth and all the birds of the air and all the creatures that move on the ground—everything that has the breath of life in it—I give every green plant for food." And it was so.

God saw all that he had made, and it was very good. And there was evening, and there was morning—the sixth day.

Thus the heavens and the earth were completed in all their vast array.

By the seventh day God had finished the work he had been doing; so on the seventh day he rested from all his work. And God blessed the seventh day and made it holy, because on it he rested from all the work of creating that he had done.

Everything, truly everything, begins here. The story of the Bible—more, the history of the universe—starts with the simple statement "In the beginning God created," and the rest of the chapter fills in what he created: stars, oceans, plants, birds, fish, mammals, and, finally, man and woman.

Genesis 1 says little about the processes God used in creation; you'll find no explanations of DNA or the scientific principles behind creation. But the opening chapter of the Bible does insist on two facts:

Creation was God's work. "And God said ... And God said ... And God said ..."— the phrase beats in cadence all the way through the chapter, a chapter that mentions the word *God* thirty times. And in this first chapter, the very first glimpse we have of God is as an artist. Butterflies, waterfalls, bottlenose dolphins, praying mantises, kangaroos—they were all his idea. This entire magnificent world we live in is the product of his creative work. All that follows in the Bible reinforces the message of Genesis 1: behind all of history, there is God.

Creation was good. Another sentence tolls softly, like a bell, throughout this chapter: "And God saw that it was good." In our day, we hear alarming reports about nature: the ozone layer, polluted oceans, vanishing species, the destruction of rain forests. Much has changed, much has been spoiled since that first moment of creation. Genesis 1 describes the world as God wanted it, before any spoiling. Whatever beauty we sense in nature today is a faint echo of that pristine state.

Captain Frank Borman, one of America's Apollo astronauts, read this chapter of Genesis on a telecast from outer space on Christmas Eve. As he gazed out of his window, he saw earth as a brightly colored ball hanging alone in the darkness of space. It looked at once awesomely beautiful and terribly fragile. It looked like the view from Genesis 1.   —PY

DAILY CONTEMPLATION

When was the last time you really noticed the beauty of the natural world? What do you notice today?

DAY 2
Genesis 2:4–25

ADAM AND EVE

This is the account of the heavens and the earth when they were created. When the LORD God made the earth and the heavens—and no shrub of the field had yet appeared on the earth and no plant of the field had yet sprung up, for the LORD God had not sent rain on the earth and there was no man to work the ground, but streams came up from the earth and watered the whole surface of the ground—the LORD God formed the man from the dust of the ground and breathed into his nostrils the breath of life, and the man became a living being.

Now the LORD God had planted a garden in the east, in Eden; and there he put the man he had formed. And the LORD God made all kinds of trees grow out of the ground—trees that were pleasing to the eye and good for food. In the middle of the garden were the tree of life and the tree of the knowledge of good and evil.

A river watering the garden flowed from Eden; from there it was separated into four headwaters. The name of the first is the Pishon; it winds through the entire land of Havilah, where there is gold. (The gold of that land is good; aromatic resin and onyx are also there.) The name of the second river is the Gihon; it winds through the entire land of Cush. The name of the third river is the Tigris; it runs along the east side of Asshur. And the fourth river is the Euphrates.

The LORD God took the man and put him in the Garden of Eden to work it and take care of it. And the LORD God commanded the man, "You are free to eat from any tree in the garden; but you must not eat from the tree of the knowledge of good and evil, for when you eat of it you will surely die."

The LORD God said, "It is not good for the man to be alone. I will make a helper suitable for him."

Now the LORD God had formed out of the ground all the beasts of the field and all the birds of the air. He brought them to the man to see what he would name them; and whatever the man called each living creature, that was its name. So the man gave names to all the livestock, the birds of the air and all the beasts of the field.

But for Adam no suitable helper was found. So the LORD God caused the man to fall into a deep sleep; and while he was sleeping, he took one of the man's ribs and closed up the place with flesh. Then the LORD God made a woman from the rib he had taken out of the man, and he brought her to the man.

The man said,

"This is now bone of my bones
    and flesh of my flesh;
she shall be called 'woman,'
    for she was taken out of man."

For this reason a man will leave his father and mother and be united to his wife, and they will become one flesh.

The man and his wife were both naked, and they felt no shame.

After presenting the cosmic view in chapter 1, Genesis repeats the story of creation, narrowing the focus to human beings. We alone, of all God's works, are made "in God's image." People have disagreed over the years on what, exactly, that phrase "image of God" means. Is it immortality? Intelligence? Creativity? Relationship? Perhaps the best way to understand is to think of "the image of God" as a mirror. God created us so that when he looked upon us, he would see reflected something of himself.

Nothing else God created contains that same image of himself. Alone of all creation, human beings received the very breath of life from God. Genesis declares that human beings, in God's eyes, possess a value far beyond other living things. Similarly, humans have value that can never be equaled—even by today's increasingly powerful computers, no matter how intelligent and lifelike.

Genesis 2 shows human history just getting under way. Marriage begins here: even in a state of perfection, Adam feels loneliness and desire, and God provides woman. From then on, marriage takes priority over all other relationships. Work begins here too: Adam is set in a role of authority over the animals and plants. Ever since, humans have had a kind of mastery over the rest of creation.

Only the slightest hint of foreboding clouds this blissful scene of Paradise. It appears in verse 17, in the form of a single negative command from God. Adam enjoys perfect freedom with this one small exception—a test of obedience.

Throughout history, artists have tried to re-create in words and images what a perfect world would look like, a world of love and beauty, a world without guilt or suffering or shame. Genesis 1–2 describes such a world. For a time in Genesis, peace reigns. When God looks at all he has created, he pays humanity its highest compliment. "Very good," he pronounces. Creation is now complete.   —PY

DAILY CONTEMPLATION

Think about a close friend or family member. In what way does this person reflect God? Does some quality or personality trait speak of what God must be like?

DAY 3   Genesis 3:1–24

THE FALL OF MAN

Now the serpent was more crafty than any of the wild animals the LORD God had made. He said to the woman, "Did God really say, 'You must not eat from any tree in the garden'?"

The woman said to the serpent, "We may eat fruit from the trees in the garden, but God did say, 'You must not eat fruit from the tree that is in the middle of the garden, and you must not touch it, or you will die.'"

"You will not surely die," the serpent said to the woman. "For God knows that when you eat of it your eyes will be opened, and you will be like God, knowing good and evil."

When the woman saw that the fruit of the tree was good for food and pleasing to the eye, and also desirable for gaining wisdom, she took some and ate it. She also gave some to her husband, who was with her, and he ate it. Then the eyes of both of them were opened, and they realized they were naked; so they sewed fig leaves together and made coverings for themselves.

Then the man and his wife heard the sound of the LORD God as he was walking in the garden in the cool of the day, and they hid from the LORD God among the trees of the garden. But the LORD God called to the man, "Where are you?"

He answered, "I heard you in the garden, and I was afraid because I was naked; so I hid."

And he said, "Who told you that you were naked? Have you eaten from the tree that I commanded you not to eat from?"

The man said, "The woman you put here with me—she gave me some fruit from the tree, and I ate it."

Then the LORD God said to the woman, "What is this you have done?"

The woman said, "The serpent deceived me, and I ate."

So the LORD God said to the serpent, "Because you have done this,

"Cursed are you above all the livestock
    and all the wild animals!
You will crawl on your belly
    and you will eat dust
    all the days of your life.
And I will put enmity
    between you and the woman,
    and between your offspring and hers;
he will crush your head,
    and you will strike his heel."

To the woman he said,

"I will greatly increase your pains in childbearing;
    with pain you will give birth to children.
Your desire will be for your husband,
    and he will rule over you."

To Adam he said, "Because you listened to your wife and ate from the tree about which I commanded you, 'You must not eat of it,'

"Cursed is the ground because of you;
    through painful toil you will eat of it
    all the days of your life.
It will produce thorns and thistles for you,
    and you will eat the plants of the field.
By the sweat of your brow
    you will eat your food

until you return to the ground,
>   since from it you were taken;
for dust you are
>   and to dust you will return."

Adam named his wife Eve, because she would become the mother of all the living.

The LORD God made garments of skin for Adam and his wife and clothed them. And the LORD God said, "The man has now become like one of us, knowing good and evil. He must not be allowed to reach out his hand and take also from the tree of life and eat, and live forever." So the LORD God banished him from the Garden of Eden to work the ground from which he had been taken. After he drove the man out, he placed on the east side of the Garden of Eden cherubim and a flaming sword flashing back and forth to guard the way to the tree of life.

The fall of man" theologians call it, but really it is more like a crash. Adam and Eve have everything a person could want in Paradise, and yet still a thought nags them: *Are we somehow missing out? Is God keeping something from us?* Like every human being who has ever lived, they cannot resist the temptation to reach for what lies beyond them.

Genesis gives few details about that first sin. Only one thing matters: God labeled one tree, just one, off-limits. Many people mistakenly assume sex is involved, but in fact something far more basic is at stake. The real issue is, Who will set the rules—the humans or God? Adam and Eve decide in favor of themselves, and the world has never been the same.

Adam and Eve react to their sin as anyone reacts to sin. They rationalize, explain themselves, and look for someone else to take the blame. They hide from each other, sensing for the first time a feeling of shame over their nakedness. Perhaps the greatest change of all, however, occurs in their relationship with God. Previously they have walked and talked with God in the Garden as a friend. Now, when they hear him, they hide.

Genesis 3 tells of other profound changes that affect the world when the creatures choose against their Creator. Suffering multiplies, work becomes harder, and a new word, *death*, enters human vocabulary. Perfection is permanently spoiled.

The underlying message of Genesis goes against some common assumptions about human history. According to these chapters, the world and humanity have not been gradually evolving toward a better state. Long ago, we wrecked against the rocks of our own pride and stubbornness. We're still bearing the consequences: all wars, all violence, all broken relationships, all grief and sadness trace back to that one monumental day in the Garden of Eden.   —PY

DAILY CONTEMPLATION

Have you felt hemmed in or stifled by any of God's commands? How have you responded to this feeling?

① Eve recognized God in the child bearing.

CAIN AND ABEL

Adam lay with his wife Eve, and she became pregnant and gave birth to Cain. She said, "With the help of the LORD I have brought forth a man." Later she gave birth to his brother Abel.

Now Abel kept flocks, and Cain worked the soil. In the course of time Cain brought some of the fruits of the soil as an offering to the LORD. But Abel brought fat portions from some of the firstborn of his flock. The LORD looked with favor on Abel and his offering, but on Cain and his offering he did not look with favor. So Cain was very angry, and his face was downcast.

Then the LORD said to Cain, "Why are you angry? Why is your face downcast? If you do what is right, will you not be accepted? But if you do not do what is right, sin is crouching at your door; it desires to have you, but you must master it."

Now Cain said to his brother Abel, "Let's go out to the field." And while they were in the field, Cain attacked his brother Abel and killed him.

Then the LORD said to Cain, "Where is your brother Abel?"

"I don't know," he replied. "Am I my brother's keeper?"

The LORD said, "What have you done? Listen! Your brother's blood cries out to me from the ground. Now you are under a curse and driven from the ground, which opened its mouth to receive your brother's blood from your hand. When you work the ground, it will no longer yield its crops for you. You will be a restless wanderer on the earth."

Cain said to the LORD, "My punishment is more than I can bear. Today you are driving me from the land, and I will be hidden from your presence; I will be a restless wanderer on the earth, and whoever finds me will kill me."

But the LORD said to him, "Not so; if anyone kills Cain, he will suffer vengeance seven times over." Then the LORD put a mark on Cain so that no one who found him would kill him. So Cain went out from the LORD's presence and lived in the land of Nod, east of Eden.

Cain lay with his wife, and she became pregnant and gave birth to Enoch. Cain was then building a city, and he named it after his son Enoch. To Enoch was born Irad, and Irad was the father of Mehujael, and Mehujael was the father of Methushael, and Methushael was the father of Lamech.

Lamech married two women, one named Adah and the other Zillah. Adah gave birth to Jabal; he was the father of those who live in tents and raise livestock. His brother's name was Jubal; he was the father of all who play the harp and flute. Zillah also had a son, Tubal-Cain, who forged all kinds of tools out of bronze and iron. Tubal-Cain's sister was Naamah.

Lamech said to his wives,

"Adah and Zillah, listen to me;
   wives of Lamech, hear my words.

I have killed a man for wounding me,
   a young man for injuring me.
If Cain is avenged seven times,
   then Lamech seventy-seven times."

Creation, the origins of man and woman, a fall into sin—in three chapters Genesis has set the stage for human history, and now that history begins to play itself out. The first childbirth—imagine the shock!—the first formal worship, the first division of labor, the first extended families, and cities and signs of culture all appear in chapter 4. But one "first" overshadows all the others: the first death of a human being, a death by murder.

It takes just one generation for sin to enter the world, and by the second generation people are already killing each other; the malignant results of the Fall spread that quickly. Cain offers a sacrifice to God with a poor attitude and then kills his brother when he learns God is more pleased with Abel's offering (see Hebrews 11:4). God steps in once again with a custom-designed punishment: Cain is to bear a mark of shame the rest of his life. The slide continues, though, for a few generations later a man named Lamech will brag about his murders.

Not all the news is bad. Civilization progresses rather quickly, with some people learning agriculture, some choosing to work with tools of bronze and iron, and some discovering music and the arts. In this way, human beings begin to fulfill the role assigned them as masters over the created world. But despite these advances, history is sliding along another track as well. Every person who follows Adam and Eve faces the same choice of whether or not to obey God's word. And, with numbing monotony, all make a choice like their original parents'. The next few chapters tell of an ever worsening spiral of rebellion and evil.   —PY

DAILY CONTEMPLATION

Look at Cain's response when God confronts him. What do you think you would say if God appeared in person to confront you about your sin?

DAY 5   Reflection

DID GOD REALLY SAY . . . ?

The Bible is God's great storybook, full of the tales of men and women who lived on earth, walked with God, experienced his love, and yet struggled in believing what he said. We see this pattern beginning right away in Genesis. God crafts the earth in all its beauty and complexity and creates man and woman, giving them all the earth. Yet Adam and Eve aren't content. They fall right into Satan's alluring trap.

"Did God really say …?" Every person who has lived since Adam and Eve has been tempted by Satan with these words. Just as the Serpent coaxed Eve with this question in Genesis 3:1, Satan uses similar reasoning with us as he tempts us to water down God's words, walk beyond his loving protection, and make our own choices. This reasoning can appear so sensible, so innocently self-supporting. We think we know what we need, and rather than going to God and asking, "Did you really say …?" we feel the urge to move ahead on our own, telling ourselves, "God did not *really* say...."

Eventually we regret ignoring God's warning and, like Adam and Eve, may suffer consequences that shape our future. If we are wise, in time we stop fighting God's guidance and gain a good ear for distinguishing between his voice and deceptive substitutes. The false promises that once appeared so sensible and hopeful lose their appeal. Only God's promises stand worthy of trust.

Although the Bible doesn't speak in specifics about every choice we must make, God's Word and a relationship with God himself are enough to help us choose God's way. We can trust that he will never deceive us, mislead us, or abandon us. This is his promise in Isaiah 41:10: "Do not fear, for I am with you; do not be dismayed, for I am your God. I will strengthen you and help you; I will uphold you with my righteous right hand."

—BQ

DAILY CONTEMPLATION

Our God, who created an earth full of wonder, who crafted the intricately beautiful human person, cares deeply and intimately about you. How have you come to know this? Spend a few moments talking with him. Tell him, "God, I want to hear what you really say...."

DAY 6   Genesis 6:1–7:24

THE FLOOD

When men began to increase in number on the earth and daughters were born to them, the sons of God saw that the daughters of men were beautiful, and they married any of them they chose. Then the LORD said, "My Spirit will not contend with man forever, for he is mortal; his days will be a hundred and twenty years."

The Nephilim were on the earth in those days—and also afterward—when the sons of God went to the daughters of men and had children by them. They were the heroes of old, men of renown.

The LORD saw how great man's wickedness on the earth had become, and that every inclination of the thoughts of his heart was only evil all the time. The LORD was grieved that he had made man on the earth, and his heart was filled with pain. So the LORD said, "I will wipe mankind, whom I have created, from the face of the earth—men and animals, and creatures that move along

the ground, and birds of the air—for I am grieved that I have made them."
But Noah found favor in the eyes of the LORD.

This is the account of Noah.

Noah was a righteous man, blameless among the people of his time, and
he walked with God. Noah had three sons: Shem, Ham and Japheth.

Now the earth was corrupt in God's sight and was full of violence. God saw
how corrupt the earth had become, for all the people on earth had corrupted
their ways. So God said to Noah, "I am going to put an end to all people, for
the earth is filled with violence because of them. I am surely going to destroy
both them and the earth. So make yourself an ark of cypress wood; make
rooms in it and coat it with pitch inside and out. This is how you are to build
it: The ark is to be 450 feet long, 75 feet wide and 45 feet high. Make a roof
for it and finish the ark to within 18 inches of the top. Put a door in the side
of the ark and make lower, middle and upper decks. I am going to bring floodwaters on the earth to destroy all life under the heavens, every creature that
has the breath of life in it. Everything on earth will perish. But I will establish
my covenant with you, and you will enter the ark—you and your sons and your
wife and your sons' wives with you. You are to bring into the ark two of all
living creatures, male and female, to keep them alive with you. Two of every
kind of bird, of every kind of animal and of every kind of creature that moves
along the ground will come to you to be kept alive. You are to take every kind
of food that is to be eaten and store it away as food for you and for them."

Noah did everything just as God commanded him.

The LORD then said to Noah, "Go into the ark, you and your whole family,
because I have found you righteous in this generation. Take with you seven of
every kind of clean animal, a male and its mate, and two of every kind of
unclean animal, a male and its mate, and also seven of every kind of bird, male
and female, to keep their various kinds alive throughout the earth. Seven days
from now I will send rain on the earth for forty days and forty nights, and I will
wipe from the face of the earth every living creature I have made."

And Noah did all that the LORD commanded him.

Noah was six hundred years old when the floodwaters came on the earth.
And Noah and his sons and his wife and his sons' wives entered the ark to
escape the waters of the flood. Pairs of clean and unclean animals, of birds and
of all creatures that move along the ground, male and female, came to Noah
and entered the ark, as God had commanded Noah. And after the seven days
the floodwaters came on the earth.

In the six hundredth year of Noah's life, on the seventeenth day of the second month—on that day all the springs of the great deep burst forth, and the
floodgates of the heavens were opened. And rain fell on the earth forty days
and forty nights.

On that very day Noah and his sons, Shem, Ham and Japheth, together with
his wife and the wives of his three sons, entered the ark. They had with them
every wild animal according to its kind, all livestock according to their kinds,
every creature that moves along the ground according to its kind and every

bird according to its kind, everything with wings. Pairs of all creatures that have the breath of life in them came to Noah and entered the ark. The animals going in were male and female of every living thing, as God had commanded Noah. Then the LORD shut him in.

For forty days the flood kept coming on the earth, and as the waters increased they lifted the ark high above the earth. The waters rose and increased greatly on the earth, and the ark floated on the surface of the water. They rose greatly on the earth, and all the high mountains under the entire heavens were covered. The waters rose and covered the mountains to a depth of more than twenty feet. Every living thing that moved on the earth perished—birds, livestock, wild animals, all the creatures that swarm over the earth, and all mankind. Everything on dry land that had the breath of life in its nostrils died. Every living thing on the face of the earth was wiped out; men and animals and the creatures that move along the ground and the birds of the air were wiped from the earth. Only Noah was left, and those with him in the ark.

The waters flooded the earth for a hundred and fifty days.

God can no longer tolerate the violence that has already spread across his world. It seems that the human experiment has failed. God, who has taken such pride in his creation, is now ready to destroy it.

Legends of a great flood exist in the records of cultures in the Middle East, in Asia, and in South America. One Babylonian document ("The Epic of Gilgamesh") has many parallels to the account in this chapter. But Genesis presents the Flood not merely as an accident of geography or climate; it is an act of God to destroy all humans who have turned their backs on him. Yet Noah's ark—a huge, ungainly boat riding out the storm—stands as a symbol: a symbol of God's mercy. God has resolved to give earth a second chance.

Genesis underscores one message above all: The first human beings on earth made a mess of things. Their rebellion brought on the downfall of all creation. But God spares Noah and his family—eight people who will birth future generations and carry on the story of God's undying love for his people.   —PY

DAILY CONTEMPLATION

Many people feel that good and evil, right and wrong, must be defined by each individual. Do you agree?

DAY 7   Genesis 8:1–22

THE LAND DRIES

God remembered Noah and all the wild animals and the livestock that were with him in the ark, and he sent a wind over the earth, and the waters receded. Now the springs of the deep and the floodgates of the heavens had been closed, and the rain had stopped falling from the sky. The water receded steadily from the earth. At the end of the hundred and fifty days the water had gone down, and on the seventeenth day of the seventh month the ark came to rest on the mountains of Ararat. The waters continued to recede until the tenth month, and on the first day of the tenth month the tops of the mountains became visible.

After forty days Noah opened the window he had made in the ark and sent out a raven, and it kept flying back and forth until the water had dried up from the earth. Then he sent out a dove to see if the water had receded from the surface of the ground. But the dove could find no place to set its feet because there was water over all the surface of the earth; so it returned to Noah in the ark. He reached out his hand and took the dove and brought it back to himself in the ark. He waited seven more days and again sent out the dove from the ark. When the dove returned to him in the evening, there in its beak was a freshly plucked olive leaf! Then Noah knew that the water had receded from the earth. He waited seven more days and sent the dove out again, but this time it did not return to him.

By the first day of the first month of Noah's six hundred and first year, the water had dried up from the earth. Noah then removed the covering from the ark and saw that the surface of the ground was dry. By the twenty-seventh day of the second month the earth was completely dry.

Then God said to Noah, "Come out of the ark, you and your wife and your sons and their wives. Bring out every kind of living creature that is with you— the birds, the animals, and all the creatures that move along the ground—so they can multiply on the earth and be fruitful and increase in number upon it."

So Noah came out, together with his sons and his wife and his sons' wives. All the animals and all the creatures that move along the ground and all the birds—everything that moves on the earth—came out of the ark, one kind after another.

Then Noah built an altar to the LORD and, taking some of all the clean animals and clean birds, he sacrificed burnt offerings on it. The LORD smelled the pleasing aroma and said in his heart: "Never again will I curse the ground because of man, even though every inclination of his heart is evil from childhood. And never again will I destroy all living creatures, as I have done.

"As long as the earth endures,
seedtime and harvest,
cold and heat,
summer and winter,
day and night
will never cease."

The gloomy tone of Genesis 7 brightens almost immediately. Genesis 8 tells of Noah and his family landing on a cleansed earth that is bringing forth new life. All the people who have so grievously offended God have died off. For the first time in years, human beings seek to please God: in his first act on land, Noah makes an offering of thanksgiving.

Noah is thankful for God's good care of him and his family as they watched the unthinkable happen to all those they had known and lived with. Noah has become the first person to go along with a plan of God's that looked absurd at the time and come out on the other side with a renewed respect and a deepened love for God.

Think of the ridicule Noah must have endured as he built an enormous boat and turned it into a zoo. Like Noah, many men and women throughout subsequent generations will have to decide whether to obey God in actions that seem senseless. Many, after obeying, will give thanksgiving just as Noah did, realizing anew that although we may not understand God's ways, we can trust and follow him in confidence. He's known to be dependable—and full of good surprises.   —BQ

DAILY CONTEMPLATION

What difficult time in your life can you look back on now with thankfulness to God for his awareness of your needs?

DAY 8   Genesis 9:1–17

GOD'S COVENANT RAINBOW

Then God blessed Noah and his sons, saying to them, "Be fruitful and increase in number and fill the earth. The fear and dread of you will fall upon all the beasts of the earth and all the birds of the air, upon every creature that moves along the ground, and upon all the fish of the sea; they are given into your hands. Everything that lives and moves will be food for you. Just as I gave you the green plants, I now give you everything.

"But you must not eat meat that has its lifeblood still in it. And for your lifeblood I will surely demand an accounting. I will demand an accounting from every animal. And from each man, too, I will demand an accounting for the life of his fellow man.

"Whoever sheds the blood of man,
    by man shall his blood be shed;
for in the image of God
    has God made man.

"As for you, be fruitful and increase in number; multiply on the earth and increase upon it."

Then God said to Noah and to his sons with him: "I now establish my covenant with you and with your descendants after you and with every living creature that was with you—the birds, the livestock and all the wild animals, all those that came out of the ark with you—every living creature on earth. I establish my covenant with you: Never again will all life be cut off by the waters of a flood; never again will there be a flood to destroy the earth."

And God said, "This is the sign of the covenant I am making between me and you and every living creature with you, a covenant for all generations to come: I have set my rainbow in the clouds, and it will be the sign of the covenant between me and the earth. Whenever I bring clouds over the earth and the rainbow appears in the clouds, I will remember my covenant between me and you and all living creatures of every kind. Never again will the waters become a flood to destroy all life. Whenever the rainbow appears in the clouds, I will see it and remember the everlasting covenant between God and all living creatures of every kind on the earth."

So God said to Noah, "This is the sign of the covenant I have established between me and all life on the earth."

God shows his pleasure in Noah by responding with a solemn promise, the first of several covenants in the Bible. The terms of the covenant reveal how deeply Adam's fall has affected all of creation. Humankind has cast a shadow across all nature, a shadow of fear and dread that will continue to spread throughout the animal kingdom. God's covenant recognizes certain sad adjustments to the original design of the world, taking for granted that human beings will continue to kill, not only the animals but also each other.

Despite these adjustments, God promises that regardless of what might happen, never again will he destroy life on such a massive scale. He vows in effect to find another way to deal with the rebellion and violence of humanity, "though every inclination of his heart is evil from childhood" (8:21).

An appropriate symbol—the rainbow—marks this first recorded covenant by God. Before he dies, even Noah will need this reminder of God's covenant in the rainbow. The last glimpse Genesis gives of Noah, later in this chapter, shows him sprawled in his tent, drunken and naked. Despite Noah's remarkable story as a man who walks radically with God, Noah too makes a mistake. He fails God and finds himself in need of God's mercy.   —PY

DAILY CONTEMPLATION

How do you react to those in your life who make mistakes and treat you wrongly?

DAY 9   Genesis 11:1–9

THE TOWER OF BABEL

Now the whole world had one language and a common speech. As men moved eastward, they found a plain in Shinar and settled there.

They said to each other, "Come, let's make bricks and bake them thoroughly." They used brick instead of stone, and tar for mortar. Then they said, "Come, let us build ourselves a city, with a tower that reaches to the heavens, so that we may make a name for ourselves and not be scattered over the face of the whole earth."

But the LORD came down to see the city and the tower that the men were building. The LORD said, "If as one people speaking the same language they have begun to do this, then nothing they plan to do will be impossible for them. Come, let us go down and confuse their language so they will not understand each other."

So the LORD scattered them from there over all the earth, and they stopped building the city. That is why it was called Babel—because there the LORD confused the language of the whole world. From there the LORD scattered them over the face of the whole earth.

Human civilization undergoes another significant change after pursuing the idea of the Tower of Babel. While attempting to take destiny into their own hands, the people of the world learn they cannot overcome God. Although they think they are all-powerful, they learn that God's ways will prevail and that humans are ultimately incapable of determining their own future.

God actually does the people a favor by confusing their language and causing them to spread throughout the earth. In this way he separates them from each other and causes them once again to realize their need for him. We catch another glimpse of a God who loves people too much to let them stray outside the realm of his love and toward their own utter destruction. —BQ

DAILY CONTEMPLATION

Has God ever revealed his great love for you by putting something in your life to show you that you needed him?

DAY 10   Reflection

GOD BECOMES A PARENT

If I had to reduce the "plot" of Genesis to one sentence, it would be something like this: God learns how to be a parent.* The disruption in Eden changed the world forever, destroying the intimacy Adam and Eve had known with God. In a kind of warm-up to history, God and human beings had to get used to each other. The humans set the pace by breaking all the rules, and God responded with individualized punishments. What did it feel like to be God? What does it feel like to be the parent of a two-year-old?

No one could accuse God of being shy to intervene in the early days. He seems a close, even hovering parent. When Adam sins, God meets with him in person, explaining that all creation will have to adjust to the choice he, Adam, has made. Just one generation later a new kind of horror—murder—appears on earth. "What have you done?" God demands of Cain. "Listen! Your brother's blood cries out to me from the ground." Once again God meets with the culprit and custom-designs a punishment.

The state of the earth and, indeed, the entire human race deteriorates toward a point of crisis which the Bible sums up in the most poignant sentence ever written: "The LORD was grieved that he had made man on the earth, and his heart was filled with pain" (6:6). Behind that one statement stands all the shock and grief God feels as a parent.

What human parent has not experienced at least a pang of such remorse? A teenage son tears away in a fit of rebellion. "I hate you!" he cries, fumbling for words that will cause the most pain. He seems bent on twisting a knife in the belly of his parents. That rejection is what God experiences, not just from one child but from the entire human race. As a result, what God has created, God destroys. All the joy of Genesis 1 vanishes under the churning waters of the Flood.

But here is Noah, that one man of faith who "walked with God." After the remorse expressed in Genesis 3–7, you can almost hear God sigh with relief as Noah, in his first act back on land, worships the God who has saved him. *At last, someone to build on.* (Years later, in a message to Ezekiel, God will mention Noah as one of his three most righteous followers.) With the whole planet freshly scrubbed and sprouting life anew, God agrees to a covenant, or contract, that binds him not just to Noah but to every living creature. It promises one thing only: that God will never again destroy all creation.

Even in that promise God limits himself. He, the sworn enemy of all evil in the universe, pledges to endure wickedness on this planet for a time—or, rather, to solve it through some means other than annihilation. Like the parent of a runaway teenager, he forces himself into the role of the Waiting Father (as Jesus' story of the Prodigal Son expresses so eloquently). Before long another mass rebellion, at a place called Babel, tests God's resolve, and he keeps his promise not to destroy.

In earliest history, then, God acts so plainly that no one can grouse about his hiddenness or silence. Yet these early interventions share one important feature: each is a punishment, a response, to human rebellion. If it is God's intention to have a mature relationship with free human beings, he certainly meets with a lot of rude setbacks. How can he ever relate to his creation as adults when they keep behaving like children?

Soon, with the coming of Abraham, God will set into motion a new plan for human history. Rather than trying to restore the whole earth at once, God will begin with a pioneer settlement, a new race set apart from all others.[1]   —PY

DAILY CONTEMPLATION

In what ways have you in the past, or are you now, responding to God as a rebellious child? Are you, like Noah, walking with God and following his guidance? Or are you, like the people of Babel, building your own methods for handling life?

THE CALL OF ABRAM

The LORD had said to Abram, "Leave your country, your people and your father's household and go to the land I will show you.

"I will make you into a great nation
  and I will bless you;
I will make your name great,
  and you will be a blessing.
I will bless those who bless you,
  and whoever curses you I will curse;
and all peoples on earth
  will be blessed through you."

So Abram left, as the LORD had told him; and Lot went with him. Abram was seventy-five years old when he set out from Haran. He took his wife Sarai, his nephew Lot, all the possessions they had accumulated and the people they had acquired in Haran, and they set out for the land of Canaan, and they arrived there.

Abram traveled through the land as far as the site of the great tree of Moreh at Shechem. At that time the Canaanites were in the land. The LORD appeared to Abram and said, "To your offspring I will give this land." So he built an altar there to the LORD, who had appeared to him.

From there he went on toward the hills east of Bethel and pitched his tent, with Bethel on the west and Ai on the east. There he built an altar to the LORD and called on the name of the LORD. Then Abram set out and continued toward the Negev.

Now there was a famine in the land, and Abram went down to Egypt to live there for a while because the famine was severe. As he was about to enter Egypt, he said to his wife Sarai, "I know what a beautiful woman you are. When the Egyptians see you, they will say, 'This is his wife.' Then they will kill me but will let you live. Say you are my sister, so that I will be treated well for your sake and my life will be spared because of you."

When Abram came to Egypt, the Egyptians saw that she was a very beautiful woman. And when Pharaoh's officials saw her, they praised her to Pharaoh, and she was taken into his palace. He treated Abram well for her sake, and Abram acquired sheep and cattle, male and female donkeys, menservants and maidservants, and camels.

But the LORD inflicted serious diseases on Pharaoh and his household because of Abram's wife Sarai. So Pharaoh summoned Abram. "What have you done to me?" he said. "Why didn't you tell me she was your wife? Why did you say, 'She is my sister,' so that I took her to be my wife? Now then, here is your wife. Take her and go!" Then Pharaoh gave orders about Abram to his men, and they sent him on his way, with his wife and everything he had.

Middle-aged and prospering financially, Abram suddenly hears a call from God to leave his comfortable life in the land of his fathers. He has no reason to leave home except that God tells him to go. Although Abram can't see the big picture at the time, God has plans to make him the father of God's chosen people, Israel. Abram will found a nation, and it all begins with these words: "Go to the land I will show you."

Probably more than any other person in the Bible, Abram characterizes faith. Because Abram makes himself available to be used by God, a nation is born that becomes the model for God's love relationship with all people. God has a plan for Abram. He asks Abram to take the first step, promising in turn to bless him and make him a blessing to others.

Abram leaves his fertile, prosperous home to journey by faith through a dry land of famine. He falters along the way, even lying about his wife in Egypt to protect himself. Early in Abram's story this great man of faith does slip, yet God remains faithful to his word and doesn't let Abram's mistake harm his bigger plan.   —BQ

DAILY CONTEMPLATION

Is God nudging you to step beyond your comfort zone in any way today?

DAY 12   Genesis 13:1–18

ABRAM AND LOT SEPARATE

Abram went up from Egypt to the Negev, with his wife and everything he had, and Lot went with him. Abram had become very wealthy in livestock and in silver and gold.

From the Negev he went from place to place until he came to Bethel, to the place between Bethel and Ai where his tent had been earlier and where he had first built an altar. There Abram called on the name of the LORD.

Now Lot, who was moving about with Abram, also had flocks and herds and tents. But the land could not support them while they stayed together, for their possessions were so great that they were not able to stay together. And quarreling arose between Abram's herdsmen and the herdsmen of Lot. The Canaanites and Perizzites were also living in the land at that time.

So Abram said to Lot, "Let's not have any quarreling between you and me, or between your herdsmen and mine, for we are brothers. Is not the whole land before you? Let's part company. If you go to the left, I'll go to the right; if you go to the right, I'll go to the left."

Lot looked up and saw that the whole plain of the Jordan was well watered, like the garden of the LORD, like the land of Egypt, toward Zoar. (This was before the LORD destroyed Sodom and Gomorrah.) So Lot chose for himself the whole plain of the Jordan and set out toward the east. The two men parted company: Abram lived in the land of Canaan, while Lot lived among the cities of the plain and pitched his tents near Sodom. Now the men of Sodom were wicked and were sinning greatly against the LORD.

The LORD said to Abram after Lot had parted from him, "Lift up your eyes from where you are and look north and south, east and west. All the land that you see I will give to you and your offspring forever. I will make your offspring like the dust of the earth, so that if anyone could count the dust, then your offspring could be counted. Go, walk through the length and breadth of the land, for I am giving it to you."

So Abram moved his tents and went to live near the great trees of Mamre at Hebron, where he built an altar to the LORD.

Like children who must decide who will get which piece of chocolate cake, Abram and Lot find they must part ways and each take for himself a portion of the land. But Abram isn't childish as he considers the situation. Rather than hurriedly claiming what might seem best, he generously lets Lot choose first. As any child would do, Lot takes what looks most appealing to him at the moment. He chooses selfishly and gets more than he bargains for. His choice of land will later prove dangerous for him and his family.

Abram has learned that he isn't responsible for bringing about God's promise. He is content to give up control and let God handle the situation. This story is a beautiful tribute to Abram's outlook of faith. By resting in God's hands, Abram allows God to work out his plan without interference. —BQ

DAILY CONTEMPLATION

What are your needs today? Can you give them up to God and trust him to provide for you?

DAY 13   Genesis 15:1–21

GOD'S COVENANT WITH ABRAM

The word of the LORD came to Abram in a vision:

"Do not be afraid, Abram.
  I am your shield,
  your very great reward."

But Abram said, "O Sovereign LORD, what can you give me since I remain childless and the one who will inherit my estate is Eliezer of Damascus?" And Abram said, "You have given me no children; so a servant in my household will be my heir."

Then the word of the LORD came to him: "This man will not be your heir, but a son coming from your own body will be your heir." He took him outside and said, "Look up at the heavens and count the stars—if indeed you can count them." Then he said to him, "So shall your offspring be."

Abram believed the LORD, and he credited it to him as righteousness.

He also said to him, "I am the LORD, who brought you out of Ur of the Chaldeans to give you this land to take possession of it."

But Abram said, "O Sovereign LORD, how can I know that I will gain possession of it?"

So the LORD said to him, "Bring me a heifer, a goat and a ram, each three years old, along with a dove and a young pigeon."

Abram brought all these to him, cut them in two and arranged the halves opposite each other; the birds, however, he did not cut in half. Then birds of prey came down on the carcasses, but Abram drove them away.

As the sun was setting, Abram fell into a deep sleep, and a thick and dreadful darkness came over him. Then the LORD said to him, "Know for certain that your descendants will be strangers in a country not their own, and they will be enslaved and mistreated four hundred years. But I will punish the nation they serve as slaves, and afterward they will come out with great possessions. You, however, will go to your fathers in peace and be buried at a good old age. In the fourth generation your descendants will come back here, for the sin of the Amorites has not yet reached its full measure."

When the sun had set and darkness had fallen, a smoking firepot with a blazing torch appeared and passed between the pieces. On that day the LORD made a covenant with Abram and said, "To your descendants I give this land, from the river of Egypt to the great river, the Euphrates—the land of the Kenites, Kenizzites, Kadmonites, Hittites, Perizzites, Rephaites, Amorites, Canaanites, Girgashites and Jebusites."

Many times God had intervened directly in human history, but almost always for the sake of punishment—in Adam's day, and Cain's, and in the days of Noah, and at Babel. After scanning these centuries of dismal failure, Genesis changes dramatically at chapter 12. It leaves the big picture of world history and settles on one lonely individual: not a great king or a wealthy landowner but a childless nomad named Abram.

It's almost impossible to exaggerate the importance of Abraham (Abram's later name) in the Bible. To the Jews he is the father of a nation, but to all Christians he represents far more. He became a singular man of faith whose relationship to God was so close that for many centuries God himself was known as "the God of Abraham."

In effect, God in Abram's day is narrowing the scope of his activity on earth by separating out one group of people he can have a unique relationship with. They will be set apart from other men and women as God's peculiar treasures, his kingdom of priests. This special group will by example teach the rest of the world the advantages of loving and serving God. And Abraham is the father of this new humanity.

Dozens of other passages in the Old Testament set forth the details of God's covenant, or contract, with his chosen people. (The word *testament* means covenant.) Genesis 15 is the first to spell out the terms of this covenant.

Here is what God promises Abraham: A *new land to live in*. Trusting God, Abraham travels hundreds of miles toward Canaan. A *large and prosperous family*. This dream obsesses Abraham and, when its fulfillment seems long in coming, tests his faith severely. A *great nation*. It takes many centuries after Abraham for this promise to come true, but finally, in the days of David and Solomon, the Hebrews at last become a nation. A *blessing to the whole world*. From the beginning, God makes clear that he has chosen the Hebrew people not as an end but as a means to the end goal of reaching other nations.* —PY

DAILY CONTEMPLATION

God chose you to be his beloved child. Is it hard for you to envision him loving you this way?

DAY 14 Genesis 16:1–16

HAGAR AND ISHMAEL

Now Sarai, Abram's wife, had borne him no children. But she had an Egyptian maidservant named Hagar; so she said to Abram, "The LORD has kept me from having children. Go, sleep with my maidservant; perhaps I can build a family through her."

Abram agreed to what Sarai said. So after Abram had been living in Canaan ten years, Sarai his wife took her Egyptian maidservant Hagar and gave her to her husband to be his wife. He slept with Hagar, and she conceived.

When she knew she was pregnant, she began to despise her mistress. Then Sarai said to Abram, "You are responsible for the wrong I am suffering. I put my servant in your arms, and now that she knows she is pregnant, she despises me. May the LORD judge between you and me."

"Your servant is in your hands," Abram said. "Do with her whatever you think best." Then Sarai mistreated Hagar; so she fled from her.

---

*You will begin to see the terms Hebrew, Israelite, and Jew used interchangeably. Each refers to the group of God's chosen people who will remain the focus of most of the Old Testament.

The angel of the LORD found Hagar near a spring in the desert; it was the spring that is beside the road to Shur. And he said, "Hagar, servant of Sarai, where have you come from, and where are you going?"

"I'm running away from my mistress Sarai," she answered.

Then the angel of the LORD told her, "Go back to your mistress and submit to her." The angel added, "I will so increase your descendants that they will be too numerous to count."

The angel of the LORD also said to her:

"You are now with child
    and you will have a son.
You shall name him Ishmael,
    for the LORD has heard of your misery.
He will be a wild donkey of a man;
    his hand will be against everyone
    and everyone's hand against him,
and he will live in hostility
    toward all his brothers."

She gave this name to the LORD who spoke to her: "You are the God who sees me," for she said, "I have now seen the One who sees me." That is why the well was called Beer Lahai Roi; it is still there, between Kadesh and Bered.

So Hagar bore Abram a son, and Abram gave the name Ishmael to the son she had borne. Abram was eighty-six years old when Hagar bore him Ishmael.

Once again Abram and his wife, Sarai (SAY-ri), wander from their walk of faith. When the child that God promised is delayed in coming, they decide to take matters into their own hands and find another way to fulfill the promise. Problems begin as soon as they act, however. Sarai and Hagar (HAY-gahr) begin to hate each other. Abram and Sarai's marriage reels from blame and jealousy. And a child is on the way whose descendants will carry hostility toward God's people for many generations.

The story of Sarai, Abram, and Hagar declares that God hears and God sees even when to us he seems absent (vv. 11, 13). He reminds those he loves that they can trust his word and wait for its fulfillment. God knows the difficulties in waiting. Our sorrows matter to him. He hears our cries and sees our troubles. Still, he asks us to wait patiently, because he *will* bring about what he has promised.   —BQ

DAILY CONTEMPLATION

What are you waiting for? How are you doing in your waiting?

THE THREE VISITORS

The LORD appeared to Abraham near the great trees of Mamre while he was sitting at the entrance to his tent in the heat of the day. Abraham looked up and saw three men standing nearby. When he saw them, he hurried from the entrance of his tent to meet them and bowed low to the ground.

He said, "If I have found favor in your eyes, my lord, do not pass your servant by. Let a little water be brought, and then you may all wash your feet and rest under this tree. Let me get you something to eat, so you can be refreshed and then go on your way—now that you have come to your servant."

"Very well," they answered, "do as you say."

So Abraham hurried into the tent to Sarah. "Quick," he said, "get three seahs of fine flour and knead it and bake some bread."

Then he ran to the herd and selected a choice, tender calf and gave it to a servant, who hurried to prepare it. He then brought some curds and milk and the calf that had been prepared, and set these before them. While they ate, he stood near them under a tree.

"Where is your wife Sarah?" they asked him.

"There, in the tent," he said.

Then the LORD said, "I will surely return to you about this time next year, and Sarah your wife will have a son."

Now Sarah was listening at the entrance to the tent, which was behind him. Abraham and Sarah were already old and well advanced in years, and Sarah was past the age of childbearing. So Sarah laughed to herself as she thought, "After I am worn out and my master is old, will I now have this pleasure?"

Then the LORD said to Abraham, "Why did Sarah laugh and say, 'Will I really have a child, now that I am old?' Is anything too hard for the LORD? I will return to you at the appointed time next year and Sarah will have a son."

Sarah was afraid, so she lied and said, "I did not laugh."

But he said, "Yes, you did laugh."

Before this chapter begins, Ishmael (ISH-may-uhl) has reached age thirteen and God has changed two people's names. God is preparing to provide the promised child to this chosen couple, and the changes in name are one more step in the fulfillment of the promise. The name Abram, meaning "exalted father," looks back to Abram's royal lineage. His new name, Abraham, "father of a multitude," looks ahead to his many descendants. Sarai becomes Sarah, meaning "princess," a fitting title for one who will produce kings.

Soon after, the Angel of the Lord and two other angels visit Abraham. This visit of God in person represents an intimate reminder of the close and ongoing relationship that God and Abraham share. Yet despite the many times God has confirmed his promise to Abraham, Sarah laughs when she hears about the son who will arrive in the next year. The prospect of pregnancy seems absurd to a woman in her nineties. But once again we learn that what is impossible for humans is possible for God. His promises are no laughing matter. —BQ

DAY 16   Reflection

GOD CALLS

Abraham's story tells us a lot about how fickle people are. One day content with what we have, the next day we want something *now*. One day filled with hope, the next day we wallow in despair. Abraham earned a reputation as a man of great faith, yet clearly he faltered a few times. Though he believed God, his own doubts and fears crept in at times and began to obscure his faith.

As we look at Abraham's stellar acts of faith—and there are more coming in the next chapters—we'll see that it is God who ultimately proves faithful. When God saves us, he calls us to a plan that uniquely fits us. As with Abraham, God is consistent in gradually unfolding his call in our lives, both during those times when we trust him and even in those times when we don't.

Sometimes, like Abraham, we may feel God has forgotten us. His provision will seem long in coming, and we may doubt whether he will ever provide. Yet, as we'll see in Abraham's life, God's plans are not vague. No matter how things look, he has not tired of us and moved on. At times he works slowly and quietly, at others quickly and unmistakably. Never, though, does he abandon us.

Abraham's story is really God's story. We learn that people will waver and fail but God will not. God reminds us again and again, in a voice that is creative and eloquent and clear, that he loves us, has a purpose for us, and will not let go of us. As we recall the story of God and Abraham today, we have the privilege of believing even more deeply than Abraham was able to, because we have seen God prove that he will finish what he started. We have seen that he can do the impossible. It was true for Abraham and is absolutely true for us. —BQ

ABRAHAM PLEADS FOR SODOM

When the men got up to leave, they looked down toward Sodom, and Abraham walked along with them to see them on their way. Then the LORD said, "Shall I hide from Abraham what I am about to do? Abraham will surely become a great and powerful nation, and all nations on earth will be blessed through him. For I have chosen him, so that he will direct his children and his household after him to keep the way of the LORD by doing what is right and just, so that the LORD will bring about for Abraham what he has promised him."

Then the LORD said, "The outcry against Sodom and Gomorrah is so great and their sin so grievous that I will go down and see if what they have done is as bad as the outcry that has reached me. If not, I will know."

The men turned away and went toward Sodom, but Abraham remained standing before the LORD. Then Abraham approached him and said: "Will you sweep away the righteous with the wicked? What if there are fifty righteous people in the city? Will you really sweep it away and not spare the place for the sake of the fifty righteous people in it? Far be it from you to do such a thing—to kill the righteous with the wicked, treating the righteous and the wicked alike. Far be it from you! Will not the Judge of all the earth do right?"

The LORD said, "If I find fifty righteous people in the city of Sodom, I will spare the whole place for their sake."

Then Abraham spoke up again: "Now that I have been so bold as to speak to the Lord, though I am nothing but dust and ashes, what if the number of the righteous is five less than fifty? Will you destroy the whole city because of five people?"

"If I find forty-five there," he said, "I will not destroy it."

Once again he spoke to him, "What if only forty are found there?"

He said, "For the sake of forty, I will not do it."

Then he said, "May the Lord not be angry, but let me speak. What if only thirty can be found there?"

He answered, "I will not do it if I find thirty there."

Abraham said, "Now that I have been so bold as to speak to the Lord, what if only twenty can be found there?"

He said, "For the sake of twenty, I will not destroy it."

Then he said, "May the Lord not be angry, but let me speak just once more. What if only ten can be found there?"

He answered, "For the sake of ten, I will not destroy it."

When the LORD had finished speaking with Abraham, he left, and Abraham returned home.

We learn more in this chapter about Abraham's character. In genuine humility and reverence he pleads with God to save all the people in Sodom (SAH-dum) and Gomorrah (guh-MOR-uh), both the righteous and the wicked, for the sake of the righteous.

Abraham feels compassion toward those who love God and face destruction. His compassion makes him bold in coming before God on behalf of these people in need. Not only does Abraham faithfully guide his own household in God's ways; he looks beyond his family to care about others, including the family of his nephew Lot, now living within Sodom. Abraham understands that sometimes the wicked must be spared with the righteous, so he entreats God to delay his punishment and spare all the people for a time.   —BQ

DAILY CONTEMPLATION

Who is in need of your prayers today?

DAY 18   Genesis 19:1–29

SODOM AND GOMORRAH DESTROYED

The two angels arrived at Sodom in the evening, and Lot was sitting in the gateway of the city. When he saw them, he got up to meet them and bowed down with his face to the ground. "My lords," he said, "please turn aside to your servant's house. You can wash your feet and spend the night and then go on your way early in the morning."

"No," they answered, "we will spend the night in the square."

But he insisted so strongly that they did go with him and entered his house. He prepared a meal for them, baking bread without yeast, and they ate. Before they had gone to bed, all the men from every part of the city of Sodom—both young and old—surrounded the house. They called to Lot, "Where are the men who came to you tonight? Bring them out to us so that we can have sex with them."

Lot went outside to meet them and shut the door behind him and said, "No, my friends. Don't do this wicked thing. Look, I have two daughters who have never slept with a man. Let me bring them out to you, and you can do what you like with them. But don't do anything to these men, for they have come under the protection of my roof."

"Get out of our way," they replied. And they said, "This fellow came here as an alien, and now he wants to play the judge! We'll treat you worse than them." They kept bringing pressure on Lot and moved forward to break down the door.

But the men inside reached out and pulled Lot back into the house and shut the door. Then they struck the men who were at the door of the house, young and old, with blindness so that they could not find the door.

The two men said to Lot, "Do you have anyone else here—sons-in-law, sons or daughters, or anyone else in the city who belongs to you? Get them out of here, because we are going to destroy this place. The outcry to the LORD against its people is so great that he has sent us to destroy it."

So Lot went out and spoke to his sons-in-law, who were pledged to marry his daughters. He said, "Hurry and get out of this place, because the LORD is about to destroy the city!" But his sons-in-law thought he was joking.

With the coming of dawn, the angels urged Lot, saying, "Hurry! Take your wife and your two daughters who are here, or you will be swept away when the city is punished."

When he hesitated, the men grasped his hand and the hands of his wife and of his two daughters and led them safely out of the city, for the LORD was merciful to them. As soon as they had brought them out, one of them said, "Flee for your lives! Don't look back, and don't stop anywhere in the plain! Flee to the mountains or you will be swept away!"

But Lot said to them, "No, my lords, please! Your servant has found favor in your eyes, and you have shown great kindness to me in sparing my life. But I can't flee to the mountains; this disaster will overtake me, and I'll die. Look, here is a town near enough to run to, and it is small. Let me flee to it—it is very small, isn't it? Then my life will be spared."

He said to him, "Very well, I will grant this request too; I will not overthrow the town you speak of. But flee there quickly, because I cannot do anything until you reach it." (That is why the town was called Zoar.)

By the time Lot reached Zoar, the sun had risen over the land. Then the LORD rained down burning sulfur on Sodom and Gomorrah—from the LORD out of the heavens. Thus he overthrew those cities and the entire plain, including all those living in the cities—and also the vegetation in the land. But Lot's wife looked back, and she became a pillar of salt.

Early the next morning Abraham got up and returned to the place where he had stood before the LORD. He looked down toward Sodom and Gomorrah, toward all the land of the plain, and he saw dense smoke rising from the land, like smoke from a furnace.

So when God destroyed the cities of the plain, he remembered Abraham, and he brought Lot out of the catastrophe that overthrew the cities where Lot had lived.

Like a photo negative, this chapter shows by contrast what Abraham is up against in his efforts to found a new and godly nation. His own nephew lives in the city of Sodom, a sordid place that looks on visiting strangers—angels, as it turns out—as prime targets for gang rape. Sexual violence is just one of Sodom's problems; Ezekiel 16:49 says that Sodom was "arrogant, overfed and unconcerned; they did not help the poor and needy."

In the midst of this story, we also see Lot's true character. Although he opposes some of the evil of Sodom, he has been drawn into its allure. His hypocrisy becomes evident when he takes hospitality much too far, offering his own daughters in exchange for the protection of his guests. Clearly, the hearts of Lot and the rest of his family have been colored by their time in Sodom.

God's patience with Sodom and Gomorrah finally runs out. Once more he steps in with direct punishment, not to destroy the whole world but to wipe out two centers of evil. In typical style, the Bible doesn't bother with scientific explanations of the destruction. Was it a volcanic eruption? The Bible does not say, and the area, now apparently at the bottom of the Dead Sea, cannot easily be investigated. Genesis stresses not how it happened but why.

According to this chapter, Lot does not learn a lesson from Sodom. Later in the chapter, in a drunken state, he commits incest with his daughters, producing two family lines that will be traditional enemies of Abraham's family, the Jews.

Jesus later uses the account of Sodom and Gomorrah as a warning to people who see his miracles but ignore them (Matthew 11). God may not always intervene so spectacularly, but this story serves as a warning that his tolerance for evil has a limit.

—PY

DAILY CONTEMPLATION

What practices common to our society do you think God considers intolerable?

DAY 19 Genesis 21:1–21

ISAAC'S BIRTH

Now the LORD was gracious to Sarah as he had said, and the LORD did for Sarah what he had promised. Sarah became pregnant and bore a son to Abraham in his old age, at the very time God had promised him. Abraham gave the name Isaac to the son Sarah bore him. When his son Isaac was eight days old, Abraham circumcised him, as God commanded him. Abraham was a hundred years old when his son Isaac was born to him.

Sarah said, "God has brought me laughter, and everyone who hears about this will laugh with me." And she added, "Who would have said to Abraham that Sarah would nurse children? Yet I have borne him a son in his old age."

The child grew and was weaned, and on the day Isaac was weaned Abraham held a great feast. But Sarah saw that the son whom Hagar the Egyptian had borne to Abraham was mocking, and she said to Abraham, "Get rid of that slave woman and her son, for that slave woman's son will never share in the inheritance with my son Isaac."

The matter distressed Abraham greatly because it concerned his son. But God said to him, "Do not be so distressed about the boy and your maidservant. Listen to whatever Sarah tells you, because it is through Isaac that your offspring will be reckoned. I will make the son of the maidservant into a nation also, because he is your offspring."

Early the next morning Abraham took some food and a skin of water and gave them to Hagar. He set them on her shoulders and then sent her off with the boy. She went on her way and wandered in the desert of Beersheba.

When the water in the skin was gone, she put the boy under one of the bushes. Then she went off and sat down nearby, about a bowshot away, for she thought, "I cannot watch the boy die." And as she sat there nearby, she began to sob.

God heard the boy crying, and the angel of God called to Hagar from heaven and said to her, "What is the matter, Hagar? Do not be afraid; God has heard the boy crying as he lies there. Lift the boy up and take him by the hand, for I will make him into a great nation."

Then God opened her eyes and she saw a well of water. So she went and filled the skin with water and gave the boy a drink.

God was with the boy as he grew up. He lived in the desert and became an archer. While he was living in the Desert of Paran, his mother got a wife for him from Egypt.

Paul, writer of the New Testament letter of Galatians (guh-LAY-shuns), discusses the deep significance of this story of Abraham and his family (Galatians 4:21–31). Paul uses the story to illustrate how Christ's coming has changed our lives. Ishmael was born by the flesh "through the slave woman," a by-product of Abraham's impatience and human effort. In contrast, Isaac was born as the result of God's promise; a gift of grace in Abraham's old age, Isaac became heir to the nation God would build. According to Paul, Ishmael represents the Old Testament time when people could be saved only by following God's law. Isaac represents the coming of Jesus, God's Promised One, the Savior.

For those who belong to Jesus, we also have become, like him, God's sons and daughters. We too are children of the promise. As Abraham sent Hagar away with her child, we must reject the idea of earning God's approval through doing good. Rather, we place our hope in Jesus. Because he loved us and died for us, we have been set free from the burden of needing to save ourselves by being good enough.   —BQ

DAILY CONTEMPLATION

In God's eyes you are a child he has wanted and specially planned for. How does this make you feel toward God?

ABRAHAM TESTED

Some time later God tested Abraham. He said to him, "Abraham!"

"Here I am," he replied.

Then God said, "Take your son, your only son, Isaac, whom you love, and go to the region of Moriah. Sacrifice him there as a burnt offering on one of the mountains I will tell you about."

Early the next morning Abraham got up and saddled his donkey. He took with him two of his servants and his son Isaac. When he had cut enough wood for the burnt offering, he set out for the place God had told him about. On the third day Abraham looked up and saw the place in the distance. He said to his servants, "Stay here with the donkey while I and the boy go over there. We will worship and then we will come back to you."

Abraham took the wood for the burnt offering and placed it on his son Isaac, and he himself carried the fire and the knife. As the two of them went on together, Isaac spoke up and said to his father Abraham, "Father?"

"Yes, my son?" Abraham replied.

"The fire and wood are here," Isaac said, "but where is the lamb for the burnt offering?"

Abraham answered, "God himself will provide the lamb for the burnt offering, my son." And the two of them went on together.

When they reached the place God had told him about, Abraham built an altar there and arranged the wood on it. He bound his son Isaac and laid him on the altar, on top of the wood. Then he reached out his hand and took the knife to slay his son. But the angel of the LORD called out to him from heaven, "Abraham! Abraham!"

"Here I am," he replied.

"Do not lay a hand on the boy," he said. "Do not do anything to him. Now I know that you fear God, because you have not withheld from me your son, your only son."

Abraham looked up and there in a thicket he saw a ram caught by its horns. He went over and took the ram and sacrificed it as a burnt offering instead of his son. So Abraham called that place The LORD Will Provide. And to this day it is said, "On the mountain of the LORD it will be provided."

The angel of the LORD called to Abraham from heaven a second time and said, "I swear by myself, declares the LORD, that because you have done this and have not withheld your son, your only son, I will surely bless you and make your descendants as numerous as the stars in the sky and as the sand on the seashore. Your descendants will take possession of the cities of their enemies, and through your offspring all nations on earth will be blessed, because you have obeyed me."

Then Abraham returned to his servants, and they set off together for Beersheba. And Abraham stayed in Beersheba.

Once more Abraham's faith faces a test. Although God has shown Abraham his overall plan for the future in spectacular fashion, the actual working out of that plan has included many bumps and pitfalls.

What does God want? He wants faith, the Bible says, which means complete trust against all odds, and Abraham finally learns that lesson. Abraham and Sarah will never live to see their descendants multiply like the stars in the sky. But they have one beloved son, whom they name Isaac, or "laughter," as if to remind them of the very absurdity, the miracle, of childbirth at their ages.

Now God presents a final test of faith, a trial so severe that it makes the others seem like kindergarten games. The Bible makes clear that God never intends to let Abraham go through with his plan of child sacrifice. (Years later, when the Israelites actually commit infant sacrifice, God will call it "something I did not command or mention, nor did it enter my mind" [Jeremiah 19:5].) All along, God has provided another sacrifice, a ram caught by its horns nearby. But Abraham does not know these things as he climbs the steep mountain with his only son. (Later, this same mountain will become home to Jerusalem, the place where God will provide his only Son as the final sacrifice for all people.)

Too many times Abraham has doubted God—this time he will obey no matter what. It has taken more than a hundred years, but Abraham finally has learned to trust. Ever since, he's been known as a man of great faith.   —PY

DAILY CONTEMPLATION

Have you ever had a "Mount Moriah experience," in which you faced extreme circumstances and needed to have great faith in God? How has God been teaching you that you can trust him?

DAY 21   Genesis 24:1–30, 50–66

ISAAC AND REBEKAH

Abraham was now old and well advanced in years, and the LORD had blessed him in every way. He said to the chief servant in his household, the one in charge of all that he had, "Put your hand under my thigh. I want you to swear by the LORD, the God of heaven and the God of earth, that you will not get a wife for my son from the daughters of the Canaanites, among whom I am living, but will go to my country and my own relatives and get a wife for my son Isaac."

The servant asked him, "What if the woman is unwilling to come back with me to this land? Shall I then take your son back to the country you came from?"

"Make sure that you do not take my son back there," Abraham said. "The LORD, the God of heaven, who brought me out of my father's household and my native land and who spoke to me and promised me on oath, saying, 'To your offspring I will give this land'—he will send his angel before you so that you can get a wife for my son from there. If the woman is unwilling to come back with you, then you will be released from this oath of mine. Only do not take my son back there." So the servant put his hand under the thigh of his master Abraham and swore an oath to him concerning this matter.

Then the servant took ten of his master's camels and left, taking with him all kinds of good things from his master. He set out for Aram Naharaim and made his way to the town of Nahor. He had the camels kneel down near the well outside the town; it was toward evening, the time the women go out to draw water.

Then he prayed, "O Lord, God of my master Abraham, give me success today, and show kindness to my master Abraham. See, I am standing beside this spring, and the daughters of the townspeople are coming out to draw water. May it be that when I say to a girl, 'Please let down your jar that I may have a drink,' and she says, 'Drink, and I'll water your camels too'—let her be the one you have chosen for your servant Isaac. By this I will know that you have shown kindness to my master."

Before he had finished praying, Rebekah came out with her jar on her shoulder. She was the daughter of Bethuel son of Milcah, who was the wife of Abraham's brother Nahor. The girl was very beautiful, a virgin; no man had ever lain with her. She went down to the spring, filled her jar and came up again.

The servant hurried to meet her and said, "Please give me a little water from your jar."

"Drink, my lord," she said, and quickly lowered the jar to her hands and gave him a drink.

After she had given him a drink, she said, "I'll draw water for your camels too, until they have finished drinking." So she quickly emptied her jar into the trough, ran back to the well to draw more water, and drew enough for all his camels. Without saying a word, the man watched her closely to learn whether or not the Lord had made his journey successful.

When the camels had finished drinking, the man took out a gold nose ring weighing a beka and two gold bracelets weighing ten shekels. Then he asked, "Whose daughter are you? Please tell me, is there room in your father's house for us to spend the night?"

She answered him, "I am the daughter of Bethuel, the son that Milcah bore to Nahor." And she added, "We have plenty of straw and fodder, as well as room for you to spend the night."

Then the man bowed down and worshiped the Lord, saying, "Praise be to the Lord, the God of my master Abraham, who has not abandoned his kindness and faithfulness to my master. As for me, the Lord has led me on the journey to the house of my master's relatives."

The girl ran and told her mother's household about these things. Now Rebekah had a brother named Laban, and he hurried out to the man at the spring. As soon as he had seen the nose ring, and the bracelets on his sister's arms, and had heard Rebekah tell what the man said to her, he went out to the man and found him standing by the camels near the spring....

Laban and Bethuel answered, "This is from the LORD; we can say nothing to you one way or the other. Here is Rebekah; take her and go, and let her become the wife of your master's son, as the LORD has directed."

When Abraham's servant heard what they said, he bowed down to the ground before the LORD. Then the servant brought out gold and silver jewelry and articles of clothing and gave them to Rebekah; he also gave costly gifts to her brother and to her mother. Then he and the men who were with him ate and drank and spent the night there.

When they got up the next morning, he said, "Send me on my way to my master."

But her brother and her mother replied, "Let the girl remain with us ten days or so; then you may go."

But he said to them, "Do not detain me, now that the LORD has granted success to my journey. Send me on my way so I may go to my master."

This story involves no words from God, no miracle, and no prophecy, but throughout the story the Bible makes clear God's intimate involvement in every aspect of bringing Isaac and Rebekah together. The events of the story testify to God's loving care in the lives of those who follow him. In its original Hebrew, the passage contains the word *hesed*, used several times to convey the "loyal love" shown by both God and his people, who cooperated in love and reverence with his plan.

God's *hesed* shows itself in the details of Isaac's life, and we can be confident that God's *hesed* goes with us too. Not only will God carry out his good plan, but he will loyally and lovingly orchestrate circumstances along the way if we walk with him in faith.   —BQ

DAILY CONTEMPLATION

How have you seen God acting out his hesed *in your life this week?*

DAY 22   Reflection

BENEATH THE SURFACE OF FAITH

What comes to mind when you think of a person of great faith—a person like Abraham? You might think of someone who is strong in a quiet way, someone sure of his or her beliefs about God and of the relationship he or she has with God. You think of someone who doesn't get ruffled too easily, who seems capable of handling anything.

Abraham fits the image. Yet he also proves that what we see on the surface is only part of the picture. Underneath, in any person of faith, we likely will find vivid images of struggles and sorrows and challenges that have consumed heart and strength. For instance, Abraham's record of difficulty began when he agreed to follow God to a foreign place. Soon he met challenges with his nephew Lot and then struggled to understand the barrenness of his marriage. A second wife and a child brought new layers of hardship. Finally, Abraham underwent an ultimate test with God's command to sacrifice his long-awaited son.

Abraham earned his reputation through the real, life-shaking struggles he encountered. He grew his faith in the soil of tough times while watching God move and direct in loving, unexpected ways.

Do you want to be a person of faith if it means learning to trust through difficult days? Perhaps a better question is, Can you learn to trust a God who is there for you in your struggles? As you cope with hard times, you, together with God, are writing a life story. The way you respond to struggles and to God determines its outcome. Are you becoming a strong person of faith who, when others probe beneath the surface, can tell of God's triumph through your tough times? —BQ

Daily Contemplation

Come to God now and talk to him about a struggle you are experiencing. Later in life, how would you like to look back on the way you coped with this difficulty? Give it to God and pray for help in being obedient. Then wait as he turns your struggle into triumph.

DAY 23
Genesis 25:19–34

Jacob and Esau

This is the account of Abraham's son Isaac.

Abraham became the father of Isaac, and Isaac was forty years old when he married Rebekah daughter of Bethuel the Aramean from Paddan Aram and sister of Laban the Aramean.

Isaac prayed to the LORD on behalf of his wife, because she was barren. The LORD answered his prayer, and his wife Rebekah became pregnant. The babies jostled each other within her, and she said, "Why is this happening to me?" So she went to inquire of the LORD.

The LORD said to her,

"Two nations are in your womb,
    and two peoples from within you will be separated;
one people will be stronger than the other,
    and the older will serve the younger."

When the time came for her to give birth, there were twin boys in her womb. The first to come out was red, and his whole body was like a hairy garment; so they named him Esau. After this, his brother came out, with his hand grasping Esau's heel; so he was named Jacob. Isaac was sixty years old when Rebekah gave birth to them.

The boys grew up, and Esau became a skillful hunter, a man of the open country, while Jacob was a quiet man, staying among the tents. Isaac, who had a taste for wild game, loved Esau, but Rebekah loved Jacob.

Once when Jacob was cooking some stew, Esau came in from the open country, famished. He said to Jacob, "Quick, let me have some of that red stew! I'm famished!" (That is why he was also called Edom.)

Jacob replied, "First sell me your birthright."

"Look, I am about to die," Esau said. "What good is the birthright to me?"

But Jacob said, "Swear to me first." So he swore an oath to him, selling his birthright to Jacob.

Then Jacob gave Esau some bread and some lentil stew. He ate and drank, and then got up and left.

So Esau despised his birthright.

God's promise of the birth of a nation marches forward here with the birth of twin boys to Rebekah and Isaac. Already conflict within the womb foreshadows the future for the nations to come from Jacob and Esau (EE-saw). The Israelites, descending from Jacob, and the Edomites, descending from Esau, will fight continuously in the coming decades.

As the two boys are born and grow, God's preference for Jacob over Esau becomes clear. Although Esau, the firstborn, is entitled to the bulk of his father's inheritance, Jacob, by scheming and trickery, foils the law of his day. Early in their story we see them model two ways of handling things of great spiritual importance. Esau, who by tradition would have inherited headship over Isaac's family, "despised his birthright" (v. 34). He treats this first of God's family blessings with contempt, seeing no great value in the spiritual inheritance due him. Esau, most concerned to satisfy his immediate physical appetite, openly reveals a lack of any spiritual hunger.

Jacob, in contrast to his brother, has a great craving for spiritual blessing. But he chooses human tactics of craft and manipulation to pursue his ambition. Although he wants the right things, Jacob wants them in order to serve himself. He focuses on his own gain rather than on God's. Later God will teach Jacob what it means to be a servant used for his higher purposes. —BQ

DAILY CONTEMPLATION

Are you more like Esau, focused on fulfilling immediate desires in the here and now, or like Jacob, focused on pursuing lasting and spiritual gain? Are you seeking spiritual things through God's help or through your own efforts?

Jacob Gets Isaac's Blessing

When Isaac was old and his eyes were so weak that he could no longer see, he called for Esau his older son and said to him, "My son."

"Here I am," he answered.

Isaac said, "I am now an old man and don't know the day of my death. Now then, get your weapons—your quiver and bow—and go out to the open country to hunt some wild game for me. Prepare me the kind of tasty food I like and bring it to me to eat, so that I may give you my blessing before I die."

Now Rebekah was listening as Isaac spoke to his son Esau. When Esau left for the open country to hunt game and bring it back, Rebekah said to her son Jacob, "Look, I overheard your father say to your brother Esau, 'Bring me some game and prepare me some tasty food to eat, so that I may give you my blessing in the presence of the LORD before I die.' Now, my son, listen carefully and do what I tell you: Go out to the flock and bring me two choice young goats, so I can prepare some tasty food for your father, just the way he likes it. Then take it to your father to eat, so that he may give you his blessing before he dies."

Jacob said to Rebekah his mother, "But my brother Esau is a hairy man, and I'm a man with smooth skin. What if my father touches me? I would appear to be tricking him and would bring down a curse on myself rather than a blessing."

His mother said to him, "My son, let the curse fall on me. Just do what I say; go and get them for me."

So he went and got them and brought them to his mother, and she prepared some tasty food, just the way his father liked it. Then Rebekah took the best clothes of Esau her older son, which she had in the house, and put them on her younger son Jacob. She also covered his hands and the smooth part of his neck with the goatskins. Then she handed to her son Jacob the tasty food and the bread she had made.

He went to his father and said, "My father."

"Yes, my son," he answered. "Who is it?"

Jacob said to his father, "I am Esau your firstborn. I have done as you told me. Please sit up and eat some of my game so that you may give me your blessing."

Isaac asked his son, "How did you find it so quickly, my son?"

"The LORD your God gave me success," he replied.

Then Isaac said to Jacob, "Come near so I can touch you, my son, to know whether you really are my son Esau or not."

Jacob went close to his father Isaac, who touched him and said, "The voice is the voice of Jacob, but the hands are the hands of Esau." He did not recognize him, for his hands were hairy like those of his brother Esau; so he blessed him. "Are you really my son Esau?" he asked.

"I am," he replied.

Then he said, "My son, bring me some of your game to eat, so that I may give you my blessing."

Jacob brought it to him and he ate; and he brought some wine and he drank. Then his father Isaac said to him, "Come here, my son, and kiss me."

So he went to him and kissed him. When Isaac caught the smell of his clothes, he blessed him and said,

"Ah, the smell of my son
    is like the smell of a field
    that the LORD has blessed.
May God give you of heaven's dew
    and of earth's richness—
    an abundance of grain and new wine.
May nations serve you
    and peoples bow down to you.
Be lord over your brothers,
    and may the sons of your mother bow down to you.
May those who curse you be cursed
    and those who bless you be blessed."

After Isaac finished blessing him and Jacob had scarcely left his father's presence, his brother Esau came in from hunting. He too prepared some tasty food and brought it to his father. Then he said to him, "My father, sit up and eat some of my game, so that you may give me your blessing."

His father Isaac asked him, "Who are you?"

"I am your son," he answered, "your firstborn, Esau."

Isaac trembled violently and said, "Who was it, then, that hunted game and brought it to me? I ate it just before you came and I blessed him—and indeed he will be blessed!"

When Esau heard his father's words, he burst out with a loud and bitter cry and said to his father, "Bless me—me too, my father!"

But he said, "Your brother came deceitfully and took your blessing."

Esau said, "Isn't he rightly named Jacob? He has deceived me these two times: He took my birthright, and now he's taken my blessing!" Then he asked, "Haven't you reserved any blessing for me?"

Isaac answered Esau, "I have made him lord over you and have made all his relatives his servants, and I have sustained him with grain and new wine. So what can I possibly do for you, my son?"

Esau said to his father, "Do you have only one blessing, my father? Bless me too, my father!" Then Esau wept aloud.

His father Isaac answered him,

"Your dwelling will be
    away from the earth's richness,
    away from the dew of heaven above.
You will live by the sword

and you will serve your brother.
But when you grow restless,
    you will throw his yoke
    from off your neck."

If Abraham is renowned for faith, his grandson Jacob is renowned for treachery. A twin, he was born with one hand grasping the heel of his brother who preceded him, and his parents memorialized that scene by giving him a name meaning "he grasps the heel," or "he deceives."

In ancient times, as we've seen, the oldest son had two clear advantages: He would receive the family birthright and the father's blessing. The *birthright*, like an inheritance document, granted the right to be in charge of the family and its property. Jacob has already taken the birthright from Esau by striking a bargain for food.

For most people of that day, the *blessing* represented a kind of magical power that conveyed prosperity from one generation to another; for Isaac, it represents far more. He is transferring to his son the covenant blessing passed down from his father Abraham, a blessing that will one day produce a whole nation of God's favored people. This chapter records one of Jacob's most elaborate tricks: a ruse to get from his tottery father the blessing that rightfully belongs to his elder brother.

As you read these stories, you might find your sympathies leaning toward poor Esau, who gets tricked out of his blessing and sells his birthright for a hot meal. But the Bible comes down clearly on the side of Jacob. Esau is blamed for "despising his birthright" (Genesis 25:34; Hebrews 12:16).

Jacob, willing to lie, cheat, and steal to get in on God's blessing, would have flunked anyone's morality test (Genesis surely does not commend those tricks—Jacob has to pay dearly for them, as we will read later on). Yet his life offers up an important lesson: God can deal with anyone, no matter how flawed, who passionately pursues him. The story of Jacob gives hope to imperfect people everywhere.   —PY

DAILY CONTEMPLATION

In Old Testament times, names like Isaac ("laughter") or Jacob ("grasper") carried great significance. Do you know what your name means? Does the description fit you? If not, what kind of description would fit you better?

DAY 25   Genesis 27:41–43; 28:10–22

JACOB'S DREAM AT BETHEL

Esau held a grudge against Jacob because of the blessing his father had given him. He said to himself, "The days of mourning for my father are near; then I will kill my brother Jacob."

When Rebekah was told what her older son Esau had said, she sent for her younger son Jacob and said to him, "Your brother Esau is consoling himself with the thought of killing you. Now then, my son, do what I say: Flee at once to my brother Laban in Haran." . . .

Jacob left Beersheba and set out for Haran. When he reached a certain place, he stopped for the night because the sun had set. Taking one of the stones there, he put it under his head and lay down to sleep. He had a dream in which he saw a stairway resting on the earth, with its top reaching to heaven, and the angels of God were ascending and descending on it. There above it stood the LORD, and he said: "I am the LORD, the God of your father Abraham and the God of Isaac. I will give you and your descendants the land on which you are lying. Your descendants will be like the dust of the earth, and you will spread out to the west and to the east, to the north and to the south. All peoples on earth will be blessed through you and your offspring. I am with you and will watch over you wherever you go, and I will bring you back to this land. I will not leave you until I have done what I have promised you."

When Jacob awoke from his sleep, he thought, "Surely the LORD is in this place, and I was not aware of it." He was afraid and said, "How awesome is this place! This is none other than the house of God; this is the gate of heaven."

Early the next morning Jacob took the stone he had placed under his head and set it up as a pillar and poured oil on top of it. He called that place Bethel, though the city used to be called Luz.

Then Jacob made a vow, saying, "If God will be with me and will watch over me on this journey I am taking and will give me food to eat and clothes to wear so that I return safely to my father's house, then the LORD will be my God and this stone that I have set up as a pillar will be God's house, and of all that you give me I will give you a tenth."

Jacob and Rebekah, by scheming, won the birthright and blessing for Jacob. But in doing so, they won for themselves something God would have given Jacob anyway, and lost much in the process. Now, as a consequence of Jacob's deception, he must flee his home to avoid his brother's wrath. Jacob will have difficult years ahead, and Rebekah will never see him again.

Despite Jacob's selfish ways, God provides a special vision at Bethel (BETH-uhl) to reassure him that God will go with him, will never leave him, and will fulfill the promises he has made to Abraham, Isaac, and now to Jacob. Jacob's response establishes a pattern that Jews and believers since have followed as a response to God's faithfulness and grace.

Prior to this vision, Jacob has viewed God as belonging to his fathers. Now, for the first time, Jacob considers that "the LORD will be my God" (v. 21). Jacob also recognizes at Bethel that all he has belongs to God. He pledges to give back ten percent of his belongings and in this way bless God and others.

Jacob is so moved by God's word to him in his vision at Bethel that he sets stones in place to memorialize his visitation from God. He thus creates a tradition for believers, affirming the importance of memorials, or milestones—physical reminders of

God's work in our lives. When we make these memorials—perhaps planting a tree, creating a wall hanging, or keeping a journal—we create a tangible memory of God's presence and his personal care for us. —BQ

DAILY CONTEMPLATION

Can you recall a time when God made one of his promises very clear to you? What kind of memorial have you made to commemorate this promise?

DAY 26
Genesis 29:1–30

JACOB MARRIES LEAH AND RACHEL

Then Jacob continued on his journey and came to the land of the eastern peoples. There he saw a well in the field, with three flocks of sheep lying near it because the flocks were watered from that well. The stone over the mouth of the well was large. When all the flocks were gathered there, the shepherds would roll the stone away from the well's mouth and water the sheep. Then they would return the stone to its place over the mouth of the well.

Jacob asked the shepherds, "My brothers, where are you from?"

"We're from Haran," they replied.

He said to them, "Do you know Laban, Nahor's grandson?"

"Yes, we know him," they answered.

Then Jacob asked them, "Is he well?"

"Yes, he is," they said, "and here comes his daughter Rachel with the sheep."

"Look," he said, "the sun is still high; it is not time for the flocks to be gathered. Water the sheep and take them back to pasture."

"We can't," they replied, "until all the flocks are gathered and the stone has been rolled away from the mouth of the well. Then we will water the sheep."

While he was still talking with them, Rachel came with her father's sheep, for she was a shepherdess. When Jacob saw Rachel daughter of Laban, his mother's brother, and Laban's sheep, he went over and rolled the stone away from the mouth of the well and watered his uncle's sheep. Then Jacob kissed Rachel and began to weep aloud. He had told Rachel that he was a relative of her father and a son of Rebekah. So she ran and told her father.

As soon as Laban heard the news about Jacob, his sister's son, he hurried to meet him. He embraced him and kissed him and brought him to his home, and there Jacob told him all these things. Then Laban said to him, "You are my own flesh and blood."

After Jacob had stayed with him for a whole month, Laban said to him, "Just because you are a relative of mine, should you work for me for nothing? Tell me what your wages should be."

Now Laban had two daughters; the name of the older was Leah, and the name of the younger was Rachel. Leah had weak eyes, but Rachel was lovely in form, and beautiful. Jacob was in love with Rachel and said, "I'll work for you seven years in return for your younger daughter Rachel."

Laban said, "It's better that I give her to you than to some other man. Stay here with me." So Jacob served seven years to get Rachel, but they seemed like only a few days to him because of his love for her.

Then Jacob said to Laban, "Give me my wife. My time is completed, and I want to lie with her."

So Laban brought together all the people of the place and gave a feast. But when evening came, he took his daughter Leah and gave her to Jacob, and Jacob lay with her. And Laban gave his servant girl Zilpah to his daughter as her maidservant.

When morning came, there was Leah! So Jacob said to Laban, "What is this you have done to me? I served you for Rachel, didn't I? Why have you deceived me?"

Laban replied, "It is not our custom here to give the younger daughter in marriage before the older one. Finish this daughter's bridal week; then we will give you the younger one also, in return for another seven years of work."

And Jacob did so. He finished the week with Leah, and then Laban gave him his daughter Rachel to be his wife. Laban gave his servant girl Bilhah to his daughter Rachel as her maidservant. Jacob lay with Rachel also, and he loved Rachel more than Leah. And he worked for Laban another seven years.

What goes around comes around." Jacob waited only seven years to experience the justice reflected in this statement. After deceiving his father and taking by dishonesty what didn't belong to him, Jacob is himself tricked into taking as a wife someone he doesn't want. If he had waited on God to provide, Jacob could have received the birthright and blessing through God's provision; he may also have received Rachel without enduring deception and hurting Leah in the process. Yet Jacob's selfishness and lack of trust bring about painful consequences. God doesn't leave Jacob, but he teaches him by allowing deception to reverberate in his own life.

This passage does show how Jacob has grown. Able to accept the circumstances and finish what he's begun, Jacob yields to God's discipline through the hand of Laban (LAY-buhn). As he does so, he learns to look to God for help, rather than to himself. —BQ

DAILY CONTEMPLATION

What circumstances in your life are difficult? Have you brought any of them upon yourself? How are you looking to God to take you through them?

JACOB'S CHILDREN

When the LORD saw that Leah was not loved, he opened her womb, but Rachel was barren. Leah became pregnant and gave birth to a son. She named him Reuben, for she said, "It is because the LORD has seen my misery. Surely my husband will love me now."

She conceived again, and when she gave birth to a son she said, "Because the LORD heard that I am not loved, he gave me this one too." So she named him Simeon.

Again she conceived, and when she gave birth to a son she said, "Now at last my husband will become attached to me, because I have borne him three sons." So he was named Levi.

She conceived again, and when she gave birth to a son she said, "This time I will praise the LORD." So she named him Judah. Then she stopped having children.

When Rachel saw that she was not bearing Jacob any children, she became jealous of her sister. So she said to Jacob, "Give me children, or I'll die!"

Jacob became angry with her and said, "Am I in the place of God, who has kept you from having children?"

Then she said, "Here is Bilhah, my maidservant. Sleep with her so that she can bear children for me and that through her I too can build a family."

So she gave him her servant Bilhah as a wife. Jacob slept with her, and she became pregnant and bore him a son. Then Rachel said, "God has vindicated me; he has listened to my plea and given me a son." Because of this she named him Dan.

Rachel's servant Bilhah conceived again and bore Jacob a second son. Then Rachel said, "I have had a great struggle with my sister, and I have won." So she named him Naphtali.

When Leah saw that she had stopped having children, she took her maidservant Zilpah and gave her to Jacob as a wife. Leah's servant Zilpah bore Jacob a son. Then Leah said, "What good fortune!" So she named him Gad.

Leah's servant Zilpah bore Jacob a second son. Then Leah said, "How happy I am! The women will call me happy." So she named him Asher.

During wheat harvest, Reuben went out into the fields and found some mandrake plants, which he brought to his mother Leah. Rachel said to Leah, "Please give me some of your son's mandrakes."

But she said to her, "Wasn't it enough that you took away my husband? Will you take my son's mandrakes too?"

"Very well," Rachel said, "he can sleep with you tonight in return for your son's mandrakes."

So when Jacob came in from the fields that evening, Leah went out to meet him. "You must sleep with me," she said. "I have hired you with my son's mandrakes." So he slept with her that night.

God listened to Leah, and she became pregnant and bore Jacob a fifth son. Then Leah said, "God has rewarded me for giving my maidservant to my husband." So she named him Issachar.

Leah conceived again and bore Jacob a sixth son. Then Leah said, "God has presented me with a precious gift. This time my husband will treat me with honor, because I have borne him six sons." So she named him Zebulun.

Some time later she gave birth to a daughter and named her Dinah.

Then God remembered Rachel; he listened to her and opened her womb. She became pregnant and gave birth to a son and said, "God has taken away my disgrace." She named him Joseph, and said, "May the LORD add to me another son."

After Rachel gave birth to Joseph, Jacob said to Laban, "Send me on my way so I can go back to my own homeland. Give me my wives and children, for whom I have served you, and I will be on my way. You know how much work I've done for you."

But Laban said to him, "If I have found favor in your eyes, please stay. I have learned by divination that the LORD has blessed me because of you." He added, "Name your wages, and I will pay them."

Jacob said to him, "You know how I have worked for you and how your livestock has fared under my care. The little you had before I came has increased greatly, and the LORD has blessed you wherever I have been. But now, when may I do something for my own household?"

"What shall I give you?" he asked.

"Don't give me anything," Jacob replied. "But if you will do this one thing for me, I will go on tending your flocks and watching over them: Let me go through all your flocks today and remove from them every speckled or spotted sheep, every dark-colored lamb and every spotted or speckled goat. They will be my wages. And my honesty will testify for me in the future, whenever you check on the wages you have paid me. Any goat in my possession that is not speckled or spotted, or any lamb that is not dark-colored, will be considered stolen."

"Agreed," said Laban. "Let it be as you have said."

Earlier chapters of Genesis told the stories of both Sarah's and Rebekah's battle with barrenness. Rachel's story reiterates God's power as Lifegiver, opener of the womb. Neither maidservants nor mandrakes, superstitiously thought to induce pregnancy, could alter a woman's barren state. God, however, bestows fertility to all these women, and they learn it is to him their hopes and prayers must be directed.

God also shows his great love and compassion for those who are unloved. Jacob clearly cares more deeply for Rachel than for Leah, and despite Leah's hopes to change his affections through having children, she will live the rest of her life in Rachel's shadow. Yet God cares about Leah's pain and blesses her with many sons. He exalts her by making her the first mother and by giving her the kingly tribe of Judah and the priestly tribe of Levi, among others, as her descendants.

Each of the twelve sons of Jacob, born to Leah, Rachel (who in Genesis 35 gives birth to Jacob's youngest son, Benjamin), Bilhah (BIL-hah), and Zilpah (ZIL-puh), will go on to head the twelve tribes of Israel. Jesus, the Messiah, will descend from the tribe of Judah, from the lineage of Leah—one rejected by man, as Christ would be also, yet loved dearly by God. —BQ

DAY 28 Reflection

GOD SHINING FROM THE SHADOWS

Genesis paints a rather unflattering picture of the third of Israel's patriarchs, or fathers. Although the first patriarchs, Abraham and Isaac, were human and made some mistakes, Jacob tops them both.

As a young man, greedy and conniving, he takes advantage of his brother and then deceives his dying father. Jacob must go on the run to escape his brother's anger; later he neglects one of his two wives, fueling the rivalry between them. Jacob hardly models for us the "spiritual giant" we would like to envision when we think of the renowned fathers of our faith.

As we look at the panorama of Jacob's life to this point, however, we see again that his story is really about God, not him. Looming in the background of Jacob's early treachery, we see a God who has higher purposes, who works out his plan despite Jacob's insistence on doing it himself. As Jacob flees, we see God in the shadows before him and surrounding him, even coming in a dream to bring comfort, reminding Jacob of the promises God still intends to keep. Then, as Jacob marries not one wife but two, we see God filling in the gaps, giving love where love is lacking.

Across the canvas of Jacob's life we see God building a nation through an inadequate man, an unloved woman, and a woman who long felt abandoned by God. God doesn't need perfect people to do the things he has planned. With supreme irony, he chooses a flawed, self-centered man to carry on the lifeline of a nation that will eventually produce the perfect Messiah, who will offer a way for all sinful people to come back to God.

Jacob's mural looks a lot like our own. Each believer is chosen by God, and once we are chosen, nothing can change God's love for us. No mistake, no matter how big, can alter the way God cares for us. And like Jacob, as we walk with God and listen to him, we gradually find our heart and our will looking more like his. —BQ

Jacob Flees from Laban

Jacob heard that Laban's sons were saying, "Jacob has taken everything our father owned and has gained all this wealth from what belonged to our father." And Jacob noticed that Laban's attitude toward him was not what it had been.

Then the LORD said to Jacob, "Go back to the land of your fathers and to your relatives, and I will be with you."

So Jacob sent word to Rachel and Leah to come out to the fields where his flocks were. He said to them, "I see that your father's attitude toward me is not what it was before, but the God of my father has been with me. You know that I've worked for your father with all my strength, yet your father has cheated me by changing my wages ten times. However, God has not allowed him to harm me. If he said, 'The speckled ones will be your wages,' then all the flocks gave birth to speckled young; and if he said, 'The streaked ones will be your wages,' then all the flocks bore streaked young. So God has taken away your father's livestock and has given them to me.

"In breeding season I once had a dream in which I looked up and saw that the male goats mating with the flock were streaked, speckled or spotted. The angel of God said to me in the dream, 'Jacob.' I answered, 'Here I am.' And he said, 'Look up and see that all the male goats mating with the flock are streaked, speckled or spotted, for I have seen all that Laban has been doing to you. I am the God of Bethel, where you anointed a pillar and where you made a vow to me. Now leave this land at once and go back to your native land.'"

Then Rachel and Leah replied, "Do we still have any share in the inheritance of our father's estate? Does he not regard us as foreigners? Not only has he sold us, but he has used up what was paid for us. Surely all the wealth that God took away from our father belongs to us and our children. So do whatever God has told you."

Then Jacob put his children and his wives on camels, and he drove all his livestock ahead of him, along with all the goods he had accumulated in Paddan Aram, to go to his father Isaac in the land of Canaan.

When Laban had gone to shear his sheep, Rachel stole her father's household gods. Moreover, Jacob deceived Laban the Aramean by not telling him he was running away. So he fled with all he had, and crossing the River, he headed for the hill country of Gilead.

God finally calls Jacob back to his own land. Jacob leaves Laban for some of the same reasons he originally came—he flees to escape the animosity directed toward him, this time from Laban and his sons. Jacob has good reason to leave, for he and his wives have been cheated by Laban. But more importantly, it is God's time for Jacob to return home.

A wordplay in the original Hebrew text stresses that while Jacob "stole away," Rachel stole the gods of her father. Jacob's dishonesty now spreads to his wife. In ancient days the possession of a family's gods was often tied to the rights of inheritance. Perhaps in taking the gods, Rachel wants to ensure that her family will inherit Laban's estate. In any case, Laban will pursue Jacob and his family, seeking to discover why they secretly left and took with them the gods he relies on for protection.   —BQ

DAILY CONTEMPLATION

Where do you turn for protection? Are you inclined, like Jacob, to turn to your own ways of protecting yourself? Or do you, like Laban and Rachel, turn to things in your life for protection? How often do you ask God to protect you?

DAY 30   Genesis 31:22–55

LABAN PURSUES JACOB

On the third day Laban was told that Jacob had fled. Taking his relatives with him, he pursued Jacob for seven days and caught up with him in the hill country of Gilead. Then God came to Laban the Aramean in a dream at night and said to him, "Be careful not to say anything to Jacob, either good or bad."

Jacob had pitched his tent in the hill country of Gilead when Laban overtook him, and Laban and his relatives camped there too. Then Laban said to Jacob, "What have you done? You've deceived me, and you've carried off my daughters like captives in war. Why did you run off secretly and deceive me? Why didn't you tell me, so I could send you away with joy and singing to the music of tambourines and harps? You didn't even let me kiss my grandchildren and my daughters good-by. You have done a foolish thing. I have the power to harm you; but last night the God of your father said to me, 'Be careful not to say anything to Jacob, either good or bad.' Now you have gone off because you longed to return to your father's house. But why did you steal my gods?"

Jacob answered Laban, "I was afraid, because I thought you would take your daughters away from me by force. But if you find anyone who has your gods, he shall not live. In the presence of our relatives, see for yourself whether there is anything of yours here with me; and if so, take it." Now Jacob did not know that Rachel had stolen the gods.

So Laban went into Jacob's tent and into Leah's tent and into the tent of the two maidservants, but he found nothing. After he came out of Leah's tent, he entered Rachel's tent. Now Rachel had taken the household gods and put them inside her camel's saddle and was sitting on them. Laban searched through everything in the tent but found nothing.

Rachel said to her father, "Don't be angry, my lord, that I cannot stand up in your presence; I'm having my period." So he searched but could not find the household gods.

Jacob was angry and took Laban to task. "What is my crime?" he asked Laban. "What sin have I committed that you hunt me down? Now that you have searched through all my goods, what have you found that belongs to your household? Put it here in front of your relatives and mine, and let them judge between the two of us.

"I have been with you for twenty years now. Your sheep and goats have not miscarried, nor have I eaten rams from your flocks. I did not bring you animals torn by wild beasts; I bore the loss myself. And you demanded payment from me for whatever was stolen by day or night. This was my situation: The heat consumed me in the daytime and the cold at night, and sleep fled from my eyes. It was like this for the twenty years I was in your household. I worked for you fourteen years for your two daughters and six years for your flocks, and you changed my wages ten times. If the God of my father, the God of Abraham and the Fear of Isaac, had not been with me, you would surely have sent me away empty-handed. But God has seen my hardship and the toil of my hands, and last night he rebuked you."

Laban answered Jacob, "The women are my daughters, the children are my children, and the flocks are my flocks. All you see is mine. Yet what can I do today about these daughters of mine, or about the children they have borne? Come now, let's make a covenant, you and I, and let it serve as a witness between us."

So Jacob took a stone and set it up as a pillar. He said to his relatives, "Gather some stones." So they took stones and piled them in a heap, and they ate there by the heap. Laban called it Jegar Sahadutha, and Jacob called it Galeed.

Laban said, "This heap is a witness between you and me today." That is why it was called Galeed. It was also called Mizpah, because he said, "May the LORD keep watch between you and me when we are away from each other. If you mistreat my daughters or if you take any wives besides my daughters, even though no one is with us, remember that God is a witness between you and me."

Laban also said to Jacob, "Here is this heap, and here is this pillar I have set up between you and me. This heap is a witness, and this pillar is a witness, that I will not go past this heap to your side to harm you and that you will not go past this heap and pillar to my side to harm me. May the God of Abraham and the God of Nahor, the God of their father, judge between us."

So Jacob took an oath in the name of the Fear of his father Isaac. He offered a sacrifice there in the hill country and invited his relatives to a meal. After they had eaten, they spent the night there.

Early the next morning Laban kissed his grandchildren and his daughters and blessed them. Then he left and returned home.

Just as Jacob has done to his own father, Rachel now lies to her father and successfully deceives him. She lies in order to protect useless gods and an inheritance she will never need. Jacob's character of deception is carried on by his new family. For his part, Laban has cheated his daughters and Jacob and now seems most concerned for his own safety, suggesting a treaty to prevent future problems.

God has spoken separately to Jacob and Laban to bring about their separation. Despite the selfish ways of both men, God protects Jacob from Laban's animosity and ensures that Jacob will reach his homeland safely. Jacob's journeying will become a model for Israel later when the nation is led out of captivity in Egypt back to Jacob's homeland of Canaan. God will deliver and protect the nation of Israel despite its imperfections, just as he is doing for Jacob.

The Israelites and eventually modern-day generations of believers will repeat again and again a pattern similar to Jacob's. Rather than trusting in God's ways, we follow our own ways and seek what we want by our own methods. We will suffer consequences; nevertheless, we will find that despite our selfish wanderings, God never leaves us.

—BQ

DAILY CONTEMPLATION

Do you reflect any character qualities of your family? What qualities are you passing on to others?

DAY 31 Genesis 32:1–21

JACOB PREPARES TO MEET ESAU

Jacob also went on his way, and the angels of God met him. When Jacob saw them, he said, "This is the camp of God!" So he named that place Mahanaim.

Jacob sent messengers ahead of him to his brother Esau in the land of Seir, the country of Edom. He instructed them: "This is what you are to say to my master Esau: 'Your servant Jacob says, I have been staying with Laban and have remained there till now. I have cattle and donkeys, sheep and goats, menservants and maidservants. Now I am sending this message to my lord, that I may find favor in your eyes.'"

When the messengers returned to Jacob, they said, "We went to your brother Esau, and now he is coming to meet you, and four hundred men are with him."

In great fear and distress Jacob divided the people who were with him into two groups, and the flocks and herds and camels as well. He thought, "If Esau comes and attacks one group, the group that is left may escape."

Then Jacob prayed, "O God of my father Abraham, God of my father Isaac, O LORD, who said to me, 'Go back to your country and your relatives, and I will make you prosper,' I am unworthy of all the kindness and faithfulness you have shown your servant. I had only my staff when I crossed this Jordan, but now I have become two groups. Save me, I pray, from the hand of my brother

Esau, for I am afraid he will come and attack me, and also the mothers with their children. But you have said, 'I will surely make you prosper and will make your descendants like the sand of the sea, which cannot be counted.'"

He spent the night there, and from what he had with him he selected a gift for his brother Esau: two hundred female goats and twenty male goats, two hundred ewes and twenty rams, thirty female camels with their young, forty cows and ten bulls, and twenty female donkeys and ten male donkeys. He put them in the care of his servants, each herd by itself, and said to his servants, "Go ahead of me, and keep some space between the herds."

He instructed the one in the lead: "When my brother Esau meets you and asks, 'To whom do you belong, and where are you going, and who owns all these animals in front of you?' then you are to say, 'They belong to your servant Jacob. They are a gift sent to my lord Esau, and he is coming behind us.'"

He also instructed the second, the third and all the others who followed the herds: "You are to say the same thing to Esau when you meet him. And be sure to say, 'Your servant Jacob is coming behind us.'" For he thought, "I will pacify him with these gifts I am sending on ahead; later, when I see him, perhaps he will receive me." So Jacob's gifts went on ahead of him, but he himself spent the night in the camp.

Jacob's deceptions have marked him as an untrustworthy, dishonest man. But in this passage we see once more that despite Jacob's character flaws, God is ultimately in charge of his future. We also glimpse a place of honesty deep inside Jacob. He knows he is "unworthy of all the kindness and faithfulness" God has shown him (v. 10). Coming home and facing pain from the past, Jacob must reach to the core of himself and his relationship with God to find the answers to his crisis.

Jacob's prayer is the prayer of every believer in a fearful situation: "Save me, I pray, . . . for I am afraid" (v. 11). This is the honesty God awaits, the prayer that releases God to do for us better than we could do for ourselves.   —BQ

DAILY CONTEMPLATION

What are you afraid of today? Have you talked to God about your fear?

DAY 32   Genesis 32:22–32

JACOB WRESTLES WITH GOD

That night Jacob got up and took his two wives, his two maidservants and his eleven sons and crossed the ford of the Jabbok. After he had sent them across the stream, he sent over all his possessions. So Jacob was left alone, and a man wrestled with him till daybreak. When the man saw that he could not overpower him, he touched the socket of Jacob's hip so that his hip was wrenched as he wrestled with the man. Then the man said, "Let me go, for it is daybreak."

But Jacob replied, "I will not let you go unless you bless me."

The man asked him, "What is your name?"

"Jacob," he answered.

Then the man said, "Your name will no longer be Jacob, but Israel, because you have struggled with God and with men and have overcome."

Jacob said, "Please tell me your name."

But he replied, "Why do you ask my name?" Then he blessed him there.

So Jacob called the place Peniel, saying, "It is because I saw God face to face, and yet my life was spared."

The sun rose above him as he passed Peniel, and he was limping because of his hip. Therefore to this day the Israelites do not eat the tendon attached to the socket of the hip, because the socket of Jacob's hip was touched near the tendon.

In Romans 9, the apostle Paul uses Jacob as an example of God's grace. Why would God use a cheating rascal like Jacob to carry out his plan of building a holy nation? "I will have mercy on whom I have mercy, and I will have compassion on whom I have compassion" (v. 15) is God's answer. Paul loved the word *grace*—it means "an undeserved gift"—because he had spent the first part of his life fighting against God's will, and yet God loved him anyway.

Two scenes in Jacob's life especially show grace at work. At two critical moments, just as he was about to lose heart, God met him in dramatic personal encounters.

The first time, Jacob was crossing a desert alone as a fugitive. Having cheated his brother out of the family birthright, he was running away from Esau and his murderous threats. Yet God came to him with bright promises, not the reproaches he deserved. Jacob had not sought God; rather, God sought him. At that tender moment, God confirmed that all the blessings he had promised Abraham would apply to Jacob, disgraced runaway.

The next encounter occurs several decades later, the night before Jacob is to attempt reconciliation with Esau. In the intervening years, Jacob has learned many hard lessons, but as he thinks about the rendezvous he trembles in fear. After pleading with God to keep his promises, he receives in response a supernatural encounter as strange as any in the Bible. Jacob, the grasper, has met a worthy opponent at last: he wrestles with God himself. After this strange night, Jacob will always walk with a limp, a permanent reminder of the struggle.

Along the way, Jacob picks up a new name, "Israel," a name that puts the final seal of God's grace on him. Jacob the cheat becomes the namesake of God's chosen people, the "Israelites." —PY

DAILY CONTEMPLATION

Not many people have such dramatic encounters with God. How has God met you at a time of need?

JACOB MEETS ESAU

Jacob looked up and there was Esau, coming with his four hundred men; so he divided the children among Leah, Rachel and the two maidservants. He put the maidservants and their children in front, Leah and her children next, and Rachel and Joseph in the rear. He himself went on ahead and bowed down to the ground seven times as he approached his brother.

But Esau ran to meet Jacob and embraced him; he threw his arms around his neck and kissed him. And they wept. Then Esau looked up and saw the women and children. "Who are these with you?" he asked.

Jacob answered, "They are the children God has graciously given your servant."

Then the maidservants and their children approached and bowed down. Next, Leah and her children came and bowed down. Last of all came Joseph and Rachel, and they too bowed down.

Esau asked, "What do you mean by all these droves I met?"

"To find favor in your eyes, my lord," he said.

But Esau said, "I already have plenty, my brother. Keep what you have for yourself."

"No, please!" said Jacob. "If I have found favor in your eyes, accept this gift from me. For to see your face is like seeing the face of God, now that you have received me favorably. Please accept the present that was brought to you, for God has been gracious to me and I have all I need." And because Jacob insisted, Esau accepted it.

Then Esau said, "Let us be on our way; I'll accompany you."

But Jacob said to him, "My lord knows that the children are tender and that I must care for the ewes and cows that are nursing their young. If they are driven hard just one day, all the animals will die. So let my lord go on ahead of his servant, while I move along slowly at the pace of the droves before me and that of the children, until I come to my lord in Seir."

Esau said, "Then let me leave some of my men with you."

"But why do that?" Jacob asked. "Just let me find favor in the eyes of my lord."

So that day Esau started on his way back to Seir. Jacob, however, went to Succoth, where he built a place for himself and made shelters for his livestock. That is why the place is called Succoth.

After Jacob came from Paddan Aram, he arrived safely at the city of Shechem in Canaan and camped within sight of the city. For a hundred pieces of silver, he bought from the sons of Hamor, the father of Shechem, the plot of ground where he pitched his tent. There he set up an altar and called it El Elohe Israel.

God answers Jacob's prayer for help in a way beyond Jacob's imagining. Not only does Esau not harm his brother; he runs open-armed to meet him. God has changed the hearts of both brothers: Esau now wants reconciliation more than revenge, and Jacob has gained humility and generosity in his time away from Esau.

In this long-awaited meeting, Jacob gets a clearer picture of the face of God than he has ever seen before. For so long Jacob wrestled with God, insisting on his own way in the course of his life. In a final wrestling match, God showed Jacob his power and once again bestowed blessing. Now, as Jacob comes home to a sibling who should hate him, he instead sees God in the face of this weeping, eager brother.

God will give believers this same picture of himself several times throughout the Bible. One who should be angry and finished with forgiveness, such as Esau, instead welcomes back another who deserves reproach. They are all pictures of God's unrelenting love for us, his children. May we, like Jacob, have the eyes to see.   —BQ

DAILY CONTEMPLATION

When has God shown you himself through the unexpected love of another person?

DAY 34 Genesis 35:1–15

JACOB RETURNS TO BETHEL

Then God said to Jacob, "Go up to Bethel and settle there, and build an altar there to God, who appeared to you when you were fleeing from your brother Esau."

So Jacob said to his household and to all who were with him, "Get rid of the foreign gods you have with you, and purify yourselves and change your clothes. Then come, let us go up to Bethel, where I will build an altar to God, who answered me in the day of my distress and who has been with me wherever I have gone." So they gave Jacob all the foreign gods they had and the rings in their ears, and Jacob buried them under the oak at Shechem. Then they set out, and the terror of God fell upon the towns all around them so that no one pursued them.

Jacob and all the people with him came to Luz (that is, Bethel) in the land of Canaan. There he built an altar, and he called the place El Bethel, because it was there that God revealed himself to him when he was fleeing from his brother.

Now Deborah, Rebekah's nurse, died and was buried under the oak below Bethel. So it was named Allon Bacuth.

After Jacob returned from Paddan Aram, God appeared to him again and blessed him. God said to him, "Your name is Jacob, but you will no longer be called Jacob; your name will be Israel." So he named him Israel.

And God said to him, "I am God Almighty; be fruitful and increase in number. A nation and a community of nations will come from you, and kings will come from your body. The land I gave to Abraham and Isaac I also give to you, and I will give this land to your descendants after you." Then God went up from him at the place where he had talked with him.

Jacob set up a stone pillar at the place where God had talked with him, and he poured out a drink offering on it; he also poured oil on it. Jacob called the place where God had talked with him Bethel.

In a sense, Jacob has come full circle. He has made mistakes, gone his own way, suffered due to his actions, and seen God's grace extended time and again to bring him back home. Now he returns to a familiar place of safety, for the continued growth of the nation God has promised.

God calls Jacob back to Bethel for Jacob to recall the journey he has traveled and to remember God's role in his life. After all Jacob has seen and experienced, he must pass on to his family the heritage of a God who has shown himself true and faithful.

As Jacob begins the journey, he recalls the vows he made to God at Bethel many years ago. He remembers the loyalty he promised God and sees his family now allowing idols to share a place with God. They must rid themselves of these objects of trust and attention. They must become pure before entering a place dedicated to the Lord.

Once again God speaks to Jacob at Bethel. Again he declares that he will fulfill what he has promised. Although Jacob has not always been faithful, God has remained faithful to him. God's promise at Bethel has not changed.   —BQ

DAILY CONTEMPLATION

Where are you in your journey with God? Are you insisting on your own way? Are you experiencing God's grace? Are you seeing some of God's promises fulfilled?

DAY 35   Reflection

WRESTLING WITH GOD

What to make of ancient Bible stories about a man who went around lying to people and then spent a dark night wrestling on a riverbank with a figure who turned out to be God? We find in these accounts some striking truths about the love of God for even the most undeserving of people. We also learn something about the process of living alongside our God, who has a plan for our lives and the power to implement it.

The image of wrestling fits well the relationship many of us have with God throughout much of our lives. Like Jacob, we get acquainted with God and make some tentative pledges to follow him. Then we carry on with life, doing whatever seems right at the moment to clear the path we've chosen for ourselves. We may consult God occasionally, sometimes in sincerity and sometimes simply going through the motions. But then we charge ahead again, like strong-willed children, insisting on doing things our way. We struggle with God again and again, not yet mature enough to realize the nature of our Opponent, and more, the nature of his victory, would we only give up the fight.

God will not force himself on us. He will let the struggle go on if we insist. Finally, if we are truly blessed, he may touch us on the hip and reveal to us the truth of our weakness. Then we realize that God has always been the winner. And we know that only when God wins can we win, too. That first shy act of acquaintance with God, those first tentative pledges we made, may have been weak, but they set in motion God's loving act of replacing our weakness with his strength.

We may wrestle with God for a while, but in time we'll stop the struggle and say to God, as Jacob did, "I will not let you go." We'll echo the words of the apostle Paul, from later in the Bible: "When I am weak, then I am strong" (2 Corinthians 12:10). —BQ

DAILY CONTEMPLATION

Are you wrestling with God? What are you trying to achieve? Ask God to help you understand yourself and what lies at the heart of your desires. Ask God to help you trust his plan and rely on his strength.

DAY 36

Genesis 37:1–36

JOSEPH'S DREAMS

Jacob lived in the land where his father had stayed, the land of Canaan. This is the account of Jacob.

Joseph, a young man of seventeen, was tending the flocks with his brothers, the sons of Bilhah and the sons of Zilpah, his father's wives, and he brought their father a bad report about them.

Now Israel loved Joseph more than any of his other sons, because he had been born to him in his old age; and he made a richly ornamented robe for him. When his brothers saw that their father loved him more than any of them, they hated him and could not speak a kind word to him.

Joseph had a dream, and when he told it to his brothers, they hated him all the more. He said to them, "Listen to this dream I had: We were binding sheaves of grain out in the field when suddenly my sheaf rose and stood upright, while your sheaves gathered around mine and bowed down to it."

His brothers said to him, "Do you intend to reign over us? Will you actually rule us?" And they hated him all the more because of his dream and what he had said.

Then he had another dream, and he told it to his brothers. "Listen," he said, "I had another dream, and this time the sun and moon and eleven stars were bowing down to me."

When he told his father as well as his brothers, his father rebuked him and said, "What is this dream you had? Will your mother and I and your brothers actually come and bow down to the ground before you?" His brothers were jealous of him, but his father kept the matter in mind.

Now his brothers had gone to graze their father's flocks near Shechem, and Israel said to Joseph, "As you know, your brothers are grazing the flocks near Shechem. Come, I am going to send you to them."

"Very well," he replied.

So he said to him, "Go and see if all is well with your brothers and with the flocks, and bring word back to me." Then he sent him off from the Valley of Hebron.

When Joseph arrived at Shechem, a man found him wandering around in the fields and asked him, "What are you looking for?"

He replied, "I'm looking for my brothers. Can you tell me where they are grazing their flocks?"

"They have moved on from here," the man answered. "I heard them say, 'Let's go to Dothan.'"

So Joseph went after his brothers and found them near Dothan. But they saw him in the distance, and before he reached them, they plotted to kill him.

"Here comes that dreamer!" they said to each other. "Come now, let's kill him and throw him into one of these cisterns and say that a ferocious animal devoured him. Then we'll see what comes of his dreams."

When Reuben heard this, he tried to rescue him from their hands. "Let's not take his life," he said. "Don't shed any blood. Throw him into this cistern here in the desert, but don't lay a hand on him." Reuben said this to rescue him from them and take him back to his father.

So when Joseph came to his brothers, they stripped him of his robe—the richly ornamented robe he was wearing—and they took him and threw him into the cistern. Now the cistern was empty; there was no water in it.

As they sat down to eat their meal, they looked up and saw a caravan of Ishmaelites coming from Gilead. Their camels were loaded with spices, balm and myrrh, and they were on their way to take them down to Egypt.

Judah said to his brothers, "What will we gain if we kill our brother and cover up his blood? Come, let's sell him to the Ishmaelites and not lay our hands on him; after all, he is our brother, our own flesh and blood." His brothers agreed.

So when the Midianite merchants came by, his brothers pulled Joseph up out of the cistern and sold him for twenty shekels of silver to the Ishmaelites, who took him to Egypt.

When Reuben returned to the cistern and saw that Joseph was not there, he tore his clothes. He went back to his brothers and said, "The boy isn't there! Where can I turn now?"

Then they got Joseph's robe, slaughtered a goat and dipped the robe in the blood. They took the ornamented robe back to their father and said, "We found this. Examine it to see whether it is your son's robe."

He recognized it and said, "It is my son's robe! Some ferocious animal has devoured him. Joseph has surely been torn to pieces."

Then Jacob tore his clothes, put on sackcloth and mourned for his son many days. All his sons and daughters came to comfort him, but he refused to be comforted. "No," he said, "in mourning will I go down to the grave to my son." So his father wept for him.

Meanwhile, the Midianites sold Joseph in Egypt to Potiphar, one of Pharaoh's officials, the captain of the guard.

Nobody fights like brothers and sisters—family closeness seems to rub salt in the wounds of relationships. Genesis tells of several great brotherly rivalries: Cain and Abel, Isaac and his half brother Ishmael, Jacob and Esau. In this last story, Joseph's story, eleven brothers line up against one.

The pace of Genesis slows down when it gets to Joseph, with the book devoting far more attention to his life story than anyone else's. Little wonder—Joseph lived one of the great adventure stories of history. A stowaway slave, and condemned prisoner, he rose to become the number two ruler of the greatest empire on earth. The saga all begins with the near-tragic event recorded in this chapter.

As his father's acknowledged favorite, Joseph seems curiously insensitive to the potential of his brothers' jealousy. He may even be flaunting status by relating two dreams of his family bowing down to him. At the least, he alienates his brothers so strongly that they decide to take revenge.

The brothers' first plan involves murder. As a last-second thought, they sell Joseph instead to traveling merchants on their way to Egypt. Neither the brothers nor Joseph's grieving father, Jacob—he swallows their story of a wild animal attack—ever expect to see him again. God, however, has other plans. Joseph's strange dreams, which got him into so much trouble at home, will prove to be his salvation in the faraway land of Egypt.   —PY

DAILY CONTEMPLATION

Have you ever experienced God bringing good out of what at first seemed like a disaster?

DAY 37   Genesis 39:1–23

JOSEPH AND POTIPHAR'S WIFE

Now Joseph had been taken down to Egypt. Potiphar, an Egyptian who was one of Pharaoh's officials, the captain of the guard, bought him from the Ishmaelites who had taken him there.

The LORD was with Joseph and he prospered, and he lived in the house of his Egyptian master. When his master saw that the LORD was with him and that the LORD gave him success in everything he did, Joseph found favor in his eyes and became his attendant. Potiphar put him in charge of his household, and he entrusted to his care everything he owned. From the time he put him in charge of his household and of all that he owned, the LORD blessed the household of the Egyptian because of Joseph. The blessing of the LORD was on everything Potiphar had, both in the house and in the field. So he left in Joseph's care everything he had; with Joseph in charge, he did not concern himself with anything except the food he ate.

Now Joseph was well-built and handsome, and after a while his master's wife took notice of Joseph and said, "Come to bed with me!"

But he refused. "With me in charge," he told her, "my master does not concern himself with anything in the house; everything he owns he has entrusted to my care. No one is greater in this house than I am. My master has withheld nothing from me except you, because you are his wife. How then could I do such a wicked thing and sin against God?" And though she spoke to Joseph day after day, he refused to go to bed with her or even be with her.

One day he went into the house to attend to his duties, and none of the household servants was inside. She caught him by his cloak and said, "Come to bed with me!" But he left his cloak in her hand and ran out of the house.

When she saw that he had left his cloak in her hand and had run out of the house, she called her household servants. "Look," she said to them, "this Hebrew has been brought to us to make sport of us! He came in here to sleep with me, but I screamed. When he heard me scream for help, he left his cloak beside me and ran out of the house."

She kept his cloak beside her until his master came home. Then she told him this story: "That Hebrew slave you brought us came to me to make sport of me. But as soon as I screamed for help, he left his cloak beside me and ran out of the house."

When his master heard the story his wife told him, saying, "This is how your slave treated me," he burned with anger. Joseph's master took him and put him in prison, the place where the king's prisoners were confined.

But while Joseph was there in the prison, the LORD was with him; he showed him kindness and granted him favor in the eyes of the prison warden. So the warden put Joseph in charge of all those held in the prison, and he was made responsible for all that was done there. The warden paid no attention to anything under Joseph's care, because the LORD was with Joseph and gave him success in whatever he did.

The LORD was with Joseph . . . " The passage begins and ends with these words, and throughout the story we are told many times that God's hand is on Joseph and every situation surrounding him. Clearly, it is God's hand that turns the heart of Potiphar (PAHT-ih-fuhr) toward Joseph. God's hand allows Joseph to prosper in all he does as a servant. Even in prison, it is God's hand that causes Joseph to find favor with the warden. Without a doubt, God is watching over Joseph and fashioning good out of unfortunate circumstances.

Only in the incident with Potiphar's wife do we find a seeming absence of God's hand at work. Did he leave Joseph for a few hours that morning? Did he decide to test Joseph's obedience? God doesn't tell us why he again allowed someone to mistreat and betray Joseph, but he does make it clear that he wasn't far away.

Through all his trials, Joseph remains faithful, refusing to give in to a short-lived pleasure that would dishonor God. In prison God reassures Joseph that he is near, showing kindness and making the situation bearable. He continues to bring Joseph success despite his captivity.

God has a big plan for Joseph. Although Joseph can't see how it will happen during his days as a servant and prisoner, he will become God's tool for helping the Israelites. Joseph has shown that he can resist temptation and wait for God to bless him. His servanthood and captivity won't be wasted. They will position him for the greater work God has planned. —BQ

DAILY CONTEMPLATION

Is a temptation calling to you, a chance for immediate gratification? Will giving in dishonor God and hinder his bigger plan for you?

DAY 38 Genesis 40:1–23

THE CUPBEARER AND THE BAKER

Some time later, the cupbearer and the baker of the king of Egypt offended their master, the king of Egypt. Pharaoh was angry with his two officials, the chief cupbearer and the chief baker, and put them in custody in the house of the captain of the guard, in the same prison where Joseph was confined. The captain of the guard assigned them to Joseph, and he attended them.

After they had been in custody for some time, each of the two men—the cupbearer and the baker of the king of Egypt, who were being held in prison—had a dream the same night, and each dream had a meaning of its own.

When Joseph came to them the next morning, he saw that they were dejected. So he asked Pharaoh's officials who were in custody with him in his master's house, "Why are your faces so sad today?"

"We both had dreams," they answered, "but there is no one to interpret them."

Then Joseph said to them, "Do not interpretations belong to God? Tell me your dreams."

So the chief cupbearer told Joseph his dream. He said to him, "In my dream I saw a vine in front of me, and on the vine were three branches. As soon as it budded, it blossomed, and its clusters ripened into grapes. Pharaoh's cup was in my hand, and I took the grapes, squeezed them into Pharaoh's cup and put the cup in his hand."

"This is what it means," Joseph said to him. "The three branches are three days. Within three days Pharaoh will lift up your head and restore you to your position, and you will put Pharaoh's cup in his hand, just as you used to do when you were his cupbearer. But when all goes well with you, remember me and show me kindness; mention me to Pharaoh and get me out of this prison. For I was forcibly carried off from the land of the Hebrews, and even here I have done nothing to deserve being put in a dungeon."

When the chief baker saw that Joseph had given a favorable interpretation, he said to Joseph, "I too had a dream: On my head were three baskets of bread. In the top basket were all kinds of baked goods for Pharaoh, but the birds were eating them out of the basket on my head."

"This is what it means," Joseph said. "The three baskets are three days. Within three days Pharaoh will lift off your head and hang you on a tree. And the birds will eat away your flesh."

Now the third day was Pharaoh's birthday, and he gave a feast for all his officials. He lifted up the heads of the chief cupbearer and the chief baker in the presence of his officials: He restored the chief cupbearer to his position, so that he once again put the cup into Pharaoh's hand, but he hanged the chief baker, just as Joseph had said to them in his interpretation.

The chief cupbearer, however, did not remember Joseph; he forgot him.

God again uses dreams to speak to Joseph about what lies in store for the future. Although the dreams of the cupbearer and the baker don't directly involve Joseph, God uses the fulfillment of the prophecies in these dreams to show Joseph that indeed God has given him the gift of interpreting dreams. Just as God brings about the events Joseph predicted for his fellow prisoners, God will in the same way bring about the future predicted in Joseph's own dreams.

The cupbearer, seemingly Joseph's ticket out of prison, lets him down by promptly forgetting Joseph once released. God, however, does not forget him. God's dream for Joseph stays alive and well. Though things look dim in the confines of the dungeon, God's plan will prove unbounded. —BQ

DAILY CONTEMPLATION

What situation in your life is looking grim today? How can you look at your situation through God's eyes?

DAY 39   Genesis 41:1, 8–43, 53–55

PHARAOH'S DREAMS

When two full years had passed, Pharaoh had a dream. . . . In the morning his mind was troubled, so he sent for all the magicians and wise men of Egypt. Pharaoh told them his dreams, but no one could interpret them for him.

Then the chief cupbearer said to Pharaoh, "Today I am reminded of my shortcomings. Pharaoh was once angry with his servants, and he imprisoned me and the chief baker in the house of the captain of the guard. Each of us had a dream the same night, and each dream had a meaning of its own. Now a young Hebrew was there with us, a servant of the captain of the guard. We told him our dreams, and he interpreted them for us, giving each man the interpretation of his dream. And things turned out exactly as he interpreted them to us: I was restored to my position, and the other man was hanged."

So Pharaoh sent for Joseph, and he was quickly brought from the dungeon. When he had shaved and changed his clothes, he came before Pharaoh.

Pharaoh said to Joseph, "I had a dream, and no one can interpret it. But I have heard it said of you that when you hear a dream you can interpret it."

"I cannot do it," Joseph replied to Pharaoh, "but God will give Pharaoh the answer he desires."

Then Pharaoh said to Joseph, "In my dream I was standing on the bank of the Nile, when out of the river there came up seven cows, fat and sleek, and they grazed among the reeds. After them, seven other cows came up—scrawny and very ugly and lean. I had never seen such ugly cows in all the land of Egypt. The lean, ugly cows ate up the seven fat cows that came up first. But even after they ate them, no one could tell that they had done so; they looked just as ugly as before. Then I woke up.

"In my dreams I also saw seven heads of grain, full and good, growing on a single stalk. After them, seven other heads sprouted—withered and thin and scorched by the east wind. The thin heads of grain swallowed up the seven good heads. I told this to the magicians, but none could explain it to me."

Then Joseph said to Pharaoh, "The dreams of Pharaoh are one and the same. God has revealed to Pharaoh what he is about to do. The seven good cows are seven years, and the seven good heads of grain are seven years; it is one and the same dream. The seven lean, ugly cows that came up afterward are seven years, and so are the seven worthless heads of grain scorched by the east wind: They are seven years of famine.

"It is just as I said to Pharaoh: God has shown Pharaoh what he is about to do. Seven years of great abundance are coming throughout the land of Egypt, but seven years of famine will follow them. Then all the abundance in Egypt will be forgotten, and the famine will ravage the land. The abundance in the land will not be remembered, because the famine that follows it will be so severe. The reason the dream was given to Pharaoh in two forms is that the matter has been firmly decided by God, and God will do it soon.

"And now let Pharaoh look for a discerning and wise man and put him in charge of the land of Egypt. Let Pharaoh appoint commissioners over the land to take a fifth of the harvest of Egypt during the seven years of abundance. They should collect all the food of these good years that are coming and store up the grain under the authority of Pharaoh, to be kept in the cities for food. This food should be held in reserve for the country, to be used during the seven years of famine that will come upon Egypt, so that the country may not be ruined by the famine."

The plan seemed good to Pharaoh and to all his officials. So Pharaoh asked them, "Can we find anyone like this man, one in whom is the spirit of God?"

Then Pharaoh said to Joseph, "Since God has made all this known to you, there is no one so discerning and wise as you. You shall be in charge of my palace, and all my people are to submit to your orders. Only with respect to the throne will I be greater than you."

So Pharaoh said to Joseph, "I hereby put you in charge of the whole land of Egypt." Then Pharaoh took his signet ring from his finger and put it on Joseph's finger. He dressed him in robes of fine linen and put a gold chain around his neck. He had him ride in a chariot as his second-in-command, and men shouted before him, "Make way!" Thus he put him in charge of the whole land of Egypt....

The seven years of abundance in Egypt came to an end, and the seven years of famine began, just as Joseph had said. There was famine in all the other lands, but in the whole land of Egypt there was food. When all Egypt began to feel the famine, the people cried to Pharaoh for food. Then Pharaoh told all the Egyptians, "Go to Joseph and do what he tells you."

Genesis provides a fascinating look at a variety of ways in which God gave guidance to his people. Sometimes, as with Abraham, he would appear spectacularly and in person, or send angelic messengers. For other people, like Jacob, the guidance came in more mysterious forms: a late-night wrestling match, a dream of a ladder reaching into heaven. For Joseph, God's guidance is indirect and probably quite mystifying.

God communicates to Joseph not through angels but mainly through dreams, weird dreams he hears about from such dubious sources as jail mates and a despotic Egyptian pharaoh (FAIR-oh). Yet because God reveals to Joseph the proper meaning of these dreams, Joseph eventually rises to prominence. Egyptians of that day were fascinated by dreams (archaeologists have unearthed lengthy textbooks on dream interpretations), and Joseph the dream interpreter soon finds himself at the top of Pharoah's government.

In Joseph's time, God mostly works behind the scenes. In fact, on the surface it often seems that Joseph gets the exact opposite of what he deserves. He explains a dream to his brothers, and they throw him in a cistern. He resists a sexual advance and lands in an Egyptian prison. He interprets another dream to save a cell mate's life, and the cell mate forgets about him.

Yet—and perhaps this is why Genesis devotes so much space to him—Joseph never stops trusting God. Joseph comes to see God's hand in the tragedies of his life. Being sold into slavery, for example, eventually turns out for good. It leads him into a powerful new career, and soon he will have the opportunity to save his own family from starvation.

—PY

DAILY CONTEMPLATION

If God has an important message for you, how does he get it across?

A Life Motto

Life isn't fair."

How many times have you been chided by these words in the face of an injustice you've encountered? How many times have you muttered them to yourself while pondering yet another unfair burden? Many of us learn this life motto at an early age. We realize as children that life just doesn't unfold in the way we'd prefer. As time moves on, we see the motto confirmed again in numerous ways. Eventually we grow hardened. Why hope for anything better?

We expect to turn to the Bible and find a way out of the unfairness that life distributes so freely. Surely, life with God must clear up the inequities of a godless world. Yet here in Joseph's story, as in many earlier stories, life isn't fair, despite God's presence.

In a world like Joseph's and ours, where God has not yet destroyed sin finally and completely, life will remain unfair. But the reality for Christians doesn't stop there. A believer's understanding of life goes far beyond a focus on fairness. It settles on God and his goodness. Life may not have been fair to Joseph, but God was abundantly good to him. In the midst of each unfair turn of events, each long night of heartache, God worked things for the good of this man he loved.

Julian of Norwich, a Benedictine nun in England who lived in a time of social unrest and fear of the Black Plague and who herself suffered a serious illness at a young age, penned the following words. "Just as our flesh is covered by clothing, . . . so are we, soul and body, covered and enclosed by the goodness of God. Yet the clothing and the flesh will pass away, but the goodness of God will always remain and will remain closer to us than our own flesh."

Life isn't fair but God is good.

—BQ

DAILY CONTEMPLATION

What struggle are you facing today that seems to be another instance of injustice? Come to God and talk about the anger you feel. Tell him of the ache in your heart. Ask for a clear view of his goodness in your life.

DAY 41   Genesis 42:1–26

Joseph's Brothers Go to Egypt

When Jacob learned that there was grain in Egypt, he said to his sons, "Why do you just keep looking at each other?" He continued, "I have heard that there is grain in Egypt. Go down there and buy some for us, so that we may live and not die."

Then ten of Joseph's brothers went down to buy grain from Egypt. But Jacob did not send Benjamin, Joseph's brother, with the others, because he was afraid that harm might come to him. So Israel's sons were among those who went to buy grain, for the famine was in the land of Canaan also.

Now Joseph was the governor of the land, the one who sold grain to all its people. So when Joseph's brothers arrived, they bowed down to him with their faces to the ground. As soon as Joseph saw his brothers, he recognized them, but he pretended to be a stranger and spoke harshly to them. "Where do you come from?" he asked.

"From the land of Canaan," they replied, "to buy food."

Although Joseph recognized his brothers, they did not recognize him. Then he remembered his dreams about them and said to them, "You are spies! You have come to see where our land is unprotected."

"No, my lord," they answered. "Your servants have come to buy food. We are all the sons of one man. Your servants are honest men, not spies."

"No!" he said to them. "You have come to see where our land is unprotected."

But they replied, "Your servants were twelve brothers, the sons of one man, who lives in the land of Canaan. The youngest is now with our father, and one is no more."

Joseph said to them, "It is just as I told you: You are spies! And this is how you will be tested: As surely as Pharaoh lives, you will not leave this place unless your youngest brother comes here. Send one of your number to get your brother; the rest of you will be kept in prison, so that your words may be tested to see if you are telling the truth. If you are not, then as surely as Pharaoh lives, you are spies!" And he put them all in custody for three days.

On the third day, Joseph said to them, "Do this and you will live, for I fear God: If you are honest men, let one of your brothers stay here in prison, while the rest of you go and take grain back for your starving households. But you must bring your youngest brother to me, so that your words may be verified and that you may not die." This they proceeded to do.

They said to one another, "Surely we are being punished because of our brother. We saw how distressed he was when he pleaded with us for his life, but we would not listen; that's why this distress has come upon us."

Reuben replied, "Didn't I tell you not to sin against the boy? But you wouldn't listen! Now we must give an accounting for his blood." They did not realize that Joseph could understand them, since he was using an interpreter.

He turned away from them and began to weep, but then turned back and spoke to them again. He had Simeon taken from them and bound before their eyes.

Joseph gave orders to fill their bags with grain, to put each man's silver back in his sack, and to give them provisions for their journey. After this was done for them, they loaded their grain on their donkeys and left.

Finally, after at least twenty years apart, Joseph and his brothers reunite—in a way. He recognizes them, but they cannot see past his new Egyptian identity. Joseph is flooded with mixed emotions. He remembers the dreams he had many years ago, and as he remembers, the urge for revenge surges up. Once the victim of their cruelty, now he controls their fate.

As his brothers are brought into a position of vulnerability, their guilt comes to light. Even though they don't recognize this governor as their brother, at last they sense they will have to pay consequences for their actions. Just as the Bible reveals the injustices of life, it also confirms that in the end people often reap what they sow. Whatever suffering may lie ahead for the brothers stands justified. They deserve to pay for what they've done.

The true character of Joseph now begins to shine. He has spent many days and nights questioning the course his life has taken. Now, as the brothers question their future, Joseph finally sees that God has brought him to a place where he can save his family from death.

After breaking down weeping, Joseph gives himself time to collect his thoughts by sending the nine home for Benjamin. Now he will see his best-loved brother, and he will have time to consider this turn of events. His brothers also will have time to reckon with their wrong. —BQ

DAILY CONTEMPLATION

When have you reaped the consequences of your actions?

DAY 42 Genesis 42:27–38

JOSEPH'S BROTHERS RETURN TO CANAAN

At the place where they stopped for the night one of them opened his sack to get feed for his donkey, and he saw his silver in the mouth of his sack. "My silver has been returned," he said to his brothers. "Here it is in my sack."

Their hearts sank and they turned to each other trembling and said, "What is this that God has done to us?"

When they came to their father Jacob in the land of Canaan, they told him all that had happened to them. They said, "The man who is lord over the land spoke harshly to us and treated us as though we were spying on the land. But we said to him, 'We are honest men; we are not spies. We were twelve brothers, sons of one father. One is no more, and the youngest is now with our father in Canaan.'

"Then the man who is lord over the land said to us, 'This is how I will know whether you are honest men: Leave one of your brothers here with me, and take food for your starving households and go. But bring your youngest brother to me so I will know that you are not spies but honest men. Then I will give your brother back to you, and you can trade in the land.'"

As they were emptying their sacks, there in each man's sack was his pouch of silver! When they and their father saw the money pouches, they were frightened. Their father Jacob said to them, "You have deprived me of my children. Joseph is no more and Simeon is no more, and now you want to take Benjamin. Everything is against me!"

Then Reuben said to his father, "You may put both of my sons to death if I do not bring him back to you. Entrust him to my care, and I will bring him back."

But Jacob said, "My son will not go down there with you; his brother is dead and he is the only one left. If harm comes to him on the journey you are taking, you will bring my gray head down to the grave in sorrow."

God uses Joseph's desire to see Benjamin as a tool to help bring about repentant hearts in the brothers. By placing silver back in their grain sacks, Joseph frames them to appear as dishonest spies. To the brothers, it seems God is acting deliberately to punish them.

In truth, God is sovereignly caring for Jacob's family, preserving them during a time of widespread famine. Through Joseph he is bringing them to the land of Egypt, where the Israelites will live for four hundred years and grow into a great nation. As they enter Egypt, their hearts must turn toward God. They must become humble before him and remember his ways. Although for a time the brothers are afraid, God is guiding their hearts back to a place of oneness with him.　　　　—BQ

DAILY CONTEMPLATION

Has fear ever turned you to God? Did God bring good out of your fear?

DAY 43　　　　　　　　　　　　　　Genesis 43:1–2, 8–31

THE SECOND JOURNEY TO EGYPT

Now the famine was still severe in the land. So when they had eaten all the grain they had brought from Egypt, their father said to them, "Go back and buy us a little more food." ...

Then Judah said to Israel his father, "Send the boy along with me and we will go at once, so that we and you and our children may live and not die. I myself will guarantee his safety; you can hold me personally responsible for him. If I do not bring him back to you and set him here before you, I will bear the blame before you all my life. As it is, if we had not delayed, we could have gone and returned twice."

Then their father Israel said to them, "If it must be, then do this: Put some of the best products of the land in your bags and take them down to the man as a gift—a little balm and a little honey, some spices and myrrh, some pistachio nuts and almonds. Take double the amount of silver with you, for you must return the silver that was put back into the mouths of your sacks. Perhaps it was a mistake. Take your brother also and go back to the man at once. And may God Almighty grant you mercy before the man so that he will let your other brother and Benjamin come back with you. As for me, if I am bereaved, I am bereaved."

So the men took the gifts and double the amount of silver, and Benjamin also. They hurried down to Egypt and presented themselves to Joseph. When Joseph saw Benjamin with them, he said to the steward of his house, "Take these men to my house, slaughter an animal and prepare dinner; they are to eat with me at noon."

The man did as Joseph told him and took the men to Joseph's house. Now the men were frightened when they were taken to his house. They thought, "We were brought here because of the silver that was put back into our sacks the first time. He wants to attack us and overpower us and seize us as slaves and take our donkeys."

So they went up to Joseph's steward and spoke to him at the entrance to the house. "Please, sir," they said, "we came down here the first time to buy food. But at the place where we stopped for the night we opened our sacks and each of us found his silver—the exact weight—in the mouth of his sack. So we have brought it back with us. We have also brought additional silver with us to buy food. We don't know who put our silver in our sacks."

"It's all right," he said. "Don't be afraid. Your God, the God of your father, has given you treasure in your sacks; I received your silver." Then he brought Simeon out to them.

The steward took the men into Joseph's house, gave them water to wash their feet and provided fodder for their donkeys. They prepared their gifts for Joseph's arrival at noon, because they had heard that they were to eat there.

When Joseph came home, they presented to him the gifts they had brought into the house, and they bowed down before him to the ground. He asked them how they were, and then he said, "How is your aged father you told me about? Is he still living?"

They replied, "Your servant our father is still alive and well." And they bowed low to pay him honor.

As he looked about and saw his brother Benjamin, his own mother's son, he asked, "Is this your youngest brother, the one you told me about?" And he said, "God be gracious to you, my son." Deeply moved at the sight of his brother, Joseph hurried out and looked for a place to weep. He went into his private room and wept there.

After he had washed his face, he came out and, controlling himself, said, "Serve the food."

Once again Jacob's sons must travel to Egypt. Some time has passed, and they have used all the grain they bought from Joseph. Despite his misgivings, Jacob can no longer put off his decision. He will risk the life of Benjamin or lose all of his family to starvation.

When the brothers arrive and are invited to dinner with Joseph, they try to explain to Joseph's steward about the silver. The steward's reply brings into focus their whole experience in Egypt. "Don't be afraid. Your God, the God of your father, has given you treasure in your sacks."

Joseph's brothers soon will learn that they have come to Egypt for much more than grain. They are to be reunited with their brother. They will receive a new home, and in this place they will grow into a treasured nation belonging to God. The silver that seemed to be a setup was actually a symbol of a people treasured by God, hidden in his hand amid the multitudes of a foreign land.   —BQ

DAILY CONTEMPLATION

What are you afraid of today? Might treasure be hidden within the thing you fear?

DAY 44   Genesis 44:1–18, 27–34

A SILVER CUP IN A SACK

Now Joseph gave these instructions to the steward of his house: "Fill the men's sacks with as much food as they can carry, and put each man's silver in the mouth of his sack. Then put my cup, the silver one, in the mouth of the youngest one's sack, along with the silver for his grain." And he did as Joseph said.

As morning dawned, the men were sent on their way with their donkeys. They had not gone far from the city when Joseph said to his steward, "Go after those men at once, and when you catch up with them, say to them, 'Why have you repaid good with evil? Isn't this the cup my master drinks from and also uses for divination? This is a wicked thing you have done.'"

When he caught up with them, he repeated these words to them. But they said to him, "Why does my lord say such things? Far be it from your servants to do anything like that! We even brought back to you from the land of Canaan the silver we found inside the mouths of our sacks. So why would we steal silver or gold from your master's house? If any of your servants is found to have it, he will die; and the rest of us will become my lord's slaves."

"Very well, then," he said, "let it be as you say. Whoever is found to have it will become my slave; the rest of you will be free from blame."

Each of them quickly lowered his sack to the ground and opened it. Then the steward proceeded to search, beginning with the oldest and ending with the youngest. And the cup was found in Benjamin's sack. At this, they tore their clothes. Then they all loaded their donkeys and returned to the city.

Joseph was still in the house when Judah and his brothers came in, and they threw themselves to the ground before him. Joseph said to them, "What is this you have done? Don't you know that a man like me can find things out by divination?"

"What can we say to my lord?" Judah replied. "What can we say? How can we prove our innocence? God has uncovered your servants' guilt. We are now my lord's slaves—we ourselves and the one who was found to have the cup."

But Joseph said, "Far be it from me to do such a thing! Only the man who was found to have the cup will become my slave. The rest of you, go back to your father in peace."

Then Judah went up to him and said: "Please, my lord, let your servant speak a word to my lord. Do not be angry with your servant, though you are equal to Pharaoh himself. . . .

"Your servant my father said to us, 'You know that my wife bore me two sons. One of them went away from me, and I said, "He has surely been torn to pieces." And I have not seen him since. If you take this one from me too and harm comes to him, you will bring my gray head down to the grave in misery.'

"So now, if the boy is not with us when I go back to your servant my father and if my father, whose life is closely bound up with the boy's life, sees that the boy isn't there, he will die. Your servants will bring the gray head of our father down to the grave in sorrow. Your servant guaranteed the boy's safety to my father. I said, 'If I do not bring him back to you, I will bear the blame before you, my father, all my life!'

"Now then, please let your servant remain here as my lord's slave in place of the boy, and let the boy return with his brothers. How can I go back to my father if the boy is not with me? No! Do not let me see the misery that would come upon my father."

Despite being reassured that they will not suffer for the silver in their sacks, Joseph's brothers must again face accusation for stealing—this time with the main suspicion resting on Benjamin. Joseph orchestrates this final trial to test his brothers' recognition of evil. If they show compassion for Benjamin and for their father, they will prove they have repented of their sin against Joseph. Then they can take part in the fulfillment of God's promises.

The brothers pass the test. Judah admits, "God has uncovered your servants' guilt." Rather than simply resigning himself to Benjamin's loss and returning home, Judah offers himself as Joseph's slave. He cares more about his father's well-being than about his own. When this becomes evident, Joseph stands ready to forgive and prepares to reveal his identity.   —BQ

DAY 45   Genesis 45:1–46:4; 47:11; 49:33; 50:14–21

JOSEPH MAKES HIMSELF KNOWN

Then Joseph could no longer control himself before all his attendants, and he cried out, "Have everyone leave my presence!" So there was no one with Joseph when he made himself known to his brothers. And he wept so loudly that the Egyptians heard him, and Pharaoh's household heard about it.

Joseph said to his brothers, "I am Joseph! Is my father still living?" But his brothers were not able to answer him, because they were terrified at his presence.

Then Joseph said to his brothers, "Come close to me." When they had done so, he said, "I am your brother Joseph, the one you sold into Egypt! And now, do not be distressed and do not be angry with yourselves for selling me here, because it was to save lives that God sent me ahead of you. For two years now there has been famine in the land, and for the next five years there will not be plowing and reaping. But God sent me ahead of you to preserve for you a remnant on earth and to save your lives by a great deliverance.

"So then, it was not you who sent me here, but God. He made me father to Pharaoh, lord of his entire household and ruler of all Egypt. Now hurry back to my father and say to him, 'This is what your son Joseph says: God has made me lord of all Egypt. Come down to me; don't delay. You shall live in the region of Goshen and be near me—you, your children and grandchildren, your flocks and herds, and all you have. I will provide for you there, because five years of famine are still to come. Otherwise you and your household and all who belong to you will become destitute.'

"You can see for yourselves, and so can my brother Benjamin, that it is really I who am speaking to you. Tell my father about all the honor accorded me in Egypt and about everything you have seen. And bring my father down here quickly."

Then he threw his arms around his brother Benjamin and wept, and Benjamin embraced him, weeping. And he kissed all his brothers and wept over them. Afterward his brothers talked with him.

When the news reached Pharaoh's palace that Joseph's brothers had come, Pharaoh and all his officials were pleased. Pharaoh said to Joseph, "Tell your brothers, 'Do this: Load your animals and return to the land of Canaan, and bring your father and your families back to me. I will give you the best of the land of Egypt and you can enjoy the fat of the land.'

"You are also directed to tell them, 'Do this: Take some carts from Egypt for your children and your wives, and get your father and come. Never mind about your belongings, because the best of all Egypt will be yours.'"

So the sons of Israel did this. Joseph gave them carts, as Pharaoh had commanded, and he also gave them provisions for their journey. To each of them he gave new clothing, but to Benjamin he gave three hundred shekels of silver and five sets of clothes. And this is what he sent to his father: ten donkeys loaded with the best things of Egypt, and ten female donkeys loaded with grain and bread and other provisions for his journey. Then he sent his brothers away, and as they were leaving he said to them, "Don't quarrel on the way!"

So they went up out of Egypt and came to their father Jacob in the land of Canaan. They told him, "Joseph is still alive! In fact, he is ruler of all Egypt." Jacob was stunned; he did not believe them. But when they told him everything Joseph had said to them, and when he saw the carts Joseph had sent to carry him back, the spirit of their father Jacob revived. And Israel said, "I'm convinced! My son Joseph is still alive. I will go and see him before I die."

So Israel set out with all that was his, and when he reached Beersheba, he offered sacrifices to the God of his father Isaac.

And God spoke to Israel in a vision at night and said, "Jacob! Jacob!"

"Here I am," he replied.

"I am God, the God of your father," he said. "Do not be afraid to go down to Egypt, for I will make you into a great nation there. I will go down to Egypt with you, and I will surely bring you back again. And Joseph's own hand will close your eyes." ...

So Joseph settled his father and his brothers in Egypt and gave them property in the best part of the land, the district of Rameses, as Pharaoh directed. ...

When Jacob had finished giving instructions to his sons, he drew his feet up into the bed, breathed his last and was gathered to his people. ...

After burying his father, Joseph returned to Egypt, together with his brothers and all the others who had gone with him to bury his father.

When Joseph's brothers saw that their father was dead, they said, "What if Joseph holds a grudge against us and pays us back for all the wrongs we did to him?" So they sent word to Joseph, saying, "Your father left these instructions before he died: 'This is what you are to say to Joseph: I ask you to forgive your brothers the sins and the wrongs they committed in treating you so badly.' Now please forgive the sins of the servants of the God of your father." When their message came to him, Joseph wept.

His brothers then came and threw themselves down before him. "We are your slaves," they said.

But Joseph said to them, "Don't be afraid. Am I in the place of God? You intended to harm me, but God intended it for good to accomplish what is now being done, the saving of many lives. So then, don't be afraid. I will provide for you and your children." And he reassured them and spoke kindly to them.

For nearly *two years* Joseph has conducted a series of elaborate tests, demanding things from his brothers, playing tricks on them, and accusing them. All these games bring his brothers confusion and fear, and also flashbacks of guilt over their treatment of him years before. Joseph accomplishes what needs to happen.

But the drama also exacts an emotional toll on Joseph. Five times he has broken into tears, once with cries loud enough to be heard in the next room. Joseph is feeling the awful strain of forgiveness. Finally, the brothers discover the stunning truth: the teenager they once sold as a slave, and nearly killed, is now the second-ranking imperial official of Egypt. He holds their fate in his hands.

Joseph, however, has no interest in revenge. At last ready to forgive, he understands now that "you intended to harm me, but God intended it for good to accomplish what is now being done, the saving of many lives." Seeing his difficult years as part of God's big picture, Joseph is free to release his anger. The brothers' reconciliation thus opens the way for the children of Israel to become one family of twelve tribes, a single nation.

The old man Jacob, back home in Palestine, hardly knows what to believe when he hears the news about his "dead" son. But, spurred on by one last personal revelation from God, he too heads off for Egypt.

A large family, a nation, a land—God promised all these to Abraham and to Isaac and to Jacob. As Genesis closes, only the first of the promises has come true: Jacob's twelve sons have produced a flock of children. The Bible makes plain that these twelve are no more holy than any other sons—eleven of them, after all, have betrayed Joseph. But from this starting point God will build his nation.   —PY

DAILY CONTEMPLATION

What makes it so hard for us to forgive others?

DAY 46   Reflection

WHY FORGIVE?

The scandal of forgiveness confronts anyone who agrees to a moral cease-fire just because someone says, "I'm sorry." When I feel wronged, I can contrive a hundred reasons against forgiveness. *He needs to learn a lesson. I'll let her stew for a while; it'll do her good. It's not up to me to make the first move.* When I finally soften to the point of granting forgiveness, it seems a capitulation, a leap from hard logic to mushy sentiment.

Why do I ever make such a leap? One factor that motivates me is that as a Christian I am commanded to, as the child of a Father who forgives. But why do any of us, Christian or unbeliever alike, choose this unnatural act? I can identify at least three pragmatic reasons.

First, forgiveness alone can halt the cycle of blame and pain, breaking the chain of ungrace. In the New Testament the most common Greek word for forgiveness means, literally, to release, to hurl away, to free yourself. If we do not transcend nature, we remain bound to the people we cannot forgive, held in their vise grip. This principle applies even when one party is wholly innocent and the other wholly to blame, for the innocent party will bear the wound until he or she can find a way to release it—and forgiveness is the only way.

For Joseph, who had borne a well-deserved grudge against his brothers, forgiveness spilled out in the form of tears and groans. These, like childbirth's, were harbingers of liberation, and through them Joseph gained at last his freedom. He named his son Manasseh, "one who causes to be forgotten."

The second great power of forgiveness is that it can loosen the stranglehold of guilt in the perpetrator. Magnanimous forgiveness allows the possibility of transformation in the guilty party. Lewis Smedes cautions that forgiveness is not the same as pardon: you may forgive one who wronged you and still insist on a just punishment for that wrong. If you can bring yourself to the point of forgiveness, though, you will release its healing power both in you and in the person who wronged you.

Forgiveness breaks the cycle of blame and loosens the stranglehold of guilt. It accomplishes these two things through a remarkable linkage, placing the forgiver on the same side as the party who did the wrong. Through it we realize we are not as different from the wrongdoer as we would like to think. "I also am other than what I imagine myself to be. To know this is forgiveness," said Simone Weil.

The gracious miracle of God's forgiveness was made possible because of the linkage that occurred when God came to earth in Christ. Somehow God had to come to terms with these creatures he desperately wanted to love—but how? Experientially, God did not know what it was like to be tempted to sin, to have a trying day. On earth, living among us, he learned what it was like. He put himself on our side.[2]   —PY

Daily Contemplation

Have you struggled with the logic of forgiveness? Is there someone in your life whom you have been unable to forgive? Ask God to soften you and guide you in how to go about forgiving. And thank him for all he has forgiven you.

PART 2

BIRTHING A NATION

THE BIRTH OF MOSES

These are the names of the sons of Israel who went to Egypt with Jacob, each with his family: Reuben, Simeon, Levi and Judah; Issachar, Zebulun and Benjamin; Dan and Naphtali; Gad and Asher. The descendants of Jacob numbered seventy in all; Joseph was already in Egypt.

Now Joseph and all his brothers and all that generation died, but the Israelites were fruitful and multiplied greatly and became exceedingly numerous, so that the land was filled with them.

Then a new king, who did not know about Joseph, came to power in Egypt. "Look," he said to his people, "the Israelites have become much too numerous for us. Come, we must deal shrewdly with them or they will become even more numerous and, if war breaks out, will join our enemies, fight against us and leave the country."

So they put slave masters over them to oppress them with forced labor, and they built Pithom and Rameses as store cities for Pharaoh. But the more they were oppressed, the more they multiplied and spread; so the Egyptians came to dread the Israelites and worked them ruthlessly. They made their lives bitter with hard labor in brick and mortar and with all kinds of work in the fields; in all their hard labor the Egyptians used them ruthlessly.

The king of Egypt said to the Hebrew midwives, whose names were Shiphrah and Puah, "When you help the Hebrew women in childbirth and observe them on the delivery stool, if it is a boy, kill him; but if it is a girl, let her live." The midwives, however, feared God and did not do what the king of Egypt had told them to do; they let the boys live. Then the king of Egypt summoned the midwives and asked them, "Why have you done this? Why have you let the boys live?"

The midwives answered Pharaoh, "Hebrew women are not like Egyptian women; they are vigorous and give birth before the midwives arrive."

So God was kind to the midwives and the people increased and became even more numerous. And because the midwives feared God, he gave them families of their own.

Then Pharaoh gave this order to all his people: "Every boy that is born you must throw into the Nile, but let every girl live."

Now a man of the house of Levi married a Levite woman, and she became pregnant and gave birth to a son. When she saw that he was a fine child, she hid him for three months. But when she could hide him no longer, she got a papyrus basket for him and coated it with tar and pitch. Then she placed the child in it and put it among the reeds along the bank of the Nile. His sister stood at a distance to see what would happen to him.

Then Pharaoh's daughter went down to the Nile to bathe, and her attendants were walking along the river bank. She saw the basket among the reeds and sent her slave girl to get it. She opened it and saw the baby. He was crying, and she felt sorry for him. "This is one of the Hebrew babies," she said.

Then his sister asked Pharaoh's daughter, "Shall I go and get one of the Hebrew women to nurse the baby for you?"

"Yes, go," she answered. And the girl went and got the baby's mother. Pharaoh's daughter said to her, "Take this baby and nurse him for me, and I will pay you." So the woman took the baby and nursed him. When the child grew older, she took him to Pharaoh's daughter and he became her son. She named him Moses, saying, "I drew him out of the water."

One day, after Moses had grown up, he went out to where his own people were and watched them at their hard labor. He saw an Egyptian beating a Hebrew, one of his own people. Glancing this way and that and seeing no one, he killed the Egyptian and hid him in the sand. The next day he went out and saw two Hebrews fighting. He asked the one in the wrong, "Why are you hitting your fellow Hebrew?"

The man said, "Who made you ruler and judge over us? Are you thinking of killing me as you killed the Egyptian?" Then Moses was afraid and thought, "What I did must have become known."

When Pharaoh heard of this, he tried to kill Moses, but Moses fled from Pharaoh and went to live in Midian.

Generations have been born and have died since Jacob's family entered Egypt. In this time, a few hundred years in all, the Israelites have grown into a multitude of people. Though they are prospering in Egypt, this is not to be their home. As tension builds between the Egyptians and Israelites, God prepares his people to leave.

The Egyptians have become ever more severe in their treatment of the Hebrew people. Now God raises up the man he has chosen to deliver his people: Moses. Unlike many other Hebrew boys who are thrown in the Nile river to die, he is placed in the river only to be saved by the family of Pharaoh himself. Moses is nurtured by his own Hebrew mother and then raised as an Egyptian child, in the process becoming highly educated and learning to speak fluently both Egyptian and Hebrew. In this unexpected way, God appropriately grooms the one he has chosen to carry out his plan. —BQ

DAILY CONTEMPLATION

In what ways has God groomed you?

DAY 48

Exodus 3:1–22

MOSES AND THE BURNING BUSH

Now Moses was tending the flock of Jethro his father-in-law, the priest of Midian, and he led the flock to the far side of the desert and came to Horeb, the mountain of God. There the angel of the LORD appeared to him in flames of fire from within a bush. Moses saw that though the bush was on fire it did not burn up. So Moses thought, "I will go over and see this strange sight— why the bush does not burn up."

When the LORD saw that he had gone over to look, God called to him from within the bush, "Moses! Moses!"

And Moses said, "Here I am."

"Do not come any closer," God said. "Take off your sandals, for the place where you are standing is holy ground." Then he said, "I am the God of your father, the God of Abraham, the God of Isaac and the God of Jacob." At this, Moses hid his face, because he was afraid to look at God.

The LORD said, "I have indeed seen the misery of my people in Egypt. I have heard them crying out because of their slave drivers, and I am concerned about their suffering. So I have come down to rescue them from the hand of the Egyptians and to bring them up out of that land into a good and spacious land, a land flowing with milk and honey—the home of the Canaanites, Hittites, Amorites, Perizzites, Hivites and Jebusites. And now the cry of the Israelites has reached me, and I have seen the way the Egyptians are oppressing them. So now, go. I am sending you to Pharaoh to bring my people the Israelites out of Egypt."

But Moses said to God, "Who am I, that I should go to Pharaoh and bring the Israelites out of Egypt?"

And God said, "I will be with you. And this will be the sign to you that it is I who have sent you: When you have brought the people out of Egypt, you will worship God on this mountain."

Moses said to God, "Suppose I go to the Israelites and say to them, 'The God of your fathers has sent me to you,' and they ask me, 'What is his name?' Then what shall I tell them?"

God said to Moses, "I AM WHO I AM. This is what you are to say to the Israelites: 'I AM has sent me to you.'"

God also said to Moses, "Say to the Israelites, 'The LORD, the God of your fathers—the God of Abraham, the God of Isaac and the God of Jacob—has sent me to you.' This is my name forever, the name by which I am to be remembered from generation to generation.

"Go, assemble the elders of Israel and say to them, 'The LORD, the God of your fathers—the God of Abraham, Isaac and Jacob—appeared to me and said: I have watched over you and have seen what has been done to you in Egypt. And I have promised to bring you up out of your misery in Egypt into the land of the Canaanites, Hittites, Amorites, Perizzites, Hivites and Jebusites—a land flowing with milk and honey.'

"The elders of Israel will listen to you. Then you and the elders are to go to the king of Egypt and say to him, 'The LORD, the God of the Hebrews, has met with us. Let us take a three-day journey into the desert to offer sacrifices to the LORD our God.' But I know that the king of Egypt will not let you go unless a mighty hand compels him. So I will stretch out my hand and strike the Egyptians with all the wonders that I will perform among them. After that, he will let you go.

"And I will make the Egyptians favorably disposed toward this people, so that when you leave you will not go empty-handed. Every woman is to ask her neighbor and any woman living in her house for articles of silver and gold and for clothing, which you will put on your sons and daughters. And so you will plunder the Egyptians."

Jacob's family has grown into a great, swarming tribe. God's plan is slowly progressing, but with one major hitch: the Hebrews now toil as slaves under a hostile pharaoh.

God's promises to Abraham, Isaac, and Jacob have been passed down to each new generation, but who believes in the covenant anymore? Daily, they feel the whips of Egyptian taskmasters. As for the vaunted Promised Land, it lies to the east somewhere, carved up under the dominion of a dozen different kings.

At last God has had enough. "I have indeed seen the misery of my people in Egypt," he says. "Now you will see what I will do." The chapters that follow record the most impressive display of God's power unleashed on earth since creation.

First, God needs a leader, and for that job he has selected Moses, a choice rich with irony. It took forty years in Egypt and then forty years in the desert to prepare Moses for the leadership role. God's announcement, or "call," is an encounter Moses will never forget: a fiery bush, a voice from nowhere, God introducing himself by name. "I am the God of Abraham, Isaac, and Jacob," he says, drawing a connection to all the promises that have gone before. And now the time for action has arrived. Moses is God's handpicked choice to lead the mob from slavery in Egypt to freedom in the Promised Land.

As this chapter shows, Moses is far from an eager recruit. Yet his own resistance to God's plan is minor compared with that put up by the Israelites . . . and the Egyptians.   —PY

DAILY CONTEMPLATION

In the past, how has God gotten your attention to let you know of a job he had for you?

DAY 49   Exodus 4:1–17

SIGNS FOR MOSES

Moses answered, "What if they do not believe me or listen to me and say, 'The LORD did not appear to you'?"

Then the LORD said to him, "What is that in your hand?"

"A staff," he replied.

The LORD said, "Throw it on the ground."

Moses threw it on the ground and it became a snake, and he ran from it. Then the LORD said to him, "Reach out your hand and take it by the tail." So Moses reached out and took hold of the snake and it turned back into a staff in his hand. "This," said the LORD, "is so that they may believe that the LORD, the God of their fathers—the God of Abraham, the God of Isaac and the God of Jacob—has appeared to you."

Then the LORD said, "Put your hand inside your cloak." So Moses put his hand into his cloak, and when he took it out, it was leprous, like snow.

"Now put it back into your cloak," he said. So Moses put his hand back into his cloak, and when he took it out, it was restored, like the rest of his flesh.

Then the LORD said, "If they do not believe you or pay attention to the first miraculous sign, they may believe the second. But if they do not believe these two signs or listen to you, take some water from the Nile and pour it on the dry ground. The water you take from the river will become blood on the ground."

Moses said to the LORD, "O Lord, I have never been eloquent, neither in the past nor since you have spoken to your servant. I am slow of speech and tongue."

The LORD said to him, "Who gave man his mouth? Who makes him deaf or mute? Who gives him sight or makes him blind? Is it not I, the LORD? Now go; I will help you speak and will teach you what to say."

But Moses said, "O Lord, please send someone else to do it."

Then the LORD's anger burned against Moses and he said, "What about your brother, Aaron the Levite? I know he can speak well. He is already on his way to meet you, and his heart will be glad when he sees you. You shall speak to him and put words in his mouth; I will help both of you speak and will teach you what to do. He will speak to the people for you, and it will be as if he were your mouth and as if you were God to him. But take this staff in your hand so you can perform miraculous signs with it."

Moses has received a big assignment from God—a job that feels much too big. As Moses continues to talk with God at the burning bush, he shrinks back from the prospect of such an enormous leadership role. For years he has lived as a reclusive shepherd, overseeing animals and keeping company with the land. Now God is asking him to enter the company of Pharaoh and then shepherd masses of Hebrew people out of the land of Egypt.

God understands Moses' initial fears and gives him three miraculous signs to help the people believe him. When Moses again doubts his abilities and asks God to find someone else, God becomes angry. Now Moses is displaying a disobedient heart. He may not feel qualified or confident, but if God has chosen him, surely God will give him the ability to do the job. Yet Moses still can't believe, and God must select Aaron as Moses' spokesperson. That accommodation, enough to calm Moses now, will later prove to be a decidedly mixed blessing.

Here on Mount Horeb (HOR-eb) God calls Moses to lead the Israelites into their next phase of life as God's people. Later Moses will again stand on Mount Horeb as God relays the Ten Commandments—the law that will govern this nation. —BQ

DAILY CONTEMPLATION

What job has God recently asked you to do? In what ways do you feel like the wrong person for the job? Can God equip you anyway?

DAY 50 Exodus 7:14–8:15

THE PLAGUES OF BLOOD AND FROGS

Then the LORD said to Moses, "Pharaoh's heart is unyielding; he refuses to let the people go. Go to Pharaoh in the morning as he goes out to the water. Wait on the bank of the Nile to meet him, and take in your hand the staff that was changed into a snake. Then say to him, 'The LORD, the God of the Hebrews, has sent me to say to you: Let my people go, so that they may worship me in the desert. But until now you have not listened. This is what the LORD says: By this you will know that I am the LORD: With the staff that is in my hand I will strike the water of the Nile, and it will be changed into blood. The fish in the Nile will die, and the river will stink; the Egyptians will not be able to drink its water.'"

The LORD said to Moses, "Tell Aaron, 'Take your staff and stretch out your hand over the waters of Egypt—over the streams and canals, over the ponds and all the reservoirs'—and they will turn to blood. Blood will be everywhere in Egypt, even in the wooden buckets and stone jars."

Moses and Aaron did just as the LORD had commanded. He raised his staff in the presence of Pharaoh and his officials and struck the water of the Nile, and all the water was changed into blood. The fish in the Nile died, and the river smelled so bad that the Egyptians could not drink its water. Blood was everywhere in Egypt.

But the Egyptian magicians did the same things by their secret arts, and Pharaoh's heart became hard; he would not listen to Moses and Aaron, just as the LORD had said. Instead, he turned and went into his palace, and did not take even this to heart. And all the Egyptians dug along the Nile to get drinking water, because they could not drink the water of the river.

Seven days passed after the LORD struck the Nile. Then the LORD said to Moses, "Go to Pharaoh and say to him, 'This is what the LORD says: Let my people go, so that they may worship me. If you refuse to let them go, I will plague your whole country with frogs. The Nile will teem with frogs. They will come up into your palace and your bedroom and onto your bed, into the houses of your officials and on your people, and into your ovens and kneading troughs. The frogs will go up on you and your people and all your officials.'"

Then the LORD said to Moses, "Tell Aaron, 'Stretch out your hand with your staff over the streams and canals and ponds, and make frogs come up on the land of Egypt.'"

So Aaron stretched out his hand over the waters of Egypt, and the frogs came up and covered the land. But the magicians did the same things by their secret arts; they also made frogs come up on the land of Egypt.

Pharaoh summoned Moses and Aaron and said, "Pray to the LORD to take the frogs away from me and my people, and I will let your people go to offer sacrifices to the LORD."

Moses said to Pharaoh, "I leave to you the honor of setting the time for me to pray for you and your officials and your people that you and your houses may be rid of the frogs, except for those that remain in the Nile."

"Tomorrow," Pharaoh said.

Moses replied, "It will be as you say, so that you may know there is no one like the LORD our God. The frogs will leave you and your houses, your officials and your people; they will remain only in the Nile."

After Moses and Aaron left Pharaoh, Moses cried out to the LORD about the frogs he had brought on Pharaoh. And the LORD did what Moses asked. The frogs died in the houses, in the courtyards and in the fields. They were piled into heaps, and the land reeked of them. But when Pharaoh saw that there was relief, he hardened his heart and would not listen to Moses and Aaron, just as the LORD had said.

Moses and Aaron have gone to Pharaoh to ask for the release of the Israelites, but as God foretold, Pharaoh will not consent. Instead, he makes life harder for the people by increasing their workload. God begins a series of ten plagues on Egypt that within a year will wear down Pharaoh's resistance and bring about the release of the Israelite people.

God first turns the water in the Nile to blood. Some Bible scholars believe that the water did not literally become blood; rather, the Nile was flooded as large quantities of red soil washed down from Ethiopia, causing the water to run as red as blood. Whatever his method, God miraculously brings about the conditions that create plagues designed to change Pharaoh's heart.

In the second plague frogs descend upon the people of Egypt, invading their kitchens and bedrooms and even crawling on their bodies. If this plague was God's intensification of a natural event, the frogs, which were abundant in the Nile, probably left the river because of the dead fish and polluted water. Pharaoh becomes bothered enough to promise the people's release if Moses prays to God for relief. But when the frogs die, Pharaoh reneges on his promise.　　　　　　　　—BQ

DAILY CONTEMPLATION

When have you seen God move through an event to change a person's heart?

DAY 51　　　　　　　　　　　　　　　　Exodus 8:16–9:7

THE PLAGUES OF GNATS, FLIES, AND LIVESTOCK

Then the LORD said to Moses, "Tell Aaron, 'Stretch out your staff and strike the dust of the ground,' and throughout the land of Egypt the dust will become gnats." They did this, and when Aaron stretched out his hand with the staff and struck the dust of the ground, gnats came upon men and animals. All the dust throughout the land of Egypt became gnats. But when the magicians tried to produce gnats by their secret arts, they could not. And the gnats were on men and animals.

The magicians said to Pharaoh, "This is the finger of God." But Pharaoh's heart was hard and he would not listen, just as the LORD had said.

Then the LORD said to Moses, "Get up early in the morning and confront Pharaoh as he goes to the water and say to him, 'This is what the LORD says: Let my people go, so that they may worship me. If you do not let my people go, I will send swarms of flies on you and your officials, on your people and into your houses. The houses of the Egyptians will be full of flies, and even the ground where they are.

"'But on that day I will deal differently with the land of Goshen, where my people live; no swarms of flies will be there, so that you will know that I, the LORD, am in this land. I will make a distinction between my people and your people. This miraculous sign will occur tomorrow.'"

And the LORD did this. Dense swarms of flies poured into Pharaoh's palace and into the houses of his officials, and throughout Egypt the land was ruined by the flies.

Then Pharaoh summoned Moses and Aaron and said, "Go, sacrifice to your God here in the land."

But Moses said, "That would not be right. The sacrifices we offer the LORD our God would be detestable to the Egyptians. And if we offer sacrifices that are detestable in their eyes, will they not stone us? We must take a three-day journey into the desert to offer sacrifices to the LORD our God, as he commands us."

Pharaoh said, "I will let you go to offer sacrifices to the LORD your God in the desert, but you must not go very far. Now pray for me."

Moses answered, "As soon as I leave you, I will pray to the LORD, and tomorrow the flies will leave Pharaoh and his officials and his people. Only be sure that Pharaoh does not act deceitfully again by not letting the people go to offer sacrifices to the LORD."

Then Moses left Pharaoh and prayed to the LORD, and the LORD did what Moses asked: The flies left Pharaoh and his officials and his people; not a fly remained. But this time also Pharaoh hardened his heart and would not let the people go.

Then the LORD said to Moses, "Go to Pharaoh and say to him, 'This is what the LORD, the God of the Hebrews, says: "Let my people go, so that they may worship me." If you refuse to let them go and continue to hold them back, the hand of the LORD will bring a terrible plague on your livestock in the field— on your horses and donkeys and camels and on your cattle and sheep and goats. But the LORD will make a distinction between the livestock of Israel and that of Egypt, so that no animal belonging to the Israelites will die.'"

The LORD set a time and said, "Tomorrow the LORD will do this in the land." And the next day the LORD did it: All the livestock of the Egyptians died, but not one animal belonging to the Israelites died. Pharaoh sent men to investigate and found that not even one of the animals of the Israelites had died. Yet his heart was unyielding and he would not let the people go.

Now God allows gnats and flies to plague the Egyptian people. The gnats may have bred in the flooded fields of Egypt, and the flies on the wet banks of the receding Nile. It's likely that the flies were a type that when full-grown would bite both animals and people. As with the frogs, Pharaoh hates the flies so much that he again promises to let the people go. But when the flies vanish, he backs down on his promise.

Next God brings a plague on all the livestock belonging to the Egyptians and left out in the fields. God spares livestock belonging to the Israelites, as well as Egyptian livestock in shelters. The flies of the earlier plague may have carried the anthrax bacteria that originated in the algae-infested Nile. Flies carrying this bacteria could easily infect livestock. Not only does this plague hurt the Egyptians economically; it also insults some of their deities. The bull and cow are considered sacred, representing Egyptian gods and goddesses. Yet despite his loss, Pharaoh remains unyielding. —BQ

DAILY CONTEMPLATION

Do you consider yourself a cooperative or stubborn person?

DAY 52 Reflection

PRAYER OF A RELUCTANT SERVANT

Dear God,

I've got to make a decision soon. I can't believe I'm even considering doing this. It's a big commitment, a huge change for me. And I'm not even sure it fits me. *Who am I, that I should go* and take this step? Of all people, why did you choose me? I really don't know if I can handle the task.

Let's imagine I say yes. How do I begin? I can't just waltz in there and assume command, as if everyone already trusts me. *What shall I tell them?* They might not accept me. Maybe they won't like me. I can't do this without their support. *What if they don't believe me?* What if they think I'm not qualified, or worse, don't want my help? I can't take being rejected, God. You know how fragile my ego is.

I can't picture myself doing this. I'm not cut out for it. *I have never been eloquent.* It's not in my nature. Why can't I stick to what I've been doing and not embarrass you or anyone else?

The more I think about it, the colder my feet get. I can't do this. It scares me, and I certainly don't need more fear in my life. I don't have what it takes for this one, God. *O Lord, please send someone else to do it.* Surely you have an alternate who will do a better job than I could ever do. . . .

You're still asking me to do it. I can't shake the sense that you're serious. You really want *me,* don't you? Forgive my arguments, Lord. I'm learning that you have a much higher view of me than I do. Thanks for your confidence. I guess we both know who's really going to get it done. I'm going to need your help, God. Yes, I'm definitely going to need your help.

Amen. —BQ

DAY 53 Exodus 9:8–35

THE PLAGUES OF BOILS AND HAIL

Then the LORD said to Moses and Aaron, "Take handfuls of soot from a furnace and have Moses toss it into the air in the presence of Pharaoh. It will become fine dust over the whole land of Egypt, and festering boils will break out on men and animals throughout the land."

So they took soot from a furnace and stood before Pharaoh. Moses tossed it into the air, and festering boils broke out on men and animals. The magicians could not stand before Moses because of the boils that were on them and on all the Egyptians. But the LORD hardened Pharaoh's heart and he would not listen to Moses and Aaron, just as the LORD had said to Moses.

Then the LORD said to Moses, "Get up early in the morning, confront Pharaoh and say to him, 'This is what the LORD, the God of the Hebrews, says: Let my people go, so that they may worship me, or this time I will send the full force of my plagues against you and against your officials and your people, so you may know that there is no one like me in all the earth. For by now I could have stretched out my hand and struck you and your people with a plague that would have wiped you off the earth. But I have raised you up for this very purpose, that I might show you my power and that my name might be proclaimed in all the earth. You still set yourself against my people and will not let them go. Therefore, at this time tomorrow I will send the worst hailstorm that has ever fallen on Egypt, from the day it was founded till now. Give an order now to bring your livestock and everything you have in the field to a place of shelter, because the hail will fall on every man and animal that has not been brought in and is still out in the field, and they will die.'"

Those officials of Pharaoh who feared the word of the LORD hurried to bring their slaves and their livestock inside. But those who ignored the word of the LORD left their slaves and livestock in the field.

Then the LORD said to Moses, "Stretch out your hand toward the sky so that hail will fall all over Egypt—on men and animals and on everything growing in the fields of Egypt." When Moses stretched out his staff toward the sky, the LORD sent thunder and hail, and lightning flashed down to the ground. So the LORD rained hail on the land of Egypt; hail fell and lightning flashed back and forth. It was the worst storm in all the land of Egypt since it had become a nation. Throughout Egypt hail struck everything in the fields—both men and animals; it beat down everything growing in the fields and stripped every tree. The only place it did not hail was the land of Goshen, where the Israelites were.

Then Pharaoh summoned Moses and Aaron. "This time I have sinned," he said to them. "The LORD is in the right, and I and my people are in the wrong. Pray to the LORD, for we have had enough thunder and hail. I will let you go; you don't have to stay any longer."

Moses replied, "When I have gone out of the city, I will spread out my hands in prayer to the LORD. The thunder will stop and there will be no more hail, so you may know that the earth is the LORD's. But I know that you and your officials still do not fear the LORD God."

(The flax and barley were destroyed, since the barley had headed and the flax was in bloom. The wheat and spelt, however, were not destroyed, because they ripen later.)

Then Moses left Pharaoh and went out of the city. He spread out his hands toward the LORD; the thunder and hail stopped, and the rain no longer poured down on the land. When Pharaoh saw that the rain and hail and thunder had stopped, he sinned again: He and his officials hardened their hearts. So Pharaoh's heart was hard and he would not let the Israelites go, just as the LORD had said through Moses.

The plague of boils is the first to directly afflict the bodies of the Egyptian people. The plague hits with no warning, incapacitating even the magicians. (The boils may have resulted from a skin anthrax similar to what plagued the livestock earlier.) Only Pharaoh remains stubbornly unmoved.

God deals with the pharoah's hardness in the next plague, telling Moses to warn Pharaoh and the people about the coming of the worst hailstorm in the history of Egypt. God mercifully cautions any who will listen and act to save their own lives and the lives of their slaves and animals. Speaking to Pharaoh, God teaches about his sovereignty. The apostle Paul quotes verse 16 in Romans 9:17 as he discusses God's freedom in using people for his purposes: "I raised you up for this very purpose, that I might display my power in you and that my name might be proclaimed in all the earth." Rather than obliterating Pharaoh and the land of Egypt, which he could easily do, God chooses to display his own power to many people through Pharaoh's hardened heart. —BQ

DAILY CONTEMPLATION

When have you sensed God's power through an event of nature?

THE PLAGUES OF LOCUSTS, DARKNESS, AND
PLAGUE ON THE FIRSTBORN

Then the LORD said to Moses, "Go to Pharaoh, for I have hardened his heart and the hearts of his officials so that I may perform these miraculous signs of mine among them that you may tell your children and grandchildren how I dealt harshly with the Egyptians and how I performed my signs among them, and that you may know that I am the LORD."

So Moses and Aaron went to Pharaoh and said to him, "This is what the LORD, the God of the Hebrews, says: 'How long will you refuse to humble yourself before me? Let my people go, so that they may worship me. If you refuse to let them go, I will bring locusts into your country tomorrow. They will cover the face of the ground so that it cannot be seen. They will devour what little you have left after the hail, including every tree that is growing in your fields. They will fill your houses and those of all your officials and all the Egyptians—something neither your fathers nor your forefathers have ever seen from the day they settled in this land till now.'" Then Moses turned and left Pharaoh.

Pharaoh's officials said to him, "How long will this man be a snare to us? Let the people go, so that they may worship the LORD their God. Do you not yet realize that Egypt is ruined?"

Then Moses and Aaron were brought back to Pharaoh. "Go, worship the LORD your God," he said. "But just who will be going?"

Moses answered, "We will go with our young and old, with our sons and daughters, and with our flocks and herds, because we are to celebrate a festival to the LORD."

Pharaoh said, "The LORD be with you—if I let you go, along with your women and children! Clearly you are bent on evil. No! Have only the men go; and worship the LORD, since that's what you have been asking for." Then Moses and Aaron were driven out of Pharaoh's presence.

And the LORD said to Moses, "Stretch out your hand over Egypt so that locusts will swarm over the land and devour everything growing in the fields, everything left by the hail."

So Moses stretched out his staff over Egypt, and the LORD made an east wind blow across the land all that day and all that night. By morning the wind had brought the locusts; they invaded all Egypt and settled down in every area of the country in great numbers. Never before had there been such a plague of locusts, nor will there ever be again. They covered all the ground until it was black. They devoured all that was left after the hail—everything growing in the fields and the fruit on the trees. Nothing green remained on tree or plant in all the land of Egypt.

Pharaoh quickly summoned Moses and Aaron and said, "I have sinned against the LORD your God and against you. Now forgive my sin once more and pray to the LORD your God to take this deadly plague away from me."

Moses then left Pharaoh and prayed to the LORD. And the LORD changed the wind to a very strong west wind, which caught up the locusts and carried them into the Red Sea. Not a locust was left anywhere in Egypt. But the LORD hardened Pharaoh's heart, and he would not let the Israelites go.

Then the LORD said to Moses, "Stretch out your hand toward the sky so that darkness will spread over Egypt—darkness that can be felt." So Moses stretched out his hand toward the sky, and total darkness covered all Egypt for three days. No one could see anyone else or leave his place for three days. Yet all the Israelites had light in the places where they lived.

Then Pharaoh summoned Moses and said, "Go, worship the LORD. Even your women and children may go with you; only leave your flocks and herds behind."

But Moses said, "You must allow us to have sacrifices and burnt offerings to present to the LORD our God. Our livestock too must go with us; not a hoof is to be left behind. We have to use some of them in worshiping the LORD our God, and until we get there we will not know what we are to use to worship the LORD."

But the LORD hardened Pharaoh's heart, and he was not willing to let them go. Pharaoh said to Moses, "Get out of my sight! Make sure you do not appear before me again! The day you see my face you will die."

"Just as you say," Moses replied, "I will never appear before you again."

Now the LORD had said to Moses, "I will bring one more plague on Pharaoh and on Egypt. After that, he will let you go from here, and when he does, he will drive you out completely. Tell the people that men and women alike are to ask their neighbors for articles of silver and gold." (The LORD made the Egyptians favorably disposed toward the people, and Moses himself was highly regarded in Egypt by Pharaoh's officials and by the people.)

So Moses said, "This is what the LORD says: 'About midnight I will go throughout Egypt. Every firstborn son in Egypt will die, from the firstborn son of Pharaoh, who sits on the throne, to the firstborn son of the slave girl, who is at her hand mill, and all the firstborn of the cattle as well. There will be loud wailing throughout Egypt—worse than there has ever been or ever will be again. But among the Israelites not a dog will bark at any man or animal.' Then you will know that the LORD makes a distinction between Egypt and Israel. All these officials of yours will come to me, bowing down before me and saying, 'Go, you and all the people who follow you!' After that I will leave." Then Moses, hot with anger, left Pharaoh.

The LORD had said to Moses, "Pharaoh will refuse to listen to you—so that my wonders may be multiplied in Egypt." Moses and Aaron performed all these wonders before Pharaoh, but the LORD hardened Pharaoh's heart, and he would not let the Israelites go out of his country.

To liberate the Israelite slaves, God stages a cosmic showdown known as the Ten Plagues, a showdown so dramatic that in modern times it strains the limits of Hollywood special effects crews just to depict it on-screen. A nation is aborning, and the task of uprooting the Israelites from Egypt calls for outside intervention.

First, the Israelites themselves have to be convinced of God's power. Somehow God has to demonstrate that he has not forgotten his chosen people, even though he has seemed silent and unconcerned. Then, too, Egypt needs convincing: no empire will let thousands of valuable slaves walk away free. Exodus asserts more than a dozen times that the plagues are given so that the Israelites and Egyptians will recognize the power of Israel's God.

An even more basic issue is at stake: God's personal credibility. Is he just one more tribal god, like the ones the Egyptians worship? The plagues are, in effect, God's open warfare against the false gods of Egypt. He declares as much: "I will bring judgment on all the gods of Egypt" (12:12). Some scholars see each plague as a targeted attack against a specific Egyptian idol. Thus, the plague on the Nile River countered the Egyptians' river god; the plague of flies, the sacred fly; the plague of darkness, the sun god Ra; and the plague on livestock, the sacred bull.

In the end, the plagues will work so effectively that thousands of slaves will leave unhindered, with the wealth of Egypt showered upon them as farewell gifts. "I am the God who brought you out of Egypt," God will remind them again and again whenever they are tempted to doubt his power or concern for them.   —PY

DAILY CONTEMPLATION

If God declared war on the "gods" of our modern society, what would they be?

DAY 55   Exodus 12:1–30

THE PASSOVER

The LORD said to Moses and Aaron in Egypt, "This month is to be for you the first month, the first month of your year. Tell the whole community of Israel that on the tenth day of this month each man is to take a lamb for his family, one for each household. If any household is too small for a whole lamb, they must share one with their nearest neighbor, having taken into account the number of people there are. You are to determine the amount of lamb needed in accordance with what each person will eat. The animals you choose must be year-old males without defect, and you may take them from the sheep or the goats. Take care of them until the fourteenth day of the month, when all the people of the community of Israel must slaughter them at twilight. Then they are to take some of the blood and put it on the sides and tops of the doorframes of the houses where they eat the lambs. That same night they are to eat the meat roasted over the fire, along with bitter herbs, and bread made without yeast. Do not eat the meat raw or cooked in water, but roast it over the fire—head, legs and inner parts. Do not leave any of it till morning; if some is left till morning, you must burn it. This is how you are to eat it: with your cloak tucked into your belt, your sandals on your feet and your staff in your hand. Eat it in haste; it is the LORD's Passover.

"On that same night I will pass through Egypt and strike down every first-born—both men and animals—and I will bring judgment on all the gods of Egypt. I am the LORD. The blood will be a sign for you on the houses where you are; and when I see the blood, I will pass over you. No destructive plague will touch you when I strike Egypt.

"This is a day you are to commemorate; for the generations to come you shall celebrate it as a festival to the LORD—a lasting ordinance. For seven days you are to eat bread made without yeast. On the first day remove the yeast from your houses, for whoever eats anything with yeast in it from the first day through the seventh must be cut off from Israel. On the first day hold a sacred assembly, and another one on the seventh day. Do no work at all on these days, except to prepare food for everyone to eat—that is all you may do.

"Celebrate the Feast of Unleavened Bread, because it was on this very day that I brought your divisions out of Egypt. Celebrate this day as a lasting ordinance for the generations to come. In the first month you are to eat bread made without yeast, from the evening of the fourteenth day until the evening of the twenty-first day. For seven days no yeast is to be found in your houses. And whoever eats anything with yeast in it must be cut off from the community of Israel, whether he is an alien or native-born. Eat nothing made with yeast. Wherever you live, you must eat unleavened bread."

Then Moses summoned all the elders of Israel and said to them, "Go at once and select the animals for your families and slaughter the Passover lamb. Take a bunch of hyssop, dip it into the blood in the basin and put some of the blood on the top and on both sides of the doorframe. Not one of you shall go out the door of his house until morning. When the LORD goes through the land to strike down the Egyptians, he will see the blood on the top and sides of the doorframe and will pass over that doorway, and he will not permit the destroyer to enter your houses and strike you down.

"Obey these instructions as a lasting ordinance for you and your descendants. When you enter the land that the LORD will give you as he promised, observe this ceremony. And when your children ask you, 'What does this ceremony mean to you?' then tell them, 'It is the Passover sacrifice to the LORD, who passed over the houses of the Israelites in Egypt and spared our homes when he struck down the Egyptians.'" Then the people bowed down and worshiped. The Israelites did just what the LORD commanded Moses and Aaron.

At midnight the LORD struck down all the firstborn in Egypt, from the first-born of Pharaoh, who sat on the throne, to the firstborn of the prisoner, who was in the dungeon, and the firstborn of all the livestock as well. Pharaoh and all his officials and all the Egyptians got up during the night, and there was loud wailing in Egypt, for there was not a house without someone dead.

Life in Egypt has been hellish. For centuries the Israelites have been held captive to people who oppress them and who worship false, powerless gods. Finally the time has come. God shows the Egyptians once and for all that those who worship any god but the true God deserve death. He spares the Israelites because he's chosen them as his own and because they use the blood of a lamb to signal they belong to him.

The story may sound vaguely familiar, not because you've heard it before but because it sets the stage for the central story of the Bible: the story of Jesus Christ, the Lamb slain to save the lives of those who love God, rescuing them out of a sinful world. Here in the Old Testament the Israelites are the people God has chosen for himself, the ones he singles out to save. As the story of God's walk with his people continues through the Bible, the group of chosen people will extend beyond this ethnic group of Jews to encompass all who follow Jesus.

Now we, as believers, share in the Passover story. Like the Israelites in Egypt, we know we're not at home in this world of pain and suffering. But we are ready to journey with God. Our hope is in the sacrifice Jesus made for us, and we're waiting to be with him always in the Promised Land. —BQ

DAILY CONTEMPLATION

What is your life like now compared with life "in Egypt," before you knew Jesus?

DAY 56 Exodus 12:31–42

THE EXODUS

During the night Pharaoh summoned Moses and Aaron and said, "Up! Leave my people, you and the Israelites! Go, worship the LORD as you have requested. Take your flocks and herds, as you have said, and go. And also bless me."

The Egyptians urged the people to hurry and leave the country. "For otherwise," they said, "we will all die!" So the people took their dough before the yeast was added, and carried it on their shoulders in kneading troughs wrapped in clothing. The Israelites did as Moses instructed and asked the Egyptians for articles of silver and gold and for clothing. The LORD had made the Egyptians favorably disposed toward the people, and they gave them what they asked for; so they plundered the Egyptians.

The Israelites journeyed from Rameses to Succoth. There were about six hundred thousand men on foot, besides women and children. Many other people went up with them, as well as large droves of livestock, both flocks and herds. With the dough they had brought from Egypt, they baked cakes of unleavened bread. The dough was without yeast because they had been driven out of Egypt and did not have time to prepare food for themselves.

Now the length of time the Israelite people lived in Egypt was 430 years. At the end of the 430 years, to the very day, all the LORD's divisions left Egypt. Because the LORD kept vigil that night to bring them out of Egypt, on this night all the Israelites are to keep vigil to honor the LORD for the generations to come.

The journey has begun. For nearly a year the Israelites have watched one plague after another besiege the Egyptian people, only to leave Pharaoh as hard-hearted as ever. Freedom has seemed improbable for a long time, God's promises clouded by the daunting circumstances. Suddenly Pharaoh is forcing them out faster than they can go.

Immediately everything changes. Literally overnight the man considered a god by his people orders the Israelites to leave, taking all their belongings. Pharaoh even asks for a blessing. As they go, the Israelites find their Egyptian neighbors only too willing to bestow going-away gifts of silver, gold, and clothing—a turn of events too good to be true.

Within hours this vast nation is heading to the desert. They discover that God will do what he says despite the odds against it. Unfortunately, the people will forget this lesson many times in the desert and even after they've reached the Promised Land. They will lose sight of a lesson that all future believers also will struggle to embrace.   —BQ

DAILY CONTEMPLATION

What circumstances are clouding your view of the plan God has for you?

DAY 57 | Exodus 13:17–14:31

CROSSING THE RED SEA

When Pharaoh let the people go, God did not lead them on the road through the Philistine country, though that was shorter. For God said, "If they face war, they might change their minds and return to Egypt." So God led the people around by the desert road toward the Red Sea. The Israelites went up out of Egypt armed for battle.

Moses took the bones of Joseph with him because Joseph had made the sons of Israel swear an oath. He had said, "God will surely come to your aid, and then you must carry my bones up with you from this place."

After leaving Succoth they camped at Etham on the edge of the desert. By day the LORD went ahead of them in a pillar of cloud to guide them on their way and by night in a pillar of fire to give them light, so that they could travel by day or night. Neither the pillar of cloud by day nor the pillar of fire by night left its place in front of the people.

Then the LORD said to Moses, "Tell the Israelites to turn back and encamp near Pi Hahiroth, between Migdol and the sea. They are to encamp by the sea, directly opposite Baal Zephon. Pharaoh will think, 'The Israelites are wandering around the land in confusion, hemmed in by the desert.' And I will harden Pharaoh's heart, and he will pursue them. But I will gain glory for myself through Pharaoh and all his army, and the Egyptians will know that I am the LORD." So the Israelites did this.

When the king of Egypt was told that the people had fled, Pharaoh and his officials changed their minds about them and said, "What have we done? We have let the Israelites go and have lost their services!" So he had his chariot made ready and took his army with him. He took six hundred of the best chariots, along with all the other chariots of Egypt, with officers over all of them. The LORD hardened the heart of Pharaoh king of Egypt, so that he pursued the Israelites, who were marching out boldly. The Egyptians—all Pharaoh's horses and chariots, horsemen and troops—pursued the Israelites and overtook them as they camped by the sea near Pi Hahiroth, opposite Baal Zephon.

As Pharaoh approached, the Israelites looked up, and there were the Egyptians, marching after them. They were terrified and cried out to the LORD. They said to Moses, "Was it because there were no graves in Egypt that you brought us to the desert to die? What have you done to us by bringing us out of Egypt? Didn't we say to you in Egypt, 'Leave us alone; let us serve the Egyptians'? It would have been better for us to serve the Egyptians than to die in the desert!"

Moses answered the people, "Do not be afraid. Stand firm and you will see the deliverance the LORD will bring you today. The Egyptians you see today you will never see again. The LORD will fight for you; you need only to be still."

Then the LORD said to Moses, "Why are you crying out to me? Tell the Israelites to move on. Raise your staff and stretch out your hand over the sea to divide the water so that the Israelites can go through the sea on dry ground. I will harden the hearts of the Egyptians so that they will go in after them. And I will gain glory through Pharaoh and all his army, through his chariots and his horsemen. The Egyptians will know that I am the LORD when I gain glory through Pharaoh, his chariots and his horsemen."

Then the angel of God, who had been traveling in front of Israel's army, withdrew and went behind them. The pillar of cloud also moved from in front and stood behind them, coming between the armies of Egypt and Israel. Throughout the night the cloud brought darkness to the one side and light to the other side; so neither went near the other all night long.

Then Moses stretched out his hand over the sea, and all that night the LORD drove the sea back with a strong east wind and turned it into dry land. The waters were divided, and the Israelites went through the sea on dry ground, with a wall of water on their right and on their left.

The Egyptians pursued them, and all Pharaoh's horses and chariots and horsemen followed them into the sea. During the last watch of the night the LORD looked down from the pillar of fire and cloud at the Egyptian army and threw it into confusion. He made the wheels of their chariots come off so that they had difficulty driving. And the Egyptians said, "Let's get away from the Israelites! The LORD is fighting for them against Egypt."

Then the LORD said to Moses, "Stretch out your hand over the sea so that the waters may flow back over the Egyptians and their chariots and horsemen." Moses stretched out his hand over the sea, and at daybreak the sea went back to its place. The Egyptians were fleeing toward it, and the LORD swept them into the sea. The water flowed back and covered the chariots and horsemen—the entire army of Pharaoh that had followed the Israelites into the sea. Not one of them survived.

But the Israelites went through the sea on dry ground, with a wall of water on their right and on their left. That day the LORD saved Israel from the hands of the Egyptians, and Israel saw the Egyptians lying dead on the shore. And when the Israelites saw the great power the LORD displayed against the Egyptians, the people feared the LORD and put their trust in him and in Moses his servant.

It doesn't take long for Pharaoh and the Egyptians to second-guess their decision to release the slaves. Soon a glittering army of chariots and horsemen is charging after the defenseless Israelites.

Nor does it take long for the Israelites to second-guess their decision to leave. At the first sight of Pharaoh's army, they quake in fear and accuse Moses of leading them to certain destruction in the desert.

As this chapter tells it, the Israelites' final confrontation with Egypt is divinely stage-managed to make a point for all time: God himself, no one else, is responsible for the Israelites' liberation. More than anything else, the account of the Exodus underscores that one indisputable fact. No Israelite armies stand against the mighty Egyptians. At the last possible minute, God arranges a spectacular rescue operation and an equally spectacular defeat of the Egyptian army. The freed captives can only respond with humility and praise; there is no room for pride. For them, independence from Egypt means dependence on God.

That pattern of depending on God will continue all through the Exodus. When the wilderness wanderers run out of water, God provides. When food supplies fail, God provides. When raiders attack, God provides. In fact, the book of Exodus shows a greater proportion of miracles—direct supernatural acts of God—than any part of the Bible except the Gospels. The psalmists will never tire of celebrating these events in music, and the prophets will later hark back to the days of the Exodus to stir the conscience of their nation. The great miracle of the Red Sea merely sets the tone for a national history that is from beginning to end an active movement of God. —PY

DAILY CONTEMPLATION

Has God ever parted a "Red Sea" in your life, to rescue you from something that would have been harmful?

SPIRITUAL AMNESIA

Now that you've read about the beginning of creation and become acquainted with the fathers of the faith, how much do you remember about the ways in which God makes his will possible in their lives?

Your recollections should include the great flood, when God saved only one family on a boat and then through them repopulated the earth. Abraham and Sarah, a couple who'd been infertile and were too old to conceive, gave birth to a son, Isaac, whose life was spared by an order from God. Twin brothers, Jacob and Esau, reunited with weeping and gifts after living apart for years due to rivalry and deception. Joseph, a son of Jacob, survived enslavement and became the wealthy governor of Egypt. Moses, a captive Hebrew who'd been raised an Egyptian, watched God rain destruction in the form of plagues and then saw God part the waters of the sea to provide an escape route.

In all these ways God kept his promises, never failing to surprise his people in working out his plans. Those coming after Moses will remember God's doings. King David finds the memories of God's acts comforting, and he declares to God, "You remain the same" (Psalm 102:27). The writer of Hebrews affirms, "Jesus Christ is the same yesterday and today and forever" (Hebrews 13:8). The God we've watched in the Bible so far is the same God the first Christians knew two thousand years ago and the same God we know today.

Why, then, don't believers do a better job of trusting? The Israelites remembered God's many feats, but sometimes they forgot. The early church remembered, too, but sometimes their memory lapsed. Believers throughout the ages have exhibited a sort of selective memory, recalling God's power and then letting fears block that memory. It's a spiritual amnesia, usually contracted by a hard knock from the world. As many Christians before us have discovered, the surest cure for forgetfulness is going back to the beginning and reminding ourselves of God's track record.

How's your memory?   —BQ

DAILY CONTEMPLATION

Spend a few moments thinking about the ways in which God has rescued you in the past. Do you need rescuing now? Thank God for the ways in which he has already come through for you, and tell him you need him now.

DAY 59   Exodus 16:1–26, 31

MANNA AND QUAIL

The whole Israelite community set out from Elim and came to the Desert of Sin, which is between Elim and Sinai, on the fifteenth day of the second month after they had come out of Egypt. In the desert the whole community grumbled against Moses and Aaron. The Israelites said to them, "If only we had died by the LORD's hand in Egypt! There we sat around pots of meat and ate all the food we wanted, but you have brought us out into this desert to starve this entire assembly to death."

Then the LORD said to Moses, "I will rain down bread from heaven for you. The people are to go out each day and gather enough for that day. In this way I will test them and see whether they will follow my instructions. On the sixth day they are to prepare what they bring in, and that is to be twice as much as they gather on the other days."

So Moses and Aaron said to all the Israelites, "In the evening you will know that it was the LORD who brought you out of Egypt, and in the morning you will see the glory of the LORD, because he has heard your grumbling against him. Who are we, that you should grumble against us?" Moses also said, "You will know that it was the LORD when he gives you meat to eat in the evening and all the bread you want in the morning, because he has heard your grumbling against him. Who are we? You are not grumbling against us, but against the LORD."

Then Moses told Aaron, "Say to the entire Israelite community, 'Come before the LORD, for he has heard your grumbling.'"

While Aaron was speaking to the whole Israelite community, they looked toward the desert, and there was the glory of the LORD appearing in the cloud.

The LORD said to Moses, "I have heard the grumbling of the Israelites. Tell them, 'At twilight you will eat meat, and in the morning you will be filled with bread. Then you will know that I am the LORD your God.'"

That evening quail came and covered the camp, and in the morning there was a layer of dew around the camp. When the dew was gone, thin flakes like frost on the ground appeared on the desert floor. When the Israelites saw it, they said to each other, "What is it?" For they did not know what it was.

Moses said to them, "It is the bread the LORD has given you to eat. This is what the LORD has commanded: 'Each one is to gather as much as he needs. Take an omer for each person you have in your tent.'"

The Israelites did as they were told; some gathered much, some little. And when they measured it by the omer, he who gathered much did not have too much, and he who gathered little did not have too little. Each one gathered as much as he needed.

Then Moses said to them, "No one is to keep any of it until morning."

However, some of them paid no attention to Moses; they kept part of it until morning, but it was full of maggots and began to smell. So Moses was angry with them.

Each morning everyone gathered as much as he needed, and when the sun grew hot, it melted away. On the sixth day, they gathered twice as much—two omers for each person—and the leaders of the community came and reported this to Moses. He said to them, "This is what the LORD commanded: 'Tomorrow is to be a day of rest, a holy Sabbath to the LORD. So bake what you want to bake and boil what you want to boil. Save whatever is left and keep it until morning.'"

So they saved it until morning, as Moses commanded, and it did not stink or get maggots in it. "Eat it today," Moses said, "because today is a Sabbath to the LORD. You will not find any of it on the ground today. Six days you are to gather it, but on the seventh day, the Sabbath, there will not be any." ...

The people of Israel called the bread manna. It was white like coriander seed and tasted like wafers made with honey.

Only weeks after they walk through a parted Red Sea and watch their Egyptian pursuers drown in the waters, the Israelites are already complaining about the death they feel is imminent. Out of food, they feel certain they'll starve. Not only does God provide an immediate and lasting food supply; he puts the Israelites on a schedule that gives them a day each week to rest and eat leftovers.

Again in this passage we see reflections of future Bible events. God provides for the Israelites in the desert by showering them with manna each morning. Jesus will teach the disciples to ask for similar provision by praying, "Give us today our daily bread" (Matthew 6:11). More importantly, Jesus will call himself "the living bread that came down from heaven" (John 6:51). Not only does God provide for our immediate physical needs; he has given us Jesus to care daily for our spirits and give us life that will last forever.   —BQ

DAILY CONTEMPLATION

What kind of "manna" do you need God to provide in the coming days?

DAY 60   Exodus 18:1–27

JETHRO VISITS MOSES

Now Jethro, the priest of Midian and father-in-law of Moses, heard of everything God had done for Moses and for his people Israel, and how the LORD had brought Israel out of Egypt.

After Moses had sent away his wife Zipporah, his father-in-law Jethro received her and her two sons. One son was named Gershom, for Moses said, "I have become an alien in a foreign land"; and the other was named Eliezer, for he said, "My father's God was my helper; he saved me from the sword of Pharaoh."

Jethro, Moses' father-in-law, together with Moses' sons and wife, came to him in the desert, where he was camped near the mountain of God. Jethro had sent word to him, "I, your father-in-law Jethro, am coming to you with your wife and her two sons."

So Moses went out to meet his father-in-law and bowed down and kissed him. They greeted each other and then went into the tent. Moses told his father-in-law about everything the LORD had done to Pharaoh and the Egyptians for Israel's sake and about all the hardships they had met along the way and how the LORD had saved them.

Jethro was delighted to hear about all the good things the LORD had done for Israel in rescuing them from the hand of the Egyptians. He said, "Praise be to the LORD, who rescued you from the hand of the Egyptians and of Pharaoh, and who rescued the people from the hand of the Egyptians. Now I know that the LORD is greater than all other gods, for he did this to those who had treated Israel arrogantly." Then Jethro, Moses' father-in-law, brought a burnt offering and other sacrifices to God, and Aaron came with all the elders of Israel to eat bread with Moses' father-in-law in the presence of God.

The next day Moses took his seat to serve as judge for the people, and they stood around him from morning till evening. When his father-in-law saw all that Moses was doing for the people, he said, "What is this you are doing for the people? Why do you alone sit as judge, while all these people stand around you from morning till evening?"

Moses answered him, "Because the people come to me to seek God's will. Whenever they have a dispute, it is brought to me, and I decide between the parties and inform them of God's decrees and laws."

Moses' father-in-law replied, "What you are doing is not good. You and these people who come to you will only wear yourselves out. The work is too heavy for you; you cannot handle it alone. Listen now to me and I will give you some advice, and may God be with you. You must be the people's representative before God and bring their disputes to him. Teach them the decrees and laws, and show them the way to live and the duties they are to perform. But select capable men from all the people—men who fear God, trustworthy men who hate dishonest gain—and appoint them as officials over thousands, hundreds, fifties and tens. Have them serve as judges for the people at all times, but have them bring every difficult case to you; the simple cases they can decide themselves. That will make your load lighter, because they will share it with you. If you do this and God so commands, you will be able to stand the strain, and all these people will go home satisfied."

Moses listened to his father-in-law and did everything he said. He chose capable men from all Israel and made them leaders of the people, officials over thousands, hundreds, fifties and tens. They served as judges for the people at all times. The difficult cases they brought to Moses, but the simple ones they decided themselves.

Then Moses sent his father-in-law on his way, and Jethro returned to his own country.

Moses' father-in-law, Jethro, becomes the first counselor to warn against becoming one of those people who do too much. God has given Moses the job of representing the people before God and teaching them how to live. But clearly Moses, who feels he must carry out his job from beginning to end, doing it all himself, needs help. God brings somebody in from the outside to let him know he'll soon wear out. God wants to spread the work to others and keep Moses fresh for what God especially wants him to do. —BQ

DAILY CONTEMPLATION

Are you doing too much? Which responsibilities has God clearly given you? Which might you need to release to someone else?

DAY 61   Exodus 19:1–6, 17–19; 20:1–17

THE TEN COMMANDMENTS

In the third month after the Israelites left Egypt—on the very day—they came to the Desert of Sinai. After they set out from Rephidim, they entered the Desert of Sinai, and Israel camped there in the desert in front of the mountain.

Then Moses went up to God, and the LORD called to him from the mountain and said, "This is what you are to say to the house of Jacob and what you are to tell the people of Israel: 'You yourselves have seen what I did to Egypt, and how I carried you on eagles' wings and brought you to myself. Now if you obey me fully and keep my covenant, then out of all nations you will be my treasured possession. Although the whole earth is mine, you will be for me a kingdom of priests and a holy nation.' These are the words you are to speak to the Israelites."

...

Then Moses led the people out of the camp to meet with God, and they stood at the foot of the mountain. Mount Sinai was covered with smoke, because the LORD descended on it in fire. The smoke billowed up from it like smoke from a furnace, the whole mountain trembled violently, and the sound of the trumpet grew louder and louder. Then Moses spoke and the voice of God answered him. . . .

And God spoke all these words:

"I am the LORD your God, who brought you out of Egypt, out of the land of slavery.

"You shall have no other gods before me.

"You shall not make for yourself an idol in the form of anything in heaven above or on the earth beneath or in the waters below. You shall not bow down to them or worship them; for I, the LORD your God, am a jealous God, punishing the children for the sin of the fathers to the third and fourth generation of those who hate me, but showing love to a thousand generations of those who love me and keep my commandments.

"You shall not misuse the name of the LORD your God, for the LORD will not hold anyone guiltless who misuses his name.

"Remember the Sabbath day by keeping it holy. Six days you shall labor and do all your work, but the seventh day is a Sabbath to the LORD your God. On it you shall not do any work, neither you, nor your son or daughter, nor your manservant or maidservant, nor your animals, nor the alien within your gates. For in six days the LORD made the heavens and the earth, the sea, and all that is in them, but he rested on the seventh day. Therefore the LORD blessed the Sabbath day and made it holy.

"Honor your father and your mother, so that you may live long in the land the LORD your God is giving you.

"You shall not murder.

"You shall not commit adultery.

"You shall not steal.

"You shall not give false testimony against your neighbor.

"You shall not covet your neighbor's house. You shall not covet your neighbor's wife, or his manservant or maidservant, his ox or donkey, or anything that belongs to your neighbor."

Nearly everyone has heard of the Ten Commandments. For most of us, they represent a central core of morality, "the basics" that God requires. But for the Israelites in the desert, the Ten Commandments represent far more—nothing less than a major breakthrough. Nations around them, who worship many different gods, live in constant fear of the gods' unpredictability. Who could tell what might anger or please them? But now God himself, Maker of the universe, is giving the Israelites a binding treaty signed in his own hand. They will always know exactly what God requires and where they stand before him.

God holds before them some wonderful guarantees: prosperity, abundant crops, victorious armies, immunity from health problems. In effect, he agrees to remove most of the problems people face in daily existence. In exchange, he asks that the Israelites obey the rules outlined in this and the next few chapters. God's original covenant with Abraham he now makes formal, and applies to a whole nation. (This middle part of Exodus is known as the Book of the Covenant, for it contains the essence of the Israelites' treaty with God.)

"Although the whole earth is mine, you will be for me a kingdom of priests and a holy nation," God said (19:5–6). He wants a nation like no other, a model society centered around a commitment to him. All the Israelites wait in anticipation as Moses climbs a dark, smoky mountain to meet with God. No one present could miss the significance of this meeting: It is marked by thunder and lightning and a loud, piercing trumpet blast and fire. The ground itself shakes, as in an earthquake.

Out of this meeting on Mount Sinai (SIE-nie) come the rules summarized here. The Bible fills in more details of the treaty, but these Ten Commandments express the kind of behavior God wants from his people. It is a day of wild hope. "We will do everything the LORD has said," the people all promise with a shout (19:8). —PY

DAILY CONTEMPLATION

What would some of the Ten Commandments say if worded positively (reading, "You shall ..." rather than, "You shall not ...")?

DAY 62   Exodus 32:1–35

THE GOLDEN CALF

When the people saw that Moses was so long in coming down from the mountain, they gathered around Aaron and said, "Come, make us gods who will go before us. As for this fellow Moses who brought us up out of Egypt, we don't know what has happened to him."

Aaron answered them, "Take off the gold earrings that your wives, your sons and your daughters are wearing, and bring them to me." So all the people took off their earrings and brought them to Aaron. He took what they handed him and made it into an idol cast in the shape of a calf, fashioning it with a tool. Then they said, "These are your gods, O Israel, who brought you up out of Egypt."

When Aaron saw this, he built an altar in front of the calf and announced, "Tomorrow there will be a festival to the LORD." So the next day the people rose early and sacrificed burnt offerings and presented fellowship offerings. Afterward they sat down to eat and drink and got up to indulge in revelry.

Then the LORD said to Moses, "Go down, because your people, whom you brought up out of Egypt, have become corrupt. They have been quick to turn away from what I commanded them and have made themselves an idol cast in the shape of a calf. They have bowed down to it and sacrificed to it and have said, 'These are your gods, O Israel, who brought you up out of Egypt.'

"I have seen these people," the LORD said to Moses, "and they are a stiff-necked people. Now leave me alone so that my anger may burn against them and that I may destroy them. Then I will make you into a great nation."

But Moses sought the favor of the LORD his God. "O LORD," he said, "why should your anger burn against your people, whom you brought out of Egypt with great power and a mighty hand? Why should the Egyptians say, 'It was with evil intent that he brought them out, to kill them in the mountains and to wipe them off the face of the earth'? Turn from your fierce anger; relent and do not bring disaster on your people. Remember your servants Abraham, Isaac and Israel, to whom you swore by your own self: 'I will make your descendants as numerous as the stars in the sky and I will give your descendants all this land I promised them, and it will be their inheritance forever.'" Then the LORD relented and did not bring on his people the disaster he had threatened.

Moses turned and went down the mountain with the two tablets of the Testimony in his hands. They were inscribed on both sides, front and back. The tablets were the work of God; the writing was the writing of God, engraved on the tablets.

When Joshua heard the noise of the people shouting, he said to Moses, "There is the sound of war in the camp."

Moses replied:

"It is not the sound of victory,
    it is not the sound of defeat;
    it is the sound of singing that I hear."

When Moses approached the camp and saw the calf and the dancing, his anger burned and he threw the tablets out of his hands, breaking them to pieces at the foot of the mountain. And he took the calf they had made and burned it in the fire; then he ground it to powder, scattered it on the water and made the Israelites drink it.

He said to Aaron, "What did these people do to you, that you led them into such great sin?"

"Do not be angry, my lord," Aaron answered. "You know how prone these people are to evil. They said to me, 'Make us gods who will go before us. As for this fellow Moses who brought us up out of Egypt, we don't know what has happened to him.' So I told them, 'Whoever has any gold jewelry, take it off.' Then they gave me the gold, and I threw it into the fire, and out came this calf!"

Moses saw that the people were running wild and that Aaron had let them get out of control and so become a laughingstock to their enemies. So he stood at the entrance to the camp and said, "Whoever is for the LORD, come to me." And all the Levites rallied to him.

Then he said to them, "This is what the LORD, the God of Israel, says: 'Each man strap a sword to his side. Go back and forth through the camp from one end to the other, each killing his brother and friend and neighbor.'" The Levites did as Moses commanded, and that day about three thousand of the people died. Then Moses said, "You have been set apart to the LORD today, for you were against your own sons and brothers, and he has blessed you this day."

The next day Moses said to the people, "You have committed a great sin. But now I will go up to the LORD; perhaps I can make atonement for your sin."

So Moses went back to the LORD and said, "Oh, what a great sin these people have committed! They have made themselves gods of gold. But now, please forgive their sin—but if not, then blot me out of the book you have written."

The LORD replied to Moses, "Whoever has sinned against me I will blot out of my book. Now go, lead the people to the place I spoke of, and my angel will go before you. However, when the time comes for me to punish, I will punish them for their sin."

And the LORD struck the people with a plague because of what they did with the calf Aaron had made.

The bright hope of Exodus 20 dies forever in Exodus 32; there is no more jarring contrast in all the Bible. For forty days Moses visits with God on Mount Sinai, receiving the terms of the covenant, or treaty, that will open up an unprecedented closeness between God and human beings. But what happens down below, at the foot of the mountain, almost defies belief.

The Israelites—people who have seen the ten plagues of Egypt, who have crossed the Red Sea on dry ground, who have drunk water from a rock, who are digesting the miracle of manna in their stomachs at this moment—these same people feel boredom or impatience or rebellion or jealousy or some such mortal urge and apparently forget all about their God. By the time Moses descends from Sinai, the Israelites, God's people, are dancing like pagans around a golden statue.

Moses is so mad that he hurls to the ground the tablets of stone signed by God himself. God is so mad that he nearly destroys the whole cantankerous nation.

This chapter has many parallels with the story of the very first human rebellion in Genesis 3. Both times, people favored by God fail to trust him and strike out instead against his clear command. Both times, the rebels devise elaborate rationalizations to explain their behavior. Both times, they forfeit special privileges and suffer harsh punishment.

It appears, for a moment, that something new in the history of humanity will take place among the Israelites: an entire nation devoted to following God. Instead, the same old story replays itself. No matter what terms God comes up with, people find ways to break them.

Only one ray of hope shines out of this dark scene. Moses, the stuttering, reluctant leader, seems to grow into his position at last. His eloquent prayers are answered, and God grants the Israelites yet another chance.　　　　　—PY

DAILY CONTEMPLATION

Why do you think the Israelites rebelled? Have you ever rebelled for a similar reason?

DAY 63　　　　　　　　　　　　　　　Reflection

TRAVELING ON GOD'S WINGS

In their first weeks growing up together as a liberated nation, the Israelites have experienced God's care—not only as Lord and Deliverer, he has loved them as

Parent. In their first stories of desert sojourn, God has also given us a lesson in parenting and being parented.

God first met the Israelites' most basic need, for food, ensuring that they would have something to eat every day and feel satisfied. Next God gave them guidance. As any parent advises a child—"Don't lift that. It's too heavy for you. I'll help"— God advised Moses and the people as to how they could work best together without wearing out. After securing their physical and emotional needs, he led the people on to the next stage of maturity, introducing a set of rules to govern the household. Without rules these children would remain aimless, but with a clear set of directives they could become grounded people, fit for serving God.

As God has cared for the Israelites, he cares for us, his children, today. He gives us food to keep us going. He guides us day to day in handling our lives. And as we make choices, we turn to God's rules as a foundation for our behavior. Like typical children, we need rules to feel loved. We need a Parent who knows better than we what is good for us.

God may come off a bit harsh and demanding in much of Exodus, but occasionally we get a glimpse of the poetry of his heart, the tenderness he feels for his people. As he prepares to give Moses the Ten Commandments, God says, "You yourselves have seen what I did to Egypt, and how I carried you on eagle's wings and brought you to myself" (19:4).

God speaks not as a distant, bellowing old man. Rather, he likens himself to a mother eagle teaching her young to fly by soaring beneath, with wings spread to catch the faltering eaglet. He doesn't leave his children in a barren place to help themselves, while calling from afar with pointless admonitions. Rather, he flies only inches underneath and often rests them by bringing them to himself.   —BQ

DAILY CONTEMPLATION

Consider the ways in which God has been a truly loving Parent to you. Can you feel him near, wings spread to lift you when you fall? Thank him now for knowing your needs and for meeting them. Thank him for loving you tenderly and rightly.

DAY 64   Leviticus 26:3–43

REWARD FOR OBEDIENCE
AND PUNISHMENT FOR DISOBEDIENCE

[The LORD said to Moses,] "If you follow my decrees and are careful to obey my commands, I will send you rain in its season, and the ground will yield its crops and the trees of the field their fruit. Your threshing will continue until grape harvest and the grape harvest will continue until planting, and you will eat all the food you want and live in safety in your land.

"I will grant peace in the land, and you will lie down and no one will make you afraid. I will remove savage beasts from the land, and the sword will not pass through your country. You will pursue your enemies, and they will fall by the sword before you. Five of you will chase a hundred, and a hundred of you will chase ten thousand, and your enemies will fall by the sword before you.

"I will look on you with favor and make you fruitful and increase your numbers, and I will keep my covenant with you. You will still be eating last year's harvest when you will have to move it out to make room for the new. I will put my dwelling place among you, and I will not abhor you. I will walk among you and be your God, and you will be my people. I am the LORD your God, who brought you out of Egypt so that you would no longer be slaves to the Egyptians; I broke the bars of your yoke and enabled you to walk with heads held high.

"But if you will not listen to me and carry out all these commands, and if you reject my decrees and abhor my laws and fail to carry out all my commands and so violate my covenant, then I will do this to you: I will bring upon you sudden terror, wasting diseases and fever that will destroy your sight and drain away your life. You will plant seed in vain, because your enemies will eat it. I will set my face against you so that you will be defeated by your enemies; those who hate you will rule over you, and you will flee even when no one is pursuing you.

"If after all this you will not listen to me, I will punish you for your sins seven times over. I will break down your stubborn pride and make the sky above you like iron and the ground beneath you like bronze. Your strength will be spent in vain, because your soil will not yield its crops, nor will the trees of the land yield their fruit.

"If you remain hostile toward me and refuse to listen to me, I will multiply your afflictions seven times over, as your sins deserve. I will send wild animals against you, and they will rob you of your children, destroy your cattle and make you so few in number that your roads will be deserted.

"If in spite of these things you do not accept my correction but continue to be hostile toward me, I myself will be hostile toward you and will afflict you for your sins seven times over. And I will bring the sword upon you to avenge the breaking of the covenant. When you withdraw into your cities, I will send a plague among you, and you will be given into enemy hands. When I cut off your supply of bread, ten women will be able to bake your bread in one oven, and they will dole out the bread by weight. You will eat, but you will not be satisfied.

"If in spite of this you still do not listen to me but continue to be hostile toward me, then in my anger I will be hostile toward you, and I myself will punish you for your sins seven times over. You will eat the flesh of your sons and the flesh of your daughters. I will destroy your high places, cut down your incense altars and pile your dead bodies on the lifeless forms of your idols, and I will abhor you. I will turn your cities into ruins and lay waste your sanctuaries, and I will take no delight in the pleasing aroma of your offerings. I will lay waste the land, so that your enemies who live there will be appalled. I will scatter you among the nations and will draw out my sword and pursue you. Your land will be laid waste, and your cities will lie in ruins. Then the land will enjoy its sabbath years all the time that it lies desolate and you are in the country of your enemies; then the land will rest and enjoy its sabbaths. All the time that it lies desolate, the land will have the rest it did not have during the sabbaths you lived in it.

"As for those of you who are left, I will make their hearts so fearful in the lands of their enemies that the sound of a windblown leaf will put them to flight. They will run as though fleeing from the sword, and they will fall, even though no one is pursuing them. They will stumble over one another as though fleeing from the sword, even though no one is pursuing them. So you will not be able to stand before your enemies. You will perish among the nations; the land of your enemies will devour you. Those of you who are left will waste away in the lands of their enemies because of their sins; also because of their fathers' sins they will waste away.

"But if they will confess their sins and the sins of their fathers—their treachery against me and their hostility toward me, which made me hostile toward them so that I sent them into the land of their enemies—then when their uncircumcised hearts are humbled and they pay for their sin, I will remember my covenant with Jacob and my covenant with Isaac and my covenant with Abraham, and I will remember the land. For the land will be deserted by them and will enjoy its sabbaths while it lies desolate without them. They will pay for their sins because they rejected my laws and abhorred my decrees."

Leviticus seems very strange to the modern world, so strange that readers intending to read the entire Bible often bog down in this book. Unlike most of the Bible, it has few stories or personalities and no poetry. It's a book of laws, crammed full of detailed rules and procedures.

Many of these individual rules, appropriate to God's goal of calling out a "separate" people, were changed in the New Testament. Yet a study of such laws can prove rewarding, for they express God's priorities on such subjects as care for the land, concern for the poor, and abuses of family and neighbors.

Although the Old Testament laws recorded in Leviticus, Exodus, Numbers, and Deuteronomy may seem long-winded, keep them in perspective. These laws—just over six hundred in all—comprise the entire set of regulations for a nation, as far as we know. (Most modern cities have more traffic laws!) And they are brief and clear. You don't have to go to law school to understand them.

The variety of the laws shows that God involves himself in every aspect of the Israelites' life. Laws against witchcraft are mixed in with laws concerning improper haircuts, tattoos, and prostitution. God is advancing his plan for the Israelites by carving out a separate culture. After four centuries in Egypt, the just-freed slaves, more Egyptian than anything else, need a comprehensive makeover. That is exactly what God gives them. (Many of the laws seem designed primarily to keep the Israelites "different" from their pagan neighbors.)

The Israelites in this Old Testament time are a unique people, unlike any other nation on earth, called by God to demonstrate holiness and purity to people around them. The reward for obeying the laws will make the Israelites the envy of the world. And if they disobey? God spells out in frightening detail the punishments they can then expect. —PY

DAILY CONTEMPLATION

Everybody has a code to live by. Where do you get yours?

THE CLOUD ABOVE THE TABERNACLE

On the day the tabernacle, the Tent of the Testimony, was set up, the cloud covered it. From evening till morning the cloud above the tabernacle looked like fire. That is how it continued to be; the cloud covered it, and at night it looked like fire. Whenever the cloud lifted from above the Tent, the Israelites set out; wherever the cloud settled, the Israelites encamped. At the Lord's command the Israelites set out, and at his command they encamped. As long as the cloud stayed over the tabernacle, they remained in camp. When the cloud remained over the tabernacle a long time, the Israelites obeyed the Lord's order and did not set out. Sometimes the cloud was over the tabernacle only a few days; at the Lord's command they would encamp, and then at his command they would set out. Sometimes the cloud stayed only from evening till morning, and when it lifted in the morning, they set out. Whether by day or by night, whenever the cloud lifted, they set out. Whether the cloud stayed over the tabernacle for two days or a month or a year, the Israelites would remain in camp and not set out; but when it lifted, they would set out. At the Lord's command they encamped, and at the Lord's command they set out. They obeyed the Lord's order, in accordance with his command through Moses.

God makes his presence obvious to the people every day through the visible symbol of a cloud. They have no doubt as to whether God is with them and directing their journey. Although God is unpredictable, sometimes stopping them only for a short time before moving them on and sometimes keeping them encamped for weeks or months, God remains continually present, a part of their daily life and travels.

The Israelite people have no reason to doubt God's care. Each day they eat manna from God and are covered by the cloud of his guidance. But soon they will again lose sight of their gratitude for his provision. —BQ

DAY 66   Numbers 11:4–23, 31–34

QUAIL FROM THE LORD

The rabble with them began to crave other food, and again the Israelites started wailing and said, "If only we had meat to eat! We remember the fish we ate in Egypt at no cost—also the cucumbers, melons, leeks, onions and garlic. But now we have lost our appetite; we never see anything but this manna!"

The manna was like coriander seed and looked like resin. The people went around gathering it, and then ground it in a handmill or crushed it in a mortar. They cooked it in a pot or made it into cakes. And it tasted like something made with olive oil. When the dew settled on the camp at night, the manna also came down.

Moses heard the people of every family wailing, each at the entrance to his tent. The LORD became exceedingly angry, and Moses was troubled. He asked the LORD, "Why have you brought this trouble on your servant? What have I done to displease you that you put the burden of all these people on me? Did I conceive all these people? Did I give them birth? Why do you tell me to carry them in my arms, as a nurse carries an infant, to the land you promised on oath to their forefathers? Where can I get meat for all these people? They keep wailing to me, 'Give us meat to eat!' I cannot carry all these people by myself; the burden is too heavy for me. If this is how you are going to treat me, put me to death right now—if I have found favor in your eyes—and do not let me face my own ruin."

The LORD said to Moses: "Bring me seventy of Israel's elders who are known to you as leaders and officials among the people. Have them come to the Tent of Meeting, that they may stand there with you. I will come down and speak with you there, and I will take of the Spirit that is on you and put the Spirit on them. They will help you carry the burden of the people so that you will not have to carry it alone.

"Tell the people: 'Consecrate yourselves in preparation for tomorrow, when you will eat meat. The LORD heard you when you wailed, "If only we had meat to eat! We were better off in Egypt!" Now the LORD will give you meat, and you will eat it. You will not eat it for just one day, or two days, or five, ten or twenty days, but for a whole month—until it comes out of your nostrils and you loathe it—because you have rejected the LORD, who is among you, and have wailed before him, saying, "Why did we ever leave Egypt?"'"

But Moses said, "Here I am among six hundred thousand men on foot, and you say, 'I will give them meat to eat for a whole month!' Would they have enough if flocks and herds were slaughtered for them? Would they have enough if all the fish in the sea were caught for them?"

The LORD answered Moses, "Is the LORD's arm too short? You will now see whether or not what I say will come true for you." ...

Now a wind went out from the LORD and drove quail in from the sea. It brought them down all around the camp to about three feet above the ground, as far as a day's walk in any direction. All that day and night and all the next day the people went out and gathered quail. No one gathered less than ten homers. Then they spread them out all around the camp. But while the meat was still between their teeth and before it could be consumed, the anger of the LORD burned against the people, and he struck them with a severe plague. Therefore the place was named Kibroth Hattaavah, because there they buried the people who had craved other food.

The book of Numbers covers a journey through the desert that should have lasted about two weeks but instead lasted forty years. When they first crossed into the Sinai Peninsula, the Israelites were bursting with a spirit of hope and adventure. Free at last from the chains of slavery, they headed toward the Promised Land. But the weeks, months, and then years of wandering in a hostile desert soon wore down all positive feelings.

With relentless honesty, Numbers tells what happens to change a short excursion into a forty-year detour. Petty things seem to bother the Israelites most, as their constant complaints about food indicate. With a few exceptions, they eat the same thing every day: *manna* (meaning literally, "What is it?"), which appears like dew on the ground each morning. A monotonous diet may seem a trivial exchange for freedom from slavery, but read their grumbling for yourself in this chapter.

The rebellion portrayed here is typical of the whole journey. And the more childishly the people act, the more their leaders are forced to respond like stern parents. Moses and God take turns getting exasperated by the Israelites' constant whining.

True, conditions are rigorous: facing a constant threat from enemy armies, the tribes have to march under a broiling sun through a desert region oppressed by snakes, scorpions, and constant drought. But the underlying issue is a simple test of faith: Will they trust God to see them through such hard circumstances? Will they follow the terms of the covenant he has signed with them and depend on his promised protection?   —PY

DAILY CONTEMPLATION

Do you ever grumble against God? If so, what tends to trigger the complaining?

MIRIAM AND AARON OPPOSE MOSES

Miriam and Aaron began to talk against Moses because of his Cushite wife, for he had married a Cushite. "Has the LORD spoken only through Moses?" they asked. "Hasn't he also spoken through us?" And the LORD heard this.

(Now Moses was a very humble man, more humble than anyone else on the face of the earth.)

At once the LORD said to Moses, Aaron and Miriam, "Come out to the Tent of Meeting, all three of you." So the three of them came out. Then the LORD came down in a pillar of cloud; he stood at the entrance to the Tent and summoned Aaron and Miriam. When both of them stepped forward,

He said, "Listen to my words:

"When a prophet of the LORD is among you,
   I reveal myself to him in visions,
   I speak to him in dreams.
But this is not true of my servant Moses;
   he is faithful in all my house.
With him I speak face to face,
   clearly and not in riddles;
   he sees the form of the LORD.
Why then were you not afraid
   to speak against my servant Moses?"

The anger of the LORD burned against them, and he left them.

When the cloud lifted from above the Tent, there stood Miriam—leprous, like snow. Aaron turned toward her and saw that she had leprosy; and he said to Moses, "Please, my lord, do not hold against us the sin we have so foolishly committed. Do not let her be like a stillborn infant coming from its mother's womb with its flesh half eaten away."

So Moses cried out to the LORD, "O God, please heal her!"

The LORD replied to Moses, "If her father had spit in her face, would she not have been in disgrace for seven days? Confine her outside the camp for seven days; after that she can be brought back." So Miriam was confined outside the camp for seven days, and the people did not move on till she was brought back.

After that, the people left Hazeroth and encamped in the Desert of Paran.

Miriam and Aaron envy their brother Moses, who has been chosen to hear God's voice in a way no other person could. God acted sovereignly and selected one man as his primary representative to the Israelites as they travel through the desert to the Promised Land. God also chose both Miriam and Aaron as leaders, yet despite Moses' humility they feel resentful that God has placed him in a position of greater authority.

This brother and sister, compelled to compare themselves with Moses, are exhibiting traits common to imperfect human nature. Seeing him to have a seemingly higher position of favor with God, they become jealous and critical. But this human nature can't be allowed to take hold. God is blessing all the people through Moses, and he will not tolerate anyone who questions his choice of caring for them. As Miriam and Aaron learn, when God clearly places someone in a position of authority, that person must be treated with respect and shown submission.   —BQ

DAILY CONTEMPLATION

Is God asking you to respect someone he has placed in a position of authority?

DAY 68   Reflection

GOD'S PUZZLING WAYS

Jigsaw puzzles bother me. I never seem able to fit the pieces together, and find myself more annoyed than amused by this pastime.

Puzzles have taught me something about my life, though. I don't always see things the way God does, and a lot of people are like me that way. God sees each part of our lives as a puzzle piece in the larger picture of a life that belongs to him and is being made ready for his purpose. God doesn't desire for us to stray from him and suffer, but even if that happens, when we come to him with a humble heart, he works our experiences into the artistry of what he has already begun.

Unfortunately, we tend to hold a small piece of jigsaw puzzle in our hands, see the dark, unattractive piece as a symbol of the whole picture, and react the way the Israelites did: "God, we're sick of this dusty old desert. If we were in Egypt, we'd have a banquet at every meal rather than this insufferable manna." But listen to the Israelites before they left Egypt: "God, we're so tired of living under the thumb of these pagan Egyptians. Can't you do something to give us our freedom? Nothing about our lives here is good."

In short, the Israelites didn't like either piece of the puzzle. Worse, they refused to see these odd-shaped events as small parts of a bigger picture God was creating for their nation. If only they had looked back at God's promises and forward to the certain fulfillment of them. If only they had clung to the certainty that their difficult circumstances were temporary, bringing them one step closer to the fullness of God's plan. Listen to how their voices might have sounded: "God, we long to be freed to live as your people in a land of our own. You've increased our numbers and saved us from famine. Thanks for the good future you've promised us." And then: "Lord, this desert trip isn't always easy. We yearn to be settled in a place with good food and water. But we are free! You are feeding and protecting us, and soon you'll bring us home."

I may not enjoy puzzles, but I'm learning that if I can take my eyes off that pesky piece that doesn't seem to fit and look at the half-finished picture, I'll see that God is fitting together something beautiful. —BQ

DAY 69   Numbers 13:1–3, 17–33

EXPLORING CANAAN

The LORD said to Moses, "Send some men to explore the land of Canaan, which I am giving to the Israelites. From each ancestral tribe send one of its leaders."

So at the LORD's command Moses sent them out from the Desert of Paran. All of them were leaders of the Israelites. . . .

When Moses sent them to explore Canaan, he said, "Go up through the Negev and on into the hill country. See what the land is like and whether the people who live there are strong or weak, few or many. What kind of land do they live in? Is it good or bad? What kind of towns do they live in? Are they unwalled or fortified? How is the soil? Is it fertile or poor? Are there trees on it or not? Do your best to bring back some of the fruit of the land." (It was the season for the first ripe grapes.)

So they went up and explored the land from the Desert of Zin as far as Rehob, toward Lebo Hamath. They went up through the Negev and came to Hebron, where Ahiman, Sheshai and Talmai, the descendants of Anak, lived. (Hebron had been built seven years before Zoan in Egypt.) When they reached the Valley of Eshcol, they cut off a branch bearing a single cluster of grapes. Two of them carried it on a pole between them, along with some pomegranates and figs. That place was called the Valley of Eshcol because of the cluster of grapes the Israelites cut off there. At the end of forty days they returned from exploring the land.

They came back to Moses and Aaron and the whole Israelite community at Kadesh in the Desert of Paran. There they reported to them and to the whole assembly and showed them the fruit of the land. They gave Moses this account: "We went into the land to which you sent us, and it does flow with milk and honey! Here is its fruit. But the people who live there are powerful, and the cities are fortified and very large. We even saw descendants of Anak there. The Amalekites live in the Negev; the Hittites, Jebusites and Amorites live in the hill country; and the Canaanites live near the sea and along the Jordan."

Then Caleb silenced the people before Moses and said, "We should go up and take possession of the land, for we can certainly do it."

But the men who had gone up with him said, "We can't attack those people; they are stronger than we are." And they spread among the Israelites a bad report about the land they had explored. They said, "The land we explored devours those living in it. All the people we saw there are of great size. We saw the Nephilim there (the descendants of Anak come from the Nephilim). We seemed like grasshoppers in our own eyes, and we looked the same to them."

Finally the Israelites approach the borders of the Promised Land. Canaan (KAY-nuhn) is inhabited by powerful groups of people who seem to have firm control of the land. Although the Israelites are ready to take possession of their homeland, the spies take one look at their opponents and wilt. It seems impossible to overcome these tribes so established and confident. In scouting out the land, the spies see Canaan and themselves only through their own limited vision.

One spy, Caleb, chooses to see Canaan through the eyes of a believer. When he looks at the land, rather than seeing strong people, he sees a God who saved Noah's family in a worldwide flood, One who saved Jacob's family from widespread famine, One who plagued Egypt until Pharaoh released the Israelites, One who parted the Red Sea to save the Israelites and drown the Egyptians, One who provided water and manna to people wandering in the desert. To Caleb, no people or cities can pose even the smallest threat to God's power.

Caleb knows that God's promise far outweighs the threat of any form of earthly power. No matter how unlikely God's way seems to those who look with this world's eyes, God will do what he has set out to do. —BQ

DAILY CONTEMPLATION

What situation do you need to see through God's eyes rather than your own?

DAY 70   Numbers 14:1–44

THE PEOPLE REBEL

That night all the people of the community raised their voices and wept aloud. All the Israelites grumbled against Moses and Aaron, and the whole assembly said to them, "If only we had died in Egypt! Or in this desert! Why is the LORD bringing us to this land only to let us fall by the sword? Our wives and children will be taken as plunder. Wouldn't it be better for us to go back to Egypt?" And they said to each other, "We should choose a leader and go back to Egypt."

Then Moses and Aaron fell facedown in front of the whole Israelite assembly gathered there. Joshua son of Nun and Caleb son of Jephunneh, who were among those who had explored the land, tore their clothes and said to the entire Israelite assembly, "The land we passed through and explored is exceedingly good. If the LORD is pleased with us, he will lead us into that land, a land flowing with milk and honey, and will give it to us. Only do not rebel against the LORD. And do not be afraid of the people of the land, because we will swallow them up. Their protection is gone, but the LORD is with us. Do not be afraid of them."

But the whole assembly talked about stoning them. Then the glory of the LORD appeared at the Tent of Meeting to all the Israelites. The LORD said to Moses, "How long will these people treat me with contempt? How long will they refuse to believe in me, in spite of all the miraculous signs I have performed among them? I will strike them down with a plague and destroy them, but I will make you into a nation greater and stronger than they."

Moses said to the LORD, "Then the Egyptians will hear about it! By your power you brought these people up from among them. And they will tell the inhabitants of this land about it. They have already heard that you, O LORD, are with these people and that you, O LORD, have been seen face to face, that your cloud stays over them, and that you go before them in a pillar of cloud by day and a pillar of fire by night. If you put these people to death all at one time, the nations who have heard this report about you will say, 'The LORD was not able to bring these people into the land he promised them on oath; so he slaughtered them in the desert.'

"Now may the Lord's strength be displayed, just as you have declared: 'The LORD is slow to anger, abounding in love and forgiving sin and rebellion. Yet he does not leave the guilty unpunished; he punishes the children for the sin of the fathers to the third and fourth generation.' In accordance with your great love, forgive the sin of these people, just as you have pardoned them from the time they left Egypt until now."

The LORD replied, "I have forgiven them, as you asked. Nevertheless, as surely as I live and as surely as the glory of the LORD fills the whole earth, not one of the men who saw my glory and the miraculous signs I performed in Egypt and in the desert but who disobeyed me and tested me ten times— not one of them will ever see the land I promised on oath to their forefathers. No one who has treated me with contempt will ever see it. But because my servant Caleb has a different spirit and follows me wholeheartedly, I will bring him into the land he went to, and his descendants will inherit it. Since the Amalekites and Canaanites are living in the valleys, turn back tomorrow and set out toward the desert along the route to the Red Sea."

The LORD said to Moses and Aaron: "How long will this wicked community grumble against me? I have heard the complaints of these grumbling Israelites. So tell them, 'As surely as I live, declares the LORD, I will do to you the very things I heard you say: In this desert your bodies will fall—every one of you twenty years old or more who was counted in the census and who has grumbled against me.

Not one of you will enter the land I swore with uplifted hand to make your home, except Caleb son of Jephunneh and Joshua son of Nun. As for your children that you said would be taken as plunder, I will bring them in to enjoy the land you have rejected. But you—your bodies will fall in this desert. Your children will be shepherds here for forty years, suffering for your unfaithfulness, until the last of your bodies lies in the desert. For forty years—one year for each of the forty days you explored the land—you will suffer for your sins and know what it is like to have me against you.' I, the LORD, have spoken, and I will surely do these things to this whole wicked community, which has banded together against me. They will meet their end in this desert; here they will die."

So the men Moses had sent to explore the land, who returned and made the whole community grumble against him by spreading a bad report about it—these men responsible for spreading the bad report about the land were struck down and died of a plague before the LORD. Of the men who went to explore the land, only Joshua son of Nun and Caleb son of Jephunneh survived.

When Moses reported this to all the Israelites, they mourned bitterly. Early the next morning they went up toward the high hill country. "We have sinned," they said. "We will go up to the place the LORD promised."

But Moses said, "Why are you disobeying the LORD's command? This will not succeed! Do not go up, because the LORD is not with you. You will be defeated by your enemies, for the Amalekites and Canaanites will face you there. Because you have turned away from the LORD, he will not be with you and you will fall by the sword."

Nevertheless, in their presumption they went up toward the high hill country, though neither Moses nor the ark of the LORD's covenant moved from the camp.

Most ancient histories record the heroic exploits of mighty warriors and unblemished leaders. The Bible, however, gives a strikingly different picture, as seen in the brutal realism of Numbers. On a dozen different occasions the Israelites lash out in despair or rise up in rebellion, plotting against their leaders and denouncing God. The spirit of revolt spreads to the priests, to the military, to Moses' family, and ultimately to Moses himself.

This chapter recounts the pivotal event of Numbers, the most decisive event since the Exodus from Egypt. The Israelites are poised on the very border of the Promised Land. If they simply trust God, they can leave the torturous desert and walk into a land abundant with food and water.

Yet despite the miracles God has already performed on their behalf, the Israelites choose to distrust him once again. Cowed by a military scouting report of potential opposition, they loudly bemoan the original decision to leave Egypt. In open mutiny, they even conspire to stone Moses and his brother Aaron.

The real object of revolt, the Israelites' God, feels spurned like a cast-off lover. Convinced at last that this band of renegades is unprepared for conquest of the Promised Land, he postpones all plans. The covenant promise of a new nation in a new land will have to wait, at least until all adults of the grumbling generation have died off. And that's why, out of the many thousands who have left Egypt, only two adults, Joshua and Caleb, survive to enter the Promised Land.

The Israelites have lost faith not only in themselves but in their God. The apostle Paul points out that these failures "happened to them as examples and were written down as warnings for us, on whom the fulfillment of the ages has come. So, if you think you are standing firm, be careful that you don't fall!" (1 Corinthians 10:11–12). —PY

DAILY CONTEMPLATION

What "giants" cause you fear? How do you respond?

DAY 71
Numbers 20:1–13; 21:4–9

WATER FROM THE ROCK; THE BRONZE SNAKE

In the first month the whole Israelite community arrived at the Desert of Zin, and they stayed at Kadesh. There Miriam died and was buried.

Now there was no water for the community, and the people gathered in opposition to Moses and Aaron. They quarreled with Moses and said, "If only we had died when our brothers fell dead before the LORD! Why did you bring the LORD's community into this desert, that we and our livestock should die here? Why did you bring us up out of Egypt to this terrible place? It has no grain or figs, grapevines or pomegranates. And there is no water to drink!"

Moses and Aaron went from the assembly to the entrance to the Tent of Meeting and fell facedown, and the glory of the LORD appeared to them. The LORD said to Moses, "Take the staff, and you and your brother Aaron gather the assembly together. Speak to that rock before their eyes and it will pour out its water. You will bring water out of the rock for the community so they and their livestock can drink."

So Moses took the staff from the LORD's presence, just as he commanded him. He and Aaron gathered the assembly together in front of the rock and Moses said to them, "Listen, you rebels, must we bring you water out of this rock?" Then Moses raised his arm and struck the rock twice with his staff. Water gushed out, and the community and their livestock drank.

But the LORD said to Moses and Aaron, "Because you did not trust in me enough to honor me as holy in the sight of the Israelites, you will not bring this community into the land I give them."

These were the waters of Meribah, where the Israelites quarreled with the LORD and where he showed himself holy among them....

They traveled from Mount Hor along the route to the Red Sea, to go around Edom. But the people grew impatient on the way; they spoke against God and against Moses, and said, "Why have you brought us up out of Egypt to die in the desert? There is no bread! There is no water! And we detest this miserable food!"

Then the LORD sent venomous snakes among them; they bit the people and many Israelites died. The people came to Moses and said, "We sinned when we spoke against the LORD and against you. Pray that the LORD will take the snakes away from us." So Moses prayed for the people.

The LORD said to Moses, "Make a snake and put it up on a pole; anyone who is bitten can look at it and live." So Moses made a bronze snake and put it up on a pole. Then when anyone was bitten by a snake and looked at the bronze snake, he lived.

Once again the people become irritated by their living conditions in the desert. Although they have seen God provide for them many times, they fall into an attitude of complaining. Moses and Aaron have endured the complaints and distrust for forty years now. They know it is nearly time to enter Canaan. Yet in these stories the people's grumbling reaches an all-time high. Fed up, Moses loses his temper and reacts in anger toward the Israelites and in disrespect toward God.

Later in the Bible God tells us that "from everyone who has been given much, much will be demanded; and from the one who has been entrusted with much, much more will be asked" (Luke 12:48). Moses and Aaron hold great positions of responsibility, and because they act in front of the people with disrespect for God, calling attention to themselves, God denies them entrance to the Promised Land.

In an offense toward God that is just as serious, the people express contempt for the manna he has provided. Crying out, "We detest this miserable food!" the Israelites thumb their noses at God's grace. By his holy nature, God must punish their disdain.

The gospel of John compares the incident with the bronze snake to the salvation of Jesus. "Just as Moses lifted up the snake in the desert, so the Son of Man must be lifted up, that everyone who believes in him may have eternal life" (John 3:14–15).

—BQ

DAILY CONTEMPLATION

What responsibilities has God given you?

DAY 72   Deuteronomy 1:1; 4:7–38

OBEDIENCE COMMANDED

These are the words Moses spoke to all Israel in the desert east of the Jordan. . . .

What other nation is so great as to have their gods near them the way the LORD our God is near us whenever we pray to him? And what other nation is so great as to have such righteous decrees and laws as this body of laws I am setting before you today?

Only be careful, and watch yourselves closely so that you do not forget the things your eyes have seen or let them slip from your heart as long as you live. Teach them to your children and to their children after them. Remember the day you stood before the LORD your God at Horeb, when he said to me, "Assemble the people before me to hear my words so that they may learn to revere me as long as they live in the land and may teach them to their children." You came near and stood at the foot of the mountain while it blazed with fire to the very heavens, with black clouds and deep darkness. Then the LORD spoke to you out of the fire. You heard the sound of words but saw no form; there was only a voice. He declared to you his covenant, the Ten Commandments, which he commanded you to follow and then wrote them on two stone tablets. And the LORD directed me at that time to teach you the decrees and laws you are to follow in the land that you are crossing the Jordan to possess.

You saw no form of any kind the day the LORD spoke to you at Horeb out of the fire. Therefore watch yourselves very carefully, so that you do not become corrupt and make for yourselves an idol, an image of any shape, whether formed like a man or a woman, or like any animal on earth or any bird that flies in the air, or like any creature that moves along the ground or any fish in the waters below. And when you look up to the sky and see the sun, the moon and the stars—all the heavenly array—do not be enticed into bowing down to them and worshiping things the LORD your God has apportioned to all the nations under heaven. But as for you, the LORD took you and brought you out of the iron-smelting furnace, out of Egypt, to be the people of his inheritance, as you now are.

The LORD was angry with me because of you, and he solemnly swore that I would not cross the Jordan and enter the good land the LORD your God is giving you as your inheritance. I will die in this land; I will not cross the Jordan; but you are about to cross over and take possession of that good land. Be careful not to forget the covenant of the LORD your God that he made with you; do not make for yourselves an idol in the form of anything the LORD your God has forbidden. For the LORD your God is a consuming fire, a jealous God.

After you have had children and grandchildren and have lived in the land a long time—if you then become corrupt and make any kind of idol, doing evil in the eyes of the LORD your God and provoking him to anger, I call heaven and earth as witnesses against you this day that you will quickly perish from the land that you are crossing the Jordan to possess. You will not live there long but will certainly be destroyed. The LORD will scatter you among the peoples, and only a few of you will survive among the nations to which the LORD will drive you. There you will worship man-made gods of wood and stone, which cannot see or hear or eat or smell. But if from there you seek the LORD your God, you will find him if you look for him with all your heart and with all your soul. When you are in distress and all these things have happened to you, then in later days you will return to the LORD your God and obey him. For the

LORD your God is a merciful God; he will not abandon or destroy you or forget the covenant with your forefathers, which he confirmed to them by oath.

Ask now about the former days, long before your time, from the day God created man on the earth; ask from one end of the heavens to the other. Has anything so great as this ever happened, or has anything like it ever been heard of? Has any other people heard the voice of God speaking out of fire, as you have, and lived? Has any god ever tried to take for himself one nation out of another nation, by testings, by miraculous signs and wonders, by war, by a mighty hand and an outstretched arm, or by great and awesome deeds, like all the things the LORD your God did for you in Egypt before your very eyes?

You were shown these things so that you might know that the LORD is God; besides him there is no other. From heaven he made you hear his voice to discipline you. On earth he showed you his great fire, and you heard his words from out of the fire. Because he loved your forefathers and chose their descendants after them, he brought you out of Egypt by his Presence and his great strength, to drive out before you nations greater and stronger than you and to bring you into their land to give it to you for your inheritance, as it is today.

Four decades later the Israelites stand at the edge of the Promised Land, spiritually and physically seasoned by their wilderness wanderings. Egypt is a faint memory from childhood. With the older generation of doubters and grumblers now dead and buried, a new generation chafes to march in and claim the land.

There at the border, the old man Moses delivers three speeches that, for their length and emotional power, have no equal in the Bible. It is his last chance to advise and inspire the people he has led for forty tumultuous years. Passionately, deliberately, tearfully, he reviews their history step by step, occasionally flaring up at a painful memory but more often pouring out the anguished love of a doting parent. An undercurrent of sadness runs through the speeches, for Moses has learned he will not join the triumph of entering Canaan.

Moses' longest speech reiterates all the laws that the Israelites have agreed to keep as their part of the covenant. Moses also recalls the hallmark day when God delivered the covenant on Mount Sinai. He remembers aloud the black clouds and deep darkness and blazing fire. *You saw no shape or form of God on that day*, he reminds them. God's presence cannot be reduced to any mere image. Moses' central message: *Never forget the lessons you learned in the desert.*

Besides all the warnings, Moses is giving a kind of pep talk, a final challenge for the Israelites to recognize their unique calling as a nation. If they follow God's laws, all the lavish benefits of the covenant will be theirs. More, every other nation will look to them and want to know their God. Moses seems incurably astonished at all God has done for him and the other Israelites, and this speech represents his last chance to communicate that sense of wonder and thanksgiving.   —PY

DAILY CONTEMPLATION

What are you learning now from God that will become a part of your history with him?

DO NOT FORGET THE LORD

Be careful to follow every command I am giving you today, so that you may live and increase and may enter and possess the land that the LORD promised on oath to your forefathers. Remember how the LORD your God led you all the way in the desert these forty years, to humble you and to test you in order to know what was in your heart, whether or not you would keep his commands. He humbled you, causing you to hunger and then feeding you with manna, which neither you nor your fathers had known, to teach you that man does not live on bread alone but on every word that comes from the mouth of the LORD. Your clothes did not wear out and your feet did not swell during these forty years. Know then in your heart that as a man disciplines his son, so the LORD your God disciplines you.

Observe the commands of the LORD your God, walking in his ways and revering him. For the LORD your God is bringing you into a good land—a land with streams and pools of water, with springs flowing in the valleys and hills; a land with wheat and barley, vines and fig trees, pomegranates, olive oil and honey; a land where bread will not be scarce and you will lack nothing; a land where the rocks are iron and you can dig copper out of the hills.

When you have eaten and are satisfied, praise the LORD your God for the good land he has given you. Be careful that you do not forget the LORD your God, failing to observe his commands, his laws and his decrees that I am giving you this day. Otherwise, when you eat and are satisfied, when you build fine houses and settle down, and when your herds and flocks grow large and your silver and gold increase and all you have is multiplied, then your heart will become proud and you will forget the LORD your God, who brought you out of Egypt, out of the land of slavery. He led you through the vast and dreadful desert, that thirsty and waterless land, with its venomous snakes and scorpions. He brought you water out of hard rock. He gave you manna to eat in the desert, something your fathers had never known, to humble and to test you so that in the end it might go well with you. You may say to yourself, "My power and the strength of my hands have produced this wealth for me." But remember the LORD your God, for it is he who gives you the ability to produce wealth, and so confirms his covenant, which he swore to your forefathers, as it is today.

If you ever forget the LORD your God and follow other gods and worship and bow down to them, I testify against you today that you will surely be destroyed. Like the nations the LORD destroyed before you, so you will be destroyed for not obeying the LORD your God.

Alexandr Solzhenitsyn says that he first learned to pray in a Siberian concentration camp. He turned to prayer because he had no other hope. Before his arrest, when things were going well, he had seldom given God a thought.

Similarly, Moses felt the Israelites had learned the habit of depending on God in the Sinai wilderness, where they had no choice; they needed his intervention each day just to eat and drink. But now, on the banks of the Jordan River, they are about to face a more difficult test of faith. After they enter the land of plenty, will they soon forget the God who has given it to them?

Desert-bred, the Israelites know little about the seductions of other cultures: the alluring sensuality, the exotic religions, the glittering wealth. Now they are preparing to march into a region known for these enticements, and Moses seems to fear the coming prosperity far more than the rigors of the desert. In the beautiful land, the Promised Land, the Israelites might put God behind them and credit themselves for their success.

"Remember!" Moses keeps urging. Remember the days of slavery in Egypt, and God's acts of liberation. Remember the trials of the vast and desolate desert, and God's faithfulness there. Remember your special calling as God's peculiar treasures.

Moses has good reason for concern, for God, who can see the future, has told him plainly what will happen: "When I have brought them into the land flowing with milk and honey, the land I promised on oath to their forefathers, and when they eat their fill and thrive, they will turn to other gods and worship them, rejecting me and breaking my covenant" (31:20). As the books following Deuteronomy relate, all of Moses' fears come true.

Ironically, as Deuteronomy shows, success may make it harder to depend on God. The Israelites prove less faithful to God after they move into the Promised Land. There is a grave danger in finally getting what you want. —PY

DAILY CONTEMPLATION

Do you think most about God when things are going well or when you are in trouble?

DAY 74 Reflection

A JEKYLL-AND-HYDE GOD?

Some of God's harshest words to the Israelite people are spoken in the last passages we've read from Deuteronomy: "The LORD your God is a consuming fire, a jealous God" (4:24). "Like the nations the LORD destroyed before you, so you will be destroyed for not obeying the LORD your God" (8:20). Yet in the same passages we find words of unmistakable tenderness and compassion: "The LORD your God is a merciful God; he will not abandon or destroy you or forget the covenant with your forefathers, which he confirmed to them by oath" (4:31).

One minute God is warning the people of the doom that awaits them if they stray from him, and the next he is welcoming them back and reassuring them of his love.

To the Israelites, God's alternating voices surely seem confusing. Who, really, is this God they serve? What is his true nature?

As we take a long look at God while reading through the Old Testament, we too may wonder about this God. We know him as One who forgives us and welcomes us into his family in love. We know him as caring and merciful. But in the Old Testament we see glimpses of a stern, unbending Power who speaks to his people in no uncertain terms about actions and consequences. He is demanding and blunt. Still, a few breaths later he gushes in willingness to forgive once more. Do we worship a Jekyll and Hyde? Is even God unsettled as to how to handle these unreliable children of his? Should we expect the same treatment from him today?

It is crucial that we, as believers, gain a right understanding of God's nature. Then we can see the big picture of God and his dealings with humanity. Then we can let go of the confusion that practically begs an explanation throughout the Old Testament.

God, in his holiness, can be compared to water—pure and life-giving. Jesus used this comparison, describing his gift of eternal life as "living water." Humans, though, are marred by sin, which is like oil, a substance incompatible with water. Try to clean oil from a stove top with a cloth and water, and the oil only smears. When oil spills in the ocean, it holds together and continues to float atop the water. Oil and water don't mix, no matter how hard one may try.

This is a picture of God and sinful people. God's character is wholly incompatible with sin. Regardless of how he feels about people who are sinners, God's nature keeps him irreversibly separated from anyone with sin. Despite his compassion and mercy, he is incapable of compromising his nature. God's love flows freely, but when his people are unfaithful and disobedient, he must cast them away.

Extend the metaphor to Jesus. He is like soap. Water and oil will never mix, but soap is one substance that can allow water to interact effectively with oil. It cleans and dissolves oil. Only through Jesus' death for all sinners was God able to cleanse away sin and draw people close to him.

God's holiness doesn't change, nor does his incompatibility with sin. But with those who have come to him through the saving gift of Christ, he can freely love and forgive and walk in relationship, without threats or punishment, despite the fact that we continue to sin. God still desires holiness in his people. He still calls for respect and loyalty. But he gives his Spirit to make it possible to fulfill his demands, and his grace to cover our failure. Through Jesus, God remains fully true to himself and fully true to the love he has always possessed for his people.   —BQ

DAILY CONTEMPLATION

Has your relationship with Jesus changed your understanding of God, and your relationship with him? Pray that in the areas in which your view of God is inappropriately stern and demanding, he will reveal the fullness of himself in his love and mercy.

Rahab and the Spies

Then Joshua son of Nun secretly sent two spies from Shittim. "Go, look over the land," he said, "especially Jericho." So they went and entered the house of a prostitute named Rahab and stayed there.

The king of Jericho was told, "Look! Some of the Israelites have come here tonight to spy out the land." So the king of Jericho sent this message to Rahab: "Bring out the men who came to you and entered your house, because they have come to spy out the whole land."

But the woman had taken the two men and hidden them. She said, "Yes, the men came to me, but I did not know where they had come from. At dusk, when it was time to close the city gate, the men left. I don't know which way they went. Go after them quickly. You may catch up with them." (But she had taken them up to the roof and hidden them under the stalks of flax she had laid out on the roof.) So the men set out in pursuit of the spies on the road that leads to the fords of the Jordan, and as soon as the pursuers had gone out, the gate was shut.

Before the spies lay down for the night, she went up on the roof and said to them, "I know that the LORD has given this land to you and that a great fear of you has fallen on us, so that all who live in this country are melting in fear because of you. We have heard how the LORD dried up the water of the Red Sea for you when you came out of Egypt, and what you did to Sihon and Og, the two kings of the Amorites east of the Jordan, whom you completely destroyed. When we heard of it, our hearts melted and everyone's courage failed because of you, for the LORD your God is God in heaven above and on the earth below. Now then, please swear to me by the LORD that you will show kindness to my family, because I have shown kindness to you. Give me a sure sign that you will spare the lives of my father and mother, my brothers and sisters, and all who belong to them, and that you will save us from death."

"Our lives for your lives!" the men assured her. "If you don't tell what we are doing, we will treat you kindly and faithfully when the LORD gives us the land."

So she let them down by a rope through the window, for the house she lived in was part of the city wall. Now she had said to them, "Go to the hills so the pursuers will not find you. Hide yourselves there three days until they return, and then go on your way."

The men said to her, "This oath you made us swear will not be binding on us unless, when we enter the land, you have tied this scarlet cord in the window through which you let us down, and unless you have brought your father and mother, your brothers and all your family into your house. If anyone goes outside your house into the street, his blood will be on his own head; we will not be responsible. As for anyone who is in the house with you, his blood will be on our head if a hand is laid on him. But if you tell what we are doing, we will be released from the oath you made us swear."

"Agreed," she replied. "Let it be as you say." So she sent them away and they departed. And she tied the scarlet cord in the window.

When they left, they went into the hills and stayed there three days, until the pursuers had searched all along the road and returned without finding them. Then the two men started back. They went down out of the hills, forded the river and came to Joshua son of Nun and told him everything that had happened to them. They said to Joshua, "The LORD has surely given the whole land into our hands; all the people are melting in fear because of us."

Often, as we have seen in the books of Exodus, Numbers, and Deuteronomy, the Israelites offer examples of what *not* to do. But the Old Testament does contain a few bright spots of hope, with the book of Joshua representing one of the brightest.

Joshua's opening scene replays an earlier scene. After listening to Moses' swan song speeches, the refugees amass again beside the Jordan River for a test of courage and faith. Are they ready to cross into the Promised Land? Forty years before, their forebears had panicked in fear. Now, without their legendary leader, Moses, would the Israelites panic again? They have no chariots or even horses, only primitive arms, an untested new leader, and the promise of God's protection.

An entirely new spirit characterizes this group, however, and the spy story in Joshua 2 expresses the difference clearly. Forty years ago, sparking a revolt among the Israelites, only two of the twelve spies held out any optimism. But the older generation with its fearful slave mentality has died off, and the new generation is now led by one of the original optimistic spies, Joshua.

This time, Joshua handpicks his own scouts, and the report they bring back makes a sharp contrast with the spy report in Numbers (13:31–33). The new scouts conclude that God has given the land of Canaan into the Israelites' hands, that all the people are fearful of the Israelites. Thus Joshua begins as a good news book, a welcome relief from the discouragement of Numbers and the fatalism of Deuteronomy. What a difference forty years has made!

The heroine of this chapter, Rahab (RAY-hab) the pagan prostitute, becomes a favorite figure in Jewish stories and is esteemed by Bible writers as well (see Hebrews 11:31 and James 2:25). She proves that God honors true faith from anyone, regardless of race or religious background. In fact, Rahab, survivor of Jericho, becomes a direct ancestress of Jesus.   —PY

DAILY CONTEMPLATION

When you confront obstacles, are you more likely to see them as problems or opportunities?

CROSSING THE JORDAN

Early in the morning Joshua and all the Israelites set out from Shittim and went to the Jordan, where they camped before crossing over. After three days the officers went throughout the camp, giving orders to the people: "When you see the ark of the covenant of the LORD your God, and the priests, who are Levites, carrying it, you are to move out from your positions and follow it. Then you will know which way to go, since you have never been this way before. But keep a distance of about a thousand yards between you and the ark; do not go near it."

Joshua told the people, "Consecrate yourselves, for tomorrow the LORD will do amazing things among you."

Joshua said to the priests, "Take up the ark of the covenant and pass on ahead of the people." So they took it up and went ahead of them.

And the LORD said to Joshua, "Today I will begin to exalt you in the eyes of all Israel, so they may know that I am with you as I was with Moses. Tell the priests who carry the ark of the covenant: 'When you reach the edge of the Jordan's waters, go and stand in the river.'"

Joshua said to the Israelites, "Come here and listen to the words of the LORD your God. This is how you will know that the living God is among you and that he will certainly drive out before you the Canaanites, Hittites, Hivites, Perizzites, Girgashites, Amorites and Jebusites. See, the ark of the covenant of the Lord of all the earth will go into the Jordan ahead of you. Now then, choose twelve men from the tribes of Israel, one from each tribe. And as soon as the priests who carry the ark of the LORD—the Lord of all the earth—set foot in the Jordan, its waters flowing downstream will be cut off and stand up in a heap."

So when the people broke camp to cross the Jordan, the priests carrying the ark of the covenant went ahead of them. Now the Jordan is at flood stage all during harvest. Yet as soon as the priests who carried the ark reached the Jordan and their feet touched the water's edge, the water from upstream stopped flowing. It piled up in a heap a great distance away, at a town called Adam in the vicinity of Zarethan, while the water flowing down to the Sea of the Arabah (the Salt Sea) was completely cut off. So the people crossed over opposite Jericho. The priests who carried the ark of the covenant of the LORD stood firm on dry ground in the middle of the Jordan, while all Israel passed by until the whole nation had completed the crossing on dry ground.

When the whole nation had finished crossing the Jordan, the LORD said to Joshua, "Choose twelve men from among the people, one from each tribe, and tell them to take up twelve stones from the middle of the Jordan from right where the priests stood and to carry them over with you and put them down at the place where you stay tonight."

So Joshua called together the twelve men he had appointed from the Israelites, one from each tribe, and said to them, "Go over before the ark of the LORD your

God into the middle of the Jordan. Each of you is to take up a stone on his shoulder, according to the number of the tribes of the Israelites, to serve as a sign among you. In the future, when your children ask you, 'What do these stones mean?' tell them that the flow of the Jordan was cut off before the ark of the covenant of the LORD. When it crossed the Jordan, the waters of the Jordan were cut off. These stones are to be a memorial to the people of Israel forever." ...

Joshua set up the twelve stones that had been in the middle of the Jordan at the spot where the priests who carried the ark of the covenant had stood. And they are there to this day. . . .

About forty thousand armed for battle crossed over before the LORD to the plains of Jericho for war. . . .

And the priests came up out of the river carrying the ark of the covenant of the LORD. No sooner had they set their feet on the dry ground than the waters of the Jordan returned to their place and ran at flood stage as before. . . .

And Joshua set up at Gilgal the twelve stones they had taken out of the Jordan. He said to the Israelites, "In the future when your descendants ask their fathers, 'What do these stones mean?' tell them, 'Israel crossed the Jordan on dry ground.' For the LORD your God dried up the Jordan before you until you had crossed over. The LORD your God did to the Jordan just what he had done to the Red Sea when he dried it up before us until we had crossed over. He did this so that all the peoples of the earth might know that the hand of the LORD is powerful and so that you might always fear the LORD your God."

The day has come to set forth into the Promised Land. As he did in the parting of the Red Sea, God shows the people that a great body of water is no obstacle. He stops up the river and dries the land, instructing the Israelites to follow behind the ark of the covenant as they cross over into Canaan.

The ark, kept in the tabernacle and regarded as the most sacred of furnishings, signifies the Lord's throne. In following the ark of the covenant across the Jordan River, the Israelites sense God himself leading them into the land he has promised. They must follow at a distance, observing a holy respect for the God that the ark represents.

When all have crossed, God determines that his people will not forget what he has done for them once again. He knows that, like the story of the Red Sea, this story will be repeated for many generations to come. Not only will the people tell the story, but they will have a visible reminder of this momentous day whenever they look at the stone memorial erected by each of the twelve tribes.

God knows human nature, as seen in the actions of his people during the last decades. He knows they are quick to forget his faithfulness and see life rather through their own eyes. He instructs Joshua to help them remember.   —BQ

DAILY CONTEMPLATION

What memorials or reminders help you recall what God has done for you?

THE FALL OF JERICHO

Now when Joshua was near Jericho, he looked up and saw a man standing in front of him with a drawn sword in his hand. Joshua went up to him and asked, "Are you for us or for our enemies?"

"Neither," he replied, "but as commander of the army of the LORD I have now come." Then Joshua fell facedown to the ground in reverence, and asked him, "What message does my Lord have for his servant?"

The commander of the LORD's army replied, "Take off your sandals, for the place where you are standing is holy." And Joshua did so.

Now Jericho was tightly shut up because of the Israelites. No one went out and no one came in.

Then the LORD said to Joshua, "See, I have delivered Jericho into your hands, along with its king and its fighting men. March around the city once with all the armed men. Do this for six days. Have seven priests carry trumpets of rams' horns in front of the ark. On the seventh day, march around the city seven times, with the priests blowing the trumpets. When you hear them sound a long blast on the trumpets, have all the people give a loud shout; then the wall of the city will collapse and the people will go up, every man straight in."

So Joshua son of Nun called the priests and said to them, "Take up the ark of the covenant of the LORD and have seven priests carry trumpets in front of it." And he ordered the people, "Advance! March around the city, with the armed guard going ahead of the ark of the LORD."

When Joshua had spoken to the people, the seven priests carrying the seven trumpets before the LORD went forward, blowing their trumpets, and the ark of the LORD's covenant followed them. The armed guard marched ahead of the priests who blew the trumpets, and the rear guard followed the ark. All this time the trumpets were sounding. But Joshua had commanded the people, "Do not give a war cry, do not raise your voices, do not say a word until the day I tell you to shout. Then shout!" So he had the ark of the LORD carried around the city, circling it once. Then the people returned to camp and spent the night there.

Joshua got up early the next morning and the priests took up the ark of the LORD. The seven priests carrying the seven trumpets went forward, marching before the ark of the LORD and blowing the trumpets. The armed men went ahead of them and the rear guard followed the ark of the LORD, while the trumpets kept sounding. So on the second day they marched around the city once and returned to the camp. They did this for six days.

On the seventh day, they got up at daybreak and marched around the city seven times in the same manner, except that on that day they circled the city seven times. The seventh time around, when the priests sounded the trumpet blast, Joshua commanded the people, "Shout! For the LORD has given you the city! The city and all that is in it are to be devoted to the LORD. Only Rahab the prostitute and all who are with her in her house shall be spared, because she hid the spies we sent. But keep away from the devoted things, so that you will not bring about your own destruction by taking any of them. Otherwise you will make the camp of Israel liable to destruction and bring trouble on it. All the silver and gold and the articles of bronze and iron are sacred to the LORD and must go into his treasury."

When the trumpets sounded, the people shouted, and at the sound of the trumpet, when the people gave a loud shout, the wall collapsed; so every man charged straight in, and they took the city. They devoted the city to the LORD and destroyed with the sword every living thing in it—men and women, young and old, cattle, sheep and donkeys.

Joshua said to the two men who had spied out the land, "Go into the prostitute's house and bring her out and all who belong to her, in accordance with your oath to her." So the young men who had done the spying went in and brought out Rahab, her father and mother and brothers and all who belonged to her. They brought out her entire family and put them in a place outside the camp of Israel.

The Israelites' abysmal failures in the Sinai Desert can be traced back to a simple matter of disobedience. Despite unmistakable divine guidance, they insisted on choosing their own way over God's. Will the new generation respond any differently? Once they have crossed into Canaan, God tests the Israelites' new resolve to follow him, and it surely strains their faith to new limits.

As for the residents of Canaan, who have long heard about the Israelites' plan to conquer the Promised Land, they brace for the worst. Citizens of Jericho, the first city in the invaders' path, barricade themselves behind stone walls and await the feared onslaught. But how do the vaunted Israelites spend their first week in Canaan? They build a stone monument to God, perform circumcision rituals, and hold a Passover celebration—not the sort of behavior you'd expect from a conquering army.

The incidents recorded in Joshua seem specially selected to strike home the point that God, no one else, is in charge. Just before the battle of Jericho, a supernatural visitor appears to Joshua to remind him of the true commander of this military campaign. And the bizarre tactics of the Israelites in besieging Jericho leave no doubt who is really in charge. An army could hardly take credit for victory when all it does is march around in circles and shout.

Jericho was probably a center for the worship of the moon god in Canaan, and so the destruction of that city—like the ten plagues on Egypt—symbolically announces an open warfare between the God of the Israelites and the region's pagan gods. Although measures against the Canaanites may seem harsh, the Bible makes clear that they have forfeited their right to the land. As Moses tells the Israelites, "It is not because of your righteousness or your integrity that you are going in to take possession of their land; but on account of the wickedness of these nations, the LORD your God will drive them out before you" (Deuteronomy 9:5). And, as the story of Rahab shows, Canaanites who turned to God were spared.   —PY

DAY 78   Joshua 7:1–26

ACHAN'S SIN

The Israelites acted unfaithfully in regard to the devoted things; Achan son of Carmi, the son of Zimri, the son of Zerah, of the tribe of Judah, took some of them. So the LORD's anger burned against Israel.

Now Joshua sent men from Jericho to Ai, which is near Beth Aven to the east of Bethel, and told them, "Go up and spy out the region." So the men went up and spied out Ai.

When they returned to Joshua, they said, "Not all the people will have to go up against Ai. Send two or three thousand men to take it and do not weary all the people, for only a few men are there." So about three thousand men went up; but they were routed by the men of Ai, who killed about thirty-six of them. They chased the Israelites from the city gate as far as the stone quarries and struck them down on the slopes. At this the hearts of the people melted and became like water.

Then Joshua tore his clothes and fell facedown to the ground before the ark of the LORD, remaining there till evening. The elders of Israel did the same, and sprinkled dust on their heads. And Joshua said, "Ah, Sovereign LORD, why did you ever bring this people across the Jordan to deliver us into the hands of the Amorites to destroy us? If only we had been content to stay on the other side of the Jordan! O Lord, what can I say, now that Israel has been routed by its enemies? The Canaanites and the other people of the country will hear about this and they will surround us and wipe out our name from the earth. What then will you do for your own great name?"

The LORD said to Joshua, "Stand up! What are you doing down on your face? Israel has sinned; they have violated my covenant, which I commanded them to keep. They have taken some of the devoted things; they have stolen, they have lied, they have put them with their own possessions. That is why the Israelites cannot stand against their enemies; they turn their backs and run because they have been made liable to destruction. I will not be with you anymore unless you destroy whatever among you is devoted to destruction.

"Go, consecrate the people. Tell them, 'Consecrate yourselves in preparation for tomorrow; for this is what the LORD, the God of Israel, says: That which is devoted is among you, O Israel. You cannot stand against your enemies until you remove it.

"'In the morning, present yourselves tribe by tribe. The tribe that the LORD takes shall come forward clan by clan; the clan that the LORD takes shall come forward family by family; and the family that the LORD takes shall come forward man by man. He who is caught with the devoted things shall be destroyed by fire, along with all that belongs to him. He has violated the covenant of the LORD and has done a disgraceful thing in Israel!'"

Early the next morning Joshua had Israel come forward by tribes, and Judah was taken. The clans of Judah came forward, and he took the Zerahites. He had the clan of the Zerahites come forward by families, and Zimri was taken. Joshua had his family come forward man by man, and Achan son of Carmi, the son of Zimri, the son of Zerah, of the tribe of Judah, was taken.

Then Joshua said to Achan, "My son, give glory to the LORD, the God of Israel, and give him the praise. Tell me what you have done; do not hide it from me."

Achan replied, "It is true! I have sinned against the LORD, the God of Israel. This is what I have done: When I saw in the plunder a beautiful robe from Babylonia, two hundred shekels of silver and a wedge of gold weighing fifty shekels, I coveted them and took them. They are hidden in the ground inside my tent, with the silver underneath."

So Joshua sent messengers, and they ran to the tent, and there it was, hidden in his tent, with the silver underneath. They took the things from the tent, brought them to Joshua and all the Israelites and spread them out before the LORD.

Then Joshua, together with all Israel, took Achan son of Zerah, the silver, the robe, the gold wedge, his sons and daughters, his cattle, donkeys and sheep, his tent and all that he had, to the Valley of Achor. Joshua said, "Why have you brought this trouble on us? The LORD will bring trouble on you today."

Then all Israel stoned him, and after they had stoned the rest, they burned them. Over Achan they heaped up a large pile of rocks, which remains to this day. Then the LORD turned from his fierce anger. Therefore that place has been called the Valley of Achor ever since.

The Bible does not record history for its own sake. Rather, it selects and highlights certain events that yield practical and spiritual lessons. For example, the book of Joshua, which spans a period of approximately seven years, devotes only a few sentences to some extensive military campaigns. But other key events, such as the fall of Jericho, get detailed coverage. That battle establishes an important pattern: The Israelites will succeed only if they rely on God, not military might.

Perhaps inevitably, the Israelites get cocky after Jericho. Since they have conquered a fortified city without firing an arrow, the next target, the puny town of Ai (AY-ie), poses no threat at all. A few thousand soldiers stroll toward Ai. A short time later those same soldiers—minus their dead and wounded—are scrambling for home, thoroughly routed.

Clearly, the juxtaposition of these two stories, Jericho and Ai, is meant to convey a lesson. If the Israelites obey God and place their trust in him, no challenge is too great to overcome. On the other hand, if they insist on their own way, no obstacle is too small to trip them up.

Significantly, Ai stood near the original site where God had appeared to Abraham and revealed the covenant centuries before. A humiliating defeat in that place shakes Joshua to the core. He dissolves in fright, earning God's stern rebuke, "Stand up! What are you doing down on your face?"

Without God's protection, Joshua realizes, the Israelites are hopelessly vulnerable. After the painful lesson of Ai, he goes back to the basics. The public exposure of Achan's sin underscores the need to follow God's orders scrupulously, even in the earthy matter of warfare. God will not tolerate any of the lying or looting typical of invading armies. —PY

DAILY CONTEMPLATION

Why would such a seemingly "little" sin, such as Achan's deceit, have such major consequences?

DAY 79
Joshua 24:1–29

THE COVENANT RENEWED AT SHECHEM

Then Joshua assembled all the tribes of Israel at Shechem. He summoned the elders, leaders, judges and officials of Israel, and they presented themselves before God.

Joshua said to all the people, "This is what the LORD, the God of Israel, says: 'Long ago your forefathers, including Terah the father of Abraham and Nahor, lived beyond the River and worshiped other gods. But I took your father Abraham from the land beyond the River and led him throughout Canaan and gave him many descendants. I gave him Isaac, and to Isaac I gave Jacob and Esau. I assigned the hill country of Seir to Esau, but Jacob and his sons went down to Egypt.

"'Then I sent Moses and Aaron, and I afflicted the Egyptians by what I did there, and I brought you out. When I brought your fathers out of Egypt, you came to the sea, and the Egyptians pursued them with chariots and horsemen as far as the Red Sea. But they cried to the LORD for help, and he put darkness between you and the Egyptians; he brought the sea over them and covered them. You saw with your own eyes what I did to the Egyptians. Then you lived in the desert for a long time.

"'I brought you to the land of the Amorites who lived east of the Jordan. They fought against you, but I gave them into your hands. I destroyed them from before you, and you took possession of their land. When Balak son of Zippor, the king of Moab, prepared to fight against Israel, he sent for Balaam son of Beor to put a curse on you. But I would not listen to Balaam, so he blessed you again and again, and I delivered you out of his hand.

"'Then you crossed the Jordan and came to Jericho. The citizens of Jericho fought against you, as did also the Amorites, Perizzites, Canaanites, Hittites, Girgashites, Hivites and Jebusites, but I gave them into your hands. I sent the hornet ahead of you, which drove them out before you—also the two Amorite kings. You did not do it with your own sword and bow. So I gave you a land on which you did not toil and cities you did not build; and you live in them and eat from vineyards and olive groves that you did not plant.'

"Now fear the LORD and serve him with all faithfulness. Throw away the gods your forefathers worshiped beyond the River and in Egypt, and serve the LORD. But if serving the LORD seems undesirable to you, then choose for yourselves this day whom you will serve, whether the gods your forefathers served beyond the River, or the gods of the Amorites, in whose land you are living. But as for me and my household, we will serve the LORD."

Then the people answered, "Far be it from us to forsake the LORD to serve other gods! It was the LORD our God himself who brought us and our fathers up out of Egypt, from that land of slavery, and performed those great signs before our eyes. He protected us on our entire journey and among all the nations through which we traveled. And the LORD drove out before us all the nations, including the Amorites, who lived in the land. We too will serve the LORD, because he is our God."

Joshua said to the people, "You are not able to serve the LORD. He is a holy God; he is a jealous God. He will not forgive your rebellion and your sins. If you forsake the LORD and serve foreign gods, he will turn and bring disaster on you and make an end of you, after he has been good to you."

But the people said to Joshua, "No! We will serve the LORD."

Then Joshua said, "You are witnesses against yourselves that you have chosen to serve the LORD."

"Yes, we are witnesses," they replied.

"Now then," said Joshua, "throw away the foreign gods that are among you and yield your hearts to the LORD, the God of Israel."

And the people said to Joshua, "We will serve the LORD our God and obey him."

On that day Joshua made a covenant for the people, and there at Shechem he drew up for them decrees and laws. And Joshua recorded these things in the Book of the Law of God. Then he took a large stone and set it up there under the oak near the holy place of the LORD.

"See!" he said to all the people. "This stone will be a witness against us. It has heard all the words the LORD has said to us. It will be a witness against you if you are untrue to your God."

Then Joshua sent the people away, each to his own inheritance.

After these things, Joshua son of Nun, the servant of the LORD, died at the age of a hundred and ten.

At the end of his life, Joshua, like Moses before him, stands before the Israelites to deliver a farewell address. Things have gone well under his leadership. The Bible gives the remarkable assessment: "Israel served the LORD throughout the lifetime of Joshua" (v. 31). And now Joshua uses his final speech to review all that God has done and to remind the people of their obligations under the covenant with God.

"I gave you a land on which you did not toil and cities you did not build"—at every point, Joshua emphasizes that *God* is the sole source of their success. He called out Abraham and blessed him with children, delivered the Israelites from slavery in Egypt, carried them across the desert. And in Joshua's own lifetime he fulfills one more promise of the covenant: he gives them the Promised Land. It is theirs to live in.

"Choose for yourselves this day whom you will serve," Joshua challenges his listeners in the stirring climax to his speech. All the people present swear their allegiance to God, the God who has kept his covenant with them. Joshua solemnly ratifies the covenant and sends the people away, then quietly prepares to die.

The book of Joshua ends with an act of deep symbolism: the Israelites finally bury the remains of Joseph. For well over four centuries those remains have been preserved in Egypt in anticipation of the Israelites' return to their homeland. And during the forty years of wilderness wanderings, the tribes have carried Joseph's bones as a treasured reminder of their past. Now, at last, Abraham's descendants have come home, and even the dead can rest in peace. —PY

DAILY CONTEMPLATION

When you experience success, whom do you tend to credit—yourself or God?

DAY 80 Reflection

CHOOSING TO LOVE GOD

Choose for yourselves this day whom you will serve . . ."

Joshua posed this challenge to the Israelite people when he was nearing death. He hoped they would choose God and then hold to their choice in the days and years ahead. Joshua knew well that a choice made today wouldn't necessarily ensure the future. The choice would have to be made each day, or it would stand no chance of enduring.

Christian authors and psychologists Gary Smalley and John Trent coined the modern-day phrase "Love is a decision" in their writing about marriage: "Contrary to popular belief, love is actually a reflection of how much we 'honor' another person—for at its core genuine love is a decision, not a feeling."[3] For love in a marriage to survive, husband and wife must *decide* to love and honor each other every day, regardless of how they feel toward each other at any particular moment. This concept is expressed in the traditional wedding vow: ". . . to have and to hold, from this day forward, for better, for worse, for richer, for poorer, in sickness and in health, to love and to cherish, till death do us part." Two people pledge—choose—to love one another for a lifetime, regardless of circumstances.

In their marriage to God, the Israelites have faced a variety of situations in which they had to choose whether or not to serve him. Rahab, though not originally an Israelite, chose God over her people. The Israelites, on the edge of the Promised Land, decided to step out into the Jordan riverbed. And instead of claiming victory for themselves, the people chose to honor God when they conquered Jericho.

One man, however, made a wrong choice. When faced with the enticing goods of the world, Achan chose them over God. He couldn't resist keeping for himself a robe, silver, and gold rather than turning them in with the rest of the plunder of Jericho.

Several times in both the Old and New Testaments, God refers to his people and the Christian church as the bride of Christ. Believers have entered into a marriage-like relationship with God. Just as in human marriages, we will only make the pledge last if we choose daily to honor God no matter what our feelings compel us to do. We'll stay true to God only if our love becomes a decision.

Whom will you love today?   —BQ

DAILY CONTEMPLATION

In your love relationship with God, how are you feeling toward him at the moment? Talk to God about your feelings. He knows them, so you can be honest. Choose to love God today despite your feelings. Ask him to help you follow through.

DAY 81   Judges 4:1–24

DEBORAH

After Ehud died, the Israelites once again did evil in the eyes of the LORD. So the LORD sold them into the hands of Jabin, a king of Canaan, who reigned in Hazor. The commander of his army was Sisera, who lived in Harosheth Haggoyim. Because he had nine hundred iron chariots and had cruelly oppressed the Israelites for twenty years, they cried to the LORD for help.

Deborah, a prophetess, the wife of Lappidoth, was leading Israel at that time. She held court under the Palm of Deborah between Ramah and Bethel in the hill country of Ephraim, and the Israelites came to her to have their disputes decided. She sent for Barak son of Abinoam from Kedesh in Naphtali and said to him, "The LORD, the God of Israel, commands you: 'Go, take with you ten thousand men of Naphtali and Zebulun and lead the way to Mount Tabor. I will lure Sisera, the commander of Jabin's army, with his chariots and his troops to the Kishon River and give him into your hands.'"

152

Barak said to her, "If you go with me, I will go; but if you don't go with me, I won't go."

"Very well," Deborah said, "I will go with you. But because of the way you are going about this, the honor will not be yours, for the LORD will hand Sisera over to a woman." So Deborah went with Barak to Kedesh, where he summoned Zebulun and Naphtali. Ten thousand men followed him, and Deborah also went with him.

Now Heber the Kenite had left the other Kenites, the descendants of Hobab, Moses' brother-in-law, and pitched his tent by the great tree in Zaanannim near Kedesh.

When they told Sisera that Barak son of Abinoam had gone up to Mount Tabor, Sisera gathered together his nine hundred iron chariots and all the men with him, from Harosheth Haggoyim to the Kishon River.

Then Deborah said to Barak, "Go! This is the day the LORD has given Sisera into your hands. Has not the LORD gone ahead of you?" So Barak went down Mount Tabor, followed by ten thousand men. At Barak's advance, the LORD routed Sisera and all his chariots and army by the sword, and Sisera abandoned his chariot and fled on foot. But Barak pursued the chariots and army as far as Harosheth Haggoyim. All the troops of Sisera fell by the sword; not a man was left.

Sisera, however, fled on foot to the tent of Jael, the wife of Heber the Kenite, because there were friendly relations between Jabin king of Hazor and the clan of Heber the Kenite.

Jael went out to meet Sisera and said to him, "Come, my lord, come right in. Don't be afraid." So he entered her tent, and she put a covering over him.

"I'm thirsty," he said. "Please give me some water." She opened a skin of milk, gave him a drink, and covered him up.

"Stand in the doorway of the tent," he told her. "If someone comes by and asks you, 'Is anyone here?' say 'No.'"

But Jael, Heber's wife, picked up a tent peg and a hammer and went quietly to him while he lay fast asleep, exhausted. She drove the peg through his temple into the ground, and he died.

Barak came by in pursuit of Sisera, and Jael went out to meet him. "Come," she said, "I will show you the man you're looking for." So he went in with her, and there lay Sisera with the tent peg through his temple—dead.

On that day God subdued Jabin, the Canaanite king, before the Israelites. And the hand of the Israelites grew stronger and stronger against Jabin, the Canaanite king, until they destroyed him.

About two hundred years have passed since God delivered the Israelites from Egypt. They have strayed from God since entering Canaan, and he has given them into the hands of the Canaanites as punishment. But God hears their cries. He uses Deborah, a prophetess and judge over the Israelites, to defeat the Canaanites.

Deborah becomes the only woman to hold a place among the twelve judges who serve Israel during their time in the Promised Land. Although she lives in a patriarchal culture, this woman possesses a prophetic gift and strong personal qualities. God chooses her to lead the people. Because Deborah walks closely with God and exhibits faith in him, he enables her to overcome the limitations imposed on a woman in her society and carry out the role he has appointed. —BQ

DAILY CONTEMPLATION

Do you feel God has asked you to do something atypical?

DAY 82   Judges 6:1, 11–40

GIDEON

Again the Israelites did evil in the eyes of the LORD, and for seven years he gave them into the hands of the Midianites. . . .

The angel of the LORD came and sat down under the oak in Ophrah that belonged to Joash the Abiezrite, where his son Gideon was threshing wheat in a winepress to keep it from the Midianites. When the angel of the LORD appeared to Gideon, he said, "The LORD is with you, mighty warrior."

"But sir," Gideon replied, "if the LORD is with us, why has all this happened to us? Where are all his wonders that our fathers told us about when they said, 'Did not the LORD bring us up out of Egypt?' But now the LORD has abandoned us and put us into the hand of Midian."

The LORD turned to him and said, "Go in the strength you have and save Israel out of Midian's hand. Am I not sending you?"

"But Lord," Gideon asked, "how can I save Israel? My clan is the weakest in Manasseh, and I am the least in my family."

The LORD answered, "I will be with you, and you will strike down all the Midianites together."

Gideon replied, "If now I have found favor in your eyes, give me a sign that it is really you talking to me. Please do not go away until I come back and bring my offering and set it before you."

And the LORD said, "I will wait until you return."

Gideon went in, prepared a young goat, and from an ephah of flour he made bread without yeast. Putting the meat in a basket and its broth in a pot, he brought them out and offered them to him under the oak.

The angel of God said to him, "Take the meat and the unleavened bread, place them on this rock, and pour out the broth." And Gideon did so. With the tip of the staff that was in his hand, the angel of the LORD touched the meat and the unleavened bread. Fire flared from the rock, consuming the meat and the bread. And the angel of the LORD disappeared. When Gideon realized that it was the angel of the LORD, he exclaimed, "Ah, Sovereign LORD! I have seen the angel of the LORD face to face!"

But the LORD said to him, "Peace! Do not be afraid. You are not going to die."

So Gideon built an altar to the LORD there and called it The LORD is Peace. To this day it stands in Ophrah of the Abiezrites.

That same night the LORD said to him, "Take the second bull from your father's herd, the one seven years old. Tear down your father's altar to Baal and cut down the Asherah pole beside it. Then build a proper kind of altar to the LORD your God on the top of this height. Using the wood of the Asherah pole that you cut down, offer the second bull as a burnt offering."

So Gideon took ten of his servants and did as the LORD told him. But because he was afraid of his family and the men of the town, he did it at night rather than in the daytime.

In the morning when the men of the town got up, there was Baal's altar, demolished, with the Asherah pole beside it cut down and the second bull sacrificed on the newly built altar!

They asked each other, "Who did this?"

When they carefully investigated, they were told, "Gideon son of Joash did it."

The men of the town demanded of Joash, "Bring out your son. He must die, because he has broken down Baal's altar and cut down the Asherah pole beside it."

But Joash replied to the hostile crowd around him, "Are you going to plead Baal's cause? Are you trying to save him? Whoever fights for him shall be put to death by morning! If Baal really is a god, he can defend himself when someone breaks down his altar." So that day they called Gideon "Jerub-Baal," saying, "Let Baal contend with him," because he broke down Baal's altar.

Now all the Midianites, Amalekites and other eastern peoples joined forces and crossed over the Jordan and camped in the Valley of Jezreel. Then the Spirit of the LORD came upon Gideon, and he blew a trumpet, summoning the Abiezrites to follow him. He sent messengers throughout Manasseh, calling them to arms, and also into Asher, Zebulun and Naphtali, so that they too went up to meet them.

Gideon said to God, "If you will save Israel by my hand as you have promised—look, I will place a wool fleece on the threshing floor. If there is dew only on the fleece and all the ground is dry, then I will know that you will save Israel by my hand, as you said." And that is what happened. Gideon rose early the next day; he squeezed the fleece and wrung out the dew—a bowlful of water.

Then Gideon said to God, "Do not be angry with me. Let me make just one more request. Allow me one more test with the fleece. This time make the fleece dry and the ground covered with dew." That night God did so. Only the fleece was dry; all the ground was covered with dew.

The good-news tone of Joshua has soured abruptly in Judges. After an initial spurt of enthusiasm, the Israelites stray far, very far, from the way God has pointed them. Ignoring Joshua's orders to clear the land, they settle in among the pagan occupants instead. These new neighbors practice an exotic religion that includes sex orgies and child sacrifice as a regular part of worship.

Just one generation later, the Israelites have lost their sense of national identity and have forgotten all about their parents' ringing vows to honor the covenant. They too are worshiping the idol Baal (BAY-uhl). Having violated virtually every moral standard, the nation slides toward chaos. The last verse of Judges sums up the scene: "Everyone did as he saw fit."

The Israelites are suffering from a leadership crisis of huge dimensions. For eighty years they have followed Moses and Joshua, two outstanding leaders who proved impossible to replace. When the twelve tribes splinter apart and retreat into separate territories, God turns to more regional leaders called judges. The term may be misleading; these are people renowned not for court cases but for their military campaigns against foreign invaders. (Today they might be called guerrillas or freedom fighters.)

Some judges, such as Deborah and the hero of this chapter, emerge as models of courage and faith. And yet a close look at the life of Gideon shows the material God must work with. His family and village worship Baal, not the Lord. In the face of God's clear direction, Gideon sputters, demands repeated proofs, uses delaying tactics, and worships at night to avoid detection. He is subject to paralyzing fears, even on the eve of battle. But God, knowing Gideon's potential, step by step brings him to the point of courage. —PY

DAILY CONTEMPLATION

How has God given you clear guidance when you've needed it?

DAY 83   Judges 7:1–25; 8:28, 33

GIDEON DEFEATS THE MIDIANITES

Early in the morning, Jerub-Baal (that is, Gideon) and all his men camped at the spring of Harod. The camp of Midian was north of them in the valley near the hill of Moreh. The LORD said to Gideon, "You have too many men for me to deliver Midian into their hands. In order that Israel may not boast against me that her own strength has saved her, announce now to the people, 'Anyone who trembles with fear may turn back and leave Mount Gilead.'" So twenty-two thousand men left, while ten thousand remained.

But the LORD said to Gideon, "There are still too many men. Take them down to the water, and I will sift them for you there. If I say, 'This one shall go with you,' he shall go; but if I say, 'This one shall not go with you,' he shall not go."

So Gideon took the men down to the water. There the LORD told him, "Separate those who lap the water with their tongues like a dog from those who kneel down to drink." Three hundred men lapped with their hands to their mouths. All the rest got down on their knees to drink.

The LORD said to Gideon, "With the three hundred men that lapped I will save you and give the Midianites into your hands. Let all the other men go, each to his own place." So Gideon sent the rest of the Israelites to their tents but kept the three hundred, who took over the provisions and trumpets of the others.

Now the camp of Midian lay below him in the valley. During that night the LORD said to Gideon, "Get up, go down against the camp, because I am going to give it into your hands. If you are afraid to attack, go down to the camp with your servant Purah and listen to what they are saying. Afterward, you will be encouraged to attack the camp." So he and Purah his servant went down to the outposts of the camp. The Midianites, the Amalekites and all the other eastern peoples had settled in the valley, thick as locusts. Their camels could no more be counted than the sand on the seashore.

Gideon arrived just as a man was telling a friend his dream. "I had a dream," he was saying. "A round loaf of barley bread came tumbling into the Midianite camp. It struck the tent with such force that the tent overturned and collapsed."

His friend responded, "This can be nothing other than the sword of Gideon son of Joash, the Israelite. God has given the Midianites and the whole camp into his hands."

When Gideon heard the dream and its interpretation, he worshiped God. He returned to the camp of Israel and called out, "Get up! The LORD has given the Midianite camp into your hands." Dividing the three hundred men into three companies, he placed trumpets and empty jars in the hands of all of them, with torches inside.

"Watch me," he told them. "Follow my lead. When I get to the edge of the camp, do exactly as I do. When I and all who are with me blow our trumpets, then from all around the camp blow yours and shout, 'For the LORD and for Gideon.'"

Gideon and the hundred men with him reached the edge of the camp at the beginning of the middle watch, just after they had changed the guard. They blew their trumpets and broke the jars that were in their hands. The three companies blew the trumpets and smashed the jars. Grasping the torches in their left hands and holding in their right hands the trumpets they were to blow, they shouted, "A sword for the LORD and for Gideon!" While each man held his position around the camp, all the Midianites ran, crying out as they fled.

When the three hundred trumpets sounded, the LORD caused the men throughout the camp to turn on each other with their swords. The army fled to Beth Shittah toward Zererah as far as the border of Abel Meholah near Tabbath. Israelites from Naphtali, Asher and all Manasseh were called out, and they pursued the Midianites. Gideon sent messengers throughout the hill country of Ephraim, saying, "Come down against the Midianites and seize the waters of the Jordan ahead of them as far as Beth Barah."

So all the men of Ephraim were called out and they took the waters of the Jordan as far as Beth Barah. They also captured two of the Midianite leaders,

Oreb and Zeeb. They killed Oreb at the rock of Oreb, and Zeeb at the wine-press of Zeeb. They pursued the Midianites and brought the heads of Oreb and Zeeb to Gideon, who was by the Jordan. . . .

Thus Midian was subdued before the Israelites and did not raise its head again. During Gideon's lifetime, the land enjoyed peace forty years. . . .

No sooner had Gideon died than the Israelites again prostituted themselves to the Baals.

Joshua won the battle of Jericho by following orders that defied all orthodox military tactics. Similarly, when the time comes for Gideon to strike a decisive blow for the Israelites, God gives instructions that would daunt a seasoned general, much less a greenhorn like Gideon. He reduces the size of Gideon's army from thirty-two thousand to three hundred men, so as to leave no doubt it is he, God of the Hebrews, who will fight this battle.

In Gideon's days the Israelites live at the mercy of marauding tribes of Bedouins, who help themselves to the produce and wealth of the local farmers. But by following God's commands, Gideon leads a great victory and frees his people from oppression.

Gideon's against-all-odds victory shows a pattern that is repeated throughout the book of Judges. At a time when women are regarded as second-class citizens, God chooses Deborah to lead. Jephthah, another judge, leads a gang of outlaws before God chooses him. In fact, this pattern appears throughout the Bible. God does not seek the people most outwardly capable, nor the most naturally "good." He works with the most unlikely material so that everyone can see the glory is his and his alone.

The apostle Paul marveled over this principle more than a thousand years later, writing, "Brothers, think of what you were when you were called. Not many of you were wise by human standards; not many were influential; not many were of noble birth. But God chose the foolish things of the world to shame the wise; God chose the weak things of the world to shame the strong. . . . Therefore, as it is written: 'Let him who boasts boast in the Lord'" (1 Corinthians 1:26–27, 31). —PY

DAILY CONTEMPLATION

Is God using you in any unlikely ways, considering your background or abilities?

DAY 84   Reflection

FOLLOW THE LEADER

You probably played the game as a child: "Follow the Leader." Kids amble one behind the other, mimicking the antics of the one in front until someone new becomes the leader.

This childhood game is not far removed from real life. Whether we realize it or not, we are much the product of the leaders we have followed. Your parents, teachers, coaches, instructors, clergy, and peers have contributed to your life more than you may know, because they have been your up-close models of living. They have been in a position to influence your actions and the direction of your life.

Deborah and Gideon did this for their people. God picked these two as his leaders and gave them a vision for freeing the people from Canaanite oppression and for restoring them once again to himself. God knew how childlike the Israelites were in their tendency to imitate the ones they followed, so in his grace he raised up two leaders who would again turn the eyes of the people to himself.

John Maxwell, Christian founder of the leadership development institute Injoy, writes, "The focus of vision must be on the leader—like leader, like people. Followers find the leader and then the vision. Leaders find the vision and then the people."[4] Maxwell confirms the situation we find in Judges: with God-focused leaders, people will adopt a vision for God's ways; without God-focused leaders, people will adopt the ways of the self-focused leaders around them, just as the Israelites did when Deborah and Gideon died.

In looking at the long history of Israel in the Old Testament, we find that their times away from God lasted longer and were more severe in the absence of God-centered leaders. A good leader is hard to find, as we'll see throughout the remainder of the Old Testament and even in the New Testament. For this reason, in the Bible God talks often about the importance of leadership.

> "Remember your leaders, who spoke the word of God to you. Consider the outcome of their way of life and imitate their faith" (Hebrews 13:7).
> "Obey your leaders and submit to their authority. They keep watch over you as men who must give an account" (Hebrews 13:17).
> "Train a child in the way he should go, and when he is old he will not turn from it (Proverbs 22:6).
> "Fathers, do not exasperate your children; instead, bring them up in the training and instruction of the Lord" (Ephesians 6:4).
> "Not many of you should presume to be teachers, my brothers, because you know that we who teach will be judged more strictly" (James 3:1).

In our lives we will lead and we will follow. When we lead, may we do it in the reverence of God and only through his guidance. When we follow, may we seek God's leaders as our models and pray for all those in positions of leadership over us. Each day, each moment, may God through his Spirit be our most respected leader.   —BQ

DAILY CONTEMPLATION

Consider for a moment the influential people in your life. How has their leadership impacted you? Thank God for those he has used to mold you in life-giving ways. Pray for God's help in areas in which you are currently leading.

THE BIRTH OF SAMSON

Again the Israelites did evil in the eyes of the LORD, so the LORD delivered them into the hands of the Philistines for forty years.

A certain man of Zorah, named Manoah, from the clan of the Danites, had a wife who was sterile and remained childless. The angel of the LORD appeared to her and said, "You are sterile and childless, but you are going to conceive and have a son. Now see to it that you drink no wine or other fermented drink and that you do not eat anything unclean, because you will conceive and give birth to a son. No razor may be used on his head, because the boy is to be a Nazirite, set apart to God from birth, and he will begin the deliverance of Israel from the hands of the Philistines."

Then the woman went to her husband and told him, "A man of God came to me. He looked like an angel of God, very awesome. I didn't ask him where he came from, and he didn't tell me his name. But he said to me, 'You will conceive and give birth to a son. Now then, drink no wine or other fermented drink and do not eat anything unclean, because the boy will be a Nazirite of God from birth until the day of his death.'"

Then Manoah prayed to the LORD: "O Lord, I beg you, let the man of God you sent to us come again to teach us how to bring up the boy who is to be born."

God heard Manoah, and the angel of God came again to the woman while she was out in the field; but her husband Manoah was not with her. The woman hurried to tell her husband, "He's here! The man who appeared to me the other day!"

Manoah got up and followed his wife. When he came to the man, he said, "Are you the one who talked to my wife?"

"I am," he said.

So Manoah asked him, "When your words are fulfilled, what is to be the rule for the boy's life and work?"

The angel of the LORD answered, "Your wife must do all that I have told her. She must not eat anything that comes from the grapevine, nor drink any wine or other fermented drink nor eat anything unclean. She must do everything I have commanded her."

Manoah said to the angel of the LORD, "We would like you to stay until we prepare a young goat for you."

The angel of the LORD replied, "Even though you detain me, I will not eat any of your food. But if you prepare a burnt offering, offer it to the LORD." (Manoah did not realize that it was the angel of the LORD.)

Then Manoah inquired of the angel of the LORD, "What is your name, so that we may honor you when your word comes true?"

He replied, "Why do you ask my name? It is beyond understanding." Then Manoah took a young goat, together with the grain offering, and sacrificed it on a rock to the LORD. And the LORD did an amazing thing while Manoah and his wife watched: As the flame blazed up from the altar toward heaven, the angel of the LORD ascended in the flame. Seeing this, Manoah and his wife fell with their faces to the ground. When the angel of the LORD did not show himself again to Manoah and his wife, Manoah realized that it was the angel of the LORD.

"We are doomed to die!" he said to his wife. "We have seen God!"

But his wife answered, "If the LORD had meant to kill us, he would not have accepted a burnt offering and grain offering from our hands, nor shown us all these things or now told us this."

The woman gave birth to a boy and named him Samson. He grew and the LORD blessed him, and the Spirit of the LORD began to stir him while he was in Mahaneh Dan, between Zorah and Eshtaol.

Again in this story we see an instance of barrenness leading to the God-appointed birth of a boy who will serve in an important way. God raises up Samson as another judge over the people of Israel. Samson will lead in a very different way from that of both Deborah and Gideon. He will be a sort of lone ranger, distracting the Philistines (fih-LIS-tins) from their conquest of Israelite territory rather than leading the people in a military overthrow, as the others have done. Samson's character qualities are different from those of Deborah and Gideon as well. He demonstrates again that God uses people with all sorts of strengths and weaknesses. —BQ

DAILY CONTEMPLATION

Has God ever surprised you with the kind of person he used in your life?

DAY 86 Judges 14:1–20

SAMSON'S MARRIAGE

Samson went down to Timnah and saw there a young Philistine woman. When he returned, he said to his father and mother, "I have seen a Philistine woman in Timnah; now get her for me as my wife."

His father and mother replied, "Isn't there an acceptable woman among your relatives or among all our people? Must you go to the uncircumcised Philistines to get a wife?"

But Samson said to his father, "Get her for me. She's the right one for me." (His parents did not know that this was from the LORD, who was seeking an occasion to confront the Philistines; for at that time they were ruling over Israel.) Samson went down to Timnah together with his father and mother. As they approached the vineyards of Timnah, suddenly a young lion came roaring toward him. The Spirit of the LORD came upon him in power so that he tore the lion apart with his bare hands as he might have torn a young goat. But he told neither his father nor his mother what he had done. Then he went down and talked with the woman, and he liked her.

Some time later, when he went back to marry her, he turned aside to look at the lion's carcass. In it was a swarm of bees and some honey, which he scooped out with his hands and ate as he went along. When he rejoined his parents, he gave them some, and they too ate it. But he did not tell them that he had taken the honey from the lion's carcass.

Now his father went down to see the woman. And Samson made a feast there, as was customary for bridegrooms. When he appeared, he was given thirty companions.

"Let me tell you a riddle," Samson said to them. "If you can give me the answer within the seven days of the feast, I will give you thirty linen garments and thirty sets of clothes. If you can't tell me the answer, you must give me thirty linen garments and thirty sets of clothes."

"Tell us your riddle," they said. "Let's hear it."

He replied,

"Out of the eater, something to eat;
    out of the strong, something sweet."

For three days they could not give the answer.

On the fourth day, they said to Samson's wife, "Coax your husband into explaining the riddle for us, or we will burn you and your father's household to death. Did you invite us here to rob us?"

Then Samson's wife threw herself on him, sobbing, "You hate me! You don't really love me. You've given my people a riddle, but you haven't told me the answer."

"I haven't even explained it to my father or mother," he replied, "so why should I explain it to you?" She cried the whole seven days of the feast. So on the seventh day he finally told her, because she continued to press him. She in turn explained the riddle to her people.

Before sunset on the seventh day the men of the town said to him,

"What is sweeter than honey?
    What is stronger than a lion?"

Samson said to them,

"If you had not plowed with my heifer,
    you would not have solved my riddle."

Then the Spirit of the LORD came upon him in power. He went down to Ashkelon, struck down thirty of their men, stripped them of their belongings and gave their clothes to those who had explained the riddle. Burning with anger, he went up to his father's house. And Samson's wife was given to the friend who had attended him at his wedding.

Samson stubbornly determines to marry a Philistine woman despite being forbidden by Mosaic law to marry any non-Israelite. Although his parents object, they do not forbid the marriage. Not only is Samson gifted with unusual strength, he also possesses a strong will. Yet just as God has given him physical strength to subdue the Philistines, God will use Samson's strong will for his own purposes. Although he doesn't desire Samson to break the law and follow his passion for a pagan woman, God overrules Samson's rebellion for the good of his people.

As Samson will continue to reveal, his unbridled passions don't bring him happiness. Nevertheless, God uses this powerful man to begin to deliver Israel.   —BQ

DAILY CONTEMPLATION

In what area has God given you special strength?

DAY 87
Judges 16:1–10, 16–30

SAMSON AND DELILAH

One day Samson went to Gaza, where he saw a prostitute. He went in to spend the night with her. The people of Gaza were told, "Samson is here!" So they surrounded the place and lay in wait for him all night at the city gate. They made no move during the night, saying, "At dawn we'll kill him."

But Samson lay there only until the middle of the night. Then he got up and took hold of the doors of the city gate, together with the two posts, and tore them loose, bar and all. He lifted them to his shoulders and carried them to the top of the hill that faces Hebron.

Some time later, he fell in love with a woman in the Valley of Sorek whose name was Delilah. The rulers of the Philistines went to her and said, "See if you can lure him into showing you the secret of his great strength and how we can overpower him so we may tie him up and subdue him. Each one of us will give you eleven hundred shekels of silver."

So Delilah said to Samson, "Tell me the secret of your great strength and how you can be tied up and subdued."

Samson answered her, "If anyone ties me with seven fresh thongs that have not been dried, I'll become as weak as any other man."

Then the rulers of the Philistines brought her seven fresh thongs that had not been dried, and she tied him with them. With men hidden in the room, she called to him, "Samson, the Philistines are upon you!" But he snapped the thongs as easily as a piece of string snaps when it comes close to a flame. So the secret of his strength was not discovered.

Then Delilah said to Samson, "You have made a fool of me; you lied to me. Come now, tell me how you can be tied." ...

With such nagging she prodded him day after day until he was tired to death.

So he told her everything. "No razor has ever been used on my head," he said, "because I have been a Nazirite set apart to God since birth. If my head were shaved, my strength would leave me, and I would become as weak as any other man."

When Delilah saw that he had told her everything, she sent word to the rulers of the Philistines, "Come back once more; he has told me everything." So the rulers of the Philistines returned with the silver in their hands. Having put him to sleep on her lap, she called a man to shave off the seven braids of his hair, and so began to subdue him. And his strength left him.

Then she called, "Samson, the Philistines are upon you!"

He awoke from his sleep and thought, "I'll go out as before and shake myself free." But he did not know that the LORD had left him.

Then the Philistines seized him, gouged out his eyes and took him down to Gaza. Binding him with bronze shackles, they set him to grinding in the prison. But the hair on his head began to grow again after it had been shaved.

Now the rulers of the Philistines assembled to offer a great sacrifice to Dagon their god and to celebrate, saying, "Our god has delivered Samson, our enemy, into our hands."

When the people saw him, they praised their god, saying,

"Our god has delivered our enemy
   into our hands,
the one who laid waste our land
   and multiplied our slain."

While they were in high spirits, they shouted, "Bring out Samson to entertain us." So they called Samson out of the prison, and he performed for them.

When they stood him among the pillars, Samson said to the servant who held his hand, "Put me where I can feel the pillars that support the temple, so that I may lean against them." Now the temple was crowded with men and women; all the rulers of the Philistines were there, and on the roof were about three thousand men and women watching Samson perform. Then Samson prayed to the LORD, "O Sovereign LORD, remember me. O God, please strengthen me just once more, and let me with one blow get revenge on the Philistines for my two eyes." Then Samson reached toward the two central pillars on which the temple stood. Bracing himself against them, his right hand on the one and his left hand on the other, Samson said, "Let me die with the Philistines!" Then he pushed with all his might, and down came the temple on the rulers and all the people in it. Thus he killed many more when he died than while he lived.

The most famous of all the judges has made an appearance toward the end of the book, and the Bible devotes four chapters to the dramatic events of his life. If Gideon shows how a person with limited potential can be greatly used by God,

Samson illustrates just the opposite: a person with enormous potential who squanders it.

When Samson enters the picture, the Israelites are once again suffering under foreign domination. An angel announces his birth, making clear that God has great things in store for Samson and wants him specially set apart.

Indeed, Samson is blessed with extraordinary supernatural gifts. When the Spirit of the Lord comes upon him, he can tackle a lion or single-handedly rout an entire army. And yet, as the stories from his youth reveal, Samson wields that strength in ways more befitting a juvenile delinquent than a spiritual leader.

Like any rebellious teenager, he chooses for a wife the kind of woman sure to cause his parents—and God—the most grief. That marriage barely survives a week, and next Samson takes up with a Philistine prostitute. This chapter describes how he, stupidly, forfeits his great strength in a dalliance with a third woman, the seductive Delilah. Samson's story is like a morality play. No one in the world could match his physical strength; just about anyone could match his moral strength. His moral lapses would seem almost incomprehensible were they not repeated by spiritual leaders in almost every generation.

In the end, Samson, the designated savior of his people, is led out to perform like a trained bear for his captors. It appears that the God of the Israelites has been soundly defeated by the pagans and their gods. But Samson, and God, have one last surprise for the Philistine oppressors.   —PY

DAILY CONTEMPLATION

In what areas are you living up to your potential? In what areas are you falling short?

DAY 88   Reflection

A STRONG NEED FOR GOD

Strength. Independence. Self-sufficiency.

Sound familiar? These traits have become the rule rather than the exception in present-day Western culture. We have absorbed subconsciously a definition for strength that excludes any show of neediness. Strong people live life on their own. When they hit bumps in the road, they grit their teeth a little harder and keep to themselves until they get past the struggle and regain control. Mental and emotional strength are the name of the game, and image is where it's at—if you look strong, you're there.

But as we see in the life of Samson, appearance and reality are two decidedly different things. Samson had physical strength, undoubtedly. In his day, physical prowess was probably the most coveted kind of strength a man or woman could have. The ability to overpower both animals and people gave Samson supreme status. Yet his physical strength couldn't overcome his sexual appetite or his weakness for ungodly women. His strength didn't enable him to make good decisions or to find joy in living.

Samson needed not only the physical strength God provided; he needed God's daily guidance. He needed God's Spirit to supply the power to resist temptation, to desire God's best, to forego instant gratification in exchange for more fulfilling choices. More than he realized, Samson needed God to meet his weakness.

We're like Samson in our need for God's strength. No matter how capable we are, we need God every day, living in us and acting through us. We need his courage and his hope, his love and his companionship. We need his salvation. We can't live without God.

When we try to live by the cool-and-collected strength of our culture, we might mask our need but we don't meet it. Underneath we are, all of us, weak. Not far beneath the surface we all have an aching place that needs God. As we live each day, we can defy our prescribed roles and reach out in our need for one another. We can speak of our need for God. And we can cry out to God daily in that need for him. Nothing could be more powerful.   —BQ

DAILY CONTEMPLATION

How aware are you of your need for others and for God? Express your need for God by repeating this prayer several times: "Lord, I need you."

DAY 89   Ruth 1:1–22

NAOMI AND RUTH

In the days when the judges ruled, there was a famine in the land, and a man from Bethlehem in Judah, together with his wife and two sons, went to live for a while in the country of Moab. The man's name was Elimelech, his wife's name Naomi, and the names of his two sons were Mahlon and Kilion. They were Ephrathites from Bethlehem, Judah. And they went to Moab and lived there.

Now Elimelech, Naomi's husband, died, and she was left with her two sons. They married Moabite women, one named Orpah and the other Ruth. After they had lived there about ten years, both Mahlon and Kilion also died, and Naomi was left without her two sons and her husband.

When she heard in Moab that the LORD had come to the aid of his people by providing food for them, Naomi and her daughters-in-law prepared to return home from there. With her two daughters-in-law she left the place where she had been living and set out on the road that would take them back to the land of Judah.

Then Naomi said to her two daughters-in-law, "Go back, each of you, to your mother's home. May the LORD show kindness to you, as you have shown to your dead and to me. May the LORD grant that each of you will find rest in the home of another husband."

Then she kissed them and they wept aloud and said to her, "We will go back with you to your people."

But Naomi said, "Return home, my daughters. Why would you come with me? Am I going to have any more sons, who could become your husbands? Return home, my daughters; I am too old to have another husband. Even if I thought there was still hope for me—even if I had a husband tonight and then gave birth to sons—would you wait until they grew up? Would you remain unmarried for them? No, my daughters. It is more bitter for me than for you, because the LORD's hand has gone out against me!"

At this they wept again. Then Orpah kissed her mother-in-law good-by, but Ruth clung to her.

"Look," said Naomi, "your sister-in-law is going back to her people and her gods. Go back with her."

But Ruth replied, "Don't urge me to leave you or to turn back from you. Where you go I will go, and where you stay I will stay. Your people will be my people and your God my God. Where you die I will die, and there I will be buried. May the LORD deal with me, be it ever so severely, if anything but death separates you and me." When Naomi realized that Ruth was determined to go with her, she stopped urging her.

So the two women went on until they came to Bethlehem. When they arrived in Bethlehem, the whole town was stirred because of them, and the women exclaimed, "Can this be Naomi?"

"Don't call me Naomi," she told them. "Call me Mara, because the Almighty has made my life very bitter. I went away full, but the LORD has brought me back empty. Why call me Naomi? The LORD has afflicted me; the Almighty has brought misfortune upon me."

So Naomi returned from Moab accompanied by Ruth the Moabitess, her daughter-in-law, arriving in Bethlehem as the barley harvest was beginning.

This charming tale about two scrappy women has nothing like the broad sweep of history found in Judges. Rather, Ruth narrows its focus to the story of one family trying to cope during chaotic, tumultuous times.

Things got so bad in Canaan, especially after a severe famine, that Naomi's Israelite family migrated into enemy territory just to survive. There, her two sons married local pagan women and settled down. Years later, after both those sons and her husband die, Naomi decides to return to the land of her birth. This book mainly tells of the stubborn loyalty of Naomi's daughter-in-law named Ruth.

Ruth and Naomi make unlikely friends. Ruth is young and strong; Naomi past middle age and brokenhearted. In addition, they come from completely different ethnic and religious backgrounds. Who would have put them together? But somewhere along the way Ruth has converted to the worship of the true God, and she insists on returning with Naomi to the land of the Israelites.

In a few brief chapters, Ruth manages to capture a slice of agrarian life in ancient times. The male-dominated society poses problems for unattached women, and these two live in harsh, trying times. Ruth serves awhile as a migrant farmworker, surviving on the "gleanings" left in the fields by the harvesters.

You can read this small book in several ways: as a tiny, elegant portrait of life in ancient times or as a record of God's faithfulness to the needy or as an inspiring story of undying friendship. Perhaps the most accurate way to read this story, however, is as a missionary story. God not only accepts Ruth, a member of the despised Moabites, into his family, but also uses her to produce Israel's greatest king. Ruth's great-grandson turns out to be David. To anyone who thought God's love was for Israelites only, Ruth's life makes a striking contradiction.   —PY

DAILY CONTEMPLATION

When has a friend gone out on a limb for you?

DAY 90   Ruth 2:1–23

RUTH MEETS BOAZ

Now Naomi had a relative on her husband's side, from the clan of Elimelech, a man of standing, whose name was Boaz.

And Ruth the Moabitess said to Naomi, "Let me go to the fields and pick up the leftover grain behind anyone in whose eyes I find favor."

Naomi said to her, "Go ahead, my daughter." So she went out and began to glean in the fields behind the harvesters. As it turned out, she found herself working in a field belonging to Boaz, who was from the clan of Elimelech.

Just then Boaz arrived from Bethlehem and greeted the harvesters, "The LORD be with you!"

"The LORD bless you!" they called back.

Boaz asked the foreman of his harvesters, "Whose young woman is that?"

The foreman replied, "She is the Moabitess who came back from Moab with Naomi. She said, 'Please let me glean and gather among the sheaves behind the harvesters.' She went into the field and has worked steadily from morning till now, except for a short rest in the shelter."

So Boaz said to Ruth, "My daughter, listen to me. Don't go and glean in another field and don't go away from here. Stay here with my servant girls. Watch the field where the men are harvesting, and follow along after the girls. I have told the men not to touch you. And whenever you are thirsty, go and get a drink from the water jars the men have filled."

At this, she bowed down with her face to the ground. She exclaimed, "Why have I found such favor in your eyes that you notice me—a foreigner?"

Boaz replied, "I've been told all about what you have done for your mother-in-law since the death of your husband—how you left your father and mother and your homeland and came to live with a people you did not know before. May the LORD repay you for what you have done. May you be richly rewarded by the LORD, the God of Israel, under whose wings you have come to take refuge."

"May I continue to find favor in your eyes, my lord," she said. "You have given me comfort and have spoken kindly to your servant—though I do not have the standing of one of your servant girls."

At mealtime Boaz said to her, "Come over here. Have some bread and dip it in the wine vinegar."

When she sat down with the harvesters, he offered her some roasted grain. She ate all she wanted and had some left over. As she got up to glean, Boaz gave orders to his men, "Even if she gathers among the sheaves, don't embarrass her. Rather, pull out some stalks for her from the bundles and leave them for her to pick up, and don't rebuke her."

So Ruth gleaned in the field until evening. Then she threshed the barley she had gathered, and it amounted to about an ephah. She carried it back to town, and her mother-in-law saw how much she had gathered. Ruth also brought out and gave her what she had left over after she had eaten enough.

Her mother-in-law asked her, "Where did you glean today? Where did you work? Blessed be the man who took notice of you!"

Then Ruth told her mother-in-law about the one at whose place she had been working. "The name of the man I worked with today is Boaz," she said.

"The LORD bless him!" Naomi said to her daughter-in-law. "He has not stopped showing his kindness to the living and the dead." She added, "That man is our close relative; he is one of our kinsman-redeemers."

Then Ruth the Moabitess said, "He even said to me, 'Stay with my workers until they finish harvesting all my grain.'"

Naomi said to Ruth her daughter-in-law, "It will be good for you, my daughter, to go with his girls, because in someone else's field you might be harmed."

So Ruth stayed close to the servant girls of Boaz to glean until the barley and wheat harvests were finished. And she lived with her mother-in-law.

God has guided Ruth to the field belonging to Boaz (BOH-az) and has blessed her with grain and the favor of her relative. In return for Ruth's faithfulness to God and to her widowed mother-in-law, God provides for her needs. Boaz tells Ruth she may continue to glean in his field.

Harvesting of barley and wheat took place from April through July, and typically the gleaners would begin gathering after the harvesters left the area. But Ruth is allowed to stay in the fields with the workers and even drink from their water jars. Boaz promises protection from the male workers.

Here in Bethlehem, where centuries later the Savior will be born, God is weaving together a way to bring his plans about. He has guided two unlikely people, Naomi and Ruth, on a journey and brought them to a town where a child will be born. This child, like the Child to come, will reaffirm God's covenant promise of love and faithfulness to his people. And in Ruth's story, as in Jesus' story, God reminds us that the world's ways are not his ways. Though life has seemed bitter to Naomi, God will turn despairing circumstances into a time of newfound joy.   —BQ

DAILY CONTEMPLATION

Whom have you met recently who has brought good to your life in an unexpected way?

DAY 91   Ruth 3:1–4:17

BOAZ MARRIES RUTH

One day Naomi her mother-in-law said to her, "My daughter, should I not try to find a home for you, where you will be well provided for? Is not Boaz, with whose servant girls you have been, a kinsman of ours? Tonight he will be winnowing barley on the threshing floor. Wash and perfume yourself, and put on your best clothes. Then go down to the threshing floor, but don't let him know you are there until he has finished eating and drinking. When he lies down, note the place where he is lying. Then go and uncover his feet and lie down. He will tell you what to do."

"I will do whatever you say," Ruth answered. So she went down to the threshing floor and did everything her mother-in-law told her to do.

When Boaz had finished eating and drinking and was in good spirits, he went over to lie down at the far end of the grain pile. Ruth approached quietly, uncovered his feet and lay down. In the middle of the night something startled the man, and he turned and discovered a woman lying at his feet.

"Who are you?" he asked.

"I am your servant Ruth," she said. "Spread the corner of your garment over me, since you are a kinsman-redeemer."

"The LORD bless you, my daughter," he replied. "This kindness is greater than that which you showed earlier: You have not run after the younger men, whether rich or poor. And now, my daughter, don't be afraid. I will do for you all you ask. All my fellow townsmen know that you are a woman of noble character. Although it is true that I am near of kin, there is a kinsman-redeemer nearer than I. Stay here for the night, and in the morning if he wants to redeem, good; let him redeem. But if he is not willing, as surely as the LORD lives I will do it. Lie here until morning."

So she lay at his feet until morning, but got up before anyone could be recognized; and he said, "Don't let it be known that a woman came to the threshing floor."

He also said, "Bring me the shawl you are wearing and hold it out." When she did so, he poured into it six measures of barley and put it on her. Then he went back to town.

When Ruth came to her mother-in-law, Naomi asked, "How did it go, my daughter?"

Then she told her everything Boaz had done for her and added, "He gave me these six measures of barley, saying, 'Don't go back to your mother-in-law empty-handed.'"

Then Naomi said, "Wait, my daughter, until you find out what happens. For the man will not rest until the matter is settled today."

Meanwhile Boaz went up to the town gate and sat there. When the kinsman-redeemer he had mentioned came along, Boaz said, "Come over here, my friend, and sit down." So he went over and sat down.

Boaz took ten of the elders of the town and said, "Sit here," and they did so. Then he said to the kinsman-redeemer, "Naomi, who has come back from Moab, is selling the piece of land that belonged to our brother Elimelech. I thought I should bring the matter to your attention and suggest that you buy it in the presence of these seated here and in the presence of the elders of my people. If you will redeem it, do so. But if you will not, tell me, so I will know. For no one has the right to do it except you, and I am next in line."

"I will redeem it," he said.

Then Boaz said, "On the day you buy the land from Naomi and from Ruth the Moabitess, you acquire the dead man's widow, in order to maintain the name of the dead with his property."

At this, the kinsman-redeemer said, "Then I cannot redeem it because I might endanger my own estate. You redeem it yourself. I cannot do it."

(Now in earlier times in Israel, for the redemption and transfer of property to become final, one party took off his sandal and gave it to the other. This was the method of legalizing transactions in Israel.)

So the kinsman-redeemer said to Boaz, "Buy it yourself." And he removed his sandal.

Then Boaz announced to the elders and all the people, "Today you are witnesses that I have bought from Naomi all the property of Elimelech, Kilion and Mahlon. I have also acquired Ruth the Moabitess, Mahlon's widow, as my wife, in order to maintain the name of the dead with his property, so that his name will not disappear from among his family or from the town records. Today you are witnesses!"

Then the elders and all those at the gate said, "We are witnesses. May the LORD make the woman who is coming into your home like Rachel and Leah, who together built up the house of Israel. May you have standing in Ephrathah and be famous in Bethlehem. Through the offspring the LORD gives you by this young woman, may your family be like that of Perez, whom Tamar bore to Judah."

So Boaz took Ruth and she became his wife. Then he went to her, and the LORD enabled her to conceive, and she gave birth to a son. The women said to Naomi: "Praise be to the LORD, who this day has not left you without a kinsman-redeemer. May he become famous throughout Israel! He will renew your life and sustain you in your old age. For your daughter-in-law, who loves you and who is better to you than seven sons, has given him birth."

Then Naomi took the child, laid him in her lap and cared for him. The women living there said, "Naomi has a son." And they named him Obed. He was the father of Jesse, the father of David.

The relationship of Ruth and Boaz grows closer in this passage. Naomi becomes a matchmaker, and Ruth doesn't shy from Naomi's bold plan. Boaz acts responsibly by letting Ruth stay with him in safety for the night and by recognizing the rights of her nearer kinsman. Honored by Ruth's willingness to marry an older man, Boaz is nevertheless ready to receive Ruth only if she becomes rightfully his.

Boaz completes the formalities necessary to take Ruth as his wife. Her nearer kinsman, who in that culture had first option, forfeits his right to Ruth and her land, probably because if she bore him a son, this son would be entitled to a share of the kinsman's current estate, causing dissension in the family. Boaz is prepared to buy the land and marry Ruth.

Though barren for ten years in Moab, Ruth conceives after marrying Boaz and gives birth to a son. Obed (OH-bed) will become the grandfather of King David and the ancestor of Jesus. Just as Boaz becomes the kinsman-redeemer for Naomi's family, Jesus Christ will become the Kinsman-Redeemer for the family of all humankind, redeeming us from death and providing hope for a future. In a small family circle in Bethlehem, God gives us a preview of how he will bring the bitterness of life on earth to an end through an unexpected but trustworthy Redeemer. —BQ

DAILY CONTEMPLATION

Can you think of someone whom God placed in your life to help you through a dark time and remind you of his promises?

DAY 92   Reflection

THE LOOKS OF A BELIEVER

How well do you fit the image of a Christian? Do you look as if you belong in a church, carrying a Bible? Maybe you can't speak God-talk. Maybe your past would embarrass a pastor. Maybe your family embarrasses you.

If you feel like an outsider despite having given your life to Christ, you're not alone. Many Christians feel the way you do, and indeed believers as far back as Ruth, and further, share those feelings. Ruth was the daughter of non-Israelite parents. Barren and recently widowed, she then chose to leave her homeland of Moab to accompany her depressed mother-in-law to another city, where the two would try to forge a new life with some extended relatives. Ruth didn't really fit in.

In fact, the plot thickens. Ruth's family traces all the way back to Lot, Abraham's nephew. As you'll recall, Lot chose the fertile land of the Jordan plain as his home, settling his family near the evil city of Sodom. Later, after God destroyed Sodom, Lot's daughters got him drunk and had sex with him. They gave birth to two sons, Moab (MOH-ab) and Ben-Ammi (ben-AM-ee), whose people later became the Moabites and the Ammonites, nations with a history of warring against Israel. And these Moabites were the people Ruth called her own.

But in marrying into Naomi's family, Ruth switched allegiance to the true God of the Hebrews. She renounced the god of the Moabites and left her home in loyalty to God and the new family he had given her. In many ways Ruth became a loner. She belonged with Naomi yet was very different from her and from the others in Bethlehem as well. She could only hope for their kindness.

Ruth did fit in with God, however. She chose to believe in him, and to God nothing else mattered. Ruth lived out her faith by making difficult choices and following through with them. She had a humble heart, and although she undertook some uncommon methods for survival—gleaning behind workers in the fields, approaching an older man in the middle of the night—she remained faithful to God.

As a Christian, you may not feel you fit the bill as you look at other Christians. But God does not care about prescribed images. The only thing that matters to God is whether you've given your life to him. God cares only about the look of your heart.   —BQ

DAILY CONTEMPLATION

In what ways do you feel different from "mainstream Christians"? Thank God that he has made you the way you are for a reason, to be used by him in a unique way.

DAY 93   1 Samuel 1:1–28

THE BIRTH OF SAMUEL

There was a certain man from Ramathaim, a Zuphite from the hill country of Ephraim, whose name was Elkanah son of Jeroham, the son of Elihu, the son of Tohu, the son of Zuph, an Ephraimite. He had two wives; one was called Hannah and the other Peninnah. Peninnah had children, but Hannah had none.

Year after year this man went up from his town to worship and sacrifice to the LORD Almighty at Shiloh, where Hophni and Phinehas, the two sons of Eli, were priests of the LORD. Whenever the day came for Elkanah to sacrifice, he would give portions of the meat to his wife Peninnah and to all her sons and daughters. But to Hannah he gave a double portion because he loved her, and the LORD had closed her womb. And because the LORD had closed her womb, her rival kept provoking her in order to irritate her. This went on year after year. Whenever Hannah went up to the house of the LORD, her rival provoked her till she wept and would not eat. Elkanah her husband would say to her, "Hannah, why are you weeping? Why don't you eat? Why are you down-hearted? Don't I mean more to you than ten sons?"

Once when they had finished eating and drinking in Shiloh, Hannah stood up. Now Eli the priest was sitting on a chair by the doorpost of the LORD's temple. In bitterness of soul Hannah wept much and prayed to the LORD. And she made a vow, saying, "O LORD Almighty, if you will only look upon your servant's misery and remember me, and not forget your servant but give her a son, then I will give him to the LORD for all the days of his life, and no razor will ever be used on his head."

As she kept on praying to the LORD, Eli observed her mouth. Hannah was praying in her heart, and her lips were moving but her voice was not heard. Eli thought she was drunk and said to her, "How long will you keep on getting drunk? Get rid of your wine."

"Not so, my lord," Hannah replied, "I am a woman who is deeply troubled. I have not been drinking wine or beer; I was pouring out my soul to the LORD. Do not take your servant for a wicked woman; I have been praying here out of my great anguish and grief."

Eli answered, "Go in peace, and may the God of Israel grant you what you have asked of him."

She said, "May your servant find favor in your eyes." Then she went her way and ate something, and her face was no longer downcast.

Early the next morning they arose and worshiped before the LORD and then went back to their home at Ramah. Elkanah lay with Hannah his wife, and the LORD remembered her. So in the course of time Hannah conceived and gave birth to a son. She named him Samuel, saying, "Because I asked the LORD for him."

When the man Elkanah went up with all his family to offer the annual sacrifice to the LORD and to fulfill his vow, Hannah did not go. She said to her husband, "After the boy is weaned, I will take him and present him before the LORD, and he will live there always."

"Do what seems best to you," Elkanah her husband told her. "Stay here until you have weaned him; only may the LORD make good his word." So the woman stayed at home and nursed her son until she had weaned him.

After he was weaned, she took the boy with her, young as he was, along with a three-year-old bull, an ephah of flour and a skin of wine, and brought him to the house of the LORD at Shiloh. When they had slaughtered the bull, they brought the boy to Eli, and she said to him, "As surely as you live, my lord, I am the woman who stood here beside you praying to the LORD. I prayed for this child, and the LORD has granted me what I asked of him. So now I give him to the LORD. For his whole life he will be given over to the LORD." And he worshiped the LORD there.

In a situation similar to that of Rachel and Leah, Hannah and Peninnah (peh-NIN-uh) become rivals for their husband's love, their competition centering around the fertility of their wombs. They live toward the end of the period of the judges, and theirs is a moral and spiritual climate grown progressively wayward and corrupt. Elkanah (el-KAY-nuh), husband to Hannah and Peninnah, lives in bigamy, a practice never sanctioned by God.

In response to Hannah's sincere prayer for a son, whom she promises to give back to the Lord, God raises up Samuel to be used as a leader of the Israelites. Samuel will serve as a judge, prophet, and priest. He will anoint Israel's first king and later will anoint King David.   —BQ

DAILY CONTEMPLATION

Have you ever made a promise to God? Have you kept it?

DAY 94   1 Samuel 2:18–21, 3:1–21

THE LORD CALLS SAMUEL

Samuel was ministering before the LORD—a boy wearing a linen ephod. Each year his mother made him a little robe and took it to him when she went up with her husband to offer the annual sacrifice. Eli would bless Elkanah and his wife, saying, "May the LORD give you children by this woman to take the place of the one she prayed for and gave to the LORD." Then they would go home. And the LORD was gracious to Hannah; she conceived and gave birth to three sons and two daughters. Meanwhile, the boy Samuel grew up in the presence of the LORD. . . .

The boy Samuel ministered before the LORD under Eli. In those days the word of the LORD was rare; there were not many visions.

One night Eli, whose eyes were becoming so weak that he could barely see, was lying down in his usual place. The lamp of God had not yet gone out, and Samuel was lying down in the temple of the LORD, where the ark of God was. Then the LORD called Samuel.

Samuel answered, "Here I am." And he ran to Eli and said, "Here I am; you called me."

But Eli said, "I did not call; go back and lie down." So he went and lay down.

Again the LORD called, "Samuel!" And Samuel got up and went to Eli and said, "Here I am; you called me."

"My son," Eli said, "I did not call; go back and lie down."

Now Samuel did not yet know the LORD: The word of the LORD had not yet been revealed to him.

The LORD called Samuel a third time, and Samuel got up and went to Eli and said, "Here I am; you called me."

Then Eli realized that the LORD was calling the boy. So Eli told Samuel, "Go and lie down, and if he calls you, say, 'Speak, LORD, for your servant is listening.'" So Samuel went and lay down in his place.

The LORD came and stood there, calling as at the other times, "Samuel! Samuel!"

Then Samuel said, "Speak, for your servant is listening."

And the LORD said to Samuel: "See, I am about to do something in Israel that will make the ears of everyone who hears of it tingle. At that time I will carry out against Eli everything I spoke against his family—from beginning to end. For I told him that I would judge his family forever because of the sin he knew about; his sons made themselves contemptible, and he failed to restrain them. Therefore, I swore to the house of Eli, 'The guilt of Eli's house will never be atoned for by sacrifice or offering.'"

Samuel lay down until morning and then opened the doors of the house of the LORD. He was afraid to tell Eli the vision, but Eli called him and said, "Samuel, my son."

Samuel answered, "Here I am."

"What was it he said to you?" Eli asked. "Do not hide it from me. May God deal with you, be it ever so severely, if you hide from me anything he told you." So Samuel told him everything, hiding nothing from him. Then Eli said, "He is the LORD; let him do what is good in his eyes."

The LORD was with Samuel as he grew up, and he let none of his words fall to the ground. And all Israel from Dan to Beersheba recognized that Samuel was attested as a prophet of the LORD. The LORD continued to appear at Shiloh, and there he revealed himself to Samuel through his word.

By the time of the judges, most terms in the Israelites' covenant with God have already been fulfilled. Abraham's descendants, twelve tribes and many thousands strong, have a land of their own. And yet something is clearly lacking: no one could begin to call the crazy quilt of tribal territories a unified "nation." In fact, throughout the judges' era the Israelites have fought each other as often as they have fought their hostile neighbors.

As this book opens, the Philistines, a traditional enemy, are exploiting the Israelites' disunity, pushing ever deeper into their territory. The Philistines have superior weapons—chariots, in particular—and Israel has neither a central administration nor a regular army to mount an effective defense. A crisis of leadership is building, one that threatens the very existence of Israel. The military weakness leads to one of the darkest days of Jewish history, when the Philistines capture the sacred ark of the covenant. Some wonder whether God has abandoned them and thus forsaken the covenant.

"In those days the word of the LORD was rare; there were not many visions," begins this chapter. But it goes on to relate how God steps in directly, as he has done with Abraham and Moses before, calling out a leader for his people. "See, I am about to do something in Israel that will make the ears of everyone who hears of it tingle," God announces. He answers the desperate prayer of Samuel, who will grow into his role as one of Israel's greatest leaders.

Ultimately, Samuel will serve the Israelites in many capacities, as both judge and prophet. A priest by training, he will also lead the nation's worship. When the need arises, he even functions as a military general, spearheading a victorious recapture of disputed territories. Finally, under God's direction, Samuel will anoint Israel's first two kings. By performing these varied roles, Samuel leaves an important legacy: he manages to unite the tribes for the first time in a century. Under his leadership, Israel comes to the very brink of nationhood. God has not forgotten the covenant after all.

—PY

DAILY CONTEMPLATION

Have you ever felt called by God for a certain task? How have you responded?

DAY 95
1 Samuel 8:1–22

ISRAEL ASKS FOR A KING

When Samuel grew old, he appointed his sons as judges for Israel. The name of his firstborn was Joel and the name of his second was Abijah, and they served at Beersheba. But his sons did not walk in his ways. They turned aside after dishonest gain and accepted bribes and perverted justice.

So all the elders of Israel gathered together and came to Samuel at Ramah. They said to him, "You are old, and your sons do not walk in your ways; now appoint a king to lead us, such as all the other nations have."

But when they said, "Give us a king to lead us," this displeased Samuel; so he prayed to the LORD. And the LORD told him: "Listen to all that the people are saying to you; it is not you they have rejected, but they have rejected me as their king. As they have done from the day I brought them up out of Egypt until this day, forsaking me and serving other gods, so they are doing to you. Now listen to them; but warn them solemnly and let them know what the king who will reign over them will do."

Samuel told all the words of the LORD to the people who were asking him for a king. He said, "This is what the king who will reign over you will do: He will take your sons and make them serve with his chariots and horses, and they will run in front of his chariots. Some he will assign to be commanders of thousands and commanders of fifties, and others to plow his ground and reap his harvest, and still others to make weapons of war and equipment for his chariots. He will take your daughters to be perfumers and cooks and bakers. He will take the best of your fields and vineyards and olive groves and give them to his attendants. He will take a tenth of your grain and of your vintage and give it to his officials and attendants. Your menservants and maidservants and the best of your cattle and donkeys he will take for his own use. He will take a tenth of your flocks, and you yourselves will become his slaves. When that day comes, you will cry out for relief from the king you have chosen, and the LORD will not answer you in that day."

But the people refused to listen to Samuel. "No!" they said. "We want a king over us. Then we will be like all the other nations, with a king to lead us and to go out before us and fight our battles."

When Samuel heard all that the people said, he repeated it before the LORD. The LORD answered, "Listen to them and give them a king."

Then Samuel said to the men of Israel, "Everyone go back to his town."

Despite Samuel's military prowess, the Philistine threat never entirely goes away. As Samuel ages, Israel needs continuing vigorous leadership, but Samuel's sons hardly measure up to the task. What can be done? Looking around them, the tribes see that virtually every other country has a king. *Aha, that's the answer,* they conclude and urge Samuel to appoint an Israelite king.

The idea of a king seems popular with everyone except Samuel and God, who sense in the request an underlying rejection of God's own leadership. Samuel warns the elders bluntly against the problems they might be inviting: tyranny, oppression, a military draft, high taxes, maybe even slavery. But the people beg for a king despite his warnings.

Does God oppose the very notion of a king? Probably not. Many years before, Moses predicted the Israelites would someday have a king (see Genesis 17:6; Deuteronomy 17:14–20), and God will eventually use the royal line to produce his own Son Jesus, King of Kings. But the Bible makes one thing clear: God opposes the people's motives, as expressed by the elders: "Then we will be like all the other nations." God does not want them to be like all the other nations. He, no human king, is the true ruler of the Israelites.   —PY

DAILY CONTEMPLATION

What do you feel in need of today? What motivates your sense of need?

DAY 96   1 Samuel 9:1–6, 14–10:8

SAMUEL ANOINTS SAUL

There was a Benjamite, a man of standing, whose name was Kish son of Abiel, the son of Zeror, the son of Becorath, the son of Aphiah of Benjamin. He had a son named Saul, an impressive young man without equal among the Israelites—a head taller than any of the others.

Now the donkeys belonging to Saul's father Kish were lost, and Kish said to his son Saul, "Take one of the servants with you and go and look for the donkeys." So he passed through the hill country of Ephraim and through the area around Shalisha, but they did not find them. They went on into the district of Shaalim, but the donkeys were not there. Then he passed through the territory of Benjamin, but they did not find them.

When they reached the district of Zuph, Saul said to the servant who was with him, "Come, let's go back, or my father will stop thinking about the donkeys and start worrying about us."

But the servant replied, "Look, in this town there is a man of God; he is highly respected, and everything he says comes true. Let's go there now. Perhaps he will tell us what way to take." . . .

They went up to the town, and as they were entering it, there was Samuel, coming toward them on his way up to the high place.

Now the day before Saul came, the LORD had revealed this to Samuel: "About this time tomorrow I will send you a man from the land of Benjamin. Anoint him leader over my people Israel; he will deliver my people from the hand of the Philistines. I have looked upon my people, for their cry has reached me."

When Samuel caught sight of Saul, the LORD said to him, "This is the man I spoke to you about; he will govern my people."

Saul approached Samuel in the gateway and asked, "Would you please tell me where the seer's house is?"

"I am the seer," Samuel replied. "Go up ahead of me to the high place, for today you are to eat with me, and in the morning I will let you go and will tell you all that is in your heart. As for the donkeys you lost three days ago, do not worry about them; they have been found. And to whom is all the desire of Israel turned, if not to you and all your father's family?"

Saul answered, "But am I not a Benjamite, from the smallest tribe of Israel, and is not my clan the least of all the clans of the tribe of Benjamin? Why do you say such a thing to me?"

Then Samuel brought Saul and his servant into the hall and seated them at the head of those who were invited—about thirty in number. Samuel said to the cook, "Bring the piece of meat I gave you, the one I told you to lay aside."

So the cook took up the leg with what was on it and set it in front of Saul. Samuel said, "Here is what has been kept for you. Eat, because it was set aside for you for this occasion, from the time I said, 'I have invited guests.'" And Saul dined with Samuel that day.

After they came down from the high place to the town, Samuel talked with Saul on the roof of his house. They rose about daybreak and Samuel called to Saul on the roof, "Get ready, and I will send you on your way." When Saul got ready, he and Samuel went outside together. As they were going down to the edge of the town, Samuel said to Saul, "Tell the servant to go on ahead of us"— and the servant did so—"but you stay here awhile, so that I may give you a message from God."

Then Samuel took a flask of oil and poured it on Saul's head and kissed him, saying, "Has not the LORD anointed you leader over his inheritance? When you leave me today, you will meet two men near Rachel's tomb, at Zelzah on the border of Benjamin. They will say to you, 'The donkeys you set out to look for have been found. And now your father has stopped thinking about them and is worried about you. He is asking, "What shall I do about my son?"'

"Then you will go on from there until you reach the great tree of Tabor. Three men going up to God at Bethel will meet you there. One will be carrying three young goats, another three loaves of bread, and another a skin of wine. They will greet you and offer you two loaves of bread, which you will accept from them.

"After that you will go to Gibeah of God, where there is a Philistine outpost. As you approach the town, you will meet a procession of prophets coming down from the high place with lyres, tambourines, flutes and harps being played before them, and they will be prophesying. The Spirit of the LORD will come upon you in power, and you will prophesy with them; and you will be changed into a different person. Once these signs are fulfilled, do whatever your hand finds to do, for God is with you.

"Go down ahead of me to Gilgal. I will surely come down to you to sacrifice burnt offerings and fellowship offerings, but you must wait seven days until I come to you and tell you what you are to do."

After the people demand a king, God chooses Saul (SAWL) for anointing. Saul is not God's best for the role of king, but God has agreed to give the people what they want, and Saul measures up, at least outwardly. Initially Saul is humble, claiming to be unworthy of such an honor. Later, however, he will lose his humility, becoming arrogant and vindictive toward any who threaten him.

From Saul we'll learn something about leadership and power. All leaders who take on a position of authority face the danger of becoming prideful and unbending. When they succumb, as does Saul, the leader loses his or her effectiveness as well as the love and support of the people.   —BQ

DAILY CONTEMPLATION

Where are you currently serving as a leader? Have you maintained a humble spirit?

DAY 97   Reflection

PASSIONATE PRAYER

Maybe you've heard the tongue-in-cheek admonition "Be careful what you pray for—you might get it."

This warning applies to the story of the Israelites' request for a king. The years of leadership by judges had plunged the nation into a period of immorality, and the people were tired of being manipulated by men who had only their own interests at heart. So they prayed for a king just like all the nations around them had. They got what they asked for—a king like all the other nations had. Soon Saul began following his own ways rather than God's.

How can we avoid the Israelites' blunder in offering our own prayers? We need to take caution in how we pray. Jesus gave us the essentials of praying in the Lord's Prayer, and they have nothing to do with speaking eloquently or religiously; they concern the attitude behind the words: "Our Father in heaven, hallowed be your name, your kingdom come, your will be done on earth as it is in heaven. . . ." (Matthew 6:9–10).

"Hallowing" God's name means that we respect him, revere him. Praying for his kingdom to come puts our heart next to God's heart, expressing that we want his big-picture plans to be fulfilled. Asking for his will to be done on earth as in heaven tells God we know that what he wants is more important and ultimately better for us than what we want. With these words, we're asking God to pray for us a better prayer than we know how to pray, and then to answer that prayer. We are opening our hands filled with needs and burning desires and placing these hands in God's.

If the people of Israel, with their need for a king, had approached God like this, God might have responded by saying, "Wait. I'll provide for your needs now in a different way. If you'll wait a little longer for a king, I'll give you the best. Right now, a king will only complicate things."

In this way God has answered many a prayer for a relationship or marriage partner, a job, a home, a child, and scores of other requests. Like the Israelites, many believers anticipate this response from God and shut their ears, insisting instead on their own way. God gives in and grants the request, allowing also the difficulties that may accompany this choice. Other believers accept God's answer and wait, only to find that their desire has changed or that God's timing and choice is abundantly better than their own would have been.

Be careful what you pray for—you might get it. Make your prayer God's prayer by offering to him your requests and then, with open hands, letting his prayer become your own.   —BQ

DAILY CONTEMPLATION

What is the desire that burns within you today? Have you been praying about this desire? Tell God that you want what is truly good for you, knowing that he knows so much better what you need.

DAY 98   1 Samuel 15:1–29

THE LORD REJECTS SAUL AS KING

Samuel said to Saul, "I am the one the LORD sent to anoint you king over his people Israel; so listen now to the message from the LORD. This is what the LORD Almighty says: 'I will punish the Amalekites for what they did to Israel when they waylaid them as they came up from Egypt. Now go, attack the Amalekites and totally destroy everything that belongs to them. Do not spare them; put to death men and women, children and infants, cattle and sheep, camels and donkeys.'"

So Saul summoned the men and mustered them at Telaim—two hundred thousand foot soldiers and ten thousand men from Judah. Saul went to the city of Amalek and set an ambush in the ravine. Then he said to the Kenites, "Go away, leave the Amalekites so that I do not destroy you along with them; for you showed kindness to all the Israelites when they came up out of Egypt." So the Kenites moved away from the Amalekites.

Then Saul attacked the Amalekites all the way from Havilah to Shur, to the east of Egypt. He took Agag king of the Amalekites alive, and all his people he totally destroyed with the sword. But Saul and the army spared Agag and the best of the sheep and cattle, the fat calves and lambs—everything that was good. These they were unwilling to destroy completely, but everything that was despised and weak they totally destroyed.

Then the word of the LORD came to Samuel: "I am grieved that I have made Saul king, because he has turned away from me and has not carried out my instructions." Samuel was troubled, and he cried out to the LORD all that night.

Early in the morning Samuel got up and went to meet Saul, but he was told, "Saul has gone to Carmel. There he has set up a monument in his own honor and has turned and gone on down to Gilgal."

When Samuel reached him, Saul said, "The LORD bless you! I have carried out the LORD's instructions."

But Samuel said, "What then is this bleating of sheep in my ears? What is this lowing of cattle that I hear?"

Saul answered, "The soldiers brought them from the Amalekites; they spared the best of the sheep and cattle to sacrifice to the LORD your God, but we totally destroyed the rest."

"Stop!" Samuel said to Saul. "Let me tell you what the LORD said to me last night."

"Tell me," Saul replied.

Samuel said, "Although you were once small in your own eyes, did you not become the head of the tribes of Israel? The LORD anointed you king over Israel. And he sent you on a mission, saying, 'Go and completely destroy those wicked people, the Amalekites; make war on them until you have wiped them out.' Why did you not obey the LORD? Why did you pounce on the plunder and do evil in the eyes of the LORD?"

"But I did obey the LORD," Saul said. "I went on the mission the LORD assigned me. I completely destroyed the Amalekites and brought back Agag their king. The soldiers took sheep and cattle from the plunder, the best of what was devoted to God, in order to sacrifice them to the LORD your God at Gilgal."

But Samuel replied:

"Does the LORD delight in burnt offerings and sacrifices
    as much as in obeying the voice of the LORD?

To obey is better than sacrifice,
> and to heed is better than the fat of rams.

For rebellion is like the sin of divination,
> and arrogance like the evil of idolatry.

Because you have rejected the word of the LORD,
> he has rejected you as king."

Then Saul said to Samuel, "I have sinned. I violated the LORD's command and your instructions. I was afraid of the people and so I gave in to them. Now I beg you, forgive my sin and come back with me, so that I may worship the LORD."

But Samuel said to him, "I will not go back with you. You have rejected the word of the LORD, and the LORD has rejected you as king over Israel!"

As Samuel turned to leave, Saul caught hold of the hem of his robe, and it tore. Samuel said to him, "The LORD has torn the kingdom of Israel from you today and has given it to one of your neighbors—to one better than you. He who is the Glory of Israel does not lie or change his mind; for he is not a man, that he should change his mind."

This story reveals the first signs of Saul's disobedience to God. Saul wages war against the Amalekites, but he takes the liberty to bend God's instructions and allow for a little extra glory for himself and a few prime animals for his herds. He takes the Amalekite king alive as a visual aid for his people, broadcasting Saul's own power. When Samuel calls him on these acts, Saul feigns innocence and claims that the animals are intended for sacrifice to the Lord. In this sequence of disobedience, Saul permanently loses God's approval. He will serve for fifteen more years as king, but in God's eyes he has already lost his position.

Although Saul entered into kingship with a humble spirit, in time he let the position go to his head, allowing pride and disobedience to replace humility. Later, fear will cause him to hold on to his place of power so tightly that he becomes irrational and destructive. Saul models the corrupting power that leadership can have over us when self-centered motives take hold. Like Saul, we all get greedy at times, taking for ourselves more than we should or maneuvering to give our good name a boost. Through God's grace we can be forgiven of our greed—but as this passage indicates, in God's eyes greed and stubbornness are no small offense. —BQ

DAILY CONTEMPLATION

What is easier for you, obedience or sacrifice?

SAMUEL ANOINTS DAVID

The LORD said to Samuel, "How long will you mourn for Saul, since I have rejected him as king over Israel? Fill your horn with oil and be on your way; I am sending you to Jesse of Bethlehem. I have chosen one of his sons to be king."

But Samuel said, "How can I go? Saul will hear about it and kill me."

The LORD said, "Take a heifer with you and say, 'I have come to sacrifice to the LORD.' Invite Jesse to the sacrifice, and I will show you what to do. You are to anoint for me the one I indicate."

Samuel did what the LORD said. When he arrived at Bethlehem, the elders of the town trembled when they met him. They asked, "Do you come in peace?"

Samuel replied, "Yes, in peace; I have come to sacrifice to the LORD. Consecrate yourselves and come to the sacrifice with me." Then he consecrated Jesse and his sons and invited them to the sacrifice.

When they arrived, Samuel saw Eliab and thought, "Surely the LORD's anointed stands here before the LORD."

But the LORD said to Samuel, "Do not consider his appearance or his height, for I have rejected him. The LORD does not look at the things man looks at. Man looks at the outward appearance, but the LORD looks at the heart."

Then Jesse called Abinadab and had him pass in front of Samuel. But Samuel said, "The LORD has not chosen this one either." Jesse then had Shammah pass by, but Samuel said, "Nor has the LORD chosen this one." Jesse had seven of his sons pass before Samuel, but Samuel said to him, "The LORD has not chosen these." So he asked Jesse, "Are these all the sons you have?"

"There is still the youngest," Jesse answered, "but he is tending the sheep."

Samuel said, "Send for him; we will not sit down until he arrives."

So he sent and had him brought in. He was ruddy, with a fine appearance and handsome features.

Then the LORD said, "Rise and anoint him; he is the one."

So Samuel took the horn of oil and anointed him in the presence of his brothers, and from that day on the Spirit of the LORD came upon David in power. Samuel then went to Ramah.

Now the Spirit of the LORD had departed from Saul, and an evil spirit from the LORD tormented him.

Saul's attendants said to him, "See, an evil spirit from God is tormenting you. Let our lord command his servants here to search for someone who can play the harp. He will play when the evil spirit from God comes upon you, and you will feel better."

So Saul said to his attendants, "Find someone who plays well and bring him to me."

One of the servants answered, "I have seen a son of Jesse of Bethlehem who knows how to play the harp. He is a brave man and a warrior. He speaks well and is a fine-looking man. And the LORD is with him."

Then Saul sent messengers to Jesse and said, "Send me your son David, who is with the sheep." So Jesse took a donkey loaded with bread, a skin of wine and a young goat and sent them with his son David to Saul.

David came to Saul and entered his service. Saul liked him very much, and David became one of his armor-bearers. Then Saul sent word to Jesse, saying, "Allow David to remain in my service, for I am pleased with him."

Whenever the spirit from God came upon Saul, David would take his harp and play. Then relief would come to Saul; he would feel better, and the evil spirit would leave him.

Israel's first king began his reign with enormous promise. Saul was a perfect physical specimen: handsome, strong, intelligent, a head taller than anyone else. Leadership qualities oozed out of him. But he failed, for one simple reason: he disobeyed God, refusing to acknowledge him as the true ruler. And without hesitation God ended that royal dynasty and looked elsewhere for a replacement.

The replacement king is utterly unlike the first king. No one has imagined royalty potential in the shepherd boy David—not even his own father. But, as God says, "Man looks at the outward appearance, but the LORD looks at the heart." David has the kind of heart God can work with. Despite his humble beginnings, despite his many flaws, he will go on to become the greatest king in the history of the Israelites.
—PY

DAILY CONTEMPLATION

Would the leadership qualities God values be an asset or a handicap to someone running for president of the United States?

DAY 100 Psalm 23:1–6

A SHEPHERD'S SONG

The LORD is my shepherd, I shall not be in want.
    He makes me lie down in green pastures,
he leads me beside quiet waters,
    he restores my soul.

He guides me in paths of righteousness
  for his name's sake.
Even though I walk
  through the valley of the shadow of death,
I will fear no evil,
  for you are with me;
your rod and your staff,
  they comfort me.

You prepare a table before me
  in the presence of my enemies.
You anoint my head with oil;
  my cup overflows.
Surely goodness and love will follow me
  all the days of my life,
and I will dwell in the house of the LORD
  forever.

David is a well-rounded human being. Although he will have enough courage to take on the likes of Goliath, a nine-foot-tall Philistine, he certainly does not fit any "macho" warrior mold. In fact, David first gains King Saul's notice for his musical, not military, skills. Initially he is brought to the army camp because his harp playing soothes the frayed nerves of the troubled king.

Almost half of the 150 psalms in the Bible are credited to David, and it seems only appropriate to read a sampling in conjunction with his life history. This famous psalm reveals at once the secret of David's poetic abilities and the secret of his faith.

In his poetry David tends to start with the scene around him—rocks, caves, stars, battlefields, sheep—and work out from that physical world to express profound thoughts about God. Psalm 23, for instance, stems from his experience as a shepherd boy. Using metaphors that emerge from the tasks of sheep herding, David composes a few beautiful stanzas of worship poetry.

The psalm captures the essence of David's trust in God. Sheep have blind, absolute trust in a leader: if a lead sheep plunges off a cliff, an entire flock will follow. That kind of unshakable trust is what David seeks in his walk with God.

Yet no one can dismiss David as having a rosy, romantic view of life. The preceding Psalm 22 shows just how tough, gritty, and ruthlessly honest he could be. Somehow David manages to make God the center of his life, regardless of circumstances—whether he feels specially comforted by God or cruelly abandoned. "Some trust in chariots and some in horses, but we trust in the name of the LORD our God," writes this soldier who spends much of his time running from chariots and horses (Psalm 20:7).

The best way to read the Psalms is to make these ancient prayers your own by speaking them directly to God. Over the years, millions of people have found comfort and inspiration by "praying" the eloquent words of Psalm 23, written by the shepherd who would be king.   —PY

DAY 101   1 Samuel 17:1, 3–7, 16–27, 32–54

DAVID AND GOLIATH

Now the Philistines gathered their forces for war and assembled at Socoh in Judah. They pitched camp at Ephes Dammim, between Socoh and Azekah.... The Philistines occupied one hill and the Israelites another, with the valley between them.

A champion named Goliath, who was from Gath, came out of the Philistine camp. He was over nine feet tall. He had a bronze helmet on his head and wore a coat of scale armor of bronze weighing five thousand shekels; on his legs he wore bronze greaves, and a bronze javelin was slung on his back. His spear shaft was like a weaver's rod, and its iron point weighed six hundred shekels. His shield bearer went ahead of him....

For forty days the Philistine came forward every morning and evening and took his stand.

Now Jesse said to his son David, "Take this ephah of roasted grain and these ten loaves of bread for your brothers and hurry to their camp. Take along these ten cheeses to the commander of their unit. See how your brothers are and bring back some assurance from them. They are with Saul and all the men of Israel in the Valley of Elah, fighting against the Philistines."

Early in the morning David left the flock with a shepherd, loaded up and set out, as Jesse had directed. He reached the camp as the army was going out to its battle positions, shouting the war cry. Israel and the Philistines were drawing up their lines facing each other. David left his things with the keeper of supplies, ran to the battle lines and greeted his brothers. As he was talking with them, Goliath, the Philistine champion from Gath, stepped out from his lines and shouted his usual defiance, and David heard it. When the Israelites saw the man, they all ran from him in great fear.

Now the Israelites had been saying, "Do you see how this man keeps coming out? He comes out to defy Israel. The king will give great wealth to the man who kills him. He will also give him his daughter in marriage and will exempt his father's family from taxes in Israel."

David asked the men standing near him, "What will be done for the man who kills this Philistine and removes this disgrace from Israel? Who is this uncircumcised Philistine that he should defy the armies of the living God?"

They repeated to him what they had been saying and told him, "This is what will be done for the man who kills him." ...

David said to Saul, "Let no one lose heart on account of this Philistine; your servant will go and fight him."

Saul replied, "You are not able to go out against this Philistine and fight him; you are only a boy, and he has been a fighting man from his youth."

But David said to Saul, "Your servant has been keeping his father's sheep. When a lion or a bear came and carried off a sheep from the flock, I went after it, struck it and rescued the sheep from its mouth. When it turned on me, I seized it by its hair, struck it and killed it. Your servant has killed both the lion and the bear; this uncircumcised Philistine will be like one of them, because he has defied the armies of the living God. The Lord who delivered me from the paw of the lion and the paw of the bear will deliver me from the hand of this Philistine."

Saul said to David, "Go, and the Lord be with you."

Then Saul dressed David in his own tunic. He put a coat of armor on him and a bronze helmet on his head. David fastened on his sword over the tunic and tried walking around, because he was not used to them.

"I cannot go in these," he said to Saul, "because I am not used to them." So he took them off. Then he took his staff in his hand, chose five smooth stones from the stream, put them in the pouch of his shepherd's bag and, with his sling in his hand, approached the Philistine.

Meanwhile, the Philistine, with his shield bearer in front of him, kept coming closer to David. He looked David over and saw that he was only a boy, ruddy and handsome, and he despised him. He said to David, "Am I a dog, that you come at me with sticks?" And the Philistine cursed David by his gods. "Come here," he said, "and I'll give your flesh to the birds of the air and the beasts of the field!"

David said to the Philistine, "You come against me with sword and spear and javelin, but I come against you in the name of the Lord Almighty, the God of the armies of Israel, whom you have defied. This day the Lord will hand you over to me, and I'll strike you down and cut off your head. Today I will give the carcasses of the Philistine army to the birds of the air and the beasts of the earth, and the whole world will know that there is a God in Israel. All those gathered here will know that it is not by sword or spear that the Lord saves; for the battle is the Lord's, and he will give all of you into our hands."

As the Philistine moved closer to attack him, David ran quickly toward the battle line to meet him. Reaching into his bag and taking out a stone, he slung it and struck the Philistine on the forehead. The stone sank into his forehead, and he fell facedown on the ground.

So David triumphed over the Philistine with a sling and a stone; without a sword in his hand he struck down the Philistine and killed him.

David ran and stood over him. He took hold of the Philistine's sword and drew it from the scabbard. After he killed him, he cut off his head with the sword.

When the Philistines saw that their hero was dead, they turned and ran. Then the men of Israel and Judah surged forward with a shout and pursued the Philistines to the entrance of Gath and to the gates of Ekron. Their dead were strewn along the Shaaraim road to Gath and Ekron. When the Israelites returned from chasing the Philistines, they plundered their camp. David took the Philistine's head and brought it to Jerusalem, and he put the Philistine's weapons in his own tent.

King David dominates much of the Old Testament and much of Jewish history. This exciting story from his boyhood, told in colorful, eyewitness detail, is one of the most famous of all Bible stories, a beacon of hope for all outsized underdogs.

David will spend the better part of a decade trying to escape the wrath of King Saul, and much of Saul's enmity probably traces back to this one scene. Saul, leader of a large army, sits in his tent, terrorized by the taunts of the colossal Goliath. Meanwhile David, a mere boy too small for a suit of armor, strides out bravely to meet Goliath's challenge. Little wonder Saul comes to resent and fear the remarkable youth.

The scenario related here is not as far-fetched as it may seem. "Single combat" or "representative" warfare was an acceptable style of settling differences in ancient times. As Tom Wolfe explains it in *The Right Stuff*, "Originally it had a magical meaning. . . . They believed that the gods determined the outcome of single combat; therefore, it was useless for the losing side to engage in a full-scale battle."[5]

During many lonely hours as a shepherd boy, David honed his slingshot skills to a state of perfection. But he takes no personal credit for the victory. "You come against me with sword and spear and javelin," he shouts to Goliath, "but I come against you in the name of the LORD Almighty, the God of the armies of Israel, whom you have defied." In the tradition of Joshua and Gideon, he places complete trust in God alone—a lesson that King Saul never learned.

Once Goliath falls, the rest of the Philistines quickly succumb. Soon the Israelites are dancing in the streets and singing this song: "Saul has slain his thousands, and David his tens of thousands." The nation is beginning to recognize in David the qualities that have marked him for potential kingship. Saul, however, is not about to relinquish his throne without a fight.   —PY

DAILY CONTEMPLATION

Are you facing any great fear or danger about which God is telling you that you can rely utterly on him?

OUTDOOR LESSONS

The heavens declare the glory of God;
    the skies proclaim the work of his hands.
Day after day they pour forth speech;
    night after night they display knowledge.
There is no speech or language
    where their voice is not heard.
Their voice goes out into all the earth,
    their words to the ends of the world.

In the heavens he has pitched a tent for the sun,
    which is like a bridegroom coming forth from his pavilion,
    like a champion rejoicing to run his course.
It rises at one end of the heavens
    and makes its circuit to the other;
    nothing is hidden from its heat.

The law of the LORD is perfect,
    reviving the soul.
The statutes of the LORD are trustworthy,
    making wise the simple.
The precepts of the LORD are right,
    giving joy to the heart.
The commands of the LORD are radiant,
    giving light to the eyes.
The fear of the LORD is pure,
    enduring forever.
The ordinances of the LORD are sure
    and altogether righteous.
They are more precious than gold,
    than much pure gold;
they are sweeter than honey,
    than honey from the comb.
By them is your servant warned;
    in keeping them there is great reward.

Who can discern his errors?
    Forgive my hidden faults.
Keep your servant also from willful sins;
    may they not rule over me.
Then will I be blameless,
    innocent of great transgression.

> May the words of my mouth and the meditation of my heart
>> be pleasing in your sight,
>> O LORD, my Rock and my Redeemer.

David lived much of his life outdoors. It's not surprising, then, that a great love, even reverence, for the natural world shows through in many of his psalms.

The Psalms present a world that fits together as a whole. At night wild animals hunt; at daybreak humans go out to work. As rain falls, nourishing crops for people and grass for cattle, it also waters the forest where wild animals live. Yet the psalmist doesn't just marvel over the complexity and beauty of nature; behind everything he sees the hand of God. The world works because an intimate, personal God watches over it. Every breath of life depends on his will. So do the weather, the winds and clouds, the very stability of the earth.

Psalm 19 combines two of David's favorite themes: God's care for the earth and his care for the chosen people of Israel. He begins with the natural world, marveling at the mantle of stars that covers the whole earth. Yet David and the Israelites, unlike their neighbors, do not worship the sun and stars as gods but rather see them as the workmanship of a great God who oversees all creation.

In the middle of the psalm, the author turns his attention from nature to the "law of the LORD." To reflect that change, the poem in Hebrew uses a different, more personal name for God. The first six verses refer to God with a general name that anyone, of any religion, might use, much like our English word **God.** But from verse seven onward, God is called **Yahweh,** the personal name revealed to Moses from the burning bush. The heavens declare the glory of God, but God's law reveals even more—his personal voice to his chosen people.

David writes some of the Psalms as a fugitive, while fleeing the wrath of King Saul. Even though God has promised him the throne of Israel, David will have to run for his life. He will have many nights of fear and many doubts, but he believes that the God who has demonstrated his faithfulness to the natural world, and to the nation David will one day govern, will show that same faithfulness in fulfilling promises to David himself.   —PY

DAILY CONTEMPLATION

Does nature reveal the glory of God to you? Does God's law—his guidelines for living—reveal to you his trustworthiness, wisdom, and rightness?

DAY 103   Reflection

FIGHTING GIANTS

Who *are the giants in my life?* I ponder as I read in fascination the story of David and Goliath. This is a delicious tale. A brave boy approaches a gargantuan ogre and without a shred of fear announces God's victory, which, sure enough, ensues. I love David's cocksure attitude, his absolute belief that God will conquer.

Not just my love of a good story captivates me as I read; what thrills me more is this vision of conquered giants.

In David's day the giant was one man who faced one boy as all the others looked on. Today countless giants haunt the lives of many around us, taking on the form of addictions, feelings of personal inadequacy or unworthiness, fear of failure, brokenness from failed relationships, guilt over past mistakes, feelings of isolation, fear of disease or death. The list goes on. In places deep inside, giants lurk, and often we are too frightened or ashamed to bring our battles into the open. Victory seems altogether too unlikely.

When I sense these fears, I return to David's story. Unlike the Disney animations that set good against evil within romping, imaginative plots, this story took place in the life of a historical king of Israel. God really did overcome. His good conquered a giant bent on evil and destruction. If God did this for David, certainly he can do it for you and me.

As I consider my inner giants, I recall Ephesians 6:12: "Our struggle is not against flesh and blood, but against the rulers, against the authorities, against the powers of this dark world and against the spiritual forces of evil in the heavenly realms." God knows well the giants that stalk our lives, forces that aim to rob us of life and vitality, thus defeating God's presence in us. But as with David, these forces don't stand a chance against God. David used a stone. Paul tells us in Ephesians to use truth, righteousness, knowledge of the Bible, faith, salvation, and prayer in our fight. We can be as confident as David was that God will conquer. It's a delicious prospect. —BQ

DAILY CONTEMPLATION

What kind of armor have you been using as you battle the giant that plagues you? Do you trust God to make the story of David your story? Ask him to increase your confidence in what he will do and show you how to fight the battle.

DAY 104   1 Samuel 18:1–9; 19:1–18

SAUL TRIES TO KILL DAVID

After David had finished talking with Saul, Jonathan became one in spirit with David, and he loved him as himself. From that day Saul kept David with him and did not let him return to his father's house. And Jonathan made a covenant with David because he loved him as himself. Jonathan took off the robe he was wearing and gave it to David, along with his tunic, and even his sword, his bow and his belt.

Whatever Saul sent him to do, David did it so successfully that Saul gave him a high rank in the army. This pleased all the people, and Saul's officers as well.

When the men were returning home after David had killed the Philistine, the women came out from all the towns of Israel to meet King Saul with singing and dancing, with joyful songs and with tambourines and lutes. As they danced, they sang:

"Saul has slain his thousands,
    and David his tens of thousands."

Saul was very angry; this refrain galled him. "They have credited David with tens of thousands," he thought, "but me with only thousands. What more can he get but the kingdom?" And from that time on Saul kept a jealous eye on David. . . .

Saul told his son Jonathan and all the attendants to kill David. But Jonathan was very fond of David and warned him, "My father Saul is looking for a chance to kill you. Be on your guard tomorrow morning; go into hiding and stay there. I will go out and stand with my father in the field where you are. I'll speak to him about you and will tell you what I find out."

Jonathan spoke well of David to Saul his father and said to him, "Let not the king do wrong to his servant David; he has not wronged you, and what he has done has benefited you greatly. He took his life in his hands when he killed the Philistine. The LORD won a great victory for all Israel, and you saw it and were glad. Why then would you do wrong to an innocent man like David by killing him for no reason?"

Saul listened to Jonathan and took this oath: "As surely as the LORD lives, David will not be put to death."

So Jonathan called David and told him the whole conversation. He brought him to Saul, and David was with Saul as before.

Once more war broke out, and David went out and fought the Philistines. He struck them with such force that they fled before him.

But an evil spirit from the LORD came upon Saul as he was sitting in his house with his spear in his hand. While David was playing the harp, Saul tried to pin him to the wall with his spear, but David eluded him as Saul drove the spear into the wall. That night David made good his escape.

Saul sent men to David's house to watch it and to kill him in the morning. But Michal, David's wife, warned him, "If you don't run for your life tonight, tomorrow you'll be killed." So Michal let David down through a window, and he fled and escaped. Then Michal took an idol and laid it on the bed, covering it with a garment and putting some goats' hair at the head.

When Saul sent the men to capture David, Michal said, "He is ill."

Then Saul sent the men back to see David and told them, "Bring him up to me in his bed so that I may kill him." But when the men entered, there was the idol in the bed, and at the head was some goats' hair.

Saul said to Michal, "Why did you deceive me like this and send my enemy away so that he escaped?"

Michal told him, "He said to me, 'Let me get away. Why should I kill you?'"

When David had fled and made his escape, he went to Samuel at Ramah and told him all that Saul had done to him. Then he and Samuel went to Naioth and stayed there.

Saul's jealousy toward David emerges in these chapters. Though God has removed his presence from Saul's life and rulership, Saul still clings to the throne. The people, however, are giving David more acclaim than Saul. Even Jonathan and Michal (MI-kuhl), Saul's children, love David. Although no one is trying to dislodge Saul, he senses his position as king slowly slipping from his grasp. Jealousy and fear overwhelm him.

After several failed attempts by Saul's men to kill David, Saul sets out to do it himself. In an ironic, almost comic scene, he is overcome by the Spirit of God and falls into an ecstatic, trancelike state that immobilizes him (19:19–24). It should be obvious that no harm Saul intends David will succeed, and little David does will fail ultimately to succeed. God continues to fulfill his purposes for the man he has chosen to found the messianic dynasty of kings. —BQ

DAILY CONTEMPLATION

Can you remember a time when you felt overpowering jealousy toward someone?

DAY 105   1 Samuel 20:4–42

DAVID AND JONATHAN

Jonathan said to David, "Whatever you want me to do, I'll do for you."

So David said, "Look, tomorrow is the New Moon festival, and I am supposed to dine with the king; but let me go and hide in the field until the evening of the day after tomorrow. If your father misses me at all, tell him, 'David earnestly asked my permission to hurry to Bethlehem, his hometown, because an annual sacrifice is being made there for his whole clan.' If he says, 'Very well,' then your servant is safe. But if he loses his temper, you can be sure that he is determined to harm me. As for you, show kindness to your servant, for you have brought him into a covenant with you before the LORD. If I am guilty, then kill me yourself! Why hand me over to your father?"

"Never!" Jonathan said. "If I had the least inkling that my father was determined to harm you, wouldn't I tell you?"

David asked, "Who will tell me if your father answers you harshly?"

"Come," Jonathan said, "let's go out into the field." So they went there together.

Then Jonathan said to David: "By the LORD, the God of Israel, I will surely sound out my father by this time the day after tomorrow! If he is favorably disposed toward you, will I not send you word and let you know? But if my father is inclined to harm you, may the LORD deal with me, be it ever so severely, if I do not let you know and send you away safely. May the LORD be with you as he has been with my father. But show me unfailing kindness like that of the LORD as long as I live, so that I may not be killed, and do not ever cut off your kindness from my family—not even when the LORD has cut off every one of David's enemies from the face of the earth."

So Jonathan made a covenant with the house of David, saying, "May the LORD call David's enemies to account." And Jonathan had David reaffirm his oath out of love for him, because he loved him as he loved himself.

Then Jonathan said to David: "Tomorrow is the New Moon festival. You will be missed, because your seat will be empty. The day after tomorrow, toward evening, go to the place where you hid when this trouble began, and wait by the stone Ezel. I will shoot three arrows to the side of it, as though I were shooting at a target. Then I will send a boy and say, 'Go, find the arrows.' If I say to him, 'Look, the arrows are on this side of you; bring them here,' then come, because, as surely as the LORD lives, you are safe; there is no danger. But if I say to the boy, 'Look, the arrows are beyond you,' then you must go, because the LORD has sent you away. And about the matter you and I discussed—remember, the LORD is witness between you and me forever."

So David hid in the field, and when the New Moon festival came, the king sat down to eat. He sat in his customary place by the wall, opposite Jonathan, and Abner sat next to Saul, but David's place was empty. Saul said nothing that day, for he thought, "Something must have happened to David to make him ceremonially unclean—surely he is unclean." But the next day, the second day of the month, David's place was empty again. Then Saul said to his son Jonathan, "Why hasn't the son of Jesse come to the meal, either yesterday or today?"

Jonathan answered, "David earnestly asked me for permission to go to Bethlehem. He said, 'Let me go, because our family is observing a sacrifice in the town and my brother has ordered me to be there. If I have found favor in your eyes, let me get away to see my brothers.' That is why he has not come to the king's table."

Saul's anger flared up at Jonathan and he said to him, "You son of a perverse and rebellious woman! Don't I know that you have sided with the son of Jesse to your own shame and to the shame of the mother who bore you? As long as the son of Jesse lives on this earth, neither you nor your kingdom will be established. Now send and bring him to me, for he must die!"

"Why should he be put to death? What has he done?" Jonathan asked his father. But Saul hurled his spear at him to kill him. Then Jonathan knew that his father intended to kill David.

Jonathan got up from the table in fierce anger; on that second day of the month he did not eat, because he was grieved at his father's shameful treatment of David.

In the morning Jonathan went out to the field for his meeting with David. He had a small boy with him, and he said to the boy, "Run and find the arrows

I shoot." As the boy ran, he shot an arrow beyond him. When the boy came to the place where Jonathan's arrow had fallen, Jonathan called out after him, "Isn't the arrow beyond you?" Then he shouted, "Hurry! Go quickly! Don't stop!" The boy picked up the arrow and returned to his master. (The boy knew nothing of all this; only Jonathan and David knew.) Then Jonathan gave his weapons to the boy and said, "Go, carry them back to town."

After the boy had gone, David got up from the south side of the stone and bowed down before Jonathan three times, with his face to the ground. Then they kissed each other and wept together—but David wept the most.

Jonathan said to David, "Go in peace, for we have sworn friendship with each other in the name of the LORD, saying, 'The LORD is witness between you and me, and between your descendants and my descendants forever.'" Then David left, and Jonathan went back to the town.

You can sense the force of David's personality by observing the effect he has on people around him. This chapter tells of an undying friendship from his early days, before the radical break with King Saul. The king's son Jonathan values friendship with David so much that he forfeits his chance at succession to the throne.

Saul reveals his true, murderous intent to Jonathan in a dramatic scene at the dinner table. Jonathan warns David, and thus begins the terrible struggle between the competing kings. Saul, the king rejected by God, lives on in luxury while David, secretly anointed as his replacement, lives in the wilderness, scrabbling to survive. Saul has a professional army; David a small band made up of family members and an assortment of outlaws.

The events of the next few years will play out the inner character of the two men. Saul knows God's will about the rightful king of Israel but will spend his life resisting it. In contrast, David will show amazing patience, waiting for the prophecy to come true. Twice when Saul accidentally falls into his hands, David refuses to kill him.

In the remainder of 1 Samuel, a long, Shakespearean-style drama unfolds. King Saul, an ancient Macbeth, has lost his grip and is clearly deteriorating. His son has sided with David; his daughter, married to David, has shifted her loyalties as well. Saul, insane with rage, turns up the heat. Can David hold on long enough to outlast him?

At times, David despairs. "One of these days I will be destroyed by the hand of Saul," he thinks (27:1). His position is desperate. David has one precious asset only: God's promise that he will be king. Although his faith in that promise is tested to the extreme, David learns to wait for God's timing. In the end, like the hero of a Shakespearean tragedy, Saul takes his own life.

Meanwhile, David inherits the throne of Israel.   —PY

DAILY CONTEMPLATION

Do you have a close same-sex friendship like David and Jonathan had?

UPS AND DOWNS

The LORD is my light and my salvation—
    whom shall I fear?
The LORD is the stronghold of my life—
    of whom shall I be afraid?
When evil men advance against me
    to devour my flesh,
when my enemies and my foes attack me,
    they will stumble and fall.
Though an army besiege me,
    my heart will not fear;
though war break out against me,
    even then will I be confident.

One thing I ask of the LORD,
    this is what I seek:
that I may dwell in the house of the LORD
    all the days of my life,
to gaze upon the beauty of the LORD
    and to seek him in his temple.
For in the day of trouble
    he will keep me safe in his dwelling;
he will hide me in the shelter of his tabernacle
    and set me high upon a rock.
Then my head will be exalted
    above the enemies who surround me;
at his tabernacle will I sacrifice with shouts of joy;
    I will sing and make music to the LORD.

Hear my voice when I call, O LORD;
    be merciful to me and answer me.
My heart says of you, "Seek his face!"
    Your face, LORD, I will seek.
Do not hide your face from me,
    do not turn your servant away in anger;
    you have been my helper.
Do not reject me or forsake me,
    O God my Savior.
Though my father and mother forsake me,
    the LORD will receive me.
Teach me your way, O LORD;
    lead me in a straight path

because of my oppressors.
Do not turn me over to the desire of my foes,
for false witnesses rise up against me,
breathing out violence.

I am still confident of this:
I will see the goodness of the LORD
in the land of the living.
Wait for the LORD;
be strong and take heart
and wait for the LORD.

The Psalms open a window into the inner life of King David. That window discloses some surprises, however. David is surely no saint, and seldom does he show the peace and serenity normally associated with "spiritual" people. In fact, he often cries out against God, blaming him when things go wrong and begging for relief.

The Psalms are not pious devotionals. They are filled with accounts of enemies who scheme and gossip and plot violence. For the psalmists, faith in God involves a constant struggle against powerful forces that often seem more real than God. The writers frequently ask, "Where are you, God? Why don't you help me?" They often feel abandoned, misused, betrayed.

As an example, consider Psalm 27, which shifts in mood with every stanza. The first stanza opens with a bold declaration of confidence in God from an author who seems downright fearless. The second stanza hints at the author's true condition: tired of running, he yearns for the day when he can rest safely in God's dwelling and rise above all his enemies. By the third stanza, all confidence has melted and the psalmist is pleading for help. The psalm ends in a calmer tone, with a word of practical advice David often had opportunity to put into practice: "Wait for the LORD."

Yet out of such trials a strong, toughened faith in God emerges. In the years when David is an outlaw from King Saul, his hideouts include a "rock" in the desert and a "stronghold." As an experienced fighter, David knows the value of such defenses. But when he writes about these days—as in this psalm—he calls God his rock and his fortress. He recognizes readily that God is the true source of his protection.

Danger will not fade away even after David becomes king. He will face unceasing hostility from enemies, as well as numerous internal rebellions and coup attempts. But David has learned a pattern of helpless dependence in the wilderness that he will practice throughout his life. —PY

DAILY CONTEMPLATION

Is your emotional life fairly even or full of peaks and valleys? What about your spiritual life?

DAVID SPARES SAUL'S LIFE

After Saul returned from pursuing the Philistines, he was told, "David is in the Desert of En Gedi." So Saul took three thousand chosen men from all Israel and set out to look for David and his men near the Crags of the Wild Goats.

He came to the sheep pens along the way; a cave was there, and Saul went in to relieve himself. David and his men were far back in the cave. The men said, "This is the day the LORD spoke of when he said to you, 'I will give your enemy into your hands for you to deal with as you wish.'" Then David crept up unnoticed and cut off a corner of Saul's robe.

Afterward, David was conscience-stricken for having cut off a corner of his robe. He said to his men, "The LORD forbid that I should do such a thing to my master, the LORD's anointed, or lift my hand against him; for he is the anointed of the LORD." With these words David rebuked his men and did not allow them to attack Saul. And Saul left the cave and went his way.

Then David went out of the cave and called out to Saul, "My lord the king!" When Saul looked behind him, David bowed down and prostrated himself with his face to the ground. He said to Saul, "Why do you listen when men say, 'David is bent on harming you'? This day you have seen with your own eyes how the LORD delivered you into my hands in the cave. Some urged me to kill you, but I spared you; I said, 'I will not lift my hand against my master, because he is the LORD's anointed.' See, my father, look at this piece of your robe in my hand! I cut off the corner of your robe but did not kill you. Now understand and recognize that I am not guilty of wrongdoing or rebellion. I have not wronged you, but you are hunting me down to take my life. May the LORD judge between you and me. And may the LORD avenge the wrongs you have done to me, but my hand will not touch you. As the old saying goes, 'From evildoers come evil deeds,' so my hand will not touch you.

"Against whom has the king of Israel come out? Whom are you pursuing? A dead dog? A flea? May the LORD be our judge and decide between us. May he consider my cause and uphold it; may he vindicate me by delivering me from your hand."

When David finished saying this, Saul asked, "Is that your voice, David my son?" And he wept aloud. "You are more righteous than I," he said. "You have treated me well, but I have treated you badly. You have just now told me of the good you did to me; the LORD delivered me into your hands, but you did not kill me. When a man finds his enemy, does he let him get away unharmed? May the LORD reward you well for the way you treated me today. I know that you will surely be king and that the kingdom of Israel will be established in your hands. Now swear to me by the LORD that you will not cut off my descendants or wipe out my name from my father's family."

So David gave his oath to Saul. Then Saul returned home, but David and his men went up to the stronghold.

No more than twenty years old, David is forced to flee to the desert of Judah and take refuge in caves and remote areas to escape the wrath of King Saul. For ten years he will live a sort of Robin Hood existence, before Saul finally dies battling the Philistines.

This passage shows one instance of David's loyalty to God while on the run. Saul is pursuing David, intent on finding and killing him. Suddenly, in a dramatic twist, David gains the chance to quickly and easily end Saul's life. But David has such a sense of reverence for the one God anointed that he can't even entertain the thought of killing this bloodthirsty man. He is committed to letting God bring justice.

The Bible records another similar incident, in which David again has the chance to take Saul's life and chooses to let him live (1 Samuel 26). In the end God will deliver the justice David has trusted him to provide. —BQ

DAILY CONTEMPLATION

What difficulty are you facing today that could tempt you to use your own methods rather than God's in seeking an escape?

DAY 108 1 Samuel 25:1–42

DAVID, NABAL, AND ABIGAIL

Now Samuel died, and all Israel assembled and mourned for him; and they buried him at his home in Ramah.

Then David moved down into the Desert of Maon. A certain man in Maon, who had property there at Carmel, was very wealthy. He had a thousand goats and three thousand sheep, which he was shearing in Carmel. His name was Nabal and his wife's name was Abigail. She was an intelligent and beautiful woman, but her husband, a Calebite, was surly and mean in his dealings.

While David was in the desert, he heard that Nabal was shearing sheep. So he sent ten young men and said to them, "Go up to Nabal at Carmel and greet him in my name. Say to him: 'Long life to you! Good health to you and your household! And good health to all that is yours!

"'Now I hear that it is sheep-shearing time. When your shepherds were with us, we did not mistreat them, and the whole time they were at Carmel nothing of theirs was missing. Ask your own servants and they will tell you. Therefore be favorable toward my young men, since we come at a festive time. Please give your servants and your son David whatever you can find for them.'"

When David's men arrived, they gave Nabal this message in David's name. Then they waited.

Nabal answered David's servants, "Who is this David? Who is this son of Jesse? Many servants are breaking away from their masters these days. Why should I take my bread and water, and the meat I have slaughtered for my shearers, and give it to men coming from who knows where?"

David's men turned around and went back. When they arrived, they reported every word. David said to his men, "Put on your swords!" So they put on their swords, and David put on his. About four hundred men went up with David, while two hundred stayed with the supplies.

One of the servants told Nabal's wife Abigail: "David sent messengers from the desert to give our master his greetings, but he hurled insults at them. Yet these men were very good to us. They did not mistreat us, and the whole time we were out in the fields near them nothing was missing. Night and day they were a wall around us all the time we were herding our sheep near them. Now think it over and see what you can do, because disaster is hanging over our master and his whole household. He is such a wicked man that no one can talk to him."

Abigail lost no time. She took two hundred loaves of bread, two skins of wine, five dressed sheep, five seahs of roasted grain, a hundred cakes of raisins and two hundred cakes of pressed figs, and loaded them on donkeys. Then she told her servants, "Go on ahead; I'll follow you." But she did not tell her husband Nabal.

As she came riding her donkey into a mountain ravine, there were David and his men descending toward her, and she met them. David had just said, "It's been useless—all my watching over this fellow's property in the desert so that nothing of his was missing. He has paid me back evil for good. May God deal with David, be it ever so severely, if by morning I leave alive one male of all who belong to him!"

When Abigail saw David, she quickly got off her donkey and bowed down before David with her face to the ground. She fell at his feet and said: "My lord, let the blame be on me alone. Please let your servant speak to you; hear what your servant has to say. May my lord pay no attention to that wicked man Nabal. He is just like his name—his name is Fool, and folly goes with him. But as for me, your servant, I did not see the men my master sent.

"Now since the LORD has kept you, my master, from bloodshed and from avenging yourself with your own hands, as surely as the LORD lives and as you live, may your enemies and all who intend to harm my master be like Nabal. And let this gift, which your servant has brought to my master, be given to the men who follow you. Please forgive your servant's offense, for the LORD will certainly make a lasting dynasty for my master, because he fights the LORD's battles. Let no wrongdoing be found in you as long as you live. Even though someone is pursuing you to take your life, the life of my master will be bound securely in the bundle of the living by the LORD your God. But the lives of your enemies he will hurl away as from the pocket of a sling. When the LORD has done for my master every good thing he promised concerning him and has appointed him leader over Israel, my master will not have on his conscience the staggering burden of needless bloodshed or of having avenged himself. And when the LORD has brought my master success, remember your servant."

David said to Abigail, "Praise be to the LORD, the God of Israel, who has sent you today to meet me. May you be blessed for your good judgment and for keeping me from bloodshed this day and from avenging myself with my own hands. Otherwise, as surely as the LORD, the God of Israel, lives, who has kept me from harming you, if you had not come quickly to meet me, not one male belonging to Nabal would have been left alive by daybreak."

Then David accepted from her hand what she had brought him and said, "Go home in peace. I have heard your words and granted your request."

When Abigail went to Nabal, he was in the house holding a banquet like that of a king. He was in high spirits and very drunk. So she told him nothing until daybreak. Then in the morning, when Nabal was sober, his wife told him all these things, and his heart failed him and he became like a stone. About ten days later, the LORD struck Nabal and he died.

When David heard that Nabal was dead, he said, "Praise be to the LORD, who has upheld my cause against Nabal for treating me with contempt. He has kept his servant from doing wrong and has brought Nabal's wrongdoing down on his own head."

Then David sent word to Abigail, asking her to become his wife. His servants went to Carmel and said to Abigail, "David has sent us to you to take you to become his wife."

She bowed down with her face to the ground and said, "Here is your maidservant, ready to serve you and wash the feet of my master's servants." Abigail quickly got on a donkey and, attended by her five maids, went with David's messengers and became his wife.

David's frustration reaches a peak in this passage, in which foolish Nabal (NAY-buhl) refuses to help David and his men in return for their prior kindness. David may well have taken Nabal's punishment into his own hands this time, but a remarkably resourceful woman named Abigail restrains him. Abigail offers another portrait of a strong woman with a deep reverence for God. Like Rahab and Ruth before her, Abigail chooses loyalty to God and God's people. She acts quickly, decisively, and wisely to prevent David from taking vengeance that belongs to God. God uses Abigail to mercifully spare David from his own violent inclination, then gives Abigail to David as a wife who will continue to support him in her strength and wisdom. —BQ

DAILY CONTEMPLATION

Whom has God put in your life to support you and give you wise counsel?

TAKING RISKS, TRUSTING GOD

Life is a risky business.

We face situational risks that stem from finances, jobs, schooling, or homes. We may also face physical risks from sports, violence, travel in cars or planes, poor eating habits, smoking, or drug use. And we encounter relational risks, especially with the people in our lives to whom we are closest—family, spouse, children, friends.

David certainly knew a life of risk. For ten years he faced every kind of risk. David's decision to spare Saul's life involved a risk that Saul could turn on David, hunting him down in a matter of hours or days. Jonathan too may easily have betrayed David out of loyalty to his father and desire for the throne. The stranger Abigail could have been deceptively seeking to save the life of her husband, setting David up for destruction. But David was right in trusting God's protection and trusting those whom God put in his life to help him. David refused to become a skeptic or a cynic.

We may have many reasons to distrust the people and situations in our lives. Sometimes our distrust protects us from making wrong decisions or relying on people who are unsafe. Yet sometimes it is not wise caution but rather improper fear that keeps us from the people and situations whereby God wishes to bless us. How can we know the difference? Like David, we must turn to God again and again, asking for the wisdom to respond properly.

David prays, "Teach me your way, O LORD; lead me in a straight path" (Psalm 27:11). We can trust God for wisdom and protection. As we do, we leave our lives open for his blessing through those people and circumstances he chooses.   —BQ

DAILY CONTEMPLATION

Where is the bulk of your distrust focused today? Do you sense God asking you to let go of your distrust and let him protect you instead? Take a moment to ask God for his wisdom and protection.

DAY 110   1 Samuel 31:3, 6; 2 Samuel 5:3; 6:1–23

KING DAVID BRINGS THE ARK TO JERUSALEM

The fighting grew fierce around Saul, and when the archers overtook him, they wounded him critically....

So Saul and his three sons and his armor-bearer and all his men died together that same day....

When all the elders of Israel had come to King David at Hebron, the king made a compact with them at Hebron before the LORD, and they anointed David king over Israel....

David again brought together out of Israel chosen men, thirty thousand in all. He and all his men set out from Baalah of Judah to bring up from there the ark of God, which is called by the Name, the name of the LORD Almighty, who is enthroned between the cherubim that are on the ark. They set the ark of God on a new cart and brought it from the house of Abinadab, which was on the hill. Uzzah and Ahio, sons of Abinadab, were guiding the new cart with the ark of God on it, and Ahio was walking in front of it. David and the whole house of Israel were celebrating with all their might before the LORD, with songs and with harps, lyres, tambourines, sistrums and cymbals.

When they came to the threshing floor of Nacon, Uzzah reached out and took hold of the ark of God, because the oxen stumbled. The LORD's anger burned against Uzzah because of his irreverent act; therefore God struck him down and he died there beside the ark of God.

Then David was angry because the LORD's wrath had broken out against Uzzah, and to this day that place is called Perez Uzzah.

David was afraid of the LORD that day and said, "How can the ark of the LORD ever come to me?" He was not willing to take the ark of the LORD to be with him in the City of David. Instead, he took it aside to the house of Obed-Edom the Gittite. The ark of the LORD remained in the house of Obed-Edom the Gittite for three months, and the LORD blessed him and his entire household.

Now King David was told, "The LORD has blessed the household of Obed-Edom and everything he has, because of the ark of God." So David went down and brought up the ark of God from the house of Obed-Edom to the City of David with rejoicing. When those who were carrying the ark of the LORD had taken six steps, he sacrificed a bull and a fattened calf. David, wearing a linen ephod, danced before the LORD with all his might, while he and the entire house of Israel brought up the ark of the LORD with shouts and the sound of trumpets.

As the ark of the LORD was entering the City of David, Michal daughter of Saul watched from a window. And when she saw King David leaping and dancing before the LORD, she despised him in her heart.

They brought the ark of the LORD and set it in its place inside the tent that David had pitched for it, and David sacrificed burnt offerings and fellowship offerings before the LORD. After he had finished sacrificing the burnt offerings and fellowship offerings, he blessed the people in the name of the LORD Almighty. Then he gave a loaf of bread, a cake of dates and a cake of raisins to each person in the whole crowd of Israelites, both men and women. And all the people went to their homes.

When David returned home to bless his household, Michal daughter of Saul came out to meet him and said, "How the king of Israel has distinguished himself today, disrobing in the sight of the slave girls of his servants as any vulgar fellow would!"

David said to Michal, "It was before the LORD, who chose me rather than your father or anyone from his house when he appointed me ruler over the LORD's people Israel—I will celebrate before the LORD. I will become even more undignified than this, and I will be humiliated in my own eyes. But by these slave girls you spoke of, I will be held in honor."

And Michal daughter of Saul had no children to the day of her death.

An unavoidable question dangles over the Bible's account of David's life. How could anyone so obviously flawed—he did, as we shall see, commit adultery and murder—be called "a man after God's own heart"? The central event in this chapter may point to an answer.

David consistently acknowledges that God, not a human king, is the true ruler of Israel, and so in one of his first official acts he sends for the sacred ark of the Lord that was captured by the Philistines half a century before. He plans to install it in Jerusalem, the new capital city he is building, as a symbol of God's reign.

It takes a few false starts to get the ark to Jerusalem. Without looking up the regulations given to Moses, the Israelites try transporting the ark on an ox cart, as the Philistines parade their gods, rather than on the shoulders of the Levites, as God has commanded. Somebody dies, David gets mad, and the ark sits in a private home for three months.

Nevertheless, when the ark finally does move to Jerusalem, to the accompaniment of a brass band and the shouts of a huge crowd, King David completely loses control. Wild with joy, he cartwheels in the streets, like an Olympic gymnast who has just won the gold medal and is out strutting his stuff.

Needless to say, the scene of a dignified king doing back flips in a scanty robe breaks every rule ever devised by a politician's image builders. David's wife, for one, is scandalized. But David sets her straight: It is God, no one else, whom he is dancing before. And, king or no, he doesn't care what anyone else thinks as long as that one-Person audience can sense his jubilation.

In short, David is a man of *passion,* and he feels more passionately about the God of Israel than about anything else in the world. The message gets through to the entire nation. As Frederick Buechner has written, "He had feet of clay like the rest of us if not more so—self-serving and deceitful, lustful and vain—but on the basis of that dance alone, you can see why it was David more than anybody else that Israel lost her heart to and why, when Jesus of Nazareth came riding into Jerusalem on his flea-bitten mule a thousand years later, it was as the Son of David that they hailed him."[6]   —PY

DAILY CONTEMPLATION

Have you ever lost control in worship? How would you respond to someone who did?

GOD'S PROMISE TO DAVID

After David was settled in his palace, he said to Nathan the prophet, "Here I am, living in a palace of cedar, while the ark of the covenant of the LORD is under a tent."

Nathan replied to David, "Whatever you have in mind, do it, for God is with you."

That night the word of God came to Nathan, saying:

"Go and tell my servant David, 'This is what the LORD says: You are not the one to build me a house to dwell in. I have not dwelt in a house from the day I brought Israel up out of Egypt to this day. I have moved from one tent site to another, from one dwelling place to another. Wherever I have moved with all the Israelites, did I ever say to any of their leaders whom I commanded to shepherd my people, "Why have you not built me a house of cedar?"'

"Now then, tell my servant David, 'This is what the LORD Almighty says: I took you from the pasture and from following the flock, to be ruler over my people Israel. I have been with you wherever you have gone, and I have cut off all your enemies from before you. Now I will make your name like the names of the greatest men of the earth. And I will provide a place for my people Israel and will plant them so that they can have a home of their own and no longer be disturbed. Wicked people will not oppress them anymore, as they did at the beginning and have done ever since the time I appointed leaders over my people Israel. I will also subdue all your enemies.

"'I declare to you that the LORD will build a house for you: When your days are over and you go to be with your fathers, I will raise up your offspring to succeed you, one of your own sons, and I will establish his kingdom. He is the one who will build a house for me, and I will establish his throne forever. I will be his father, and he will be my son. I will never take my love away from him, as I took it away from your predecessor. I will set him over my house and my kingdom forever; his throne will be established forever.'"

Nathan reported to David all the words of this entire revelation.

Then King David went in and sat before the LORD, and he said:

"Who am I, O LORD God, and what is my family, that you have brought me this far? And as if this were not enough in your sight, O God, you have spoken about the future of the house of your servant. You have looked on me as though I were the most exalted of men, O LORD God.

"What more can David say to you for honoring your servant? For you know your servant, O LORD. For the sake of your servant and according to your will, you have done this great thing and made known all these great promises.

"There is no one like you, O LORD, and there is no God but you, as we have heard with our own ears. And who is like your people Israel—the one nation on earth whose God went out to redeem a people for himself, and to make a name for yourself, and to perform great and awesome wonders by driving out nations from before your people, whom you redeemed from Egypt? You made your people Israel your very own forever, and you, O LORD, have become their God.

"And now, LORD, let the promise you have made concerning your servant and his house be established forever. Do as you promised, so that it will be established and that your name will be great forever. Then men will say, 'The LORD Almighty, the God over Israel, is Israel's God!' And the house of your servant David will be established before you.

"You, my God, have revealed to your servant that you will build a house for him. So your servant has found courage to pray to you. O LORD, you are God! You have promised these good things to your servant. Now you have been pleased to bless the house of your servant, that it may continue forever in your sight; for you, O LORD, have blessed it, and it will be blessed forever."

After bringing the ark of God to Jerusalem, David begins to dream of building a splendid home for it, a temple devoted to the God of the Israelites. In a day when pagan temples rank among the wonders of the world, he thinks it only fitting to lavish the wealth of his kingdom on a "house" for the true God. But God makes clear that David is not the one to build such a temple. Elsewhere (1 Chronicles 22:8), the Bible states the reason: as a warrior, David will shed much blood during his time on the throne, and God wants his house built by a man of peace. That task will fall on David's son.

Although God vetoes the plan to build a temple, he grants David far more. Harking back to his covenant with the Israelites, he promises—in a tender play on words—to build a "house" out of David's descendants that will last forever. Whatever his reservations about the Israelites' demand for a king, God has fully "adopted" the king as his representative within the nation. In a typically humble response, David erupts in a prayer of astonished thanksgiving.

This promise, given in an intimate exchange between God and David, sows the seed for what will become a longtime hope of the Jews: a royal "Messiah," or Anointed One. Saul's dynasty ends just as it began; David's will continue through a long line of kings and culminate in God's own Son, to be born into David's lineage in Bethlehem, the City of David. Has God's promise been fulfilled? The fact that even in modern times people still pore over the lives of David and other kings of tiny Israel—though far grander, more impressive kings have faded from history—and recognize one descendant as the true Messiah should give a hint.

(Note: The books of Samuel, Kings, and Chronicles often overlap, telling the same history from different perspectives. This chapter from 1 Chronicles repeats almost word for word the seventh chapter of 2 Samuel.) —PY

DAILY CONTEMPLATION

What have you wanted to do for God?

THE GOODNESS OF GOD

Praise the LORD, O my soul;
　　all my inmost being, praise his holy name.
Praise the LORD, O my soul,
　　and forget not all his benefits—
who forgives all your sins
　　and heals all your diseases,
who redeems your life from the pit
　　and crowns you with love and compassion,
who satisfies your desires with good things
　　so that your youth is renewed like the eagle's.

The LORD works righteousness
　　and justice for all the oppressed.

He made known his ways to Moses,
　　his deeds to the people of Israel:
The LORD is compassionate and gracious,
　　slow to anger, abounding in love.
He will not always accuse,
　　nor will he harbor his anger forever;
he does not treat us as our sins deserve
　　or repay us according to our iniquities.
For as high as the heavens are above the earth,
　　so great is his love for those who fear him;
as far as the east is from the west,
　　so far has he removed our transgressions from us.
As a father has compassion on his children,
　　so the LORD has compassion on those who fear him;
for he knows how we are formed,
　　he remembers that we are dust.
As for man, his days are like grass,
　　he flourishes like a flower of the field;
the wind blows over it and it is gone,
　　and its place remembers it no more.
But from everlasting to everlasting
　　the LORD's love is with those who fear him,
　　and his righteousness with their children's children—
with those who keep his covenant
　　and remember to obey his precepts.

The LORD has established his throne in heaven,
　　and his kingdom rules over all.

Praise the LORD, you his angels,
>   you mighty ones who do his bidding,
>   who obey his word.
Praise the LORD, all his heavenly hosts,
>   you his servants who do his will.
Praise the LORD, all his works
>   everywhere in his dominion.

Praise the LORD, O my soul.

David never gets over a sense of **astonishment** at all God has done for him. As he grows older and reviews his life, he realizes that, despite the hardships, God has always delivered him "from the pit." God has kept his promises. In gratitude, David writes many psalms praising God for his past faithfulness. The king serves, in effect, as a national reservoir of memory for his people, helping the whole nation remember God's benefits.

When the Israelites praise God, their thoughts center on God's actions in freeing them from slavery and leading them into a land of their own. Their psalms are like history lessons, designed to summon up the past, especially the hallmark days of deliverance under Moses. They study those days in the Torah, or five books of Moses, and write songs to commemorate them.

The memories aren't all positive, and the Israelites' songs can be brutally frank about the ancestors' rebellions, complaints, and lack of gratitude. Yet they have one great, happy reason to rejoice: God has kept his promise to love them. To psalm writers like David, the events of Israel's history are unmistakable signs of God's grace. They have done nothing to deserve God's love, and yet he has showered love on them.

This psalm could be titled "The Goodness of God." It reviews the dark times of illness and oppression, of sin and rebellion, and then it points with amazement to the remarkable ways in which God transformed all those dark times. God understands and will not overwhelm human weakness: "He knows how we are formed, he remembers that we are dust." More, despite our failings, he has in store for us an unfathomable eternity of love.

David has one loud message to celebrate: We do not get what we deserve. We get far more. The psalm ends in a burst of praise, starting with the grand sweep of the universe and spiraling back to the setting of the very first verse—David praising God in his inmost being.   —PY

DAILY CONTEMPLATION

When you review your past, do you tend to focus on the victories or the failures?

DAVID AND BATHSHEBA

In the spring, at the time when kings go off to war, David sent Joab out with the king's men and the whole Israelite army. They destroyed the Ammonites and besieged Rabbah. But David remained in Jerusalem.

One evening David got up from his bed and walked around on the roof of the palace. From the roof he saw a woman bathing. The woman was very beautiful, and David sent someone to find out about her. The man said, "Isn't this Bathsheba, the daughter of Eliam and the wife of Uriah the Hittite?" Then David sent messengers to get her. She came to him, and he slept with her. (She had purified herself from her uncleanness.) Then she went back home. The woman conceived and sent word to David, saying, "I am pregnant."

So David sent this word to Joab: "Send me Uriah the Hittite." And Joab sent him to David. When Uriah came to him, David asked him how Joab was, how the soldiers were and how the war was going. Then David said to Uriah, "Go down to your house and wash your feet." So Uriah left the palace, and a gift from the king was sent after him. But Uriah slept at the entrance to the palace with all his master's servants and did not go down to his house.

When David was told, "Uriah did not go home," he asked him, "Haven't you just come from a distance? Why didn't you go home?"

Uriah said to David, "The ark and Israel and Judah are staying in tents, and my master Joab and my lord's men are camped in the open fields. How could I go to my house to eat and drink and lie with my wife? As surely as you live, I will not do such a thing!"

Then David said to him, "Stay here one more day, and tomorrow I will send you back." So Uriah remained in Jerusalem that day and the next. At David's invitation, he ate and drank with him, and David made him drunk. But in the evening Uriah went out to sleep on his mat among his master's servants; he did not go home.

In the morning David wrote a letter to Joab and sent it with Uriah. In it he wrote, "Put Uriah in the front line where the fighting is fiercest. Then withdraw from him so he will be struck down and die."

So while Joab had the city under siege, he put Uriah at a place where he knew the strongest defenders were. When the men of the city came out and fought against Joab, some of the men in David's army fell; moreover, Uriah the Hittite died.

Joab sent David a full account of the battle. He instructed the messenger: "When you have finished giving the king this account of the battle, the king's anger may flare up, and he may ask you, 'Why did you get so close to the city to fight? Didn't you know they would shoot arrows from the wall? Who killed Abimelech son of Jerub-Besheth? Didn't a woman throw an upper millstone on him from the wall, so that he died in Thebez? Why did you get so close to the wall?' If he asks you this, then say to him, 'Also, your servant Uriah the Hittite is dead.'"

The messenger set out, and when he arrived he told David everything Joab had sent him to say. The messenger said to David, "The men overpowered us and came out against us in the open, but we drove them back to the entrance to the city gate. Then the archers shot arrows at your servants from the wall, and some of the king's men died. Moreover, your servant Uriah the Hittite is dead."

David told the messenger, "Say this to Joab: 'Don't let this upset you; the sword devours one as well as another. Press the attack against the city and destroy it.' Say this to encourage Joab."

When Uriah's wife heard that her husband was dead, she mourned for him. After the time of mourning was over, David had her brought to his house, and she became his wife and bore him a son. But the thing David had done displeased the LORD.

It is the simplest story in the world, this tale of David and Bathsheba (bath-SHEE-bah): man sees woman, man sleeps with woman, woman gets pregnant. Nothing unusual there. Every year the tabloids broadcast modern variations on the same theme. Substitute a politician—or evangelist—for the king, and a beauty queen for Bathsheba. What else is new?

The scandal doesn't especially shock David's Israelite subjects. Like most people, they are resigned to the fact that the people on top who make the rules often don't bother to live by them. Lots of leaders in history have followed this course, taking the spoils they want, the money they want, the privileges they want. The Romans had a phrase for such behavior, *rex lex*—the king is law—rather than *lex rex*—the law is king.

Bathsheba's pregnancy complicates the picture somewhat. Today, a leader in David's situation might destroy the evidence with an abortion. David has his own cover-up plan. It starts as a clever attempt to deceive, making Bathsheba's husband appear as the likely father. Uriah's (yoor-I-uh) scruples, however, put King David to shame, or should. What ensues is a classic case of "One crime leads to another." In the end, David, the man after God's own heart, breaks the sixth, seventh, ninth, and tenth commandments. For his loyalty, David's soldier Uriah gets the reward of murder, and many other Israelites fall with him.

This story shows David at his most Machiavellian: cold as iron, ruthless in use of his power. Even so, not a word of protest is filed. What the king wants the king gets, no questions asked. Such is life.

After a mourning period, Bathsheba moves into the palace and David marries her. By now many people must have surmised what has happened—the servants know, at any rate—but the Bible doesn't report that any of them protest. The story of David's infidelity might have ended here, and probably would have, except for one portentous sentence at the close of this chapter. It says merely, "The thing David had done displeased the LORD." —PY

211

DAY 114   Reflection

SIN AND GOD'S LOVE THROUGH THE

EYES OF AN UNBELIEVER

We live in a postmodern culture. Postmodernism holds that right and wrong are defined individually—no one standard of right and wrong exists that all must adhere to. "My right may be your wrong, and that's perfectly all right." This perspective has become so ingrained in our culture that it is akin to a law of nature.

Christians, though, believe that the Bible is the overarching standard of right and wrong, the final authority. God's words are set down in the Bible. It stands as the only true and reliable guidebook for living this life and preparing for eternity.

David knew God's law well, as given through Moses. During most of his life this shepherd-at-heart followed God's law, aware that God's rules are the boundaries that keep us, God's sheep, within the pastures that are richest and most fulfilling. But David shut his eyes to God's law on the evening he spied Bathsheba on a nearby roof. His unchecked passion propelled him into making a big mistake, and we'll see that he suffered much heartache as a result. Sin, wildly fun for a while, always brings pain in the end.

Like David, we each make mistakes. Some of them we make in ignorance before becoming believers; others we make while knowing well the wrong we are doing. Often our mistakes bring difficult consequences. But as we look at how tenderly God cares for us, we can echo David's words in Psalm 103: "He does not treat us as our sins deserve or repay us according to our iniquities" (v. 10). The price we pay for sin does not even approach the price we owe, all because of the payment Jesus made in our place.

Only with this understanding can we reach out to those in our postmodern culture who lack a center of authority. When unbelievers come to know God's deep love for them, they can begin to understand the love he's shown through the guidelines in his Word, the Bible. And they can learn that what Jesus did out of love for us, he also did for them. They too can see the Bible as a long, long story of God's immeasurable love.   —BQ

DAILY CONTEMPLATION

When has God spared you from your own mistakes? How has he surprised you with blessing beyond your dreams? Ask God to help you tell others about his love for you in spite of your mistakes.

Nathan Rebukes David

The Lord sent Nathan to David. When he came to him, he said, "There were two men in a certain town, one rich and the other poor. The rich man had a very large number of sheep and cattle, but the poor man had nothing except one little ewe lamb he had bought. He raised it, and it grew up with him and his children. It shared his food, drank from his cup and even slept in his arms. It was like a daughter to him.

"Now a traveler came to the rich man, but the rich man refrained from taking one of his own sheep or cattle to prepare a meal for the traveler who had come to him. Instead, he took the ewe lamb that belonged to the poor man and prepared it for the one who had come to him."

David burned with anger against the man and said to Nathan, "As surely as the Lord lives, the man who did this deserves to die! He must pay for that lamb four times over, because he did such a thing and had no pity."

Then Nathan said to David, "You are the man! This is what the Lord, the God of Israel, says: 'I anointed you king over Israel, and I delivered you from the hand of Saul. I gave your master's house to you, and your master's wives into your arms. I gave you the house of Israel and Judah. And if all this had been too little, I would have given you even more. Why did you despise the word of the Lord by doing what is evil in his eyes? You struck down Uriah the Hittite with the sword and took his wife to be your own. You killed him with the sword of the Ammonites. Now, therefore, the sword will never depart from your house, because you despised me and took the wife of Uriah the Hittite to be your own.'

"This is what the Lord says: 'Out of your own household I am going to bring calamity upon you. Before your very eyes I will take your wives and give them to one who is close to you, and he will lie with your wives in broad daylight. You did it in secret, but I will do this thing in broad daylight before all Israel.'"

Then David said to Nathan, "I have sinned against the Lord."

Nathan replied, "The Lord has taken away your sin. You are not going to die. But because by doing this you have made the enemies of the Lord show utter contempt, the son born to you will die."

After Nathan had gone home, the Lord struck the child that Uriah's wife had borne to David, and he became ill. David pleaded with God for the child. He fasted and went into his house and spent the nights lying on the ground. The elders of his household stood beside him to get him up from the ground, but he refused, and he would not eat any food with them.

On the seventh day the child died. David's servants were afraid to tell him that the child was dead, for they thought, "While the child was still living, we spoke to David but he would not listen to us. How can we tell him the child is dead? He may do something desperate."

David noticed that his servants were whispering among themselves and he realized the child was dead. "Is the child dead?" he asked.

"Yes," they replied, "he is dead."

Then David got up from the ground. After he had washed, put on lotions and changed his clothes, he went into the house of the LORD and worshiped. Then he went to his own house, and at his request they served him food, and he ate.

His servants asked him, "Why are you acting this way? While the child was alive, you fasted and wept, but now that the child is dead, you get up and eat!"

He answered, "While the child was still alive, I fasted and wept. I thought, 'Who knows? The LORD may be gracious to me and let the child live.' But now that he is dead, why should I fast? Can I bring him back again? I will go to him, but he will not return to me."

Then David comforted his wife Bathsheba, and he went to her and lay with her. She gave birth to a son, and they named him Solomon. The LORD loved him; and because the LORD loved him, he sent word through Nathan the prophet to name him Jedidiah.

All over the globe today people who live under the thumb of tyrants ask the question, Who holds the ruler accountable? From the beginning God established Israel as *his* kingdom, with its ruler as his representative, not the final authority. And after David's great sin, God sends the prophet Nathan to confront the king.

It was Nathan who conveyed to the king God's lavish promise to establish David's "house" (1 Chronicles 17). This time he comes with a heartrending tale of poverty, greed, and injustice. He presents the case to David, the highest judge in Israel, for a verdict. David knows exactly how to decide such a case: the man deserves to die! When he says so, Nathan delivers his own devastating verdict, "You are the man!"

In this dramatic scene David's greatness shows itself. He could have had Nathan killed. Or he could have laughed and thrown him out of the palace. Instead, David says to Nathan, "I have sinned against the LORD," immediately admitting guilt and acknowledging God as the true ruler.

To appreciate David's confession, you only have to think of the response of leaders "caught in the act" in our own time: Richard Nixon grudgingly admitting, "Mistakes were made"; a parade of officials marching before the Senate during the Irangate hearings with alibis, excuses, and rationalizations; Bill Clinton initially denying well-substantiated charges of womanizing. But King David sees at once the heart of the issue. He has sinned not just against Uriah and his country but against the Lord.

David is a great king partly because he does not act with the normal pride of a great king. Confronted with the truth, he repents. Forgiveness comes in an instant, but the consequences of David's actions will plague the kingdom for a generation. For one thing, he has lost moral authority within his own family. Over the next few years, one of David's sons will rape his sister, and another will kill his brother and launch a coup against David himself. King David has left a legacy of abuse of power, and not all his successors will be as quick to repent. —PY

DAILY CONTEMPLATION

How do you instinctively react when someone confronts you about wrongdoing?

TRUE CONFESSION

Have mercy on me, O God,
  according to your unfailing love;
according to your great compassion
  blot out my transgressions.
Wash away all my iniquity
  and cleanse me from my sin.

For I know my transgressions,
  and my sin is always before me.
Against you, you only, have I sinned
  and done what is evil in your sight,
so that you are proved right when you speak
  and justified when you judge.
Surely I was sinful at birth,
  sinful from the time my mother conceived me.
Surely you desire truth in the inner parts;
  you teach me wisdom in the inmost place.

Cleanse me with hyssop, and I will be clean;
  wash me, and I will be whiter than snow.
Let me hear joy and gladness;
  let the bones you have crushed rejoice.
Hide your face from my sins
  and blot out all my iniquity.

Create in me a pure heart, O God,
  and renew a steadfast spirit within me.
Do not cast me from your presence
  or take your Holy Spirit from me.
Restore to me the joy of your salvation
  and grant me a willing spirit, to sustain me.

Then I will teach transgressors your ways,
  and sinners will turn back to you.
Save me from bloodguilt, O God,
  the God who saves me,
  and my tongue will sing of your righteousness.
O Lord, open my lips,
  and my mouth will declare your praise.
You do not delight in sacrifice, or I would bring it;
  you do not take pleasure in burnt offerings.
The sacrifices of God are a broken spirit;
  a broken and contrite heart,
  O God, you will not despise.

This poem of remembrance may well be the most impressive outcome of David's sordid affair with Bathsheba. It is one thing for a king to confess a moral lapse in private to a prophet. It is quite another for him to compose a detailed account of that confession to be sung throughout the land!

All nations have heroes, but Israel may be alone in making epic literature about its greatest hero's failings. This eloquent psalm, possibly used in worship services as a guide for confession, shows that Israel ultimately remembered David more for his devotion to God than for his political achievements.

Step by step, the psalm takes the reader (or singer) through the stages of repentance. It describes the constant mental replays—"Oh, if only I had a chance to do it over"—the gnawing guilt, the shame, and finally the hope for a new beginning that springs from true repentance.

David lives under Old Testament law, which prescribes a harsh punishment for his crimes: death by stoning. But in a remarkable way this psalm transcends the rigid formulas of law and reveals the true nature of sin as a broken *relationship* with God. "Against you, you only, have I sinned," David cries out. He sees that no ritual sacrifices or religious ceremonies will cause his guilt to vanish; the sacrifices God wants are "a broken spirit, a broken and contrite heart." Those, David has.

In the midst of his prayer, David looks for possible good that might come out of his tragedy and sees a glimmer of light. He prays for God to use his experience as a moral lesson for others. Perhaps, by reading his story of sin, they might avoid the same pitfalls, or by reading his confession they might gain hope in forgiveness. David's prayer is fully answered and becomes his greatest legacy as king. The best king of Israel has fallen the farthest. But neither he, nor anyone, can fall beyond the reach of God's love and forgiveness. —PY

DAILY CONTEMPLATION

Would you lose respect for a leader if he or she admitted failures this openly?

DAY 117
Psalm 139:1–24

DAVID'S SPIRITUAL SECRET

O LORD, you have searched me
and you know me.
You know when I sit and when I rise;
you perceive my thoughts from afar.
You discern my going out and my lying down;
you are familiar with all my ways.

Before a word is on my tongue
　　you know it completely, O LORD.

You hem me in—behind and before;
　　you have laid your hand upon me.
Such knowledge is too wonderful for me,
　　too lofty for me to attain.

Where can I go from your Spirit?
　　Where can I flee from your presence?
If I go up to the heavens, you are there;
　　if I make my bed in the depths, you are there.
If I rise on the wings of the dawn,
　　if I settle on the far side of the sea,
even there your hand will guide me,
　　your right hand will hold me fast.

If I say, "Surely the darkness will hide me
　　and the light become night around me,"
even the darkness will not be dark to you;
　　the night will shine like the day,
　　for darkness is as light to you.

For you created my inmost being;
　　you knit me together in my mother's womb.
I praise you because I am fearfully and wonderfully made;
　　your works are wonderful,
　　I know that full well.
My frame was not hidden from you
　　when I was made in the secret place.
When I was woven together in the depths of the earth,
　　your eyes saw my unformed body.
All the days ordained for me
　　were written in your book
　　before one of them came to be.

How precious to me are your thoughts, O God!
　　How vast is the sum of them!
Were I to count them,
　　they would outnumber the grains of sand.
When I awake,
　　I am still with you.

If only you would slay the wicked, O God!
　　Away from me, you bloodthirsty men!
They speak of you with evil intent;
　　your adversaries misuse your name.
Do I not hate those who hate you, O LORD,
　　and abhor those who rise up against you?

I have nothing but hatred for them;
  I count them my enemies.

Search me, O God, and know my heart;
  test me and know my anxious thoughts.
See if there is any offensive way in me,
  and lead me in the way everlasting.

In the end David—lusty, vengeful King David—gains a reputation as a friend of God. For a time in Israel, Jehovah (or Yahweh) is known as "the God of David"; the two are that closely identified. What is David's secret? This majestic psalm hints at an answer.

Mainly, Psalm 139 reveals the **intimacy** that exists between David and his God. Although his exploits—killing wild animals bare-handed, felling Goliath, surviving Saul's onslaughts, routing the Philistines—make him a hero in his nation's eyes, David always finds a way to make God the one on center stage. Throughout his life David believes, truly believes, that the spiritual world is every bit as real as his physical world of swords and spears and caves and thrones.

The Psalms form a record of David's conscious effort to subject his own daily life to the reality of that spiritual world beyond him. Whatever the phrase "practicing the presence of God" means, David experiences it. He intentionally involves God in every detail of his life.

David firmly believes he **matters** to God. After one narrow escape he writes, "[God] rescued me because he delighted in me" (Psalm 18:19). Another time he argues, in so many words, "What good will it do you if I die, Lord? Who will praise you then?" (Psalm 30). And this psalm, 139, beautifully expresses David's sense of wonder at God's love and concern.

Reading David's psalms, with all their emotional peaks and valleys, it may even seem that he writes them as a form of spiritual therapy, a way of talking himself into faith when his spirit and emotions are wavering. Now, centuries later, we can use these very same prayers as steps of faith, a path to lead us from an obsession with ourselves to the actual presence of God. —PY

DAILY CONTEMPLATION

How do you practice the presence of God in your life? Read Psalm 139 again and make it your prayer to God.

DAY 118   Reflection

PRACTICING HIS PRESENCE

God is always with us. He's always focused on us, always thinking about us, always aware of what we're doing, thinking, and feeling. Never for a second does he turn his attention from us. And all of his attention flows from a burning, passionate love for us that never grows cold, never tires.

If we in turn make God the center of our attention, we can be in a continual love relationship with God that will give us perspective on everything in life and fill the deepest needs of our souls. David understood God's constant presence and in return was often present to God. His understanding of God's nearness helped him to walk more closely with God.

Another man has helped believers understand this concept more fully. Brother Lawrence lived in a Carmelite monastery in France during the seventeenth century, working in the kitchen of the monastery until he died at age eighty. His work held no special significance by this earth's standards, but Brother Lawrence transformed his work in a way that has left an impact on thousands who have come after him. During his years serving in the kitchen, Brother Lawrence grew in what he called "practicing the presence of God."

> I beheld him in my heart as my Father and as my God. I worshiped him as often as I could, keeping my mind in his holy presence and recalling it back to God as often as I found it had wandered from him. . . . I make it my business only to persevere in his holy presence wherein I keep myself by a simple attention and a general fond regard to God, which I refer to as an *actual presence* of God. Or, to put it another way, an habitual, silent, and secret conversation of the soul with God. . . . In short, by often repeating these acts they become **habitual,** and the presence of God becomes something that comes naturally to us.[7]

David and Brother Lawrence were earthy people with human weaknesses and wandering hearts, yet through discipline and a real love for God, they discovered that it is possible to form a habit of being consciously present to God.

The apostle Paul, writing to church friends, asked them to "pray continually; give thanks in all circumstances, for this is God's will for you in Christ Jesus" (1 Thessalonians 5:17–18). Paul knew that the inner practice of sitting with God, sensing him and whispering to him, sometimes with words and sometimes just with the language of our hearts, not only is possible but is God's will for you.　　　　　　—BQ

DAILY CONTEMPLATION

How often during the day are you aware of God's presence? How often do you pray? Ask God to help turn your mind to him often during the day, in both times of quiet and times of activity.

DAY 119　　　　　　　1 Kings 1:28–30; 3:1–28

SOLOMON ASKS FOR WISDOM

King David said, "Call in Bathsheba." So she came into the king's presence and stood before him.

The king then took an oath: "As surely as the LORD lives, who has delivered me out of every trouble, I will surely carry out today what I swore to you by the LORD, the God of Israel: Solomon your son shall be king after me, and he will sit on my throne in my place." ...

Solomon made an alliance with Pharaoh king of Egypt and married his daughter. He brought her to the City of David until he finished building his palace and the temple of the LORD, and the wall around Jerusalem. The people, however, were still sacrificing at the high places, because a temple had not yet been built for the Name of the LORD. Solomon showed his love for the LORD by walking according to the statutes of his father David, except that he offered sacrifices and burned incense on the high places.

The king went to Gibeon to offer sacrifices, for that was the most important high place, and Solomon offered a thousand burnt offerings on that altar. At Gibeon the LORD appeared to Solomon during the night in a dream, and God said, "Ask for whatever you want me to give you."

Solomon answered, "You have shown great kindness to your servant, my father David, because he was faithful to you and righteous and upright in heart. You have continued this great kindness to him and have given him a son to sit on his throne this very day.

"Now, O LORD my God, you have made your servant king in place of my father David. But I am only a little child and do not know how to carry out my duties. Your servant is here among the people you have chosen, a great people, too numerous to count or number. So give your servant a discerning heart to govern your people and to distinguish between right and wrong. For who is able to govern this great people of yours?"

The Lord was pleased that Solomon had asked for this. So God said to him, "Since you have asked for this and not for long life or wealth for yourself, nor have asked for the death of your enemies but for discernment in administering justice, I will do what you have asked. I will give you a wise and discerning heart, so that there will never have been anyone like you, nor will there ever be. Moreover, I will give you what you have not asked for—both riches and honor—so that in your lifetime you will have no equal among kings. And if you walk in my ways and obey my statutes and commands as David your father did, I will give you a long life." Then Solomon awoke—and he realized it had been a dream.

He returned to Jerusalem, stood before the ark of the Lord's covenant and sacrificed burnt offerings and fellowship offerings. Then he gave a feast for all his court.

Now two prostitutes came to the king and stood before him. One of them said, "My lord, this woman and I live in the same house. I had a baby while she was there with me. The third day after my child was born, this woman also had a baby. We were alone; there was no one in the house but the two of us.

"During the night this woman's son died because she lay on him. So she got up in the middle of the night and took my son from my side while I your servant was asleep. She put him by her breast and put her dead son by my breast. The next morning, I got up to nurse my son—and he was dead! But when I looked at him closely in the morning light, I saw that it wasn't the son I had borne."

The other woman said, "No! The living one is my son; the dead one is yours."

But the first one insisted, "No! The dead one is yours; the living one is mine." And so they argued before the king.

The king said, "This one says, 'My son is alive and your son is dead,' while that one says, 'No! Your son is dead and mine is alive.'"

Then the king said, "Bring me a sword." So they brought a sword for the king. He then gave an order: "Cut the living child in two and give half to one and half to the other."

The woman whose son was alive was filled with compassion for her son and said to the king, "Please, my lord, give her the living baby! Don't kill him!"

But the other said, "Neither I nor you shall have him. Cut him in two!"

Then the king gave his ruling: "Give the living baby to the first woman. Do not kill him; she is his mother."

When all Israel heard the verdict the king had given, they held the king in awe, because they saw that he had wisdom from God to administer justice.

The first half of 1 Kings describes a man who gets life handed to him on a silver platter. The favored son of King David and Queen Bathsheba, young Solomon grows up in the royal palace. God lavishes special gifts on Solomon. In an incredible dream sequence, young Solomon actually gets the opportunity every child secretly longs for. God offers him any wish—long life, riches, anything at all—and when Solomon chooses wisdom, God adds bonus gifts of wealth, honor, and peace. Early on, the precocious prince astounds others with his talent for songwriting and natural history.

A mere teenager when he takes over the throne of Israel, Solomon soon becomes the richest, most impressive ruler of his time. In Jerusalem, silver is as common as stones (10:27). And a fleet of trading ships brings exotica for the king's private collections—apes and baboons from Africa, and ivory and gold by the ton. He is called the wisest man in the world, and kings and queens travel hundreds of miles to meet him. They leave dazzled by the genius of Israel's king and by the prosperity of his nation.

Israel reaches its Golden Age under King Solomon, a shining moment of tranquillity in its long, tormented history. Almost all the Promised Land lies in Solomon's domain, and the nation is at peace. Literature and culture flourish. Of the common people, the Bible reports simply that "they ate, they drank and they were happy" (4:20).

However, even in the happy days, danger signs appear. King Solomon makes a shrewd political alliance with Pharaoh of Egypt. Already he is looking to military strength, rather than to God, for security. In addition, Solomon has a passion for foreign-born women. Over time, he marries princesses from Moab, Ammon, Edom, Sidon, and other nations—seven hundred wives in all, and three hundred concubines! Eventually, to please his wives, Solomon will take a final, terrible step of building altars to all their gods. —PY

DAILY CONTEMPLATION

What are your God-given abilities? Do you tend to use those gifts to serve God?

DAY 120
1 Kings 6:1, 38; 8:1–34

THE ARK BROUGHT TO THE TEMPLE

In the four hundred and eightieth year after the Israelites had come out of Egypt, in the fourth year of Solomon's reign over Israel, in the month of Ziv, the second month, he began to build the temple of the LORD....

In the eleventh year in the month of Bul, the eighth month, the temple was finished in all its details according to its specifications. He had spent seven years building it....

Then King Solomon summoned into his presence at Jerusalem the elders of Israel, all the heads of the tribes and the chiefs of the Israelite families, to bring up the ark of the LORD's covenant from Zion, the City of David. All the men of Israel came together to King Solomon at the time of the festival in the month of Ethanim, the seventh month.

When all the elders of Israel had arrived, the priests took up the ark, and they brought up the ark of the LORD and the Tent of Meeting and all the sacred furnishings in it. The priests and Levites carried them up, and King Solomon and the entire assembly of Israel that had gathered about him were before the ark, sacrificing so many sheep and cattle that they could not be recorded or counted.

The priests then brought the ark of the LORD's covenant to its place in the inner sanctuary of the temple, the Most Holy Place, and put it beneath the wings of the cherubim. The cherubim spread their wings over the place of the ark and overshadowed the ark and its carrying poles. These poles were so long that their ends could be seen from the Holy Place in front of the inner sanctuary, but not from outside the Holy Place; and they are still there today. There was nothing in the ark except the two stone tablets that Moses had placed in it at Horeb, where the LORD made a covenant with the Israelites after they came out of Egypt.

When the priests withdrew from the Holy Place, the cloud filled the temple of the LORD. And the priests could not perform their service because of the cloud, for the glory of the LORD filled his temple.

Then Solomon said, "The LORD has said that he would dwell in a dark cloud; I have indeed built a magnificent temple for you, a place for you to dwell forever."

While the whole assembly of Israel was standing there, the king turned around and blessed them. Then he said:

"Praise be to the LORD, the God of Israel, who with his own hand has fulfilled what he promised with his own mouth to my father David. For he said, 'Since the day I brought my people Israel out of Egypt, I have not chosen a city in any tribe of Israel to have a temple built for my Name to be there, but I have chosen David to rule my people Israel.'

"My father David had it in his heart to build a temple for the Name of the LORD, the God of Israel. But the LORD said to my father David, 'Because it was in your heart to build a temple for my Name, you did well to have this in your heart. Nevertheless, you are not the one to build the temple, but your son, who is your own flesh and blood—he is the one who will build the temple for my Name.'

"The LORD has kept the promise he made: I have succeeded David my father and now I sit on the throne of Israel, just as the LORD promised, and I have built the temple for the Name of the LORD, the God of Israel. I have provided a place there for the ark, in which is the covenant of the LORD that he made with our fathers when he brought them out of Egypt."

Then Solomon stood before the altar of the LORD in front of the whole assembly of Israel, spread out his hands toward heaven and said:

"O LORD, God of Israel, there is no God like you in heaven above or on earth below—you who keep your covenant of love with your servants who continue wholeheartedly in your way. You have kept your promise to your servant David my father; with your mouth you have promised and with your hand you have fulfilled it—as it is today.

"Now LORD, God of Israel, keep for your servant David my father the promises you made to him when you said, 'You shall never fail to have a man to sit before me on the throne of Israel, if only your sons are careful in all they do to walk before me as you have done.' And now, O God of Israel, let your word that you promised your servant David my father come true.

"But will God really dwell on earth? The heavens, even the highest heaven, cannot contain you. How much less this temple I have built! Yet give attention to your servant's prayer and his plea for mercy, O LORD my God. Hear the cry and the prayer that your servant is praying in your presence this day. May your eyes be open toward this temple night and day, this place of which you said, 'My Name shall be there,' so that you will hear the prayer your servant prays toward this place. Hear the supplication of your servant and of your people Israel when they pray toward this place. Hear from heaven, your dwelling place, and when you hear, forgive.

"When a man wrongs his neighbor and is required to take an oath and he comes and swears the oath before your altar in this temple, then hear from heaven and act. Judge between your servants, condemning the guilty and bringing down on his own head what he has done. Declare the innocent not guilty, and so establish his innocence.

"When your people Israel have been defeated by an enemy because they have sinned against you, and when they turn back to you and confess your name, praying and making supplication to you in this temple, then hear from heaven and forgive the sin of your people Israel and bring them back to the land you gave to their fathers."

Of Solomon's many accomplishments, one looms large above the rest. He spares no expense in building a place for God to dwell, and Solomon's temple, fashioned by two hundred thousand workmen, soon ranks as one of the wonders of the world. From a distance, it shines like a snowcapped mountain. Inside, all the walls, and even the floors, are plated with pure gold.

In many ways the scene in this chapter represents the high-water mark of the entire Old Testament, the fulfillment of God's covenant with Israel. Solomon calls the nation together to dedicate the temple to God, and as thousands of people look on in a huge public ceremony, the glory of the Lord comes down to fill the temple. Even the priests are driven back by the mighty force.

God is making Solomon's temple the center of his activity on earth, and the crowd spontaneously decides to stay another two weeks to celebrate. Kneeling on a bronze platform, Solomon prays aloud, "I have indeed built a magnificent temple for you, a place for you to dwell forever." Then he catches himself in astonishment. "But will God really dwell on earth? The heavens, even the highest heaven, cannot contain you. How much less this temple I have built!"

God has done it! His promises to Abraham and Moses have finally come true. In one of the most magnificent prayers ever prayed, Solomon reviews the history of the covenant and asks God to seal that agreement with his presence in the temple. God responds: "I have heard the prayer and plea you have made before me; I have consecrated this temple. . . . My eyes and my heart will always be there" (9:3).

The Israelites now have land, a nation with secure boundaries, and a gleaming symbol of God's presence among them. All this comes to pass in a land rich with silver and gold. On the famous day of the temple dedication, everyone sees the fire and the cloud of his presence. No one can doubt God's faithfulness.   —PY

DAILY CONTEMPLATION

What promise of God are you waiting on?

DAY 121   Psalm 84:1–12

MORE THAN A BUILDING

How lovely is your dwelling place,
    O Lord Almighty!
My soul yearns, even faints,
    for the courts of the Lord;
my heart and my flesh cry out
    for the living God.

Even the sparrow has found a home,
  and the swallow a nest for herself,
  where she may have her young—
a place near your altar,
  O LORD Almighty, my King and my God.
Blessed are those who dwell in your house;
  they are ever praising you.

Blessed are those whose strength is in you,
  who have set their hearts on pilgrimage.
As they pass through the Valley of Baca,
  they make it a place of springs;
  the autumn rains also cover it with pools.
They go from strength to strength,
  till each appears before God in Zion.

Hear my prayer, O LORD God Almighty;
  listen to me, O God of Jacob.
Look upon our shield, O God;
  look with favor on your anointed one.

Better is one day in your courts
  than a thousand elsewhere;
I would rather be a doorkeeper in the house of my God
  than dwell in the tents of the wicked.
For the LORD God is a sun and shield;
  the LORD bestows favor and honor;
no good thing does he withhold
  from those whose walk is blameless.

O LORD Almighty,
  blessed is the man who trusts in you.

It is almost impossible to exaggerate the significance of the temple for Jews throughout history. They took pride in its beautiful architecture (as people today might honor the Notre Dame cathedral), but the temple was far more than a grand symbol. Israel's entire national religious life centered around this building, the house of God.

Faithful Jews turned and faced the temple daily in prayer. Each year they made pilgrimages there to celebrate three great festivals honoring God's covenant with them. The Israelites even came to believe that the temple magically protected them against foreign invasion. As long as the temple stood, some said, no foreign armies could enter Jerusalem—a belief the prophet Jeremiah roundly condemned.

This psalm captures some of the intense feelings about the temple. It is written by one of the "Sons of Korah," a priestly choir established by King David to provide music for worship. As the writer travels to the temple on pilgrimage, his joy and anticipation make the desert surroundings seem almost like an oasis. Perhaps using a little humor, he claims to envy the sparrows and swallows that build nests inside the walls of the temple and thus get to live there permanently. He sings, "Better is one day in your courts than a thousand elsewhere."

The object of the psalmist's enthusiasm, the glorious temple built by Solomon, stood for about 380 years, occasionally falling into disrepair. Destroyed by the Babylonians, it was partially rebuilt under the leadership of Ezra and Nehemiah and then reconstructed by King Herod in Jesus' time. Jesus, who also made pilgrimages to the temple, walked on "Solomon's Porch," and the early church met on the temple grounds.

Herod's temple eventually fell to the Romans, and years later the Moslems built a mosque on the site. But the temple has never lost its sacred significance for the Jews, and even today some in Israel propose rebuilding the temple.

In the days since Jesus' resurrection, we who have received salvation through Christ are the temples of God. He now dwells in our bodies rather than in a physical construct. —PY

DAILY CONTEMPLATION

Is worshiping God dull or exciting for you? Why? Read Psalm 84 again as a prayer to God for the continued living presence of his Spirit in you.

DAY 122   1 Kings 10:1–13

THE QUEEN OF SHEBA VISITS SOLOMON

When the queen of Sheba heard about the fame of Solomon and his relation to the name of the LORD, she came to test him with hard questions. Arriving at Jerusalem with a very great caravan—with camels carrying spices, large quantities of gold, and precious stones—she came to Solomon and talked with him about all that she had on her mind. Solomon answered all her questions; nothing was too hard for the king to explain to her. When the queen of Sheba saw all the wisdom of Solomon and the palace he had built, the food on his table, the seating of his officials, the attending servants in their robes, his cupbearers, and the burnt offerings he made at the temple of the LORD, she was overwhelmed.

She said to the king, "The report I heard in my own country about your achievements and your wisdom is true. But I did not believe these things until I came and saw with my own eyes. Indeed, not even half was told me; in wisdom and wealth you have far exceeded the report I heard. How happy your men must be! How happy your officials, who continually stand before you and hear your wisdom! Praise be to the LORD your God, who has delighted in you and placed you on the throne of Israel. Because of the LORD's eternal love for Israel, he has made you king, to maintain justice and righteousness."

And she gave the king 120 talents of gold, large quantities of spices, and precious stones. Never again were so many spices brought in as those the queen of Sheba gave to King Solomon.

(Hiram's ships brought gold from Ophir; and from there they brought great cargoes of almugwood and precious stones. The king used the almugwood to make supports for the temple of the LORD and for the royal palace, and to make harps and lyres for the musicians. So much almugwood has never been imported or seen since that day.)

King Solomon gave the queen of Sheba all she desired and asked for, besides what he had given her out of his royal bounty. Then she left and returned with her retinue to her own country.

This passage gives a glimpse of just one of the world rulers who came to see Solomon's magnificent kingdom firsthand and to observe his wisdom. The queen of Sheba (SHEE-buh) does not go away disappointed. Rather, what she sees overwhelms her. Solomon's reign of wisdom and wealth exceeds anything she expects. It seems obvious even to this queen, likely a pagan ruler and wealthy in her own right, that the Lord of Solomon loves him and has chosen to bless Israel through Solomon's leadership.

Sheba was located south of Israel and Arabia in the country now called Yemen, bordering the Indian Ocean to the south. The queen's words to Solomon indicate that God has revealed to her, one outside the chosen nation of Israel, that God has an "eternal love for Israel" (v. 9).

Jesus will later remember the queen of Sheba and compare her with the people of his time. "The Queen of the South will rise at the judgment with the men of this generation and condemn them; for she came from the ends of the earth to listen to Solomon's wisdom, and now one greater than Solomon is here," Jesus said (Luke 11:31). So impressed was the queen with Solomon's riches and wisdom that she traveled a great distance and brought him costly gifts. How much more should all those in Jesus' day have yearned to follow Jesus, who offered true riches and perfect wisdom.   —BQ

DAILY CONTEMPLATION

How much effort are you expending in seeking Jesus?

DAY 123   1 Kings 10:23–11:13

SOLOMON'S SPLENDOR, SOLOMON'S WIVES

King Solomon was greater in riches and wisdom than all the other kings of the earth. The whole world sought audience with Solomon to hear the wisdom God had put in his heart. Year after year, everyone who came brought a gift— articles of silver and gold, robes, weapons and spices, and horses and mules.

Solomon accumulated chariots and horses; he had fourteen hundred chariots and twelve thousand horses, which he kept in the chariot cities and also with him in Jerusalem. The king made silver as common in Jerusalem as stones, and cedar as plentiful as sycamore-fig trees in the foothills. Solomon's horses were imported from Egypt and from Kue—the royal merchants purchased them from Kue. They imported a chariot from Egypt for six hundred shekels of silver, and a horse for a hundred and fifty. They also exported them to all the kings of the Hittites and of the Arameans.

King Solomon, however, loved many foreign women besides Pharaoh's daughter—Moabites, Ammonites, Edomites, Sidonians and Hittites. They were from nations about which the LORD had told the Israelites, "You must not intermarry with them, because they will surely turn your hearts after their gods." Nevertheless, Solomon held fast to them in love. He had seven hundred wives of royal birth and three hundred concubines, and his wives led him astray. As Solomon grew old, his wives turned his heart after other gods, and his heart was not fully devoted to the LORD his God, as the heart of David his father had been. He followed Ashtoreth the goddess of the Sidonians, and Molech the detestable god of the Ammonites. So Solomon did evil in the eyes of the LORD; he did not follow the LORD completely, as David his father had done.

On a hill east of Jerusalem, Solomon built a high place for Chemosh the detestable god of Moab, and for Molech the detestable god of the Ammonites. He did the same for all his foreign wives, who burned incense and offered sacrifices to their gods.

The LORD became angry with Solomon because his heart had turned away from the LORD, the God of Israel, who had appeared to him twice. Although he had forbidden Solomon to follow other gods, Solomon did not keep the LORD's command. So the LORD said to Solomon, "Since this is your attitude and you have not kept my covenant and my decrees, which I commanded you, I will most certainly tear the kingdom away from you and give it to one of your subordinates. Nevertheless, for the sake of David your father, I will not do it during your lifetime. I will tear it out of the hand of your son. Yet I will not tear the whole kingdom from him, but will give him one tribe for the sake of David my servant and for the sake of Jerusalem, which I have chosen."

Part of God's law to the Israelites reads, "The king, moreover, must not acquire great numbers of horses for himself or make the people return to Egypt to get more of them, for the LORD has told you, 'You are not to go back that way again.' He must not take many wives, or his heart will be led astray. He must not accumulate large amounts of silver and gold" (Deuteronomy 17:16–17).

Clearly, God has warned Israel against the very patterns Solomon falls into. He imports horses from Egypt. He takes seven hundred wives and nearly half as many mistresses. And he accumulates more silver and gold than any other king on earth. He also amasses rich clothing, spices, horses, mules, and apes and baboons, which may have been fashionable pets for royalty at the time (1 Kings 10:22).

God has specifically warned that many horses, an abundance of wives, and great wealth will harm Israel rather than help her. When Israel purchases horses to assist in battle, the nation's confidence will turn to its own power rather than to God for victory. When the nation grows wealthy, it will lose its sense of need for God. When the king surrounds himself with foreign wives, many of whom remain loyal to false gods, his heart will turn toward their loyalties.

In all these forms of disobedience, Solomon and Israel grieve God more deeply than David ever did. Israel has chosen not to love God with all its heart (Deuteronomy 6:5). —BQ

DAILY CONTEMPLATION

How might our nation resemble Israel during Solomon's reign?

DAY 124   Reflection

LOSING SIGHT OF GOD

"Don't go back that way again" (Deuteronomy 17:16).

With his accumulation of horses, women, and riches, Solomon put himself in a position where he could conquer anyone, enjoy exotic sex at a moment's notice, and delight in the acclaim of all who valued wealth. In the eyes of his world Solomon had it all.

Yet while he was focused on his wealth and enjoying his popularity, Solomon was gradually drifting "back that way again." God had warned the Israelites in the desert, after freeing them from Egypt and leading them toward the Promised Land, not to return to the ways of Egypt. He had liberated them from the false promises of Egypt and had led them instead to a place where they could, through his power and blessing, enjoy true pleasure in life. In the Promised Land they would experience a full life with God as he continued to build their nation and care for them.

It didn't take long for the Israelites' hearts to start going "back that way again." The very son of David, who had heard from God himself and possessed more wisdom than anyone ever, could not see that in straying back toward security, seduction, and wealth, he was betraying the One who had given him life. He was forfeiting the deeper pleasures God offered, in favor of cheap counterfeits. The world deceived even Solomon. In the end he found himself worshiping Ashtoreth, a goddess of sex and fertility, and Molech, a god whose worship involved child sacrifice, a practice that God had strictly forbidden (Leviticus 18:21).

It's easy to lose sight of God. It's tempting to grow comfortable in this world, to enjoy God's gifts and then begin to believe that in them, rather than in God, lie our security and delight. Just as God warned Israel not to return to the ways of Egypt, he reminds us that he has freed us from the lies of this world.

We may never be as wise as Solomon, but we can understand the truth he missed. Only God can save us and bring us lasting joy. Earthly strength will not save, sex

cannot satisfy, and possessions cannot hold a candle to God's approval and blessing. Why go back that way again?   —BQ

DAY 125   Song of Songs 2:1–17

UNCOMMON SONG

Beloved
I am a rose of Sharon,
    a lily of the valleys.

Lover
Like a lily among thorns
    is my darling among the maidens.

Beloved
Like an apple tree among the trees of the forest
    is my lover among the young men.
I delight to sit in his shade,
    and his fruit is sweet to my taste.
He has taken me to the banquet hall,
    and his banner over me is love.
Strengthen me with raisins,
    refresh me with apples,
    for I am faint with love.
His left arm is under my head,
    and his right arm embraces me.
Daughters of Jerusalem, I charge you
    by the gazelles and by the does of the field:
Do not arouse or awaken love
    until it so desires.

Listen! My lover!
    Look! Here he comes,
leaping across the mountains,
    bounding over the hills.
My lover is like a gazelle or a young stag.
    Look! There he stands behind our wall,

gazing through the windows,
　　peering through the lattice.
My lover spoke and said to me,
　　"Arise, my darling,
　　my beautiful one, and come with me.
See! The winter is past;
　　the rains are over and gone.
Flowers appear on the earth;
　　the season of singing has come,
the cooing of doves
　　is heard in our land.
The fig tree forms its early fruit;
　　the blossoming vines spread their fragrance.
Arise, come, my darling;
　　my beautiful one, come with me."

Lover
My dove in the clefts of the rock,
　　in the hiding places on the mountainside,
show me your face,
　　let me hear your voice;
for your voice is sweet,
　　and your face is lovely.
Catch for us the foxes,
　　the little foxes
that ruin the vineyards,
　　our vineyards that are in bloom.

Beloved
My lover is mine and I am his;
　　he browses among the lilies.
Until the day breaks
　　and the shadows flee,
turn, my lover,
　　and be like a gazelle
or like a young stag
　　on the rugged hills.

Without doubt more songs have been written about romantic love than any other subject. And, to many people's surprise, the Bible itself contains an explicit love song—complete with erotic lyrics.

Solomon, with all his wives and mistresses, was a devoted student of romance. Ultimately, he fell victim to an obsession with it that caused him much grief. But the Song of Songs (also known as the Song of Solomon) celebrates a high form of beautiful love. It shows no embarrassment about lovers enjoying each other's bodies and openly expressing that enjoyment.

Not everyone has felt comfortable with the frankness of this book. In medieval Spain, Saint Teresa of Avila led a campaign to remove all copies of Song of Songs from the Bible and burn them in public bonfires. Priests and teachers who refused were removed from their jobs and even imprisoned.

Over the centuries, many others have tried to read the song as though it had nothing to do with physical lovers, seeing it instead as an allegory of love between God and his people. But nowadays most scholars believe that the poem was intended to be taken at face value, as a celebration of love between two newlyweds.

These lovers look without shame on one another and tell each other what they feel. They revel in the sensuous: the beauty of nature, the scent of perfumes and spices. They are explicit and erotic. Yet Song of Songs creates a very different atmosphere than most modern love songs. It harks back to the original love in the Garden of Eden, when man and woman were naked and unashamed. You sense no shame or guilt; you feel that God himself smiles upon their love.   —PY

DAILY CONTEMPLATION

What did you learn about romantic love from your parents or teachers when you were growing up?

DAY 126   Song of Songs 3:7–4:16

THE WEDDING

Beloved
Look! It is Solomon's carriage,
    escorted by sixty warriors,
    the noblest of Israel,
all of them wearing the sword,
    all experienced in battle,
each with his sword at his side,
    prepared for the terrors of the night.
King Solomon made for himself the carriage;
    he made it of wood from Lebanon.
Its posts he made of silver,
    its base of gold.
Its seat was upholstered with purple,
    its interior lovingly inlaid
    by the daughters of Jerusalem.
Come out, you daughters of Zion,
    and look at King Solomon wearing the crown,
    the crown with which his mother crowned him

on the day of his wedding,
the day his heart rejoiced.

Lover
How beautiful you are, my darling!
Oh, how beautiful!
Your eyes behind your veil are doves.
Your hair is like a flock of goats
descending from Mount Gilead.
Your teeth are like a flock of sheep just shorn,
coming up from the washing.
Each has its twin;
not one of them is alone.
Your lips are like a scarlet ribbon;
your mouth is lovely.
Your temples behind your veil
are like the halves of a pomegranate.
Your neck is like the tower of David,
built with elegance;
on it hang a thousand shields,
all of them shields of warriors.
Your two breasts are like two fawns,
like twin fawns of a gazelle
that browse among the lilies.
Until the day breaks
and the shadows flee,
I will go to the mountain of myrrh
and to the hill of incense.
All beautiful you are, my darling;
there is no flaw in you.

Come with me from Lebanon, my bride,
come with me from Lebanon.
Descend from the crest of Amana,
from the top of Senir, the summit of Hermon,
from the lions' dens
and the mountain haunts of the leopards.
You have stolen my heart, my sister, my bride;
you have stolen my heart
with one glance of your eyes,
with one jewel of your necklace.
How delightful is your love, my sister, my bride!
How much more pleasing is your love than wine,
and the fragrance of your perfume than any spice!
Your lips drop sweetness as the honeycomb, my bride;
milk and honey are under your tongue.

The fragrance of your garments is like that of Lebanon.
You are a garden locked up, my sister, my bride;
 you are a spring enclosed, a sealed fountain.
Your plants are an orchard of pomegranates
 with choice fruits,
 with henna and nard,
 nard and saffron,
 calamus and cinnamon,
 with every kind of incense tree,
 with myrrh and aloes
 and all the finest spices.
You are a garden fountain,
 a well of flowing water
 streaming down from Lebanon.

Beloved
Awake, north wind,
 and come, south wind!
Blow on my garden,
 that its fragrance may spread abroad.
Let my lover come into his garden
 and taste its choice fruits.

Solomon's Song of Songs progresses from the courtship of two lovers to their wedding night—today's passage—to maturation in their marriage.

The custom in ancient Israel, still practiced in the Middle East today, is for the groom to lead a procession to his bride's home for the wedding ceremony. After the ceremony, the couple consummate their marriage with a beautiful wedding night together, each lavishing love on the other. Solomon's praise for his bride's physical beauty echoes the praise of every loving groom or bride for his or her new spouse.

Although Solomon's beloved has a dark complexion (1:5)—a trait that in her day was less desirable than a light complexion—Solomon finds her beautiful. Later the beloved will praise the beauty she finds in her lover (ch. 5). As today's passage ends, the bride invites her new husband to come and enjoy her fully. She gives herself to him, like a tree offering its ripened fruit. —BQ

DAILY CONTEMPLATION

Did you grow up believing sex to be a beautiful and fulfilling part of marriage, or were you taught differently?

MATURING MARRIAGE

Beloved
If only you were to me like a brother,
   who was nursed at my mother's breasts!
Then, if I found you outside,
   I would kiss you,
   and no one would despise me.
I would lead you
   and bring you to my mother's house—
   she who has taught me.
I would give you spiced wine to drink,
   the nectar of my pomegranates.
His left arm is under my head
   and his right arm embraces me.
Daughters of Jerusalem, I charge you:
   Do not arouse or awaken love
   until it so desires.

Friends
Who is this coming up from the desert
   leaning on her lover?

Beloved
Under the apple tree I roused you;
   there your mother conceived you,
   there she who was in labor gave you birth.
Place me like a seal over your heart,
   like a seal on your arm;
for love is as strong as death,
   its jealousy unyielding as the grave.
It burns like blazing fire,
   like a mighty flame.
Many waters cannot quench love;
   rivers cannot wash it away.
If one were to give
   all the wealth of his house for love,
   it would be utterly scorned. . . .

Lover
You who dwell in the gardens
   with friends in attendance,
   let me hear your voice!

Beloved
Come away, my lover,
    and be like a gazelle
or like a young stag
    on the spice-laden mountains.

This last chapter of the Song of Songs portrays the lovers enjoying a maturing marriage that has sustained trials yet still possesses loving, passionate intimacy. The culture of Solomon's day frowns on public displays of affection between husband and wife. Here in the first verses, the beloved expresses her desire to display affection for her husband as a sister would be allowed to do for a brother. In a playful manner, the wife speaks of herself as a sister, a mother, and earlier as a friend (5:16) to her lover. Clearly, this couple shares a multifaceted relationship in which each meets various needs of the other.

As the couple emerges from the desert in verse 5, we see a picture of two who have overcome trials in their marriage. Earlier they dealt with the insecurity of the beloved (1:5), "foxes" (2:15) representing obstacles or temptations that threaten their relationship, and indifference on the part of the beloved toward her husband (5:2–7). In the image of coming up out of the desert, the song suggests that the couple has worked to overcome the disharmony that became a part of life between a husband and wife when sin entered the world (Genesis 3:16).

The song goes on to express the great power that love holds over a person. The beloved tells of her desire to be her husband's most valued possession. Once love takes hold, its power can bring a heightened energy for life or it can bring destruction. If its passion is not kindled and preserved, jealousy will burn with a destructive force. Ultimately, love is a priceless gift from God that must be treasured and protected.

In the final two verses of the song, the lovers recall their days of courtship, expressing a love for each other still strong and intimate while also playful and passionate. The husband and wife have lived out a committed relationship with one another that in all its phases reflects God's intentions for marriage.   —BQ

DAILY CONTEMPLATION

Do you know a couple who embody the marriage described in Song of Songs?

DAY 128   Reflection

LOVING GOD'S WAY

So how did Solomon get the privilege of having his song on marital love make it into the Bible—he of the **seven hundred** wives and **three hundred** mistresses? Did God overlook his polygamy and adultery? Do Don Juans and Casanovas have the most to teach about love and passion?

Some scholars believe that Solomon wrote the Song of Songs after his marriage to his first wife, before he began accumulating hundreds of others. If so, it fits his pattern. Solomon could not control his appetites. When he found something good—horses, buildings, gold, wives—he hoarded it like a child with secret treasures.

Or maybe Solomon wrote the song when old and tired of his harem of women. Looking back on his life—as in his musings of Ecclesiastes—perhaps he saw the errors in his ways and recalled a time of innocence when his marriage reflected God's plan for a man and a woman.

Whatever the reason why God chose Solomon to author this most beautiful of love songs, it's clear that God gave us the song to teach us about loving. Throughout, the Song of Songs presents romantic love as a powerful, living force within us. How strong? Think of a blazing fire, a thirst that cannot be quenched, a boulder that can't be washed away by the river. Love is consuming and unchangeable. Sound like God's love for us?

God intended love to have this power over us. It unites us and stokes the energies needed to care for another in all the happenings of life. Solomon alluded to this in a proverb: "Above all else, guard your heart, for it is the wellspring of life" (Proverbs 4:23).

Solomon's song celebrates the life-giving power of love, with sex as the ultimate expression of this love. Sex becomes the fulfillment of a loving relationship that through marital union will only keep growing. As the final gift of two people to one another, sex joins lives together for the duration of their time on earth.

The Bible, a realistic book, never downplays the force of sex. This act reaches to our emotions and wills, influencing everything we do and even the person we are. Although the beauty of sex may feel right at an earlier time, the feeling won't last if it isn't happening within a marriage relationship. Rather than bringing energy to life, this intimate act will drain us and begin to consume us.

God illustrates in Song of Songs that within the right context, every part of a romantic, loving relationship is a gift from him. He also warns repeatedly, "Do not arouse or awaken love until it so desires" (2:7). Because love is a wonderful gift, many desire to marry and thus experience it. But love cannot be bought or forced. Although within marriage love requires commitment and work, no amount of effort can make love happen in the beginning.

As we reflect on God's gift of love, we can celebrate his passionate, pursuing love of us. The romantic love we experience here on earth is merely a taste of the love God has for us and will reveal fully in eternity. "Now I know in part; then I shall know fully, even as I am fully known" (1 Corinthians 13:12).　　　—BQ

DAILY CONTEMPLATION

Are you in a romantic relationship now? Are you seeking one? Are you questioning God's will for a relationship? Express to God your desire to love as he has intended, and ask for wisdom in the choices you make about love.

LIFE ADVICE

Listen, my sons, to a father's instruction;
  pay attention and gain understanding.
I give you sound learning,
  so do not forsake my teaching.
When I was a boy in my father's house,
  still tender, and an only child of my mother,
he taught me and said,
  "Lay hold of my words with all your heart;
  keep my commands and you will live.
Get wisdom, get understanding;
  do not forget my words or swerve from them.
Do not forsake wisdom, and she will protect you;
  love her, and she will watch over you.
Wisdom is supreme; therefore get wisdom.
  Though it cost all you have, get understanding.
Esteem her, and she will exalt you;
  embrace her, and she will honor you.
She will set a garland of grace on your head
  and present you with a crown of splendor."

Listen, my son, accept what I say,
  and the years of your life will be many.
I guide you in the way of wisdom
  and lead you along straight paths.
When you walk, your steps will not be hampered;
  when you run, you will not stumble.
Hold on to instruction, do not let it go;
  guard it well, for it is your life.
Do not set foot on the path of the wicked
  or walk in the way of evil men.
Avoid it, do not travel on it;
  turn from it and go on your way.
For they cannot sleep till they do evil;
  they are robbed of slumber till they make someone fall.
They eat the bread of wickedness
  and drink the wine of violence.

The path of the righteous is like the first gleam of dawn,
  shining ever brighter till the full light of day.
But the way of the wicked is like deep darkness;
  they do not know what makes them stumble.

My son, pay attention to what I say;
    listen closely to my words.
Do not let them out of your sight,
    keep them within your heart;
for they are life to those who find them
    and health to a man's whole body.
Above all else, guard your heart,
    for it is the wellspring of life.
Put away perversity from your mouth;
    keep corrupt talk far from your lips.
Let your eyes look straight ahead,
    fix your gaze directly before you.
Make level paths for your feet
    and take only ways that are firm.
Do not swerve to the right or the left;
    keep your foot from evil.

The happy days of Solomon's reign do not last. In a pointed editorial aside, the author of 1 Kings notes that after building the temple, Solomon spends twice as much time and energy on the construction of his own palace (7:1). He proves unable to control his extravagant appetite in any area: wealth, power, romance, political intrigue. He seems obsessed with a desire to outdo anyone who has ever lived, and gradually his devotion to God slips away. First Kings gives this summation of Solomon's days, "So Solomon did evil in the eyes of the LORD; he did not follow the LORD completely, as David his father had done" (11:6).

Yet, although Solomon ultimately fails to please God, he does use his enormous talent for much good. In the arts, he creates many fine works, among them several books of biblical literature. Inspired by God's supernatural gift of wisdom, he composes 1,005 songs and 3,000 proverbs—many of which are collected in the book of Proverbs.

This representative chapter captures the tone of the book of Proverbs: a wise old man, surrounded by eager young admirers, coyly unveils to them the secrets of his life. (A modern parallel: millions of Americans will buy the latest how-to book by a famous sports figure or business executive—*Maybe it will help me achieve that same kind of success,* they think.)

Before revealing his secrets, however, the author of Proverbs wants to get one thing straight. The wisdom he is teaching cannot be reduced to a series of "Don't do this; do that" rules. There is no formula for "one-minute wisdom"; true wisdom demands a lifelong quest. The rewards of such a life, however, will repay any sacrifice, "though it cost all you have."

As the author contrasts "the path of the righteous" with "the way of the wicked," one cannot help wondering how Solomon might have fared if he had consistently followed his own advice. Now his time is passing; he can only hope to convey that hard-bitten wisdom to future generations. —PY

DAY 130   Proverbs 10:1–23

HOW TO READ PROVERBS

The proverbs of Solomon:

A wise son brings joy to his father,
    but a foolish son grief to his mother.

Ill-gotten treasures are of no value,
    but righteousness delivers from death.

The LORD does not let the righteous go hungry
    but he thwarts the craving of the wicked.

Lazy hands make a man poor,
    but diligent hands bring wealth.

He who gathers crops in summer is a wise son,
    but he who sleeps during harvest is a disgraceful son.

Blessings crown the head of the righteous,
    but violence overwhelms the mouth of the wicked.

The memory of the righteous will be a blessing,
    but the name of the wicked will rot.

The wise in heart accept commands,
    but a chattering fool comes to ruin.

The man of integrity walks securely,
    but he who takes crooked paths will be found out.

He who winks maliciously causes grief,
    and a chattering fool comes to ruin.

The mouth of the righteous is a fountain of life,
    but violence overwhelms the mouth of the wicked.

Hatred stirs up dissension,
    but love covers over all wrongs.

Wisdom is found on the lips of the discerning,
    but a rod is for the back of him who lacks judgment.

Wise men store up knowledge,
    but the mouth of a fool invites ruin.

The wealth of the rich is their fortified city,
　　but poverty is the ruin of the poor.

The wages of the righteous bring them life,
　　but the income of the wicked brings them punishment.

He who heeds discipline shows the way to life,
　　but whoever ignores correction leads others astray.

He who conceals his hatred has lying lips,
　　and whoever spreads slander is a fool.

When words are many, sin is not absent,
　　but he who holds his tongue is wise.

The tongue of the righteous is choice silver,
　　but the heart of the wicked is of little value.

The lips of the righteous nourish many,
　　but fools die for lack of judgment.

The blessing of the LORD brings wealth,
　　and he adds no trouble to it.

A fool finds pleasure in evil conduct,
　　but a man of understanding delights in wisdom.

Solomon had the ability to express his great wisdom in a very down-to-earth way. As a result, the book of Proverbs reads like a collection of folksy, commonsense advice. The practical guidance, intended to help you make your way in the world, skips from topic to topic. It comments on small issues as well as large: blabber-mouthing, wearing out your welcome with neighbors, being unbearably cheerful too early in the morning.

Anybody can find exceptions to the generalities in Proverbs. For instance, Proverbs 10:4 says, "Lazy hands make a man poor, but diligent hands bring wealth." Yet farmers who work diligently may go hungry during a drought, and lazy dreamers sometimes hit the lottery jackpot. Proverbs simply tells how life works most of the time; it gives the rule, not the exceptions. Normally, people who are godly, moral, hardworking, and wise will succeed in life. Fools and scoffers, though they appear successful, will pay a long-term price for their lifestyles.

The advice in Proverbs usually takes the form of a brief, pungent "one-liner," so the book requires a different kind of reading than others in the Bible. It's hard to read several chapters in a row. Some people have made a practice of reading one chapter of Proverbs each day. With thirty-one chapters, the book can be read through once each month. The proverbs are meant to be taken in small doses, savored, digested, and gradually absorbed.

Many proverbs are written in a style called "parallelism," a word that describes the tendency of Hebrew poetry to repeat a thought in a slightly different way. In one such form, "synonymous parallelism," the second half of the proverb underscores and embellishes the message of the first half (10:10). In another form, "antithetical parallelism," a thought is followed by its opposite. In both kinds of parallelism, the trick is to compare each phrase with its pair in the other half of the proverb. For instance, in 10:4 "diligent hands" pairs with its opposite, "lazy hands," and "bring wealth" is the opposite of "make a man poor." Sometimes these comparisons bare subtle shades of meaning. —PY

DAILY CONTEMPLATION

Which of the proverbs in this chapter apply most directly to you?

DAY 131 A Proverbs Sampler

WORDS ABOUT WORDS

Proverbs on the Importance of Words

The mouth of the righteous is a fountain of life,
  but violence overwhelms the mouth of the wicked....

The tongue of the righteous is choice silver,
  but the heart of the wicked is of little value. (10:11, 12)
From the fruit of his lips a man is filled with good things
  as surely as the work of his hands rewards him. (12:14)
The tongue that brings healing is a tree of life,
  but a deceitful tongue crushes the spirit. (15:4)
A rebuke impresses a man of discernment
  more than a hundred lashes a fool. (17:10)
The tongue has the power of life and death,
  and those who love it will eat its fruit. (18:21)
A word aptly spoken
  is like apples of gold in settings of silver. (25:11)

Proverbs on the Wrong Way to Speak

There are six things the LORD hates,
  seven that are detestable to him:
  haughty eyes,
  a lying tongue,
  hands that shed innocent blood,
  a heart that devises wicked schemes,
  feet that are quick to rush into evil,
  a false witness who pours out lies
  and a man who stirs up dissension among brothers. (6:16–19)
With his mouth the godless destroys his neighbor,
  but through knowledge the righteous escape....

A man who lacks judgment derides his neighbor,
   but a man of understanding holds his tongue.

A gossip betrays a confidence,
   but a trustworthy man keeps a secret. (11:9, 12–13)
Reckless words pierce like a sword,
   but the tongue of the wise brings healing. (12:18)
He who guards his lips guards his life,
   but he who speaks rashly will come to ruin. (13:3)
The words of a gossip are like choice morsels;
   they go down to a man's inmost parts....

He who answers before listening—
   that is his folly and his shame. (18:8, 13)
Like a coating of glaze over earthenware
   are fervent lips with an evil heart.

A malicious man disguises himself with his lips,
   but in his heart he harbors deceit.
Though his speech is charming, do not believe him,
   for seven abominations fill his heart.
His malice may be concealed by deception,
   but his wickedness will be exposed in the assembly.

If a man digs a pit, he will fall into it;
   if a man rolls a stone, it will roll back on him.

A lying tongue hates those it hurts,
   and a flattering mouth works ruin. (26:23–28)

Proverbs on the Right Way to Speak

Wise men store up knowledge,
   but the mouth of a fool invites ruin....

The lips of the righteous nourish many,
   but fools die for lack of judgment....

The lips of the righteous know what is fitting,
   but the mouth of the wicked only what is perverse. (10:14, 21, 32)
An anxious heart weighs a man down,
   but a kind word cheers him up. (12:25)
A gentle answer turns away wrath,
   but a harsh word stirs up anger....

A man finds joy in giving an apt reply—
   and how good is a timely word!...

The heart of the righteous weighs its answers,
   but the mouth of the wicked gushes evil. (15:1, 23, 28)
Kings take pleasure in honest lips;
   they value a man who speaks the truth....

A wise man's heart guides his mouth,
and his lips promote instruction.

Pleasant words are a honeycomb,
sweet to the soul and healing to the bones. (16:13, 23–24)
A man of knowledge uses words with restraint,
and a man of understanding is even-tempered.

Even a fool is thought wise if he keeps silent,
and discerning if he holds his tongue. (17:27–28)
Better is open rebuke
than hidden love.

Wounds from a friend can be trusted,
but an enemy multiplies kisses. (27:5–6)
He who rebukes a man will in the end gain more favor
than he who has a flattering tongue. (28:23)

Proverbs on the Dangers of Words

When words are many, sin is not absent,
but he who holds his tongue is wise. (10:19)
All hard work brings a profit,
but mere talk leads only to poverty. (14:23)

Who is the wisest person you know? Probably you'll come up with an elderly person, full of life experience, with a wry twist of humor and a colorful way of putting things. Solomon must have been like that, and he passed down his observations about life in elegant, witty nuggets of insight.

Solomon did not sit around all day spouting proverbs in topical sequence. Most likely, those that survive in this book were assembled late in his life, in no strict order. Thus reading Proverbs may at first remind you of reading the dictionary: you'll encounter short, self-contained items in a long list with little or no connection between them.

Even though the one-liners in Proverbs move quickly (and apparently randomly) from one subject to another, there is an overall objective behind the disorder. If you spend enough time in Proverbs, you will gain a subtle and practical understanding of life. Familiar themes keep showing up: the use and abuse of the tongue, wealth and poverty, keeping and losing one's temper, laziness, and hard work.

Yet for all its wisdom, Proverbs may well be the most abused book in the Bible. People often quote the proverbs as if they were absolute promises from God or rigid rules for living, when in fact few of them should be read that way. It's best to study the whole book to get its overall point of view on a subject.

The reading plan of this book does not allow time for such in-depth study. However, the preceding sampler of proverbs, all dealing with the power of words, shows how such a study might work. Taken together, these proverbs present a wise, balanced view of conversation. They reveal the explosive power—for good or for evil—of ordinary words. —PY

DAY 132   Ecclesiastes 3:1–22

A TIME FOR EVERYTHING

There is a time for everything,
  and a season for every activity under heaven:

  a time to be born and a time to die,
  a time to plant and a time to uproot,
  a time to kill and a time to heal,
  a time to tear down and a time to build,
  a time to weep and a time to laugh,
  a time to mourn and a time to dance,
  a time to scatter stones and a time to gather them,
  a time to embrace and a time to refrain,
  a time to search and a time to give up,
  a time to keep and a time to throw away,
  a time to tear and a time to mend,
  a time to be silent and a time to speak,
  a time to love and a time to hate,
  a time for war and a time for peace.

What does the worker gain from his toil? I have seen the burden God has laid on men. He has made everything beautiful in its time. He has also set eternity in the hearts of men; yet they cannot fathom what God has done from beginning to end. I know that there is nothing better for men than to be happy and do good while they live. That everyone may eat and drink, and find satisfaction in all his toil—this is the gift of God. I know that everything God does will endure forever; nothing can be added to it and nothing taken from it. God does it so that men will revere him.

Whatever is has already been,
  and what will be has been before;
  and God will call the past to account.

And I saw something else under the sun:

In the place of judgment—wickedness was there,
  in the place of justice—wickedness was there.

  I thought in my heart,

"God will bring to judgment
    both the righteous and the wicked,
for there will be a time for every activity,
    a time for every deed."

I also thought, "As for men, God tests them so that they may see that they are like the animals. Man's fate is like that of the animals; the same fate awaits them both: As one dies, so dies the other. All have the same breath; man has no advantage over the animal. Everything is meaningless. All go to the same place; all come from dust, and to dust all return. Who knows if the spirit of man rises upward and if the spirit of the animal goes down into the earth?"

So I saw that there is nothing better for a man than to enjoy his work, because that is his lot. For who can bring him to see what will happen after him?

People surprised to find a book like Song of Songs in the Bible may be knocked flat by the book of Ecclesiastes. "Meaningless! Meaningless! Everything is meaningless!" cries the author of this bleak capitulation of despair (1:2).

Although Ecclesiastes mentions no author by name, it contains broad hints that King Solomon was, if not its author, then at least its inspiration. It tells the story of the richest, wisest, most famous man in the world, who follows every pleasure impulse as far as it can lead him. This man, "the Teacher," finally collapses in regret and despair; he has squandered his life.

This early chapter gives a capsule summary of the book, beginning with an elegant poem about time and proceeding from there into musings about life typical of the Teacher's search for meaning. The author concludes that God has laid a "burden" on humanity that keeps us from finding ultimate satisfaction on earth. After a lifetime spent in the pursuit of pleasure, the Teacher asks, "Is that all there is?" Even the rare moments of peace and satisfaction he found were easily spoiled by the onrushing threat of death. According to the Teacher, life doesn't make sense outside of God, and will in fact never fully make sense because we are not God.

But God has also "set eternity in the hearts of men." We feel longings for something more: pleasures that will last forever, love that won't go sour, fulfillment, not boredom, from our work.

The Teacher thus dangles between two states, feeling a steady drag toward despair but also a tug toward something higher. Much like a personal journal, the book of Ecclesiastes records his search for balance. The tension does not resolve in this chapter, and some readers wonder if it resolves at all. But Ecclesiastes ends with one final word of advice, the summation of all the Teacher's wisdom: "Fear God and keep his commandments, for this is the whole duty of man" (12:13).   —PY

DAILY CONTEMPLATION

The Teacher is painfully honest about his doubts and his despair. What portions of this chapter do you especially identify with?

KEYS TO BECOMING WISE

Solomon had no corner on wisdom. He may have been the wisest person to live, but he wasn't the only one with wisdom. His father, David, wrote about wisdom before Solomon was born. David in fact gives us the two most important cornerstones for acquiring wisdom: "You teach me wisdom in the inmost place" (Psalm 51:6) and "The statutes of the LORD are trustworthy, making wise the simple" (Psalm 19:7). Wisdom comes straight from God to those in relationship with him, and following God's guidelines for living is the first step in moving from unwise to wise. Another psalmist echoes David's words: "The fear of the LORD is the beginning of wisdom" (Psalm 111:10).

Solomon writes more extensively about wisdom in Proverbs. He affirms that yes, "the LORD gives wisdom" (Proverbs 2:6). It was through his own request to God that he had received his wisdom. Then he gives several attitudes and actions that are key in gaining wisdom. The first involves humility. "With humility comes wisdom," he says (Proverbs 11:12). People who are quick to promote themselves aren't wise and won't become wise. When we're concerned with elevating ourselves in the eyes of others, we aim to determine our own destiny rather than letting God determine it, and this desire can never walk hand in hand with wisdom.

Solomon also writes about accepting advice and correction: "Wisdom is found in those who take advice" (Proverbs 13:10); "The rod of correction imparts wisdom" (Proverbs 29:15). When we're willing and able to accept wisdom from others, through both advice and criticism, we'll gain it much more quickly than in trying to find it on our own.

People in our lives play a big role in making us wise or unwise. The choices we make in friends and in how we allot our time reflect how concerned we are with gaining wisdom. "He who walks with the wise grows wise," Solomon says (Proverbs 13:20). The people with whom we surround ourselves impact who we become. For example, it is those who know Jesus intimately who will carry us into greater wisdom through him.

The way we interact with people in our lives provides another key to wisdom. The words we use, the things we say, usher us deeper into wisdom or farther from it. Spouting off at the mouth usually results in regret. But when we choose our words carefully, knowing the impact they can have on other people and ourselves, we're displaying a heart that desires wisdom. "A wise man's heart guides his mouth," Solomon says (Proverbs 16:23).

Where we place our energy and commitment represents the final key to wisdom. "He who wins souls is wise," Solomon says (Proverbs 11:30). This is the final evidence of one who wants the things Jesus wants, who desires the same outlook on life he has. We can choose to focus our lives on ourselves and our interests or on God and his interests, which involve other people. If we focus on God, we will make time for those who need to know Jesus. For a person growing in wisdom, this becomes a passion that is never quenched.

According to David and Solomon, wisdom can be had by all who seek it in the right way, regardless of age. It's never too late. "Wisdom is supreme" and "more precious than rubies," says Solomon (Proverbs 4:7; 8:11). Who wouldn't want to find it? Only the unwise. —BQ

DAILY CONTEMPLATION

Where are you in possessing Solomon's keys to wisdom? Do you need to ask God for wisdom or for a commitment to his guidelines? Do you need to work on being humble, accepting advice or criticism, finding wise friends, controlling your words? How much do you care about drawing other people to Jesus? Ask God to help you move further toward wisdom.

DAY 134
1 Kings 12:1–24

ISRAEL REBELS AGAINST REHOBOAM

Rehoboam went to Shechem, for all the Israelites had gone there to make him king. When Jeroboam son of Nebat heard this (he was still in Egypt, where he had fled from King Solomon), he returned from Egypt. So they sent for Jeroboam, and he and the whole assembly of Israel went to Rehoboam and said to him: "Your father put a heavy yoke on us, but now lighten the harsh labor and the heavy yoke he put on us, and we will serve you."

Rehoboam answered, "Go away for three days and then come back to me." So the people went away.

Then King Rehoboam consulted the elders who had served his father Solomon during his lifetime. "How would you advise me to answer these people?" he asked.

They replied, "If today you will be a servant to these people and serve them and give them a favorable answer, they will always be your servants."

But Rehoboam rejected the advice the elders gave him and consulted the young men who had grown up with him and were serving him. He asked them, "What is your advice? How should we answer these people who say to me, 'Lighten the yoke your father put on us'?"

The young men who had grown up with him replied, "Tell these people who have said to you, 'Your father put a heavy yoke on us, but make our yoke lighter'—tell them, 'My little finger is thicker than my father's waist. My father laid on you a heavy yoke; I will make it even heavier. My father scourged you with whips; I will scourge you with scorpions.'"

Three days later Jeroboam and all the people returned to Rehoboam, as the king had said, "Come back to me in three days." The king answered the people harshly. Rejecting the advice given him by the elders, he followed the advice of the young men and said, "My father made your yoke heavy; I will make it even heavier. My father scourged you with whips; I will scourge you with scorpions." So the king did not listen to the people, for this turn of events was from the LORD, to fulfill the word the LORD had spoken to Jeroboam son of Nebat through Ahijah the Shilonite.

When all Israel saw that the king refused to listen to them, they answered the king:

> "What share do we have in David,
>   what part in Jesse's son?
> To your tents, O Israel!
>   Look after your own house, O David!"

So the Israelites went home. But as for the Israelites who were living in the towns of Judah, Rehoboam still ruled over them.

King Rehoboam sent out Adoniram, who was in charge of forced labor, but all Israel stoned him to death. King Rehoboam, however, managed to get into his chariot and escape to Jerusalem. So Israel has been in rebellion against the house of David to this day.

When all the Israelites heard that Jeroboam had returned, they sent and called him to the assembly and made him king over all Israel. Only the tribe of Judah remained loyal to the house of David.

When Rehoboam arrived in Jerusalem, he mustered the whole house of Judah and the tribe of Benjamin—a hundred and eighty thousand fighting men—to make war against the house of Israel and to regain the kingdom for Rehoboam son of Solomon.

But this word of God came to Shemaiah the man of God: "Say to Rehoboam son of Solomon king of Judah, to the whole house of Judah and Benjamin, and to the rest of the people, 'This is what the LORD says: Do not go up to fight against your brothers, the Israelites. Go home, every one of you, for this is my doing.'" So they obeyed the word of the LORD and went home again, as the LORD had ordered.

Under the leadership of David and Solomon, the nation of Israel finally becomes strong and prosperous. But even in their success, the twelve tribes display ongoing antagonism. Jealousy over land allotments, and claims of superiority, threaten to split them apart. And in the end Solomon's weaknesses seriously erode the kingdom. His lavish public projects lay a heavy tax burden on the citizens of Israel and force him to conscript some of them as virtual slaves. His moral failures undermine the spiritual unity of the nation, and the brief, shining vision of a covenant nation gradually fades away. After Solomon's death, Israel splits in two in 931 B.C. and slides toward ruin.

In a story reminiscent of Saul and David's early days, God makes known through a prophet his intentions to remove part of the kingdom of Israel from the hands of Rehoboam (REE-huh-BOH-uhm), Solomon's son and rightful heir to the throne, and give it to Jeroboam (JAIR-uh-BOH-uhm), a palace official. Like David, Jeroboam must go on the run after receiving the prophecy, because Solomon tries to kill him. When

Solomon dies, the prophecy comes true. Rehoboam's greed for power turns all but the southern tribes of Judah and Benjamin against him. Jeroboam is crowned king of Israel, the northern kingdom, and Rehoboam rules over the southern kingdom of Judah.   —BQ

DAILY CONTEMPLATION

Are you more focused on outward success, as was Rehoboam, or on the growth of your inner life with God?

PART 3

THE NORTHERN KINGDOM—ISRAEL

DAY 135   1 Kings 17:1–24

THE WIDOW AT ZAREPHATH

Now Elijah the Tishbite, from Tishbe in Gilead, said to Ahab, "As the LORD, the God of Israel, lives, whom I serve, there will be neither dew nor rain in the next few years except at my word."

Then the word of the LORD came to Elijah: "Leave here, turn eastward and hide in the Kerith Ravine, east of the Jordan. You will drink from the brook, and I have ordered the ravens to feed you there."

So he did what the LORD had told him. He went to the Kerith Ravine, east of the Jordan, and stayed there. The ravens brought him bread and meat in the morning and bread and meat in the evening, and he drank from the brook.

Some time later the brook dried up because there had been no rain in the land. Then the word of the LORD came to him: "Go at once to Zarephath of Sidon and stay there. I have commanded a widow in that place to supply you with food." So he went to Zarephath. When he came to the town gate, a widow was there gathering sticks. He called to her and asked, "Would you bring me a little water in a jar so I may have a drink?" As she was going to get it, he called, "And bring me, please, a piece of bread."

"As surely as the LORD your God lives," she replied, "I don't have any bread—only a handful of flour in a jar and a little oil in a jug. I am gathering a few sticks to take home and make a meal for myself and my son, that we may eat it—and die."

Elijah said to her, "Don't be afraid. Go home and do as you have said. But first make a small cake of bread for me from what you have and bring it to me, and then make something for yourself and your son. For this is what the LORD, the God of Israel, says: 'The jar of flour will not be used up and the jug of oil will not run dry until the day the LORD gives rain on the land.'"

She went away and did as Elijah had told her. So there was food every day for Elijah and for the woman and her family. For the jar of flour was not used up and the jug of oil did not run dry, in keeping with the word of the LORD spoken by Elijah.

Some time later the son of the woman who owned the house became ill. He grew worse and worse, and finally stopped breathing. She said to Elijah, "What do you have against me, man of God? Did you come to remind me of my sin and kill my son?"

"Give me your son," Elijah replied. He took him from her arms, carried him to the upper room where he was staying, and laid him on his bed. Then he cried out to the LORD, "O LORD my God, have you brought tragedy also upon this widow I am staying with, by causing her son to die?" Then he stretched himself out on the boy three times and cried to the LORD, "O LORD my God, let this boy's life return to him!"

The LORD heard Elijah's cry, and the boy's life returned to him, and he lived. Elijah picked up the child and carried him down from the room into the house. He gave him to his mother and said, "Look, your son is alive!"

Then the woman said to Elijah, "Now I know that you are a man of God and that the word of the LORD from your mouth is the truth."

Israel has split into the northern and southern kingdoms of Israel and Judah. The remaining part of the Old Testament can prove especially confusing: the two nations will have thirty-nine rulers between them, and a couple dozen prophets besides. To avoid getting hopelessly lost, keep these basic facts in mind: *Israel* is the breakaway northern kingdom, with a capital city of Samaria. All its rulers will prove unfaithful to God. *Judah* is the southern kingdom, with its capital in Jerusalem. In general its rulers, descendants of David, will remain more faithful to God and his covenant, and consequently Judah survives 136 years longer.

Although the Bible discusses all thirty-nine rulers by name, after Solomon stories of the kings speed up into a forgettable blur. God turns instead to his prophets.

Elijah, the wildest and woolliest prophet of all, first makes an appearance in this chapter. He illustrates better than anyone else the decisive change: where King Solomon had worn jewelry and fine clothes and lived luxuriously in a gilded palace, Elijah wears a diaper-like covering of black camel's hair, sleeps in the wilderness, and has to beg—or pray—for handouts. He comes on the scene when Israel (the northern kingdom) is thriving politically but floundering spiritually. Queen Jezebel has just launched a murderous campaign to eliminate all true prophets of God and replace them with a thousand handpicked pagan priests.

This chapter shows glimpses of Elijah during his fugitive days. Although he is a moody prophet, subject to bouts of depression and self-doubt, he clearly has God on his side. The tender story of his healing of a widow's son shows that God has not forgotten the "little people." The salvation of Israel will depend on how well they listen to prophets like Elijah.

—PY

DAILY CONTEMPLATION

How has God reminded you this week that he cares about what matters to you?

DAY 136   1 Kings 18:15–40

ELIJAH ON MOUNT CARMEL

Elijah said, "As the LORD Almighty lives, whom I serve, I will surely present myself to Ahab today."

So Obadiah went to meet Ahab and told him, and Ahab went to meet Elijah. When he saw Elijah, he said to him, "Is that you, you troubler of Israel?"

"I have not made trouble for Israel," Elijah replied. "But you and your father's family have. You have abandoned the LORD's commands and have followed the Baals. Now summon the people from all over Israel to meet me on Mount Carmel. And bring the four hundred and fifty prophets of Baal and the four hundred prophets of Asherah, who eat at Jezebel's table."

So Ahab sent word throughout all Israel and assembled the prophets on Mount Carmel. Elijah went before the people and said, "How long will you waver between two opinions? If the LORD is God, follow him; but if Baal is God, follow him."

But the people said nothing.

Then Elijah said to them, "I am the only one of the LORD's prophets left, but Baal has four hundred and fifty prophets. Get two bulls for us. Let them choose one for themselves, and let them cut it into pieces and put it on the wood but not set fire to it. I will prepare the other bull and put it on the wood but not set fire to it. Then you call on the name of your god, and I will call on the name of the LORD. The god who answers by fire—he is God."

Then all the people said, "What you say is good."

Elijah said to the prophets of Baal, "Choose one of the bulls and prepare it first, since there are so many of you. Call on the name of your god, but do not light the fire." So they took the bull given them and prepared it.

Then they called on the name of Baal from morning till noon. "O Baal, answer us!" they shouted. But there was no response; no one answered. And they danced around the altar they had made.

At noon Elijah began to taunt them. "Shout louder!" he said. "Surely he is a god! Perhaps he is deep in thought, or busy, or traveling. Maybe he is sleeping and must be awakened." So they shouted louder and slashed themselves with swords and spears, as was their custom, until their blood flowed. Midday passed, and they continued their frantic prophesying until the time for the evening sacrifice. But there was no response, no one answered, no one paid attention.

Then Elijah said to all the people, "Come here to me." They came to him, and he repaired the altar of the LORD, which was in ruins. Elijah took twelve stones, one for each of the tribes descended from Jacob, to whom the word of the LORD had come, saying, "Your name shall be Israel." With the stones he built an altar in the name of the LORD, and he dug a trench around it large enough to hold two seahs of seed. He arranged the wood, cut the bull into pieces and laid it on the wood. Then he said to them, "Fill four large jars with water and pour it on the offering and on the wood."

"Do it again," he said, and they did it again.

"Do it a third time," he ordered, and they did it the third time. The water ran down around the altar and even filled the trench.

At the time of sacrifice, the prophet Elijah stepped forward and prayed: "O LORD, God of Abraham, Isaac and Israel, let it be known today that you are God in Israel and that I am your servant and have done all these things at your command. Answer me, O LORD, answer me, so these people will know that you, O LORD, are God, and that you are turning their hearts back again."

Then the fire of the LORD fell and burned up the sacrifice, the wood, the stones and the soil, and also licked up the water in the trench.

When all the people saw this, they fell prostrate and cried, "The LORD—he is God! The LORD—he is God!"

Then Elijah commanded them, "Seize the prophets of Baal. Don't let anyone get away!" They seized them, and Elijah had them brought down to the Kishon Valley and slaughtered there.

In ancient Africa, tribes would sometimes fight their battles single-combat style. Great armies lined up across from each other, waving their weapons menacingly and hurling insults back and forth. When tribal hatred reached a kind of critical mass, two warriors—only two—stepped forward to fight on behalf of all the rest. Whoever drew first blood would prove the gods were on his side, and his opponent's army would surrender. Something like single-combat warfare takes place at a moment of deep crisis in Israel. As usual, the prophet Elijah occupies center stage.

Elijah journeys across Israel to a rugged mountain to confront his pagan enemies. Few scenes in history can match the one that transpires on windswept Mount Carmel (KAR-muhl). On one side stands a resplendent array of 850 prophets of Baal and Asherah (uh-SHEER-uh); on the other stands a lone, bedraggled desert prophet of God. Elijah lets the pagan prophets have first turn. As they dance around an altar beseeching their gods, he sits back, enjoys the show, and taunts them to frenzy. "Maybe your god is traveling, or sleeping," he yells, and the priests slash themselves with swords until the blood runs.

Elijah may be outnumbered, but he proves a worthy adversary. When his time comes, he works the crowd like a master magician. He stacks the odds against a miracle by dousing the site with twelve large jars of water—the most precious commodity in Israel after a three-year drought. Just when it seems Elijah is perpetrating a huge national joke, the miracle happens: fire falls from heaven. The crowd drops to the ground in fear and awe. The heat is enough to melt even the stones and soil, and flames lick water from the trenches as if it were fuel.

Elijah's very name means "The Lord is my God," and, in the final analysis, the showdown on Mount Carmel is no contest at all. Elijah goes on to orchestrate one of the greatest outbreaks of miracles in biblical history. It is as if God is sounding a loud, unmistakable final warning to the North—a warning they fail to heed.   —PY

DAILY CONTEMPLATION

In Old Testament times God was known to reveal himself in occasional spectacular public displays. Even if his power in your life hasn't been as showy, can you think of one instance in which it was clear to you that God was moving against all odds?

DAY 137   1 Kings 19:1–18

THE LORD APPEARS TO ELIJAH

Now Ahab told Jezebel everything Elijah had done and how he had killed all the prophets with the sword. So Jezebel sent a messenger to Elijah to say, "May the gods deal with me, be it ever so severely, if by this time tomorrow I do not make your life like that of one of them."

Elijah was afraid and ran for his life. When he came to Beersheba in Judah, he left his servant there, while he himself went a day's journey into the desert. He came to a broom tree, sat down under it and prayed that he might die. "I have had enough, LORD," he said. "Take my life; I am no better than my ancestors." Then he lay down under the tree and fell asleep.

All at once an angel touched him and said, "Get up and eat." He looked around, and there by his head was a cake of bread baked over hot coals, and a jar of water. He ate and drank and then lay down again.

The angel of the LORD came back a second time and touched him and said, "Get up and eat, for the journey is too much for you." So he got up and ate and drank. Strengthened by that food, he traveled forty days and forty nights until he reached Horeb, the mountain of God. There he went into a cave and spent the night.

And the word of the LORD came to him: "What are you doing here, Elijah?"

He replied, "I have been very zealous for the LORD God Almighty. The Israelites have rejected your covenant, broken down your altars, and put your prophets to death with the sword. I am the only one left, and now they are trying to kill me too."

The LORD said, "Go out and stand on the mountain in the presence of the LORD, for the LORD is about to pass by."

Then a great and powerful wind tore the mountains apart and shattered the rocks before the LORD, but the LORD was not in the wind. After the wind there was an earthquake, but the LORD was not in the earthquake. After the earthquake came a fire, but the LORD was not in the fire. And after the fire came a gentle whisper. When Elijah heard it, he pulled his cloak over his face and went out and stood at the mouth of the cave.

Then a voice said to him, "What are you doing here, Elijah?"

He replied, "I have been very zealous for the LORD God Almighty. The Israelites have rejected your covenant, broken down your altars, and put your prophets to death with the sword. I am the only one left, and now they are trying to kill me too."

The LORD said to him, "Go back the way you came, and go to the Desert of Damascus. When you get there, anoint Hazael king over Aram. Also, anoint Jehu son of Nimshi king over Israel, and anoint Elisha son of Shaphat from Abel Meholah to succeed you as prophet. Jehu will put to death any who escape the sword of Hazael, and Elisha will put to death any who escape the sword of Jehu. Yet I reserve seven thousand in Israel—all whose knees have not bowed down to Baal and all whose mouths have not kissed him."

Despite God's clear display of power on Mount Carmel, Elijah becomes terrified when Ahab's (AY-hab) wife Jezebel vows to kill him. God has just rained down fire from heaven and brought about the slaughter of hundreds of Baal prophets, but Elijah is emotionally drained and when the threat comes, it looms larger than the obvious truth of God's greater power. Elijah loves God and has been faithful in carrying out God's work, but even this great man falters in his faith. Letting fear take hold, on impulse he sets out on a long and unnecessary journey.

Nevertheless, God acts tenderly toward Elijah, even sending an angel to care for his needs. "Get up and eat. The journey is too much for you"—God gently nourishes one who in his weakness has become exhausted. In a journey that should have taken only fourteen days on foot, Elijah travels for forty, with God sustaining him along the way.

When he arrives at Mount Horeb—the mountain where God revealed himself to Moses and formed a covenant with Israel—Elijah reveals that he feels alone in his loyalty to God. He has seen other prophets of God killed and feels sure he will be next. His vision is still one-sided. The great victories God has wrought through Elijah have become buried under feelings of fear and failure. This time God speaks not through a startling event but through a quiet whisper. Elijah has seen God's spectacular displays; now he needs to hear God's gentle voice. God will use Elijah in new ways—ways that will be easier on the prophet and will continue to reassure him of his place as God's loved servant.

—BQ

DAILY CONTEMPLATION

When have you needed God to pick you up and care for you?

ELIJAH TAKEN UP TO HEAVEN

When the LORD was about to take Elijah up to heaven in a whirlwind, Elijah and Elisha were on their way from Gilgal. Elijah said to Elisha, "Stay here; the LORD has sent me to Bethel."

But Elisha said, "As surely as the LORD lives and as you live, I will not leave you." So they went down to Bethel.

The company of the prophets at Bethel came out to Elisha and asked, "Do you know that the LORD is going to take your master from you today?"

"Yes, I know," Elisha replied, "but do not speak of it."

Then Elijah said to him, "Stay here, Elisha; the LORD has sent me to Jericho."

And he replied, "As surely as the LORD lives and as you live, I will not leave you." So they went to Jericho.

The company of the prophets at Jericho went up to Elisha and asked him, "Do you know that the LORD is going to take your master from you today?"

"Yes, I know," he replied, "but do not speak of it."

Then Elijah said to him, "Stay here; the LORD has sent me to the Jordan."

And he replied, "As surely as the LORD lives and as you live, I will not leave you." So the two of them walked on.

Fifty men of the company of the prophets went and stood at a distance, facing the place where Elijah and Elisha had stopped at the Jordan. Elijah took his cloak, rolled it up and struck the water with it. The water divided to the right and to the left, and the two of them crossed over on dry ground.

When they had crossed, Elijah said to Elisha, "Tell me, what can I do for you before I am taken from you?"

"Let me inherit a double portion of your spirit," Elisha replied.

"You have asked a difficult thing," Elijah said, "yet if you see me when I am taken from you, it will be yours—otherwise not."

As they were walking along and talking together, suddenly a chariot of fire and horses of fire appeared and separated the two of them, and Elijah went up to heaven in a whirlwind. Elisha saw this and cried out, "My father! My father! The chariots and horsemen of Israel!" And Elisha saw him no more. Then he took hold of his own clothes and tore them apart.

He picked up the cloak that had fallen from Elijah and went back and stood on the bank of the Jordan. Then he took the cloak that had fallen from him and struck the water with it. "Where now is the LORD, the God of Elijah?" he asked. When he struck the water, it divided to the right and to the left, and he crossed over.

The company of the prophets from Jericho, who were watching, said, "The spirit of Elijah is resting on Elisha." And they went to meet him and bowed to the ground before him. "Look," they said, "we your servants have fifty able men.

Let them go and look for your master. Perhaps the Spirit of the LORD has picked him up and set him down on some mountain or in some valley."

"No," Elisha replied, "do not send them."

But they persisted until he was too ashamed to refuse. So he said, "Send them." And they sent fifty men, who searched for three days but did not find him. When they returned to Elisha, who was staying in Jericho, he said to them, "Didn't I tell you not to go?"

God had given Elijah and Elisha to one another as teacher and student and as partners who could support each other. The time, however, has come for Elijah to leave the earth and for Elisha to carry on his ministry. Only once before has God taken someone to heaven apart from death. Enoch was the first (Genesis 5:24). Now in a show of honor for a prophet who has served God well through a period of Israel's idolatry, God sends escorts to carry Elijah into his presence.

Elisha, a devoted spiritual son, takes up Elijah's deserted cloak and assumes the mantle of God-given authority that has passed to him. Having seen Elijah's departure, he now receives the double portion of his spirit as promised.　　—BQ

DAILY CONTEMPLATION

Whom has God placed in your life as a support and spiritual partner?

DAY 139 　　　　　　　　　　　　　　　　　　Reflection

HEARING GOD'S VOICE

At times Elijah acted without any apparent indication that he heard God's voice. He simply seemed to know what God wanted him to do. He told the widow her flour would not run out. He called on God to send fire from heaven and consume the altar. Both were clearly God's will. At other times God spoke clearly and directly to Elijah. He heard God's audible voice question him in a cave, and later God merely whispered to him. Elijah heard God speak in many ways. Was he specially gifted, or can anyone who walks with God expect to hear him clearly?

In *The Christian's Secret of a Happy Life,* Hannah Whitall Smith teaches that beyond a doubt we can still hear God's voice. Smith explains that God speaks through the Scriptures, providential circumstances, the convictions of our higher judgment, and the inward impressions of the Holy Spirit on our minds. "His voice will always be in harmony with itself, no matter how many different ways he may speak," she explains. "The voices may be many, the message can be but one. If God tells me in one voice to do or to leave undone anything, He cannot possibly tell me the opposite in another voice. If there is a contradiction in the voices, the speakers cannot be the same."[8]

The Bible gives us guidance on much of what we will encounter in life. As we become familiar with the Bible, we can make decisions that fall in line with God's voice found there. Smith gives one caution: "It is essential, however, in this connection to remember that the Bible is a book of principles, and not a book of disjointed aphorisms. Isolated texts may often be made to sanction things to which the principles of Scripture are totally opposed."[9]

Sometimes we will feel a need for more specific direction than what the Bible can provide. Then we must look also at how our circumstances are working to lead us one way or another, at our common sense "enlightened by the Spirit of God," and at any strong sense the Holy Spirit seems to be impressing upon us. "If any one of these tests fail, it is not safe to proceed, but you must wait in quiet trust until the Lord shows you the point of harmony, which He surely will, sooner or later, if it is His voice that is speaking."[10]

Smith reminds us that sometimes we will hear voices other than God's. These could come from the strong opinions of others around us, from our own moodiness or emotional state, or from spiritual enemies who would like to mislead us. We don't need to fear these voices, but we should be careful about letting them guide us. It's important to take time to discern whether we indeed hear God's voice.

We can trust God to make his voice clear if we are willing to hear it and to be patient in waiting until God makes us sure. "Take all your present perplexities, then, to the Lord. Tell Him you only want to know and obey His voice, and ask Him to make it plain to you. Promise Him that you will obey, whatever it may be. Believe implicitly that He is guiding you, according to His word. In all doubtful things, wait for clear light. Look and listen for His voice continually; and the moment you are sure of it, then, but not until then, yield an immediate obedience. Trust Him to make you forget the impression if it is not His will; and if it continues, and is in harmony with all His other voices, do not be afraid to obey."[11]　　　—BQ

DAILY CONTEMPLATION

In which areas of your life do you need to hear God's voice? Ask God to help you hear him clearly and then to obey him completely.

DAY 140   2 Kings 4:1–36

THE WIDOW'S OIL; THE SHUNAMMITE'S

SON RESTORED TO LIFE

The wife of a man from the company of the prophets cried out to Elisha, "Your servant my husband is dead, and you know that he revered the LORD. But now his creditor is coming to take my two boys as his slaves."

Elisha replied to her, "How can I help you? Tell me, what do you have in your house?"

"Your servant has nothing there at all," she said, "except a little oil."

Elisha said, "Go around and ask all your neighbors for empty jars. Don't ask for just a few. Then go inside and shut the door behind you and your sons. Pour oil into all the jars, and as each is filled, put it to one side."

She left him and afterward shut the door behind her and her sons. They brought the jars to her and she kept pouring. When all the jars were full, she said to her son, "Bring me another one."

But he replied, "There is not a jar left." Then the oil stopped flowing.

She went and told the man of God, and he said, "Go, sell the oil and pay your debts. You and your sons can live on what is left."

One day Elisha went to Shunem. And a well-to-do woman was there, who urged him to stay for a meal. So whenever he came by, he stopped there to eat. She said to her husband, "I know that this man who often comes our way is a holy man of God. Let's make a small room on the roof and put in it a bed and a table, a chair and a lamp for him. Then he can stay there whenever he comes to us."

One day when Elisha came, he went up to his room and lay down there. He said to his servant Gehazi, "Call the Shunammite." So he called her, and she stood before him. Elisha said to him, "Tell her, 'You have gone to all this trouble for us. Now what can be done for you? Can we speak on your behalf to the king or the commander of the army?'"

She replied, "I have a home among my own people."

"What can be done for her?" Elisha asked.

Gehazi said, "Well, she has no son and her husband is old."

Then Elisha said, "Call her." So he called her, and she stood in the doorway. "About this time next year," Elisha said, "you will hold a son in your arms."

"No, my lord," she objected. "Don't mislead your servant, O man of God!"

But the woman became pregnant, and the next year about that same time she gave birth to a son, just as Elisha had told her.

The child grew, and one day he went out to his father, who was with the reapers. "My head! My head!" he said to his father.

His father told a servant, "Carry him to his mother." After the servant had lifted him up and carried him to his mother, the boy sat on her lap until noon, and then he died. She went up and laid him on the bed of the man of God, then shut the door and went out.

She called her husband and said, "Please send me one of the servants and a donkey so I can go to the man of God quickly and return."

"Why go to him today?" he asked. "It's not the New Moon or the Sabbath."

"It's all right," she said.

She saddled the donkey and said to her servant, "Lead on; don't slow down for me unless I tell you." So she set out and came to the man of God at Mount Carmel.

When he saw her in the distance, the man of God said to his servant Gehazi, "Look! There's the Shunammite! Run to meet her and ask her, 'Are you all right? Is your husband all right? Is your child all right?'"

"Everything is all right," she said.

When she reached the man of God at the mountain, she took hold of his feet. Gehazi came over to push her away, but the man of God said, "Leave her alone! She is in bitter distress, but the LORD has hidden it from me and has not told me why."

"Did I ask you for a son, my lord?" she said. "Didn't I tell you, 'Don't raise my hopes'?"

Elisha said to Gehazi, "Tuck your cloak into your belt, take my staff in your hand and run. If you meet anyone, do not greet him, and if anyone greets you, do not answer. Lay my staff on the boy's face."

But the child's mother said, "As surely as the LORD lives and as you live, I will not leave you." So he got up and followed her.

Gehazi went on ahead and laid the staff on the boy's face, but there was no sound or response. So Gehazi went back to meet Elisha and told him, "The boy has not awakened."

When Elisha reached the house, there was the boy lying dead on his couch. He went in, shut the door on the two of them and prayed to the LORD. Then he got on the bed and lay upon the boy, mouth to mouth, eyes to eyes, hands to hands. As he stretched himself out upon him, the boy's body grew warm. Elisha turned away and walked back and forth in the room and then got on the bed and stretched out upon him once more. The boy sneezed seven times and opened his eyes.

Elisha summoned Gehazi and said, "Call the Shunammite." And he did. When she came, he said, "Take your son."

Today's stories demonstrate God's love for those who remain faithful to him in Israel. Although much of the nation has turned to Baal worship, some continue following God and honoring his prophets. God clearly cares for women, who were considered inferior in most Near Eastern societies of the time. God holds no gender bias in his concern for those who honor him.

In these stories both women demonstrate a strong faith in God's power to help them. The first, a widow, is doubly in need. Not only does she lack a husband to provide for her; she is the widow of a prophet and has been left with little. God provides in a way neither she nor anyone around her would have guessed.

The second woman, a Shunammite, professes her faith in God at a moment of crisis. She feels deceived and disappointed at receiving a son only to lose him again, yet she knows that God is greater than her disappointment. Even in her grief she acts on her belief. Most likely, the Shunammite woman's story of her son's birth and his return to life spread throughout Israel. Once more God shows his sovereignty over the popular Baal, hailed as god of fertility.   —BQ

DAY 141   2 Kings 5:1–27

NAAMAN HEALED OF LEPROSY

Now Naaman was commander of the army of the king of Aram. He was a great man in the sight of his master and highly regarded, because through him the LORD had given victory to Aram. He was a valiant soldier, but he had leprosy.

Now bands from Aram had gone out and had taken captive a young girl from Israel, and she served Naaman's wife. She said to her mistress, "If only my master would see the prophet who is in Samaria! He would cure him of his leprosy."

Naaman went to his master and told him what the girl from Israel had said. "By all means, go," the king of Aram replied. "I will send a letter to the king of Israel." So Naaman left, taking with him ten talents of silver, six thousand shekels of gold and ten sets of clothing. The letter that he took to the king of Israel read: "With this letter I am sending my servant Naaman to you so that you may cure him of his leprosy."

As soon as the king of Israel read the letter, he tore his robes and said, "Am I God? Can I kill and bring back to life? Why does this fellow send someone to me to be cured of his leprosy? See how he is trying to pick a quarrel with me!"

When Elisha the man of God heard that the king of Israel had torn his robes, he sent him this message: "Why have you torn your robes? Have the man come to me and he will know that there is a prophet in Israel." So Naaman went with his horses and chariots and stopped at the door of Elisha's house. Elisha sent a messenger to say to him, "Go, wash yourself seven times in the Jordan, and your flesh will be restored and you will be cleansed."

But Naaman went away angry and said, "I thought that he would surely come out to me and stand and call on the name of the LORD his God, wave his hand over the spot and cure me of my leprosy. Are not Abana and Pharpar, the rivers of Damascus, better than any of the waters of Israel? Couldn't I wash in them and be cleansed?" So he turned and went off in a rage.

Naaman's servants went to him and said, "My father, if the prophet had told you to do some great thing, would you not have done it? How much more, then, when he tells you, 'Wash and be cleansed'!" So he went down and dipped himself in the Jordan seven times, as the man of God had told him, and his flesh was restored and became clean like that of a young boy.

Then Naaman and all his attendants went back to the man of God. He stood before him and said, "Now I know that there is no God in all the world except in Israel. Please accept now a gift from your servant."

The prophet answered, "As surely as the LORD lives, whom I serve, I will not accept a thing." And even though Naaman urged him, he refused.

"If you will not," said Naaman, "please let me, your servant, be given as much earth as a pair of mules can carry, for your servant will never again make burnt offerings and sacrifices to any other god but the LORD. But may the LORD forgive your servant for this one thing: When my master enters the temple of Rimmon to bow down and he is leaning on my arm and I bow there also— when I bow down in the temple of Rimmon, may the LORD forgive your servant for this."

"Go in peace," Elisha said.

After Naaman had traveled some distance, Gehazi, the servant of Elisha the man of God, said to himself, "My master was too easy on Naaman, this Aramean, by not accepting from him what he brought. As surely as the LORD lives, I will run after him and get something from him."

So Gehazi hurried after Naaman. When Naaman saw him running toward him, he got down from the chariot to meet him. "Is everything all right?" he asked.

"Everything is all right," Gehazi answered. "My master sent me to say, 'Two young men from the company of the prophets have just come to me from the hill country of Ephraim. Please give them a talent of silver and two sets of clothing.'"

"By all means, take two talents," said Naaman. He urged Gehazi to accept them, and then tied up the two talents of silver in two bags, with two sets of clothing. He gave them to two of his servants, and they carried them ahead of Gehazi. When Gehazi came to the hill, he took the things from the servants and put them away in the house. He sent the men away and they left. Then he went in and stood before his master Elisha.

"Where have you been, Gehazi?" Elisha asked.

"Your servant didn't go anywhere," Gehazi answered.

But Elisha said to him, "Was not my spirit with you when the man got down from his chariot to meet you? Is this the time to take money, or to accept clothes, olive groves, vineyards, flocks, herds, or menservants and maidservants? Naaman's leprosy will cling to you and to your descendants forever." Then Gehazi went from Elisha's presence and he was leprous, as white as snow.

While Elijah was a loner, and often a fugitive, and preached a stern message of judgment, Elisha lives among common people and stresses life, hope, and God's grace.

Elisha lives a colorful life: he leads a school of prophets, serves as a military spy, advises kings, and even anoints revolutionaries. Easily recognizable with his bald head and wooden walking staff, he becomes a famous figure in Israel, especially as reports of his miracles spread. Elisha asked for a double portion of Elijah's spirit, and the Bible pointedly records about twice as many miracles performed by Elisha. Many of these miracles prefigure the miracles Jesus himself will later perform; they show God caring for the needs of poor and outcast people.

In this chapter Elisha is seen offering assistance to a high-ranking enemy general. Naaman's (NAY-uh-muhn) pilgrimage shows how far Elisha's fame has spread. A pagan king agrees to seek help from God's prophet in order to get a general's health restored.

Elisha's brusque treatment of generals and kings contrasts sharply with the tenderness he shows toward the poor and oppressed. The bizarre procedure he prescribes, along with his refusal to take payment, offends Naaman. Elisha, however, is making it clear that healing comes not through magical powers or a shaman's secret technique but through God—and God requires obedience and humility even of five-star generals with piles of gold.

Jesus will refer to this story at the beginning of his ministry (Luke 4:27). He makes the same point as Elisha: Don't try to "box in" God. He is to be obeyed, on his own terms, not manipulated. —PY

DAILY CONTEMPLATION

One writer has defined the Christian life as "living by God's surprises." Has God ever surprised you?

DAY 142   2 Kings 6:8–23

ELISHA AND THE CHARIOTS OF FIRE

Now the king of Aram was at war with Israel. After conferring with his officers, he said, "I will set up my camp in such and such a place."

The man of God sent word to the king of Israel: "Beware of passing that place, because the Arameans are going down there." So the king of Israel checked on the place indicated by the man of God. Time and again Elisha warned the king, so that he was on his guard in such places.

This enraged the king of Aram. He summoned his officers and demanded of them, "Will you not tell me which of us is on the side of the king of Israel?"

"None of us, my lord the king," said one of his officers, "but Elisha, the prophet who is in Israel, tells the king of Israel the very words you speak in your bedroom."

"Go, find out where he is," the king ordered, "so I can send men and capture him." The report came back: "He is in Dothan." Then he sent horses and chariots and a strong force there. They went by night and surrounded the city.

When the servant of the man of God got up and went out early the next morning, an army with horses and chariots had surrounded the city. "Oh, my lord, what shall we do?" the servant asked.

"Don't be afraid," the prophet answered. "Those who are with us are more than those who are with them."

And Elisha prayed, "O LORD, open his eyes so he may see." Then the LORD opened the servant's eyes, and he looked and saw the hills full of horses and chariots of fire all around Elisha.

As the enemy came down toward him, Elisha prayed to the LORD, "Strike these people with blindness." So he struck them with blindness, as Elisha had asked.

Elisha told them, "This is not the road and this is not the city. Follow me, and I will lead you to the man you are looking for." And he led them to Samaria.

After they entered the city, Elisha said, "LORD, open the eyes of these men so they can see." Then the LORD opened their eyes and they looked, and there they were, inside Samaria.

When the king of Israel saw them, he asked Elisha, "Shall I kill them, my father? Shall I kill them?"

"Do not kill them," he answered. "Would you kill men you have captured with your own sword or bow? Set food and water before them so that they may eat and drink and then go back to their master." So he prepared a great feast for them, and after they had finished eating and drinking, he sent them away, and they returned to their master. So the bands from Aram stopped raiding Israel's territory.

Israel and its neighbor Aram (AIR-uhm) were sometimes at war with each other and other times at peace during Elisha's ministry. God uses even wartime to make himself known to the nations. Through Elisha, God has miraculously reversed a widow's financial situation, brought life to a childless woman and a dead boy, and healed a man from leprosy. Now he blinds an entire army and sends them home in peace after treating them to a feast. In a passage that speaks of no one by name except Elisha and the Lord, we see God demonstrating once more that his presence is greater than any other force.

In most cases we do not have eyes to see the army from heaven aligned for us as we encounter battles, but this time Elisha's servant gets a moment's glimpse into that spiritual reality. Upon seeing the horses and chariots of fire, he watches as God routs the opposing army and even blesses them before peacefully sending them home. God has once again kept watch over his people and spared many lives. Through Elisha he reveals his power and his love to his children again and again, desiring as always to draw them once more to his side. —BQ

DAILY CONTEMPLATION

What battle have you faced in the past in which God came through in a powerful way?

GREATER IS GOD IN US

Jim Cymbala, longtime pastor of the Brooklyn Tabernacle in New York City, tells a story of his cry to God in the early days of the church. He had just begun as substitute pastor to this small, inner-city congregation—if you could call it a congregation. Services drew about twenty people, most of whom were poor and some vagrant. He tells of the church's lack of funds to pay the mortgage his first month there.

That Monday, my day off, I remember praying, "Lord, you have to help me. I don't know much—but I do know that we have to pay this mortgage."

I went to church on Tuesday. *Well, maybe someone will send some money out of the blue,* I told myself, *like what happened so often with George Mueller and his orphanage back in England—he just prayed and a letter or a visitor would arrive to meet his need.*

The mail came that day—and there was nothing but bills and fliers.

Now I was trapped. I went upstairs, sat at my little desk, put my head down, and began to cry. "God," I sobbed, "what can I do? We can't even pay the mortgage." . . .

I called out to the Lord for a full hour or so. Eventually, I dried my tears— and a new thought came. *Wait a minute! Besides the mail slot in the front door, the church also has a post office box. I'll go across the street and see what's there. Surely God will answer my prayer!*

With renewed confidence, I walked across the street, crossed the post office lobby, and twirled the knob on the little box. I peered inside . . .

Nothing.

As I stepped back into the sunshine, trucks roared down Atlantic Avenue. If one had flattened me just then, I wouldn't have felt any lower. Was God abandoning us? Was I doing something that displeased him? I trudged wearily back across the street to the little building.

As I unlocked the door, I was met with another surprise. There on the foyer floor was something that hadn't been there just three minutes earlier: a simple white envelope. No address, no stamp—nothing. Just a white envelope.

With trembling hands I opened it to find . . . *two $50 bills.*

I began shouting all by myself in the empty church. "God, you came through! You came through!" We had $160 in the bank, and with this $100 we could make the mortgage payment. My soul let out a deep "Hallelujah!" What a lesson for a disheartened young pastor.

To this day I don't know where that money came from. I only know it was a sign to me that God was near—and faithful.[12]

This miracle was only the beginning for Cymbala. He took on the full-time pastorate of the Brooklyn Tabernacle and in twenty-five years watched God build the church to a congregation of six thousand each Sunday. Money couldn't hold God back. The seemingly hopeless situation of the homeless, drug addicts, prostitutes, and transvestites didn't keep God's Spirit down. Steadily he drew these needy people to himself and to each other to establish a place of healing in the middle of New York City.

"Those who are with us are greater than those who are with them." Satan loves to get us in situations in which hope seems lost. But, like Elisha, we have God's horses and chariots encircling us in the times when we cry out in despair. Next time the cry of Elisha's servant passes your lips—"Oh, Lord, what will I do?"—take a look, in your mind's eye, at the battalion standing ready for you. God's strength is more real than the despair you are feeling. —BQ

Daily Contemplation

What battle do you face? Ask God for help in seeing the forces of heaven that are standing guard and ready to fight for you.

DAY 144   Joel 2:1–2, 10–19

Rend Your Heart

Blow the trumpet in Zion;
    sound the alarm on my holy hill.
Let all who live in the land tremble,
    for the day of the LORD is coming.
It is close at hand—
    a day of darkness and gloom,
    a day of clouds and blackness.
Like dawn spreading across the mountains
    a large and mighty army comes,
such as never was of old
    nor ever will be in ages to come....

Before them the earth shakes,
    the sky trembles,
the sun and moon are darkened,
    and the stars no longer shine.
The LORD thunders
    at the head of his army;
his forces are beyond number,
    and mighty are those who obey his command.
The day of the LORD is great;

it is dreadful.
Who can endure it?

"Even now," declares the LORD,
"return to me with all your heart,
with fasting and weeping and mourning."

Rend your heart
and not your garments.
Return to the LORD your God,
for he is gracious and compassionate,
slow to anger and abounding in love,
and he relents from sending calamity.
Who knows? He may turn and have pity
and leave behind a blessing—
grain offerings and drink offerings
for the LORD your God.

Blow the trumpet in Zion,
declare a holy fast,
call a sacred assembly.
Gather the people,
consecrate the assembly;
bring together the elders,
gather the children,
those nursing at the breast.
Let the bridegroom leave his room
and the bride her chamber.
Let the priests, who minister before the LORD,
weep between the temple porch and the altar.
Let them say, "Spare your people, O LORD.
Do not make your inheritance an object of scorn,
a byword among the nations.
Why should they say among the peoples,
'Where is their God?'"

Then the LORD will be jealous for his land
and take pity on his people.
The LORD will reply to them:
"I am sending you grain, new wine and oil,
enough to satisfy you fully;
never again will I make you
an object of scorn to the nations.

Scenes from the lives of Elijah and Elisha—fire on Mount Carmel, the widow's oil, Naaman's healing, the chariots of fire—are among the most familiar of Old Testament stories. But the prophets who follow them perform few miracles, relying less on spectacular displays of power and more on the power of the Word.

The prophet Joel provides a brief introduction to the style of the writing prophets. No one knows for sure when he delivered his messages—they could have come anywhere within a four-century span. No one is even sure whether he lived in Israel of the north or Judah of the south. But in gripping prose he warns his people of a terrible disaster to come. This chapter captures as well as any the essential message of all the prophets.

A day of judgment. Nearly every prophet begins with words meant to inspire fear and dread. Some warn of invading armies, and some of natural disasters. For example, Joel paints vivid pictures of an army of locusts. The locusts could symbolically represent human armies but may also be taken literally. People who have lived through a locust invasion never forget the experience.

A call to repentance. The prophets raise alarm with good reason, for they see such disasters as a consequence of their nation's unfaithfulness to God. They urgently call on their people to turn from their evil ways. Joel 2:13 could stand as a single, eloquent summary of the heart of the prophets' message.

A future of hope. Every biblical prophet, no matter how dour, gets around to a word of hope. Taken together, they tell of a time when God will make right everything wrong with the earth, a time when The World As It Is will finally match The World As God Wants It.

Joel 2 is a fine capsule summary of this threefold message.   —PY

DAILY CONTEMPLATION

Did you ever rend your heart before God? Do you think this is something a person does once or regularly?

DAY 145   Jonah 1:1–2:10

JONAH FLEES FROM THE LORD

The word of the LORD came to Jonah son of Amittai: "Go to the great city of Nineveh and preach against it, because its wickedness has come up before me."

But Jonah ran away from the LORD and headed for Tarshish. He went down to Joppa, where he found a ship bound for that port. After paying the fare, he went aboard and sailed for Tarshish to flee from the LORD.

Then the LORD sent a great wind on the sea, and such a violent storm arose that the ship threatened to break up. All the sailors were afraid and each cried out to his own god. And they threw the cargo into the sea to lighten the ship.

But Jonah had gone below deck, where he lay down and fell into a deep sleep. The captain went to him and said, "How can you sleep? Get up and call on your god! Maybe he will take notice of us, and we will not perish."

Then the sailors said to each other, "Come, let us cast lots to find out who is responsible for this calamity." They cast lots and the lot fell on Jonah.

So they asked him, "Tell us, who is responsible for making all this trouble for us? What do you do? Where do you come from? What is your country? From what people are you?"

He answered, "I am a Hebrew and I worship the LORD, the God of heaven, who made the sea and the land."

This terrified them and they asked, "What have you done?" (They knew he was running away from the LORD, because he had already told them so.)

The sea was getting rougher and rougher. So they asked him, "What should we do to you to make the sea calm down for us?"

"Pick me up and throw me into the sea," he replied, "and it will become calm. I know that it is my fault that this great storm has come upon you."

Instead, the men did their best to row back to land. But they could not, for the sea grew even wilder than before. Then they cried to the LORD, "O LORD, please do not let us die for taking this man's life. Do not hold us accountable for killing an innocent man, for you, O LORD, have done as you pleased." Then they took Jonah and threw him overboard, and the raging sea grew calm. At this the men greatly feared the LORD, and they offered a sacrifice to the LORD and made vows to him.

But the LORD provided a great fish to swallow Jonah, and Jonah was inside the fish three days and three nights.

From inside the fish Jonah prayed to the LORD his God. He said:

"In my distress I called to the LORD,
    and he answered me.
From the depths of the grave I called for help,
    and you listened to my cry.
You hurled me into the deep,
    into the very heart of the seas,
    and the currents swirled about me;
all your waves and breakers
    swept over me.
I said, 'I have been banished
    from your sight;
yet I will look again
    toward your holy temple.'
The engulfing waters threatened me,
    the deep surrounded me;
    seaweed was wrapped around my head.
To the roots of the mountains I sank down;
    the earth beneath barred me in forever.
But you brought my life up from the pit,
    O LORD my God.

"When my life was ebbing away,
    I remembered you, LORD,

and my prayer rose to you,
  to your holy temple.

"Those who cling to worthless idols
  forfeit the grace that could be theirs.
But I, with a song of thanksgiving,
  will sacrifice to you.
What I have vowed I will make good.
  Salvation comes from the LORD."

And the LORD commanded the fish, and it vomited Jonah onto dry land.

In one of the most illustrative stories of the Old Testament, a reluctant prophet runs from God's call and receives a most mysterious comeuppance. God tells Jonah to go to the great city of Nineveh (NIN-uh-vuh) in neighboring Assyria and preach to the people about their wickedness.

Such a task may sound unpleasant, but Jonah has deeper reasons for refusing to go. He discerns that God is not simply full of anger and vindictiveness toward people outside of God's chosen nation but has a heart big enough to love these wicked people if they will simply repent. Sensing God's compassion, Jonah reacts with the heart of a jealous son. No matter that God has offered him and his people eternity; Jonah can't stand the thought of allowing others into that future.

Jonah has barely begun to run when God puts a stop to the game. Jonah faces death at sea, then spends three days in the depths, and finally walks the earth once again—an experience representative of that of Jesus, God's Son.

Some have suggested that Jonah's story is too fantastic to be true, but others have noted that a Mediterranean sperm whale can swallow a man whole, and that its laryngeal pouch could hold enough air for a person to survive a few days. Regardless of natural explanations, the Bible presents the story of Jonah as a miraculous event displaying God's compassion both on his servant in Israel and on people outside of Israel.

Ezekiel declares that God takes "no pleasure in the death of the wicked, but [desires] rather that they turn from their ways and live" (Ezekiel 33:11). To those in Israel who joyfully claimed God's blessings for themselves but were quick to wish God's wrath upon their enemies, God makes a sobering revelation. Here in Jonah we see further glimpses of God's love for Gentiles—a love he will openly proclaim after his Son's final sacrifice.   —BQ

DAILY CONTEMPLATION

Do you tend to reflect more of Jonah's jealousy or God's compassion for sinful people who need God?

JONAH GOES TO NINEVEH

Then the word of the LORD came to Jonah a second time: "Go to the great city of Nineveh and proclaim to it the message I give you."

Jonah obeyed the word of the LORD and went to Nineveh. Now Nineveh was a very important city—a visit required three days. On the first day, Jonah started into the city. He proclaimed: "Forty more days and Nineveh will be overturned." The Ninevites believed God. They declared a fast, and all of them, from the greatest to the least, put on sackcloth.

When the news reached the king of Nineveh, he rose from his throne, took off his royal robes, covered himself with sackcloth and sat down in the dust. Then he issued a proclamation in Nineveh:

"By the decree of the king and his nobles:

Do not let any man or beast, herd or flock, taste anything; do not let them eat or drink. But let man and beast be covered with sackcloth. Let everyone call urgently on God. Let them give up their evil ways and their violence. Who knows? God may yet relent and with compassion turn from his fierce anger so that we will not perish."

When God saw what they did and how they turned from their evil ways, he had compassion and did not bring upon them the destruction he had threatened.

But Jonah was greatly displeased and became angry. He prayed to the LORD, "O LORD, is this not what I said when I was still at home? That is why I was so quick to flee to Tarshish. I knew that you are a gracious and compassionate God, slow to anger and abounding in love, a God who relents from sending calamity. Now, O LORD, take away my life, for it is better for me to die than to live."

But the LORD replied, "Have you any right to be angry?"

Jonah went out and sat down at a place east of the city. There he made himself a shelter, sat in its shade and waited to see what would happen to the city. Then the LORD God provided a vine and made it grow up over Jonah to give shade for his head to ease his discomfort, and Jonah was very happy about the vine. But at dawn the next day God provided a worm, which chewed the vine so that it withered. When the sun rose, God provided a scorching east wind, and the sun blazed on Jonah's head so that he grew faint. He wanted to die, and said, "It would be better for me to die than to live."

But God said to Jonah, "Do you have a right to be angry about the vine?"

"I do," he said. "I am angry enough to die."

But the LORD said, "You have been concerned about this vine, though you did not tend it or make it grow. It sprang up overnight and died overnight. But Nineveh has more than a hundred and twenty thousand people who cannot tell their right hand from their left, and many cattle as well. Should I not be concerned about that great city?"

Jonah's journey to Nineveh, complete with ocean storm and detour in the belly of a whale, often becomes the focus of the account of Jonah. As a result, readers miss the central point, the reason for Jonah's misadventures in the first place. He is rebelling against God's mercy. Jonah offers a true-life study of how hard it is to follow the biblical command "Love your enemies." While many people admire that command, few find it easy to put into practice.

Jonah has understandable reason to balk at God's orders to preach in Nineveh, for that city in his day is the capital of an empire renowned for its cruelty. Assyrian soldiers have no qualms about "scorched earth" military tactics; typically, after destroying an enemy's fields and cities they slaughter the conquered peoples or hammer iron hooks through their noses or lower lips and lead them away as slaves. Jonah wants no part in giving such bullies a chance to repent. Amazingly, though, God loves Nineveh and wants to save the city, not destroy it. He knows the people are ripe for change.

The book of Jonah powerfully expresses God's yearning to forgive, and these two brief chapters fill in the lesser-known details of Jonah's mission. To the prophet's disgust, a simple announcement of doom sparks a spiritual revival in pagan Nineveh. And Jonah, sulking under a shriveled vine, admits he has suspected God's soft heart all along. He could not trust God—could not, that is, trust him to be harsh and unrelenting toward Nineveh. As Robert Frost summed up the book, "After Jonah, you could never trust God not to be merciful again."

The book also reveals God's ultimate purpose for his chosen people: he wants them, like Jonah, to reach out to other people and demonstrate his love and forgiveness. Nineveh's wholehearted response puts the Israelites to shame, for not once have they responded to a prophet as these Assyrians have.   —PY

DAILY CONTEMPLATION

Have you ever consciously tried to love the "enemies" in your life?

DAY 147   Reflection

WORKING WITH GOD

Following God calls for hard work. His love and blessings may be easy to receive, but when obedience to God requires us to do something contrary to our human nature, a conflict sets in that tests our commitment. God desires his holiness to take root in us, and he can use precisely these trials of the will to make us more like himself.

As with Jonah, our greatest trials come when we feel threatened or hurt by others yet sense God's heart willing us to love anyway with a power that overcomes our fear and dislike. God sets the pattern: despite countless reasons to dislike us, his heart of love overcomes his dislike and he opens his arms to us. Can we allow that supernatural love to spill into our hearts and then flow into the lives of those we dislike?

Corrie ten Boom tells of an ultimate test of her willingness to let God love through her a person she had every reason to hate. She was speaking about God's forgiveness to a crowd at a church in Munich, Germany, in 1947. Corrie and her sister, Betsie, had only a few years earlier been imprisoned in the Ravensbrück concentration camp for concealing Jews in their home during the Nazi occupation of Holland. Corrie had watched her sister die a slow, painful death in the camp.

Now as Corrie stood watching people file out of the church, solemn after her challenging message, Corrie found herself being tested to the core. She spotted in the crowd a man wearing a nondescript hat and overcoat. In a flash she recalled the same face framed in a skull-and-crossboned cap and blue uniform—the garb of a Nazi guard. Suddenly she was back in the huge room at Ravensbrück, filing naked with her sister and the other prisoners past this same set of eyes. Although he didn't seem to recognize her, she had no doubt about his identity.

The man congratulated her on the message and expressed his relief at knowing his sins were, in her words, at the bottom of the sea. Corrie fumbled with her purse rather than taking his hand. This was the first time she had been confronted face to face with one of her captors. The man went on to explain that he had been a guard at Ravensbrück, the camp she had spoken of in her talk. And then he revealed that he had become a believer in Christ since the war. He'd accepted God's forgiveness, but could he have Corrie's forgiveness, he wondered? Again he extended his hand.

She froze, thoughts of Betsie's agonizing death running through her mind. How could she with the shake of a hand simply erase what had happened? She had to do it. Along with the images of Betsie came the words of Jesus, "If you forgive men when they sin against you, your heavenly Father will also forgive you. But if you do not forgive men their sins, your Father will not forgive your sins" (Matthew 6:14–15). Corrie knew that not only does God require forgiveness; it is the only way to rebuild life after tragedy. Those who nursed bitterness toward the Nazis were trapped in their hatred and consumed by it. She also knew that forgiveness is an affair of the will rather than the heart. We may not feel like forgiving, but we can make a decision to forgive and trust God to supply the feelings in time.

She lifted her hand and prayed for help. As she did, a warmth traveled down her arm and filled her. Blinking back the tears, Corrie offered heartfelt words of forgiveness, sensing God's love gripping her more intensely than ever before. His love not only supplied what she lacked; it filled her in a greater way than she could have imagined.[13]   —BQ

DAILY CONTEMPLATION

Who has been most difficult for you to forgive and love? How would you feel if this person reached out a hand and asked for your forgiveness? Do you want to forgive even if he or she doesn't request it? Ask God for help in forgiving and loving despite your feelings (and in the realization that love does not always require us to be in relationship with a person).

ISRAEL HAS NOT RETURNED TO GOD

The words of Amos, one of the shepherds of Tekoa—what he saw concerning Israel two years before the earthquake, when Uzziah was king of Judah and Jeroboam son of Jehoash was king of Israel....

Hear this word, you cows of Bashan on Mount Samaria,
  you women who oppress the poor and crush the needy
  and say to your husbands, "Bring us some drinks!"
The Sovereign LORD has sworn by his holiness:
  "The time will surely come
when you will be taken away with hooks,
  the last of you with fishhooks.
You will each go straight out
  through breaks in the wall,
  and you will be cast out toward Harmon,"
    declares the LORD.
"Go to Bethel and sin;
  go to Gilgal and sin yet more.
Bring your sacrifices every morning,
  your tithes every three years.
Burn leavened bread as a thank offering
  and brag about your freewill offerings—
boast about them, you Israelites,
  for this is what you love to do,"
    declares the Sovereign LORD.
"I gave you empty stomachs in every city
  and lack of bread in every town,
  yet you have not returned to me,"
    declares the LORD.

"I also withheld rain from you
  when the harvest was still three months away.
I sent rain on one town,
  but withheld it from another.
One field had rain;
  another had none and dried up.
People staggered from town to town for water
  but did not get enough to drink,
  yet you have not returned to me,"
    declares the LORD.

"Many times I struck your gardens and vineyards,
  I struck them with blight and mildew.

275

Locusts devoured your fig and olive trees,
    yet you have not returned to me,"
      declares the LORD.

"I sent plagues among you
    as I did to Egypt.
I killed your young men with the sword,
    along with your captured horses.
I filled your nostrils with the stench of your camps,
    yet you have not returned to me,"
      declares the LORD.

"I overthrew some of you
    as I overthrew Sodom and Gomorrah.
You were like a burning stick snatched from the fire,
    yet you have not returned to me,"
      declares the LORD.

"Therefore this is what I will do to you, Israel,
    and because I will do this to you,
    prepare to meet your God, O Israel."

He who forms the mountains,
    creates the wind,
    and reveals his thoughts to man,
he who turns dawn to darkness,
    and treads the high places of the earth—
    the LORD God Almighty is his name.

Biblical prophets represent a wide spectrum of social backgrounds and personality types, but modern-day cartoonists tend to perpetuate a single stereotyped image. And the fact is, Amos fits the stereotype. He is the kind to stand on street corners with a signboard and rail against the whole miserable world.

Ironically, Amos appears on the scene when Israel, the northern kingdom, is booming. They have beaten back all their traditional enemies and even invaded neighboring Judah, taking land and prisoners. For a change, the government is stable: King Jeroboam II presides over a half century of prosperity and strength. People are too busy enjoying the good life to listen to the rantings of a prophet, and for precisely that reason Amos speaks in italics and exclamation points.

Unlike Jonah, Amos is not a professional prophet. He is a man of the land, a shepherd and a tender of sycamore trees. A migrant to Israel from the South, he speaks with a rural accent and is probably the butt of many jokes by city sophisticates.

Amos the peasant cannot get over what he finds in the northern cities. The luxurious lifestyles shock him: gorgeous couches, beds of carved ivory, summer homes, top-grade meat, fine wine. It seems obvious to Amos that this extravagance is built on a foundation of injustice: oppression of the poor, slavery, dishonest business practices, court bribes, privilege bought with money.

Lulled into security by their powerful, victorious army, the Israelites think they are safe for generations. But, as Amos warns, Israel cannot forever push God into a small corner of their lives, to be brought out like a magic charm whenever they need him.

"Prepare to meet your God, O Israel!" Amos shouts from the street corners, but those words have about as much impact in his day as they do in ours. Nevertheless, the prophet's warnings prove true: in a remarkably short time, Israel will fall apart. A mere thirty years after Jeroboam II's reign, the northern kingdom of Israel ceases to exist.

Amos is not a comfortable book to read—its message hits too close to our own time, when nations judge success by the size of gross national product and military forces. For that reason alone, it deserves a close look. —PY

DAILY CONTEMPLATION

What parallels do you see between Amos's time and our own?

DAY 149 Hosea 1:1–3:5

HOSEA'S WIFE AND CHILDREN

The word of the LORD that came to Hosea son of Beeri during the reigns of Uzziah, Jotham, Ahaz and Hezekiah, kings of Judah, and during the reign of Jeroboam son of Jehoash king of Israel:

When the LORD began to speak through Hosea, the LORD said to him, "Go, take to yourself an adulterous wife and children of unfaithfulness, because the land is guilty of the vilest adultery in departing from the LORD." So he married Gomer daughter of Diblaim, and she conceived and bore him a son.

Then the LORD said to Hosea, "Call him Jezreel, because I will soon punish the house of Jehu for the massacre at Jezreel, and I will put an end to the kingdom of Israel. In that day I will break Israel's bow in the Valley of Jezreel."

Gomer conceived again and gave birth to a daughter. Then the LORD said to Hosea, "Call her Lo-Ruhamah, for I will no longer show love to the house of Israel, that I should at all forgive them. Yet I will show love to the house of Judah; and I will save them—not by bow, sword or battle, or by horses and horsemen, but by the LORD their God."

After she had weaned Lo-Ruhamah, Gomer had another son. Then the LORD said, "Call him Lo-Ammi, for you are not my people, and I am not your God.

"Yet the Israelites will be like the sand on the seashore, which cannot be measured or counted. In the place where it was said to them, 'You are not my people,' they will be called 'sons of the living God.' The people of Judah and the people of Israel will be reunited, and they will appoint one leader and will come up out of the land, for great will be the day of Jezreel.

"Say of your brothers, 'My people,' and of your sisters, 'My loved one.'

"Rebuke your mother, rebuke her,
for she is not my wife,
and I am not her husband.
Let her remove the adulterous look from her face
and the unfaithfulness from between her breasts.
Otherwise I will strip her naked
and make her as bare as on the day she was born;
I will make her like a desert,
turn her into a parched land,
and slay her with thirst.
I will not show my love to her children,
because they are the children of adultery.
Their mother has been unfaithful
and has conceived them in disgrace.
She said, 'I will go after my lovers,
who give me my food and my water,
my wool and my linen, my oil and my drink.'
Therefore I will block her path with thornbushes;
I will wall her in so that she cannot find her way.
She will chase after her lovers but not catch them;
she will look for them but not find them.
Then she will say,
'I will go back to my husband as at first,
for then I was better off than now.'
She has not acknowledged that I was the one
who gave her the grain, the new wine and oil,
who lavished on her the silver and gold—
which they used for Baal.

"Therefore I will take away my grain when it ripens,
and my new wine when it is ready.
I will take back my wool and my linen,
intended to cover her nakedness.
So now I will expose her lewdness
before the eyes of her lovers;
no one will take her out of my hands.
I will stop all her celebrations:
her yearly festivals, her New Moons,
her Sabbath days—all her appointed feasts.
I will ruin her vines and her fig trees,
which she said were her pay from her lovers;
I will make them a thicket,
and wild animals will devour them.
I will punish her for the days
she burned incense to the Baals;

she decked herself with rings and jewelry,
>   and went after her lovers,
>   but me she forgot,"
>   declares the LORD.

"Therefore I am now going to allure her;
>   I will lead her into the desert
>   and speak tenderly to her.
There I will give her back her vineyards,
>   and will make the Valley of Achor a door of hope.
There she will sing as in the days of her youth,
>   as in the day she came up out of Egypt.

"In that day," declares the LORD,
>   "you will call me 'my husband';
>   you will no longer call me 'my master.'
I will remove the names of the Baals from her lips;
>   no longer will their names be invoked.
In that day I will make a covenant for them
>   with the beasts of the field and the birds of the air
>   and the creatures that move along the ground.
Bow and sword and battle
>   I will abolish from the land,
>   so that all may lie down in safety.
I will betroth you to me forever;
>   I will betroth you in righteousness and justice,
>   in love and compassion.
I will betroth you in faithfulness,
>   and you will acknowledge the LORD.
"In that day I will respond,"
>   declares the LORD—
"I will respond to the skies,
>   and they will respond to the earth;
and the earth will respond to the grain,
>   the new wine and oil,
>   and they will respond to Jezreel.
I will plant her for myself in the land;
>   I will show my love to the one I called 'Not my loved one.'
I will say to those called 'Not my people,' 'You are my people';
>   and they will say, 'You are my God.'"

The LORD said to me, "Go, show your love to your wife again, though she is loved by another and is an adulteress. Love her as the LORD loves the Israelites, though they turn to other gods and love the sacred raisin cakes."

So I bought her for fifteen shekels of silver and about a homer and a lethek of barley. Then I told her, "You are to live with me many days; you must not be a prostitute or be intimate with any man, and I will live with you."

For the Israelites will live many days without king or prince, without sacrifice or sacred stones, without ephod or idol. Afterward the Israelites will return and seek the LORD their God and David their king. They will come trembling to the LORD and to his blessings in the last days.

God sent prophets to Israel and Judah to meet the need of the moment. When people were cocky, self-indulgent, and spiritually deaf, a screamer like Amos appeared on the scene. But suffering people called for another tone. Just a few years after Amos, as Israel was breaking apart and sliding toward chaos, a word from God came to Hosea (hoh-ZAY-uh). To a shattered nation, Hosea brings a hope-filled message of grace and forgiveness.

Most books of the prophets focus on the audience and all the things they've done wrong. Hosea, in contrast, shines the spotlight on God. What is it like to be God? How must he feel when his chosen people reject him and go panting after false gods? As if words alone are too weak to convey his passion, God asks the brave prophet Hosea to act out a living parable. He marries a loose woman named Gomer, who, true to form, soon runs away and commits adultery. Only by living out that drama could Hosea understand, and then express, something of how Israel's rebuke feels to God.

After all that Gomer has done, God instructs Hosea simply to invite her back and forgive her. The pattern hopelessly repeats itself. Gomer bears two children—but is Hosea really their father? According to the Mosaic law, he should turn his adulterous wife out on the street or have her tried in court. What Hosea does, and God does, is unheard of.

Hosea is one of the most emotional books in the Bible, an outpouring of suffering love from God's heart. Read aloud, this chapter sounds like a fight between a husband and wife overheard through thin walls. The book of Hosea, in fact, represents the first time God's covenant with Israel has been described in terms of marriage. It shows that God longs for his people with the tenderness and hunger that a lover feels toward his bride.

In the covenant, Israel agreed to love and obey God no matter what, "till death do us part." But as they prosper in the new land, that flame of love dies. The old covenant is fractured. As Hosea tells it, the death of their love breaks God's heart. God can only promise another chance, with a new covenant at a future time when "you will call me 'my husband'; you will no longer call me 'my master.'"   —PY

DAILY CONTEMPLATION

Hosea describes various stages in Israel's relationship to God: courtship, engagement, newly married, unfaithfulness, separation. What stage are you in with God?

GOD'S LOVE FOR ISRAEL

"When Israel was a child, I loved him,
    and out of Egypt I called my son.
But the more I called Israel,
    the further they went from me.
They sacrificed to the Baals
    and they burned incense to images.
It was I who taught Ephraim to walk,
    taking them by the arms;
but they did not realize
    it was I who healed them.
I led them with cords of human kindness,
    with ties of love;
I lifted the yoke from their neck
    and bent down to feed them.

"Will they not return to Egypt
    and will not Assyria rule over them
    because they refuse to repent?
Swords will flash in their cities,
    will destroy the bars of their gates
    and put an end to their plans.
My people are determined to turn from me.
    Even if they call to the Most High,
    he will by no means exalt them.

"How can I give you up, Ephraim?
    How can I hand you over, Israel?
How can I treat you like Admah?
    How can I make you like Zeboiim?
My heart is changed within me;
    all my compassion is aroused.
I will not carry out my fierce anger,
    nor will I turn and devastate Ephraim.
For I am God, and not man—
    the Holy One among you.
    I will not come in wrath.
They will follow the LORD;
    he will roar like a lion.
When he roars,
    his children will come trembling from the west.
They will come trembling

> like birds from Egypt,
> like doves from Assyria.
> I will settle them in their homes,"
> declares the LORD.

Many people carry around the image of God as an impersonal force, something akin to the law of gravity. Hosea portrays almost the opposite: a God of passion and fury and tears and love. A God in mourning over Israel's rejection of him.

God uses Hosea's unhappy story to illustrate his own whipsaw emotions. That first blush of love when he found Israel, he says, was like finding grapes in the desert. But as Israel breaks his trust again and again, he has to endure the awful shame of a wounded lover. God's words carry a tone surprisingly like self-pity: "I am like a moth to Ephraim [EE-free-uhm], like rot to the people of Judah" (5:12).

The powerful image of a jilted lover explains why, in a chapter like Hosea 11, God's emotions seem to vacillate so. He is preparing to obliterate Israel—wait, now he is weeping, holding out open arms—no, he is sternly pronouncing judgment again. Those shifting moods seem hopelessly irrational, except to anyone who has been jilted by a lover.

Is there a more powerful human feeling than that of betrayal? Ask a high school girl whose boyfriend has just dumped her for a pretty cheerleader. Or tune your radio to a country-western station and listen to the lyrics of infidelity. Or check out the murders reported in the daily newspaper, an amazing number of which trace back to a fight with an estranged lover. Hosea and God demonstrate in living color exactly what it is like to love someone desperately and get nothing in return. Not even God, with all his power, can force a human being to love him.

Virtually every chapter of Hosea talks about the "prostitution" or "adultery" of God's people. God the lover will not share his bride with anyone else. Yet, amazingly, even when she turns her back on him, he sticks with her. He is willing to suffer, in hope that someday she will change. Hosea proves that God longs not to punish but to love.

—PY

DAILY CONTEMPLATION

What is your strongest memory of feeling betrayed?

DAY 151   2 Kings 17:1–2, 6–9, 16–23, 35–41

ISRAEL EXILED BECAUSE OF SIN

In the twelfth year of Ahaz king of Judah, Hoshea son of Elah became king of Israel in Samaria, and he reigned nine years. He did evil in the eyes of the LORD, but not like the kings of Israel who preceded him....

In the ninth year of Hoshea, the king of Assyria captured Samaria and deported the Israelites to Assyria. He settled them in Halah, in Gozan on the Habor River and in the towns of the Medes.

All this took place because the Israelites had sinned against the LORD their God, who had brought them up out of Egypt from under the power of Pharaoh king of Egypt. They worshiped other gods and followed the practices of the nations the LORD had driven out before them, as well as the practices that the kings of Israel had introduced. The Israelites secretly did things against the LORD their God that were not right....

They forsook all the commands of the LORD their God and made for themselves two idols cast in the shape of calves, and an Asherah pole. They bowed down to all the starry hosts, and they worshiped Baal. They sacrificed their sons and daughters in the fire. They practiced divination and sorcery and sold themselves to do evil in the eyes of the LORD, provoking him to anger.

So the Lord was very angry with Israel and removed them from his presence. Only the tribe of Judah was left, and even Judah did not keep the commands of the Lord their God. They followed the practices Israel had introduced. Therefore the Lord rejected all the people of Israel; he afflicted them and gave them into the hands of plunderers, until he thrust them from his presence.

When he tore Israel away from the house of David, they made Jeroboam son of Nebat their king. Jeroboam enticed Israel away from following the LORD and caused them to commit a great sin. The Israelites persisted in all the sins of Jeroboam and did not turn away from them until the LORD removed them from his presence, as he had warned through all his servants the prophets. So the people of Israel were taken from their homeland into exile in Assyria, and they are still there....

When the LORD made a covenant with the Israelites, he commanded them: "Do not worship any other gods or bow down to them, serve them or sacrifice to them. But the LORD, who brought you up out of Egypt with mighty power and outstretched arm, is the one you must worship. To him you shall bow down and to him offer sacrifices. You must always be careful to keep the decrees and ordinances, the laws and commands he wrote for you. Do not worship other gods. Do not forget the covenant I have made with you, and do not worship other gods. Rather, worship the LORD your God; it is he who will deliver you from the hand of all your enemies."

They would not listen, however, but persisted in their former practices. Even while these people were worshiping the LORD, they were serving their idols. To this day their children and grandchildren continue to do as their fathers did.

An impressive lineup of prophets all tried their hand at convincing Israel to change its ways. But neither the miracles of Elijah and Elisha nor the shouts of Amos nor the impassioned pleas of Hosea had much effect. When times of trouble came, the nation turned toward the gods of their neighbors and frantically signed up military allies; they never turned wholeheartedly to God.

The Day of Judgment so harrowingly foretold by the prophets is here recorded in the flat, matter-of-fact language of history. The end for the northern kingdom of Israel comes when Israel's kings, against all the prophets' advice, seek to purchase political protection, first from Assyria and then from Egypt. Discovering the double cross, Assyria sends an army against Israel.

In early wars Assyrian conquerors exterminated their enemies, but in later years they adopted the technique of deporting their victims and replacing them with foreigners from other conquered territories. The radical disruption of their societies tended to keep conquered peoples from regrouping and rising up as a new threat. In keeping with that policy, Assyria deports 27,290 captives from the land of Israel, dispersing the "ten lost tribes of Israel."

These émigrés the Assyrians replace with foreigners who form a new identity as "Samaritans," a group that will exist in New Testament times and in fact can still be found in modern Israel. Samaritan settlers combine their native religions with some reverence for the true God.

After this chapter, the Bible's attention turns south toward Judah, the collective name for the two surviving tribes of Israelites. Why does the Assyrian tragedy happen? Second Kings diagnoses idolatry as the chief cause of Israel's moral collapse. Unfortunately, the practice has already gained a foothold in the southern kingdom as well.   —PY

DAILY CONTEMPLATION

What kind of idolatry might believers today fall into? The worship of possessions? People? Ideas? Image?

DAY 152   Reflection

GOD'S LOVE STORY

Everything beautiful and right—even embarrassingly so—about Solomon's Song of Songs is turned around in the book of Hosea and in Israel's continuing story in 2 Kings. Song of Songs was a celebration of blossoming love between a newly married man and woman. Hosea is a lament over married love gone sour and crushed by repeated unfaithfulness.

If ever we wonder whether God could understand the thrill of new love, we need only read the Song of Songs. God preserved this song for the Bible to let us know that not only does he understand; he also rejoices in new and enduring love between a man and a woman. This love is part of his plan, and he delights in it as deeply as we do.

If we wonder whether God could know the depths of pain we feel when betrayed or rejected, we have only to read Hosea. This oft-forgotten book of the Old Testament can provide words of empathy and solidarity to believers shaken by another's unfaithfulness. Not only does God understand such pain; he actually endured it.

If God has the capacity to love far beyond our limited ability, he also has the capacity to hurt from betrayal more deeply than we could ever hurt. We cannot grasp all God has given to his people, a gift that includes the sacrifice of his Son, and to have that gift rejected again and again has caused him indescribable pain. God knows the cries that escape from the wordless places within us—our cries are the faint echoes of his own.

Each time we suffer in a relationship that should be filled with love and life, God embraces us and reminds us that he understands our pain intimately, personally. In this pain we move closer to him with a new appreciation of his faithful love. —BQ

DAILY CONTEMPLATION

Whose rejection or betrayal is hurting you? Ask God for the help you need in coping with your feelings. As you pray, thank God for this promise to you: "Great is our Lord, and mighty in power; his understanding has no limit" (Psalm 147:5).

PART 4

THE SOUTHERN KINGDOM—JUDAH

DAY 153 2 Chronicles 20:1–30

JEHOSHAPHAT DEFEATS MOAB AND AMMON

The Moabites and Ammonites with some of the Meunites came to make war on Jehoshaphat.

Some men came and told Jehoshaphat, "A vast army is coming against you from Edom, from the other side of the Sea. It is already in Hazazon Tamar" (that is, En Gedi). Alarmed, Jehoshaphat resolved to inquire of the LORD, and he proclaimed a fast for all Judah. The people of Judah came together to seek help from the LORD; indeed, they came from every town in Judah to seek him.

Then Jehoshaphat stood up in the assembly of Judah and Jerusalem at the temple of the LORD in the front of the new courtyard and said:

"O LORD, God of our fathers, are you not the God who is in heaven? You rule over all the kingdoms of the nations. Power and might are in your hand, and no one can withstand you. O our God, did you not drive out the inhabitants of this land before your people Israel and give it forever to the descendants of Abraham your friend? They have lived in it and have built in it a sanctuary for your Name, saying, 'If calamity comes upon us, whether the sword of judgment, or plague or famine, we will stand in your presence before this temple that bears your Name and will cry out to you in our distress, and you will hear us and save us.'

"But now here are men from Ammon, Moab and Mount Seir, whose territory you would not allow Israel to invade when they came from Egypt; so they turned away from them and did not destroy them. See how they are repaying us by coming to drive us out of the possession you gave us as an inheritance. O our God, will you not judge them? For we have no power to face this vast army that is attacking us. We do not know what to do, but our eyes are upon you."

All the men of Judah, with their wives and children and little ones, stood there before the LORD.

Then the Spirit of the LORD came upon Jahaziel son of Zechariah, the son of Benaiah, the son of Jeiel, the son of Mattaniah, a Levite and descendant of Asaph, as he stood in the assembly.

He said: "Listen, King Jehoshaphat and all who live in Judah and Jerusalem! This is what the LORD says to you: 'Do not be afraid or discouraged because of this vast army. For the battle is not yours, but God's. Tomorrow march down against them. They will be climbing up by the Pass of Ziz, and you will find them at the end of the gorge in the Desert of Jeruel. You will not have to fight this battle. Take up your positions; stand firm and see the deliverance the LORD will give you, O Judah and Jerusalem. Do not be afraid; do not be discouraged. Go out to face them tomorrow, and the LORD will be with you.'"

Jehoshaphat bowed with his face to the ground, and all the people of Judah and Jerusalem fell down in worship before the LORD. Then some Levites from the Kohathites and Korahites stood up and praised the LORD, the God of Israel, with very loud voice.

Early in the morning they left for the Desert of Tekoa. As they set out, Jehoshaphat stood and said, "Listen to me, Judah and people of Jerusalem! Have faith in the LORD your God and you will be upheld; have faith in his prophets and you will be successful." After consulting the people, Jehoshaphat appointed men to sing to the LORD and to praise him for the splendor of his holiness as they went out at the head of the army, saying:

"Give thanks to the LORD,
for his love endures forever."

As they began to sing and praise, the LORD set ambushes against the men of Ammon and Moab and Mount Seir who were invading Judah, and they were defeated. The men of Ammon and Moab rose up against the men from Mount Seir to destroy and annihilate them. After they finished slaughtering the men from Seir, they helped to destroy one another.

When the men of Judah came to the place that overlooks the desert and looked toward the vast army, they saw only dead bodies lying on the ground; no one had escaped. So Jehoshaphat and his men went to carry off their plunder, and they found among them a great amount of equipment and clothing and also articles of value—more than they could take away. There was so much plunder that it took three days to collect it. On the fourth day they assembled in the Valley of Beracah, where they praised the LORD. This is why it is called the Valley of Beracah to this day.

Then, led by Jehoshaphat, all the men of Judah and Jerusalem returned joyfully to Jerusalem, for the LORD had given them cause to rejoice over their enemies. They entered Jerusalem and went to the temple of the LORD with harps and lutes and trumpets.

The fear of God came upon all the kingdoms of the countries when they heard how the LORD had fought against the enemies of Israel. And the kingdom of Jehoshaphat was at peace, for his God had given him rest on every side.

So far our readings have sampled the two-hundred-year history of Israel, which began sliding away from God from the very first days of its birth as a nation. But the Bible devotes far more space to the kings and prophets of the southern kingdom. Of the nineteen men and one woman who rule Judah, at least a handful demonstrate a quality of spiritual leadership unmatched in the northern kingdom. Judah proves more faithful in living up to the covenant with God, and chiefly for that reason it outlasts Israel by nearly a century and a half.

This chapter tells of the extraordinary king named Jehoshaphat, one of Judah's early rulers. No ruler of Judah had a wholly peaceful reign, and as a result much of the action in 2 Chronicles takes place, like this story, on a battlefield. Here is the book's philosophy of war in a nutshell: *If you trust in your own military might or that of powerful neighbors, you will lose. Instead, humble yourself and rely totally on God—regardless of the odds against you.*

As the kings of Judah demonstrate with monotonous regularity, it takes uncommon courage to rely on God alone at a moment of great peril. Even the best of them dip into the royal treasury to purchase help from neighboring allies. But King Jehoshaphat provides a textbook example of the proper response. When invading armies threaten, he calls the entire nation together in a giant prayer meeting. On the day of battle, he sends a choir in front of his army to sing praises to God.

Jehoshaphat's tactics may seem more suitable for a church service than a battlefield, but they work. The enemy forces all turn against each other, and Judah's army marches home victorious.

This bright moment of national faith shines out from a very mottled historical record. By his public prayer and personal example, King Jehoshaphat shows what can happen when a leader places complete trust in God.　　　　—PY

DAILY CONTEMPLATION

Do you know of a leader who has this kind of trust in God?

# DAY 154 	Micah 1:1; 6:1–16

THE LORD'S CASE AGAINST ISRAEL

The word of the LORD that came to Micah of Moresheth during the reigns of Jotham, Ahaz and Hezekiah, kings of Judah—the vision he saw concerning Samaria and Jerusalem. . . .

Listen to what the LORD says:

"Stand up, plead your case before the mountains;
    let the hills hear what you have to say.
Hear, O mountains, the LORD's accusation;
    listen, you everlasting foundations of the earth.
For the LORD has a case against his people;
    he is lodging a charge against Israel.

"My people, what have I done to you?
    How have I burdened you? Answer me.
I brought you up out of Egypt
    and redeemed you from the land of slavery.
I sent Moses to lead you,
    also Aaron and Miriam.
My people, remember
    what Balak king of Moab counseled
    and what Balaam son of Beor answered.
Remember your journey from Shittim to Gilgal,
    that you may know the righteous acts of the LORD."

With what shall I come before the LORD
    and bow down before the exalted God?
Shall I come before him with burnt offerings,
    with calves a year old?
Will the LORD be pleased with thousands of rams,
    with ten thousand rivers of oil?
Shall I offer my firstborn for my transgression,
    the fruit of my body for the sin of my soul?
He has showed you, O man, what is good.
    And what does the LORD require of you?
To act justly and to love mercy
    and to walk humbly with your God.

Listen! The LORD is calling to the city—
    and to fear your name is wisdom—
    "Heed the rod and the One who appointed it.
Am I still to forget, O wicked house,
    your ill-gotten treasures
    and the short ephah, which is accursed?
Shall I acquit a man with dishonest scales,
    with a bag of false weights?
Her rich men are violent;
    her people are liars
    and their tongues speak deceitfully.
Therefore, I have begun to destroy you,
    to ruin you because of your sins.

You will eat but not be satisfied;
> your stomach will still be empty.
You will store up but save nothing,
> because what you save I will give to the sword.
You will plant but not harvest;
> you will press olives but not use the oil on yourselves,
> you will crush grapes but not drink the wine.
You have observed the statutes of Omri
> and all the practices of Ahab's house,
> and you have followed their traditions.
Therefore I will give you over to ruin
> and your people to derision;
> you will bear the scorn of the nations."

Not every king of Judah has Jehoshaphat's faith and courage. As the years grind on, the same decadence that has characterized the northern kingdom of Israel spreads like an epidemic through Judah. Other parts of the Bible detail Judah's faults: one notorious king, Ahaz (AY-haz), sets up foreign altars, offers his own children in human sacrifice, and shutters the Lord's temple. Along with the religious corruption comes every other kind of sin: dishonesty, greed, bribery, injustice.

Around the same time Amos is blasting Israel in the north, another country preacher, Micah (MI-kuh), is called by God to deliver similar words of warning to Judah. Micah, a prophet who gets emotionally caught up in his message, lives in tumultuous times. At one point, Judah loses a hundred and twenty thousand soldiers in a single day (2 Chronicles 28:6). The nation watches in fear as Assyria, the chief power of the day, brutally smashes the northern kingdom. What will keep Judah from a similar fate? That very prospect of judgment is what makes Micah "howl like a jackal and moan like an owl" (1:8).

Chapter 6 of the book of Micah opens with an impassioned plea from God. "My people, what have I done to you?" God asks. He reviews the history of his chosen people, reminding them of his great works on their behalf. In his rhetorical response, Micah makes clear that God desires true, heartfelt changes, not just a veneer of religion: "What does the LORD require of you? To act justly and to love mercy and to walk humbly with your God."

Micah concludes darkly that his people, afflicted with the same sickness as their relatives to the north, will meet the same end. Even so, Micah sees light ahead. Amid graphic predictions of destruction, Micah gives clear predictions of the Messiah, the future leader from the tiny town of Bethlehem who will offer new hope to the earth (5:2).   —PY

DAILY CONTEMPLATION

How would you feel about adopting these words from Micah as a life motto: "To act justly and to love mercy and to walk humbly with your God"? Would anything have to change in your life?

HEZEKIAH CELEBRATES PASSOVER

Hezekiah sent word to all Israel and Judah and also wrote letters to Ephraim and Manasseh, inviting them to come to the temple of the LORD in Jerusalem and celebrate the Passover to the LORD, the God of Israel. The king and his officials and the whole assembly in Jerusalem decided to celebrate the Passover in the second month. They had not been able to celebrate it at the regular time because not enough priests had consecrated themselves and the people had not assembled in Jerusalem. The plan seemed right both to the king and to the whole assembly. They decided to send a proclamation throughout Israel, from Beersheba to Dan, calling the people to come to Jerusalem and celebrate the Passover to the LORD, the God of Israel. It had not been celebrated in large numbers according to what was written.

At the king's command, couriers went throughout Israel and Judah with letters from the king and from his officials, which read:

"People of Israel, return to the LORD, the God of Abraham, Isaac and Israel, that he may return to you who are left, who have escaped from the hand of the kings of Assyria. Do not be like your fathers and brothers, who were unfaithful to the LORD, the God of their fathers, so that he made them an object of horror, as you see. Do not be stiff-necked, as your fathers were; submit to the LORD. Come to the sanctuary, which he has consecrated forever. Serve the LORD your God, so that his fierce anger will turn away from you. If you return to the LORD, then your brothers and your children will be shown compassion by their captors and will come back to this land, for the LORD your God is gracious and compassionate. He will not turn his face from you if you return to him."

The couriers went from town to town in Ephraim and Manasseh, as far as Zebulun, but the people scorned and ridiculed them. Nevertheless, some men of Asher, Manasseh and Zebulun humbled themselves and went to Jerusalem. Also in Judah the hand of God was on the people to give them unity of mind to carry out what the king and his officials had ordered, following the word of the LORD.

A very large crowd of people assembled in Jerusalem to celebrate the Feast of Unleavened Bread in the second month. They removed the altars in Jerusalem and cleared away the incense altars and threw them into the Kidron Valley.

They slaughtered the Passover lamb on the fourteenth day of the second month. The priests and the Levites were ashamed and consecrated themselves and brought burnt offerings to the temple of the LORD. Then they took up their regular positions as prescribed in the Law of Moses the man of God. The priests sprinkled the blood handed to them by the Levites. Since many in the crowd had not consecrated themselves, the Levites had to kill the Passover lambs for all those who were not ceremonially clean and could not consecrate their lambs to the LORD. Although most of the many people who came from Ephraim, Manasseh, Issachar and Zebulun had not purified themselves, yet they ate the Passover, contrary to what was written. But Hezekiah prayed for them, saying, "May the LORD, who is good, pardon everyone who sets his heart on seeking God—the LORD, the God of his fathers—even if he is not clean according to the rules of the sanctuary." And the LORD heard Hezekiah and healed the people.

The Israelites who were present in Jerusalem celebrated the Feast of Unleavened Bread for seven days with great rejoicing, while the Levites and priests sang to the LORD every day, accompanied by the LORD's instruments of praise.

Hezekiah spoke encouragingly to all the Levites, who showed good understanding of the service of the LORD. For the seven days they ate their assigned portion and offered fellowship offerings and praised the LORD, the God of their fathers.

The whole assembly then agreed to celebrate the festival seven more days; so for another seven days they celebrated joyfully. Hezekiah king of Judah provided a thousand bulls and seven thousand sheep and goats for the assembly, and the officials provided them with a thousand bulls and ten thousand sheep and goats. A great number of priests consecrated themselves. The entire assembly of Judah rejoiced, along with the priests and Levites and all who had assembled from Israel, including the aliens who had come from Israel and those who lived in Judah. There was great joy in Jerusalem, for since the days of Solomon son of David king of Israel there had been nothing like this in Jerusalem. The priests and the Levites stood to bless the people, and God heard them, for their prayer reached heaven, his holy dwelling place.

Toward the end of Micah's career, just as the situation in Judah is deteriorating, another great king takes the throne. In fact, 2 Chronicles spends more time on Hezekiah (HEZ-uh-KI-uh) than on anyone else. The very first year of his reign he leads a program to restore the temple, which has fallen into disrepair from lack of use. Hezekiah turns the tables on Judah's priests: he stands in the temple square and delivers a rousing sermon to *them.*

When Hezekiah decides to sponsor a huge religious festival, the idea at first meets with scorn and ridicule. But a king's proclamation carries certain weight, and the nation finally does come together in a remarkable scene of happiness and unity. Hezekiah even sends "missionary" couriers to the devastated lands to the north, and some survivors of the Assyrian scourge make their way to Jerusalem.

This chapter closely resembles 1 Kings 8 and its story of Solomon's dedication of the temple. Hezekiah is intent on renewing the covenant with God in hopes of forestalling God's judgment. The details of the festival celebration show just how badly Judah has neglected the covenant: there is a shortage of priests, and Hezekiah has to bend the rules or not enough worshipers will be properly purified.

It is no accident that Hezekiah organizes his festival around the Passover. That day marks the birth of a nation, when God freed his people from slavery in Egypt. In a real sense, the Passover sealed the covenant, and Hezekiah is determined to remind the nation of its heritage.

Despite the initial skepticism, the people of Judah get caught up in the celebration and, as in Solomon's day, spontaneously decide to stay another seven days. "There was great joy in Jerusalem," the Bible reports, "for since the days of Solomon son of David king of Israel there had been nothing like this in Jerusalem."   —PY

DAILY CONTEMPLATION

What spiritual event you have attended has had the greatest impact on you? Did you get the feeling God was honored at this event?

DAY 156   Isaiah 1:1; 6:1–13

ISAIAH'S COMMISSION

The vision concerning Judah and Jerusalem that Isaiah son of Amoz saw during the reigns of Uzziah, Jotham, Ahaz and Hezekiah, kings of Judah....

In the year that King Uzziah died, I saw the Lord seated on a throne, high and exalted, and the train of his robe filled the temple. Above him were seraphs, each with six wings: With two wings they covered their faces, with two they covered their feet, and with two they were flying. And they were calling to one another:

"Holy, holy, holy is the LORD Almighty;
    the whole earth is full of his glory."

At the sound of their voices the doorposts and thresholds shook and the temple was filled with smoke.

"Woe to me!" I cried. "I am ruined! For I am a man of unclean lips, and I live among a people of unclean lips, and my eyes have seen the King, the LORD Almighty."

Then one of the seraphs flew to me with a live coal in his hand, which he had taken with tongs from the altar. With it he touched my mouth and said, "See, this has touched your lips; your guilt is taken away and your sin atoned for."

Then I heard the voice of the Lord saying, "Whom shall I send? And who will go for us?"

And I said, "Here am I. Send me!"

He said, "Go and tell this people:

"'Be ever hearing, but never understanding;
    be ever seeing, but never perceiving.'

Make the heart of this people calloused;
　　make their ears dull
　　and close their eyes.
Otherwise they might see with their eyes,
　　hear with their ears,
　　understand with their hearts,
and turn and be healed."

Then I said, "For how long, O Lord?"
And he answered:

"Until the cities lie ruined
　　and without inhabitant,
until the houses are left deserted
　　and the fields ruined and ravaged,
until the LORD has sent everyone far away
　　and the land is utterly forsaken.
And though a tenth remains in the land,
　　it will again be laid waste.
But as the terebinth and oak
　　leave stumps when they are cut down,
　　so the holy seed will be the stump in the land."

This chapter flashes back to a scene that took place two decades before Hezekiah became king. The prophet Isaiah, a giant of Jewish history, received a direct, dramatic call from God, as recounted in this chapter.

As Isaiah begins his work, Judah seems strong and wealthy. Yet Isaiah sees signs of grave danger—the very same signs that alarm his contemporary, the prophet Micah. Men go around drunk; women care more about their clothes than about their neighbors' hunger. People give lip service to God and keep up the outward appearance of religion but little more.

External dangers loom even larger: on all sides, monster empires are burgeoning. The nation of Judah, says Isaiah, stands at a crossroads. It can either regain its footing or begin a dangerous slide downward.

Two kings, Jotham (JAH-thuhm) and Ahaz, pay Isaiah little heed. Nevertheless, in a remarkable turnaround, the new king Hezekiah makes Isaiah one of his most trusted advisers. In any moment of crisis, he calls upon the prophet.

Not every prophet blasts the establishment from street corners. Isaiah spends his days in the corridors of power, offering political advice and helping set the course of his nation. Although he sometimes stands alone against a crowd of contrary advisers, he never tempers his message. Isaiah outlasts four kings, but he finally offends one beyond repair. Tradition records that the last, King Manasseh, has Isaiah killed by fastening him between two planks of wood and sawing his body in half.

It seems likely that much of Hezekiah's zeal for reform traces back to the influence of the prophet Isaiah. The divine call recorded in this chapter shows where Isaiah got the courage and commitment that made him such an important force in Judah's history.
　　　　　　　　　　　　　　　　　　　　　　　　　　　　　　　　—PY

DAY 157   Isaiah 25:1–26:6

PRAISE TO THE LORD

O LORD, you are my God;
    I will exalt you and praise your name,
for in perfect faithfulness
    you have done marvelous things,
    things planned long ago.
You have made the city a heap of rubble,
    the fortified town a ruin,
the foreigners' stronghold a city no more;
    it will never be rebuilt.
Therefore strong peoples will honor you;
    cities of ruthless nations will revere you.
You have been a refuge for the poor,
    a refuge for the needy in his distress,
a shelter from the storm
    and a shade from the heat.
For the breath of the ruthless
    is like a storm driving against a wall
    and like the heat of the desert.
You silence the uproar of foreigners;
    as heat is reduced by the shadow of a cloud,
    so the song of the ruthless is stilled.

On this mountain the LORD Almighty will prepare
    a feast of rich food for all peoples,
a banquet of aged wine—
    the best of meats and the finest of wines.
On this mountain he will destroy
    the shroud that enfolds all peoples,
the sheet that covers all nations;
    he will swallow up death forever.
The Sovereign LORD will wipe away the tears
    from all faces;
he will remove the disgrace of his people

from all the earth.
The LORD has spoken.
In that day they will say,
"Surely this is our God;
   we trusted in him, and he saved us.
This is the LORD, we trusted in him;
   let us rejoice and be glad in his salvation."

The hand of the LORD will rest on this mountain;
   but Moab will be trampled under him
   as straw is trampled down in the manure.
They will spread out their hands in it,
   as a swimmer spreads out his hands to swim.
God will bring down their pride
   despite the cleverness of their hands.
He will bring down your high fortified walls
   and lay them low;
he will bring them down to the ground,
   to the very dust.

In that day this song will be sung in the land of Judah:

We have a strong city;
   God makes salvation
   its walls and ramparts.
Open the gates
   that the righteous nation may enter,
   the nation that keeps faith.
You will keep in perfect peace
   him whose mind is steadfast,
   because he trusts in you.
Trust in the LORD forever,
   for the LORD, the LORD, is the Rock eternal.
He humbles those who dwell on high,
   he lays the lofty city low;
he levels it to the ground
   and casts it down to the dust.
Feet trample it down—
   the feet of the oppressed,
   the footsteps of the poor.

In addition to his role as adviser to kings, Isaiah was a writer of enormous talent. No other biblical author can match his rich vocabulary and use of imagery, and the New Testament quotes him more than all the other prophets combined. Many of his majestic phrases have become a familiar part of the English vocabulary.

Using his great ability, Isaiah tries to awaken Judah from its spiritual slump. Like most of the prophets, he preaches a two-part message of **judgment** to come unless people radically change their ways; and *hope* in a future when God will restore not only the Israelites but the whole world.

During the period when Judah is fat, self-indulgent, and reveling in luxury, warns of a reckoning day. But later, when Jerusalem is surrounded by foreign troops, Isaiah offers stirring words of hope. World-class tyrants don't intimidate Isaiah; he knows that God can toss them aside like twigs.

Isaiah summons up latent human longings for a better world. He has no doubt that God will one day transform this pockmarked planet into a new earth that has no tears, no pain, no death. In the future world as pictured by Isaiah, wild animals will lie beside each other in peace. Weapons will be melted into farm tools.

At a given point in history, God may appear powerless or blithely unconcerned about the violence and evil that plague this planet. The people of Jerusalem certainly question his concern in the face of the Assyrian invasion. Isaiah gives them a local message of hope: entrust your future to God alone. And he expands that message to encompass the entire world.

Isaiah 24–27 gives a preview of the end of all history. First will come a difficult time, when God purifies the stained earth. Like a woman in childbirth, the earth will undergo pain and struggle. But what follows next will be a future life so wonderful, we can scarcely imagine it. —PY

DAILY CONTEMPLATION

What gives you hope about the future?

DAY 158   Reflection

READY TO BE USED BY GOD

God has created you with a unique personality, a one-of-a-kind life perspective, specific talents, and particular circumstances, all with the purpose of using you for something that only you can step forward and accomplish. Because you are uniquely equipped, your service to God will fulfill the deepest part of you.

Isaiah, for instance, stood specially poised for his work in several ways. Living in Jerusalem, he had regular, privileged contact with Judah's kings. He was married to a prophetess and had two sons. Isaiah lived at a time when powerful neighbors threatened both Israel and Judah, and God was withdrawing his help because of the people's repeated unfaithfulness. God used Isaiah to bring bold prophetic warnings to his nation, as well as eloquent visions of future blessing.

As he delivered his prophecy, Isaiah skillfully painted pictures with words that would endure for centuries and be used by Jesus and many New Testament writers. Isaiah's faithfulness to his unique calling rendered an important service both for God and for us.

Before he could serve, however, Isaiah needed a right understanding of himself and God. In his vision, Isaiah had the opportunity to see God in all his majesty. This sight struck Isaiah with the reality of his own sin and unworthiness to stand before a holy God. Now God could touch Isaiah's lips with a hot coal in a symbolic gesture, purifying him and preparing him for service.

"Whom shall I send? And who will go for us?" God asked, priming Isaiah for the answer only he could offer. God was asking Isaiah to tell the people they desperately needed God's forgiveness and leadership, despite their blindness toward their need.

"Here am I. Send me!" Isaiah replied. He was ready to let God take everything he had and use everything he was, for God's own purposes.

Each of us has a purpose different from Isaiah's, but the process God will use as he prepares us will be the same. God will give us a greater understanding of his almighty power and glory. He will help us to see our great need for his cleansing and guidance. He will purify us and ask if we are willing to be used. Then we can be ready to answer with heartfelt words, "Here am I. Send me!"

Nothing will bring greater satisfaction than joining God in the work for which he has made us. Author Richard Foster affirms, "Service that flows out of our inward person is life, and joy and peace."[14]   —BQ

DAILY CONTEMPLATION

How well do you know yourself? Have you learned how God wants to use you? Ask God for a revelation of his greatness and your sinfulness, and tell him of your desire to be made ready to serve him.

DAY 159   2 Chronicles 32:1–31

SENNACHERIB THREATENS JERUSALEM

After all that Hezekiah had so faithfully done, Sennacherib king of Assyria came and invaded Judah. He laid siege to the fortified cities, thinking to conquer them for himself. When Hezekiah saw that Sennacherib had come and that he intended to make war on Jerusalem, he consulted with his officials and military staff about blocking off the water from the springs outside the city, and they helped him. A large force of men assembled, and they blocked all the springs and the stream that flowed through the land. "Why should the kings of Assyria come and find plenty of water?" they said. Then he worked hard repairing all the broken sections of the wall and building towers on it. He built another wall outside that one and reinforced the supporting terraces of the City of David. He also made large numbers of weapons and shields.

He appointed military officers over the people and assembled them before him in the square at the city gate and encouraged them with these words: "Be strong and courageous. Do not be afraid or discouraged because of the king of Assyria and the vast army with him, for there is a greater power with us than with him. With him is only the arm of flesh, but with us is the LORD our God to help us and to fight our battles." And the people gained confidence from what Hezekiah the king of Judah said.

Later, when Sennacherib king of Assyria and all his forces were laying siege to Lachish, he sent his officers to Jerusalem with this message for Hezekiah king of Judah and for all the people of Judah who were there:

"This is what Sennacherib king of Assyria says: On what are you basing your confidence, that you remain in Jerusalem under siege? When Hezekiah says, 'The LORD our God will save us from the hand of the king of Assyria,' he is misleading you, to let you die of hunger and thirst. Did not Hezekiah himself remove this god's high places and altars, saying to Judah and Jerusalem, 'You must worship before one altar and burn sacrifices on it'?

"Do you not know what I and my fathers have done to all the peoples of the other lands? Were the gods of those nations ever able to deliver their land from my hand? Who of all the gods of these nations that my fathers destroyed has been able to save his people from me? How then can your god deliver you from my hand? Now do not let Hezekiah deceive you and mislead you like this. Do not believe him, for no god of any nation or kingdom has been able to deliver his people from my hand or the hand of my fathers. How much less will your god deliver you from my hand!"

Sennacherib's officers spoke further against the LORD God and against his servant Hezekiah. The king also wrote letters insulting the LORD, the God of Israel, and saying this against him: "Just as the gods of the peoples of the other lands did not rescue their people from my hand, so the god of Hezekiah will not rescue his people from my hand." Then they called out in Hebrew to the people of Jerusalem who were on the wall, to terrify them and make them afraid in order to capture the city. They spoke about the God of Jerusalem as they did about the gods of the other peoples of the world—the work of men's hands.

King Hezekiah and the prophet Isaiah son of Amoz cried out in prayer to heaven about this. And the LORD sent an angel, who annihilated all the fighting men and the leaders and officers in the camp of the Assyrian king. So he withdrew to his own land in disgrace. And when he went into the temple of his god, some of his sons cut him down with the sword.

So the LORD saved Hezekiah and the people of Jerusalem from the hand of Sennacherib king of Assyria and from the hand of all others. He took care of them on every side. Many brought offerings to Jerusalem for the LORD and valuable gifts for Hezekiah king of Judah. From then on he was highly regarded by all the nations.

In those days Hezekiah became ill and was at the point of death. He prayed to the LORD, who answered him and gave him a miraculous sign. But Hezekiah's heart was proud and he did not respond to the kindness shown him; therefore the LORD's wrath was on him and on Judah and Jerusalem. Then Hezekiah repented of the pride of his heart, as did the people of Jerusalem; therefore the LORD's wrath did not come upon them during the days of Hezekiah.

Hezekiah had very great riches and honor, and he made treasuries for his silver and gold and for his precious stones, spices, shields and all kinds of valuables. He also made buildings to store the harvest of grain, new wine and oil; and he made stalls for various kinds of cattle, and pens for the flocks. He built villages and acquired great numbers of flocks and herds, for God had given him very great riches.

It was Hezekiah who blocked the upper outlet of the Gihon spring and channeled the water down to the west side of the City of David. He succeeded in everything he undertook. But when envoys were sent by the rulers of Babylon to ask him about the miraculous sign that had occurred in the land, God left him to test him and to know everything that was in his heart.

It is the greatest crisis that Hezekiah and Isaiah ever faced. The very survival of Judah is in peril. Assyria, ever thirsty for more conquests, has just rolled into Judah, leveling forty-six walled cities and taking 200,150 captives. The Assyrian king demands huge sums of money from Hezekiah, whom he mockingly describes in his annals as "a bird in a cage." Hezekiah may as well be in a cage, for siege armies completely surround his city.

Cowering behind his city's walls, Hezekiah once more turns to Isaiah for advice. Should he surrender? Negotiate? Outside, the Assyrians are directing a barrage of propaganda at Jerusalem's demoralized citizens. They scoff at Israelite hopes for a miracle from God. No gods have helped any other nation withstand the Assyrian juggernaut.

Isaiah, however, refuses to panic. Against all odds, he calmly advises prayer and reliance on the power of God. *Have faith,* he says. *Don't surrender and don't fear. Assyria will return home, wounded.*

Jerusalem looks like a doomed city during the siege by Assyria. But two things happen to fulfill Isaiah's prophecy. First, a great plague strikes the Assyrians (Isaiah 37), a plague also recorded by the historian Herodotus. Later, the murder of Assyria's leader brings internal chaos to that country and cancels out the Assyrian threat.

The miraculous deliverance saves Judah, but only temporarily. In his latter days, Hezekiah foolishly flaunts his country's wealth before envoys from Babylon, a rising power in the east. The citizens of Judah grow proud as well; they become convinced that Jerusalem, God's city, is indestructible—a belief that will be proved tragically false.   —PY

DAILY CONTEMPLATION

Why might God sometimes seem close to you and sometimes seem more distant? What does he care most about when he looks at your heart?

THE LORD'S ANGER AGAINST NINEVEH

An oracle concerning Nineveh. The book of the vision of Nahum the Elkoshite.

The LORD is a jealous and avenging God;
    the LORD takes vengeance and is filled with wrath.
The LORD takes vengeance on his foes
    and maintains his wrath against his enemies.
The LORD is slow to anger and great in power;
    the LORD will not leave the guilty unpunished.
His way is in the whirlwind and the storm,
    and clouds are the dust of his feet.
He rebukes the sea and dries it up;
    he makes all the rivers run dry.
Bashan and Carmel wither
    and the blossoms of Lebanon fade.
The mountains quake before him
    and the hills melt away.
The earth trembles at his presence,
    the world and all who live in it.
Who can withstand his indignation?
    Who can endure his fierce anger?
His wrath is poured out like fire;
    the rocks are shattered before him.

The LORD is good,
    a refuge in times of trouble.
He cares for those who trust in him,
    but with an overwhelming flood
he will make an end of Nineveh;
    he will pursue his foes into darkness.

Whatever they plot against the LORD
    he will bring to an end;
    trouble will not come a second time.
They will be entangled among thorns
    and drunk from their wine;
    they will be consumed like dry stubble.
From you, O Nineveh, has one come forth
    who plots evil against the LORD
    and counsels wickedness.

    This is what the LORD says:

"Although they have allies and are numerous,
    they will be cut off and pass away.

Although I have afflicted you, O Judah,
    I will afflict you no more.
Now I will break their yoke from your neck
    and tear your shackles away."

The LORD has given a command concerning you, Nineveh:
    "You will have no descendants to bear your name.
I will destroy the carved images and cast idols
    that are in the temple of your gods.
I will prepare your grave,
    for you are vile."

Look, there on the mountains,
    the feet of one who brings good news,
    who proclaims peace!
Celebrate your festivals, O Judah,
    and fulfill your vows.
No more will the wicked invade you;
    they will be completely destroyed.

Nahum (NAY-hum) has one distinct advantage over most biblical prophets: he is addressing an enemy. Prophets like Micah and Isaiah sometimes collapsed in grief as they thought about the judgments that would befall their own people. But Nahum lowers the boom on Assyria, a nation that has just obliterated the northern kingdom of Israel and, except for God's miraculous intervention in Hezekiah's day, would have done the same to Nahum's homeland of Judah.

Assyria is an easy enemy to hate—something along the line of Hitler's Germany. Its soldiers decimate cities, lead captives away with hooks in their noses, and plow salt into fertile ground. In fact, Assyria's very obnoxiousness lies at the heart of what Nahum has to say.

A question nags at the citizens of Judah, who have experienced the full force of Assyria's "endless cruelty." Assyria has trampled a huge path of destruction from the region of modern-day Turkey down the Persian Gulf all the way to Egypt. Judah, in contrast, is a tiny vassal state barely clinging to existence. Why would God hold Judah accountable but allow Assyria to go unpunished?

Nahum brashly predicts that even mighty Assyria will meet its end. Its people repented once, in Jonah's day, but have reverted to old patterns that will bring on God's judgment. Undoubtedly, the people of Judah applaud Nahum's prophecies—but who can believe them? Assyria, the most powerful empire in the world for two hundred years, will not simply disappear.

Nahum delivers these prophecies sometime around 700 B.C. In 612 B.C. Nineveh, the last Assyrian stronghold, falls to the Babylonians and Persians. Over time a carpet of grass will cover the pile of rubble marking what has been the greatest city of its time. Years later, both Alexander the Great and Napoleon will camp nearby, with no clue that a city has ever been there.

Like all the biblical prophets, Nahum sees beyond the intimidating forces of history. He knows that behind the rise and fall of empires an even greater force is at work, determining the ultimate outcome. Though God's justice may seem slow, nothing can finally escape it.   —PY

DAY 161   Zephaniah 1:1; 3:1–5, 8–13, 16–20

THE FUTURE OF JERUSALEM

The word of the LORD that came to Zephaniah son of Cushi, the son of Gedaliah, the son of Amariah, the son of Hezekiah, during the reign of Josiah son of Amon king of Judah: . . .

Woe to the city of oppressors,
    rebellious and defiled!
She obeys no one,
    she accepts no correction.
She does not trust in the LORD,
    she does not draw near to her God.
Her officials are roaring lions,
    her rulers are evening wolves,
    who leave nothing for the morning.
Her prophets are arrogant;
    they are treacherous men.
Her priests profane the sanctuary
    and do violence to the law.
The LORD within her is righteous;
    he does no wrong.
Morning by morning he dispenses his justice,
    and every new day he does not fail,
    yet the unrighteous know no shame. . . .

Therefore wait for me," declares the LORD,
    "for the day I will stand up to testify.
I have decided to assemble the nations,
    to gather the kingdoms
and to pour out my wrath on them—
    all my fierce anger.
The whole world will be consumed
    by the fire of my jealous anger.

"Then will I purify the lips of the peoples,
    that all of them may call on the name of the LORD
    and serve him shoulder to shoulder.
From beyond the rivers of Cush
    my worshipers, my scattered people,
    will bring me offerings.
On that day you will not be put to shame
    for all the wrongs you have done to me,
because I will remove from this city
    those who rejoice in their pride.
Never again will you be haughty
    on my holy hill.
But I will leave within you
    the meek and humble,
    who trust in the name of the LORD.
The remnant of Israel will do no wrong;
    they will speak no lies,
    nor will deceit be found in their mouths.
They will eat and lie down
    and no one will make them afraid." ...

On that day they will say to Jerusalem,
    "Do not fear, O Zion;
    do not let your hands hang limp.
The LORD your God is with you,
    he is mighty to save.
He will take great delight in you,
    he will quiet you with his love,
    he will rejoice over you with singing."

"The sorrows for the appointed feasts
    I will remove from you;
    they are a burden and a reproach to you.
At that time I will deal
    with all who oppressed you;
I will rescue the lame
    and gather those who have been scattered.
I will give them praise and honor
    in every land where they were put to shame.
At that time I will gather you;
    at that time I will bring you home.
I will give you honor and praise
    among all the peoples of the earth
when I restore your fortunes
    before your very eyes,"
        says the LORD.

Through the influence of prophets like Micah and Isaiah, King Hezekiah helped set the land of Judah back on course. However, Hezekiah's death vacated the throne for Manasseh (muh-NAS-uh), who proved to be one of Judah's all-time worst kings. In his fifty-year reign—the longest of any king of Israel or Judah—Manasseh reversed all the good that Hezekiah had accomplished.

An unabashed tyrant, Manasseh filled the streets of Jerusalem with blood. He made child sacrifice common practice, built astrology altars in God's temple, and encouraged male prostitution as part of religious ritual. By the time he died, very few reminders of the covenant with God remained in Judah. Public shrines abounded, and storefronts in Jerusalem were advertising household gods, mediums, and spiritists. God's chosen people were out-paganizing the pagans.

The next king, Amon (UH-muhn), started out in his father's footsteps, but this time his own officials rose up in revolt and assassinated him after two years. The nation of Judah, cut loose from its moorings, was drifting toward total anarchy. And Josiah, the pint-size prince crowned by Amon's supporters, hardly gives much reason for optimism.

In the early days of Josiah's reign, the prophet Zephaniah (ZEF-uh-NI-uh) speaks out against the decadence spreading throughout Judah. Other prophets have come from peasant stock; Zephaniah proudly traces his ancestry back to King Hezekiah. Yet, unlike others of high social standing, he doesn't try to defend the upper classes. Rather, he accuses them of chief responsibility for the decay in Judah. The officials, the priests, the rulers, the judges, even the prophets—these are the targets of Zephaniah's rage.

The leaders of Judah are pointing the entire nation on a course of self-destruction. Unless they reverse directions, Jerusalem will face the same fate as many of its fallen neighbors. —PY

DAILY CONTEMPLATION

When you have plenty of money and life seems easy, do you tend to move closer to God or farther from him?

DAY 162   2 Kings 22:1–23:3

JOSIAH RENEWS THE COVENANT

Josiah was eight years old when he became king, and he reigned in Jerusalem thirty-one years. His mother's name was Jedidah daughter of Adaiah; she was from Bozkath. He did what was right in the eyes of the LORD and walked in all the ways of his father David, not turning aside to the right or to the left.

In the eighteenth year of his reign, King Josiah sent the secretary, Shaphan son of Azaliah, the son of Meshullam, to the temple of the LORD. He said: "Go up to Hilkiah the high priest and have him get ready the money that has been brought into the temple of the LORD, which the doorkeepers have collected from the people. Have them entrust it to the men appointed to supervise the work on the temple. And have these men pay the workers who repair the temple of the LORD—the carpenters, the builders and the masons. Also have them purchase timber and dressed stone to repair the temple. But they need not account for the money entrusted to them, because they are acting faithfully."

Hilkiah the high priest said to Shaphan the secretary, "I have found the Book of the Law in the temple of the LORD." He gave it to Shaphan, who read it. Then Shaphan the secretary went to the king and reported to him: "Your officials have paid out the money that was in the temple of the LORD and have entrusted it to the workers and supervisors at the temple." Then Shaphan the secretary informed the king, "Hilkiah the priest has given me a book." And Shaphan read from it in the presence of the king.

When the king heard the words of the Book of the Law, he tore his robes. He gave these orders to Hilkiah the priest, Ahikam son of Shaphan, Acbor son of Micaiah, Shaphan the secretary and Asaiah the king's attendant: "Go and inquire of the LORD for me and for the people and for all Judah about what is written in this book that has been found. Great is the LORD's anger that burns against us because our fathers have not obeyed the words of this book; they have not acted in accordance with all that is written there concerning us."

Hilkiah the priest, Ahikam, Acbor, Shaphan and Asaiah went to speak to the prophetess Huldah, who was the wife of Shallum son of Tikvah, the son of Harhas, keeper of the wardrobe. She lived in Jerusalem, in the Second District.

She said to them, "This is what the LORD, the God of Israel, says: Tell the man who sent you to me, 'This is what the LORD says: I am going to bring disaster on this place and its people, according to everything written in the book the king of Judah has read. Because they have forsaken me and burned incense to other gods and provoked me to anger by all the idols their hands have made, my anger will burn against this place and will not be quenched.' Tell the king of Judah, who sent you to inquire of the LORD, 'This is what the LORD, the God of Israel, says concerning the words you heard: Because your heart was responsive and you humbled yourself before the LORD when you heard what I have spoken against this place and its people, that they would become accursed and laid waste, and because you tore your robes and wept in my presence, I have heard you, declares the LORD. Therefore I will gather you to your fathers, and you will be buried in peace. Your eyes will not see all the disaster I am going to bring on this place.'"

So they took her answer back to the king.

Then the king called together all the elders of Judah and Jerusalem. He went up to the temple of the LORD with the men of Judah, the people of Jerusalem, the priests and the prophets—all the people from the least to the greatest. He read in their hearing all the words of the Book of the Covenant, which had been found in the temple of the LORD. The king stood by the pillar and renewed the covenant in the presence of the LORD—to follow the LORD and keep his commands, regulations and decrees with all his heart and all his soul, thus confirming the words of the covenant written in this book. Then all the people pledged themselves to the covenant.

The Bible does not record what specific effect Zephaniah's words had within Judah. But it does give a thrilling account of a turnaround that occurred during his days, led by King Josiah.

King Josiah took over at the age of eight, in the midst of a crisis seemingly beyond all healing. Josiah, however, is no ordinary eight-year-old. Raised by a wicked king in a wicked time, he somehow emerges with a spiritual vision that has no equal. Against the odds, Josiah steers his nation back toward God.

Josiah devotes much time and energy to a favorite public works project: repairing the temple. And one busy day, as carpenters saw new joists and beams, and masons carve new stones for the temple walls, and workmen haul off rubble from the idols Josiah has smashed—in the midst of that din and clutter, a priest makes an amazing discovery. He finds a scroll that looks like—*could it be?*—the Book of the Covenant, the original record of the agreement between the Israelites and their God. (Most scholars believe the scroll contained part or all of the book of Deuteronomy.)

The neglect of such an important document, long buried and forgotten, shows the extent of Judah's slide away from God. And Josiah's response shows the depth of his commitment. Hearing those sacred words for the first time, he tears his robes in shame and repentance. And after a prophetess confirms the scroll's authenticity, Josiah pledges himself and his nation to the terms of the long-lost covenant.

This chapter tells the story of the dramatic discovery, and the next tells of Josiah's fervent campaign to call his nation back to God. His actions will change the landscape of Judah and stave off certain destruction. All this comes about because a young king takes seriously the words of God.　　　　　　　　　　　—PY

DAILY CONTEMPLATION

When have you experienced an awakening similar to King Josiah's?

DAY 163   Reflection

WHAT DOES IT TAKE TO BE FAITHFUL?

The story of Josiah offers great inspiration. Descended from a father and grandfather who modeled corrupt, God-hating leadership, Josiah nevertheless broke the mold and turned a nation's loyalties around. As no other king had done, Josiah turned to God "with all his heart and with all his soul and with all his strength" (2 Kings 23:25). Yet as time wore on, Josiah made a mistake that cost him his life and put Judah in the hands of a powerless ruler who answered to Egypt. Though Josiah was committed to obeying God, at some point he faltered, and his decision cost everything.

Why do Israel and Judah fail so consistently? Why does even Josiah go astray eventually? Are all believers doomed to start out well and fizzle at the finish?

In Israel and Judah's case, they lacked long-term obedience. They worshiped God one year and abandoned him the next. They got in trouble and turned to him, then got delivered and reverted to their own ways. Like a car out of alignment, they kept veering off the road and into the path of the world around them.

We face the same challenge. We too find it difficult to stick with something over the long haul, to grow stronger in commitment rather than weaker. We generally are not accustomed to pursuing "a long obedience in the same direction," explains author, professor, and former pastor Eugene Peterson. "We assume that if something can be done at all, it can be done quickly and efficiently. Our attention spans have been conditioned by thirty-second commercials. Our sense of reality has been flattened by thirty-page abridgments. . . . Everyone is in a hurry. . . . They are impatient for results. They have adopted the lifestyle of a tourist and only want the high points."[15]

This sets believers up for a fall. We can't develop a relationship with God once and be done. We can't achieve spiritual maturity in a few weeks or months and then move on to more exciting adventures. A believer's life with God holds depths that can't be reached in a lifetime of walking with him, and even more that we will only experience in eternity. But we *can* go a lot deeper with God here on earth, living in a way that guards us from repeating the pattern of the Israelites.

Peterson writes, "In going against the stream of the world's ways there are two biblical designations for people of faith that are extremely useful: *disciple* and *pilgrim*. *Disciple (mathetes)* says we are people who spend our lives apprenticed to our master, Jesus Christ. We are in a growing, learning relationship always. . . . *Pilgrim (parepidemos)* tells us we are people who spend our lives going someplace, going to God, and whose path for getting there is the way, Jesus Christ."[16]

As disciples, we walk daily with Jesus and learn from him. And the more we learn of him, the more we see how much we don't know. The relationship continually opens new worlds and, as we stay with it, our love for him will grow deeper and deeper. As pilgrims, we will encounter a multitude of experiences and emotions. Through it all, Jesus is the goal of our journey; he is also our companion, traveling and guiding through each landscape.

We can be faithful if we commit to a long obedience in the direction of Jesus Christ.   —BQ

DAILY CONTEMPLATION

Do you tend to persevere, staying determined and focused, or do you tire easily of one pursuit and move on to another? How is this tendency affecting your pursuit of God? Ask God to help you be faithful to the end.

ISRAEL FORSAKES GOD

The words of Jeremiah son of Hilkiah, one of the priests at Anathoth in the territory of Benjamin. The word of the LORD came to him in the thirteenth year of the reign of Josiah son of Amon king of Judah, and through the reign of Jehoiakim son of Josiah king of Judah, down to the fifth month of the eleventh year of Zedekiah son of Josiah king of Judah, when the people of Jerusalem went into exile. . . .

"Go and proclaim in the hearing of Jerusalem:

"'I remember the devotion of your youth,
     how as a bride you loved me
and followed me through the desert,
     through a land not sown.
Israel was holy to the LORD,
     the firstfruits of his harvest;
all who devoured her were held guilty,
     and disaster overtook them,'"
       declares the LORD.

Hear the word of the LORD, O house of Jacob,
     all you clans of the house of Israel.

     This is what the LORD says:

"What fault did your fathers find in me,
     that they strayed so far from me?
They followed worthless idols
     and became worthless themselves.
They did not ask, 'Where is the LORD,
     who brought us up out of Egypt
and led us through the barren wilderness,
     through a land of deserts and rifts,
a land of drought and darkness,
     a land where no one travels and no one lives?'
I brought you into a fertile land
     to eat its fruit and rich produce.
But you came and defiled my land
     and made my inheritance detestable.
The priests did not ask,
     'Where is the LORD?'
Those who deal with the law did not know me;
     the leaders rebelled against me.
The prophets prophesied by Baal,
     following worthless idols. . . .

"Has a nation ever changed its gods?
    (Yet they are not gods at all.)
But my people have exchanged their Glory
    for worthless idols.
Be appalled at this, O heavens,
    and shudder with great horror,"
      declares the LORD.
"My people have committed two sins:
They have forsaken me,
    the spring of living water,
and have dug their own cisterns,
    broken cisterns that cannot hold water.
Is Israel a servant, a slave by birth?
    Why then has he become plunder? . . .

"Long ago you broke off your yoke
    and tore off your bonds;
    you said, 'I will not serve you!'
Indeed, on every high hill
    and under every spreading tree
    you lay down as a prostitute.
I had planted you like a choice vine
    of sound and reliable stock.
How then did you turn against me
    into a corrupt, wild vine?
Although you wash yourself with soda
    and use an abundance of soap,
    the stain of your guilt is still before me,"
      declares the Sovereign LORD.
"How can you say, 'I am not defiled;
    I have not run after the Baals'?
See how you behaved in the valley;
    consider what you have done.
You are a swift she-camel
    running here and there,
a wild donkey accustomed to the desert,
    sniffing the wind in her craving—
    in her heat who can restrain her?
Any males that pursue her need not tire themselves;
    at mating time they will find her.
Do not run until your feet are bare
    and your throat is dry.
But you said, 'It's no use!
    I love foreign gods,
    and I must go after them.'

> "As a thief is disgraced when he is caught,
>   so the house of Israel is disgraced—
> they, their kings and their officials,
>   their priests and their prophets.
> They say to wood, 'You are my father,'
>   and to stone, 'You gave me birth.'
> They have turned their backs to me
>   and not their faces;
> yet when they are in trouble, they say,
>   'Come and save us!'"

Zephaniah was not the only prophet active during King Josiah's days. Just as Josiah is reaching adulthood, the doleful voice of Jeremiah begins to be heard in the streets of Jerusalem. Later, Jeremiah's messages are collected into a book that is the Bible's longest and easily its most passionate. Jeremiah is subject to violent swings of mood, and his book reflects that same emotional temperament. The English word *jeremiad,* which means "a long complaint," conveys something of the tone of this prophet.

This chapter, full of strong images and rhetorical blasts, typifies Jeremiah's style. He uses sexual imagery to present Judah's crisis as a kind of lover's quarrel between God and Judah. She is like a prostitute who lies down under every spreading tree; like a rutting she-camel; like a donkey in heat driven wild with desire.

But what is the object of Judah's desire? Incredibly, she is trading the glory of God for worthless idols of wood and stone. God, the wounded lover, cannot comprehend his people's actions, and neither can Jeremiah.

Jeremiah has two main complaints against Judah: she prostitutes herself both through idol worship and through alliances with foreign nations. When a military threat looms, Judah turns to empires like Assyria, Egypt, or Babylon for help, not to God.

Josiah, one of Judah's all-time best kings, leads a mostly successful campaign to rid the nation of idols. But even Josiah succumbs to the temptation of foreign entanglements. Against Jeremiah's counsel, he leads an ill-advised march against Egyptian armies. Josiah dies in that battle, and his death shocks the nation. A grieving Jeremiah writes laments in honor of the great king.

Judah will never recover from Josiah's fatal mistake. Egypt installs a puppet king over Judah, and from then on no one has the ability to rally Judah's religious or political strength. Jeremiah lives through the reigns of four weakling kings, and the messages collected in this book heap scorn upon them.   —PY

DAILY CONTEMPLATION

To whom do you show the most consistent loyalty? Are you loyal to God?

DEATH, FAMINE, SWORD

Then the LORD said to me: "Even if Moses and Samuel were to stand before me, my heart would not go out to this people. Send them away from my presence! Let them go!

And if they ask you, 'Where shall we go?' tell them, 'This is what the LORD says:

"'Those destined for death, to death;
those for the sword, to the sword;
those for starvation, to starvation;
those for captivity, to captivity.'

"I will send four kinds of destroyers against them," declares the LORD, "the sword to kill and the dogs to drag away and the birds of the air and the beasts of the earth to devour and destroy. I will make them abhorrent to all the kingdoms of the earth because of what Manasseh son of Hezekiah king of Judah did in Jerusalem.

"Who will have pity on you, O Jerusalem?
Who will mourn for you?
Who will stop to ask how you are?
You have rejected me," declares the LORD.
"You keep on backsliding.
So I will lay hands on you and destroy you;
I can no longer show compassion." . . .

You understand, O LORD;
remember me and care for me.
Avenge me on my persecutors.
You are long-suffering—do not take me away;
think of how I suffer reproach for your sake.
When your words came, I ate them;
they were my joy and my heart's delight,
for I bear your name,
O LORD God Almighty.
I never sat in the company of revelers,
never made merry with them;
I sat alone because your hand was on me
and you had filled me with indignation.
Why is my pain unending
and my wound grievous and incurable?
Will you be to me like a deceptive brook,
like a spring that fails?

Therefore this is what the LORD says:

"If you repent, I will restore you
> that you may serve me;
if you utter worthy, not worthless, words,
> you will be my spokesman.
Let this people turn to you,
> but you must not turn to them.
I will make you a wall to this people,
> a fortified wall of bronze;
they will fight against you
> but will not overcome you,
for I am with you
> to rescue and save you,"
> > declares the LORD.
"I will save you from the hands of the wicked
> and redeem you from the grasp of the cruel."

For most of his life Jeremiah has to deliver a gloomy message, and no one feels the weight of that message more than he. "Since my people are crushed, I am crushed; I mourn, and horror grips me.... Oh, that my head were a spring of water and my eyes a fountain of tears!" (8:21; 9:1). That spirit comes through so strongly in his writings that Jeremiah has become known as "the Weeping Prophet."

More than Judah's future causes Jeremiah alarm; he fears for his own personal safety. From the very beginning he argues with God about his assignment as a prophet. God makes harsh demands on Jeremiah, and he responds to those demands in typical fashion: by whining, complaining, feeling sorry for himself, and even lashing out against God's cruelty. The book includes a remarkable series of conversations—more like arguments—in which Jeremiah tells God exactly how he feels.

This chapter includes one such conversation with God. Quotation marks surround God's speeches: he begins by pronouncing judgment on the nation of Judah. But at verse 10 Jeremiah butts in with his agenda. What will people think of a prophet delivering a message like that? His name is a national swear word already. He'd be better off unborn. To him, God seems unreliable, like a brook that dries up, a spring that fails.

Despite Jeremiah's fits and protests, God never gives up on him. He promises to make the weepy prophet "a fortified wall of bronze," able to stand against the whole land. Likewise, Jeremiah, for all his diatribes, never gives up on God. The word of God is inside him and he can't stop talking about it. "But if I say, 'I will not mention him or speak any more in his name,' his word is in my heart like a fire, a fire shut up in my bones. I am weary of holding it in; indeed, I cannot" (20:9).   —PY

DAILY CONTEMPLATION

What complaints would you bring to God? Do you, like Jeremiah, ever feel unappreciated by God?

RESTORATION OF ISRAEL

"They will come and shout for joy on the heights of Zion;
    they will rejoice in the bounty of the LORD—
the grain, the new wine and the oil,
    the young of the flocks and herds.
They will be like a well-watered garden,
    and they will sorrow no more.
Then maidens will dance and be glad,
    young men and old as well.
I will turn their mourning into gladness;
    I will give them comfort and joy instead of sorrow.
I will satisfy the priests with abundance,
    and my people will be filled with my bounty,"
       declares the LORD.

This is what the LORD says:

"A voice is heard in Ramah,
    mourning and great weeping,
Rachel weeping for her children
    and refusing to be comforted,
    because her children are no more." . . .

This is what the LORD Almighty, the God of Israel, says: "When I bring them back from captivity, the people in the land of Judah and in its towns will once again use these words: 'The LORD bless you, O righteous dwelling, O sacred mountain.' People will live together in Judah and all its towns—farmers and those who move about with their flocks. I will refresh the weary and satisfy the faint."

At this I awoke and looked around. My sleep had been pleasant to me.

"The days are coming," declares the LORD, "when I will plant the house of Israel and the house of Judah with the offspring of men and of animals. Just as I watched over them to uproot and tear down, and to overthrow, destroy and bring disaster, so I will watch over them to build and to plant," declares the LORD. "In those days people will no longer say,

'The fathers have eaten sour grapes,
    and the children's teeth are set on edge.'
Instead, everyone will die for his own sin; whoever eats sour grapes—his
    own teeth will be set on edge.
"The time is coming," declares the Lord,
    "when I will make a new covenant
with the house of Israel
    and with the house of Judah.

It will not be like the covenant
    I made with their forefathers
when I took them by the hand
    to lead them out of Egypt,
because they broke my covenant,
    though I was a husband to them,"
      declares the LORD.
"This is the covenant I will make with the house of Israel
    after that time," declares the LORD.
"I will put my law in their minds
    and write it on their hearts.
I will be their God,
    and they will be my people.
No longer will a man teach his neighbor,
    or a man his brother, saying, 'Know the LORD,'
because they will all know me,
    from the least of them to the greatest,"
      declares the LORD.
"For I will forgive their wickedness
    and will remember their sins no more."

Trained as a priest, Jeremiah learned at an early age the story of the covenant between God and his chosen people. Yet he also knew the more recent history of ten Israelite tribes being dispersed by the Assyrians. Suddenly he is ordered to prophesy that the two surviving tribes in Judah will undergo a similar trial. In Jeremiah's own lifetime, Babylonian armies will desecrate the holy city of Jerusalem and take captive many more Israelites.

Has God abandoned the covenant? Has he cast aside his chosen people? In this chapter, Jeremiah receives a dream sequence that hints at an answer. He sees that a "remnant" will survive the Babylonian invasion. God has not permanently rejected his people but is allowing them to go through temporary punishment for the sake of purging. Moreover, God promises that the future of the Israelites will be far grander than anything in the past.

Bible interpreters disagree on the full meaning of these promises. Some things are clear: For example, God promises a "new covenant" to replace and improve on the old, broken one. Hebrews 8 quotes a key passage from this chapter in Jeremiah and applies the prophecy to Jesus, who made possible the new covenant and its grand forgiveness.

But what of the predictions that seem to apply, geographically, to the land of Palestine? Some of the exiled Israelites, led by Ezra (EZ-ruh) and Nehemiah, will eventually return from captivity in Babylon, but that sparse resettlement of a devastated land hardly calls to mind the glorious new society described here. Jewish scholars disagree on the meaning: some point to the modern-day state of Israel as a direct fulfillment of this prophecy, while others violently disagree. And some Christian theologians believe that these promises, under the new covenant, apply to the church in a more general sense and not to the Jewish race and its settlement of the land.

Jeremiah does not get a detailed blueprint of future history, but he does get a resounding confirmation of how God feels about his people. —PY

DAY 167
Jeremiah 38:1–28

JEREMIAH THROWN INTO A CISTERN

Shephatiah son of Mattan, Gedaliah son of Pashhur, Jehucal son of Shelemiah, and Pashhur son of Malkijah heard what Jeremiah was telling all the people when he said, "This is what the LORD says: 'Whoever stays in this city will die by the sword, famine or plague, but whoever goes over to the Babylonians will live. He will escape with his life; he will live.' And this is what the LORD says: 'This city will certainly be handed over to the army of the king of Babylon, who will capture it.'"

Then the officials said to the king, "This man should be put to death. He is discouraging the soldiers who are left in this city, as well as all the people, by the things he is saying to them. This man is not seeking the good of these people but their ruin."

"He is in your hands," King Zedekiah answered. "The king can do nothing to oppose you."

So they took Jeremiah and put him into the cistern of Malkijah, the king's son, which was in the courtyard of the guard. They lowered Jeremiah by ropes into the cistern; it had no water in it, only mud, and Jeremiah sank down into the mud.

But Ebed-Melech, a Cushite, an official in the royal palace, heard that they had put Jeremiah into the cistern. While the king was sitting in the Benjamin Gate, Ebed-Melech went out of the palace and said to him, "My lord the king, these men have acted wickedly in all they have done to Jeremiah the prophet. They have thrown him into a cistern, where he will starve to death when there is no longer any bread in the city."

Then the king commanded Ebed-Melech the Cushite, "Take thirty men from here with you and lift Jeremiah the prophet out of the cistern before he dies."

So Ebed-Melech took the men with him and went to a room under the treasury in the palace. He took some old rags and worn-out clothes from there and let them down with ropes to Jeremiah in the cistern. Ebed-Melech the Cushite said to Jeremiah, "Put these old rags and worn-out clothes under your arms to pad the ropes." Jeremiah did so, and they pulled him up with the ropes and lifted him out of the cistern. And Jeremiah remained in the courtyard of the guard.

Then King Zedekiah sent for Jeremiah the prophet and had him brought to the third entrance to the temple of the LORD. "I am going to ask you something," the king said to Jeremiah. "Do not hide anything from me."

Jeremiah said to Zedekiah, "If I give you an answer, will you not kill me? Even if I did give you counsel, you would not listen to me."

But King Zedekiah swore this oath secretly to Jeremiah: "As surely as the LORD lives, who has given us breath, I will neither kill you nor hand you over to those who are seeking your life."

Then Jeremiah said to Zedekiah, "This is what the LORD God Almighty, the God of Israel, says: 'If you surrender to the officers of the king of Babylon, your life will be spared and this city will not be burned down; you and your family will live. But if you will not surrender to the officers of the king of Babylon, this city will be handed over to the Babylonians and they will burn it down; you yourself will not escape from their hands.'"

King Zedekiah said to Jeremiah, "I am afraid of the Jews who have gone over to the Babylonians, for the Babylonians may hand me over to them and they will mistreat me."

"They will not hand you over," Jeremiah replied. "Obey the LORD by doing what I tell you. Then it will go well with you, and your life will be spared. But if you refuse to surrender, this is what the LORD has revealed to me: All the women left in the palace of the king of Judah will be brought out to the officials of the king of Babylon. Those women will say to you:

"'They misled you and overcame you—
   those trusted friends of yours.
Your feet are sunk in the mud;
   your friends have deserted you.'

"All your wives and children will be brought out to the Babylonians. You yourself will not escape from their hands but will be captured by the king of Babylon; and this city will be burned down."

Then Zedekiah said to Jeremiah, "Do not let anyone know about this conversation, or you may die. If the officials hear that I talked with you, and they come to you and say, 'Tell us what you said to the king and what the king said to you; do not hide it from us or we will kill you,' then tell them, 'I was pleading with the king not to send me back to Jonathan's house to die there.'"

All the officials did come to Jeremiah and question him, and he told them everything the king had ordered him to say. So they said no more to him, for no one had heard his conversation with the king.

And Jeremiah remained in the courtyard of the guard until the day Jerusalem was captured.

Jeremiah has good reason for being a weeping, balky prophet. Four kings succeeded Josiah, but each of them served as puppet for a larger empire, and each of them gave the prophet Jeremiah a hard time. One king scheduled a private reading of Jeremiah's prophecies in his winter apartment. As each scroll was read, the king casually hacked it to pieces with a knife and tossed it into the fireplace (36:23). On other occasions the prophet himself was beaten and put in stocks, or locked in a dungeon or, as this chapter relates, thrown in a well. The best state Jeremiah could hope for was house arrest or confinement in the king's courtyard.

The mistreatment, however, only serves to harden Jeremiah's resolve. He curses his tormentors even as they release him from the stocks. Evidently, he reserves his fears and doubts for God's ears alone.

The events in this chapter take place in Jerusalem, in the midst of a terrible two-year siege by the Babylonians. The city's starving residents, barely clinging to survival, have resorted to cannibalism. City officials are frantically trying to improve morale and whip up courage. Little wonder they object to Jeremiah's dour advice: "We're going to lose anyway—might as well defect over the walls or open the gates and let the Babylonians in."

The following chapter (39) tells of Jeremiah's prophecies coming true. Babylon's army does breach the walls and then captures and tortures the weak king Zedekiah. The conquerors treat Jeremiah with respect, however, having heard of his counsel to surrender.

Not long after the fall of Jerusalem, a gang of Israelites rebel against their captors and run to Egypt, with the angry prophet in tow. They think they have reached safety. But in his last recorded words, Jeremiah, a browbeaten seventy-year-old, announces that those refugees will meet a tragic end. They ignore him—just like everyone else in Jeremiah's hapless career.   —PY

DAILY CONTEMPLATION

When have you felt as if everyone were out to get you? Can you identify with Jeremiah's feelings?

DAY 168   Reflection

SERVING FROM A SENSITIVE SPIRIT

The prophet Jeremiah had a tough life. God used him in a significant way to speak his words of both punishment and hope to the people of Judah, but much of the time Jeremiah struggled with his role. For the most part the people didn't like him. Regarding him as a traitor, they beat him and locked him in a dungeon. After conveying a message that was hard to deliver, Jeremiah found that the lack of positive response made his life even more difficult.

Jeremiah's temperament, sensitive and seemingly moody, did not help. He's been called the Weeping Prophet for good reason. Anyone would weep in Jeremiah's circumstances, seeing his people and holy city fall into the hands of another nation. But not only did he weep; Jeremiah also complained to God and loudly bemoaned his lot in life. Against the people, Jeremiah retaliated with curses.

What can we learn from this prophet, who was so clearly loved and chosen by God for important work yet struggled so intensely? God told Jeremiah, "Before I formed you in the womb I knew you, before you were born I set you apart; I appointed you as a prophet to the nations" (1:5). Despite his frequent outbursts, Jeremiah loved God, too, and he embraced the truth of the message he delivered. "When your words came, I ate them; they were my joy and my heart's delight" (15:16).

We see in Jeremiah's life that following God faithfully and doing his work won't always be easy. We may suffer, experience unfair treatment, and feel unpopular. Jesus said that if he himself got such treatment, his followers should expect the same (John 15:20). When we feel discouraged, as Jeremiah did, we can be honest with God. We can reveal our questions and even voice our complaints. God can handle our true feelings. Maybe God chose Jeremiah, and chooses people today who have sensitive spirits, precisely because he needs those with soft hearts to complete the special assignments he is giving.

Yet as we mature in our walk with God, we can hope and pray to reach a place of deepened trust and fulfillment in the place he has put us. Struggles are never easy, and physical pain never pleasant. Yet as God hears our cries and shares our pain, he can also bring us to a place of oneness with him, where we can rise above the hard times and sense God's presence and promises as more real than even our physical surroundings. This ability comes only through God and through time spent training ourselves, as disciples in the presence of God, to trust and rely on him rather than our outward circumstances.

Jeremiah reveals that God cherishes his children who are temperamental and emotional. He walks closely with them and continues to give his hand of guidance and protection. We also learn from Jeremiah that God's promises are fulfilled in the end. He will care for us and remain faithful throughout our lifetime. We can trust him, and we can ask for his help in making that trust affect the way we react to our circumstances. We have a choice—to live controlled only by our human emotions or to let God embrace and transcend those emotions, giving us his own mind and heart.   —BQ

DAILY CONTEMPLATION

How do you react to suffering? Ask God to help you mature in your relationship with Jesus. "Consider it pure joy, my brothers, whenever you face trials of many kinds, because you know that the testing of your faith develops perseverance. Perseverance must finish its work so that you may be mature and complete, not lacking anything" (James 1:2–4).

HABAKKUK'S COMPLAINT

The oracle that Habakkuk the prophet received.

How long, O LORD, must I call for help,
    but you do not listen?
Or cry out to you, "Violence!"
    but you do not save?
Why do you make me look at injustice?
    Why do you tolerate wrong?
Destruction and violence are before me;
    there is strife, and conflict abounds.
Therefore the law is paralyzed,
    and justice never prevails.
The wicked hem in the righteous,
    so that justice is perverted.

"Look at the nations and watch—
    and be utterly amazed.
For I am going to do something in your days
    that you would not believe,
    even if you were told.
I am raising up the Babylonians,
    that ruthless and impetuous people,
who sweep across the whole earth
    to seize dwelling places not their own." . . .

O LORD, are you not from everlasting?
    My God, my Holy One, we will not die.
O LORD, you have appointed them to execute judgment;
    O Rock, you have ordained them to punish.
Your eyes are too pure to look on evil;
    you cannot tolerate wrong.
Why then do you tolerate the treacherous?
    Why are you silent while the wicked
swallow up those more righteous than themselves?
You have made men like fish in the sea,
    like sea creatures that have no ruler.
The wicked foe pulls all of them up with hooks,
    he catches them in his net,
he gathers them up in his dragnet;
    and so he rejoices and is glad.
Therefore he sacrifices to his net
    and burns incense to his dragnet,

for by his net he lives in luxury
and enjoys the choicest food.
Is he to keep on emptying his net,
destroying nations without mercy?

Everyone has a built-in sense of justice. If a careless driver runs down a small child and nonchalantly drives on, other drivers will follow in hot pursuit. **He can't get away with that!** We may disagree on specific rules of fairness, but we all follow some inner code.

And, frankly, much of the time life seems unfair. What child "deserves" to grow up in the slums of Calcutta, or Rio de Janeiro, or the East Bronx? Why should people like Adolf Hitler, Joseph Stalin, and Saddam Hussein get away with tyrannizing millions of people? Why are some kind, gentle people struck down in the prime of life while other, meaner people live into cantankerous old age?

We all ask different versions of such questions. And the prophet named Habakkuk (huh-BAK-uhk) asked them of God directly—and got a no-holds-barred reply. Habakkuk does not mince words. He demands that God explain why he isn't responding to the injustice, violence, and evil that the prophet can see around him.

God answers with the same message he has told Jeremiah, that he will send the Babylonians to punish Judah. But such words hardly reassure Habakkuk, for the Babylonians are ruthless, savage people. Can this be justice—using an even more evil nation to punish Judah?

The book of Habakkuk does not solve the problem of evil. But Habakkuk's conversations with God convince him of one certainty: God has not lost control. As a God of justice, he cannot let evil win. First, he will deal with the Babylonians on their own terms. Then, later, he will intervene with great force, shaking the very foundations of the earth until no sign of injustice remains.

"The earth will be filled with the knowledge of the glory of the LORD, as the waters cover the sea," God promises Habakkuk (2:14). A glimpse of that powerful glory changes the prophet's attitude from outrage to joy. In the course of his "debate" with God, Habakkuk learns new lessons about faith, which are beautifully expressed in the last chapter. God's answers so satisfy Habakkuk that his book, which begins with a complaint, ends with one of the most beautiful songs in the Bible.   —PY

DAILY CONTEMPLATION

Can you think of an instance in your life in which, after some doubt-ful times, you eventually saw God deliver justice?

HIS COMPASSIONS NEVER FAIL

I am the man who has seen affliction
    by the rod of his wrath.
He has driven me away and made me walk
    in darkness rather than light;
indeed, he has turned his hand against me
    again and again, all day long.

He has made my skin and my flesh grow old
    and has broken my bones.
He has besieged me and surrounded me
    with bitterness and hardship.
He has made me dwell in darkness
    like those long dead.

He has walled me in so I cannot escape;
    he has weighed me down with chains.
Even when I call out or cry for help,
    he shuts out my prayer.
He has barred my way with blocks of stone;
    he has made my paths crooked.

Like a bear lying in wait,
    like a lion in hiding,
he dragged me from the path and mangled me
    and left me without help.
He drew his bow
    and made me the target for his arrows.

He pierced my heart
    with arrows from his quiver.
I became the laughingstock of all my people;
    they mock me in song all day long.
He has filled me with bitter herbs
    and sated me with gall.

He has broken my teeth with gravel;
    he has trampled me in the dust.
I have been deprived of peace;
    I have forgotten what prosperity is.
So I say, "My splendor is gone
    and all that I had hoped from the LORD."

I remember my affliction and my wandering,
    the bitterness and the gall.

I well remember them,
and my soul is downcast within me.
Yet this I call to mind
and therefore I have hope:

Because of the LORD's great love we are not consumed,
for his compassions never fail.
They are new every morning;
great is your faithfulness.
I say to myself, "The LORD is my portion;
therefore I will wait for him."

The LORD is good to those whose hope is in him,
to the one who seeks him;
it is good to wait quietly
for the salvation of the LORD.
It is good for a man to bear the yoke
while he is young.

Let him sit alone in silence,
for the LORD has laid it on him.
Let him bury his face in the dust—
there may yet be hope.
Let him offer his cheek to one who would strike him,
and let him be filled with disgrace.

For men are not cast off
by the Lord forever.
Though he brings grief, he will show compassion,
so great is his unfailing love.
For he does not willingly bring affliction
or grief to the children of men.

To crush underfoot
all prisoners in the land,
to deny a man his rights
before the Most High,
to deprive a man of justice—
would not the Lord see such things?

Who can speak and have it happen
if the Lord has not decreed it?
Is it not from the mouth of the Most High
that both calamities and good things come?
Why should any living man complain
when punished for his sins?

Let us examine our ways and test them,
and let us return to the LORD.

I am the man who has seen affliction . . ." this chapter begins, and that doleful sentence captures the tone of this entire book. Judah's king is now shackled and blinded, his sons the princes slaughtered. Jerusalem—the capital city, the holy city—is no more. The poet writes this book in a state of dazed grief. He wanders the empty streets, piled high with corpses, and tries to make sense of a tragedy that defies all comprehension.

But beyond the human tragedy, a different kind of distress gnaws at the author. Babylonian soldiers have entered the temple—pagans in the Most Holy Place!— looted it, then burned it to the ground. The dream of the covenant died on that day. Historians record that as the Babylonians entered the temple, they swept the empty air with their spears, seeking the unseen Jewish God. But they found nothing. God had given up; he had fled the premises. Jews still mourn the event: each year on the anniversary of the day the temple was destroyed, the Orthodox read the book of Lamentations aloud.

The tone of this anonymous book may sound familiar, for the prophet Jeremiah is the likely author. He is an old man, with shriveled skin and broken bones. He has been hunted, jailed, tortured, thrown in a pit and left for dead. Yet nothing can match the grief he feels now as he stares not at his own wounds but at the gaping wounds of Jerusalem.

God is an enemy, the prophet concludes, in an outburst familiar to any reader of Jeremiah. He lets his venom spill out. And yet, in the middle of this dark chapter, the author remembers what he once learned about God in the brighter, happier times. He recalls the goodness of God, the love, the compassion. In the midst of this bleak book come words that a writer later crafted into a hymn: "Great Is Thy Faithfulness." At the moment of terrible tragedy, those qualities of God may seem very far away—but where else can we turn? As Lamentations shows, without God's hope, there is no hope.   —PY

DAILY CONTEMPLATION

In your darkest times, do your thoughts turn to God? What helps you find relief?

DAY 171   Obadiah 1, 8–12, 15–18

YOUR DEEDS WILL RETURN

The vision of Obadiah.

This is what the Sovereign LORD says about Edom—

We have heard a message from the LORD:
    An envoy was sent to the nations to say,

"Rise, and let us go against her for battle"...

"In that day," declares the LORD,
    "will I not destroy the wise men of Edom,
    men of understanding in the mountains of Esau?
Your warriors, O Teman, will be terrified,
    and everyone in Esau's mountains
    will be cut down in the slaughter.
Because of the violence against your brother Jacob,
    you will be covered with shame;
    you will be destroyed forever.
On the day you stood aloof
    while strangers carried off his wealth
and foreigners entered his gates
    and cast lots for Jerusalem,
    you were like one of them.
You should not look down on your brother
    in the day of his misfortune,
nor rejoice over the people of Judah
    in the day of their destruction,
nor boast so much
    in the day of their trouble....

"The day of the LORD is near
    for all nations.
As you have done, it will be done to you;
    your deeds will return upon your own head.
Just as you drank on my holy hill,
    so all the nations will drink continually;
they will drink and drink
    and be as if they had never been.
But on Mount Zion will be deliverance;
    it will be holy,
and the house of Jacob
    will possess its inheritance.
The house of Jacob will be a fire
    and the house of Joseph a flame;
the house of Esau will be stubble,
    and they will set it on fire and consume it.
There will be no survivors
    from the house of Esau."
      The LORD has spoken.

Remember, O LORD, what the Edomites did on the day Jerusalem fell. 'Tear it down,' they cried, 'tear it down to its foundations!'" (Psalm 137:7). Survivors of the sacking of Jerusalem would never forget the reactions of their neighbors the Edomites, who had watched the carnage with open glee. The Edomites cheered the conquering Babylonian army, looted the fleeing refugees, and helped plunder Jerusalem. Psalm 137, one of the saddest passages in the Bible, voices the Israelites' acrid bitterness over this offense.

To rub salt in Judah's wounds, the Edomites are actually distant relatives. Their nation traces back to the feud between twin brothers Jacob and Esau. While Jacob fathered the Israelites, Esau, having traded away his birthright for a meal, moved to desolate mountain country and founded the nation of Edom (EE-duhm). The twins' descendants continued the quarrel for hundreds of years, and now the Edomites are gloating over the Israelites' calamity. True sons of Esau, they think primarily of the immediate gain available to them from plunder.

The Edomites' attitude contrasts sharply with the sorrow expressed in the book of Lamentations. And Obadiah, the shortest book in the Old Testament, makes clear that the Edomites will pay for their callousness and cruelty: "As you have done, it will be done to you." Those who have betrayed Judah will be repaid with treachery from their own allies.

Obadiah predicts opposite futures for Israel and Edom. According to him, downtrodden Israel will rise again, but Edom will disappear from the face of the earth. History will bear out the latter prediction in 70 A.D., when Roman legions destroy the last remnant of Edomites during a siege of Jerusalem.   —PY

DAILY CONTEMPLATION

Edom was basing its security on its strategic location "on the heights" and "in the clefts of the rocks." On what do you base your security?

DAY 172   Reflection

TO LOVE OR LEAVE UNBELIEVERS?

How are God's people supposed to live when they're surrounded by unbelievers?

It finally happened to Judah. Like Israel, Judah lost its land and its freedom as an independent nation of God. The people were deported to Babylon and forced to make new lives in a foreign society. Now, worshiping the true God—suddenly a more attractive pursuit—became more difficult. Surrounded by the worship of false gods and by worldly religions, the Jews had to learn to live *in* the world without being *of* the world.

Richard Mouw, president of Fuller Seminary, writes,

When the children of Israel were taken off to Babylon as captives, they faced some serious questions about civility. For a long time they had been living in their own land, with familiar rulers and institutions. They had experienced the unity of a people who were committed (officially at least!) to obeying the will of God in all aspects of their lives.

But they were aliens in a strange environment, surrounded by a pervasively pagan culture. Psalm 137 records their poignant plea: "How could we sing the Lord's song in a foreign land?" (v. 4). God answered their query through the prophet Jeremiah. You are to settle into the land for the long haul, the prophet told the people: construct homes to live in, raise crops, get married and have children; "multiply there, and do not decrease" (Jer. 29:4–6). And then a very important "policy statement" is added: "But seek the welfare of the city where I have sent you into exile, and pray to the Lord on its behalf, for in its welfare you will find your welfare" (v. 7).[17]

God was telling the people not to deplore their new neighbors but to care for them, to engage with them, to seek their good. God hates the worship of false gods and despises religions that serve the self rather than God, but he doesn't hate the people themselves. Repeatedly God reminds us through the prophets that he hates wickedness but does not hate the wicked. He desires that all people come to him and be saved. The Bible itself is a long message of God's love and forgiveness for those who don't deserve him.

Like the people of Judah, we live in a society in which many don't follow God. We may at times feel tempted to ignore them or treat them in a condescending manner, but that isn't God's way. Just as he stresses the importance of holding firmly to our beliefs without compromising, he also stresses the need for us to love others with the love he has shown us.

Mouw explains,

> God is telling the Israelites—and us—that neither indifference nor hostility is a proper way of treating our pagan neighbors. We must seek their welfare. Indeed, it is in pursuing the well-being of others that we realize our own well-being. When Christians fail to measure up to the standards of kindness and gentleness, we are not the people God meant us to be.[18]

Before Jesus died, in prayer he voiced God's greatest desire. "As you sent me into the world, I have sent them into the world. . . . May they be brought to complete unity to let the world know that you sent me and have loved them even as you have loved me" (John 17:18, 23). God delights not in punishing sin but in bringing sinners to himself. He has chosen to use us to live out that message.   —BQ

DAILY CONTEMPLATION

What is your attitude toward those who don't follow Jesus? Do you struggle more in speaking to them about your beliefs or in treating them with love and kindness? Pray that the apostle Peter's words would become real in your life: "Always be prepared to give an answer to everyone who asks you to give the reason for the hope that you have. But do this with gentleness and respect" (1 Peter 3:15).

PART 5

STARTING OVER—IN EXILE AND RETURNING FROM EXILE

DAY 173 Ezekiel 1:1–28

THE LIVING CREATURES AND THE GLORY OF THE LORD

In the thirtieth year, in the fourth month on the fifth day, while I was among the exiles by the Kebar River, the heavens were opened and I saw visions of God.

On the fifth of the month—it was the fifth year of the exile of King Jehoiachin—the word of the LORD came to Ezekiel the priest, the son of Buzi, by the Kebar River in the land of the Babylonians. There the hand of the LORD was upon him.

I looked, and I saw a windstorm coming out of the north—an immense cloud with flashing lightning and surrounded by brilliant light. The center of the fire looked like glowing metal, and in the fire was what looked like four living creatures. In appearance their form was that of a man, but each of them had four faces and four wings. Their legs were straight; their feet were like those of a calf and gleamed like burnished bronze. Under their wings on their four sides they had the hands of a man. All four of them had faces and wings, and their wings touched one another. Each one went straight ahead; they did not turn as they moved.

Their faces looked like this: Each of the four had the face of a man, and on the right side each had the face of a lion, and on the left the face of an ox; each also had the face of an eagle. Such were their faces. Their wings were spread out upward; each had two wings, one touching the wing of another creature on either side, and two wings covering its body. Each one went straight ahead. Wherever the spirit would go, they would go, without turning as they went. The appearance of the living creatures was like burning coals of fire or like torches. Fire moved back and forth among the creatures; it was bright, and lightning flashed out of it. The creatures sped back and forth like flashes of lightning.

As I looked at the living creatures, I saw a wheel on the ground beside each creature with its four faces. This was the appearance and structure of the wheels: They sparkled like chrysolite, and all four looked alike. Each appeared to be made like a wheel intersecting a wheel. As they moved, they would go in any one of the four directions the creatures faced; the wheels did not turn about as the creatures went. Their rims were high and awesome, and all four rims were full of eyes all around.

When the living creatures moved, the wheels beside them moved; and when the living creatures rose from the ground, the wheels also rose. Wherever the spirit would go, they would go, and the wheels would rise along with them, because the spirit of the living creatures was in the wheels. When the creatures moved, they also moved; when the creatures stood still, they also stood still; and when the creatures rose from the ground, the wheels rose along with them, because the spirit of the living creatures was in the wheels.

Spread out above the heads of the living creatures was what looked like an expanse, sparkling like ice, and awesome. Under the expanse their wings were stretched out one toward the other, and each had two wings covering its body. When the creatures moved, I heard the sound of their wings, like the roar of rushing waters, like the voice of the Almighty, like the tumult of an army. When they stood still, they lowered their wings.

Then there came a voice from above the expanse over their heads as they stood with lowered wings. Above the expanse over their heads was what looked like a throne of sapphire, and high above on the throne was a figure like that of a man. I saw that from what appeared to be his waist up he looked like glowing metal, as if full of fire, and that from there down he looked like fire; and brilliant light surrounded him. Like the appearance of a rainbow in the clouds on a rainy day, so was the radiance around him.

This was the appearance of the likeness of the glory of the LORD. When I saw it, I fell facedown, and I heard the voice of one speaking.

About the same time that Jeremiah, Habakkuk, and Obadiah are prophesying in Judah, a man named Ezekiel (ee-ZEE-kee-uhl) receives a dramatic call to minister to their unfortunate countrymen in exile. The Babylonian army has been plundering Judah for twenty years before the fall of Jerusalem, and Ezekiel is among the first wave of captives taken to Babylon, nearly five hundred miles away. There he lives with the Israelites in a refugee settlement beside a river.

Like refugees everywhere, those in Babylon long for nothing more than a chance to return to their homeland. They receive letters of advice and comfort from the prophet Jeremiah. They cringe at reports of rebellion by Judah's kings, fearful that any rebellion might arouse the wrath of Babylon. They wonder anxiously whether their beleaguered nation can survive.

Uprooted, dispirited people such as these need a strong, authoritative voice, and in Ezekiel they get exactly that. As a young man in training for the priesthood, he found his career plans interrupted by the foreign deportations. *What good is a priest in Babylon when the temple is in Jerusalem?* he must have wondered. God summons Ezekiel to a new role, as prophet to the Jews in exile.

Ezekiel begins with a description so unearthly that some have suggested the prophet saw a UFO. Indeed, there are similarities: glowing lights, quick movements, inhuman figures. But there are differences too in this account of a "close encounter." This majestic being was not mysteriously rushing off to disappear. He wanted to be known by everyone. And he had chosen the prophet Ezekiel as the one privileged to make him known.

Confronted with such splendor, Ezekiel falls on his face. But the Spirit of God raises him to his feet and gives him an assignment. After this vision, Ezekiel will never again wonder about a question that often bothers the other refugees: Has God abandoned them? Ezekiel's encounter of the closest kind convinces him permanently that God still cares about his people—even the exiles in Babylon.   —PY

DAILY CONTEMPLATION

Have you ever felt abandoned by God? What helped?

DAY 174   Ezekiel 2:1–5, 9–3:3, 10–27

EZEKIEL'S CALL

He said to me, "Son of man, stand up on your feet and I will speak to you." As he spoke, the Spirit came into me and raised me to my feet, and I heard him speaking to me.

He said: "Son of man, I am sending you to the Israelites, to a rebellious nation that has rebelled against me; they and their fathers have been in revolt against me to this very day. The people to whom I am sending you are obstinate and stubborn. Say to them, 'This is what the Sovereign LORD says.' And whether they listen or fail to listen—for they are a rebellious house—they will know that a prophet has been among them." ...

Then I looked, and I saw a hand stretched out to me. In it was a scroll, which he unrolled before me. On both sides of it were written words of lament and mourning and woe.

And he said to me, "Son of man, eat what is before you, eat this scroll; then go and speak to the house of Israel." So I opened my mouth, and he gave me the scroll to eat.

Then he said to me, "Son of man, eat this scroll I am giving you and fill your stomach with it." So I ate it, and it tasted as sweet as honey in my mouth....

And he said to me, "Son of man, listen carefully and take to heart all the words I speak to you. Go now to your countrymen in exile and speak to them. Say to them, 'This is what the Sovereign LORD says,' whether they listen or fail to listen."

Then the Spirit lifted me up, and I heard behind me a loud rumbling sound— May the glory of the LORD be praised in his dwelling place!—the sound of the wings of the living creatures brushing against each other and the sound of the wheels beside them, a loud rumbling sound. The Spirit then lifted me up and took me away, and I went in bitterness and in the anger of my spirit, with the strong hand of the LORD upon me. I came to the exiles who lived at Tel Abib near the Kebar River. And there, where they were living, I sat among them for seven days—overwhelmed.

At the end of seven days the word of the LORD came to me: "Son of man, I have made you a watchman for the house of Israel; so hear the word I speak and give them warning from me. When I say to a wicked man, 'You will surely die,' and you do not warn him or speak out to dissuade him from his evil ways in order to save his life, that wicked man will die for his sin, and I will hold you accountable for his blood. But if you do warn the wicked man and he does not turn from his wickedness or from his evil ways, he will die for his sin; but you will have saved yourself.

"Again, when a righteous man turns from his righteousness and does evil, and I put a stumbling block before him, he will die. Since you did not warn him, he will die for his sin. The righteous things he did will not be remembered, and I will hold you accountable for his blood. But if you do warn the righteous man not to sin and he does not sin, he will surely live because he took warning, and you will have saved yourself."

The hand of the LORD was upon me there, and he said to me, "Get up and go out to the plain, and there I will speak to you." So I got up and went out to the plain. And the glory of the LORD was standing there, like the glory I had seen by the Kebar River, and I fell facedown.

Then the Spirit came into me and raised me to my feet. He spoke to me and said: "Go, shut yourself inside your house. And you, son of man, they will tie with ropes; you will be bound so that you cannot go out among the people. I will make your tongue stick to the roof of your mouth so that you will be silent and unable to rebuke them, though they are a rebellious house. But when I speak to you, I will open your mouth and you shall say to them, 'This is what the Sovereign LORD says.' Whoever will listen let him listen, and whoever will refuse let him refuse; for they are a rebellious house."

Orthodox Jewish rabbis forbid anyone under the age of thirty to read the first three chapters of Ezekiel. No young person, they reason, is ready for such a direct encounter with the glory of the Lord. Indeed, Ezekiel himself barely survives the experience. He falls on his face repeatedly and is knocked speechless for seven days.

Such exalted revelations are part of God's training regimen, a process of toughening up the prophet for a demanding task. With Isaiah sawn in two and Jeremiah thrown in a well, the prophets of Judah have plenty of reason for alarm. What might befall Ezekiel as he takes the word of God to an ornery people in the heart of enemy territory? Thus from the beginning God gives Ezekiel an experience he will never forget or doubt, no matter what difficulties he may confront.

God warns Ezekiel that few Israelites, if any, will listen to his message. He will have to become as stubborn and unyielding as the audience he addresses. As a result, Ezekiel lives a lonely life. People think of him as a dreamy storyteller and scoff at his pessimistic predictions of Jerusalem's fall. Still, despite the negative tone of his prophecies, Ezekiel never once loses hope. He can see past the tragedies of the present day to a future time when God will restore his people and his temple.

Ezekiel's faith cannot be shaken, because he has received a vision of the glory of the Lord. Due to his priestly training, he undoubtedly recognizes the light, the fire, and the glow—Israelites have seen those images in the pillar of fire in the wilderness, and in the cloud that descended into Solomon's temple. Now the nation is in shambles, its chief citizens in exile. But even here, in Babylon, the glory of the Lord appears to Ezekiel. This experience alone gives him the courage he will need to fight off the enemies that surround him.   —PY

DAILY CONTEMPLATION

What obstacles do you face when you try to talk to people about God?

DAY 175   Ezekiel 4:1–17

SIEGE OF JERUSALEM SYMBOLIZED

"Now, son of man, take a clay tablet, put it in front of you and draw the city of Jerusalem on it. Then lay siege to it: Erect siege works against it, build a ramp up to it, set up camps against it and put battering rams around it. Then take an iron pan, place it as an iron wall between you and the city and turn your face toward it. It will be under siege, and you shall besiege it. This will be a sign to the house of Israel.

"Then lie on your left side and put the sin of the house of Israel upon yourself. You are to bear their sin for the number of days you lie on your side. I have assigned you the same number of days as the years of their sin. So for 390 days you will bear the sin of the house of Israel.

"After you have finished this, lie down again, this time on your right side, and bear the sin of the house of Judah. I have assigned you 40 days, a day for each year. Turn your face toward the siege of Jerusalem and with bared arm prophesy against her. I will tie you up with ropes so that you cannot turn from one side to the other until you have finished the days of your siege.

333

"Take wheat and barley, beans and lentils, millet and spelt; put them in a storage jar and use them to make bread for yourself. You are to eat it during the 390 days you lie on your side. Weigh out twenty shekels of food to eat each day and eat it at set times. Also measure out a sixth of a hin of water and drink it at set times. Eat the food as you would a barley cake; bake it in the sight of the people, using human excrement for fuel." The LORD said, "In this way the people of Israel will eat defiled food among the nations where I will drive them."

Then I said, "Not so, Sovereign LORD! I have never defiled myself. From my youth until now I have never eaten anything found dead or torn by wild animals. No unclean meat has ever entered my mouth."

"Very well," he said, "I will let you bake your bread over cow manure instead of human excrement."

He then said to me: "Son of man, I will cut off the supply of food in Jerusalem. The people will eat rationed food in anxiety and drink rationed water in despair, for food and water will be scarce. They will be appalled at the sight of each other and will waste away because of their sin."

When someone asked Flannery O'Connor why she populated her novels with such exaggerated, eccentric characters, she replied, "To the hard of hearing you shout, and for the almost-blind you draw large and startling figures." The same answer may help explain the oddities of Ezekiel. He too faces a stubborn, dense audience with little tolerance for his message. And God instructs him to use some bizarre methods to get that message across.

The book records twelve public "object lessons" acted out by the prophet. For example, one year he lies on his side every day, bound by ropes and facing a clay model of Jerusalem. Strange? When a car is headed toward the edge of a cliff, you may scream and gesture so wildly that people think you insane. So it is with Ezekiel, who will do anything to force people to pay attention.

The first part of Ezekiel mainly concerns the political situation back in the homeland of Judah. False prophets are assuring the exiles that God would never allow his temple or holy city to be destroyed. Ezekiel blasts these phony optimists and broadcasts God's plan of judgment in strong words and public protests. He takes no great delight in the doomsday message. Twice, seeing the future, he falls down, crying out in horror (9:8; 11:13). In this chapter, when God tells him to cook food on human excrement as a symbolic act, he is too shocked to agree.

Ezekiel delivers an undiluted message from God, presented in a way that the Israelites cannot ignore. Ezekiel's exaggerated style says much about the One who gives him orders. God will not let go of his people until he has done all in his power to turn them around. No device is too undignified, no carnival ploy too corny, as long as he has the slightest hope of breaking through. "As surely as I live, declares the Sovereign LORD, I take no pleasure in the death of the wicked, but rather that they turn from their ways and live. Turn! Turn from your evil ways! Why will you die, O house of Israel?" (33:11).   —PY

DAY 176   Ezekiel 37:1–28

THE VALLEY OF DRY BONES

The hand of the LORD was upon me, and he brought me out by the Spirit of the LORD and set me in the middle of a valley; it was full of bones. He led me back and forth among them, and I saw a great many bones on the floor of the valley, bones that were very dry. He asked me, "Son of man, can these bones live?"

I said, "O Sovereign LORD, you alone know."

Then he said to me, "Prophesy to these bones and say to them, 'Dry bones, hear the word of the LORD! This is what the Sovereign LORD says to these bones: I will make breath enter you, and you will come to life. I will attach tendons to you and make flesh come upon you and cover you with skin; I will put breath in you, and you will come to life. Then you will know that I am the LORD.'"

So I prophesied as I was commanded. And as I was prophesying, there was a noise, a rattling sound, and the bones came together, bone to bone. I looked, and tendons and flesh appeared on them and skin covered them, but there was no breath in them.

Then he said to me, "Prophesy to the breath; prophesy, son of man, and say to it, 'This is what the Sovereign LORD says: Come from the four winds, O breath, and breathe into these slain, that they may live.'" So I prophesied as he commanded me, and breath entered them; they came to life and stood up on their feet—a vast army.

Then he said to me: "Son of man, these bones are the whole house of Israel. They say, 'Our bones are dried up and our hope is gone; we are cut off.' Therefore prophesy and say to them: 'This is what the Sovereign LORD says: O my people, I am going to open your graves and bring you up from them; I will bring you back to the land of Israel. Then you, my people, will know that I am the LORD, when I open your graves and bring you up from them. I will put my Spirit in you and you will live, and I will settle you in your own land. Then you will know that I the LORD have spoken, and I have done it, declares the LORD.'"

The word of the LORD came to me: "Son of man, take a stick of wood and write on it, 'Belonging to Judah and the Israelites associated with him.' Then take another stick of wood, and write on it, 'Ephraim's stick, belonging to Joseph and all the house of Israel associated with him.' Join them together into one stick so that they will become one in your hand.

"When your countrymen ask you, 'Won't you tell us what you mean by this?' say to them, 'This is what the Sovereign LORD says: I am going to take the stick of Joseph—which is in Ephraim's hand—and of the Israelite tribes associated with him, and join it to Judah's stick, making them a single stick of wood, and they will become one in my hand.' Hold before their eyes the sticks you have written on and say to them, 'This is what the Sovereign LORD says: I will take the Israelites out of the nations where they have gone. I will gather them from all around and bring them back into their own land. I will make them one nation in the land, on the mountains of Israel. There will be one king over all of them and they will never again be two nations or be divided into two kingdoms. They will no longer defile themselves with their idols and vile images or with any of their offenses, for I will save them from all their sinful backsliding, and I will cleanse them. They will be my people, and I will be their God.

"'My servant David will be king over them, and they will all have one shepherd. They will follow my laws and be careful to keep my decrees. They will live in the land I gave to my servant Jacob, the land where your fathers lived. They and their children and their children's children will live there forever, and David my servant will be their prince forever. I will make a covenant of peace with them; it will be an everlasting covenant. I will establish them and increase their numbers, and I will put my sanctuary among them forever. My dwelling place will be with them; I will be their God, and they will be my people. Then the nations will know that I the LORD make Israel holy, when my sanctuary is among them forever.'"

Why would Jerusalem be destroyed? Why would all Judah's enemies come to a violent end? So that they would "know that I am the LORD." This is the phrase echoed more than sixty times in the book of Ezekiel. In a sudden change of tone, God uses that same phrase to explain why he will bring about a time of future happiness.

After all the gloom, Ezekiel at last gets to pronounce words of great joy and hope. In the early days, he alone prophesied doom, and no one listened. Then for a period of seven years he maintained a virtual silence. But now he opens his mouth again, and bright words of hope issue forth.

Ezekiel experiences a sudden surge in popularity among the exiles, since only he has predicted current events accurately. As people flock to hear his words, he scolds them for their unchanged hearts, then confirms the rumor of good news to come.

No part of Ezekiel captures that message of hope more effectively than this startling vision of the valley of dry bones. Like a graveyard of scattered, bleached bones coming gloriously to life, the deadest of the dead will live.

Ezekiel's original audience is still trying to absorb the staggering news that the temple has been razed, with God apparently departed. But Ezekiel assures them God has not given up; the split kingdoms of Judah and Israel will join together again at last. God is coming back to his home, to live with his people.

The book ends with a shining vision of a new Jerusalem arising from the ruins of the old. Scholars disagree on whether Ezekiel's words apply literally, or symbolically, to the nation of Israel. But it is clear that the good news will affect the whole world. The triumphant name of that new city says it all: "And the name of the city from that time on will be: THE LORD IS THERE." —PY

DAY 177 Reflection

GOD'S BIZARRE WAYS OF LOVING

The story of Ezekiel gives us a picture of God that is one of the most startling in all the Bible. Through Ezekiel we see a God who is willing to go to any lengths to get his message across to people he loves—even if they have skulls so thick as to keep them from believing the future he has for them.

Using an array of outrageous symbolism, God warns the people about the upcoming destruction of Jerusalem. Ezekiel must draw a picture of Jerusalem under siege and then lay on his side for a year while eating food cooked on cow dung. He must shave his head and burn some of the hair, strike some with a sword, scatter some to the wind, and tuck some in his cloak. He must clap his hands and stamp his feet while prophesying the consequences of Israel's wicked behavior. He must wail, preaching doom and destruction. He must pack his belongings and crawl out of his house through a hole in the wall. He must tremble in front of the people while eating and drinking. Then when Ezekiel's wife dies, he must not mourn. All this to illustrate to the people God's distress over their sin, and the consequences they will experience.

God will later change the message to one of hope, walking Ezekiel through a detailed plan of a new temple. He plans to forgive and cleanse the people, putting a new heart within them and establishing a peace that will reign forever.

In the book of Ezekiel, God speaks with intense and passionate language. He doesn't use simple metaphors or illustrations to get his point across; he uses the bizarre behavior of a prophet who comes off looking psychotic. God shows little concern with presenting a controlled image here. If he controls his response any longer, his people won't get the message they will soon be desperate to hear.

Today God is still willing to go to any length to help us experience his truth and love. Authors Brent Curtis and John Eldredge write about God as a wild pursuer engaging us in a sacred romance with himself. "How is God wooing us through flat tires, bounced checks, and rained-out picnics?" they ask. "What is he after as we face cancer, sexual struggles, and abandonment?"[19]

"Our Story is written by God who is more than author, he is the romantic lead in our personal dramas," they conclude. "He created us for himself and now he is moving heaven and earth to restore us to his side. His wooing seems wild because he seeks to free our heart from the attachments and addictions we've chosen."[20]

God acts as a lover who seeks in every situation to bring his beloved to himself. God is so wild about us that he uses whatever strategy will intimately fit us and draw us to himself. "We lose heart when we lose the eternal Romance," Curtis and Eldredge write, "which reminds us that God sought to bring us into his sacred circle from all eternity, and . . . despite our rejection of him, he pursues us still."[21]   —BQ

DAILY CONTEMPLATION

Can you see times in your life when God was romancing you, even in seemingly bizarre or unconventional ways? If you can recognize this romance in your life, thank God now for loving you so passionately. If you can't, ask God for the eyes to recognize his pursuit.

DAY 178
Daniel 1:1–21

DANIEL'S TRAINING IN BABYLON

In the third year of the reign of Jehoiakim king of Judah, Nebuchadnezzar king of Babylon came to Jerusalem and besieged it. And the Lord delivered Jehoiakim king of Judah into his hand, along with some of the articles from the temple of God. These he carried off to the temple of his god in Babylonia and put in the treasure house of his god.

Then the king ordered Ashpenaz, chief of his court officials, to bring in some of the Israelites from the royal family and the nobility—young men without any physical defect, handsome, showing aptitude for every kind of learning, well informed, quick to understand, and qualified to serve in the king's palace. He was to teach them the language and literature of the Babylonians. The king assigned them a daily amount of food and wine from the king's table. They were to be trained for three years, and after that they were to enter the king's service.

Among these were some from Judah: Daniel, Hananiah, Mishael and Azariah. The chief official gave them new names: to Daniel, the name Belteshazzar; to Hananiah, Shadrach; to Mishael, Meshach; and to Azariah, Abednego.

But Daniel resolved not to defile himself with the royal food and wine, and he asked the chief official for permission not to defile himself this way. Now God had caused the official to show favor and sympathy to Daniel, but the official told Daniel, "I am afraid of my lord the king, who has assigned your food and drink. Why should he see you looking worse than the other young men your age? The king would then have my head because of you."

Daniel then said to the guard whom the chief official had appointed over Daniel, Hananiah, Mishael and Azariah, "Please test your servants for ten days: Give us nothing but vegetables to eat and water to drink. Then compare our appearance with that of the young men who eat the royal food, and treat your servants in accordance with what you see." So he agreed to this and tested them for ten days.

At the end of the ten days they looked healthier and better nourished than any of the young men who ate the royal food. So the guard took away their choice food and the wine they were to drink and gave them vegetables instead.

To these four young men God gave knowledge and understanding of all kinds of literature and learning. And Daniel could understand visions and dreams of all kinds.

At the end of the time set by the king to bring them in, the chief official presented them to Nebuchadnezzar. The king talked with them, and he found none equal to Daniel, Hananiah, Mishael and Azariah; so they entered the king's service. In every matter of wisdom and understanding about which the king questioned them, he found them ten times better than all the magicians and enchanters in his whole kingdom.

And Daniel remained there until the first year of King Cyrus.

Whereas Ezekiel spent his days preaching (and acting out) sermons to the Jewish exiles, Daniel was recruited for a job in the king's palace.

In fact, Daniel's life in the palace more closely resembles that of the ancient character Joseph, who also rose to a position of prominence in a foreign government. As this chapter underscores, Daniel achieves success without bending his own principles of integrity. Somehow he manages to thrive in an environment marked by ambition and intrigue, while still holding to his high-minded Jewish ideals.

The Babylonians do their best to purge the young Jews of their heritage. They force on them new, pagan names and ply them with wine and food that has been offered to idols. Even the study course for diplomats-in-training is distasteful to a Jew: it covers sorcery, magic, and a pagan, multigod religion. Daniel and his three friends overcome these obstacles and excel enough to attract the attention of the king, who has to take notice: the four are more impressive than anyone else in the kingdom.

Taken together, the biblical prophets offer not one but many models of how a person can serve both God and the state. On the one extreme stand men like Amos and Elijah, who, as outsiders, railed against the evils of society. Others, such as Jeremiah and Nathan, gave occasional counsel to kings but kept a safe distance. Isaiah and Samuel, however, became the official advisors of kings. And in this book the prophet Daniel shows that a person can keep pure even while working within a tyrannical regime.

For at least sixty-six years Daniel serves pagan kings with great diligence and resourcefulness. Yet he never once compromises his faith, even when threatened with death. The Bible offers no better model of how to live among people who do not share or respect your beliefs.   —PY

DAILY CONTEMPLATION

When have you taken a difficult or unpopular stand as a matter of integrity?

NEBUCHADNEZZAR'S DREAM

In the second year of his reign, Nebuchadnezzar had dreams; his mind was troubled and he could not sleep. So the king summoned the magicians, enchanters, sorcerers and astrologers to tell him what he had dreamed. When they came in and stood before the king, he said to them, "I have had a dream that troubles me and I want to know what it means."

Then the astrologers answered the king in Aramaic, "O king, live forever! Tell your servants the dream, and we will interpret it."

The king replied to the astrologers, "This is what I have firmly decided: If you do not tell me what my dream was and interpret it, I will have you cut into pieces and your houses turned into piles of rubble. But if you tell me the dream and explain it, you will receive from me gifts and rewards and great honor. So tell me the dream and interpret it for me."

Once more they replied, "Let the king tell his servants the dream, and we will interpret it."

Then the king answered, "I am certain that you are trying to gain time, because you realize that this is what I have firmly decided: If you do not tell me the dream, there is just one penalty for you. You have conspired to tell me misleading and wicked things, hoping the situation will change. So then, tell me the dream, and I will know that you can interpret it for me."

The astrologers answered the king, "There is not a man on earth who can do what the king asks! No king, however great and mighty, has ever asked such a thing of any magician or enchanter or astrologer. What the king asks is too difficult. No one can reveal it to the king except the gods, and they do not live among men."

This made the king so angry and furious that he ordered the execution of all the wise men of Babylon. So the decree was issued to put the wise men to death, and men were sent to look for Daniel and his friends to put them to death.

When Arioch, the commander of the king's guard, had gone out to put to death the wise men of Babylon, Daniel spoke to him with wisdom and tact. He asked the king's officer, "Why did the king issue such a harsh decree?" Arioch then explained the matter to Daniel. At this, Daniel went in to the king and asked for time, so that he might interpret the dream for him.

Then Daniel returned to his house and explained the matter to his friends Hananiah, Mishael and Azariah. He urged them to plead for mercy from the God of heaven concerning this mystery, so that he and his friends might not be executed with the rest of the wise men of Babylon. During the night the mystery was revealed to Daniel in a vision. Then Daniel praised the God of heaven and said:

"Praise be to the name of God for ever and ever;
    wisdom and power are his.
He changes times and seasons;
    he sets up kings and deposes them.
He gives wisdom to the wise
    and knowledge to the discerning.
He reveals deep and hidden things;
    he knows what lies in darkness,
    and light dwells with him.
I thank and praise you, O God of my fathers:
    You have given me wisdom and power,
you have made known to me what we asked of you,
    you have made known to us the dream of the king."

Whether to remind his own people of his power or to proclaim it to Gentile nations, God frequently creates a crisis in the lives of high-profile people in the Old Testament and allows his followers to resolve it through him. Here God positions Daniel, Hananiah (HAN-uh-NI-uh), Mishael (MISH-ee-uhl), and Azariah (AZ-uh-RI-uh) in close proximity to the king and then gives them the opportunity to do what none of the wisest in Babylon can do.

Even the astrologers admit that only the gods could do what the king demands. They are almost right. Only the one true God can know a person's dream. And although the pagan gods don't live among men, God does. Four men who are slated to die will give the proof. Once again God will proclaim to his chosen people and the Babylonians that he reigns. For all their mystique and show, sorcerers, magicians, and astrologers can only offer empty promises when arrayed against the God of heaven.   —BQ

DAILY CONTEMPLATION

When have you recently been reminded of God's power through his actions in another person's life?

DAY 180   Daniel 2:24–49

DANIEL INTERPRETS THE DREAM

Then Daniel went to Arioch, whom the king had appointed to execute the wise men of Babylon, and said to him, "Do not execute the wise men of Babylon. Take me to the king, and I will interpret his dream for him."

Arioch took Daniel to the king at once and said, "I have found a man among the exiles from Judah who can tell the king what his dream means."

The king asked Daniel (also called Belteshazzar), "Are you able to tell me what I saw in my dream and interpret it?"

Daniel replied, "No wise man, enchanter, magician or diviner can explain to the king the mystery he has asked about, but there is a God in heaven who reveals mysteries. He has shown King Nebuchadnezzar what will happen in days to come. Your dream and the visions that passed through your mind as you lay on your bed are these:

"As you were lying there, O king, your mind turned to things to come, and the revealer of mysteries showed you what is going to happen. As for me, this mystery has been revealed to me, not because I have greater wisdom than other living men, but so that you, O king, may know the interpretation and that you may understand what went through your mind.

"You looked, O king, and there before you stood a large statue—an enormous, dazzling statue, awesome in appearance. The head of the statue was made of pure gold, its chest and arms of silver, its belly and thighs of bronze, its legs of iron, its feet partly of iron and partly of baked clay. While you were watching, a rock was cut out, but not by human hands. It struck the statue on its feet of iron and clay and smashed them. Then the iron, the clay, the bronze, the silver and the gold were broken to pieces at the same time and became like chaff on a threshing floor in the summer. The wind swept them away without leaving a trace. But the rock that struck the statue became a huge mountain and filled the whole earth.

"This was the dream, and now we will interpret it to the king. You, O king, are the king of kings. The God of heaven has given you dominion and power and might and glory; in your hands he has placed mankind and the beasts of the field and the birds of the air. Wherever they live, he has made you ruler over them all. You are that head of gold.

"After you, another kingdom will rise, inferior to yours. Next, a third kingdom, one of bronze, will rule over the whole earth. Finally, there will be a fourth kingdom, strong as iron—for iron breaks and smashes everything—and as iron breaks things to pieces, so it will crush and break all the others. Just as you saw that the feet and toes were partly of baked clay and partly of iron, so this will be a divided kingdom; yet it will have some of the strength of iron in it, even as you saw iron mixed with clay. As the toes were partly iron and partly clay, so this kingdom will be partly strong and partly brittle. And just as you saw the iron mixed with baked clay, so the people will be a mixture and will not remain united, any more than iron mixes with clay.

"In the time of those kings, the God of heaven will set up a kingdom that will never be destroyed, nor will it be left to another people. It will crush all those kingdoms and bring them to an end, but it will itself endure forever. This is the meaning of the vision of the rock cut out of a mountain, but not by human hands—a rock that broke the iron, the bronze, the clay, the silver and the gold to pieces.

"The great God has shown the king what will take place in the future. The dream is true and the interpretation is trustworthy."

Then King Nebuchadnezzar fell prostrate before Daniel and paid him honor and ordered that an offering and incense be presented to him. The king said to

Daniel, "Surely your God is the God of gods and the Lord of kings and a revealer of mysteries, for you were able to reveal this mystery."

Then the king placed Daniel in a high position and lavished many gifts on him. He made him ruler over the entire province of Babylon and placed him in charge of all its wise men. Moreover, at Daniel's request the king appointed Shadrach, Meshach and Abednego administrators over the province of Babylon, while Daniel himself remained at the royal court.

God not only shows his power through Daniel's interpretation of the king's dream; he also reveals the future of the Near East and of God's own eternal kingdom. The statue in Nebuchadnezzar's (NEB-uh-kuhd-NEZ-urh) dream represents the Gentile kingdoms that will rule over the land of Palestine and the people of Israel. The gold head represents the Neo-Babylonian empire; the silver chest and arms, the Medo-Persian empire; the bronze belly and thighs, the Greek empire; and the iron legs and feet, the Roman empire. The metals represent the decreasing power and grandeur of the empires and also symbolize increasing toughness, with each empire lasting longer than the preceding one.

The four kingdoms will be destroyed not by another earthly power but by the coming of Jesus Christ, the rock that strikes the statue and causes it to crumble. When Christ returns a second time, he will rule over all kingdoms of the world, inaugurating a messianic reign to last for eternity. —BQ

DAILY CONTEMPLATION

What "kingdom" of today are you eager for Jesus to overthrow? The influence of a political or social group? The repressive government of a particular nation? A destructive cultural trend?

DAY 181

Daniel 3:1–29

THE IMAGE OF GOLD AND THE FIERY FURNACE

King Nebuchadnezzar made an image of gold, ninety feet high and nine feet wide, and set it up on the plain of Dura in the province of Babylon. He then summoned the satraps, prefects, governors, advisers, treasurers, judges, magistrates and all the other provincial officials to come to the dedication of the image he had set up. So the satraps, prefects, governors, advisers, treasurers, judges, magistrates and all the other provincial officials assembled for the dedication of the image that King Nebuchadnezzar had set up, and they stood before it.

Then the herald loudly proclaimed, "This is what you are commanded to do, O peoples, nations and men of every language: As soon as you hear the sound of the horn, flute, zither, lyre, harp, pipes and all kinds of music, you must fall down and worship the image of gold that King Nebuchadnezzar has set up. Whoever does not fall down and worship will immediately be thrown into a blazing furnace."

Therefore, as soon as they heard the sound of the horn, flute, zither, lyre, harp and all kinds of music, all the peoples, nations and men of every language fell down and worshiped the image of gold that King Nebuchadnezzar had set up.

At this time some astrologers came forward and denounced the Jews. They said to King Nebuchadnezzar, "O king, live forever! You have issued a decree, O king, that everyone who hears the sound of the horn, flute, zither, lyre, harp, pipes and all kinds of music must fall down and worship the image of gold, and that whoever does not fall down and worship will be thrown into a blazing furnace. But there are some Jews whom you have set over the affairs of the province of Babylon—Shadrach, Meshach and Abednego—who pay no attention to you, O king. They neither serve your gods nor worship the image of gold you have set up."

Furious with rage, Nebuchadnezzar summoned Shadrach, Meshach and Abednego. So these men were brought before the king, and Nebuchadnezzar said to them, "Is it true, Shadrach, Meshach and Abednego, that you do not serve my gods or worship the image of gold I have set up? Now when you hear the sound of the horn, flute, zither, lyre, harp, pipes and all kinds of music, if you are ready to fall down and worship the image I made, very good. But if you do not worship it, you will be thrown immediately into a blazing furnace. Then what god will be able to rescue you from my hand?"

Shadrach, Meshach and Abednego replied to the king, "O Nebuchadnezzar, we do not need to defend ourselves before you in this matter. If we are thrown into the blazing furnace, the God we serve is able to save us from it, and he will rescue us from your hand, O king. But even if he does not, we want you to know, O king, that we will not serve your gods or worship the image of gold you have set up."

Then Nebuchadnezzar was furious with Shadrach, Meshach and Abednego, and his attitude toward them changed. He ordered the furnace heated seven times hotter than usual and commanded some of the strongest soldiers in his army to tie up Shadrach, Meshach and Abednego and throw them into the blazing furnace. So these men, wearing their robes, trousers, turbans and other clothes, were bound and thrown into the blazing furnace. The king's command was so urgent and the furnace so hot that the flames of the fire killed the soldiers who took up Shadrach, Meshach and Abednego, and these three men, firmly tied, fell into the blazing furnace.

Then King Nebuchadnezzar leaped to his feet in amazement and asked his advisers, "Weren't there three men that we tied up and threw into the fire?"

They replied, "Certainly, O king."

He said, "Look! I see four men walking around in the fire, unbound and unharmed, and the fourth looks like a son of the gods."

Nebuchadnezzar then approached the opening of the blazing furnace and shouted, "Shadrach, Meshach and Abednego, servants of the Most High God, come out! Come here!"

So Shadrach, Meshach and Abednego came out of the fire, and the satraps, prefects, governors and royal advisers crowded around them. They saw that the fire had not harmed their bodies, nor was a hair of their heads singed; their robes were not scorched, and there was no smell of fire on them.

Then Nebuchadnezzar said, "Praise be to the God of Shadrach, Meshach and Abednego, who has sent his angel and rescued his servants! They trusted in him and defied the king's command and were willing to give up their lives rather than serve or worship any god except their own God. Therefore I decree that the people of any nation or language who say anything against the God of Shadrach, Meshach and Abednego be cut into pieces and their houses be turned into piles of rubble, for no other god can save in this way."

Stories from Daniel have become famous, and in fact any of the first six chapters would make a script for a thriller. In this story Daniel's three friends see Nebuchadnezzar's decree as a bottom-line issue of spiritual integrity that brings their dual loyalties into irreconcilable conflict. In this instance, they cannot serve both the kingdom of God and the kingdom of Babylon. There can be no compromise.

Idolatry is in fact Judah's stubborn sin that has brought on the Babylonian punishment in the first place. The Jews can never expect God's blessing if they choose to bow down to Nebuchadnezzar and his gold image. The uncompromising response of Daniel's friends shows that the Babylonian captivity is having a "refiner's fire" effect on a whole generation of Jewish exiles.

The book of Daniel makes for exciting reading because, at this most precarious time in Israelite history, God lets loose with a burst of miraculous activity: supernatural dreams, handwriting on the wall, rescues from a fiery furnace and a lions' den. Not since Elisha's day have the Israelites seen such signs and wonders.

The story of the fiery furnace has a happy ending, far beyond anything the three courageous Jews might have hoped for. Not only do they survive; the event ensures that Nebuchadnezzar will treat the Jewish religion with tolerance throughout his reign.

The Israelites are still thinking of God in terms of their own small community, but God has never intended for his blessings to stop with the Jews. When he first revealed the covenant to Abraham, he promised that Abraham's offspring would bless the whole earth (Genesis 12:3). Ironically, at a time of deep humiliation, while living as unwilling captives in Babylon, the Jews begin to convince others that their God deserves honor. The proclamations by Nebuchadnezzar and later Darius (Daniel 6:26–27) honor God more than anything a king of Judah has done in years.   —PY

DAILY CONTEMPLATION

What do you learn about faith from the reply of Daniel's friends (Daniel 3:16–18)?

THE WRITING ON THE WALL

King Belshazzar gave a great banquet for a thousand of his nobles and drank wine with them. While Belshazzar was drinking his wine, he gave orders to bring in the gold and silver goblets that Nebuchadnezzar his father had taken from the temple in Jerusalem, so that the king and his nobles, his wives and his concubines might drink from them. So they brought in the gold goblets that had been taken from the temple of God in Jerusalem, and the king and his nobles, his wives and his concubines drank from them. As they drank the wine, they praised the gods of gold and silver, of bronze, iron, wood and stone.

Suddenly the fingers of a human hand appeared and wrote on the plaster of the wall, near the lampstand in the royal palace. The king watched the hand as it wrote. His face turned pale and he was so frightened that his knees knocked together and his legs gave way.

The king called out for the enchanters, astrologers and diviners to be brought and said to these wise men of Babylon, "Whoever reads this writing and tells me what it means will be clothed in purple and have a gold chain placed around his neck, and he will be made the third highest ruler in the kingdom."

Then all the king's wise men came in, but they could not read the writing or tell the king what it meant. So King Belshazzar became even more terrified and his face grew more pale. His nobles were baffled.

The queen, hearing the voices of the king and his nobles, came into the banquet hall. "O king, live forever!" she said. "Don't be alarmed! Don't look so pale! There is a man in your kingdom who has the spirit of the holy gods in him. In the time of your father he was found to have insight and intelligence and wisdom like that of the gods. King Nebuchadnezzar your father—your father the king, I say—appointed him chief of the magicians, enchanters, astrologers and diviners. This man Daniel, whom the king called Belteshazzar, was found to have a keen mind and knowledge and understanding, and also the ability to interpret dreams, explain riddles and solve difficult problems. Call for Daniel, and he will tell you what the writing means."

So Daniel was brought before the king, and the king said to him, "Are you Daniel, one of the exiles my father the king brought from Judah? I have heard that the spirit of the gods is in you and that you have insight, intelligence and outstanding wisdom. The wise men and enchanters were brought before me to read this writing and tell me what it means, but they could not explain it. Now I have heard that you are able to give interpretations and to solve difficult problems. If you can read this writing and tell me what it means, you will be clothed in purple and have a gold chain placed around your neck, and you will be made the third highest ruler in the kingdom."

Then Daniel answered the king, "You may keep your gifts for yourself and give your rewards to someone else. Nevertheless, I will read the writing for the king and tell him what it means.

"O king, the Most High God gave your father Nebuchadnezzar sovereignty and greatness and glory and splendor. Because of the high position he gave him, all the peoples and nations and men of every language dreaded and feared him. Those the king wanted to put to death, he put to death; those he wanted to spare, he spared; those he wanted to promote, he promoted; and those he wanted to humble, he humbled. But when his heart became arrogant and hardened with pride, he was deposed from his royal throne and stripped of his glory. He was driven away from people and given the mind of an animal; he lived with the wild donkeys and ate grass like cattle; and his body was drenched with the dew of heaven, until he acknowledged that the Most High God is sovereign over the kingdoms of men and sets over them anyone he wishes.

"But you his son, O Belshazzar, have not humbled yourself, though you knew all this. Instead, you have set yourself up against the Lord of heaven. You had the goblets from his temple brought to you, and you and your nobles, your wives and your concubines drank wine from them. You praised the gods of silver and gold, of bronze, iron, wood and stone, which cannot see or hear or understand. But you did not honor the God who holds in his hand your life and all your ways. Therefore he sent the hand that wrote the inscription.

"This is the inscription that was written:

MENE, MENE, TEKEL, PARSIN

"This is what these words mean:

Mene: God has numbered the days of your reign and brought it to an end.

Tekel: You have been weighed on the scales and found wanting.

Peres: Your kingdom is divided and given to the Medes and Persians."

Then at Belshazzar's command, Daniel was clothed in purple, a gold chain was placed around his neck, and he was proclaimed the third highest ruler in the kingdom.

That very night Belshazzar, king of the Babylonians, was slain.

A miracle may make someone sit up and take notice, but it surely does not guarantee long-term change. Despite Nebuchadnezzar's newfound enthusiasm for the God of the Hebrews, in time he apparently forgot all about his religious zeal.

The king's son Belshazzar (bel-SHAZ-uhr), who grew up in the midst of the flurry of miracles, has an even shorter memory. Chapter 5 introduces the new king at a state orgy as he boozes it up with a thousand nobles and assorted women. They are carousing in a kind of "hurricane party" to show their disdain over reports of enemy armies advancing on the capital. The party even includes a religious element, after a fashion: they worship idols and use sacred relics stolen from the temple in Jerusalem to hold their wine.

Belshazzar's raucous party provides the setting for a scene straight out of a horror film: human fingers, eerily disconnected from any hand, write a message on the wall.

The king trembles and turns pale, but it takes the queen to remember the supernatural gifts of an old Jewish prophet. Daniel hasn't changed a bit over the years. He respectfully declines the king's bribes but interprets the dream anyway, after delivering an impromptu sermon.

That night, Daniel gets another high-ranking appointment to the government of a tyrant. But the job doesn't last long. The same night, Babylon falls victim to a sneak attack, and Darius the Mede takes over the kingdom.

A phrase has come down from this story—"the handwriting on the wall"—to signify a final warning just before the end. The prophets of Israel and Judah tried to interpret God's "handwriting" for their countrymen, with little success, and God used Babylon to punish them. Now Babylon, having ignored the warnings of a spiritual giant like Daniel, is itself due for punishment. They have ignored handwriting on the wall long enough.
—PY

DAILY CONTEMPLATION

Has God ever used "handwriting on the wall" in your life?

DAY 183 Daniel 6:1–26

DANIEL IN THE DEN OF LIONS

It pleased Darius to appoint 120 satraps to rule throughout the kingdom, with three administrators over them, one of whom was Daniel. The satraps were made accountable to them so that the king might not suffer loss. Now Daniel so distinguished himself among the administrators and the satraps by his exceptional qualities that the king planned to set him over the whole kingdom. At this, the administrators and the satraps tried to find grounds for charges against Daniel in his conduct of government affairs, but they were unable to do so. They could find no corruption in him, because he was trustworthy and neither corrupt nor negligent. Finally these men said, "We will never find any basis for charges against this man Daniel unless it has something to do with the law of his God."

So the administrators and the satraps went as a group to the king and said: "O King Darius, live forever! The royal administrators, prefects, satraps, advisers and governors have all agreed that the king should issue an edict and enforce the decree that anyone who prays to any god or man during the next thirty days, except to you, O king, shall be thrown into the lions' den. Now, O king, issue the decree and put it in writing so that it cannot be altered—in accordance with the laws of the Medes and Persians, which cannot be repealed." So King Darius put the decree in writing.

Now when Daniel learned that the decree had been published, he went home to his upstairs room where the windows opened toward Jerusalem.

Three times a day he got down on his knees and prayed, giving thanks to his God, just as he had done before. Then these men went as a group and found Daniel praying and asking God for help. So they went to the king and spoke to him about his royal decree: "Did you not publish a decree that during the next thirty days anyone who prays to any god or man except to you, O king, would be thrown into the lions' den?"

The king answered, "The decree stands—in accordance with the laws of the Medes and Persians, which cannot be repealed."

Then they said to the king, "Daniel, who is one of the exiles from Judah, pays no attention to you, O king, or to the decree you put in writing. He still prays three times a day." When the king heard this, he was greatly distressed; he was determined to rescue Daniel and made every effort until sundown to save him.

Then the men went as a group to the king and said to him, "Remember, O king, that according to the law of the Medes and Persians no decree or edict that the king issues can be changed."

So the king gave the order, and they brought Daniel and threw him into the lions' den. The king said to Daniel, "May your God, whom you serve continually, rescue you!"

A stone was brought and placed over the mouth of the den, and the king sealed it with his own signet ring and with the rings of his nobles, so that Daniel's situation might not be changed. Then the king returned to his palace and spent the night without eating and without any entertainment being brought to him. And he could not sleep.

At the first light of dawn, the king got up and hurried to the lions' den. When he came near the den, he called to Daniel in an anguished voice, "Daniel, servant of the living God, has your God, whom you serve continually, been able to rescue you from the lions?"

Daniel answered, "O king, live forever! My God sent his angel, and he shut the mouths of the lions. They have not hurt me, because I was found innocent in his sight. Nor have I ever done any wrong before you, O king."

The king was overjoyed and gave orders to lift Daniel out of the den. And when Daniel was lifted from the den, no wound was found on him, because he had trusted in his God.

At the king's command, the men who had falsely accused Daniel were brought in and thrown into the lions' den, along with their wives and children. And before they reached the floor of the den, the lions overpowered them and crushed all their bones.

Then King Darius wrote to all the peoples, nations and men of every language throughout the land:

"May you prosper greatly!

"I issue a decree that in every part of my kingdom people must fear and reverence the God of Daniel."

After six decades of service, Daniel finally faces a situation like his three friends in the fiery furnace faced—an unresolvable conflict between the law of God and the law of the land. During those years Daniel has lost much of his Jewish heritage and has even taken on a Babylonian name. Yet, although he can hardly worship God in the way he wishes, at the temple in Jerusalem, his devotion to God never wavers. In defiance of a king's new law, the old prophet keeps pointing himself toward Jerusalem three times a day in prayer.

The story of Daniel in the lions' den has special meaning for both Jews and Christians because, sadly, history has repeated itself so often. The Roman Empire, Stalin's Russia, Hitler's Germany, China—they've all taken their turn at restricting worship, yet the church has survived, and even thrived, during times of intense persecution. Not everyone who undergoes religious persecution receives miraculous deliverance like Daniel's. But, all together, the martyrs have given a witness to the watching world that true faith cannot be stamped out, no matter what the penalty.

A miracle spares Daniel's life; an even greater miracle takes place in those around him. Stirred by Daniel's faith, the Persian ruler issues a proclamation that everyone in his kingdom must fear and reverence "the God of Daniel." Soon, the same empire that has passed laws against Jewish worship will escort the Jewish exiles back to their homeland and allow them to rebuild the temple.

The harsh times in Babylon have their effect on the Jewish community as well. Led by the examples of people such as Daniel, they begin a new practice of meeting together in "synagogues" to study the law and to pray. And they will return to Palestine purged of the sin that has brought them so much anguish: Jews never again will be known to practice idolatry. The refining fire has done its work.   —PY

DAILY CONTEMPLATION

Has God used a "refining fire" to teach you or cleanse you from sin?

DAY 184   Reflection

AN EXCELLENT EXAMPLE

If you want a biblical person to model yourself after, Daniel is one excellent choice, mainly because of his strength of character. The Bible tells of many weak people who made mistakes and were still used by God. Daniel was one of the rare people who, as far as we know, made no great mistakes. According to all the Bible tells us, his commitment to God remained strong and steady, and he lived out that commitment for everyone to see.

"It's too late," you may sigh. "I've already made big mistakes, and I'll likely never become a Daniel." No matter what your past holds, you can pursue excellence of the kind Daniel exhibited. Ted Engstrom, president emeritus of World Vision and author of the book **The Pursuit of Excellence,** writes, "Striving for excellence in our work, whatever it is, is not only our Christian duty, but a basic form of Christian witness. And our nonverbal communication speaks so loudly that people often cannot hear a single word we say."[22]

Our actions speak for us about our caliber. Who we are reflects to others something of what it means to be a believer. In the way we live our lives, we, often unknowingly, tell unbelievers something about following God.

Take a look at Daniel's actions. In the beginning of the book we see Daniel declining the expensive food and wine offered him. Because this food has first been sacrificed to idols, Daniel's principles won't allow him to enjoy such a repast. He politely asks the guard to give him and his men a chance to eat only vegetables and water, trusting that God will keep them healthy.

Then, when he interprets a dream for the king, Daniel first acknowledges that he possesses no more wisdom than other men. He is able to interpret the dream simply because the king needs to know and understand it and God has chosen to reveal its meaning through Daniel. Daniel has no concern for promoting himself. He cares rather about the duty at hand.

Later, when another king comes to power and asks Daniel to read some strange writing on a wall, Daniel turns down the gifts and rewards offered yet agrees to interpret the writing anyway. Again he knows God has given him a job to do, and taking rewards from an ungodly king would compromise Daniel's own devotion to God.

Under yet another king, Daniel "so distinguished himself among the administrators and the satraps by his exceptional qualities that the king planned to set him over the whole kingdom" (6:3). They could find nothing wrong with Daniel, "because he was trustworthy and neither corrupt nor negligent" (6:4). Once more Daniel's excellence shines through in his actions. The jealous people around him soon conclude they can only pin something on him if it sets up a conflict with God's law.

Finally, when Daniel survives a night on the verge of death, he doesn't complain about the king throwing him into the lions' den but instead honors the king and focuses on God. "O king, live forever! My God sent his angel, and he shut the mouths of the lions" (6:21–22).

Daniel may have been born into a noble family, but he wasn't born into excellence. That he earned for himself. John Gardner, in *The Pursuit of Excellence,* explains, "Some people have greatness thrust upon them. Very few have excellence thrust upon them.... They achieve it. They do not achieve it unwittingly by 'doing what comes naturally' and they don't stumble into it in the course of amusing themselves. All excellence involves discipline and tenacity of purpose."[23]

Daniel did show discipline. He knew his purpose and held to it over the long haul. Daniel was committed to doing things God's way, and he never lost sight of that commitment. —BQ

DAILY CONTEMPLATION

How much do you think about excellence in day-to-day life? How concerned are you with doing your best and acting consistently? Ask God to help develop, or continue developing, an inner fortitude in you that helps you hold to the person you are through Jesus and find honor in God's eyes.

REBUILDING THE ALTAR

When the seventh month came and the Israelites had settled in their towns, the people assembled as one man in Jerusalem. Then Jeshua son of Jozadak and his fellow priests and Zerubbabel son of Shealtiel and his associates began to build the altar of the God of Israel to sacrifice burnt offerings on it, in accordance with what is written in the Law of Moses the man of God. Despite their fear of the peoples around them, they built the altar on its foundation and sacrificed burnt offerings on it to the LORD, both the morning and evening sacrifices. Then in accordance with what is written, they celebrated the Feast of Tabernacles with the required number of burnt offerings prescribed for each day. After that, they presented the regular burnt offerings, the New Moon sacrifices and the sacrifices for all the appointed sacred feasts of the LORD, as well as those brought as freewill offerings to the LORD. On the first day of the seventh month they began to offer burnt offerings to the LORD, though the foundation of the LORD's temple had not yet been laid.

Then they gave money to the masons and carpenters, and gave food and drink and oil to the people of Sidon and Tyre, so that they would bring cedar logs by sea from Lebanon to Joppa, as authorized by Cyrus king of Persia.

In the second month of the second year after their arrival at the house of God in Jerusalem, Zerubbabel son of Shealtiel, Jeshua son of Jozadak and the rest of their brothers (the priests and the Levites and all who had returned from the captivity to Jerusalem) began the work, appointing Levites twenty years of age and older to supervise the building of the house of the LORD. Jeshua and his sons and brothers and Kadmiel and his sons (descendants of Hodaviah) and the sons of Henadad and their sons and brothers— all Levites—joined together in supervising those working on the house of God.

When the builders laid the foundation of the temple of the LORD, the priests in their vestments and with trumpets, and the Levites (the sons of Asaph) with cymbals, took their places to praise the LORD, as prescribed by David king of Israel. With praise and thanksgiving they sang to the LORD:

"He is good;
    his love to Israel endures forever."

And all the people gave a great shout of praise to the LORD, because the foundation of the house of the LORD was laid. But many of the older priests and Levites and family heads, who had seen the former temple, wept aloud when they saw the foundation of this temple being laid, while many others shouted for joy. No one could distinguish the sound of the shouts of joy from the sound of weeping, because the people made so much noise. And the sound was heard far away.

When the enemies of Judah and Benjamin heard that the exiles were building a temple for the LORD, the God of Israel, they came to Zerubbabel and to the heads of the families and said, "Let us help you build because, like you, we seek your God and have been sacrificing to him since the time of Esarhaddon king of Assyria, who brought us here."

But Zerubbabel, Jeshua and the rest of the heads of the families of Israel answered, "You have no part with us in building a temple to our God. We alone will build it for the LORD, the God of Israel, as King Cyrus, the king of Persia, commanded us."

Then the peoples around them set out to discourage the people of Judah and make them afraid to go on building. They hired counselors to work against them and frustrate their plans during the entire reign of Cyrus king of Persia and down to the reign of Darius king of Persia.

For more than half a century Jewish exiles, among them Daniel and Ezekiel, were held captive in Babylon. Some, like Daniel, prospered in the foreign land; but no true Israelite ever felt totally at peace there. Always, a longing gnawed inside, a longing for home and for the temple of God. As one poet in exile wrote, "If I forget you, O Jerusalem, may my right hand forget its skill. May my tongue cling to the roof of my mouth if I do not remember you, if I do not consider Jerusalem my highest joy" (Psalm 137:5–6).

Daniel's new boss, in keeping with the Persian policy of religious tolerance, granted permission for the first wave of Jewish exiles to return to Jerusalem, and the book of Ezra tells their story. The sight that greets the returning exiles in Jerusalem makes them very sad: The city is a ghost town, burned and pillaged by the conquering Babylonians. The temple of God is a mound of rubble.

The settlers go to work at once, setting temple reconstruction as their highest priority. They have hope: the Persians have even given back the pilfered silver and gold temple articles. When the Jews finally lay the foundation, the sound of their shouting can be heard from far away. The temple, after all, is the place where they will meet God and, as such, symbolizes a new start with him.

Yet the shouts of joy mingle with loud cries of weeping as well. The older returnees, those who remember Solomon's temple in all its splendor, weep at the comparison. They have lost political independence and need permission from a foreign government just to rebuild the temple. The Jews have regained only a tiny portion of their former territory. They are very far from the glory days of David and Solomon.

The book of Ezra thus introduces a new period in the Israelites' history—a period in which they become more like a "church" than a nation. Their leaders focus energy not on fighting enemy armies but on fighting sin and spiritual compromise. They fear repeating the mistakes that have sent them into exile.   —PY

DAILY CONTEMPLATION

In your spiritual life, what are you fighting? Sin? Spiritual compromise? Repeat of past mistakes? Lack of trust in God?

A CALL TO BUILD THE HOUSE OF THE LORD

In the second year of King Darius, on the first day of the sixth month, the word of the LORD came through the prophet Haggai to Zerubbabel son of Shealtiel, governor of Judah, and to Joshua son of Jehozadak, the high priest:

This is what the LORD Almighty says: "These people say, 'The time has not yet come for the LORD's house to be built.'"

Then the word of the LORD came through the prophet Haggai: "Is it a time for you yourselves to be living in your paneled houses, while this house remains a ruin?"

Now this is what the LORD Almighty says: "Give careful thought to your ways. You have planted much, but have harvested little. You eat, but never have enough. You drink, but never have your fill. You put on clothes, but are not warm. You earn wages, only to put them in a purse with holes in it."

This is what the LORD Almighty says: "Give careful thought to your ways. Go up into the mountains and bring down timber and build the house, so that I may take pleasure in it and be honored," says the LORD. "You expected much, but see, it turned out to be little. What you brought home, I blew away. Why?" declares the LORD Almighty. "Because of my house, which remains a ruin, while each of you is busy with his own house. Therefore, because of you the heavens have withheld their dew and the earth its crops. I called for a drought on the fields and the mountains, on the grain, the new wine, the oil and whatever the ground produces, on men and cattle, and on the labor of your hands."

Then Zerubbabel son of Shealtiel, Joshua son of Jehozadak, the high priest, and the whole remnant of the people obeyed the voice of the LORD their God and the message of the prophet Haggai, because the LORD their God had sent him. And the people feared the LORD.

Then Haggai, the LORD's messenger, gave this message of the LORD to the people: "I am with you," declares the LORD. So the LORD stirred up the spirit of Zerubbabel son of Shealtiel, governor of Judah, and the spirit of Joshua son of Jehozadak, the high priest, and the spirit of the whole remnant of the people. They came and began to work on the house of the LORD Almighty, their God, on the twenty-fourth day of the sixth month in the second year of King Darius.

On the twenty-first day of the seventh month, the word of the LORD came through the prophet Haggai: "Speak to Zerubbabel son of Shealtiel, governor of Judah, to Joshua son of Jehozadak, the high priest, and to the remnant of the people. Ask them, 'Who of you is left who saw this house in its former glory? How does it look to you now? Does it not seem to you like nothing? But now be strong, O Zerubbabel,' declares the LORD. 'Be strong, O Joshua son of Jehozadak, the high priest. Be strong, all you people of the land,' declares the LORD, 'and work. For I am with you,' declares the LORD Almighty.

'This is what I covenanted with you when you came out of Egypt. And my Spirit remains among you. Do not fear.'"

The burst of energy described in Ezra does not last long. Opposition soon arises among the tribes bordering Israel, who do not look kindly on the resurgence of a traditional enemy. The temple project especially alarms them, in view of all the stories they have heard about the miraculous power of Israel's God. And surely, they reason, a rebuilt temple will only inflame the Israelites' religious zeal. Even Israel's protector, Persia, begins to waver on its promises to the Jews.

In the face of this stiff opposition, the Jews lose enthusiasm, or rather redirect their enthusiasm toward other projects. Just a few years after the exiles' return, work on the temple grinds to a halt. The Jews begin to concentrate instead on building their own homes and regaining their former prosperity. They have forgotten the original motive for returning to Jerusalem.

About twenty years after the first migration, a prophet named Haggai (HAG-i) appears in Jerusalem to confront the growing apathy and confusion. He does not rage like Jeremiah or act out public object lessons like Ezekiel. He simply urges these pioneers to give careful thought to their situation. "Is it a time for you yourselves to be living in your paneled houses, while this house [the temple] remains a ruin?" he asks.

Haggai puts things simply and logically. The settlers have worked hard, but what has it earned them? Their crops are unsuccessful. Their money disappears as soon as they earn it. Haggai's diagnosis: mistaken priorities. The Israelites need to put God first, and for starters that means rebuilding his temple. God's reputation is at stake. If the temple symbolizes God's presence, how can he be properly honored when his house lies in ruins?

A statement made by Jesus years later summarizes Haggai's message well: "Do not worry, saying, 'What shall we eat?' or 'What shall we drink?' or 'What shall we wear?' ... But seek first his [God's] kingdom and his righteousness, and all these things will be given to you as well" (Matthew 6:31, 33). Amazingly, Haggai strikes an immediate chord of response in his audience. Prophets before him, such as Amos, Isaiah, or Jeremiah, spoke for decades without seeing such a heartfelt reaction. —PY

DAILY CONTEMPLATION

What tends to distract you from spiritual priorities today?

DAY 187

Zechariah 8:1–23

THE LORD PROMISES TO BLESS JERUSALEM

Again the word of the LORD Almighty came to me. This is what the LORD Almighty says: "I am very jealous for Zion; I am burning with jealousy for her."

This is what the LORD says:"I will return to Zion and dwell in Jerusalem. Then Jerusalem will be called the City of Truth, and the mountain of the LORD Almighty will be called the Holy Mountain."

This is what the LORD Almighty says:"Once again men and women of ripe old age will sit in the streets of Jerusalem, each with cane in hand because of his age. The city streets will be filled with boys and girls playing there."

This is what the LORD Almighty says:"It may seem marvelous to the remnant of this people at that time, but will it seem marvelous to me?" declares the LORD Almighty.

This is what the LORD Almighty says:"I will save my people from the countries of the east and the west. I will bring them back to live in Jerusalem; they will be my people, and I will be faithful and righteous to them as their God."

This is what the LORD Almighty says:"You who now hear these words spoken by the prophets who were there when the foundation was laid for the house of the LORD Almighty, let your hands be strong so that the temple may be built. Before that time there were no wages for man or beast. No one could go about his business safely because of his enemy, for I had turned every man against his neighbor. But now I will not deal with the remnant of this people as I did in the past," declares the LORD Almighty.

"The seed will grow well, the vine will yield its fruit, the ground will produce its crops, and the heavens will drop their dew. I will give all these things as an inheritance to the remnant of this people. As you have been an object of cursing among the nations, O Judah and Israel, so will I save you, and you will be a blessing. Do not be afraid, but let your hands be strong."

This is what the LORD Almighty says:"Just as I had determined to bring disaster upon you and showed no pity when your fathers angered me," says the LORD Almighty, "so now I have determined to do good again to Jerusalem and Judah. Do not be afraid. These are the things you are to do: Speak the truth to each other, and render true and sound judgment in your courts; do not plot evil against your neighbor, and do not love to swear falsely. I hate all this," declares the LORD.

Again the word of the LORD Almighty came to me. This is what the LORD Almighty says:"The fasts of the fourth, fifth, seventh and tenth months will become joyful and glad occasions and happy festivals for Judah. Therefore love truth and peace."

This is what the LORD Almighty says:"Many peoples and the inhabitants of many cities will yet come, and the inhabitants of one city will go to another and say, 'Let us go at once to entreat the LORD and seek the LORD Almighty. I myself am going.' And many peoples and powerful nations will come to Jerusalem to seek the LORD Almighty and to entreat him."

This is what the LORD Almighty says:"In those days ten men from all languages and nations will take firm hold of one Jew by the hem of his robe and say, 'Let us go with you, because we have heard that God is with you.'"

Another, younger prophet named Zechariah (ZEK-uh-RI-uh) joins Haggai in his campaign to lift the spirits of the settlers in Jerusalem (Ezra 5:1 lists both these prophets by name). The two have a similar message but a different approach. Whereas Haggai asks the Jews to look around at their current conditions and then make some needed changes, Zechariah calls them to look beyond the present and envision a new Jerusalem, a "City of Truth."

At the time, the pioneers are focusing on immediate goals: the next planting of crops, basic shelter for their families, repopulating the deserted city. Zechariah lifts their sights toward a far more glorious future, when Jerusalem will be a light to the world and people from many nations will stream to the city "because we have heard that God is with you." The prophet gives his prescription for reaching such a state: the new society must be built on justice, honesty, integrity, and peace.

It will take years to rebuild the city of Jerusalem, and centuries for Israel to regain some form of political independence. The Jews who labor so hard must ask themselves often, "Is this all God has in mind for us?" Zechariah replies with a resounding "No!" He insists that the small refugee community in fact holds the key to the world's future: their new beginning will lead the way to a Messiah who will bring hope to the whole earth.

Following Haggai's lead, Zechariah seizes upon the need to rebuild the temple as a vital first step. These prophets see that as long as the temple lies in ruins, Israel's distinctive character as a people of God is suspect. Together, the two men have a remarkable effect on their countrymen. At their urging, the Jews organize to build again and within four years complete the temple, giving the nation a central reminder of its original covenant with God. —PY

DAILY CONTEMPLATION

When was the last time you asked, "Is this all God has in mind for me?"

DAY 188   Nehemiah 1:1–4, 11; 2:1–20

ARTAXERXES SENDS NEHEMIAH TO JERUSALEM

The words of Nehemiah son of Hacaliah:

In the month of Kislev in the twentieth year, while I was in the citadel of Susa, Hanani, one of my brothers, came from Judah with some other men, and I questioned them about the Jewish remnant that survived the exile, and also about Jerusalem.

They said to me, "Those who survived the exile and are back in the province are in great trouble and disgrace. The wall of Jerusalem is broken down, and its gates have been burned with fire."

When I heard these things, I sat down and wept. For some days I mourned and fasted and prayed before the God of heaven. . . .

"O Lord, let your ear be attentive to the prayer of this your servant and to the prayer of your servants who delight in revering your name. Give your servant success today by granting him favor in the presence of this man."

I was cupbearer to the king.

In the month of Nisan in the twentieth year of King Artaxerxes, when wine was brought for him, I took the wine and gave it to the king. I had not been sad in his presence before; so the king asked me, "Why does your face look so sad when you are not ill? This can be nothing but sadness of heart."

I was very much afraid, but I said to the king, "May the king live forever! Why should my face not look sad when the city where my fathers are buried lies in ruins, and its gates have been destroyed by fire?"

The king said to me, "What is it you want?"

Then I prayed to the God of heaven, and I answered the king, "If it pleases the king and if your servant has found favor in his sight, let him send me to the city in Judah where my fathers are buried so that I can rebuild it."

Then the king, with the queen sitting beside him, asked me, "How long will your journey take, and when will you get back?" It pleased the king to send me; so I set a time.

I also said to him, "If it pleases the king, may I have letters to the governors of Trans-Euphrates, so that they will provide me safe-conduct until I arrive in Judah? And may I have a letter to Asaph, keeper of the king's forest, so he will give me timber to make beams for the gates of the citadel by the temple and for the city wall and for the residence I will occupy?" And because the gracious hand of my God was upon me, the king granted my requests. So I went to the governors of Trans-Euphrates and gave them the king's letters. The king had also sent army officers and cavalry with me.

When Sanballat the Horonite and Tobiah the Ammonite official heard about this, they were very much disturbed that someone had come to promote the welfare of the Israelites.

I went to Jerusalem, and after staying there three days I set out during the night with a few men. I had not told anyone what my God had put in my heart to do for Jerusalem. There were no mounts with me except the one I was riding on.

By night I went out through the Valley Gate toward the Jackal Well and the Dung Gate, examining the walls of Jerusalem, which had been broken down, and its gates, which had been destroyed by fire. Then I moved on toward the Fountain Gate and the King's Pool, but there was not enough room for my mount to get through; so I went up the valley by night, examining the wall. Finally, I turned back and reentered through the Valley Gate. The officials did not know where I had gone or what I was doing, because as yet I had said nothing to the Jews or the priests or nobles or officials or any others who would be doing the work.

Then I said to them, "You see the trouble we are in: Jerusalem lies in ruins, and its gates have been burned with fire. Come, let us rebuild the wall of Jerusalem, and we will no longer be in disgrace." I also told them about the gracious hand of my God upon me and what the king had said to me.

They replied, "Let us start rebuilding." So they began this good work.

But when Sanballat the Horonite, Tobiah the Ammonite official and Geshem the Arab heard about it, they mocked and ridiculed us. "What is this you are doing?" they asked. "Are you rebelling against the king?"

I answered them by saying, "The God of heaven will give us success. We his servants will start rebuilding, but as for you, you have no share in Jerusalem or any claim or historic right to it."

Sixty-five years have passed. The Jews have a temple in Jerusalem, yes, but very little beyond that. The holy city is sparsely occupied; most Jews have settled in the outlying villages and towns rather than inside its walls. Indeed, with all the intermarriage and mixing with foreigners, the entire community seems on the verge of losing its unique identity. The Jews' cultural and religious heritage is slipping away.

What can stop the downhill slide? One man, a Jewish exile who has stayed behind in Babylon, has an idea. Like Daniel before him, Nehemiah (NEE-uh-MI-uh) has risen in the ranks of a foreign government (Persia) and is prospering. Nevertheless, his heart is with his countrymen back in Jerusalem, and when he hears the dismaying reports from that city, he feels compelled to act. He obtains the king's permission to lead an expedition to Jerusalem with the goal of rebuilding the city's wall.

In an age when nomadic warriors pose a constant danger, a wall offers a city its only security. It was for lack of a wall that the Jews scattered among their neighbors and are now facing permanent assimilation into other cultures. By constructing a wall, Nehemiah can help make Jerusalem into a sacred city again and protect its residents by controlling who else comes and goes.

Nehemiah stands in a long line of remarkable Israelite leaders such as Moses, Samuel, David, Hezekiah, and Josiah. Strictly speaking, he is not a prophet, although he is surely a man of God. He does not act without prayer, and he does not pray without acting. Although he has enormous skills in management and leadership, he does not seek after earthly status—if he did, he would never have left Persia.

Nehemiah improvises as he goes, meeting each new challenge with a combination of business savvy, courage, and dependence on God. He mobilizes work crews, fights off opposition, reforms the court system, purifies religious practices, and, when necessary, rallies the troops with stirring speeches. And he does all this while "on leave" from his responsibilities as statesman in the Persian court.   —PY

DAILY CONTEMPLATION

Do you see any secrets of success in this record of Nehemiah's actions?

EZRA READS THE LAW

The priests, the Levites, the gatekeepers, the singers and the temple servants, along with certain of the people and the rest of the Israelites, settled in their own towns.

When the seventh month came and the Israelites had settled in their towns, all the people assembled as one man in the square before the Water Gate. They told Ezra the scribe to bring out the Book of the Law of Moses, which the LORD had commanded for Israel.

So on the first day of the seventh month Ezra the priest brought the Law before the assembly, which was made up of men and women and all who were able to understand. He read it aloud from daybreak till noon as he faced the square before the Water Gate in the presence of the men, women and others who could understand. And all the people listened attentively to the Book of the Law.

Ezra the scribe stood on a high wooden platform built for the occasion. Beside him on his right stood Mattithiah, Shema, Anaiah, Uriah, Hilkiah and Maaseiah; and on his left were Pedaiah, Mishael, Malkijah, Hashum, Hashbaddanah, Zechariah and Meshullam.

Ezra opened the book. All the people could see him because he was standing above them; and as he opened it, the people all stood up. Ezra praised the LORD, the great God; and all the people lifted their hands and responded, "Amen! Amen!" Then they bowed down and worshiped the LORD with their faces to the ground.

The Levites—Jeshua, Bani, Sherebiah, Jamin, Akkub, Shabbethai, Hodiah, Maaseiah, Kelita, Azariah, Jozabad, Hanan and Pelaiah—instructed the people in the Law while the people were standing there. They read from the Book of the Law of God, making it clear and giving the meaning so that the people could understand what was being read.

Then Nehemiah the governor, Ezra the priest and scribe, and the Levites who were instructing the people said to them all, "This day is sacred to the LORD your God. Do not mourn or weep." For all the people had been weeping as they listened to the words of the Law.

Nehemiah said, "Go and enjoy choice food and sweet drinks, and send some to those who have nothing prepared. This day is sacred to our Lord. Do not grieve, for the joy of the LORD is your strength."

The Levites calmed all the people, saying, "Be still, for this is a sacred day. Do not grieve."

Then all the people went away to eat and drink, to send portions of food and to celebrate with great joy, because they now understood the words that had been made known to them.

On the second day of the month, the heads of all the families, along with the priests and the Levites, gathered around Ezra the scribe to give attention to the words of the Law. They found written in the Law, which the LORD had commanded through Moses, that the Israelites were to live in booths during the feast of the seventh month and that they should proclaim this word and spread it throughout their towns and in Jerusalem: "Go out into the hill country and bring back branches from olive and wild olive trees, and from myrtles, palms and shade trees, to make booths"—as it is written.

So the people went out and brought back branches and built themselves booths on their own roofs, in their courtyards, in the courts of the house of God and in the square by the Water Gate and the one by the Gate of Ephraim. The whole company that had returned from exile built booths and lived in them. From the days of Joshua son of Nun until that day, the Israelites had not celebrated it like this. And their joy was very great.

Day after day, from the first day to the last, Ezra read from the Book of the Law of God. They celebrated the feast for seven days, and on the eighth day, in accordance with the regulation, there was an assembly.

Nehemiah alone is an impressive leader, but when paired with Ezra (EZ-ruh), he is downright indomitable. The two make a perfect combination. Nehemiah, emboldened by good political connections, inspires others with his hands-on management style and his fearless optimism. Ezra leads more by moral force than by personality. He can trace his priestly lineage all the way back to Moses' brother Aaron, and he seems singularly determined to restore integrity to that office.

On his arrival in Jerusalem some years before, Ezra was shocked by the Jews' spiritual apathy. Rather than mounting a soapbox and scolding them for their failures, he tore his hair and beard, threw himself on the ground, and began a fast of repentance (see Ezra 9). His remarkable display of contrition so startled the Jewish settlers that they all agreed to repent and change their ways. Ezra had that kind of moral influence over people.

The action in this chapter takes place after Nehemiah has completed the arduous task of repairing the wall. The Jews, safe at last from their enemies, gather together in hopes of regaining some sense of national identity. As spiritual leader, Ezra addresses the huge crowd. He stands on a newly built platform and begins to read from a document nearly one thousand years old, the scroll that contains the Israelites' original covenant with God.

As Ezra reads the ancient words, a sound of weeping begins to rise, spreading through the multitude. The Bible does not explain the reason for the tears. Are the people feeling guilt over their long history of breaking that covenant? Or nostalgia over the favored days when Israel had full independence? Whatever the reason, this is no time for tears. Nehemiah and Ezra send out orders to prepare for a huge feast and celebration. God wants joy, not mourning. His chosen people are being rebuilt, just as surely as the stone walls of Jerusalem have been rebuilt.

The central image of this chapter—a lone figure atop a wooden platform reading from a scroll—comes to symbolize the Jewish race. They are becoming "people of the Book." The Jews have not regained the territory and splendor their nation once enjoyed under David and Solomon. The temple they have painstakingly constructed will eventually fall to looters, just like the one it replaced. But they will never forget the lesson of Ezra. He becomes the prototype for a new leader of the Jews: the scribe, a student of Scripture. —PY

DAY 190   Reflection

BUILDING GOD INTO OUR LIVES

Who and what have you built into your life?

Whether consciously or not, we all build space into our lives for the people and things most important to us. A glance at your calendar over the last weeks and months will reveal the things in your life that hold the highest priority. How often does God appear in the pages of your calendar? How much of a priority does the reading and study of his Word represent? Do appointments with God get scheduled as often as business lunches and visits to the hair salon?

For many years the people of Israel and Judah increasingly let other people and pursuits take priority over their worship of God and attention to his Word. Eventually they almost completely lost their knowledge of the law. God didn't force himself on them; rather, he let them walk away and stay away for a long time. Only by experiencing life without him would they remember who they really needed and wanted.

Through Ezra, Haggai, Zechariah, and Nehemiah, the Israelite people understood again their deep-seated need for walking closely with God and living by his Word. They celebrated with great joy upon hearing the law again for the first time, "because they now understood the words that had been made known to them" (Nehemiah 8:12). Hearing God again helped them find sense in living. God's Word gave them guidance for the present and hope for the future. The people understood, as David had, that "your word is a lamp to my feet and a light for my path" (Psalm 119:105).

In rebuilding the temple and the city of Jerusalem, the Israelite people declared they were once more building God into their lives. They needed him, needed to live near to his holiness and close to his teaching. Apart from him they would have no real joy.

Today it's not a sacred building or a particular city or a priest or scribe that defines God's presence in our lives. Jesus changed the physical nature of that presence. Now we find God's Spirit dwelling inside us. Each believer has become a living, breathing temple of God. We need to work at staying in touch with God, however. We must be intentional about building God a prominent place in our lives.

God's Word serves as our foundation. Never will we outgrow our need for studying the Bible. Never can we know it well enough. Stone by stone, reading and learning, we build God an enduring home in our hearts. —BQ

DAY 191   Esther 1:1–22

QUEEN VASHTI DEPOSED

This is what happened during the time of Xerxes, the Xerxes who ruled over 127 provinces stretching from India to Cush: At that time King Xerxes reigned from his royal throne in the citadel of Susa, and in the third year of his reign he gave a banquet for all his nobles and officials. The military leaders of Persia and Media, the princes, and the nobles of the provinces were present.

For a full 180 days he displayed the vast wealth of his kingdom and the splendor and glory of his majesty. When these days were over, the king gave a banquet, lasting seven days, in the enclosed garden of the king's palace, for all the people from the least to the greatest, who were in the citadel of Susa. The garden had hangings of white and blue linen, fastened with cords of white linen and purple material to silver rings on marble pillars. There were couches of gold and silver on a mosaic pavement of porphyry, marble, mother-of-pearl and other costly stones. Wine was served in goblets of gold, each one different from the other, and the royal wine was abundant, in keeping with the king's liberality. By the king's command each guest was allowed to drink in his own way, for the king instructed all the wine stewards to serve each man what he wished.

Queen Vashti also gave a banquet for the women in the royal palace of King Xerxes.

On the seventh day, when King Xerxes was in high spirits from wine, he commanded the seven eunuchs who served him—Mehuman, Biztha, Harbona, Bigtha, Abagtha, Zethar and Carcas—to bring before him Queen Vashti, wearing her royal crown, in order to display her beauty to the people and nobles, for she was lovely to look at. But when the attendants delivered the king's command, Queen Vashti refused to come. Then the king became furious and burned with anger.

Since it was customary for the king to consult experts in matters of law and justice, he spoke with the wise men who understood the times and were closest to the king—Carshena, Shethar, Admatha, Tarshish, Meres, Marsena and Memucan, the seven nobles of Persia and Media who had special access to the king and were highest in the kingdom.

"According to law, what must be done to Queen Vashti?" he asked. "She has not obeyed the command of King Xerxes that the eunuchs have taken to her."

Then Memucan replied in the presence of the king and the nobles, "Queen Vashti has done wrong, not only against the king but also against all the nobles and the peoples of all the provinces of King Xerxes. For the queen's conduct will become known to all the women, and so they will despise their husbands and say, 'King Xerxes commanded Queen Vashti to be brought before him, but she would not come.' This very day the Persian and Median women of the nobility who have heard about the queen's conduct will respond to all the king's nobles in the same way. There will be no end of disrespect and discord.

"Therefore, if it pleases the king, let him issue a royal decree and let it be written in the laws of Persia and Media, which cannot be repealed, that Vashti is never again to enter the presence of King Xerxes. Also let the king give her royal position to someone else who is better than she. Then when the king's edict is proclaimed throughout all his vast realm, all the women will respect their husbands, from the least to the greatest."

The king and his nobles were pleased with this advice, so the king did as Memucan proposed. He sent dispatches to all parts of the kingdom, to each province in its own script and to each people in its own language, proclaiming in each people's tongue that every man should be ruler over his own household.

Not every Jewish exile takes the opportunity to return to the homeland. Some have put down roots during the half century of Babylonian captivity, and when the more tolerant Persian regime takes over, many of these decide to stay. (Communities of Jews in present-day Iraq and Syria trace their ancestry to this group of exiles.)

This adventure story concerns two such Jews who stay behind, a beautiful woman named Esther and her cousin Mordecai (MOHR-duh-ki). Before Israel entered into captivity in Babylon, Isaiah and Jeremiah prophesied, urging the people to come out of Babylon after seventy years' captivity. They encouraged the Israelites of the future to return to the land where God would fulfill his covenant promises. Although Esther and Mordecai do not follow these instructions, God reminds his people through the book of Esther that he will keep his promises and preserve them, whether they live in Jerusalem, surrounded by powerful nations, or in the midst of the Babylonian empire.   —BQ

DAILY CONTEMPLATION

What situation in your life causes you to need God's reassurance that he will care for you and preserve you?

ESTHER MADE QUEEN

Later when the anger of King Xerxes had subsided, he remembered Vashti and what she had done and what he had decreed about her. Then the king's personal attendants proposed, "Let a search be made for beautiful young virgins for the king. Let the king appoint commissioners in every province of his realm to bring all these beautiful girls into the harem at the citadel of Susa. Let them be placed under the care of Hegai, the king's eunuch, who is in charge of the women; and let beauty treatments be given to them. Then let the girl who pleases the king be queen instead of Vashti." This advice appealed to the king, and he followed it.

Now there was in the citadel of Susa a Jew of the tribe of Benjamin, named Mordecai son of Jair, the son of Shimei, the son of Kish, who had been carried into exile from Jerusalem by Nebuchadnezzar king of Babylon, among those taken captive with Jehoiachin king of Judah. Mordecai had a cousin named Hadassah, whom he had brought up because she had neither father nor mother. This girl, who was also known as Esther, was lovely in form and features, and Mordecai had taken her as his own daughter when her father and mother died.

When the king's order and edict had been proclaimed, many girls were brought to the citadel of Susa and put under the care of Hegai. Esther also was taken to the king's palace and entrusted to Hegai, who had charge of the harem. The girl pleased him and won his favor. Immediately he provided her with her beauty treatments and special food. He assigned to her seven maids selected from the king's palace and moved her and her maids into the best place in the harem.

Esther had not revealed her nationality and family background, because Mordecai had forbidden her to do so. Every day he walked back and forth near the courtyard of the harem to find out how Esther was and what was happening to her.

Before a girl's turn came to go in to King Xerxes, she had to complete twelve months of beauty treatments prescribed for the women, six months with oil of myrrh and six with perfumes and cosmetics. And this is how she would go to the king: Anything she wanted was given her to take with her from the harem to the king's palace. In the evening she would go there and in the morning return to another part of the harem to the care of Shaashgaz, the king's eunuch who was in charge of the concubines. She would not return to the king unless he was pleased with her and summoned her by name.

When the turn came for Esther (the girl Mordecai had adopted, the daughter of his uncle Abihail) to go to the king, she asked for nothing other than what Hegai, the king's eunuch who was in charge of the harem, suggested. And Esther won the favor of everyone who saw her. She was taken to King Xerxes in the royal residence in the tenth month, the month of Tebeth, in the seventh year of his reign.

Now the king was attracted to Esther more than to any of the other women, and she won his favor and approval more than any of the other virgins. So he set a royal crown on her head and made her queen instead of Vashti. And the king gave a great banquet, Esther's banquet, for all his nobles and officials. He proclaimed a holiday throughout the provinces and distributed gifts with royal liberality.

When the virgins were assembled a second time, Mordecai was sitting at the king's gate. But Esther had kept secret her family background and nationality just as Mordecai had told her to do, for she continued to follow Mordecai's instructions as she had done when he was bringing her up.

During the time Mordecai was sitting at the king's gate, Bigthana and Teresh, two of the king's officers who guarded the doorway, became angry and conspired to assassinate King Xerxes. But Mordecai found out about the plot and told Queen Esther, who in turn reported it to the king, giving credit to Mordecai. And when the report was investigated and found to be true, the two officials were hanged on a gallows. All this was recorded in the book of the annals in the presence of the king.

Esther's story begins with intrigue as she enters into the running for Queen Vashti's (VASH-ti) replacement. Esther handles her position in the royal palace very differently than Daniel did, however. Whereas Daniel refused to eat food from the king's table because it would be considered unclean by Jewish law, Esther accepts the special food she is given, likely has sexual relations with a man not her husband, and then marries this unbeliever—all actions forbidden in God's law.

We don't know how much of the law they were familiar with, and we don't know exactly why Esther and Mordecai chose not to return to Jerusalem. But rather than condoning Esther's actions, God uses the book of Esther to remind his people that he can protect and use them whatever their situation. His grace shines through, illuminating once more his great love for his people. —BQ

DAILY CONTEMPLATION

How have you seen God's grace in your life despite a past mistake?

DAY 193

Esther 3:1–4:17

HAMAN'S PLOT AND MOREDECAI'S PLAN

After these events, King Xerxes honored Haman son of Hammedatha, the Agagite, elevating him and giving him a seat of honor higher than that of all the other nobles. All the royal officials at the king's gate knelt down and paid honor to Haman, for the king had commanded this concerning him. But Mordecai would not kneel down or pay him honor.

Then the royal officials at the king's gate asked Mordecai, "Why do you disobey the king's command?" Day after day they spoke to him but he refused to comply. Therefore they told Haman about it to see whether Mordecai's behavior would be tolerated, for he had told them he was a Jew.

When Haman saw that Mordecai would not kneel down or pay him honor, he was enraged. Yet having learned who Mordecai's people were, he scorned the idea of killing only Mordecai. Instead Haman looked for a way to destroy all Mordecai's people, the Jews, throughout the whole kingdom of Xerxes.

In the twelfth year of King Xerxes, in the first month, the month of Nisan, they cast the pur (that is, the lot) in the presence of Haman to select a day and month. And the lot fell on the twelfth month, the month of Adar.

Then Haman said to King Xerxes, "There is a certain people dispersed and scattered among the peoples in all the provinces of your kingdom whose customs are different from those of all other people and who do not obey the king's laws; it is not in the king's best interest to tolerate them. If it pleases the king, let a decree be issued to destroy them, and I will put ten thousand talents of silver into the royal treasury for the men who carry out this business."

So the king took his signet ring from his finger and gave it to Haman son of Hammedatha, the Agagite, the enemy of the Jews. "Keep the money," the king said to Haman, "and do with the people as you please."

Then on the thirteenth day of the first month the royal secretaries were summoned. They wrote out in the script of each province and in the language of each people all Haman's orders to the king's satraps, the governors of the various provinces and the nobles of the various peoples. These were written in the name of King Xerxes himself and sealed with his own ring. Dispatches were sent by couriers to all the king's provinces with the order to destroy, kill and annihilate all the Jews—young and old, women and little children—on a single day, the thirteenth day of the twelfth month, the month of Adar, and to plunder their goods. A copy of the text of the edict was to be issued as law in every province and made known to the people of every nationality so they would be ready for that day.

Spurred on by the king's command, the couriers went out, and the edict was issued in the citadel of Susa. The king and Haman sat down to drink, but the city of Susa was bewildered.

When Mordecai learned of all that had been done, he tore his clothes, put on sackcloth and ashes, and went out into the city, wailing loudly and bitterly. But he went only as far as the king's gate, because no one clothed in sackcloth was allowed to enter it. In every province to which the edict and order of the king came, there was great mourning among the Jews, with fasting, weeping and wailing. Many lay in sackcloth and ashes.

When Esther's maids and eunuchs came and told her about Mordecai, she was in great distress. She sent clothes for him to put on instead of his sackcloth, but he would not accept them. Then Esther summoned Hathach, one of the king's eunuchs assigned to attend her, and ordered him to find out what was troubling Mordecai and why.

So Hathach went out to Mordecai in the open square of the city in front of the king's gate. Mordecai told him everything that had happened to him, including the exact amount of money Haman had promised to pay into the royal treasury for the destruction of the Jews. He also gave him a copy of the text of the edict for their annihilation, which had been published in Susa, to show to Esther and explain it to her, and he told him to urge her to go into the king's presence to beg for mercy and plead with him for her people.

Hathach went back and reported to Esther what Mordecai had said. Then she instructed him to say to Mordecai, "All the king's officials and the people of the royal provinces know that for any man or woman who approaches the king in the inner court without being summoned the king has but one law: that he be put to death. The only exception to this is for the king to extend the gold scepter to him and spare his life. But thirty days have passed since I was called to go to the king."

When Esther's words were reported to Mordecai, he sent back this answer: "Do not think that because you are in the king's house you alone of all the Jews will escape. For if you remain silent at this time, relief and deliverance for the Jews will arise from another place, but you and your father's family will perish. And who knows but that you have come to royal position for such a time as this?"

Then Esther sent this reply to Mordecai: "Go, gather together all the Jews who are in Susa, and fast for me. Do not eat or drink for three days, night or day. I and my maids will fast as you do. When this is done, I will go to the king, even though it is against the law. And if I perish, I perish."

So Mordecai went away and carried out all of Esther's instructions.

The Jews in Persia face a grave crisis. Their success has attracted so much jealousy that a powerful man is leading a conspiracy to kill every Jew in the land. Tragically, the underlying "plot" of Esther is an old and familiar one to Jews, for throughout history—Roman campaigns, medieval Jew-hunts, Russian pogroms, Hitler's "final solution"—no other group has faced such a constant threat of extermination.

Although the book of Esther never once mentions the word **God,** the story highlights the many "coincidences" that work together on the Jews' behalf. By the "accident" of her beauty and the "accident" of the former queen's dismissal, Esther has risen from obscurity to become queen of the Persian Empire. She alone, of all the Jews, has access to the king. As her cousin Mordecai puts it, "Who knows but that you have come to royal position for such a time as this?"

Yet in Esther's day a queen does not easily stand up to her husband—especially a husband like Xerxes (ZERK-seez), who has already summarily dismissed one queen for insubordination. By intervening for the sake of her race, Esther might be putting her own life in jeopardy.

Esther's story is a thrilling chapter in the story of God's love for the Jews. While no other group has been so persecuted, no other group has shown the Jews' ability to overcome adversity. How? Esther reveals God's exquisite timing—combined with the courage of individuals who "happen" to be in the right place at the right time. —PY

DAILY CONTEMPLATION

Someone has called coincidences "God's way of working anonymously." Do you tend to give God credit for the coincidences in your life?

DAY 194
Esther 5:1–6:14

ESTHER'S REQUEST TO THE KING

On the third day Esther put on her royal robes and stood in the inner court of the palace, in front of the king's hall. The king was sitting on his royal throne in the hall, facing the entrance. When he saw Queen Esther standing in the court, he was pleased with her and held out to her the gold scepter that was in his hand. So Esther approached and touched the tip of the scepter.

Then the king asked, "What is it, Queen Esther? What is your request? Even up to half the kingdom, it will be given you."

"If it pleases the king," replied Esther, "let the king, together with Haman, come today to a banquet I have prepared for him."

"Bring Haman at once," the king said, "so that we may do what Esther asks."

So the king and Haman went to the banquet Esther had prepared. As they were drinking wine, the king again asked Esther, "Now what is your petition? It will be given you. And what is your request? Even up to half the kingdom, it will be granted."

Esther replied, "My petition and my request is this: If the king regards me with favor and if it pleases the king to grant my petition and fulfill my request, let the king and Haman come tomorrow to the banquet I will prepare for them. Then I will answer the king's question."

Haman went out that day happy and in high spirits. But when he saw Mordecai at the king's gate and observed that he neither rose nor showed fear in his presence, he was filled with rage against Mordecai. Nevertheless, Haman restrained himself and went home.

Calling together his friends and Zeresh, his wife, Haman boasted to them about his vast wealth, his many sons, and all the ways the king had honored him and how he had elevated him above the other nobles and officials. "And that's not all," Haman added. "I'm the only person Queen Esther invited to accompany the king to the banquet she gave. And she has invited me along with the king tomorrow. But all this gives me no satisfaction as long as I see that Jew Mordecai sitting at the king's gate."

His wife Zeresh and all his friends said to him, "Have a gallows built, seventy-five feet high, and ask the king in the morning to have Mordecai hanged on it. Then go with the king to the dinner and be happy." This suggestion delighted Haman, and he had the gallows built.

That night the king could not sleep; so he ordered the book of the chronicles, the record of his reign, to be brought in and read to him. It was found recorded there that Mordecai had exposed Bigthana and Teresh, two of the king's officers who guarded the doorway, who had conspired to assassinate King Xerxes.

"What honor and recognition has Mordecai received for this?" the king asked.

"Nothing has been done for him," his attendants answered.

The king said, "Who is in the court?" Now Haman had just entered the outer court of the palace to speak to the king about hanging Mordecai on the gallows he had erected for him.

His attendants answered, "Haman is standing in the court."

"Bring him in," the king ordered.

When Haman entered, the king asked him, "What should be done for the man the king delights to honor?"

Now Haman thought to himself, "Who is there that the king would rather honor than me?" So he answered the king, "For the man the king delights to honor, have them bring a royal robe the king has worn and a horse the king has ridden, one with a royal crest placed on its head. Then let the robe and horse be entrusted to one of the king's most noble princes. Let them robe the man the king delights to honor, and lead him on the horse through the city streets, proclaiming before him, 'This is what is done for the man the king delights to honor!'"

"Go at once," the king commanded Haman. "Get the robe and the horse and do just as you have suggested for Mordecai the Jew, who sits at the king's gate. Do not neglect anything you have recommended."

So Haman got the robe and the horse. He robed Mordecai, and led him on horseback through the city streets, proclaiming before him, "This is what is done for the man the king delights to honor!"

Afterward Mordecai returned to the king's gate. But Haman rushed home, with his head covered in grief, and told Zeresh his wife and all his friends everything that had happened to him.

His advisers and his wife Zeresh said to him, "Since Mordecai, before whom your downfall has started, is of Jewish origin, you cannot stand against him—you will surely come to ruin!" While they were still talking with him, the king's eunuchs arrived and hurried Haman away to the banquet Esther had prepared.

In one of the epic stories of the Bible, God clearly reverses the flow of history and brings justice and honor to his people. Everything points to the destruction of Jews, even of Mordecai and Esther. The evil are favored and the good are overlooked. But grim as the circumstances appear, God has not lost control. Through what seems crazy happenstance, God elevates Mordecai and humiliates Haman.

The story is too good to be true—the stuff of fairy tales. But God, the author of history, proves himself capable of creating a true tale to beat all. After everything the Jewish people have experienced in recent decades of exile and rebuilding, Esther's story brings a strong reminder that nothing is impossible with God—there's no force too strong, no position too sure, to prevent his will from prevailing. Indeed God, a miracle worker, delights in weaving his miracles into the everyday happenings of life. Esther reminds us that we can never be sure when God will move to turn a situation around through some sort of baffling and curious coincidence.   —BQ

DAILY CONTEMPLATION

When was the last time you suspected God might have something to do with a fortunate coincidence in your life?

DAY 195   Esther 7:1–8:8, 11–17

HAMAN HANGED

So the king and Haman went to dine with Queen Esther, and as they were drinking wine on that second day, the king again asked, "Queen Esther, what is your petition? It will be given you. What is your request? Even up to half the kingdom, it will be granted."

Then Queen Esther answered, "If I have found favor with you, O king, and if it pleases your majesty, grant me my life—this is my petition. And spare my people—this is my request. For I and my people have been sold for destruction and slaughter and annihilation. If we had merely been sold as male and female slaves, I would have kept quiet, because no such distress would justify disturbing the king."

King Xerxes asked Queen Esther, "Who is he? Where is the man who has dared to do such a thing?"

Esther said, "The adversary and enemy is this vile Haman."

Then Haman was terrified before the king and queen. The king got up in a rage, left his wine and went out into the palace garden. But Haman, realizing that the king had already decided his fate, stayed behind to beg Queen Esther for his life.

Just as the king returned from the palace garden to the banquet hall, Haman was falling on the couch where Esther was reclining.

The king exclaimed, "Will he even molest the queen while she is with me in the house?"

As soon as the word left the king's mouth, they covered Haman's face. Then Harbona, one of the eunuchs attending the king, said, "A gallows seventy-five feet high stands by Haman's house. He had it made for Mordecai, who spoke up to help the king."

The king said, "Hang him on it!" So they hanged Haman on the gallows he had prepared for Mordecai. Then the king's fury subsided.

That same day King Xerxes gave Queen Esther the estate of Haman, the enemy of the Jews. And Mordecai came into the presence of the king, for Esther had told how he was related to her. The king took off his signet ring, which he had reclaimed from Haman, and presented it to Mordecai. And Esther appointed him over Haman's estate.

Esther again pleaded with the king, falling at his feet and weeping. She begged him to put an end to the evil plan of Haman the Agagite, which he had devised against the Jews. Then the king extended the gold scepter to Esther and she arose and stood before him.

"If it pleases the king," she said, "and if he regards me with favor and thinks it the right thing to do, and if he is pleased with me, let an order be written overruling the dispatches that Haman son of Hammedatha, the Agagite, devised and wrote to destroy the Jews in all the king's provinces. For how can I bear to see disaster fall on my people? How can I bear to see the destruction of my family?"

King Xerxes replied to Queen Esther and to Mordecai the Jew, "Because Haman attacked the Jews, I have given his estate to Esther, and they have hanged him on the gallows. Now write another decree in the king's name in behalf of the Jews as seems best to you, and seal it with the king's signet ring— for no document written in the king's name and sealed with his ring can be revoked." ...

The king's edict granted the Jews in every city the right to assemble and protect themselves; to destroy, kill and annihilate any armed force of any nationality or province that might attack them and their women and children; and to plunder the property of their enemies. The day appointed for the Jews to do this in all the provinces of King Xerxes was the thirteenth day of the twelfth month, the month of Adar. A copy of the text of the edict was to be issued as law in every province and made known to the people of every nationality so that the Jews would be ready on that day to avenge themselves on their enemies.

The couriers, riding the royal horses, raced out, spurred on by the king's command. And the edict was also issued in the citadel of Susa.

Mordecai left the king's presence wearing royal garments of blue and white, a large crown of gold and a purple robe of fine linen. And the city of Susa held a joyous celebration. For the Jews it was a time of happiness and joy, gladness and honor. In every province and in every city, wherever the edict of the king went, there was joy and gladness among the Jews, with feasting and celebrating. And many people of other nationalities became Jews because fear of the Jews had seized them.

God finishes Esther's story in a royal fashion. The king grants all of her requests, taking Mordecai into the palace and sparing the Jews from mandated destruction. To cap off the story, many Gentiles become Jews, turning to the God who has awed them and evoked their respect. Not only does God save his own people; he turns others to himself and makes a way for them to enter into relationship with him. He cares not only about justice but about mercy toward those who need to know him.

In yet another unforgettable Old Testament account, God expresses his deep love for people who, though imperfect, show courage in carrying out his plan. In their faithfulness they find his unending forgiveness and care. —BQ

DAY 196   Reflection

GOD'S STRATEGIC WAYS

When was the last time you were in the right place at the right time?

People tell stories about getting jobs, meeting spouses, winning prizes, and finding bargains, all because they were in the right place at the right time. Often these seemingly accidental strokes of good fortune are explained with the words "It was meant to be." If the job offer is given, it was meant to be. If the relationship flourishes, it was meant to be. On the converse, if the job falls through or the relationship sours, it wasn't meant to be.

What lies behind these words? Are we speaking in a roundabout way of God's hand in our lives? Or are we attributing our successes and failures to the more general and impersonal hand of fate?

Esther had several such fortunate experiences. She was selected as a contestant to become queen, then won the king's favor and became royalty. She was in the palace at the time a plot to kill the Jews developed. She waited for a second banquet to present her request to the king, unknowingly giving him time to read about Mordecai's act of saving his life. Continually Esther found herself in the right place at the right time to save her people. Her circumstances were more than "meant to be." They were brought about by a sovereign God who had a plan for Esther's life and for the lives of his people.

We serve the same God as did the Jews of Esther's day. God tells us, "I the LORD do not change" (Malachi 3:6). His ways of moving in our lives may look somewhat different from his ways of moving in the Old Testament, but God has not changed, nor have his purposes. Just as he had a plan for his people then, he has a plan for those who belong to him now. We can trust that whenever we find ourselves in the right place at the right time, God's hand is present.

"Every good and perfect gift is from above, coming down from the Father of the heavenly lights, who does not change like shifting shadows" (James 1:17). We can thank God for each stroke of good fortune, each providential gift. Sometimes they are simple blessings. Other times they are his strategic ways of fulfilling the bigger purposes he has for us. —BQ

DAY 197

Malachi 2:17–3:18

ROBBING GOD

You have wearied the LORD with your words.

"How have we wearied him?" you ask.

By saying, "All who do evil are good in the eyes of the LORD, and he is pleased with them" or "Where is the God of justice?"

"See, I will send my messenger, who will prepare the way before me. Then suddenly the Lord you are seeking will come to his temple; the messenger of the covenant, whom you desire, will come," says the LORD Almighty.

But who can endure the day of his coming? Who can stand when he appears? For he will be like a refiner's fire or a launderer's soap. He will sit as a refiner and purifier of silver; he will purify the Levites and refine them like gold and silver. Then the LORD will have men who will bring offerings in righteousness, and the offerings of Judah and Jerusalem will be acceptable to the LORD, as in days gone by, as in former years.

"So I will come near to you for judgment. I will be quick to testify against sorcerers, adulterers and perjurers, against those who defraud laborers of their wages, who oppress the widows and the fatherless, and deprive aliens of justice, but do not fear me," says the LORD Almighty.

"I the LORD do not change. So you, O descendants of Jacob, are not destroyed. Ever since the time of your forefathers you have turned away from my decrees and have not kept them. Return to me, and I will return to you," says the LORD Almighty.

"But you ask, 'How are we to return?'

"Will a man rob God? Yet you rob me.

"But you ask, 'How do we rob you?'

"In tithes and offerings. You are under a curse—the whole nation of you—because you are robbing me. Bring the whole tithe into the storehouse, that there may be food in my house. Test me in this," says the LORD Almighty, "and see if I will not throw open the floodgates of heaven and pour out so much blessing that you will not have room enough for it. I will prevent pests from devouring your crops, and the vines in your fields will not cast their fruit," says the LORD Almighty. "Then all the nations will call you blessed, for yours will be a delightful land," says the LORD Almighty.

"You have said harsh things against me," says the LORD.

"Yet you ask, 'What have we said against you?'

"You have said, 'It is futile to serve God. What did we gain by carrying out his requirements and going about like mourners before the LORD Almighty? But now we call the arrogant blessed. Certainly the evildoers prosper, and even those who challenge God escape.'"

Then those who feared the LORD talked with each other, and the LORD listened and heard. A scroll of remembrance was written in his presence concerning those who feared the LORD and honored his name.

"They will be mine," says the LORD Almighty, "in the day when I make up my treasured possession. I will spare them, just as in compassion a man spares his son who serves him. And you will again see the distinction between the righteous and the wicked, between those who serve God and those who do not."

Malachi (MAL-uh-ki) is the last Old Testament voice, and his book serves as a good prelude to the next four hundred years of biblical silence. From the Israelites' point of view, those four centuries could be termed "the era of lowered expectations." They have returned to the land, but that land remains a backwater province under the domination of several imperial armies. The grand future of triumph and world peace described by the prophets seems a distant pipe dream. Even the restored temple causes stabs of nostalgic pain: it hardly rivals Solomon's majestic building, and no one has seen God's glory descend on this new temple as it did in Solomon's day.

A general malaise sets in among the Jews, a low-grade disappointment with God that shows in their complaints and also in their actions. They are not "big" sinners like the people before the Exile, who practiced child sacrifice and brought idols into the temple. They go through the motions of their religion but have lost contact with the God whom the religion is all about.

Malachi is written in the form of a dialogue, with the "children" of Israel bringing their grievances to God, the Father. They are questioning God's love and his fairness. One gripe bothers them more than any: following God has not brought the anticipated reward.

In reply, Malachi calls his people to rise above their selfishness and to trust the God of the covenant; he has not abandoned his treasured possession. "Test me in this," says God, "and see if I will not throw open the floodgates of heaven and pour out so much blessing that you will not have room enough for it" (3:10).

At least some of Malachi's message will take hold. During the next four hundred years, reform movements like the Pharisees become increasingly devoted to keeping the law. Unfortunately, many of them will cling fiercely to that law even when Jesus, the "messenger of the covenant" prophesied by Malachi, brings a new message of forgiveness and grace. —PY

DAILY CONTEMPLATION

When was the last time you questioned God's love and fairness? Did God prove himself to you?

PART 6

CRIES OF PAIN

Job 1:1–3, 6–2:10

JOB IS TESTED

In the land of Uz there lived a man whose name was Job. This man was blameless and upright; he feared God and shunned evil. He had seven sons and three daughters, and he owned seven thousand sheep, three thousand camels, five hundred yoke of oxen and five hundred donkeys, and had a large number of servants. He was the greatest man among all the people of the East....

One day the angels came to present themselves before the LORD, and Satan also came with them. The LORD said to Satan, "Where have you come from?"

Satan answered the LORD, "From roaming through the earth and going back and forth in it."

Then the LORD said to Satan, "Have you considered my servant Job? There is no one on earth like him; he is blameless and upright, a man who fears God and shuns evil."

"Does Job fear God for nothing?" Satan replied. "Have you not put a hedge around him and his household and everything he has? You have blessed the work of his hands, so that his flocks and herds are spread throughout the land. But stretch out your hand and strike everything he has, and he will surely curse you to your face."

The LORD said to Satan, "Very well, then, everything he has is in your hands, but on the man himself do not lay a finger."

Then Satan went out from the presence of the LORD.

One day when Job's sons and daughters were feasting and drinking wine at the oldest brother's house, a messenger came to Job and said, "The oxen were plowing and the donkeys were grazing nearby, and the Sabeans attacked and carried them off. They put the servants to the sword, and I am the only one who has escaped to tell you!"

While he was still speaking, another messenger came and said, "The fire of God fell from the sky and burned up the sheep and the servants, and I am the only one who has escaped to tell you!"

While he was still speaking, another messenger came and said, "The Chaldeans formed three raiding parties and swept down on your camels and carried them off. They put the servants to the sword, and I am the only one who has escaped to tell you!"

While he was still speaking, yet another messenger came and said, "Your sons and daughters were feasting and drinking wine at the oldest brother's house, when suddenly a mighty wind swept in from the desert and struck the four corners of the house. It collapsed on them and they are dead, and I am the only one who has escaped to tell you!"

At this, Job got up and tore his robe and shaved his head. Then he fell to the ground in worship and said:

"Naked I came from my mother's womb,
    and naked I will depart.
The LORD gave and the LORD has taken away;
    may the name of the LORD be praised."

In all this, Job did not sin by charging God with wrongdoing.

On another day the angels came to present themselves before the LORD, and Satan also came with them to present himself before him. And the LORD said to Satan, "Where have you come from?"

Satan answered the LORD, "From roaming through the earth and going back and forth in it."

Then the LORD said to Satan, "Have you considered my servant Job? There is no one on earth like him; he is blameless and upright, a man who fears God and shuns evil. And he still maintains his integrity, though you incited me against him to ruin him without any reason."

"Skin for skin!" Satan replied. "A man will give all he has for his own life. But stretch out your hand and strike his flesh and bones, and he will surely curse you to your face."

The LORD said to Satan, "Very well, then, he is in your hands; but you must spare his life."

So Satan went out from the presence of the LORD and afflicted Job with painful sores from the soles of his feet to the top of his head. Then Job took a piece of broken pottery and scraped himself with it as he sat among the ashes.

His wife said to him, "Are you still holding on to your integrity? Curse God and die!"

He replied, "You are talking like a foolish woman. Shall we accept good from God, and not trouble?"

In all this, Job did not sin in what he said.

One book of the Bible is virtually ageless. It relates the story of Job (JOHB), a rich "patriarch" who could have lived in Abraham's time but whose story was probably reduced to this poetic form hundreds of years later, during Israel's literary Golden Age. Regardless, the book raises questions so urgent and universal that it speaks to every era.

In the period between the Old and New Testaments, the book of Job becomes a favorite of the Jews (as proved by the ancient commentaries archaeologists have unearthed). His story centers around a question that has haunted the Jews from the earliest days, when they were first chosen as God's covenant people. Somehow they expected better treatment. Job has the courage to voice the question aloud—**Is God unfair?**—and no one has asked that question more eloquently or profoundly.

The book seems meant to explore the outer limits of unfairness. Job, the most upright, outstanding man in all the earth, must endure the worst calamities. He suffers unbearable punishment—but for what? What has he done wrong?

The book reads like a detective story in which the readers know far more than the central characters. The very first chapter answers Job's main concern: he has done nothing to deserve such suffering. We, the readers, know that, but nobody tells Job and his friends. As the prologue reveals, Job is involved in a cosmic test, a contest proposed in heaven but staged on earth.

People in Malachi's day had asked, "What do we gain by following God?" and that question gets at the heart of Job's test. Satan claims that people love God only because of his good gifts. According to Satan, no one would ever follow God apart from some selfish gain. **Of course** Job is blameless and upright; he is also rich and healthy. Remove those good things from Job's life, Satan challenges, and Job's faith will melt away along with his riches and health.

God's reputation is on the line in this book, resting suspensefully on the response of a devastated, miserable man. Will Job continue to trust God, even as his world crashes down around him? Will he believe in a God of justice, even when life seems grotesquely unfair?   —PY

> ## DAILY CONTEMPLATION
>
> *When have you questioned why bad things happen to good people?*

DAY 199   Job 38:1–7, 19–41

THE LORD SPEAKS

Then the LORD answered Job out of the storm. He said:

"Who is this that darkens my counsel
  with words without knowledge?

Brace yourself like a man;
    I will question you,
    and you shall answer me.

"Where were you when I laid the earth's foundation?
    Tell me, if you understand.
Who marked off its dimensions? Surely you know!
    Who stretched a measuring line across it?
On what were its footings set,
    or who laid its cornerstone—
while the morning stars sang together
    and all the angels shouted for joy? . . .

"What is the way to the abode of light?
    And where does darkness reside?
Can you take them to their places?
    Do you know the paths to their dwellings?
Surely you know, for you were already born!
    You have lived so many years!

"Have you entered the storehouses of the snow
    or seen the storehouses of the hail,
which I reserve for times of trouble,
    for days of war and battle?
What is the way to the place where the lightning is dispersed,
    or the place where the east winds are scattered over the earth?
Who cuts a channel for the torrents of rain,
    and a path for the thunderstorm,
to water a land where no man lives,
    a desert with no one in it,
to satisfy a desolate wasteland
    and make it sprout with grass?
Does the rain have a father?
    Who fathers the drops of dew?
From whose womb comes the ice?
    Who gives birth to the frost from the heavens
when the waters become hard as stone,
    when the surface of the deep is frozen?

"Can you bind the beautiful Pleiades?
    Can you loose the cords of Orion?
Can you bring forth the constellations in their seasons
    or lead out the Bear with its cubs?
Do you know the laws of the heavens?
    Can you set up God's dominion over the earth?

"Can you raise your voice to the clouds
    and cover yourself with a flood of water?

Do you send the lightning bolts on their way?
  Do they report to you, 'Here we are'?
Who endowed the heart with wisdom
  or gave understanding to the mind?
Who has the wisdom to count the clouds?
  Who can tip over the water jars of the heavens
when the dust becomes hard
  and the clods of earth stick together?

"Do you hunt the prey for the lioness
  and satisfy the hunger of the lions
when they crouch in their dens
  or lie in wait in a thicket?
Who provides food for the raven
  when its young cry out to God
  and wander about for lack of food?"

It seems a travesty to skip thirty-five chapters and rush to the conclusion, for those middle chapters of Job express the human dilemma as well as it has ever been expressed. Like all grieving persons, Job drifts on emotional currents, alternately whining, exploding, cajoling, and collapsing into self-pity. Sometimes he agrees with his friends, who blame Job himself for his suffering, and sometimes he violently disagrees. Occasionally, in the midst of deepest despair, he comes up with a statement of brilliant hope.

Nearly every argument on the problem of pain appears somewhere in the book of Job, but the arguing never seems to help Job much. His is a crisis of relationship more than a crisis of intellectual doubt. **Can he trust God?** Job wants one thing above all else: an appearance by the one Person who can explain his miserable fate. He wants to meet God himself, face to face.

Eventually, as this chapter relates, Job gets his wish. God shows up in person. He times his entrance with perfect irony, just as Job's friend Elihu (el-LI-hoo) is expounding on why Job has no right to expect a visit from God.

No one—not Job, nor any of his friends—is prepared for what God has to say. Job has saved up a long list of questions, but it is God, not Job, who asks the questions. "Brace yourself like a man," he begins; "I will question you, and you shall answer me." Brushing aside thirty-five chapters' worth of debates on the problem of pain, God plunges instead into a majestic poem on the wonders of the natural world. He guides Job through the gallery of creation, pointing out with pride such favorites as mountain goats, wild donkeys, ostriches, and eagles (ch. 39).

Above all, God's speech defines the vast difference between a God of all creation and one puny man like Job. "Do you have an arm like God's?" he asks at one point (40:9). God reels off natural phenomena—the solar system, constellations, thunderstorms, wild animals—that Job cannot begin to explain. God's point is obvious: *If you can't comprehend the visible world you live in, how dare you expect to comprehend a world you cannot even see!*   —PY

DAILY CONTEMPLATION

Does God's reply to Job surprise you? In Job's place, what kind of answer would you have wanted from God?

DAY 200   Job 42:1–17

JOB IS RESTORED

Then Job replied to the Lord:

"I know that you can do all things;
  no plan of yours can be thwarted.
You asked, 'Who is this that obscures my counsel without knowledge?'
  Surely I spoke of things I did not understand,
  things too wonderful for me to know.

"You said, 'Listen now, and I will speak;
  I will question you,
  and you shall answer me.'
My ears had heard of you
  but now my eyes have seen you.
Therefore I despise myself
  and repent in dust and ashes."

After the LORD had said these things to Job, he said to Eliphaz the Temanite, "I am angry with you and your two friends, because you have not spoken of me what is right, as my servant Job has. So now take seven bulls and seven rams and go to my servant Job and sacrifice a burnt offering for yourselves. My servant Job will pray for you, and I will accept his prayer and not deal with you according to your folly. You have not spoken of me what is right, as my servant Job has." So Eliphaz the Temanite, Bildad the Shuhite and Zophar the Naamathite did what the LORD told them; and the LORD accepted Job's prayer.

After Job had prayed for his friends, the LORD made him prosperous again and gave him twice as much as he had before. All his brothers and sisters and everyone who had known him before came and ate with him in his house. They comforted and consoled him over all the trouble the LORD had brought upon him, and each one gave him a piece of silver and a gold ring.

The LORD blessed the latter part of Job's life more than the first. He had fourteen thousand sheep, six thousand camels, a thousand yoke of oxen and a thousand donkeys. And he also had seven sons and three daughters. The first daughter he named Jemimah, the second Keziah and the third Keren-Happuch. Nowhere in all the land were there found women as beautiful as

Job's daughters, and their father granted them an inheritance along with their brothers.

After this, Job lived a hundred and forty years; he saw his children and their children to the fourth generation. And so he died, old and full of years.

What God says is not nearly so important as the mere fact that he shows up. His presence spectacularly answers Job's biggest question: Is anybody out there? "Surely I spoke of things I did not understand," Job confesses, "things too wonderful for me to know." Catching sight of the big picture at last, Job repents in dust and ashes.

God has some words of correction for Job. No one, not Job and especially not his friends, has the evidence needed to make judgments about how he runs the world. But mainly God praises Job, calling him "my servant." (Ezekiel 14:14 mentions Job in God's list of the finest human examples of righteousness.)

Satan wagered with God that Job would "surely curse you to your face" (1:11). He lost. Despite all that happens, Job does not curse God. He clings to his belief in a just God even though everything in his experience seems to contradict it. Significantly, Job speaks his contrite words *before* any of his losses have been restored, while still sitting in a pile of ashes, naked, covered with sores. He has learned to believe even in the dark, with no hope of reward.

The book of Job ends with some surprising twists. Job's friends, who spouted all the right pieties and clichés, have to plead for forgiveness. Job, who raged and cried out, receives twice as much as he ever had before: fourteen thousand sheep, six thousand camels, one thousand donkeys, and ten new children.

The book of Job will give much comfort to Jews during the harsh period between the Old and New Testaments. It demonstrates the important lesson that not all suffering comes as punishment; a person's trials may in fact be used to win a great spiritual victory. And the happy ending of Job also echoes the promises of the prophets, awakening hopes for a future time of peace and restoration.

Christians, looking back, see yet another message in Job, who stands as an early prototype of the Messiah. Job, the best man of his day, suffered terribly; Jesus, a perfect man, would suffer even more.   —PY

DAILY CONTEMPLATION

Have you experienced any Job-like trials in your life? What were the results?

DAY 201   Reflection

LOVING GOD FREELY

On the surface, the book of Job centers on the problem of suffering. Underneath, a different issue is at stake: the doctrine of human freedom. Job had to endure undeserved suffering in order to demonstrate that God is ultimately interested in freely given love.

The contest posed between Satan and God was no trivial exercise. Satan's accusation that Job loved God only because "you have put a hedge around him," stands as an attack on God's character. It implies that God is not worthy of love in himself; faithful people like Job follow him only because they are "bribed" to do so. Job's response when all the props of faith were removed would prove or disprove Satan's challenge.

To understand this issue of human freedom, it may help to imagine a world in which everyone truly does get what he or she deserves. That imaginary world has a certain appeal. It would be just and consistent, and everyone would clearly know what God expected. Fairness would reign. There is, however, one huge problem with such a tidy world: it's not at all what God wants to accomplish on earth. He wants from us love, freely given love, and we dare not underestimate the premium God places on that love. Freely given love is so important to God that he allows our planet to be a cancer of evil in his universe—for a time.

If this world ran according to fixed, perfectly fair rules, there would be no true freedom. We would act rightly because of our own immediate gain, and selfish motives would taint every act of goodness. In contrast, the Christian virtues described in the Bible develop when we choose God and his ways in spite of temptation or impulses to do otherwise.

Throughout the Bible, an analogy that illustrates the relationship between God and his people keeps surfacing. God, the husband, is pictured as wooing the bride to himself. He wants her love. If the world were constructed so that every sin earned a punishment and every good deed a reward, the parallel would not hold. The closest analogue to that relationship would be a kept woman, who is pampered and bribed and locked away in a room so that the lover can be sure of her faithfulness. God does not "keep" his people. He loves us, gives himself to us, and eagerly awaits our free response.

God wants us to choose to love him freely, even when that choice involves pain, because we are committed to *him,* not to our own good feelings and rewards. He wants us to cleave to him, as Job did, even when we have every reason to deny him hotly. Job clung to God's justice when he was the best example in history of God's apparent injustice. He did not seek the Giver because of his gifts; when all gifts were removed, he still sought the Giver.[24] —PY

DAILY CONTEMPLATION

In times of suffering, do you cling to your love for God or accuse him of tormenting you? Talk with God about your attitude toward suffering. Let him know you want your love for him to be bigger than anger or dismay over your circumstances. Ask him to help you hold to your love even in the most difficult times.

COMFORT FOR GOD'S PEOPLE

A voice says, "Cry out."
  And I said, "What shall I cry?"
"All men are like grass,
  and all their glory is like the flowers of the field.
The grass withers and the flowers fall,
  because the breath of the LORD blows on them.
  Surely the people are grass.
The grass withers and the flowers fall,
  but the word of our God stands forever."

You who bring good tidings to Zion,
  go up on a high mountain.
You who bring good tidings to Jerusalem,
  lift up your voice with a shout,
lift it up, do not be afraid;
  say to the towns of Judah,
  "Here is your God!"
See, the Sovereign LORD comes with power,
  and his arm rules for him.
See, his reward is with him,
  and his recompense accompanies him.
He tends his flock like a shepherd:
  He gathers the lambs in his arms
and carries them close to his heart;
  he gently leads those that have young. . . .

Surely the nations are like a drop in a bucket;
  they are regarded as dust on the scales;
  he weighs the islands as though they were fine dust. . . .

To whom, then, will you compare God?
  What image will you compare him to?
As for an idol, a craftsman casts it,
  and a goldsmith overlays it with gold
  and fashions silver chains for it.
A man too poor to present such an offering
  selects wood that will not rot.
He looks for a skilled craftsman
  to set up an idol that will not topple.

Do you not know?
  Have you not heard?

Has it not been told you from the beginning?
    Have you not understood since the earth was founded?
He sits enthroned above the circle of the earth,
    and its people are like grasshoppers.
He stretches out the heavens like a canopy,
    and spreads them out like a tent to live in.
He brings princes to naught
    and reduces the rulers of this world to nothing.
No sooner are they planted,
    no sooner are they sown,
    no sooner do they take root in the ground,
than he blows on them and they wither,
    and a whirlwind sweeps them away like chaff. . . .

Why do you say, O Jacob,
    and complain, O Israel,
"My way is hidden from the LORD;
    my cause is disregarded by my God"?
Do you not know?
    Have you not heard?
The LORD is the everlasting God,
    the Creator of the ends of the earth.
He will not grow tired or weary,
    and his understanding no one can fathom.
He gives strength to the weary
    and increases the power of the weak.
Even youths grow tired and weary,
    and young men stumble and fall;
but those who hope in the LORD
    will renew their strength.
They will soar on wings like eagles;
    they will run and not grow weary,
    they will walk and not be faint.

The book of Job concerns the sufferings of one man. The prophets of Israel and Judah speak to the sufferings of an entire race. Most of the Jews at the end of the Old Testament are scattered across the Middle East, dispersed by Assyrian and Babylonian armies. The minority who have returned to Jerusalem live under the total domination of a foreign government in Persia. The same questions Job asked while scratching himself with shards of pottery, the Jews ask now about their race. Has God abandoned them? Will they have a future?

The Jews' hope for the future centers in a Messiah, who has been promised by almost all the prophets. After Malachi, as the years drag on, the Jews scour the scrolls of these prophets, seeking clues into their destiny. Of all the prophets, Isaiah gives perhaps the clearest picture of what the Jews can expect. His earlier messages blast his nation's sin and unfaithfulness. But beginning with chapter 40, Isaiah shifts into a new key. Gone are the bleak predictions of judgment. Instead, a message of hope and joy and light breaks in. "Speak tenderly to Jerusalem, and proclaim to her that her hard service has been completed..." (40:2).

According to Isaiah, what happened to Judah was not God's defeat. God has in mind a new thing, a plan far more wonderful than anything seen before. The book of Isaiah explains why the future holds hope—not just for the Jews but for the whole world. A mysterious figure called "the servant" will, through his suffering, provide a means of rescue. Later, in a faraway time, God will usher in peace for all in a new heaven and new earth.

Chapter 40 introduces this last section of Isaiah with the sweeping declaration that God reigns over all. In many ways, these soaring words restate in a global sense God's personal message to Job. "Surely the nations are like a drop in a bucket.... He sits enthroned above the circle of the earth, and its people are like grasshoppers." God shows himself master of nature, of history—indeed, of the entire universe.   —PY

DAILY CONTEMPLATION

What do Isaiah's words "Those who hope in the LORD will renew their strength" mean to you today?

DAY 203 Isaiah 52:1–15

THE CUP OF THE LORD'S WRATH

Awake, awake, O Zion,
    clothe yourself with strength.
Put on your garments of splendor,
    O Jerusalem, the holy city.
The uncircumcised and defiled
    will not enter you again.
Shake off your dust;
    rise up, sit enthroned, O Jerusalem.
Free yourself from the chains on your neck,
    O captive Daughter of Zion.
    For this is what the LORD says:
"You were sold for nothing,
    and without money you will be redeemed."
    For this is what the Sovereign LORD says:
"At first my people went down to Egypt to live;
    lately, Assyria has oppressed them.
    "And now what do I have here?" declares the LORD.
"For my people have been taken away for nothing,

and those who rule them mock,"
   declares the LORD.
"And all day long
   my name is constantly blasphemed.
Therefore my people will know my name;
   therefore in that day they will know
that it is I who foretold it.
   Yes, it is I."

How beautiful on the mountains
   are the feet of those who bring good news,
who proclaim peace,
   who bring good tidings,
   who proclaim salvation,
who say to Zion,
   "Your God reigns!"
Listen! Your watchmen lift up their voices;
   together they shout for joy.
When the LORD returns to Zion,
   they will see it with their own eyes.
Burst into songs of joy together,
   you ruins of Jerusalem,
for the LORD has comforted his people,
   he has redeemed Jerusalem.
The LORD will lay bare his holy arm
   in the sight of all the nations,
and all the ends of the earth will see
   the salvation of our God.

Depart, depart, go out from there!
   Touch no unclean thing!
Come out from it and be pure,
   you who carry the vessels of the LORD.
But you will not leave in haste
   or go in flight;
for the LORD will go before you,
   the God of Israel will be your rear guard.

See, my servant will act wisely;
   he will be raised and lifted up and highly exalted.
Just as there were many who were appalled at him—
   his appearance was so disfigured beyond that of any man
   and his form marred beyond human likeness—
so will he sprinkle many nations,
   and kings will shut their mouths because of him.
For what they were not told, they will see,
   and what they have not heard, they will understand.

Isaiah's four songs about a "suffering servant" are among the richest, and most closely studied, passages in the Old Testament. The first part of the chapter stirs anticipation for a glorious time when God will restore Jerusalem and prove to all, "Your God reigns!" It looks as if Israel will gain revenge on their enemies at last.

But the author explains how God will "redeem Jerusalem" by introducing the mysterious figure of the suffering servant, whose appearance was "disfigured beyond that of any man." Who is this suffering servant? And how will such a wounded person bring about a great victory?

Jewish scholars puzzled over these passages for centuries. What exactly did the prophet mean? Some of the servant songs refer to the nation of Israel as a whole, but passages like this one portray the servant as a specific individual, a great leader who suffers terribly. Although Isaiah holds him up as the deliverer of all humankind, he resembles more a tragic figure than a hero.

Some Jewish scholars speculated the prophet was describing himself or perhaps a colleague, such as Jeremiah. Still others focused their hopes on a Messiah to come. In general, however, the idea of the suffering servant never really caught on among the Jewish nation. They longed for a victorious Messiah, not a suffering one.

The image of the suffering servant went underground, as it were, lying dormant for centuries. Then, in a dramatic scene early in his ministry, Jesus quoted from one of Isaiah's servant passages. After reading aloud in the synagogue, Jesus "rolled up the scroll, gave it back to the attendant and sat down. The eyes of everyone in the synagogue were fastened on him, and he began by saying to them, 'Today this scripture is fulfilled in your hearing'" (Luke 4:20–21).

At last, a link snapped into place for some, but not all, of Jesus' listeners. The Messiah had come at last—not as a conquering general but as a carpenter's son from Nazareth. —PY

DAILY CONTEMPLATION

What kind of Savior were you looking for when you found Jesus?

DAY 204   Isaiah 53:1–12

THE SUFFERING AND GLORY OF THE SERVANT

Who has believed our message
  and to whom has the arm of the LORD been revealed?
He grew up before him like a tender shoot,
  and like a root out of dry ground.
He had no beauty or majesty to attract us to him,
  nothing in his appearance that we should desire him.

He was despised and rejected by men,
    a man of sorrows, and familiar with suffering.
Like one from whom men hide their faces
    he was despised, and we esteemed him not.

Surely he took up our infirmities
    and carried our sorrows,
yet we considered him stricken by God,
    smitten by him, and afflicted.
But he was pierced for our transgressions,
    he was crushed for our iniquities;
the punishment that brought us peace was upon him,
    and by his wounds we are healed.
We all, like sheep, have gone astray,
    each of us has turned to his own way;
and the LORD has laid on him
    the iniquity of us all.

He was oppressed and afflicted,
    yet he did not open his mouth;
he was led like a lamb to the slaughter,
    and as a sheep before her shearers is silent,
    so he did not open his mouth.
By oppression and judgment he was taken away.
    And who can speak of his descendants?
For he was cut off from the land of the living;
    for the transgression of my people he was stricken.
He was assigned a grave with the wicked,
    and with the rich in his death,
though he had done no violence,
    nor was any deceit in his mouth.

Yet it was the LORD's will to crush him and cause him to suffer,
    and though the LORD makes his life a guilt offering,
he will see his offspring and prolong his days,
    and the will of the LORD will prosper in his hand.
After the suffering of his soul,
    he will see the light of life and be satisfied;
by his knowledge my righteous servant will justify many,
    and he will bear their iniquities.
Therefore I will give him a portion among the great,
    and he will divide the spoils with the strong,
because he poured out his life unto death,
    and was numbered with the transgressors.
For he bore the sin of many,
    and made intercession for the transgressors.

New Testament writers leave no doubt as to the identity of the suffering servant: at least ten times they apply Isaiah's four songs directly to Jesus (for example, Matthew 8:17, Luke 22:37, 1 Peter 2:22–24). In one instance, Philip corrects an Ethiopian official who wonders if the suffering servant refers to an ancient prophet (Acts 8:26–35).

Isaiah 53 reads almost like an eyewitness account of Jesus' last days on earth. The physical description—the Bible contains no other physical description of Jesus—is shocking. The servant "had no beauty or majesty to attract us to him"; he was "like one from whom men hide their faces." As this chapter foretells, Jesus did not "open his mouth" to answer his accusers at his trial. He left no descendants. He was cut off in the prime of life and, thanks to a gracious friend, was buried in a rich man's tomb. But that was not the end. After three days he saw "the light of life."

According to Isaiah, the servant died for a very specific purpose: "He was pierced for our transgressions." He took on pain for the sake of others, for *our* sakes. His wounds, an apparent defeat, made possible a great victory. His death sealed a future triumph when all that is wrong on earth will be set right. Significantly, the book of Isaiah does not end with the suffering servant image but goes on to describe that wonderful life in a new heaven and new earth. But the time of travail was a necessary first step, for the servant absorbed in himself the punishment that was due for all the evils of the world.

Isaiah 53 forms an underlying foundation for much New Testament theology. In addition, these detailed prophecies, recorded many centuries before Jesus' birth, offer convincing proof that God is revealing his plan for the ages through the ancient prophets. He has not permanently severed his covenant with the Jews. Rather, out of Jewish roots—King David's own stock—he will bring forth a new king, a king like no other, to reclaim all the earth.   —PY

DAILY CONTEMPLATION

Who in your life needs to hear about the Messiah, Jesus, prophesied here in Isaiah?

DAY 205   Isaiah 55:1–13

INVITATION TO THE THIRSTY

> "Come, all you who are thirsty,
>   come to the waters;
> and you who have no money,
>   come, buy and eat!
> Come, buy wine and milk

without money and without cost.
Why spend money on what is not bread,
    and your labor on what does not satisfy?
Listen, listen to me, and eat what is good,
    and your soul will delight in the richest of fare.
Give ear and come to me;
    hear me, that your soul may live.
I will make an everlasting covenant with you,
    my faithful love promised to David.
See, I have made him a witness to the peoples,
    a leader and commander of the peoples.
Surely you will summon nations you know not,
    and nations that do not know you will hasten to you,
because of the LORD your God,
    the Holy One of Israel,
    for he has endowed you with splendor."

Seek the LORD while he may be found;
    call on him while he is near.
Let the wicked forsake his way
    and the evil man his thoughts.
Let him turn to the LORD, and he will have mercy on him,
    and to our God, for he will freely pardon.

"For my thoughts are not your thoughts,
    neither are your ways my ways,"
    declares the LORD.
"As the heavens are higher than the earth,
    so are my ways higher than your ways
    and my thoughts than your thoughts.
As the rain and the snow
    come down from heaven,
and do not return to it
    without watering the earth
and making it bud and flourish,
    so that it yields seed for the sower and bread for the eater,
so is my word that goes out from my mouth:
    It will not return to me empty,
but will accomplish what I desire
    and achieve the purpose for which I sent it.
You will go out in joy
    and be led forth in peace;
the mountains and hills
    will burst into song before you,
and all the trees of the field
    will clap their hands.

> Instead of the thornbush will grow the pine tree,
> and instead of briers the myrtle will grow.
> This will be for the LORD's renown,
> for an everlasting sign,
> which will not be destroyed."

Isaiah has seen a glimpse of the future, and that glimpse convinces him that good news lies ahead. No invading armies, no terrible calamities can interfere with God's final purpose for the earth.

"For a brief moment I abandoned you, but with deep compassion I will bring you back," God says to Israel (54:7). Isaiah foretells a time when the ruined holy city, rebuilt, will achieve an unprecedented level of greatness. Yet the promise in these chapters goes far beyond what has ever been realized in Jerusalem. It merges into a vision of a future state where sin and sorrow no longer exist and we live in final peace with God.

The last part of Isaiah, addressed to a people facing deep despair, opens the door for the Jews to become a gift to all people. According to Isaiah, word about God will go out to nations nearby and faraway and to distant islands that have never heard of him (66:18–21). This prophecy sees fulfillment in Jesus, who recruits disciples to carry his message worldwide. Through his life and death, the suffering servant indeed introduces the gospel to the entire world.

In this and other soaring chapters, Isaiah describes the future with such eloquence that New Testament books like Revelation cannot improve on the language; they merely quote Isaiah. Whatever longings we feel on earth—for peace, for an end to suffering, for an unspoiled planet—will someday be fulfilled. Isaiah assures us that one day our very best dreams, all of them, will come true.

We may not understand the process the world must go through to arrive at that future time: "'For my thoughts are not your thoughts, neither are your ways my ways,' declares the LORD." But, as this chapter makes clear, God's covenant with his people is everlasting. Nothing can cancel it.

As the decades, even centuries, pass, empires—Babylon, Persia, Egypt, Greece, Syria, Rome—rise and fall, their armies chasing each other across the plains of Palestine. Each new empire subjugates the Jews with ease. Sometimes the entire race verges on extinction. Four centuries separate the last words of the prophets in the Old Testament and the first words of Matthew in the New Testament—"the four hundred silent years," they are called. Does God care? Is he even alive? In desperation the common people wait for a Messiah; they have no other hope. —PY

DAILY CONTEMPLATION

What would you most like to see changed in the world? Does Isaiah speak to that change?

JESUS, OUR HIGHEST CHOICE, OUR GREATEST PROMISE

What are your deep-down hopes, your most cherished dreams? Isaiah has given us, as well as the beleaguered people of Israel, a vision of hope for the future. Sickness and sorrow, oppression and injustice are not the final reality for those who walk with God. Isaiah proclaims strength for the weary, joy and peace for believers, and God's power one day revealed to everyone in every nation. Ours is a future replete with goodness and promise.

Isaiah paints a revelation from God meant not only to clue us in to this future but also to impact our lives in the present. For this reason, Isaiah pleads with believers to make choices in keeping with our future. Despite the presence of God in our world today, we know only a shadow of the redeemed world that awaits us. We live with the mistaken values of a human race fallen to sin. Many of the goals and aspirations of the people of our world are merely counterfeits of the lasting reality God has set in place. Our pursuits are often centered on, in Isaiah's words, spending money on what is not bread, and labor on what does not satisfy.

Author and futures consultant Tom Sine writes, "We have bought into an image of the better future that equates happiness with acquisition. We have really come to believe that the more we accumulate in our garages, ring up on our charge cards, and invest in the newest novelties, the happier we will be."[25] Especially for believers in the Western world, this pattern of acquisition has become the norm. There is a real danger that the pursuit of possessions can distract our souls. We await a future that holds extravagance with which the material things of this world pale in comparison. Yet as we are drawn into the world's pursuits, we lose all sight of what brings authentic joy.

We find—and we see in those around us—that the world's quest is never satisfying. In fact, often in direct proportion, those who are most successful at the quest are the most dissatisfied. Sine notes the words of British missionary and author Lesslie Newbigin: "Technology continues to forge ahead with more and more brilliant achievements; but the novels, the drama and the general literature of the West are full of nihilism and despair."[26]

"Listen, listen to me," Isaiah pleads. "Eat what is good, and your soul will delight in the richest of fare" (Isaiah 55:2). Only Jesus can offer food that will fill us and satisfy us. Believers have learned this secret, and God has given us power to make the secret known to all who need the Bread of Life.

"Our vocation is not the preservation and advancement of the present order, but cooperation with God in the inbreaking of a radical new one," Sine writes. "Never has it been more urgent for people of faith and people of concern to question the visions and values to which we have given our lives and to begin to dream new dreams while there is yet time."[27]
—BQ

DAILY CONTEMPLATION

What are your dreams? How do you spend your money and your labor? Talk with God about your pursuits and ask him to help you dream his dreams. Ask him to make Isaiah's vision for the present and the future more of an abiding vision in your life.

PART 7

A SURPRISING MESSIAH

DAY 207 Luke 1:5–52

THE BIRTHS OF JOHN THE BAPTIST
AND JESUS FORETOLD

In the time of Herod king of Judea there was a priest named Zechariah, who belonged to the priestly division of Abijah; his wife Elizabeth was also a descendant of Aaron. Both of them were upright in the sight of God, observing all the Lord's commandments and regulations blamelessly. But they had no children, because Elizabeth was barren; and they were both well along in years.

Once when Zechariah's division was on duty and he was serving as priest before God, he was chosen by lot, according to the custom of the priesthood, to go into the temple of the Lord and burn incense. And when the time for the burning of incense came, all the assembled worshipers were praying outside.

Then an angel of the Lord appeared to him, standing at the right side of the altar of incense. When Zechariah saw him, he was startled and was gripped with fear. But the angel said to him: "Do not be afraid, Zechariah; your prayer has been heard. Your wife Elizabeth will bear you a son, and you are to give him the name John. He will be a joy and delight to you, and many will rejoice because of his birth, for he will be great in the sight of the Lord. He is never to take wine or other fermented drink, and he will be filled with the Holy Spirit even from birth. Many of the people of Israel will he bring back to the Lord their God. And he will go on before the Lord, in the spirit and power of Elijah, to turn the hearts of the fathers to their children and the disobedient to the wisdom of the righteous—to make ready a people prepared for the Lord."

Zechariah asked the angel, "How can I be sure of this? I am an old man and my wife is well along in years."

The angel answered, "I am Gabriel. I stand in the presence of God, and I have been sent to speak to you and to tell you this good news. And now you will be silent and not able to speak until the day this happens, because you did not believe my words, which will come true at their proper time."

Meanwhile, the people were waiting for Zechariah and wondering why he stayed so long in the temple. When he came out, he could not speak to them. They realized he had seen a vision in the temple, for he kept making signs to them but remained unable to speak.

When his time of service was completed, he returned home. After this his wife Elizabeth became pregnant and for five months remained in seclusion. "The Lord has done this for me," she said. "In these days he has shown his favor and taken away my disgrace among the people."

In the sixth month, God sent the angel Gabriel to Nazareth, a town in Galilee, to a virgin pledged to be married to a man named Joseph, a descendant of David. The virgin's name was Mary. The angel went to her and said, "Greetings, you who are highly favored! The Lord is with you."

Mary was greatly troubled at his words and wondered what kind of greeting this might be. But the angel said to her, "Do not be afraid, Mary, you have found favor with God. You will be with child and give birth to a son, and you are to give him the name Jesus. He will be great and will be called the Son of the Most High. The Lord God will give him the throne of his father David, and he will reign over the house of Jacob forever; his kingdom will never end."

"How will this be," Mary asked the angel, "since I am a virgin?"

The angel answered, "The Holy Spirit will come upon you, and the power of the Most High will overshadow you. So the holy one to be born will be called the Son of God. Even Elizabeth your relative is going to have a child in her old age, and she who was said to be barren is in her sixth month. For nothing is impossible with God."

"I am the Lord's servant," Mary answered. "May it be to me as you have said." Then the angel left her.

At that time Mary got ready and hurried to a town in the hill country of Judea, where she entered Zechariah's home and greeted Elizabeth. When Elizabeth heard Mary's greeting, the baby leaped in her womb, and Elizabeth was filled with the Holy Spirit. In a loud voice she exclaimed: "Blessed are you among women, and blessed is the child you will bear! But why am I so favored, that the mother of my Lord should come to me? As soon as the sound of your greeting reached my ears, the baby in my womb leaped for joy. Blessed is she who has believed that what the Lord has said to her will be accomplished!"

And Mary said:

"My soul glorifies the Lord
and my spirit rejoices in God my Savior,
for he has been mindful
of the humble state of his servant.
From now on all generations will call me blessed,
for the Mighty One has done great things for me—
holy is his name.
His mercy extends to those who fear him,
from generation to generation.
He has performed mighty deeds with his arm;
he has scattered those who are proud in their inmost thoughts.
He has brought down rulers from their thrones
but has lifted up the humble."

Does any human emotion run as deep as hope? Fairy tales, for example, pass down from generation to generation a belief in the impossibly happy ending, an irrepressible sense that in the end the forces of evil will lose the struggle and the brave and good will somehow triumph.

For the Jews in Palestine at the dawn of the first millennium, all hope seems like a fairy tale. As Middle Eastern empires rise and fall, the tiny nation of Israel can never break free from the domination of greater powers. No prophet has spoken to them in four hundred years. At the end of the Old Testament, God is in hiding. He has long threatened to hide his face, and as he does so, a dark shadow falls across the planet.

For four centuries, the four hundred years of God's silence, the Jews wait and wonder. God seems passive, unconcerned, and deaf to their prayers. Only one hope remains, the ancient promise of a Messiah; on that promise the Jews stake everything. And then something momentous happens. The birth of a baby is announced— a birth unlike any that have come before.

You can catch the excitement just by reading the reactions of people in this chapter. The way Luke tells it, events surrounding Jesus' birth resemble a joy-filled musical. Characters crowd into the scene: a white-haired great uncle, an astonished virgin, a tottery old prophetess (Luke 2). They all smile broadly and, as likely as not, burst into song. Once Mary overcomes the shock from seeing an angel, she lets loose with a beautiful hymn. Even an unborn cousin kicks for joy inside his mother's womb.

Luke takes care to make direct connections to Old Testament promises of a Messiah; the angel Gabriel even calls John the Baptist an "Elijah" sent to prepare the way for the Lord. Clearly, something is brewing on planet Earth. Among dreary, defeated villagers in a remote corner of the Roman Empire, something climactically good is breaking out.   —PY

DAILY CONTEMPLATION

If an angel appeared to you, would you respond like Zechariah or like Mary?

An Angel Appears to Joseph

A record of the genealogy of Jesus Christ the son of David, the
   son of Abraham:
Abraham was the father of Isaac,
Isaac the father of Jacob,
Jacob the father of Judah and his brothers,
Judah the father of Perez and Zerah, whose mother was Tamar,
Perez the father of Hezron,
Hezron the father of Ram,
Ram the father of Amminadab,
Amminadab the father of Nahshon,
Nahshon the father of Salmon,
Salmon the father of Boaz, whose mother was Rahab,
Boaz the father of Obed, whose mother was Ruth,
Obed the father of Jesse,
and Jesse the father of King David.
David was the father of Solomon, whose mother had been Uriah's wife,
Solomon the father of Rehoboam,
Rehoboam the father of Abijah,
Abijah the father of Asa,
Asa the father of Jehoshaphat,
Jehoshaphat the father of Jehoram,
Jehoram the father of Uzziah,
Uzziah the father of Jotham,
Jotham the father of Ahaz,
Ahaz the father of Hezekiah,
Hezekiah the father of Manasseh,
Manasseh the father of Amon,
Amon the father of Josiah,
and Josiah the father of Jeconiah and his brothers at the time of the exile to
   Babylon.
After the exile to Babylon:
Jeconiah was the father of Shealtiel,
Shealtiel the father of Zerubbabel,
Zerubbabel the father of Abiud,
Abiud the father of Eliakim,
Eliakim the father of Azor,
Azor the father of Zadok,
Zadok the father of Akim,
Akim the father of Eliud,
Eliud the father of Eleazar,
Eleazar the father of Matthan,
Matthan the father of Jacob,
and Jacob the father of Joseph, the husband of Mary, of whom was born Jesus,
   who is called Christ.

Thus there were fourteen generations in all from Abraham to David, fourteen from David to the exile to Babylon, and fourteen from the exile to the Christ.

This is how the birth of Jesus Christ came about: His mother Mary was pledged to be married to Joseph, but before they came together, she was found to be with child through the Holy Spirit. Because Joseph her husband was a righteous man and did not want to expose her to public disgrace, he had in mind to divorce her quietly.

But after he had considered this, an angel of the Lord appeared to him in a dream and said, "Joseph son of David, do not be afraid to take Mary home as your wife, because what is conceived in her is from the Holy Spirit. She will give birth to a son, and you are to give him the name Jesus, because he will save his people from their sins."

All this took place to fulfill what the Lord had said through the prophet: "The virgin will be with child and will give birth to a son, and they will call him Immanuel"—which means, "God with us."

When Joseph woke up, he did what the angel of the Lord had commanded him and took Mary home as his wife. But he had no union with her until she gave birth to a son. And he gave him the name Jesus.

Matthew, the author of this gospel, was a Jewish tax collector who became one of Jesus' twelve disciples. In the first passage of this gospel Matthew reveals that he is writing mainly to the Jews, who will be especially concerned about the ancestry of Jesus. The prophesied Messiah would come from the line of David, and unless the Jews see this to be true, they will not believe in Jesus as that Messiah.

Glance back at the genealogy and you'll see many familiar names: Abraham, Isaac, Jacob, Judah, Boaz, Rahab, Ruth, David, and Solomon. Through the line of his legal father, Joseph, Jesus does indeed trace back to David and to Abraham. Notice the women listed in the genealogy. The only ones who appear are those with questionable backgrounds. Tamar (TAY-mar) and Rahab were prostitutes. Ruth was a foreigner, and Bathsheba, Uriah's wife, committed adultery with David. Perhaps God wants to remind the Jews that many of both the men and the women in the Savior's line were imperfect people who experienced God's grace and despite their faults were used by God to produce the Messiah.

Jesus' closest relatives, Mary and Joseph, each need great faith to bring Jesus finally into the world. Matthew focuses in this chapter on Joseph. Seven hundred years earlier God had prophesied through Isaiah that "the virgin will be with child and will give birth to a son, and will call him Immanuel" (Isaiah 7:14). Now the prophesy is being realized, and Joseph has been chosen to fill the role of father, even though he will not physically conceive the child. In faith, Joseph cuts short the expected one-year betrothal period and brings Mary immediately into his home. He marries her and cares for her during her pregnancy. No doubt the couple become the object of gossip and disrespect, which is just the beginning of a lifetime of misunderstanding awaiting their son Jesus.   —BQ

DAY 209

Luke 1:57–80

THE BIRTH OF JOHN THE BAPTIST

When it was time for Elizabeth to have her baby, she gave birth to a son. Her neighbors and relatives heard that the Lord had shown her great mercy, and they shared her joy.

On the eighth day they came to circumcise the child, and they were going to name him after his father Zechariah, but his mother spoke up and said, "No! He is to be called John."

They said to her, "There is no one among your relatives who has that name."

Then they made signs to his father, to find out what he would like to name the child. He asked for a writing tablet, and to everyone's astonishment he wrote, "His name is John." Immediately his mouth was opened and his tongue was loosed, and he began to speak, praising God. The neighbors were all filled with awe, and throughout the hill country of Judea people were talking about all these things. Everyone who heard this wondered about it, asking, "What then is this child going to be?" For the Lord's hand was with him.

His father Zechariah was filled with the Holy Spirit and prophesied:

"Praise be to the Lord, the God of Israel,
　because he has come and has redeemed his people.
He has raised up a horn of salvation for us
　in the house of his servant David
(as he said through his holy prophets of long ago),
salvation from our enemies
　and from the hand of all who hate us—
to show mercy to our fathers
　and to remember his holy covenant,
　the oath he swore to our father Abraham:
to rescue us from the hand of our enemies,
　and to enable us to serve him without fear
　in holiness and righteousness before him all our days.

And you, my child, will be called a prophet of the Most High;
　for you will go on before the Lord to prepare the way for him,
to give his people the knowledge of salvation
　through the forgiveness of their sins,
because of the tender mercy of our God,

by which the rising sun will come to us from heaven
>>to shine on those living in darkness
>>>and in the shadow of death,
>>to guide our feet into the path of peace."

And the child grew and became strong in spirit; and he lived in the desert until he appeared publicly to Israel.

As did Matthew in the first chapter of his gospel, Luke also demonstrates that everything surrounding the coming of Jesus falls in line with the Old Testament prophecies of the Messiah.

The prophet Malachi announced that God would send "my messenger, who will prepare the way before me" (Malachi 3:1). He compared this messenger to Elijah, saying, "See, I will send you the prophet Elijah before that great and dreadful day of the LORD comes" (Malachi 4:5). Earlier in this chapter of Luke, an angel appears to Zechariah, John's father, and in announcing John's coming birth declares that John will "go on before the Lord" and minister "in the spirit and power of Elijah" (v. 17).

Prophecy finds fulfillment in the birth of John. Just as Elijah brought a message of judgment and redemption, so John will be a powerful forerunner announcing the coming of the awaited Messiah, ultimate Judge and Redeemer. Just as Elijah prepared for his ministry in a desolate area, so John lives in the desert until his ministry begins. He will not fit the image of a typical Jewish holy man, donning rich robes and frequenting the temple. His style is only fitting, for he precedes a Savior who does not match the expectations of a waiting Jewish world. John will succeed in getting the attention of many people, and Jesus will fulfill the promises with which many are familiar but too few understand. —BQ

DAILY CONTEMPLATION

How do you respond when God does something unconventional in your life?

DAY 210 Luke 2:1–40

THE BIRTH OF JESUS

In those days Caesar Augustus issued a decree that a census should be taken of the entire Roman world. (This was the first census that took place while Quirinius was governor of Syria.) And everyone went to his own town to register.

So Joseph also went up from the town of Nazareth in Galilee to Judea, to Bethlehem the town of David, because he belonged to the house and line of David. He went there to register with Mary, who was pledged to be married to him and was expecting a child. While they were there, the time came for the baby to be born, and she gave birth to her firstborn, a son. She wrapped him in cloths and placed him in a manger, because there was no room for them in the inn.

And there were shepherds living out in the fields nearby, keeping watch over their flocks at night. An angel of the Lord appeared to them, and the glory of the Lord shone around them, and they were terrified. But the angel said to them, "Do not be afraid. I bring you good news of great joy that will be for all the people. Today in the town of David a Savior has been born to you; he is Christ the Lord. This will be a sign to you: You will find a baby wrapped in cloths and lying in a manger."

Suddenly a great company of the heavenly host appeared with the angel, praising God and saying,

"Glory to God in the highest,
and on earth peace to men on whom his favor rests."

When the angels had left them and gone into heaven, the shepherds said to one another, "Let's go to Bethlehem and see this thing that has happened, which the Lord has told us about."

So they hurried off and found Mary and Joseph, and the baby, who was lying in the manger. When they had seen him, they spread the word concerning what had been told them about this child, and all who heard it were amazed at what the shepherds said to them. But Mary treasured up all these things and pondered them in her heart. The shepherds returned, glorifying and praising God for all the things they had heard and seen, which were just as they had been told.

On the eighth day, when it was time to circumcise him, he was named Jesus, the name the angel had given him before he had been conceived.

When the time of their purification according to the Law of Moses had been completed, Joseph and Mary took him to Jerusalem to present him to the Lord (as it is written in the Law of the Lord, "Every firstborn male is to be consecrated to the Lord"), and to offer a sacrifice in keeping with what is said in the Law of the Lord: "a pair of doves or two young pigeons."

Now there was a man in Jerusalem called Simeon, who was righteous and devout. He was waiting for the consolation of Israel, and the Holy Spirit was upon him. It had been revealed to him by the Holy Spirit that he would not die before he had seen the Lord's Christ. Moved by the Spirit, he went into the temple courts. When the parents brought in the child Jesus to do for him what the custom of the Law required, Simeon took him in his arms and praised God, saying:

"Sovereign Lord, as you have promised,
you now dismiss your servant in peace.
For my eyes have seen your salvation,
which you have prepared in the sight of all people,

a light for revelation to the Gentiles
and for glory to your people Israel."

The child's father and mother marveled at what was said about him. Then Simeon blessed them and said to Mary, his mother: "This child is destined to cause the falling and rising of many in Israel, and to be a sign that will be spoken against, so that the thoughts of many hearts will be revealed. And a sword will pierce your own soul too."

There was also a prophetess, Anna, the daughter of Phanuel, of the tribe of Asher. She was very old; she had lived with her husband seven years after her marriage, and then was a widow until she was eighty-four. She never left the temple but worshiped night and day, fasting and praying. Coming up to them at that very moment, she gave thanks to God and spoke about the child to all who were looking forward to the redemption of Jerusalem.

When Joseph and Mary had done everything required by the Law of the Lord, they returned to Galilee to their own town of Nazareth. And the child grew and became strong; he was filled with wisdom, and the grace of God was upon him.

Nearly every time an angel appears in the Bible, the first words he says are "Don't be afraid!" Little wonder. When the supernatural makes contact with planet Earth, it usually leaves the human observers flat on their faces, in catatonic fear. But Luke tells of God making an appearance on earth in a form that does not frighten. In Jesus, born in a barn and laid in a feeding trough, God finds at last a mode of approach that we need not fear. What could be less scary than a newborn baby?

Imagine becoming a baby again: giving up language and muscle coordination and the ability to eat solid food and control your bladder. That gives just a hint of the "emptying" that God goes through.

According to the Bible, on earth Jesus is both God and man. As God, he can work miracles, forgive sins, conquer death, and predict the future. Jesus does all that, provoking awe in the people around him. But for Jews accustomed to images of God as a bright cloud or pillar of fire, Jesus also causes much confusion. How could a baby in Bethlehem, a carpenter's son, a man from Nazareth, be the Messiah from God? Jesus' skin gets in the way.

Puzzled skeptics will stalk Jesus throughout his ministry. But this chapter shows that God confirms Jesus' identity from his earliest days. A group of shepherds in a field have no doubt—they hear the message of good news straight from a choir of angels. And an old prophet and prophetess recognize him also. Even the skeptical teachers in the temple are amazed.

Why does God empty himself and take on human form? The Bible gives many reasons, some densely theological and some quite practical. The upcoming scene of Jesus as an adolescent lecturing rabbis in the temple gives one clue. For the first time, ordinary people can hold a conversation, a debate, with God in visible form. Jesus can talk to anyone—his parents, a rabbi, a poor widow—without first having to announce, "Don't be afraid!" In Jesus, God comes close.   —PY

DAY 211

THE WORD BECAME FLESH

In the beginning was the Word, and the Word was with God, and the Word was God. He was with God in the beginning.

Through him all things were made; without him nothing was made that has been made. In him was life, and that life was the light of men. The light shines in the darkness, but the darkness has not understood it.

There came a man who was sent from God; his name was John. He came as a witness to testify concerning that light, so that through him all men might believe. He himself was not the light; he came only as a witness to the light. The true light that gives light to every man was coming into the world.

He was in the world, and though the world was made through him, the world did not recognize him. He came to that which was his own, but his own did not receive him. Yet to all who received him, to those who believed in his name, he gave the right to become children of God—children born not of natural descent, nor of human decision or a husband's will, but born of God.

The Word became flesh and made his dwelling among us. We have seen his glory, the glory of the One and Only, who came from the Father, full of grace and truth.

John testifies concerning him. He cries out, saying, "This was he of whom I said, 'He who comes after me has surpassed me because he was before me.'" From the fullness of his grace we have all received one blessing after another. For the law was given through Moses; grace and truth came through Jesus Christ. No one has ever seen God, but God the One and Only, who is at the Father's side, has made him known.

From the beginning of his gospel John is writing about one person: Jesus. He doesn't begin with a narrative, as Mark and Luke have done. Rather, he chooses to open his account by reaching back to the beginning of time to reveal the eternity of Jesus in his relationship to God the Father.

The passage is beautiful and filled with important theology, although in some places difficult to understand. For example, John's initial reference to Christ as "the Word" can be confusing. Greeks used this term, *logos*, to refer to the spoken and unspoken word, the reason of the mind. When speaking of the universe, the Greeks used *logos*, or *word*, to describe the rational principle that governs all things. Jews, on the other hand, used *Word* in reference to God. Therefore John's description of Jesus as the Word is appropriate for both Jews and Greeks. Jesus, John declares, is the source of all reason, the only one with true understanding and the capacity to rule. Jesus is the final word. He is God.

Jesus was with God in the beginning and he is God. This Messiah Jesus was not, as many claim, just a good man or a messenger from God. He is God's Son while simultaneously being God himself. Present at the creation of the world, he is also living today.

Jesus as a distinct being yet one with God seems contradictory. But that is the mystery of the Trinity—one God in three persons, Father, Son, and Holy Spirit. As part of this triune Godhead, Jesus fills the role of uniting us with God. Our eternal future depends not on our biological family nor on the arbitrary decisions of our parents but simply on our belief in his name. In Jesus we are released from the need to follow God's law to be saved and instead are saved through his grace and truth. Jesus offers us the love of God in all its fullness.   —BQ

DAILY CONTEMPLATION

Who did you believe Jesus to be before you came to know him?

DAY 212   Reflection

JESUS, OUR PICTURE OF GOD

What is it about Jesus that makes Christianity unique among all other religions? What sets Jesus apart from other religious greats in world history?

John gives us the answer in the first chapter of his gospel. He calls Jesus "the Word" and declares that Jesus both was with God and was God. Then John explains that Jesus, the Word, "became flesh and made his dwelling among us . . . , full of grace and truth" (1:14). As he walked the earth in the flesh of a man, Jesus embodied the fullness of God. In his words and actions, Jesus in human form revealed God in a way God had never revealed himself before. Not only did Jesus exhibit the *truth* found only in God; he displayed the *grace* that defines God and sets him apart from any other purported deity from any time or place.

The book *What's So Amazing About Grace?* tells a story about British author and scholar C. S. Lewis.

> During a British conference on comparative religions, experts from around the world debated what, if any, belief was unique to the Christian faith. They began eliminating possibilities. Incarnation? Other religions had different versions of gods appearing in human forms. Resurrection? Again, other religions had accounts of return from death. The debate went on for some time until C. S. Lewis wandered into the room. "What's the rumpus about?" he asked, and heard in reply that his colleagues were discussing

Christianity's unique contribution among world religions. Lewis responded, "Oh, that's easy. It's grace."

After some discussion, the conferees had to agree. The notion of God's love coming to us free of charge, no strings attached, seems to go against every instinct of humanity. The Buddhist eight-fold path, the Hindu doctrine of *karma*, the Jewish covenant, and Muslim code of law—each of these offers a way to earn approval. Only Christianity dares to make God's love unconditional.[28]

Before Jesus came, God exhibited his grace time and time again to the Israelite people by forgiving them for disobeying and turning their backs on him. God even showed grace toward Gentiles—people like Rahab, Ruth, and Persians of Esther's day who turned to him. But his standard for salvation hadn't changed. Adherence to the law was still necessary for people to qualify to live for eternity in the presence of a holy God.

Early in the Old Testament, however, God was already planning to make a way for people to come to him apart from the law. No one in the Old Testament kept the law perfectly as God required, so only faith would ultimately qualify a person for heaven. Salvation was possible only because of the yet-to-be-completed sacrifice of Christ. Jesus was God's way of paying sin's debt once and for all, and his death on the cross gives us the greatest picture of God's grace and his love for us.

God has every reason to walk away from us because of our failures at loving him well. Instead, through Jesus, he walks toward us and forever silences our pleas for mercy. Jesus is our picture of a holy, loving God who draws believers near once and forever.

—BQ

DAILY CONTEMPLATION

How well do you know Jesus? How much has your understanding of Jesus transformed the way you see God? Talk to Jesus about your desire to get to know him better. Ask him to help you see God more clearly in the days ahead as we look at Jesus' life in the Gospels.

DAY 213
Matthew 2:1–23

THE VISIT OF THE MAGI, ESCAPE TO EGYPT,

AND RETURN TO NAZARETH

After Jesus was born in Bethlehem in Judea, during the time of King Herod, Magi from the east came to Jerusalem and asked, "Where is the one who has been born king of the Jews? We saw his star in the east and have come to worship him."

When King Herod heard this he was disturbed, and all Jerusalem with him. When he had called together all the people's chief priests and teachers of the law, he asked them where the Christ was to be born. "In Bethlehem in Judea," they replied, "for this is what the prophet has written:

"'But you, Bethlehem, in the land of Judah,
    are by no means least among the rulers of Judah;
for out of you will come a ruler
    who will be the shepherd of my people Israel.'"

Then Herod called the Magi secretly and found out from them the exact time the star had appeared. He sent them to Bethlehem and said, "Go and make a careful search for the child. As soon as you find him, report to me, so that I too may go and worship him."

After they had heard the king, they went on their way, and the star they had seen in the east went ahead of them until it stopped over the place where the child was. When they saw the star, they were overjoyed. On coming to the house, they saw the child with his mother Mary, and they bowed down and worshiped him. Then they opened their treasures and presented him with gifts of gold and of incense and of myrrh. And having been warned in a dream not to go back to Herod, they returned to their country by another route.

When they had gone, an angel of the Lord appeared to Joseph in a dream. "Get up," he said, "take the child and his mother and escape to Egypt. Stay there until I tell you, for Herod is going to search for the child to kill him."

So he got up, took the child and his mother during the night and left for Egypt, where he stayed until the death of Herod. And so was fulfilled what the Lord had said through the prophet: "Out of Egypt I called my son."

When Herod realized that he had been outwitted by the Magi, he was furious, and he gave orders to kill all the boys in Bethlehem and its vicinity who were two years old and under, in accordance with the time he had learned from the Magi. Then what was said through the prophet Jeremiah was fulfilled:

"A voice is heard in Ramah,
    weeping and great mourning,
Rachel weeping for her children
    and refusing to be comforted,
because they are no more."

After Herod died, an angel of the Lord appeared in a dream to Joseph in Egypt and said, "Get up, take the child and his mother and go to the land of Israel, for those who were trying to take the child's life are dead."

So he got up, took the child and his mother and went to the land of Israel. But when he heard that Archelaus was reigning in Judea in place of his father Herod, he was afraid to go there. Having been warned in a dream, he withdrew to the district of Galilee, and he went and lived in a town called Nazareth. So was fulfilled what was said through the prophets: "He will be called a Nazarene."

Not just a few select Jews recognize Jesus as the Messiah early on. Even some non-Jewish astronomers travel a great distance to worship the newborn King of the Jews. Tradition tells us three Magi made the trip, although no one is certain how many actually came. Whatever their number, they came prepared with special gifts. Theirs was no casual journey.

Some have speculated that the gifts the Magi brought were symbolic, not merely expensive offerings. Perhaps these precious gifts reflected the character of the Child's life, with the gold representing his deity or purity, the incense his fragrant life, and the myrrh his sacrifice and death (myrrh was used for embalming).

After receiving the acclaim of foreign visitors, Jesus' parents learn of the first threat to his life. Herod the Great, on the throne at the time of Jesus' birth, has a reputation for cruelty not only toward Jews but even toward his own family. During his lifetime he puts to death, among others, a few of his wives and several of his own children. Herod's son Archelaus (ahr-kuh-LAY-uhs) takes over one region after Herod's death and follows in his father's footsteps of tyranny and murder. (Eventually he will go insane, possibly a result of close family intermarriages.)

A few years after Jesus' birth, Joseph avoids the dangers of Archelaus and returns with his family to Nazareth, a town in Galilee ruled by another, more capable son of Herod. Joseph and Mary had left Nazareth to register for the census in Bethlehem. Now they again make the town of Nazareth their home, despite its unlikely setting for an up-and-coming Messiah.

As the military post of the north for Roman soldiers, Nazareth has earned the Jews' disdain. Jewish residents of Nazareth are thought to be sympathizers with the enemy, Rome. This reputation will help color Jesus' reputation. A later disciple, Nathanael, will first react to Jesus in reference to his Nazarene status. "Can anything good come from there?" (John 1:46). As a Nazarene, Jesus fulfills Old Testament prophecy speaking of his lowliness and the contempt many Israelites will feel toward him.　　—BQ

DAILY CONTEMPLATION

Can you identify in any way with the rejection Jesus felt because of the place he called home?

DAY 214　　　　　　　Luke 2:41–52; Matthew 3:1–12

THE BOY JESUS AT THE TEMPLE;
JOHN THE BAPTIST PREPARES THE WAY

Every year his parents went to Jerusalem for the Feast of the Passover. When he was twelve years old, they went up to the Feast, according to the custom. After the Feast was over, while his parents were returning home, the boy Jesus stayed behind in Jerusalem, but they were unaware of it. Thinking he was in their company, they traveled on for a day. Then they began looking for him among their relatives and friends. When they did not find him, they went back to Jerusalem to look for him. After three days they found him in the temple courts, sitting among the teachers, listening to them and asking them questions. Everyone who heard him was amazed at his understanding and his answers. When his parents saw him, they were astonished. His mother said to him, "Son, why have you treated us like this? Your father and I have been anxiously searching for you."

"Why were you searching for me?" he asked. "Didn't you know I had to be in my Father's house?" But they did not understand what he was saying to them.

Then he went down to Nazareth with them and was obedient to them. But his mother treasured all these things in her heart. And Jesus grew in wisdom and stature, and in favor with God and men. . . .

In those days John the Baptist came, preaching in the Desert of Judea and saying, "Repent, for the kingdom of heaven is near." This is he who was spoken of through the prophet Isaiah:

"A voice of one calling in the desert,
'Prepare the way for the Lord,
    make straight paths for him.'"

John's clothes were made of camel's hair, and he had a leather belt around his waist. His food was locusts and wild honey. People went out to him from Jerusalem and all Judea and the whole region of the Jordan. Confessing their sins, they were baptized by him in the Jordan River.

But when he saw many of the Pharisees and Sadducees coming to where he was baptizing, he said to them: "You brood of vipers! Who warned you to flee from the coming wrath? Produce fruit in keeping with repentance. And do not think you can say to yourselves, 'We have Abraham as our father.' I tell you that out of these stones God can raise up children for Abraham. The ax is already at the root of the trees, and every tree that does not produce good fruit will be cut down and thrown into the fire.

"I baptize you with water for repentance. But after me will come one who is more powerful than I, whose sandals I am not fit to carry. He will baptize you with the Holy Spirit and with fire. His winnowing fork is in his hand, and he will clear his threshing floor, gathering his wheat into the barn and burning up the chaff with unquenchable fire."

At twelve Jesus already understands his purpose on earth, focusing even at this young age on revealing the intent of his Father. Lingering at the temple in Jerusalem despite his parents' departure may appear insensitive. As Jesus sees it, though, he is merely concentrating on pleasing his Father in heaven and completing the mission he has been sent to accomplish.

His cousin John the Baptist knows exactly why Jesus has been sent. As he prepares people for Jesus' ministry, he encounters two religious groups who will question Jesus throughout his public life. The Pharisees (FAIR-uh-sees) are a legalistic group who keep themselves separate from other Jews in a belief that they, more than any others, succeed in keeping the written law of Moses and the unwritten tradition of the Jewish elders. The Pharisees pride themselves on their knowledge of the law and Scriptures. Yet, as both John and Jesus point out, they are often hypocritical in their adherence to the law, accusing others yet rationalizing their own sinful behavior. The Sadducees (SAD-yoo-sees) concern themselves with the world and the political realm. Theologically unorthodox, they deny belief in such matters as angels, spirits, and the resurrection of the dead.

John addresses the mistaken assumption among many of the Pharisees and Sadducees that as children of Abraham they will automatically enter the kingdom of God. John cries a different message: "Repent, for the kingdom of heaven is near." Only through repentance can a person be saved. Lineage won't do it, and no amount of knowledge, status, or good behavior will suffice. In fact, these things are irrelevant. God requires a repentant heart and a new mind for his ways.

Many will reject Jesus for these reasons. They would rather cling to belief in their own goodness or hold to a previously conceived personal understanding of God. Jesus will have no patience with their stubbornness, continuing to offer them a place in his kingdom only if they will accept the message he has come to embody.   —BQ

DAILY CONTEMPLATION

Has it been hard for you to accept that Jesus is more concerned about your repentant heart than about your knowledge or your good deeds?

DAY 215   Mark 1:9–45

JESUS IS BAPTIZED, TEMPTED, AND

BEGINS HIS WORK

At that time Jesus came from Nazareth in Galilee and was baptized by John in the Jordan. As Jesus was coming up out of the water, he saw heaven being torn open and the Spirit descending on him like a dove. And a voice came from heaven: "You are my Son, whom I love; with you I am well pleased."

At once the Spirit sent him out into the desert, and he was in the desert forty days, being tempted by Satan. He was with the wild animals, and angels attended him.

412

After John was put in prison, Jesus went into Galilee, proclaiming the good news of God. "The time has come," he said. "The kingdom of God is near. Repent and believe the good news!"

As Jesus walked beside the Sea of Galilee, he saw Simon and his brother Andrew casting a net into the lake, for they were fishermen. "Come, follow me," Jesus said, "and I will make you fishers of men." At once they left their nets and followed him.

When he had gone a little farther, he saw James son of Zebedee and his brother John in a boat, preparing their nets. Without delay he called them, and they left their father Zebedee in the boat with the hired men and followed him.

They went to Capernaum, and when the Sabbath came, Jesus went into the synagogue and began to teach. The people were amazed at his teaching, because he taught them as one who had authority, not as the teachers of the law. Just then a man in their synagogue who was possessed by an evil spirit cried out, "What do you want with us, Jesus of Nazareth? Have you come to destroy us? I know who you are—the Holy One of God!"

"Be quiet!" said Jesus sternly. "Come out of him!" The evil spirit shook the man violently and came out of him with a shriek.

The people were all so amazed that they asked each other, "What is this? A new teaching—and with authority! He even gives orders to evil spirits and they obey him." News about him spread quickly over the whole region of Galilee.

As soon as they left the synagogue, they went with James and John to the home of Simon and Andrew. Simon's mother-in-law was in bed with a fever, and they told Jesus about her. So he went to her, took her hand and helped her up. The fever left her and she began to wait on them.

That evening after sunset the people brought to Jesus all the sick and demon-possessed. The whole town gathered at the door, and Jesus healed many who had various diseases. He also drove out many demons, but he would not let the demons speak because they knew who he was.

Very early in the morning, while it was still dark, Jesus got up, left the house and went off to a solitary place, where he prayed. Simon and his companions went to look for him, and when they found him, they exclaimed: "Everyone is looking for you!"

Jesus replied, "Let us go somewhere else—to the nearby villages—so I can preach there also. That is why I have come." So he traveled throughout Galilee, preaching in their synagogues and driving out demons.

A man with leprosy came to him and begged him on his knees, "If you are willing, you can make me clean."

Filled with compassion, Jesus reached out his hand and touched the man. "I am willing," he said. "Be clean!" Immediately the leprosy left him and he was cured.

Jesus sent him away at once with a strong warning: "See that you don't tell this to anyone. But go, show yourself to the priest and offer the sacrifices that Moses commanded for your cleansing, as a testimony to them."

Instead he went out and began to talk freely, spreading the news. As a result, Jesus could no longer enter a town openly but stayed outside in lonely places. Yet the people still came to him from everywhere.

Although the four gospels all cover basically the same ground, each one looks at Jesus' life from a unique angle. Matthew and Luke both begin with three chapters of historical background, taking pains to verify Jesus' Old Testament connections. Mark, however, plunges right in to report on Jesus' ministry, covering his baptism and temptation, the calling of the disciples, and a series of miracles in the first chapter alone.

Mark reads like a newspaper account, jam-packed with action, and with little room left over for parables, speeches, or editorial comments. Thus the book gives an ideal "bird's-eye view" of Jesus' life. Its style—simple sentences without complicated transitions or long speeches—makes understanding easier.

After John the Baptist fans enthusiasm for Jesus—so much enthusiasm, in fact, that John lands in jail—Jesus openly announces his ministry. He has some surprises in store for the eager audience. For one thing, Jesus goes not to Jerusalem, the natural center of activity for any aspiring leader, but to small towns in the hill country of Galilee.

In other ways too Jesus does not fit the expected image of a prophet. His cousin John personifies the severe ascetic image: he lives in a desert, eats insects, and preaches a harsh message of judgment. But Jesus lives in the midst of people, dines in their homes, and brings a message of "the good news of God."

When Jesus begins healing people, however, his reputation swells overnight. Mark shows stadium-size crowds pressing around Jesus so tightly that he has to plan escape routes. News of his miraculous powers spreads even when he tries to hush it up. Wherever Jesus goes, the crowds follow, buzzing about his remarkable life. "Is he the Holy One of God?" "Is he mad?" "Isn't this the carpenter's boy?" The word is out.   —PY

DAILY CONTEMPLATION

Considering what you have read about Jesus so far, what characteristic about him surprises you most?

DAY 216
Matthew 4:1–11

THE TEMPTATION OF JESUS

Then Jesus was led by the Spirit into the desert to be tempted by the devil. After fasting forty days and forty nights, he was hungry. The tempter came to him and said, "If you are the Son of God, tell these stones to become bread."

Jesus answered, "It is written: 'Man does not live on bread alone, but on every word that comes from the mouth of God.'"

Then the devil took him to the holy city and had him stand on the highest point of the temple. "If you are the Son of God," he said, "throw yourself down. For it is written:

> "'He will command his angels concerning you,
>   and they will lift you up in their hands,
> so that you will not strike your foot against a stone.'"

Jesus answered him, "It is also written: 'Do not put the Lord your God to the test.'"

Again, the devil took him to a very high mountain and showed him all the kingdoms of the world and their splendor. "All this I will give you," he said, "if you will bow down and worship me."

Jesus said to him, "Away from me, Satan! For it is written: 'Worship the Lord your God, and serve him only.'"

Then the devil left him, and angels came and attended him.

The story of Jesus' temptation brings to mind two Old Testament stories. Whereas Jesus is tempted for forty days in the desert, the Israelites wandered forty years in the desert. Moses described God's purpose in the Israelite's wanderings: "to humble you and to test you in order to know what was in your heart, whether or not you would keep his commands" (Deuteronomy 8:2). Although the Israelites failed their test, Jesus shows himself to be a true Israelite. He endures, staying faithful to God and his purposes.

Jesus' temptation also reflects an earlier scene—Eve's encounter with Satan in the Garden of Eden. Although God tested Israel to try their loyalty to him, it was Satan who tempted Eve to do evil. More than simply a negative force or influence, Satan acted as a living being with both Eve and Jesus, using the same tactics he uses with us today. He makes an appeal to the physical appetite, to the human desire for personal gain, and to the human longing for a quick and easy path to power or prestige.

Jesus believes the Scriptures he quotes in resisting Satan. He knows that only God can satisfy our hunger, that God's gain is more important than personal gain, and that worship of God must take the place of any quest for personal position or power. In standing against Satan's proposals, Jesus shows he is qualified to be the Savior of all who receive him. He understands what we experience, and he can help us when we are being tempted.   —BQ

DAILY CONTEMPLATION

What has been your most recent temptation? Does it resemble any of Jesus' three temptations?

DAY 217   Reflection

JESUS' PATTERN OF RESTRAINT

As I look back on the three temptations, I see that Satan proposed an enticing improvement. He tempted Jesus toward the good parts of being human without the bad: to savor the taste of bread without being subject to the fixed rules of hunger and of agriculture, to confront risk with no real danger, to enjoy fame and power without the prospect of painful rejection—in short, to wear a crown but not a cross. (The temptation that Jesus resisted, many of us, his followers, still long for.)

The temptation in the desert reveals a profound difference between God's power and Satan's power. Satan has the power to coerce, to dazzle, to force obedience, to destroy. Humans have learned much from that power, and governments draw deeply from its reservoir. With a bullwhip or a billy club or an AK-47, human beings can force other human beings to do just about anything they want. Satan's power is external and coercive.

God's power, in contrast, is internal and noncoercive. "You would not enslave man by a miracle, and craved faith given freely, not based on miracle," said the Inquisitor to Jesus in Dostoevsky's novel *The Brothers Karamazov.* Such power may seem at times like weakness. In its commitment to transform gently from the inside out and in its relentless dependence on human choice, God's power may resemble a kind of abdication. As every parent and every lover knows, love can be rendered powerless if the beloved chooses to spurn it.

Sometimes, I concede, I wish that God used a heavier touch. My faith suffers from too much freedom, too many temptations to disbelieve. At times I want God to overwhelm me, to overcome my doubts with certainty, to give final proofs of his existence and his concern.

I want God to take a more active role in my personal history too. I want quick and spectacular answers to my prayers, healing for my diseases, protection and safety for my loved ones. I want a God without ambiguity, one to whom I can point for the sake of my doubting friends.

When I think these thoughts, I recognize in myself a thin, hollow echo of the challenge that Satan hurled at Jesus two thousand years ago. God resists those temptations now as Jesus resisted them on earth, settling instead for a slower, gentler way.

As I survey the rest of Jesus' life, I see that the pattern of restraint established in the desert persisted throughout his life. I never sense Jesus twisting a person's arm. Rather, he stated the consequences of a choice, then threw the decision back to the other party. He answered a wealthy man's question with uncompromising words and then let him walk away. Mark pointedly adds this comment: "Jesus looked at him and loved him" (Mark 10:21). Jesus had a realistic view of how the world would respond to him: "Because of the increase of wickedness, the love of most will grow cold" (Matthew 24:12).

When I examine myself, I find that I too am vulnerable to the Temptation. I lack the willpower to resist shortcut solutions to human needs. I lack the patience to allow God to work in a slow, "gentlemanly" way. I want to seize control myself, to compel others to help accomplish the causes I believe in. I am willing to trade away certain freedoms for the guarantee of safety and protection. I am willing to trade away even more for the chance to realize my ambitions.

When I feel those temptations rising within me, I return to the story of Jesus and Satan in the desert. Jesus' resistance against Satan's temptations preserved for me the very freedom I exercise when I face my own temptations. I pray for the same trust and patience that Jesus showed. And I rejoice that, as Hebrews said, "We do not have a high priest who is unable to sympathize with our weaknesses, but we have one who has been tempted in every way, just as we are—yet was without sin. . . . Because he himself suffered when he was tempted, he is able to help those who are being tempted" (Hebrews 4:15; 2:18).[29]   —PY

DAILY CONTEMPLATION

What kinds of temptations seem to nag you most frequently? Can you look back and see Jesus' pattern of restraint in your life? Thank Jesus for drawing you to him gently, without coercion. Ask for his Spirit to increasingly pervade you as you fight the temptation to wear a crown but not a cross.

DAY 218   John 2:1–11

JESUS CHANGES WATER TO WINE

On the third day a wedding took place at Cana in Galilee. Jesus' mother was there, and Jesus and his disciples had also been invited to the wedding. When the wine was gone, Jesus' mother said to him, "They have no more wine."

"Dear woman, why do you involve me?" Jesus replied. "My time has not yet come."

His mother said to the servants, "Do whatever he tells you."

Nearby stood six stone water jars, the kind used by the Jews for ceremonial washing, each holding from twenty to thirty gallons.

Jesus said to the servants, "Fill the jars with water"; so they filled them to the brim.

Then he told them, "Now draw some out and take it to the master of the banquet."

They did so, and the master of the banquet tasted the water that had been turned into wine. He did not realize where it had come from, though the servants who had drawn the water knew. Then he called the bridegroom aside and said, "Everyone brings out the choice wine first and then the cheaper wine after the guests have had too much to drink; but you have saved the best till now."

This, the first of his miraculous signs, Jesus performed at Cana in Galilee. He thus revealed his glory, and his disciples put their faith in him.

John tells the story of Jesus' first miracle, and the following story makes it clear that, as with all his miracles, Jesus performed more than magic. His miracles joined the natural world with God's supernatural power and brought results that even today are impacting our world.

Dr. Richard Eby tells about his father, an employee with General Electric in the early 1900s, and some modern-day repercussions of Jesus' first miracle. In 1908 the president of G.E. believed that the future of America would depend on vast voltages of electrical energy. At the time, proper insulators, or bushings, had not yet been developed, and without them grand-scale electricity was impossible. Eugene Eby, a young engineer, was given the job of solving the problem.

Many months of research and trial and error produced no answers. Eby and his staff were unable to identify a type of porcelain insulator that could withstand the surge of electricity produced by lightning storms that daily would hit electric sub-stations and cross-country tension lines. Every bushing they developed was quickly destroyed even with the zap of a man-made bolt of lightning.

One Saturday morning at breakfast, Eby felt suddenly hopeful. He and his staff of engineers, mechanics, test operators, chemists, and porcelain specialists had been ready to give up. Exhausted, they were no closer to finding a solution. But the night before, Eby told his family, he'd told God in prayer that he would have to provide an answer or else let the problem of electricity remain unsolved.

When he'd woken in the morning, Eby had opened his Bible and let it fall to the story of Jesus' first miracle. Reading this familiar passage again, he began to think like an engineer. Jesus used six large pots and his power to change the water to wine. The pots held twenty to thirty gallons each; such pottery would have to be very strong. Furthermore, in the chemical change of water to alcohol, millions of volts would be needed to rearrange the molecules, as if bombs were exploding in the pots as the miracle occurred. Yet the pots withstood all the pressure.

Eby had no clear answers, he told his family, but the next day he would give his staff a month's vacation and await further insight.

A month later no answers had come. A wire arrived from President Hoover in the White House, addressing the topic of the Boulder Dam, later to be renamed the Hoover Dam. Its construction well under way, it promised to be the world's greatest dam. But it would prove useless as a power source apart from adequate bushings. The problem was urgent and needed a quick resolution.

Eby made a phone call to his Schenectady office, where a Mr. Cermak headed the porcelain research. Cermak had just returned from a trip to Europe and Egypt, and in the course of small talk mentioned that while in Egypt he learned of a tomb that had just been opened, housing the remains of King Tut. Touring the tomb, Cermak said, he had pocketed a small "souvenir" while the guard's back was turned. Business talk followed, with discussion of the president's orders, but no solutions became apparent.

That night Eby couldn't shake a feeling that some connection was waiting to be made. In the dark hours of the morning he knew he needed to phone Cermak immediately. Sure enough, the souvenir Cermak took was a piece of pottery, probably from some kind of pitcher, roughly three thousand years old, dating further back than Jesus' time on earth. Cermak agreed to test its composition right away.

Two weeks later in the lightning lab, Eby, with his son standing by, tested a newly formed bushing made from the same material as the Tut pottery. An electric volt that shook the building didn't budge the bushing. President Hoover was notified. The dam would work. It would become the largest power plant, and the world would have its answer to grand-scale electricity.[30]   —BQ

DAILY CONTEMPLATION

When has God used an experience from your past to affect your future unexpectedly yet profoundly?

DAY 219   John 3:1–21

JESUS TEACHES NICODEMUS

Now there was a man of the Pharisees named Nicodemus, a member of the Jewish ruling council. He came to Jesus at night and said, "Rabbi, we know you are a teacher who has come from God. For no one could perform the miraculous signs you are doing if God were not with him."

In reply Jesus declared, "I tell you the truth, no one can see the kingdom of God unless he is born again."

"How can a man be born when he is old?" Nicodemus asked. "Surely he cannot enter a second time into his mother's womb to be born!"

Jesus answered, "I tell you the truth, no one can enter the kingdom of God unless he is born of water and the Spirit. Flesh gives birth to flesh, but the Spirit gives birth to spirit. You should not be surprised at my saying, 'You must be born again.' The wind blows wherever it pleases. You hear its sound, but you cannot tell where it comes from or where it is going. So it is with everyone born of the Spirit."

"How can this be?" Nicodemus asked.

"You are Israel's teacher," said Jesus, "and do you not understand these things? I tell you the truth, we speak of what we know, and we testify to what we have seen, but still you people do not accept our testimony. I have spoken to you of earthly things and you do not believe; how then will you believe if I speak of heavenly things? No one has ever gone into heaven except the one who came from heaven—the Son of Man. Just as Moses lifted up the snake in the desert, so the Son of Man must be lifted up, that everyone who believes in him may have eternal life.

"For God so loved the world that he gave his one and only Son, that whoever believes in him shall not perish but have eternal life. For God did not send his Son into the world to condemn the world, but to save the world through him. Whoever believes in him is not condemned, but whoever does not believe stands condemned already because he has not believed in the name of God's one and only Son. This is the verdict: Light has come into the world, but men loved darkness instead of light because their deeds were evil. Everyone who does evil hates the light, and will not come into the light for fear that his deeds will be exposed. But whoever lives by the truth comes into the light, so that it may be seen plainly that what he has done has been done through God."

A simultaneous reading of John 3 and Mark 2 (scheduled for day 224) reveals a chief difference between Mark's and John's gospels. Mark gives the panoramic view: action, crowds, short scenes spliced together to create an overall impact. John tightens the camera angle, closing in on a few individual faces—a woman at a well, a blind man, a member of the Jewish ruling council—to compose a more intimate, in-depth portrait.

A simple word or phrase with a profound meaning—that is the style of Jesus' teaching as presented in John. No biblical author uses simpler, more commonplace words: *water, world, light, life, birth, love, truth.* Yet John uses them with such depth and skill that hundreds of authors since have tried to plumb their meaning.

Take this conversation with Nicodemus (NIK-uh-DEE-muhs), for instance. He comes to Jesus at night, in order to avoid detection. He risks his reputation and safety even by meeting with Jesus, whom his fellow Pharisees have sworn to kill. But Nicodemus has questions, burning questions, the most important questions anyone could ask: *Who are you, Jesus? Have you really come from God?* Jesus responds with the image of a second birth, in words that have become some of the most familiar in the Bible.

Evidently, some of Jesus' words to Nicodemus sink in. Later he will stand up for Jesus at the Jewish ruling council and, after the Crucifixion, help prepare Jesus' body for burial.

John follows this conversation with a report from John the Baptist. People are questioning him too about the new teacher across the river who is drawing all the crowds. In words that echo Jesus' own, John the Baptist confirms that Jesus holds the keys to eternal life. He is indeed the one John has come to herald: "He must become greater; I must become less" (John 3:30).   —PY

DAILY CONTEMPLATION

How did you interpret the phrase "born again" before you became a believer? How do your nonbelieving friends interpret this phrase?

DAY 220   John 4:1–30, 39–42

JESUS TALKS WITH A SAMARITAN WOMAN

The Pharisees heard that Jesus was gaining and baptizing more disciples than John, although in fact it was not Jesus who baptized, but his disciples.

When the Lord learned of this, he left Judea and went back once more to Galilee.

Now he had to go through Samaria. So he came to a town in Samaria called Sychar, near the plot of ground Jacob had given to his son Joseph. Jacob's well was there, and Jesus, tired as he was from the journey, sat down by the well. It was about the sixth hour.

When a Samaritan woman came to draw water, Jesus said to her, "Will you give me a drink?" (His disciples had gone into the town to buy food.)

The Samaritan woman said to him, "You are a Jew and I am a Samaritan woman. How can you ask me for a drink?" (For Jews do not associate with Samaritans.)

Jesus answered her, "If you knew the gift of God and who it is that asks you for a drink, you would have asked him and he would have given you living water."

"Sir," the woman said, "you have nothing to draw with and the well is deep. Where can you get this living water? Are you greater than our father Jacob, who gave us the well and drank from it himself, as did also his sons and his flocks and herds?"

Jesus answered, "Everyone who drinks this water will be thirsty again, but whoever drinks the water I give him will never thirst. Indeed, the water I give him will become in him a spring of water welling up to eternal life."

The woman said to him, "Sir, give me this water so that I won't get thirsty and have to keep coming here to draw water."

He told her, "Go, call your husband and come back."

"I have no husband," she replied.

Jesus said to her, "You are right when you say you have no husband. The fact is, you have had five husbands, and the man you now have is not your husband. What you have just said is quite true."

"Sir," the woman said, "I can see that you are a prophet. Our fathers worshiped on this mountain, but you Jews claim that the place where we must worship is in Jerusalem."

Jesus declared, "Believe me, woman, a time is coming when you will worship the Father neither on this mountain nor in Jerusalem. You Samaritans worship what you do not know; we worship what we do know, for salvation is from the Jews. Yet a time is coming and has now come when the true worshipers will worship the Father in spirit and truth, for they are the kind of worshipers the Father seeks. God is spirit, and his worshipers must worship in spirit and in truth."

The woman said, "I know that Messiah" (called Christ) "is coming. When he comes, he will explain everything to us."

Then Jesus declared, "I who speak to you am he."

Just then his disciples returned and were surprised to find him talking with a woman. But no one asked, "What do you want?" or "Why are you talking with her?"

Then, leaving her water jar, the woman went back to the town and said to the people, "Come, see a man who told me everything I ever did. Could this be the Christ?" They came out of the town and made their way toward him....

Many of the Samaritans from that town believed in him because of the woman's testimony, "He told me everything I ever did." So when the Samaritans came to him, they urged him to stay with them, and he stayed two days. And because of his words many more became believers.

They said to the woman, "We no longer believe just because of what you said; now we have heard for ourselves, and we know that this man really is the Savior of the world."

In ways not so obvious today, Jesus' actions in this story border on outrageous. The Jews of Jesus' day, you see, have nothing but contempt for Samaritans, a half-breed minority. When Assyria conquered the northern kingdom of Israel in 722 B.C., overrunning its capital, Samaria, most Jews were deported and replaced with other conquered peoples. These new settlers intermarried with remaining Jews and adopted some of Israel's religious practices, combining them with worship of their own gods. For this reason, the Jews came to despise the "impostor" Samaritans.

Because of their hatred, the Jews of Jesus' day shun contact with Samaritans. Deliberately avoiding the shortest route from Judea to Galilee, through Samaria, the Jews often cross over the Jordan River to the east side and travel north or south through Perea in order to bypass Samaria. Not Jesus. He chooses to travel directly through Samaria, and en route he upsets yet another Jewish tradition. In talking with the Samaritan woman, Jesus also defies a prejudice that frowns on conversation between men and women.

Jesus reveals his identity as Messiah, and this Samaritan woman becomes the first to hear him speak of himself so clearly. In Jewish territories Jesus must use care in revealing himself, so as not to incite political friction too quickly. But here in Samaria political danger remains low. In speaking openly to the woman and others in town, Jesus again expresses his great love for people outside the Jewish community. —BQ

DAILY CONTEMPLATION

What kind of thirst has Jesus quenched in your life?

DAY 221   Luke 4:14–30

JESUS REJECTED AT NAZARETH

Jesus returned to Galilee in the power of the Spirit, and news about him spread through the whole countryside. He taught in their synagogues, and everyone praised him.

He went to Nazareth, where he had been brought up, and on the Sabbath day he went into the synagogue, as was his custom. And he stood up to read. The scroll of the prophet Isaiah was handed to him. Unrolling it, he found the place where it is written:

> "The Spirit of the Lord is on me,
>> because he has anointed me
>> to preach good news to the poor.
> He has sent me to proclaim freedom for the prisoners
>> and recovery of sight for the blind,
> to release the oppressed,
>> to proclaim the year of the Lord's favor."

Then he rolled up the scroll, gave it back to the attendant and sat down. The eyes of everyone in the synagogue were fastened on him, and he began by saying to them, "Today this scripture is fulfilled in your hearing."

All spoke well of him and were amazed at the gracious words that came from his lips. "Isn't this Joseph's son?" they asked.

Jesus said to them, "Surely you will quote this proverb to me: 'Physician, heal yourself! Do here in your hometown what we have heard that you did in Capernaum.'"

"I tell you the truth," he continued, "no prophet is accepted in his hometown. I assure you that there were many widows in Israel in Elijah's time, when the sky was shut for three and a half years and there was a severe famine throughout the land. Yet Elijah was not sent to any of them, but to a widow in Zarephath in the region of Sidon. And there were many in Israel with leprosy in the time of Elisha the prophet, yet not one of them was cleansed—only Naaman the Syrian."

All the people in the synagogue were furious when they heard this. They got up, drove him out of the town, and took him to the brow of the hill on which the town was built, in order to throw him down the cliff. But he walked right through the crowd and went on his way.

Jesus' homecoming nearly sparks a riot when he reveals who he is and who he came to help. Jesus has returned to Galilee, visiting his hometown of Nazareth. In this dramatic scene he identifies himself as the Messiah whom Isaiah has prophesied to all nations. But the people can see only Joseph's son standing before them. His wisdom and authority impress them, yet how could one so familiar—just recently a boy playing in the nearby streets—be the Promised One of God?

Jesus senses their doubt and it comes as no surprise. He knows the similar rejection Elijah and Elisha experienced in Israel. As those prophets turned elsewhere, Jesus proclaims, he too will turn aside and care for Gentiles when his own people reject him. —BQ

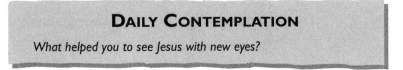

DAILY CONTEMPLATION

What helped you to see Jesus with new eyes?

JESUS CAME FOR ALL PEOPLE

It's hard to peg Jesus' taste in friends. Already it seems clear that he came to reach out to a varied group of people. In one instance he met with the most Jewish of Jews: Nicodemus, a teacher, a Pharisee, and a member of the Sanhedrin (san-HEE-druhn), the Jewish ruling council comprising only seventy members. Jesus also cared for a Samaritan woman and many in her town. He healed outcasts such as a man with an evil spirit and one with leprosy. He called common fishermen and a tax collector—one from a profession considered dishonest by the Jews—to be part of his closest circle.

Jesus came to let all people know of the love of God reaching fulfillment through his presence on earth. He came to tell us that our lives are precious to God, valuable into eternity. Jesus is looking not for a particular appearance or life story but for a heart that recognizes its need for him. Belief in Jesus and salvation through him are all that matter.

When we give our lives to him, Jesus' love for all people will become a part of our own hearts. Mother Teresa, founder of the Missionaries of Charity, spoke often about extending Jesus' love to everyone, beginning with those immediately surrounding us. "When you know how much God is in love with you then you can only live your life radiating that love. I always say that love starts at home: family first, and then your own town or city. It is easy to love people who are far away but it is not always so easy to love those who live with us or right next to us. I do not agree with the big way of doing things—love needs to start with an individual. To get to love a person, you must contact that person, become close. Everyone needs love. All must know that they're wanted and that they are important to God."[31]

Often it seems we decide whom we want to love and then keep ourselves mentally and emotionally detached from others, especially if they seem unattractive or unable to give back to us. But that isn't Jesus' way. He came not just for the rich but for the poor, not just for the Jews but for everyone else, not just for the healthy but for the sick, not just for the "together" but for the outcasts. And he came for ones most undeserving—the egotistical, the self-righteous, the cheaters, the obnoxious, the ones who know all the answers.

When Jesus comes again, he will know his followers by the way they have cared for others. "I tell you the truth, whatever you did for one of the least of these brothers of mine, you did for me" (Matthew 25:40). Mother Teresa reflects that "the least of these" includes "the hungry and the lonely, not only for food but for the Word of God; the thirsty and the ignorant, not only for water but also for knowledge, peace, truth, justice, and love; the naked and the unloved, not only for clothes but also for human dignity; the unwanted, the unborn child; the racially discriminated against; the homeless and abandoned, not only for a shelter made of bricks, but for a heart that understands, that covers, that loves; the sick, the dying destitutes, and the captives, not only in body but also in mind and spirit: all those who have lost all hope

and faith in life, the alcoholics and drug addicts and all those who have lost God
... and who have lost all hope in the power of the Spirit."[32]   —BQ

DAILY CONTEMPLATION

*Who are the people most difficult for you to love? Who are you
afraid to love? Ask God to reveal to you how you can begin to love
these people, and ask him to make Jesus' love for them real in you.*

DAY 223   Luke 5:1–11

THE CALLING OF THE FIRST DISCIPLES

One day as Jesus was standing by the Lake of Gennesaret, with the people
crowding around him and listening to the word of God, he saw at the water's
edge two boats, left there by the fishermen, who were washing their nets.
He got into one of the boats, the one belonging to Simon, and asked him to
put out a little from shore. Then he sat down and taught the people from the
boat.

When he had finished speaking, he said to Simon, "Put out into deep water,
and let down the nets for a catch."

Simon answered, "Master, we've worked hard all night and haven't caught
anything. But because you say so, I will let down the nets."

When they had done so, they caught such a large number of fish that their
nets began to break. So they signaled their partners in the other boat to come
and help them, and they came and filled both boats so full that they began to
sink.

When Simon Peter saw this, he fell at Jesus' knees and said, "Go away from
me, Lord; I am a sinful man!" For he and all his companions were astonished
at the catch of fish they had taken, and so were James and John, the sons of
Zebedee, Simon's partners.

Then Jesus said to Simon, "Don't be afraid; from now on you will catch
men." So they pulled their boats up on shore, left everything and followed
him.

Jesus now begins to assemble an official following. Other gospel passages record Jesus
in contact with Simon Peter and other disciples prior to this call on the shores of
Gennesaret (geh-NES-uh-ret), indicating that these men have been loosely following
Jesus. As he moves into the full swing of his ministry, Jesus demonstrates his authority once more and calls them to leave their fishnets and follow him.

Jesus isn't asking these men simply to tag along after him and marvel at his teaching and miracles. He is calling them to join in relationship with him, be filled with
his Spirit, and carry on his ministry. They become the first believers to be mentored

by God in the person of Christ. Privileged to know Jesus more intimately than anyone during his time on earth, they will go on to lead the early church after Jesus' death. Some will write parts of the New Testament.

Jesus calls believers today to follow him as well. Although we lack his physical presence, he remains present to us through the Bible and through his living Spirit. Still today he asks us to drop our nets into deep water and trust for his provision. As he meets our needs, Jesus calls us to put down the things that preoccupy us and to turn our attention to him. He will use us, as he used the twelve disciples, to catch up men and women in his message of hope and new life. —BQ

DAILY CONTEMPLATION

How is Jesus using you right now as his disciple?

DAY 224 Mark 2:1–28

JESUS MEETS OPPOSITION

A few days later, when Jesus again entered Capernaum, the people heard that he had come home. So many gathered that there was no room left, not even outside the door, and he preached the word to them. Some men came, bringing to him a paralytic, carried by four of them. Since they could not get him to Jesus because of the crowd, they made an opening in the roof above Jesus and, after digging through it, lowered the mat the paralyzed man was lying on. When Jesus saw their faith, he said to the paralytic, "Son, your sins are forgiven."

Now some teachers of the law were sitting there, thinking to themselves, "Why does this fellow talk like that? He's blaspheming! Who can forgive sins but God alone?"

Immediately Jesus knew in his spirit that this was what they were thinking in their hearts, and he said to them, "Why are you thinking these things? Which is easier: to say to the paralytic, 'Your sins are forgiven,' or to say, 'Get up, take your mat and walk'? But that you may know that the Son of Man has authority on earth to forgive sins . . ." He said to the paralytic, "I tell you, get up, take your mat and go home." He got up, took his mat and walked out in full view of them all. This amazed everyone and they praised God, saying, "We have never seen anything like this!"

Once again Jesus went out beside the lake. A large crowd came to him, and he began to teach them. As he walked along, he saw Levi son of Alphaeus sitting at the tax collector's booth. "Follow me," Jesus told him, and Levi got up and followed him.

While Jesus was having dinner at Levi's house, many tax collectors and "sinners" were eating with him and his disciples, for there were many who followed him. When the teachers of the law who were Pharisees saw him eating with the "sinners" and tax collectors, they asked his disciples: "Why does he eat with tax collectors and 'sinners'?"

On hearing this, Jesus said to them, "It is not the healthy who need a doctor, but the sick. I have not come to call the righteous, but sinners."

Now John's disciples and the Pharisees were fasting. Some people came and asked Jesus, "How is it that John's disciples and the disciples of the Pharisees are fasting, but yours are not?"

Jesus answered, "How can the guests of the bridegroom fast while he is with them? They cannot, so long as they have him with them. But the time will come when the bridegroom will be taken from them, and on that day they will fast.

"No one sews a patch of unshrunk cloth on an old garment. If he does, the new piece will pull away from the old, making the tear worse. And no one pours new wine into old wineskins. If he does, the wine will burst the skins, and both the wine and the wineskins will be ruined. No, he pours new wine into new wineskins."

One Sabbath Jesus was going through the grainfields, and as his disciples walked along, they began to pick some heads of grain. The Pharisees said to him, "Look, why are they doing what is unlawful on the Sabbath?"

He answered, "Have you never read what David did when he and his companions were hungry and in need? In the days of Abiathar the high priest, he entered the house of God and ate the consecrated bread, which is lawful only for priests to eat. And he also gave some to his companions."

Then he said to them, "The Sabbath was made for man, not man for the Sabbath. So the Son of Man is Lord even of the Sabbath."

When a new leader starts making waves, opposition surely follows. While on earth, Jesus makes an extravagant claim: he claims to be the Messiah, sent from God. And opposition to him springs up soon after the wild surge of popularity in Galilee. This chapter tells of three different criticisms that people will make against Jesus throughout his life.

He blasphemes. The teachers of the law are scandalized by Jesus' forgiving sins. "Who can forgive sins but God alone?" they mutter. Jesus readily agrees that only God can forgive sins—that is his point, exactly.

Throughout his life, Jesus faces strongest opposition from the most pious followers of Old Testament law; they can never accept that the awesome, distant God of Israel could take up residence inside a human body. Eventually, they have Jesus executed for making that claim. (People who accept Jesus as a "good man and enlightened teacher" today often overlook the scenes where Jesus blatantly identifies himself with God. When the Pharisees react violently to Jesus in his day, it is because they have heard him correctly—they simply refuse to believe him.)

He keeps disreputable company. Jesus shows a distinct preference for the most unseemly sort of people. He offends politicians and religious leaders by calling them names. Even after becoming famous, he dines with an outcast tax collector and his low-life friends. On hearing the gossip about this strange behavior, Jesus says simply,

"It is not the healthy who need a doctor, but the sick. I have not come to call the righteous, but sinners."

He goes against tradition. To the Pharisees, it seems Jesus' disciples are playing fast and loose with the holy Sabbath. Jesus' response: It's time for a new cloth; the old one has been patched together long enough. Before long, he will introduce the "new covenant." God has some major changes in store for the human race, and the narrow, confining covenant with the Israelites simply can't hold all those changes.   —PY

DAILY CONTEMPLATION

What attracts you most to Jesus: that he is frank about who he is, that he spends time with outcasts, or that he goes against tradition in revealing God? What troubles you most?

DAY 225

JESUS TEACHES AND HEALS

Another time he went into the synagogue, and a man with a shriveled hand was there. Some of them were looking for a reason to accuse Jesus, so they watched him closely to see if he would heal him on the Sabbath. Jesus said to the man with the shriveled hand, "Stand up in front of everyone."

Then Jesus asked them, "Which is lawful on the Sabbath: to do good or to do evil, to save life or to kill?" But they remained silent.

He looked around at them in anger and, deeply distressed at their stubborn hearts, said to the man, "Stretch out your hand." He stretched it out, and his hand was completely restored. Then the Pharisees went out and began to plot with the Herodians how they might kill Jesus.

Jesus withdrew with his disciples to the lake, and a large crowd from Galilee followed. When they heard all he was doing, many people came to him from Judea, Jerusalem, Idumea, and the regions across the Jordan and around Tyre and Sidon. Because of the crowd he told his disciples to have a small boat ready for him, to keep the people from crowding him. For he had healed many, so that those with diseases were pushing forward to touch him. Whenever the evil spirits saw him, they fell down before him and cried out, "You are the Son of God." But he gave them strict orders not to tell who he was.

Jesus went up on a mountainside and called to him those he wanted, and they came to him. He appointed twelve—designating them apostles—that they might be with him and that he might send them out to preach and to have authority to drive out demons. These are the twelve he appointed: Simon (to whom he gave the name Peter); James son of Zebedee and his brother John (to them he gave the name Boanerges, which means Sons of Thunder); Andrew,

Philip, Bartholomew, Matthew, Thomas, James son of Alphaeus, Thaddaeus, Simon the Zealot and Judas Iscariot, who betrayed him.

Then Jesus entered a house, and again a crowd gathered, so that he and his disciples were not even able to eat. When his family heard about this, they went to take charge of him, for they said, "He is out of his mind."

And the teachers of the law who came down from Jerusalem said, "He is possessed by Beelzebub! By the prince of demons he is driving out demons."

So Jesus called them and spoke to them in parables: "How can Satan drive out Satan? If a kingdom is divided against itself, that kingdom cannot stand. If a house is divided against itself, that house cannot stand. And if Satan opposes himself and is divided, he cannot stand; his end has come. In fact, no one can enter a strong man's house and carry off his possessions unless he first ties up the strong man. Then he can rob his house. I tell you the truth, all the sins and blasphemies of men will be forgiven them. But whoever blasphemes against the Holy Spirit will never be forgiven; he is guilty of an eternal sin."

He said this because they were saying, "He has an evil spirit."

Then Jesus' mother and brothers arrived. Standing outside, they sent someone in to call him. A crowd was sitting around him, and they told him, "Your mother and brothers are outside looking for you."

"Who are my mother and my brothers?" he asked.

Then he looked at those seated in a circle around him and said, "Here are my mother and my brothers! Whoever does God's will is my brother and sister and mother."

The Gospels record some three dozen miracles performed by Jesus, and he states plainly why he does them: "Believe me when I say that I am in the Father and the Father is in me; or at least believe on the evidence of the miracles themselves" (John 14:11). They serve as convincing proofs that he is the Messiah, the Son of God.

Large crowds flock from far away as word of Jesus' power spreads. Some people come for healing, others just to witness the extraordinary phenomena. Who but a messenger from God could perform such works? Yet Jesus himself has an odd ambivalence toward miracles. He never does "tricks" on demand, like a magician. "A wicked and adulterous generation looks for a miraculous sign," he says to those who seek a display of magic (Matthew 16:4).

Jesus seems not to trust miracles to produce the kind of faith he is interested in. Mark reports that on seven separate occasions he warns a person just healed, "Tell no one!" He is suspicious of the popular acclaim that his miracles stir up, for he has a hard message of obedience and sacrifice, and miracles tend to attract gawkers and sensation seekers.

Mainly, Jesus uses his powers in compassionate response to human needs. Every time someone asks directly, he heals. When his disciples grow frightened on a stormy lake, he walks to them across the water or calms the wind. When his audience gets hungry he feeds them, and when wedding guests grow thirsty he makes wine.

Much like people today, Jesus' contemporaries look for ways to explain away his powers, even when faced with irrefutable evidence. Here, the Pharisees seek to credit the miracles to Satan's power. On another occasion they arrange a formal tribunal, complete with judges and witnesses, to examine a man Jesus has healed. The man's parents confirm his story ("One thing I do know. I was blind but now I see!"), but still the doubters hurl insults and throw him out of court (John 9).

In short, the crowd's mixed responses bear out Jesus' suspicions about the limited value of miracles. They rarely create faith but rather affirm it in true seekers. —PY

DAILY CONTEMPLATION

If you were to ask Jesus for one miracle today, what would it be? Do you have a hard time believing that Jesus has as much compassion for your need as he had for the people he encountered when he was on earth?

DAY 226 Mark 4:1–41

THE PARABLE OF THE SOWER AND OTHER PARABLES; JESUS CALMS THE STORM

Again Jesus began to teach by the lake. The crowd that gathered around him was so large that he got into a boat and sat in it out on the lake, while all the people were along the shore at the water's edge. He taught them many things by parables, and in his teaching said: "Listen! A farmer went out to sow his seed. As he was scattering the seed, some fell along the path, and the birds came and ate it up. Some fell on rocky places, where it did not have much soil. It sprang up quickly, because the soil was shallow. But when the sun came up, the plants were scorched, and they withered because they had no root. Other seed fell among thorns, which grew up and choked the plants, so that they did not bear grain. Still other seed fell on good soil. It came up, grew and produced a crop, multiplying thirty, sixty, or even a hundred times."

Then Jesus said, "He who has ears to hear, let him hear."

When he was alone, the Twelve and the others around him asked him about the parables. He told them, "The secret of the kingdom of God has been given to you. But to those on the outside everything is said in parables so that,

"'they may be ever seeing but never perceiving,
 and ever hearing but never understanding;
otherwise they might turn and be forgiven!'"

Then Jesus said to them, "Don't you understand this parable? How then will you understand any parable? The farmer sows the word. Some people are like seed along the path, where the word is sown. As soon as they hear it, Satan comes and takes away the word that was sown in them. Others, like seed sown on rocky places, hear the word and at once receive it with joy. But since they have no root, they last only a short time. When trouble or persecution comes because of the word, they quickly fall away. Still others, like seed sown among thorns, hear the word; but the worries of this life, the deceitfulness of wealth and the desires for other things come in and choke the word, making it unfruitful. Others, like seed sown on good soil, hear the word, accept it, and produce a crop—thirty, sixty or even a hundred times what was sown."

He said to them, "Do you bring in a lamp to put it under a bowl or a bed? Instead, don't you put it on its stand? For whatever is hidden is meant to be disclosed, and whatever is concealed is meant to be brought out into the open. If anyone has ears to hear, let him hear."

"Consider carefully what you hear," he continued. "With the measure you use, it will be measured to you—and even more. Whoever has will be given more; whoever does not have, even what he has will be taken from him."

He also said, "This is what the kingdom of God is like. A man scatters seed on the ground. Night and day, whether he sleeps or gets up, the seed sprouts and grows, though he does not know how. All by itself the soil produces grain—first the stalk, then the head, then the full kernel in the head. As soon as the grain is ripe, he puts the sickle to it, because the harvest has come."

Again he said, "What shall we say the kingdom of God is like, or what parable shall we use to describe it? It is like a mustard seed, which is the smallest seed you plant in the ground. Yet when planted, it grows and becomes the largest of all garden plants, with such big branches that the birds of the air can perch in its shade."

With many similar parables Jesus spoke the word to them, as much as they could understand. He did not say anything to them without using a parable. But when he was alone with his own disciples, he explained everything.

That day when evening came, he said to his disciples, "Let us go over to the other side." Leaving the crowd behind, they took him along, just as he was, in the boat. There were also other boats with him. A furious squall came up, and the waves broke over the boat, so that it was nearly swamped. Jesus was in the stern, sleeping on a cushion. The disciples woke him and said to him, "Teacher, don't you care if we drown?"

He got up, rebuked the wind and said to the waves, "Quiet! Be still!" Then the wind died down and it was completely calm.

He said to his disciples, "Why are you so afraid? Do you still have no faith?"

They were terrified and asked each other, "Who is this? Even the wind and the waves obey him!"

The story about the sower of seed summarizes well the mixed results Jesus himself gets while on earth. We who live two thousand years later, with such events as Christmas and Easter marked plainly on our calendars, may easily miss the sheer incredulity that greets Jesus in the flesh.

Neighbors have watched him play in the streets with their own children; Jesus is simply too familiar for them to believe he was sent from God. "Isn't this the carpenter?" they ask. "Isn't this Mary's son and the brother of James, Joseph, Judas and Simon? . . . What's this wisdom that has been given him, that he even does miracles!" (Mark 6:3, 2).

Not even Jesus' family can easily reconcile the wondrous and the ordinary. Mark casually mentions that one time Jesus' mother and brothers arrive to take charge of him because they have concluded, "He is out of his mind" (3:21). Neither can common people make up their minds about Jesus. They judge him "raving mad" (John 10:20) one moment, then forcibly try to crown him king the next.

The scribes and Pharisees, who pore over the Prophets, should have the clearest notion of what the Messiah will look like. But no group causes Jesus more trouble. They criticize his theology, his lifestyle, and his choice of friends. When he performs miracles, they attribute his power to Satan and demons.

When a storm nearly capsizes the boat transporting Jesus, he yells into the wind, "Quiet! Be still!" The disciples shrink back in terror. What kind of person can shout down the weather, as if correcting an unruly child? That scene helps convince them Jesus is unlike anyone else on earth. Yet it suggests a reason for their confusion about him. Jesus has, after all, fallen asleep in the boat from sheer fatigue, a symptom of his human frailty.

The early church will argue for three centuries about exactly what happened when God became man, but their creeds will do little to dispel the sense of mystery. In a way, Jesus is just like everyone else—he has a race, an occupation, a family background, a body shape. In a way, he is something entirely new in the history of the universe. In between those two statements lies the mystery that never completely goes away.   —PY

DAILY CONTEMPLATION

In Jesus' story of the sower and the soil, what soil best represents your response to the gospel?

DAY 227   Mark 5:1–42

JESUS HEALS A DEMON-POSSESSED MAN,
A DEAD GIRL, AND A SICK WOMAN

They went across the lake to the region of the Gerasenes. When Jesus got out of the boat, a man with an evil spirit came from the tombs to meet him. This man lived in the tombs, and no one could bind him any more, not even with a chain. For he had often been chained hand and foot, but he tore the

432

chains apart and broke the irons on his feet. No one was strong enough to subdue him. Night and day among the tombs and in the hills he would cry out and cut himself with stones.

When he saw Jesus from a distance, he ran and fell on his knees in front of him. He shouted at the top of his voice, "What do you want with me, Jesus, Son of the Most High God? Swear to God that you won't torture me!" For Jesus had said to him, "Come out of this man, you evil spirit!"

Then Jesus asked him, "What is your name?"

"My name is Legion," he replied, "for we are many." And he begged Jesus again and again not to send them out of the area.

A large herd of pigs was feeding on the nearby hillside. The demons begged Jesus, "Send us among the pigs; allow us to go into them." He gave them permission, and the evil spirits came out and went into the pigs. The herd, about two thousand in number, rushed down the steep bank into the lake and were drowned.

Those tending the pigs ran off and reported this in the town and countryside, and the people went out to see what had happened. When they came to Jesus, they saw the man who had been possessed by the legion of demons, sitting there, dressed and in his right mind; and they were afraid. Those who had seen it told the people what had happened to the demon-possessed man—and told about the pigs as well. Then the people began to plead with Jesus to leave their region.

As Jesus was getting into the boat, the man who had been demon-possessed begged to go with him. Jesus did not let him, but said, "Go home to your family and tell them how much the Lord has done for you, and how he has had mercy on you." So the man went away and began to tell in the Decapolis how much Jesus had done for him. And all the people were amazed.

When Jesus had again crossed over by boat to the other side of the lake, a large crowd gathered around him while he was by the lake. Then one of the synagogue rulers, named Jairus, came there. Seeing Jesus, he fell at his feet and pleaded earnestly with him, "My little daughter is dying. Please come and put your hands on her so that she will be healed and live." So Jesus went with him.

A large crowd followed and pressed around him. And a woman was there who had been subject to bleeding for twelve years. She had suffered a great deal under the care of many doctors and had spent all she had, yet instead of getting better she grew worse. When she heard about Jesus, she came up behind him in the crowd and touched his cloak, because she thought, "If I just touch his clothes, I will be healed." Immediately her bleeding stopped and she felt in her body that she was freed from her suffering.

At once Jesus realized that power had gone out from him. He turned around in the crowd and asked, "Who touched my clothes?"

"You see the people crowding against you," his disciples answered, "and yet you can ask, 'Who touched me?'"

But Jesus kept looking around to see who had done it. Then the woman, knowing what had happened to her, came and fell at his feet and, trembling with fear, told him the whole truth. He said to her, "Daughter, your faith has healed you. Go in peace and be freed from your suffering."

While Jesus was still speaking, some men came from the house of Jairus, the synagogue ruler. "Your daughter is dead," they said. "Why bother the teacher any more?"

Ignoring what they said, Jesus told the synagogue ruler, "Don't be afraid; just believe."

He did not let anyone follow him except Peter, James and John the brother of James. When they came to the home of the synagogue ruler, Jesus saw a commotion, with people crying and wailing loudly. He went in and said to them, "Why all this commotion and wailing? The child is not dead but asleep." But they laughed at him.

After he put them all out, he took the child's father and mother and the disciples who were with him, and went in where the child was. He took her by the hand and said to her, "Talitha koum!" (which means, "Little girl, I say to you, get up!"). Immediately the girl stood up and walked around (she was twelve years old). At this they were completely astonished.

At one point some of the controversy about Jesus even affects John the Baptist, the prophet who more than anyone has raised the people's hopes about a Messiah. It is he who has baptized Jesus and pronounced him the Son of God. But two years later, as he languishes on death row, John the Baptist himself begins to wonder. He sends Jesus a direct question: "Are you the one who was to come, or should we expect someone else?" (Luke 7:20).

This is Jesus' reply: "Go back and report to John what you have seen and heard: The blind receive sight, the lame walk, those who have leprosy are cured, the deaf hear, the dead are raised, and the good news is preached to the poor. Blessed is the man who does not fall away on account of me" (Luke 7:22–23). Clearly, Jesus sees his miracles of healing as important proofs of who he is.

The healings do something else as well: they overturn common notions about how God views sick people. During Jesus' lifetime, Pharisees teach a very strict principle (along the lines of Job's friends' beliefs) that all suffering comes from sin. They judge a deranged or demon-possessed person as permanently cursed by God. They see God's hand of punishment in natural disasters, birth defects, and such long-term conditions as blindness and paralysis. Leprosy victims are unclean, excluded even from worship.

But Jesus contradicts such teaching. This chapter shows him curing a demon-possessed man, touching and healing an "unclean" woman, and resurrecting a child. On other occasions, he directly refutes the doctrine about sin and suffering. He denies that a man's blindness comes from his own or his parents' sin, and he dismisses the common opinion that tragedies happen to those who deserve them (see John 9 and Luke 13).

Jesus does not heal everyone on earth or even in Palestine. But his treatment of the sick and needy shows they are especially loved, not cursed, by God. The healings also provide a "sign" of what will happen in the future, when all diseases, and even death, will be destroyed.   —PY

DAILY CONTEMPLATION

Were you ever made to feel that in an illness or time of suffering you got what you deserved?

DAY 228   Reflection

JESUS DESIRES TO TOUCH AND HEAL

J esus had a big heart. The Gospels are filled with stories of his touch on those who suffered blindness, leprosy, paralysis, bleeding, evil spirits, deafness, and other unspecified illnesses. He healed to confirm to the people his claim that he was God incarnate. But just as importantly, he healed because he had compassion on the ones who suffered.

This picture of the tender, sympathetic Jesus can sometimes, in hurried reading of the Gospels, get lost among his more difficult teaching and his often harsh words to those who feigned real love for God. Jesus' care for the common people may come across on a printed page as less passionate than his indictment of hypocrisy and unbelief, but to many people of his day, Jesus' actions spoke volumes. His love was more real to them than any other characteristic he displayed.

If Jesus was truly the tenderhearted God we see in the Gospels, surely his heart has not changed. Does he desire to touch and heal today as he did then? Author Catherine Marshall asked this question as she lay confined to bed with tuberculosis for more than two years. In taking a close look at the Bible, she began to understand the truth about the Jesus of two thousand years ago and the Jesus of today.

> One of my initial, joyous discoveries about Jesus' will is that having Himself created these awesomely constructed bodies of ours, of *course* He wants us to be well. All over the gospels is Jesus' positive zest for healing the diseased or the handicapped or the blind. In fact, he drew vicious criticism from the religious authorities because He could not wait even 24 hours to heal certain sufferers, thus unabashedly proceeding to break the Jewish Sabbath law, since in Jewish law, healing was "work."

> And Scripture makes it plain that Jesus is "the same yesterday, today, and forever," projecting into the future ages the same power He had while on earth in the flesh, and specifically passing on that power to future disciples who accept His full Lordship....

> Since this very different message from Scripture was living water for my thirsty spirit and needy body, I received it with overwhelming eagerness.[33]

435

Marshall struggled for many more months after this discovery before finally experiencing clear lungs and a return to health. This foundational truth of Jesus' deep compassion sustained her as she searched the Bible and her own heart for the things God would reveal to her during her illness. She later wrote, "Jesus came to earth to show us the Father's will. He who created the incredible human body still heals today, but not as a divine magician. We need to seek His way, His timing, and the lessons He wants us to learn along the way."[34]

Marshall would later learn, in the death of her young husband, the respected pastor Peter Marshall, that Jesus does not always bring physical healing. Yet even then his compassion endures. "Most important of all, He had shown me through more than two years of illness that I would always need Him every day for the rest of my life and more, throughout eternity. . . . Christ is still the greatest Physician to the spirit."[35]

—BQ

DAILY CONTEMPLATION

Are you in need of healing from Jesus right now? Let Jesus reach out and touch you, lovingly assuring you of how much he cares about your need. Let the truth of his deep love for you fill your mind and body. Ask for healing in his time and his way as he continues to teach you about himself.

DAY 229

Matthew 5:1–48

THE BEATITUDES AND THE SERMON ON THE MOUNT

Now when he saw the crowds, he went up on a mountainside and sat down. His disciples came to him, and he began to teach them, saying:

"Blessed are the poor in spirit,
   for theirs is the kingdom of heaven.
Blessed are those who mourn,
   for they will be comforted.
Blessed are the meek,
   for they will inherit the earth.
Blessed are those who hunger and thirst for righteousness,
   for they will be filled.
Blessed are the merciful,
   for they will be shown mercy.
Blessed are the pure in heart,
   for they will see God.
Blessed are the peacemakers,
   for they will be called sons of God.

Blessed are those who are persecuted because of righteousness,
for theirs is the kingdom of heaven.

"Blessed are you when people insult you, persecute you and falsely say all kinds of evil against you because of me. Rejoice and be glad, because great is your reward in heaven, for in the same way they persecuted the prophets who were before you.

"You are the salt of the earth. But if the salt loses its saltiness, how can it be made salty again? It is no longer good for anything, except to be thrown out and trampled by men.

"You are the light of the world. A city on a hill cannot be hidden. Neither do people light a lamp and put it under a bowl. Instead they put it on its stand, and it gives light to everyone in the house. In the same way, let your light shine before men, that they may see your good deeds and praise your Father in heaven.

"Do not think that I have come to abolish the Law or the Prophets; I have not come to abolish them but to fulfill them. I tell you the truth, until heaven and earth disappear, not the smallest letter, not the least stroke of a pen, will by any means disappear from the Law until everything is accomplished. Anyone who breaks one of the least of these commandments and teaches others to do the same will be called least in the kingdom of heaven, but whoever practices and teaches these commands will be called great in the kingdom of heaven. For I tell you that unless your righteousness surpasses that of the Pharisees and the teachers of the law, you will certainly not enter the kingdom of heaven.

"You have heard that it was said to the people long ago, 'Do not murder, and anyone who murders will be subject to judgment.' But I tell you that anyone who is angry with his brother will be subject to judgment. Again, anyone who says to his brother, 'Raca,' is answerable to the Sanhedrin. But anyone who says, 'You fool!' will be in danger of the fire of hell.

"Therefore, if you are offering your gift at the altar and there remember that your brother has something against you, leave your gift there in front of the altar. First go and be reconciled to your brother; then come and offer your gift.

"Settle matters quickly with your adversary who is taking you to court. Do it while you are still with him on the way, or he may hand you over to the judge, and the judge may hand you over to the officer, and you may be thrown into prison. I tell you the truth, you will not get out until you have paid the last penny.

"You have heard that it was said, 'Do not commit adultery.' But I tell you that anyone who looks at a woman lustfully has already committed adultery with her in his heart. If your right eye causes you to sin, gouge it out and throw it away. It is better for you to lose one part of your body than for your whole body to be thrown into hell. And if your right hand causes you to sin, cut it off and throw it away. It is better for you to lose one part of your body than for your whole body to go into hell.

"It has been said, 'Anyone who divorces his wife must give her a certificate of divorce.' But I tell you that anyone who divorces his wife, except for marital unfaithfulness, causes her to become an adulteress, and anyone who marries the divorced woman commits adultery.

"Again, you have heard that it was said to the people long ago, 'Do not break your oath, but keep the oaths you have made to the Lord.' But I tell you, Do not swear at all: either by heaven, for it is God's throne; or by the earth, for it is his footstool; or by Jerusalem, for it is the city of the Great King. And do not swear by your head, for you cannot make even one hair white or black. Simply let your 'Yes' be 'Yes,' and your 'No,' 'No'; anything beyond this comes from the evil one.

"You have heard that it was said, 'Eye for eye, and tooth for tooth.' But I tell you, Do not resist an evil person. If someone strikes you on the right cheek, turn to him the other also. And if someone wants to sue you and take your tunic, let him have your cloak as well. If someone forces you to go one mile, go with him two miles. Give to the one who asks you, and do not turn away from the one who wants to borrow from you.

"You have heard that it was said, 'Love your neighbor and hate your enemy.' But I tell you: Love your enemies and pray for those who persecute you, that you may be sons of your Father in heaven. He causes his sun to rise on the evil and the good, and sends rain on the righteous and the unrighteous. If you love those who love you, what reward will you get? Are not even the tax collectors doing that? And if you greet only your brothers, what are you doing more than others? Do not even pagans do that? Be perfect, therefore, as your heavenly Father is perfect."

If Jesus had avoided one emotionally charged word, *kingdom*, everything might have been different. Whenever he said it, images would dance in the minds of his audience: bright banners, glittering armies, the gold and ivory of Solomon's day, the nation of Israel restored to glory. Jesus often used this word that quickened the pulse of Israel, starting with his very first message, "Repent, for the kingdom of heaven is near" (4:17).

By boldly comparing himself to Solomon, Israel's most powerful king (12:42), Jesus taps into the reservoir of his nation's deepest longings. More, he claims that the promises of the prophets are coming true in him. What is about to happen, he says, is a new thing and will far surpass anything from the past: "For I tell you that many prophets and kings wanted to see what you see but did not see it, and to hear what you hear but did not hear it" (Luke 10:24).

The expectations raised by such statements lead to confusion and, finally, angry rejection. Disappointment displaces the initial excitement over Jesus' miracles when he fails to restore the long-awaited kingdom. For, as it turns out, the word *kingdom* means one thing to the crowd and quite another to Jesus.

Winds of change are blowing through Israel as Jesus speaks. Armed and well-organized, guerrilla fighters called Zealots are spoiling for a fight against oppressive

Rome. But the signal for revolt never comes. To their dismay, it gradually becomes clear that Jesus is not talking about a political or military kingdom.

Jesus indicates that we live in a visible world of families and people and cities and nations, "the kingdom of this world." But he calls for people to commit their lives to an *invisible* kingdom, the "kingdom of heaven," more important and more valuable than anything in the visible world.

Success in the kingdom of heaven involves a great reversal of values, as seen in this major address, the Sermon on the Mount. "Blessed are the poor in spirit," Jesus says, and also those who mourn, and the meek, and those who hunger and thirst, and the persecuted . . . "for theirs is the kingdom of heaven." Status in this world is no guarantee of status in the kingdom of heaven.   —PY

DAILY CONTEMPLATION

Are you more focused on achieving success in the kingdom of this world or in the kingdom of heaven?

DAY 230   Matthew 6:1–34

THE SERMON ON THE MOUNT, CONTINUED

"Be careful not to do your 'acts of righteousness' before men, to be seen by them. If you do, you will have no reward from your Father in heaven.

"So when you give to the needy, do not announce it with trumpets, as the hypocrites do in the synagogues and on the streets, to be honored by men. I tell you the truth, they have received their reward in full. But when you give to the needy, do not let your left hand know what your right hand is doing, so that your giving may be in secret. Then your Father, who sees what is done in secret, will reward you.

"And when you pray, do not be like the hypocrites, for they love to pray standing in the synagogues and on the street corners to be seen by men. I tell you the truth, they have received their reward in full. But when you pray, go into your room, close the door and pray to your Father, who is unseen. Then your Father, who sees what is done in secret, will reward you. And when you pray, do not keep on babbling like pagans, for they think they will be heard because of their many words. Do not be like them, for your Father knows what you need before you ask him.

"This, then, is how you should pray:

"'Our Father in heaven,
hallowed be your name,
your kingdom come,
your will be done

on earth as it is in heaven.
Give us today our daily bread.
Forgive us our debts,
    as we also have forgiven our debtors.
And lead us not into temptation,
but deliver us from the evil one.'

For if you forgive men when they sin against you, your heavenly Father will also forgive you. But if you do not forgive men their sins, your Father will not forgive your sins.

"When you fast, do not look somber as the hypocrites do, for they disfigure their faces to show men they are fasting. I tell you the truth, they have received their reward in full. But when you fast, put oil on your head and wash your face, so that it will not be obvious to men that you are fasting, but only to your Father, who is unseen; and your Father, who sees what is done in secret, will reward you.

"Do not store up for yourselves treasures on earth, where moth and rust destroy, and where thieves break in and steal. But store up for yourselves treasures in heaven, where moth and rust do not destroy, and where thieves do not break in and steal. For where your treasure is, there your heart will be also.

"The eye is the lamp of the body. If your eyes are good, your whole body will be full of light. But if your eyes are bad, your whole body will be full of darkness. If then the light within you is darkness, how great is that darkness!

"No one can serve two masters. Either he will hate the one and love the other, or he will be devoted to the one and despise the other. You cannot serve both God and Money.

"Therefore I tell you, do not worry about your life, what you will eat or drink; or about your body, what you will wear. Is not life more important than food, and the body more important than clothes? Look at the birds of the air; they do not sow or reap or store away in barns, and yet your heavenly Father feeds them. Are you not much more valuable than they? Who of you by worrying can add a single hour to his life?

"And why do you worry about clothes? See how the lilies of the field grow. They do not labor or spin. Yet I tell you that not even Solomon in all his splendor was dressed like one of these. If that is how God clothes the grass of the field, which is here today and tomorrow is thrown into the fire, will he not much more clothe you, O you of little faith? So do not worry, saying, 'What shall we eat?' or 'What shall we drink?' or 'What shall we wear?' For the pagans run after all these things, and your heavenly Father knows that you need them. But seek first his kingdom and his righteousness, and all these things will be given to you as well. Therefore do not worry about tomorrow, for tomorrow will worry about itself. Each day has enough trouble of its own."

Matthew 6, a continuation of the Sermon on the Mount, contains the Lord's Prayer, perhaps the most famous prayer of all. Jesus gives it as a model of prayer, and it captures well the message of the kingdom: "Your kingdom come, your will be done on earth as it is in heaven." Jesus seeks to bring the two worlds together, and the Sermon on the Mount explains how.

At first glance, some of the advice may seem downright foolish: Give to everyone who asks, love your enemies, turn the other cheek, grant interest-free loans, don't worry about clothes or food. Can such idealism ever work in the "real," or visible, world? That is Jesus' point precisely: Break your obsession with safety, security, thriftiness, self-righteousness. Depend instead on the Father, letting him take care of the personal injustices that come your way, trusting him to look after your daily needs. In a nutshell, the message of the kingdom is this: Live for God and not other people.

The message applies to rewards as well. Most of us look to friends and colleagues for our rewards: a slap on the back, a hero medal, applause, a lavish compliment. But according to Jesus, by far the more important rewards await us after death. Therefore, the most significant human acts of all may be carried out in secret, seen by no one but God.

As Jesus explains it, we are accumulating a kind of savings account, "storing up treasures" in heaven rather than on earth—treasures so great that they will pay back any amount of suffering in this life. The Old Testament has dropped a few scant hints about an afterlife, but Jesus speaks plainly about a place where "the righteous will shine like the sun in the kingdom of their Father" (13:43).

In their quest for a kingdom, the Jews of Jesus' day have been looking for signs of God's approval in this life, primarily through prosperity and political power. Beginning with this speech, Jesus changes the focus to the life to come. He discounts success in this visible world. Invest in the future life, he cautions—after all, rust, a thief, or a lowly insect can destroy all else that we accumulate.   —PY

DAILY CONTEMPLATION

Of the people you know, who best puts the principles of the Sermon on the Mount into practice?

DAY 231   Matthew 7:1–29

THE SERMON ON THE MOUNT, CONTINUED

"Do not judge, or you too will be judged. For in the same way you judge others, you will be judged, and with the measure you use, it will be measured to you.

"Why do you look at the speck of sawdust in your brother's eye and pay no attention to the plank in your own eye? How can you say to your brother, 'Let me take the speck out of your eye,' when all the time there is a plank in your own eye? You hypocrite, first take the plank out of your own eye, and then you will see clearly to remove the speck from your brother's eye.

"Do not give dogs what is sacred; do not throw your pearls to pigs. If you do, they may trample them under their feet, and then turn and tear you to pieces.

"Ask and it will be given to you; seek and you will find; knock and the door will be opened to you. For everyone who asks receives; he who seeks finds; and to him who knocks, the door will be opened.

"Which of you, if his son asks for bread, will give him a stone? Or if he asks for a fish, will give him a snake? If you, then, though you are evil, know how to give good gifts to your children, how much more will your Father in heaven give good gifts to those who ask him! So in everything, do to others what you would have them do to you, for this sums up the Law and the Prophets.

"Enter through the narrow gate. For wide is the gate and broad is the road that leads to destruction, and many enter through it. But small is the gate and narrow the road that leads to life, and only a few find it.

"Watch out for false prophets. They come to you in sheep's clothing, but inwardly they are ferocious wolves. By their fruit you will recognize them. Do people pick grapes from thornbushes, or figs from thistles? Likewise every good tree bears good fruit, but a bad tree bears bad fruit. A good tree cannot bear bad fruit, and a bad tree cannot bear good fruit. Every tree that does not bear good fruit is cut down and thrown into the fire. Thus, by their fruit you will recognize them.

"Not everyone who says to me, 'Lord, Lord,' will enter the kingdom of heaven, but only he who does the will of my Father who is in heaven. Many will say to me on that day, 'Lord, Lord, did we not prophesy in your name, and in your name drive out demons and perform many miracles?' Then I will tell them plainly, 'I never knew you. Away from me, you evildoers!'

"Therefore everyone who hears these words of mine and puts them into practice is like a wise man who built his house on the rock. The rain came down, the streams rose, and the winds blew and beat against that house; yet it did not fall, because it had its foundation on the rock. But everyone who hears these words of mine and does not put them into practice is like a foolish man who built his house on sand. The rain came down, the streams rose, and the winds blew and beat against that house, and it fell with a great crash."

When Jesus had finished saying these things, the crowds were amazed at his teaching, because he taught as one who had authority, and not as their teachers of the law.

Painting several more familiar images to illustrate his teaching, Jesus completes his Sermon on the Mount in this passage. At the end lies an illustration that reveals the purpose of the entire sermon. Jesus' followers, those who hear the sermon in person and those who have read it since, will build a life foundation either on the promises of this world or on the promises of God. They will rely on the ways of the world or on the ways of Christ.

Pharisees make up a large portion of Jesus' hillside audience. They are banking on a self-produced righteousness to usher them to heaven. Pleasure seekers also stay to hear Jesus. Living for the satisfactions of the moment, they trust earthly pleasures to build for them an attractive present and future life. Others who listen truly seek God, searching for the way to follow him. They will choose the small gate and narrow road Jesus identifies. He describes these people throughout his sermon. Rather than following the impulsive tendencies of human nature, they will seek to let his radical ways infiltrate their lives.

These God seekers will pay much more attention to their own faults than to others'. Although they will be concerned enough to correct others, they will make sure their own lives are in order first. They will talk to God as to their true Father, comfortable and confident that he delights in hearing their needs. And they will follow only those who show the fruit of God's Spirit in their lives. Mere words or signs will never take the place of a visible relationship with Jesus. On Jesus, the Rock, the people of God will build for themselves a long-standing house, a shelter in the storms of this life and a home forever in the presence of the King. —BQ

DAILY CONTEMPLATION

What can you see in yourself that resembles a Pharisee, a pleasure seeker, and a God seeker?

DAY 232 Reflection

SEEING THROUGH GOD'S EYES

The Sermon on the Mount haunted my adolescence. I would read a book like Charles Sheldon's *In His Steps*, solemnly vow to act "as Jesus would act," and turn to Matthew 5–7 for guidance. What to make of such advice? Should I offer myself to be pummeled by the motorcycle-riding "hoods" in school? Tear out my tongue after speaking a harsh word to my brother?

Now that I am an adult, the crisis of the Sermon on the Mount still has not gone away. Though I have tried at times to dismiss it as rhetorical excess, the more I study Jesus, the more I realize that the statements contained here lie at the heart of his message. If I fail to understand his teaching, I fail to understand him.

To begin, are the Beatitudes true? Gradually I have come to recognize them as important truths. To me, they apply on at least three levels.

Dangled promises. The Beatitudes are not merely Jesus' hollow words of consolation to the unfortunates. For convicts in the Soviet Gulag, and slaves in America, and Christians in Roman cages awaiting their turn with the wild beasts, the promise of reward has been a source of hope. It keeps you alive. It allows you to believe in a just God after all.

The Great Reversal. I have also come to believe that the Beatitudes describe the present as well as the future. They neatly contrast how to succeed in the kingdom of heaven with how to succeed in the kingdom of this world. The Beatitudes express quite plainly that God views the world through a different set of lenses.

Psychological reality. The Beatitudes reveal that what brings us success in the kingdom of heaven also benefits us most in this life here and now. I would rather spend time among the servants of this world than among the stars. The servants clearly emerge as the favored ones, the graced ones. They possess qualities of depth and richness and even joy that I have not found elsewhere. Somehow, as Jesus promises, in the process of losing their lives, they find them.

The Beatitudes represent only the first step toward understanding the Sermon on the Mount. Long after I came to recognize the enduring truth of the Beatitudes, I still brooded over the uncompromising harshness of the rest of Jesus' sermon. "Be perfect, therefore, as your heavenly Father is perfect," Jesus said (Matthew 5:48), his statement tucked almost casually between commands to love enemies and give away money. Be perfect like God? Whatever did he mean?

Ultimately I found a key to understanding the Sermon on the Mount in an unlikely place: the writings of two nineteenth-century Russian novelists, Tolstoy and Dostoevsky.

From Tolstoy I learned a deep respect for God's inflexible, absolute ideal. Tolstoy strove to follow the Sermon on the Mount literally. Sometimes he accomplished great good. His philosophy of nonviolence, lifted directly from the Sermon on the Mount, had an impact that long outlived him, in ideological descendants like Gandhi and Martin Luther King Jr. Yet his intensity soon caused his family to feel like victims of his quest for holiness.

Tolstoy failed to practice what he preached, and he never found peace. Despite his failures, though, Tolstoy's relentless pursuit of authentic faith has made an indelible impression on me. Having grown up with many whom, in my arrogance of youth, I considered frauds, Tolstoy as an author accomplished for me the most difficult of tasks: to make good as believable and appealing as evil.

Fyodor Dostoevsky was the opposite of Tolstoy in every way, but he got one thing right: his novels communicate grace and forgiveness with a Tolstoyan force. He spent ten years in exile poring over the New Testament and emerged with unshakable Christian convictions. In prison he came to believe that only through being loved is a human being capable of love. He went on to write about grace in his novels.

These two authors helped me come to terms with a central paradox of the Christian life. From Tolstoy I learned the need to look inside, to the kingdom of God that is within me. I saw how miserably I had failed the high ideals of the gospel. From Dostoevsky I learned the full extent of grace. Not only the kingdom of God is within me; Christ himself dwells there. There is only one way for us to resolve the tension between the high ideals of the gospel and the grim reality of ourselves: to accept that we will never measure up, but that we do not have to. We are judged by the righteousness of the Christ who lives within, not our own.

Why did Jesus give us the Sermon on the Mount? Not to burden us but to tell us what God is like. He gave us God's ideal to teach us that we should never stop striving yet also to show us that none of us will ever reach that ideal.[36]   —PY

DAILY CONTEMPLATION

In what ways do you struggle in living out God's ideals? Ask forgiveness for the ways in which you fail to live up to those ideals, and thank him for always holding out grace. Ask Jesus to make his life more and more evident in you.

DAY 233   Matthew 11:25–30; Luke 11:1–13

REST FOR THE WEARY; JESUS' TEACHING ON PRAYER

At that time Jesus said, "I praise you, Father, Lord of heaven and earth, because you have hidden these things from the wise and learned, and revealed them to little children. Yes, Father, for this was your good pleasure.

"All things have been committed to me by my Father. No one knows the Son except the Father, and no one knows the Father except the Son and those to whom the Son chooses to reveal him.

"Come to me, all you who are weary and burdened, and I will give you rest. Take my yoke upon you and learn from me, for I am gentle and humble in heart, and you will find rest for your souls. For my yoke is easy and my burden is light." ...

One day Jesus was praying in a certain place. When he finished, one of his disciples said to him, "Lord, teach us to pray, just as John taught his disciples."

He said to them, "When you pray, say:

"'Father,
hallowed be your name,
your kingdom come.
Give us each day our daily bread.
Forgive us our sins,
     for we also forgive everyone who sins against us.
And lead us not into temptation.'"

Then he said to them, "Suppose one of you has a friend, and he goes to him at midnight and says, 'Friend, lend me three loaves of bread, because a friend of mine on a journey has come to me, and I have nothing to set before him.'

"Then the one inside answers, 'Don't bother me. The door is already locked, and my children are with me in bed. I can't get up and give you anything.' I tell you, though he will not get up and give him the bread because he is his friend, yet because of the man's boldness he will get up and give him as much as he needs.

"So I say to you: Ask and it will be given to you; seek and you will find; knock and the door will be opened to you. For everyone who asks receives; he who seeks finds; and to him who knocks, the door will be opened.

"Which of you fathers, if your son asks for a fish, will give him a snake instead? Or if he asks for an egg, will give him a scorpion? If you then, though you are evil, know how to give good gifts to your children, how much more will your Father in heaven give the Holy Spirit to those who ask him!"

Jesus brings a message of love and of the better life his love will bring, holding out hope to people who face struggles daily, people who are weary of the cares of life. He offers what can be found nowhere else: rest for the soul.

Following Jesus isn't meant to be a burden, he reveals with compassion. By coming to him, we can finally find relief from the concerns that weigh on us. He responds in gentleness, with a humble heart. Jesus, almighty God, shows kindness toward those who draw near to him.

In a passage reminiscent of the Sermon on the Mount, Jesus again teaches his followers how to pray, using simple statements and requests. Prayer need not be impressive and eloquent; Jesus teaches rather that it should involve approaching God with a reverent attitude, placing our will alongside his, and asking humbly for God to meet our daily needs, forgive our sins, and keep us from situations wherein we might sin.

Though perfect and holy, Jesus retains a heart humble and compassionate toward us. He teaches us that with this knowledge, we can talk with God the Father in humble confidence, recognizing our weakness and need for him, as children speaking to a loving parent. —BQ

DAILY CONTEMPLATION

When you pray to God, which emotion do you usually feel the most: fear, awkwardness, a sense of distance, comfort, relief, love?

DAY 234   Matthew 13:24–58

PARABLE OF THE WEEDS, MUSTARD SEED, AND OTHERS

Jesus told them another parable: "The kingdom of heaven is like a man who sowed good seed in his field. But while everyone was sleeping, his enemy came and sowed weeds among the wheat, and went away. When the wheat sprouted and formed heads, then the weeds also appeared.

"The owner's servants came to him and said, 'Sir, didn't you sow good seed in your field? Where then did the weeds come from?'

"'An enemy did this,' he replied.

"The servants asked him, 'Do you want us to go and pull them up?'

"'No,' he answered, 'because while you are pulling the weeds, you may root up the wheat with them. Let both grow together until the harvest. At that time I will tell the harvesters: First collect the weeds and tie them in bundles to be burned; then gather the wheat and bring it into my barn.'"

446

He told them another parable: "The kingdom of heaven is like a mustard seed, which a man took and planted in his field. Though it is the smallest of all your seeds, yet when it grows, it is the largest of garden plants and becomes a tree, so that the birds of the air come and perch in its branches."

He told them still another parable: "The kingdom of heaven is like yeast that a woman took and mixed into a large amount of flour until it worked all through the dough."

Jesus spoke all these things to the crowd in parables; he did not say anything to them without using a parable. So was fulfilled what was spoken through the prophet:

"I will open my mouth in parables,
    I will utter things hidden since the creation of the world."

Then he left the crowd and went into the house. His disciples came to him and said, "Explain to us the parable of the weeds in the field."

He answered, "The one who sowed the good seed is the Son of Man. The field is the world, and the good seed stands for the sons of the kingdom. The weeds are the sons of the evil one, and the enemy who sows them is the devil. The harvest is the end of the age, and the harvesters are angels.

"As the weeds are pulled up and burned in the fire, so it will be at the end of the age. The Son of Man will send out his angels, and they will weed out of his kingdom everything that causes sin and all who do evil. They will throw them into the fiery furnace, where there will be weeping and gnashing of teeth. Then the righteous will shine like the sun in the kingdom of their Father. He who has ears, let him hear.

"The kingdom of heaven is like treasure hidden in a field. When a man found it, he hid it again, and then in his joy went and sold all he had and bought that field.

"Again, the kingdom of heaven is like a merchant looking for fine pearls. When he found one of great value, he went away and sold everything he had and bought it.

"Once again, the kingdom of heaven is like a net that was let down into the lake and caught all kinds of fish. When it was full, the fishermen pulled it up on the shore. Then they sat down and collected the good fish in baskets, but threw the bad away. This is how it will be at the end of the age. The angels will come and separate the wicked from the righteous and throw them into the fiery furnace, where there will be weeping and gnashing of teeth.

"Have you understood all these things?" Jesus asked.

"Yes," they replied.

He said to them, "Therefore every teacher of the law who has been instructed about the kingdom of heaven is like the owner of a house who brings out of his storeroom new treasures as well as old."

When Jesus had finished these parables, he moved on from there. Coming to his hometown, he began teaching the people in their synagogue, and they were amazed. "Where did this man get this wisdom and these miraculous powers?" they asked. "Isn't this the carpenter's son? Isn't his mother's name Mary, and aren't his brothers James, Joseph, Simon and Judas? Aren't all his sisters with us? Where then did this man get all these things?" And they took offense at him.

But Jesus said to them, "Only in his hometown and in his own house is a prophet without honor."

And he did not do many miracles there because of their lack of faith.

Writers have long marveled at Jesus' skill in communicating profound truth through parables—short, simple, everyday stories with a moral.

The parables serve Jesus' purposes perfectly. When he first tells the stories in this chapter, he is floating offshore in a boat, shouting to the large crowds that have gathered. Because the stories concern their daily lives—farming, baking bread, hunting buried treasure, fishing—he is able to hold their attention. And yet the parables simultaneously allow Jesus to train his disciples "privately"; later on, he can take the disciples aside and explain the deeper meaning.

As Jesus tells his disciples, parables also help to winnow the audience. Spectators seeking entertainment can go home with a few stories to mull over, but more serious inquirers will need to come back for further interpretation. Parables also help preserve his message: Years later, as people reflect on what Jesus taught, his parables will come to mind in vivid detail.

Matthew 13 collects several of Jesus' stories about the "kingdom of heaven." Although Jesus never concisely defines the term, he gives many clues about the nature of his kingdom. Unlike, say, Greece or China or Spain, it has no geographical boundaries and can't be charted on a map. Its followers live right among their enemies, not separated from them by a moat or a wall. Still Jesus predicts that the kingdom will show remarkable growth even in an evil environment bent on its destruction.

In summary, the kingdom of heaven consists of the rule of God in the world. It comprises people of all races and from all nations who loyally follow God's will on earth. The disciples, accustomed to more traditional images of power and leadership, can't quite grasp Jesus' concept of the kingdom. They keep asking him to explain his parables even as they jockey vainly for status. Not until he dies and then comes back do they comprehend his mission on earth. —PY

DAILY CONTEMPLATION

When do you most feel like wheat among weeds, a follower of Jesus living among forces that seek to smother the gospel?

JOHN THE BAPTIST BEHEADED; JESUS FEEDS FIVE THOUSAND;
JESUS WALKS ON WATER

King Herod heard about this, for Jesus' name had become well known. Some were saying, "John the Baptist has been raised from the dead, and that is why miraculous powers are at work in him."

Others said, "He is Elijah."

And still others claimed, "He is a prophet, like one of the prophets of long ago."

But when Herod heard this, he said, "John, the man I beheaded, has been raised from the dead!"

For Herod himself had given orders to have John arrested, and he had him bound and put in prison. He did this because of Herodias, his brother Philip's wife, whom he had married. For John had been saying to Herod, "It is not lawful for you to have your brother's wife." So Herodias nursed a grudge against John and wanted to kill him. But she was not able to, because Herod feared John and protected him, knowing him to be a righteous and holy man. When Herod heard John, he was greatly puzzled; yet he liked to listen to him.

Finally the opportune time came. On his birthday Herod gave a banquet for his high officials and military commanders and the leading men of Galilee. When the daughter of Herodias came in and danced, she pleased Herod and his dinner guests.

The king said to the girl, "Ask me for anything you want, and I'll give it to you." And he promised her with an oath, "Whatever you ask I will give you, up to half my kingdom."

She went out and said to her mother, "What shall I ask for?"

"The head of John the Baptist," she answered.

At once the girl hurried in to the king with the request: "I want you to give me right now the head of John the Baptist on a platter."

The king was greatly distressed, but because of his oaths and his dinner guests, he did not want to refuse her. So he immediately sent an executioner with orders to bring John's head. The man went, beheaded John in the prison, and brought back his head on a platter. He presented it to the girl, and she gave it to her mother. On hearing of this, John's disciples came and took his body and laid it in a tomb.

The apostles gathered around Jesus and reported to him all they had done and taught. Then, because so many people were coming and going that they did not even have a chance to eat, he said to them, "Come with me by yourselves to a quiet place and get some rest."

So they went away by themselves in a boat to a solitary place. But many who saw them leaving recognized them and ran on foot from all the towns and got there ahead of them. When Jesus landed and saw a large crowd, he had compassion on them, because they were like sheep without a shepherd. So he began teaching them many things.

By this time it was late in the day, so his disciples came to him. "This is a remote place," they said, "and it's already very late. Send the people away so they can go to the surrounding countryside and villages and buy themselves something to eat."

But he answered, "You give them something to eat."

They said to him, "That would take eight months of a man's wages! Are we to go and spend that much on bread and give it to them to eat?"

"How many loaves do you have?" he asked. "Go and see."

When they found out, they said, "Five—and two fish."

Then Jesus directed them to have all the people sit down in groups on the green grass. So they sat down in groups of hundreds and fifties. Taking the five loaves and the two fish and looking up to heaven, he gave thanks and broke the loaves. Then he gave them to his disciples to set before the people. He also divided the two fish among them all. They all ate and were satisfied, and the disciples picked up twelve basketfuls of broken pieces of bread and fish. The number of the men who had eaten was five thousand.

Immediately Jesus made his disciples get into the boat and go on ahead of him to Bethsaida, while he dismissed the crowd. After leaving them, he went up on a mountainside to pray.

When evening came, the boat was in the middle of the lake, and he was alone on land. He saw the disciples straining at the oars, because the wind was against them. About the fourth watch of the night he went out to them, walking on the lake. He was about to pass by them, but when they saw him walking on the lake, they thought he was a ghost. They cried out, because they all saw him and were terrified.

Immediately he spoke to them and said, "Take courage! It is I. Don't be afraid." Then he climbed into the boat with them, and the wind died down. They were completely amazed, for they had not understood about the loaves; their hearts were hardened.

When they had crossed over, they landed at Gennesaret and anchored there. As soon as they got out of the boat, people recognized Jesus. They ran throughout that whole region and carried the sick on mats to wherever they heard he was. And wherever he went—into villages, towns or countryside—they placed the sick in the marketplaces. They begged him to let them touch even the edge of his cloak, and all who touched him were healed.

This chapter brings together scenes that illustrate very different kinds of power in the two kingdoms. Herod, ruler of Galilee, personifies one type. Rich and ruthless, he has legions of Roman soldiers to carry out his every command. He leaves impressive monuments all over Palestine. Mark tells how Herod uses power: he steals his brother's wife, locks up John the Baptist, and then has the prophet beheaded as a party trick. Killing John isn't Herod's preference, but he feels the need to honor a careless vow in order to protect his image.

Jesus too is a leader—a king, in fact—but one who breaks stereotypes. Though possessing undeniable power, he uses that power compassionately, to feed the hungry and heal the sick. At the beginning of his ministry, Jesus declined a tempting offer of glory and territory, and after that he seems to give no thought to cultivating an image of power or importance. He spends his time telling stories, not raising an army. He seeks to please God, not to satisfy people's false expectations.

Herod has built a lavish palace in Jesus' home province of Galilee, but Jesus carefully avoids that fashionable area. As Herod wines and dines prominent guests in the resort town of Tiberias, Jesus roams the countryside with his ragtag followers. He too serves a banquet, of sorts, to five thousand unexpected guests. His simple message of love, forgiveness, and healing has its own kind of power. Mark tells of crowds chasing Jesus around a lake, running to fetch their sick friends, pressing in close to touch the Teacher.

Jesus contemptuously dismisses Herod as "that fox." But as talk about Jesus spreads, Herod longs for a chance to meet him. Eventually he'll get his chance, at Jesus' trial. Eager to see a miracle, Herod uses charm, ridicule, and military force to try to coax some response from Jesus. He fails—Jesus never succumbs to that kind of power.   —PY

DAILY CONTEMPLATION

To which kind of power are most people attracted? To which kind are you attracted?

DAY 236   Luke 16:1–31

THE PARABLE OF THE SHREWD MANAGER;
THE RICH MAN AND LAZARUS

Jesus told his disciples: "There was a rich man whose manager was accused of wasting his possessions. So he called him in and asked him, 'What is this I hear about you? Give an account of your management, because you cannot be manager any longer.'

"The manager said to himself, 'What shall I do now? My master is taking away my job. I'm not strong enough to dig, and I'm ashamed to beg—I know what I'll do so that, when I lose my job here, people will welcome me into their houses.'

"So he called in each one of his master's debtors. He asked the first, 'How much do you owe my master?'

"'Eight hundred gallons of olive oil,' he replied.

"The manager told him, 'Take your bill, sit down quickly, and make it four hundred.'

"Then he asked the second, 'And how much do you owe?'"

"'A thousand bushels of wheat,' he replied.

"He told him, 'Take your bill and make it eight hundred.'

"The master commended the dishonest manager because he had acted shrewdly. For the people of this world are more shrewd in dealing with their own kind than are the people of the light. I tell you, use worldly wealth to gain friends for yourselves, so that when it is gone, you will be welcomed into eternal dwellings.

"Whoever can be trusted with very little can also be trusted with much, and whoever is dishonest with very little will also be dishonest with much. So if you have not been trustworthy in handling worldly wealth, who will trust you with true riches? And if you have not been trustworthy with someone else's property, who will give you property of your own?

"No servant can serve two masters. Either he will hate the one and love the other, or he will be devoted to the one and despise the other. You cannot serve both God and Money."

The Pharisees, who loved money, heard all this and were sneering at Jesus. He said to them, "You are the ones who justify yourselves in the eyes of men, but God knows your hearts. What is highly valued among men is detestable in God's sight.

"The Law and the Prophets were proclaimed until John. Since that time, the good news of the kingdom of God is being preached, and everyone is forcing his way into it. It is easier for heaven and earth to disappear than for the least stroke of a pen to drop out of the Law.

"Anyone who divorces his wife and marries another woman commits adultery, and the man who marries a divorced woman commits adultery.

"There was a rich man who was dressed in purple and fine linen and lived in luxury every day. At his gate was laid a beggar named Lazarus, covered with sores and longing to eat what fell from the rich man's table. Even the dogs came and licked his sores.

"The time came when the beggar died and the angels carried him to Abraham's side. The rich man also died and was buried. In hell, where he was in torment, he looked up and saw Abraham far away, with Lazarus by his side. So he called to him, 'Father Abraham, have pity on me and send Lazarus to dip the tip of his finger in water and cool my tongue, because I am in agony in this fire.'

"But Abraham replied, 'Son, remember that in your lifetime you received your good things, while Lazarus received bad things, but now he is comforted here and you are in agony. And besides all this, between us and you a great chasm has been fixed, so that those who want to go from here to you cannot, nor can anyone cross over from there to us.'

"He answered, 'Then I beg you, father, send Lazarus to my father's house, for I have five brothers. Let him warn them, so that they will not also come to this place of torment.'

"Abraham replied, 'They have Moses and the Prophets; let them listen to them.'

"'No, father Abraham,' he said, 'but if someone from the dead goes to them, they will repent.'

"He said to him, 'If they do not listen to Moses and the Prophets, they will not be convinced even if someone rises from the dead.'"

A story is told about Rabbi Joseph Schneerson, a Hasidic leader during the early days of Russian communism. The rabbi spent much time in jail, persecuted for his faith. One morning in 1927, as he prayed in a Leningrad synagogue, secret police rushed in and arrested him. They took him to a police station and worked him over, demanding that he give up his religious activities. He refused. The interrogator brandished a gun in his face and said, "This little toy has made many a man change his mind." Rabbi Schneerson answered, "This little toy can intimidate only that kind of man who has many gods and but one world. Because I have only one God and two worlds, I am not impressed by this little toy."

The theme of "two worlds," or two kingdoms, emerges often in Jesus' teaching, and two stories in this chapter draw a sharp distinction between the two worlds. "What is highly valued among men is detestable in God's sight," Jesus says, commenting on the first story. The second story, of the rich man and Lazarus (LAZ-uh-ruhs), elaborates on that difference in values between the two worlds. The rich man prospers in this world yet neglects to make any provision for eternal life and thus suffers the consequences. Meanwhile a half-starved beggar, who by any standard would be judged a failure in this life, receives an eternal reward.

Jesus tells such stories to a Jewish audience with a tradition of wealthy patriarchs, strong kings, and victorious heroes. But Jesus keeps emphasizing his stunning reversal of values. People who have little value in this world (the poor, the persecuted—people like Lazarus) may in fact have great stature in God's kingdom. Consistently he presents the visible world as a place to invest for the future, to store up treasure for the life to come.

In a question that brings the two worlds starkly together, Jesus asks, "What good will it be for a man if he gains the whole world, yet forfeits his soul?" (Matthew 16:26).   —PY

DAILY CONTEMPLATION

How would you rate yourself, using the standards of success and failure in this world? What if you used Jesus' standards?

THE PARABLE OF THE RICH FOOL;

TEACHINGS ON WORRY AND WATCHFULNESS

Someone in the crowd said to him, "Teacher, tell my brother to divide the inheritance with me."

Jesus replied, "Man, who appointed me a judge or an arbiter between you?" Then he said to them, "Watch out! Be on your guard against all kinds of greed; a man's life does not consist in the abundance of his possessions."

And he told them this parable: "The ground of a certain rich man produced a good crop. He thought to himself, 'What shall I do? I have no place to store my crops.'

"Then he said, 'This is what I'll do. I will tear down my barns and build bigger ones, and there I will store all my grain and my goods. And I'll say to myself, "You have plenty of good things laid up for many years. Take life easy; eat, drink and be merry."'

"But God said to him, 'You fool! This very night your life will be demanded from you. Then who will get what you have prepared for yourself?'

"This is how it will be with anyone who stores up things for himself but is not rich toward God."

Then Jesus said to his disciples: "Therefore I tell you, do not worry about your life, what you will eat; or about your body, what you will wear. Life is more than food, and the body more than clothes. Consider the ravens: They do not sow or reap, they have no storeroom or barn; yet God feeds them. And how much more valuable you are than birds! Who of you by worrying can add a single hour to his life? Since you cannot do this very little thing, why do you worry about the rest?

"Consider how the lilies grow. They do not labor or spin. Yet I tell you, not even Solomon in all his splendor was dressed like one of these. If that is how God clothes the grass of the field, which is here today, and tomorrow is thrown into the fire, how much more will he clothe you, O you of little faith! And do not set your heart on what you will eat or drink; do not worry about it. For the pagan world runs after all such things, and your Father knows that you need them. But seek his kingdom, and these things will be given to you as well.

"Do not be afraid, little flock, for your Father has been pleased to give you the kingdom. Sell your possessions and give to the poor. Provide purses for yourselves that will not wear out, a treasure in heaven that will not be exhausted, where no thief comes near and no moth destroys. For where your treasure is, there your heart will be also.

"Be dressed ready for service and keep your lamps burning, like men waiting for their master to return from a wedding banquet, so that when he comes and knocks they can immediately open the door for him. It will be good for those servants whose master finds them watching when he comes. I tell you the truth, he will dress himself to serve, will have them recline at the table and will come and wait on them. It will be good for those servants whose master finds them ready, even if he comes in the second or third watch of the night. But understand this: If the owner of the house had known at what hour the thief was coming, he would not have let his house be broken into. You also must be ready, because the Son of Man will come at an hour when you do not expect him."

Peter asked, "Lord, are you telling this parable to us, or to everyone?"

The Lord answered, "Who then is the faithful and wise manager, whom the master puts in charge of his servants to give them their food allowance at the proper time? It will be good for that servant whom the master finds doing so when he returns. I tell you the truth, he will put him in charge of all his possessions. But suppose the servant says to himself, 'My master is taking a long time in coming,' and he then begins to beat the menservants and maidservants and to eat and drink and get drunk. The master of that servant will come on a day when he does not expect him and at an hour he is not aware of. He will cut him to pieces and assign him a place with the unbelievers.

"That servant who knows his master's will and does not get ready or does not do what his master wants will be beaten with many blows. But the one who does not know and does things deserving punishment will be beaten with few blows. From everyone who has been given much, much will be demanded; and from the one who has been entrusted with much, much more will be asked."

Jesus has more to say on money than almost any other topic. Yet two thousand years later Christians have trouble agreeing on exactly what he *does* say. One reason is that he rarely gives "practical" advice. He avoids comment on specific economic systems and, as in this chapter, refuses to get involved in personal disputes about finances. Jesus sees money primarily as a *spiritual* force.

One pastor boils down money issues into three questions:

1. How did you get it? (Did it involve injustice, cheating, oppression of the poor?)
2. What are you doing with it? (Are you hoarding it? Exploiting others? Wasting it on needless luxuries?)
3. What is it doing to you?

Although Jesus speaks to all three of these issues, he concentrates on the last one. As he explains it, money operates much like idolatry. It can catch hold and dominate a person's life, diverting attention away from God. Jesus challenges people to break free of money's power—even if it means giving it all away.

This chapter offers a good summary of Jesus' attitude toward money. He does not condemn all possessions (" . . . your Father knows that you need [food, drink, and clothes]"). But he strongly warns against putting faith in money to secure the future.

As his story of the rich man shows, money will ultimately fail to solve life's biggest problems.

Jesus urges his listeners to seek treasure in the kingdom of God, for such treasure can benefit them in this life and the next one too. "Do not worry," he says. Rather, trust God to provide your basic needs. To emphasize his point, he brings up the example of King Solomon, the richest man in the Old Testament. To most nationalistic Jews, Solomon is a hero, but Jesus sees him in a different light: Solomon's wealth has long since vanished—and even in his prime he was no more impressive than a common wildflower. Better to trust in the God who lavishes care on the whole earth than to spend your life worrying about money and possessions. —PY

DAILY CONTEMPLATION

How do you fit together Jesus' teaching and our culture's emphasis on financial security for the future?

DAY 238   Reflection

GOD'S LOVING NATURE

A saying goes, "The clothes make the man," and another, "Dress for success." They are among the prescriptions given for making it in the world. Jesus offered another plan. "Do not worry about your life, what you will eat; or about your body, what you will wear. Life is more than food, and the body more than clothes," he said (Luke 12:23), going on to illustrate that nothing we can do for ourselves compares with what God can do for us. Worries are needless if only we will see how God cares for the details of our lives.

Take nature, for instance. According to Jesus, no garment of clothing could match the splendor of a wildflower. Nothing made with human hands can match the beauty God lavishes on the natural world. Nature itself is a message from God, his proclamation of love and care for all he created.

A man named John Muir agreed. Living a century ago, Muir spent most of his life so enamored with nature's beauty that he virtually made his home in the wilds, roaming frequently both summer and winter without even a backpack through parts of Canada, the South, and the western United States. Journals preserve the sentiments of this man who in his lifetime helped save the Grand Canyon and other wilderness areas. Muir's writings speak often of, among other loves, his enchantment with wildflowers: "The radiant, honeyful corollas, touching and overlapping, and rising above one another glowed in the living light like a sunset sky—one sheet of purple and gold, with the bright Sacramento [River] pouring through the midst of it from the north. . . ."[37]

The study of botany deepened Muir's awe for God's creation. "Like everybody else I was always fond of flowers, attracted by their external beauty and purity. Now my eyes were opened to their inner beauty, all alike revealing glorious traces of the thoughts of.God, and leading on and on into the infinite cosmos."[38]

While his skills as an inventor could have made him a millionaire, Muir chose instead to enjoy the land's wealth, spending countless hours and days traveling afoot and observing. "I have not yet in all my wanderings found a single person so free as myself," he mused. "When in the woods I sit at times for hours watching birds or squirrels or looking down into the faces of flowers without suffering any feeling of haste."[39]

A black-and-white photograph of Muir captures him seated on a rock outcropping gazing into the reflections falling across a mountain lake. The picture mirrors God's intense and present love for a creation that day after day, moment by moment, receives care and attention, God's uninterrupted gaze. "How much more valuable you are than birds!" Jesus cries. "How much more will he clothe you!" If God's Spirit roams the world with such devotion and delight, caring more than anything else for the people of his creation, should we doubt that he will meet our needs? Should we fear not "making it"?   —BQ

DAILY CONTEMPLATION

What are your worries today? Imagine God gazing on your life with affection and deep love, seeing also the ripples of anxiety disturbing your spirit. Ask him to calm your fears. Ask for his help in trusting, letting go of worry and instead enjoying the attention and care he lavishes on you.

DAY 239   Luke 18:1–30

JESUS TEACHES AND HEALS, AND
WELCOMES THE CHILDREN

Then Jesus told his disciples a parable to show them that they should always pray and not give up. He said: "In a certain town there was a judge who neither feared God nor cared about men. And there was a widow in that town who kept coming to him with the plea, 'Grant me justice against my adversary.'

"For some time he refused. But finally he said to himself, 'Even though I don't fear God or care about men, yet because this widow keeps bothering me, I will see that she gets justice, so that she won't eventually wear me out with her coming!'"

And the Lord said, "Listen to what the unjust judge says. And will not God bring about justice for his chosen ones, who cry out to him day and night? Will he keep putting them off? I tell you, he will see that they get justice, and quickly. However, when the Son of Man comes, will he find faith on the earth?"

To some who were confident of their own righteousness and looked down on everybody else, Jesus told this parable: "Two men went up to the temple to pray, one a Pharisee and the other a tax collector. The Pharisee stood up and prayed about himself: 'God, I thank you that I am not like other men—robbers, evildoers, adulterers—or even like this tax collector. I fast twice a week and give a tenth of all I get.'

"But the tax collector stood at a distance. He would not even look up to heaven, but beat his breast and said, 'God, have mercy on me, a sinner.'

"I tell you that this man, rather than the other, went home justified before God. For everyone who exalts himself will be humbled, and he who humbles himself will be exalted."

People were also bringing babies to Jesus to have him touch them. When the disciples saw this, they rebuked them. But Jesus called the children to him and said, "Let the little children come to me, and do not hinder them, for the kingdom of God belongs to such as these. I tell you the truth, anyone who will not receive the kingdom of God like a little child will never enter it."

A certain ruler asked him, "Good teacher, what must I do to inherit eternal life?"

"Why do you call me good?" Jesus answered. "No one is good—except God alone. You know the commandments: 'Do not commit adultery, do not murder, do not steal, do not give false testimony, honor your father and mother.'"

"All these I have kept since I was a boy," he said.

When Jesus heard this, he said to him, "You still lack one thing. Sell everything you have and give to the poor, and you will have treasure in heaven. Then come, follow me."

When he heard this, he became very sad, because he was a man of great wealth. Jesus looked at him and said, "How hard it is for the rich to enter the kingdom of God! Indeed, it is easier for a camel to go through the eye of a needle than for a rich man to enter the kingdom of God."

Those who heard this asked, "Who then can be saved?"

Jesus replied, "What is impossible with men is possible with God."

Peter said to him, "We have left all we had to follow you!"

"I tell you the truth," Jesus said to them, "no one who has left home or wife or brothers or parents or children for the sake of the kingdom of God will fail to receive many times as much in this age and, in the age to come, eternal life."

A series of vignettes in this chapter reinforces the message about money and about two worlds. In Luke's typical style, the stories feature underdogs: a mistreated widow, a despised tax collector, little children, a blind beggar (vv. 35–43). A rich man makes an appearance, but, like the rich man in the story of Lazarus, only as a negative example.

Even Jesus' closest disciples have trouble swallowing his teaching that money represents a grave danger. Yet Jesus sternly warns that wealth can keep people from the kingdom of God by tempting them to depend on themselves rather than on God.

The story of the Pharisee and the tax collector expands that message. Not only wealth but *any* form of pride or self-dependence tends to lead away from God.

An effort to become "holy," for example, may accomplish just the opposite if it produces spiritual pride and a feeling of superiority. Human beings have an incurable tendency to feed their own egos, to take credit, to compete. The way to God, said Jesus, is just the opposite: trust God like a little child, admit wrong, let go.

Jesus reveals the key to true success in the very first story in this collection, a parable to illustrate why we "should always pray and not give up." The persistent widow endures much frustration and apparent injustice before the judge finally grants her request. Similarly, Jesus implies, we may go through desert periods when it looks as if God is ignoring our heartfelt requests. But in the end God himself will settle accounts. And all those whose faith holds firm, even in the hard times, will see justice.   —PY

DAILY CONTEMPLATION

In what area of your life do you most tend to want to feed your ego and compete? How have you seen this tendency lead you away from God?

DAY 240   John 5:1–47

THE HEALING AT THE POOL; LIFE THROUGH THE SON

Some time later, Jesus went up to Jerusalem for a feast of the Jews. Now there is in Jerusalem near the Sheep Gate a pool, which in Aramaic is called Bethesda and which is surrounded by five covered colonnades. Here a great number of disabled people used to lie—the blind, the lame, the paralyzed. One who was there had been an invalid for thirty-eight years. When Jesus saw him lying there and learned that he had been in this condition for a long time, he asked him, "Do you want to get well?"

"Sir," the invalid replied, "I have no one to help me into the pool when the water is stirred. While I am trying to get in, someone else goes down ahead of me."

Then Jesus said to him, "Get up! Pick up your mat and walk." At once the man was cured; he picked up his mat and walked.

The day on which this took place was a Sabbath, and so the Jews said to the man who had been healed, "It is the Sabbath; the law forbids you to carry your mat."

But he replied, "The man who made me well said to me, 'Pick up your mat and walk.'"

So they asked him, "Who is this fellow who told you to pick it up and walk?"

The man who was healed had no idea who it was, for Jesus had slipped away into the crowd that was there.

Later Jesus found him at the temple and said to him, "See, you are well again. Stop sinning or something worse may happen to you." The man went away and told the Jews that it was Jesus who had made him well.

So, because Jesus was doing these things on the Sabbath, the Jews persecuted him. Jesus said to them, "My Father is always at his work to this very day, and I, too, am working." For this reason the Jews tried all the harder to kill him; not only was he breaking the Sabbath, but he was even calling God his own Father, making himself equal with God.

Jesus gave them this answer: "I tell you the truth, the Son can do nothing by himself; he can do only what he sees his Father doing, because whatever the Father does the Son also does. For the Father loves the Son and shows him all he does. Yes, to your amazement he will show him even greater things than these. For just as the Father raises the dead and gives them life, even so the Son gives life to whom he is pleased to give it. Moreover, the Father judges no one, but has entrusted all judgment to the Son, that all may honor the Son just as they honor the Father. He who does not honor the Son does not honor the Father, who sent him.

"I tell you the truth, whoever hears my word and believes him who sent me has eternal life and will not be condemned; he has crossed over from death to life. I tell you the truth, a time is coming and has now come when the dead will hear the voice of the Son of God and those who hear will live. For as the Father has life in himself, so he has granted the Son to have life in himself. And he has given him authority to judge because he is the Son of Man.

"Do not be amazed at this, for a time is coming when all who are in their graves will hear his voice and come out—those who have done good will rise to live, and those who have done evil will rise to be condemned. By myself I can do nothing; I judge only as I hear, and my judgment is just, for I seek not to please myself but him who sent me.

"If I testify about myself, my testimony is not valid. There is another who testifies in my favor, and I know that his testimony about me is valid.

"You have sent to John and he has testified to the truth. Not that I accept human testimony; but I mention it that you may be saved. John was a lamp that burned and gave light, and you chose for a time to enjoy his light.

"I have testimony weightier than that of John. For the very work that the Father has given me to finish, and which I am doing, testifies that the Father has sent me. And the Father who sent me has himself testified concerning me. You have never heard his voice nor seen his form, nor does his word dwell in you, for you do not believe the one he sent. You diligently study the Scriptures because you think that by them you possess eternal life. These are the Scriptures that testify about me, yet you refuse to come to me to have life.

"I do not accept praise from men, but I know you. I know that you do not have the love of God in your hearts. I have come in my Father's name, and you do not accept me; but if someone else comes in his own name, you will accept him. How can you believe if you accept praise from one another, yet make no effort to obtain the praise that comes from the only God?

"But do not think I will accuse you before the Father. Your accuser is Moses, on whom your hopes are set. If you believed Moses, you would believe me, for he wrote about me. But since you do not believe what he wrote, how are you going to believe what I say?"

According to tradition of Jesus' day, invalids who lay near the Pool of Bethesda would be healed if they made it first into the pool when an angel came and stirred the waters. This superstition was not from God, who would never create such a contest for those suffering illness. Yet despite the misguided beliefs of the invalids, Jesus feels compassion for them and chooses to heal one.

After making the crippled man walk, Jesus lets him know that life can get much worse than suffering as an invalid. The man's eternal life is in question. If he doesn't turn to God, he will experience permanent suffering in eternity.

Facing opposition once more to his work of healing on the Sabbath, Jesus explains to his detractors who he is and how God has made himself known before their eyes. He opens the door for any who will listen and soften their hearts to the truth he preaches. Those who hear and believe will have eternal life, he explains. They will pass, like invalids suddenly healed, from death to life.   —BQ

DAILY CONTEMPLATION

What did it take to make you hear and believe Jesus as your Savior?

DAY 241   Matthew 20:1–16

THE PARABLE OF THE WORKERS IN THE VINEYARD

"The kingdom of heaven is like a landowner who went out early in the morning to hire men to work in his vineyard. He agreed to pay them a denarius for the day and sent them into his vineyard.

"About the third hour he went out and saw others standing in the marketplace doing nothing. He told them, 'You also go and work in my vineyard, and I will pay you whatever is right.' So they went.

"He went out again about the sixth hour and the ninth hour and did the same thing. About the eleventh hour he went out and found still others standing around. He asked them, 'Why have you been standing here all day long doing nothing?'

"'Because no one has hired us,' they answered.

"He said to them, 'You also go and work in my vineyard.'

"When evening came, the owner of the vineyard said to his foreman, 'Call the workers and pay them their wages, beginning with the last ones hired and going on to the first.'

"The workers who were hired about the eleventh hour came and each received a denarius. So when those came who were hired first, they expected to receive more. But each one of them also received a denarius. When they received it, they began to grumble against the landowner. 'These men who were hired last worked only one hour,' they said, 'and you have made them equal to us who have borne the burden of the work and the heat of the day.'

"But he answered one of them, 'Friend, I am not being unfair to you. Didn't you agree to work for a denarius? Take your pay and go. I want to give the man who was hired last the same as I gave you. Don't I have the right to do what I want with my own money? Or are you envious because I am generous?'

"So the last will be first, and the first will be last."

In this parable Jesus teaches about an issue close to the heart of every person: fairness. By nature we expect reward proportionate to what we have earned. We'll accept more, of course, but if given less we will usually balk or protest. Although life can throw curves that ignore completely the rules of fairness, we expect that when dealing with rational beings, especially God, fairness should prevail.

God has his own definition of what is fair, Jesus teaches. His generosity may take us by surprise. God is sovereign, so nothing can happen that is beyond his control and will. Above all, God is good—his mind and will are perfect and right at all times, in all things—so we can trust his choices.

Although our deepest selves cling to the longing for a fair and predictable faith, we can do no better than to continually lay this desire down in the hands of a God whose actions are more gracious toward us than we could ever deserve.   —BQ

DAILY CONTEMPLATION

When was the last time you questioned God about an unfairness you experienced?

DAY 242   Matthew 25:1–30

THE PARABLE OF THE TEN VIRGINS AND THE
PARABLE OF THE TALENTS

"At that time the kingdom of heaven will be like ten virgins who took their lamps and went out to meet the bridegroom. Five of them were foolish and five were wise. The foolish ones took their lamps but did not take any oil with them. The wise, however, took oil in jars along with their lamps. The bridegroom was a long time in coming, and they all became drowsy and fell asleep.

"At midnight the cry rang out: 'Here's the bridegroom! Come out to meet him!'

"Then all the virgins woke up and trimmed their lamps. The foolish ones said to the wise, 'Give us some of your oil; our lamps are going out.'

"'No,' they replied, 'there may not be enough for both us and you. Instead, go to those who sell oil and buy some for yourselves.'

"But while they were on their way to buy the oil, the bridegroom arrived. The virgins who were ready went in with him to the wedding banquet. And the door was shut.

"Later the others also came. 'Sir! Sir!' they said. 'Open the door for us!'

"But he replied, 'I tell you the truth, I don't know you.'

"Therefore keep watch, because you do not know the day or the hour.

"Again, it will be like a man going on a journey, who called his servants and entrusted his property to them. To one he gave five talents of money, to another two talents, and to another one talent, each according to his ability. Then he went on his journey. The man who had received the five talents went at once and put his money to work and gained five more. So also, the one with the two talents gained two more. But the man who had received the one talent went off, dug a hole in the ground and hid his master's money.

"After a long time the master of those servants returned and settled accounts with them. The man who had received the five talents brought the other five. 'Master,' he said, 'you entrusted me with five talents. See, I have gained five more.'

"His master replied, 'Well done, good and faithful servant! You have been faithful with a few things; I will put you in charge of many things. Come and share your master's happiness!'

"The man with the two talents also came. 'Master,' he said, 'you entrusted me with two talents; see, I have gained two more.'

"His master replied, 'Well done, good and faithful servant! You have been faithful with a few things; I will put you in charge of many things. Come and share your master's happiness!'

"Then the man who had received the one talent came. 'Master,' he said, 'I knew that you are a hard man, harvesting where you have not sown and gathering where you have not scattered seed. So I was afraid and went out and hid your talent in the ground. See, here is what belongs to you.'

"His master replied, 'You wicked, lazy servant! So you knew that I harvest where I have not sown and gather where I have not scattered seed? Well then, you should have put my money on deposit with the bankers, so that when I returned I would have received it back with interest.

"'Take the talent from him and give it to the one who has the ten talents. For everyone who has will be given more, and he will have an abundance. Whoever does not have, even what he has will be taken from him. And throw that worthless servant outside, into the darkness, where there will be weeping and gnashing of teeth.'"

A parable of a simple wedding carries with it a serious message. Some Bible scholars believe that the parable of the ten virgins speaks specifically about the Jewish people during the time of trials just before Jesus' second coming. They will know of Christ's imminent return, but only some will choose to enter relationship with him while there is still time.

Whether this parable speaks to the Jews or to all people, it stands as an awesome reminder that a day will come for all when Jesus calls believers to eternity with him and releases unbelievers to hell. Some like to believe they have ample time to get their spiritual lives in order, but they risk being caught off guard and as a result, like the virgins, will remain in darkness when Jesus comes for those who have the Light.

In a similar vein, the parable of the talents teaches believers that God holds us responsible for the work he has given us to do until Jesus' return. The kingdom of God is real, Jesus stresses. Those who don't take seriously the impact their lives now have for eternity will face lasting regret.   —BQ

DAILY CONTEMPLATION

What is the work of preparation or kingdom building that God has given you to do?

DAY 243   Reflection

LIVING WITH MYSTERY

Sometimes Jesus seemed to speak a little above our heads, making it difficult to interpret his parables and teaching. Yet he also told us to be like little children, whom he extolled above all other people. "The kingdom of God belongs to such as these. I tell you the truth, anyone who will not receive the kingdom of God like a little child will never enter it" (Luke 18:16–17). How can those who think like children ever hope to understand such a Teacher?

For a clue, think of the delight and intrigue children show toward mystery. Whether marveling at a magic show or watching a butterfly emerge from a caterpillar's cocoon, fascination marks a child's world. Rather than demanding complete understanding in life, they are thrilled with glimpses of truth that leave broad places for unexplained yet fascinating possibility. Children aren't dumb. They have an uncanny sense for truth and falsehood. Yet they happily let many of the details remain in the haze that casts a rosy glow to their world.

Dr. Ravi Zacharias, an Indian-born speaker, apologist, and author, explains that for many of us, our too-adult approach to life has robbed us of a belief in truths that can only be approached by a mind large enough—or childlike enough—for mystery. "We pursue [the] quest for knowledge to a degree that demands the removal of all mystery, even from life's most sublime intimations. We want no part of a God who denies us the slightest bit of information on any matter to which we feel we are entitled."[40]

Although we may seek understanding for good reason, he explains, taking our need for understanding too far can prove self-centered and blasphemous. "In leaving the bounteous world of our childhood, we have not merely walked out of fairyland; we have brazenly wandered into a barren desert bereft of wonder and meaning, supposedly having torn away the horizon of our infinitude and seen nothing there. The quest was understandable, the departure legitimate; but the journey was wrongheaded."[41]

As we lose our captivation with the mystery of God and his truths, we also lose our sense of gratitude to God. At such moments it helps to turn to children, who brim with gratitude for even the trivial things they receive. When we lose the fascination of a child, we lose the heart of gratitude that keeps us brimming with life.

The loss is tragic, because we also lose all hope of finding any deeply and wildly satisfying hope. Our souls yearn for a wonder that reaches beyond the dimensions of our finite minds, and if we don't allow a wonder toward God, we'll search for it elsewhere, in false gods. "I say to you with emphasis that the *older you get, the more it takes to fill your heart with wonder, and only God is big enough to do that,*" Zacharias stresses.[42]

"How do you find wonder?" he asks. "May I suggest to you, dear friend, that it is not in argument, nor is it in mere dogma. It is not even found in the church. There is a clue to meaning in our experiences—that clue is in relationships. The centerpiece of history, says the Bible, is Christ Himself, and you will find unending wonder in a relationship with Him. . . . The answer to the search for wonder is in a relationship with Christ. Jesus Christ went beyond fantasy: He pointed to truth."[43]

Rather than balking at Jesus' teachings, we can embrace them and let them whisk us nearer the Father of mystery. Our faith depends on it. One day all will be revealed, and the fullness of truth we discover will surpass what our minds can imagine. —BQ

DAILY CONTEMPLATION

Which of God's mysteries have occupied your mind? Come to God now and hold them before him, thanking him that he is big enough to hold your awe. Thank him for the truths he will keep revealing as you live in relationship with Jesus.

DAY 244   Matthew 25:31–46

THE SHEEP AND THE GOATS

"When the Son of Man comes in his glory, and all the angels with him, he will sit on his throne in heavenly glory. All the nations will be gathered before him, and he will separate the people one from another as a shepherd separates the sheep from the goats. He will put the sheep on his right and the goats on his left.

"Then the King will say to those on his right, 'Come, you who are blessed by my Father; take your inheritance, the kingdom prepared for you since the creation of the world. For I was hungry and you gave me something to eat, I was thirsty and you gave me something to drink, I was a stranger and you invited me in, I needed clothes and you clothed me, I was sick and you looked after me, I was in prison and you came to visit me.'

"Then the righteous will answer him, 'Lord, when did we see you hungry and feed you, or thirsty and give you something to drink? When did we see you a stranger and invite you in, or needing clothes and clothe you? When did we see you sick or in prison and go to visit you?'

"The King will reply, 'I tell you the truth, whatever you did for one of the least of these brothers of mine, you did for me.'

"Then he will say to those on his left, 'Depart from me, you who are cursed, into the eternal fire prepared for the devil and his angels. For I was hungry and you gave me nothing to eat, I was thirsty and you gave me nothing to drink, I was a stranger and you did not invite me in, I needed clothes and you did not clothe me, I was sick and in prison and you did not look after me.'

"They also will answer, 'Lord, when did we see you hungry or thirsty or a stranger or needing clothes or sick or in prison, and did not help you?'

"He will reply, 'I tell you the truth, whatever you did not do for one of the least of these, you did not do for me.'

"Then they will go away to eternal punishment, but the righteous to eternal life."

Using another simple parable, Jesus explains the coming day of judgment, when he will separate those who have genuinely loved him from those who have not. Jesus uses the parable to make clear the direct correlation between loving him and loving others in need. Love for Jesus is not simply an inward feeling that issues from us to his Spirit. If true love, it will manifest itself in caring for people toward whom Christ feels compassion. That same love he showed for every kind of person while here on earth will become a living love that flows from him through us and touches others.

Jesus does not imply that a list of good deeds will save us in the end. The Bible is clear—we are saved by grace through our faith in him. But here he tells us that the proof of our love is how we care for others. Our faith saves us, and our faith also compels us to help people in need. Each one we help, Jesus explains, carries a part of himself. In loving them, we are directly loving him.   —BQ

DAILY CONTEMPLATION

Whom have you helped lately who was hungry, thirsty, lonely, unclothed, sick, or in prison?

THE PARABLE OF THE GREAT BANQUET;

THE COST OF BEING A DISCIPLE

One of those at the table with him ... said to Jesus, "Blessed is the man who will eat at the feast in the kingdom of God."

Jesus replied: "A certain man was preparing a great banquet and invited many guests. At the time of the banquet he sent his servant to tell those who had been invited, 'Come, for everything is now ready.'

"But they all alike began to make excuses. The first said, 'I have just bought a field, and I must go and see it. Please excuse me.'

"Another said, 'I have just bought five yoke of oxen, and I'm on my way to try them out. Please excuse me.'

"Still another said, 'I just got married, so I can't come.'

"The servant came back and reported this to his master. Then the owner of the house became angry and ordered his servant, 'Go out quickly into the streets and alleys of the town and bring in the poor, the crippled, the blind and the lame.'

"'Sir,' the servant said, 'what you ordered has been done, but there is still room.'

"Then the master told his servant, 'Go out to the roads and country lanes and make them come in, so that my house will be full. I tell you, not one of those men who were invited will get a taste of my banquet.'"

Large crowds were traveling with Jesus, and turning to them he said: "If anyone comes to me and does not hate his father and mother, his wife and children, his brothers and sisters—yes, even his own life—he cannot be my disciple. And anyone who does not carry his cross and follow me cannot be my disciple.

"Suppose one of you wants to build a tower. Will he not first sit down and estimate the cost to see if he has enough money to complete it? For if he lays the foundation and is not able to finish it, everyone who sees it will ridicule him, saying, 'This fellow began to build and was not able to finish.'

"Or suppose a king is about to go to war against another king. Will he not first sit down and consider whether he is able with ten thousand men to oppose the one coming against him with twenty thousand? If he is not able, he will send a delegation while the other is still a long way off and will ask for terms of peace. In the same way, any of you who does not give up everything he has cannot be my disciple.

"Salt is good, but if it loses its saltiness, how can it be made salty again? It is fit neither for the soil nor for the manure pile; it is thrown out.

"He who has ears to hear, let him hear."

Jesus told several parables about the coming day when God will judge believers and unbelievers. Some people in his parables were unprepared for his second coming, some didn't invest in God's kingdom while here on earth, and some didn't exhibit a genuine love for him by caring for others.

In this parable, Jesus tells of people who at first accepted an invitation to God's kingdom, then let other priorities crowd God out of their lives. Once again Jesus teaches that not all will enter his kingdom. Those who take for granted what he offers will eventually lose the chance to dine with him in eternity—at a banquet far more appealing than anything the earth offers.

Faith will cost believers something here on earth, Jesus cautions. Much of his teaching has focused on God's love and faithfulness. Following Christ leads to fulfillment and peace that we can find nowhere else. Yet following him may also, for a time, bring encounters with difficulty, heartache, and sacrifice.

For instance, Jesus takes priority even over our families. Although he teaches us to love and honor family, he asks us to love him more. If we must choose one over the other, Jesus must come first. It's a commitment not to be taken lightly nor in ignorance and may involve rejection or persecution by others. Nonetheless, if we choose to follow him, the rewards will far exceed the suffering. —BQ

DAILY CONTEMPLATION

What cost have you had to pay for being a disciple of Jesus?

PART 8

RESPONSES TO JESUS

DAY 246

THE PARABLES OF THE LOST SHEEP AND
THE LOST COIN

Now the tax collectors and "sinners" were all gathering around to hear him. But the Pharisees and the teachers of the law muttered, "This man welcomes sinners and eats with them."

Then Jesus told them this parable: "Suppose one of you has a hundred sheep and loses one of them. Does he not leave the ninety-nine in the open country and go after the lost sheep until he finds it? And when he finds it, he joyfully puts it on his shoulders and goes home. Then he calls his friends and neighbors together and says, 'Rejoice with me; I have found my lost sheep.' I tell you that in the same way there will be more rejoicing in heaven over one sinner who repents than over ninety-nine righteous persons who do not need to repent.

"Or suppose a woman has ten silver coins and loses one. Does she not light a lamp, sweep the house and search carefully until she finds it? And when she finds it, she calls her friends and neighbors together and says, 'Rejoice with me; I have found my lost coin.' In the same way, I tell you, there is rejoicing in the presence of the angels of God over one sinner who repents."

This passage relays two of three parables Jesus tells about the lost. As in previous stories, the Pharisees and teachers of the law are again the target of his teaching. They may consider themselves the spiritual ones worthy of God's attention and approval, but they earn Jesus' rebuke because in his eyes they are as lost as those in the crowds he encounters on the hillsides.

Jesus repeated one message throughout his time on earth: no one is righteous. All are sinners in need of God's forgiveness and grace, and only repentant sinners will have a place in God's kingdom. Those who recognize their sin and come to God for salvation become like the lost sheep who is found. The Shepherd and all heaven rejoice. Probably Jesus is speaking tongue in cheek when he compares the sinner who repents with the ninety-nine righteous who do not need to repent. The ninety-nine probably represent the Pharisees, who do not recognize their need for repentance. If they too genuinely turned to him, God's rejoicing would be great indeed.

Carrying a similar message, the parable of the lost coin illustrates how God values those who don't know him. The Pharisees might disapprove of Jesus' attention to tax collectors and sinners, but God approves. He sent his Son to earth for these very people and wants them to be found. —BQ

DAILY CONTEMPLATION

When did you lose something important and then find it again?

DAY 247
Luke 15:11–32

THE PARABLE OF THE LOST SON (PRODIGAL)

Jesus continued: "There was a man who had two sons. The younger one said to his father, 'Father, give me my share of the estate.' So he divided his property between them.

"Not long after that, the younger son got together all he had, set off for a distant country and there squandered his wealth in wild living. After he had spent everything, there was a severe famine in that whole country, and he began to be in need. So he went and hired himself out to a citizen of that country, who sent him to his fields to feed pigs. He longed to fill his stomach with the pods that the pigs were eating, but no one gave him anything.

"When he came to his senses, he said, 'How many of my father's hired men have food to spare, and here I am starving to death! I will set out and go back to my father and say to him: Father, I have sinned against heaven and against you. I am no longer worthy to be called your son; make me like one of your hired men.' So he got up and went to his father.

"But while he was still a long way off, his father saw him and was filled with compassion for him; he ran to his son, threw his arms around him and kissed him.

470

"The son said to him, 'Father, I have sinned against heaven and against you. I am no longer worthy to be called your son.'

"But the father said to his servants, 'Quick! Bring the best robe and put it on him. Put a ring on his finger and sandals on his feet. Bring the fattened calf and kill it. Let's have a feast and celebrate. For this son of mine was dead and is alive again; he was lost and is found.' So they began to celebrate.

"Meanwhile, the older son was in the field. When he came near the house, he heard music and dancing. So he called one of the servants and asked him what was going on. 'Your brother has come,' he replied, 'and your father has killed the fattened calf because he has him back safe and sound.'

"The older brother became angry and refused to go in. So his father went out and pleaded with him. But he answered his father, 'Look! All these years I've been slaving for you and never disobeyed your orders. Yet you never gave me even a young goat so I could celebrate with my friends. But when this son of yours who has squandered your property with prostitutes comes home, you kill the fattened calf for him!'

"'My son,' the father said, 'you are always with me, and everything I have is yours. But we had to celebrate and be glad, because this brother of yours was dead and is alive again; he was lost and is found.'"

The chief priests, the teachers of the law and the leaders among the people were trying to kill him. Yet they could not find any way to do it, because all the people hung on his words" (Luke 19:47–48). Using simple, homespun images, Jesus expresses profound truths in a way that holds his audience captive. His parables, or concise short stories, have won high praise even from literary experts who do not accept their message. Some of the most famous of these parables, including the three in Luke 15, appear only in Luke's gospel.

Although trained as a physician, Luke demonstrates great skill as a writer. The introduction to his book mentions that he carefully investigated reports from eyewitnesses before writing the book that bears his name. Using the finest Greek found in the New Testament, he brings characters and scenes vividly to life.

Luke especially excels at conveying the plight of the poor and the outcast. Women, largely ignored by ancient historians, play a large role in his book (he introduces thirteen mentioned nowhere else), as do children. It may seem strange that a man belonging to the upper class would emerge as a champion of the underdog—evidently, Jesus' own compassion has affected Luke deeply.

The three stories in Luke 15 all stir up feelings for the underdog. A shepherd scours the hillside in a frantic search for a missing sheep. A woman turns her house upside down over a lost silver coin. And a runaway son thumbs his nose at a life of comfort and ends up half-starved in a pigpen. In a few brief sentences, the parables tug at feelings of loss and remorse that lie buried just beneath the surface in all of us. And yet all three parables end the same: spectacular good news floods in to replace the sadness, and partying breaks out.

The word *gospel* itself comes from the Old English word *godspell*. It means, simply, "good news"—a message that Luke never loses sight of. Even for the saddest story, there can be a happy ending after all. —PY

DAY 248
Luke 19:1–10

ZACCHAEUS THE TAX COLLECTOR

Jesus entered Jericho and was passing through. A man was there by the name of Zacchaeus; he was a chief tax collector and was wealthy. He wanted to see who Jesus was, but being a short man he could not, because of the crowd. So he ran ahead and climbed a sycamore-fig tree to see him, since Jesus was coming that way.

When Jesus reached the spot, he looked up and said to him, "Zacchaeus, come down immediately. I must stay at your house today." So he came down at once and welcomed him gladly.

All the people saw this and began to mutter, "He has gone to be the guest of a 'sinner.'"

But Zacchaeus stood up and said to the Lord, "Look, Lord! Here and now I give half of my possessions to the poor, and if I have cheated anybody out of anything, I will pay back four times the amount."

Jesus said to him, "Today salvation has come to this house, because this man, too, is a son of Abraham. For the Son of Man came to seek and to save what was lost."

Zacchaeus (za-KEE-uhs) is an underdog of sorts, although the people of his day resent rather than pity him. A rich exploiter of his neighbors, Zacchaeus would seem an unlikely target for Jesus' love and attention. Not only a tax collector, Zacchaeus is a chief tax collector, probably in charge of a group of collectors and very wealthy. Members of his profession have a reputation for cheating people and getting rich off the profits. Zacchaeus, like Matthew, ranks at the bottom in the eyes of the Jewish people.

Yet Jesus sees past the surface, to the heart of a man in need of salvation. Zacchaeus's response shows that not only does he qualify as a Jew by heritage, but he also has the faith of Abraham and a heart eager for the Messiah. Jesus looks past outward appearances to care for even the most hopeless unbeliever. His love reveals that every person, no matter how unlikely, has the potential of coming to him.   —BQ

DAILY CONTEMPLATION

Who in your life needs Jesus but seems most unlikely to ever receive him?

JESUS THE BREAD OF LIFE;

MANY DISCIPLES DESERT JESUS

Once the crowd realized that neither Jesus nor his disciples were there, they got into the boats and went to Capernaum in search of Jesus.

When they found him on the other side of the lake, they asked him, "Rabbi, when did you get here?"

Jesus answered, "I tell you the truth, you are looking for me, not because you saw miraculous signs but because you ate the loaves and had your fill. Do not work for food that spoils, but for food that endures to eternal life, which the Son of Man will give you. On him God the Father has placed his seal of approval."

Then they asked him, "What must we do to do the works God requires?"

Jesus answered, "The work of God is this: to believe in the one he has sent."

So they asked him, "What miraculous sign then will you give that we may see it and believe you? What will you do? Our forefathers ate the manna in the desert; as it is written: 'He gave them bread from heaven to eat.'"

Jesus said to them, "I tell you the truth, it is not Moses who has given you the bread from heaven, but it is my Father who gives you the true bread from heaven. For the bread of God is he who comes down from heaven and gives life to the world."

"Sir," they said, "from now on give us this bread."

Then Jesus declared, "I am the bread of life. He who comes to me will never go hungry, and he who believes in me will never be thirsty. But as I told you, you have seen me and still you do not believe. All that the Father gives me will come to me, and whoever comes to me I will never drive away. For I have come down from heaven not to do my will but to do the will of him who sent me. And this is the will of him who sent me, that I shall lose none of all that he has given me, but raise them up at the last day. For my Father's will is that everyone who looks to the Son and believes in him shall have eternal life, and I will raise him up at the last day."

At this the Jews began to grumble about him because he said, "I am the bread that came down from heaven." They said, "Is this not Jesus, the son of Joseph, whose father and mother we know? How can he now say, 'I came down from heaven'?"

"Stop grumbling among yourselves," Jesus answered. "No one can come to me unless the Father who sent me draws him, and I will raise him up at the last day. It is written in the Prophets: 'They will all be taught by God.' Everyone who listens to the Father and learns from him comes to me. No one has seen the Father except the one who is from God; only he has seen the Father. I tell you the truth, he who believes has everlasting life. I am the bread of life.

Your forefathers ate the manna in the desert, yet they died. But here is the bread that comes down from heaven, which a man may eat and not die. I am the living bread that came down from heaven. If anyone eats of this bread, he will live forever. This bread is my flesh, which I will give for the life of the world."

Then the Jews began to argue sharply among themselves, "How can this man give us his flesh to eat?"

Jesus said to them, "I tell you the truth, unless you eat the flesh of the Son of Man and drink his blood, you have no life in you. Whoever eats my flesh and drinks my blood has eternal life, and I will raise him up at the last day. For my flesh is real food and my blood is real drink. Whoever eats my flesh and drinks my blood remains in me, and I in him. Just as the living Father sent me and I live because of the Father, so the one who feeds on me will live because of me. This is the bread that came down from heaven. Your forefathers ate manna and died, but he who feeds on this bread will live forever." He said this while teaching in the synagogue in Capernaum.

On hearing it, many of his disciples said, "This is a hard teaching. Who can accept it?"

Aware that his disciples were grumbling about this, Jesus said to them, "Does this offend you? What if you see the Son of Man ascend to where he was before! The Spirit gives life; the flesh counts for nothing. The words I have spoken to you are spirit and they are life. Yet there are some of you who do not believe." For Jesus had known from the beginning which of them did not believe and who would betray him. He went on to say, "This is why I told you that no one can come to me unless the Father has enabled him."

From this time many of his disciples turned back and no longer followed him.

"You do not want to leave too, do you?" Jesus asked the Twelve.

Simon Peter answered him, "Lord, to whom shall we go? You have the words of eternal life. We believe and know that you are the Holy One of God."

Then Jesus replied, "Have I not chosen you, the Twelve? Yet one of you is a devil!" (He meant Judas, the son of Simon Iscariot, who, though one of the Twelve, was later to betray him.)

All four gospels include an account of the feeding of the five thousand, but John adds the most detail, describing the effect of the miracle on the ordinary people who saw it. At first, dazzled by the miracle, they forcibly try to crown Jesus king. When he, characteristically, slips away, the persistent crowd commandeers boats and sails across a lake in pursuit.

The next day when the crowds catch up with him, Jesus meets them with a blunt warning: "I tell you the truth, you are looking for me, not because you saw miraculous signs but because you ate the loaves and had your fill. Do not work for food that spoils, but for food that endures to eternal life, which the Son of Man will give you."

That response shows why Jesus distrusts sensation-seeking crowds: they care far more for physical spectacle than for spiritual truth. And what happens next certainly bears out his suspicion. As he is interpreting the spiritual meaning of the miracle, all the enthusiasm of the previous day melts away. The crowd grows downright restless when he openly avows his true identity as the one sent from God. They cannot reconcile such exalted claims ("I have come down from heaven") with their knowledge that he is a local man, whose mother and father they know.

Jesus uses the miracle they have seen firsthand as a way of introducing his topic of the bread of life (his words are later applied to the Lord's Supper, or the Eucharist). But in the end the people in the crowd—who have proof of Jesus' supernatural power digesting in their bellies—abandon him, unbelieving. Many of his disciples turn back, too, never to follow him again.   —PY

DAILY CONTEMPLATION

Have you ever taken offense at Jesus? Why?

DAY 250   John 8:2–11

THE WOMAN CAUGHT IN ADULTERY

At dawn [Jesus] appeared again in the temple courts, where all the people gathered around him, and he sat down to teach them. The teachers of the law and the Pharisees brought in a woman caught in adultery. They made her stand before the group and said to Jesus, "Teacher, this woman was caught in the act of adultery. In the Law Moses commanded us to stone such women. Now what do you say?" They were using this question as a trap, in order to have a basis for accusing him.

But Jesus bent down and started to write on the ground with his finger. When they kept on questioning him, he straightened up and said to them, "If any one of you is without sin, let him be the first to throw a stone at her." Again he stooped down and wrote on the ground.

At this, those who heard began to go away one at a time, the older ones first, until only Jesus was left, with the woman still standing there. Jesus straightened up and asked her, "Woman, where are they? Has no one condemned you?"

"No one, sir," she said.

"Then neither do I condemn you," Jesus declared. "Go now and leave your life of sin."

This story, one of the most memorable in the Gospels, is not found in the earliest and most reliable manuscripts of John. Some manuscripts place the story in Luke, and others don't include the story anywhere. Many Bible scholars believe the story is authentic nonetheless. Surely it gives us another reliable glimpse of Jesus' heart.

Once again Jesus shows compassion toward an underdog. His attention to women in his ministry is unusual in itself, especially for the Jewish culture of that day. Many of the gospel stories tell of Jesus' friendship with women and his attention to their physical, emotional, and spiritual needs. Far ahead of his time, Jesus treats women as equally worthy.

In this story he cares for a woman who has committed sexual sin. According to the law, both she and her partner deserve death. But Romans do not allow Jews to carry out death sentences, so the Pharisees try to trap Jesus between Jewish and Roman regulations.

Jesus will not be duped by conniving, heartless legalists. He cuts to the core of the matter: sin. God gave his law to define sin and to punish it, and because she broke the law, the adulteress deserves punishment. Yet God's law encompasses more than sexual sin. No person is guiltless in the face of the law, and no one should know that fact better than these legal experts. Jesus puts them in their place, proclaiming that his Father's business is vastly different—more merciful—from the business they have taken upon themselves in the guise of acting in the Father's name.

Jesus came to convict of sin, yes, but also to offer a way out through himself. The Pharisees, on the other hand, remain stuck in a self-made maze called law.   —BQ

DAILY CONTEMPLATION

Do you tend to categorize sin, considering some sins better than others, and some worse?

DAY 251   Reflection

FINDING JESUS

Inside all of us is a yearning that only God can meet. The African bishop Saint Augustine once wrote, "Thou hast made us for Thyself, and the heart of man is restless until it finds its rest in Thee." French mathematician, philosopher, and scientist Blaise Pascal wrote, "Inside of every man is a God-shaped vacuum."

Whether or not we are in tune with our need for God, he stands as the only one who can fill us completely. Jesus spoke of God's filling this way: "I am the bread of life. He who comes to me will never go hungry, and he who believes in me will never be thirsty" (John 6:35). Jesus meets a need even more basic than that of physical hunger—the need for bread that satisfies forever. Jesus can satisfy us now and promise us eternal life.

Often we find ourselves most aware of our need for Jesus in times of struggle. With our senses sharpened by the raw edges of pain, life takes on fresh perspective. The incidentals fall away, and we see that God is a part of everything that really matters. If we don't have union with him, life holds no hope. We will continue to hunger and thirst.

The death of a friend or loved one, or the prospect of our own death, dramatically brings us face to face with that God-shaped vacuum inside. In a very different way, so does the monotonous pursuit of everyday life. Without God to fill the days with more than routine, life becomes heavy, our souls restless. What is the point? What gives life meaning?

Any circumstance of life, in the end, gives occasion to a yearning for God. In good times or bad we need him—in youth and old age, in sickness and in health. Without God we'll stay empty. Why then doesn't every person turn to God? Why do many still resist him, and many others continue to search, looking everywhere but to God?

John 6 gives one insight. After hearing Jesus reveal himself as the Bread of Life, many of his disciples responded, "This is a hard teaching. Who can accept it?" (v. 60). Why follow a God who became man and died a humiliating death? Why follow a God who asks us to give up our lives for him? Why follow One we don't understand? In each case Jesus responds, "No one can come to me unless the Father has enabled him" (v. 65). He explains that in the very act of sensing our need and responding to him, we need God's help. In a seeming dichotomy, we have the free will to consider and choose Jesus, yet we need God's help in doing even that.

Those who have found the solution to that God-shaped vacuum can thank God for enabling us to see and respond to his love. As we pray for family and friends who have yet to accept the love of Jesus, we pray for God's help. They too need his enabling to respond.   —BQ

DAILY CONTEMPLATION

Can you put a finger on what it was that finally turned your heart to Jesus? Can you detect any help from God in that process? Thank God for enabling you to see your need and accept Jesus' love. Name the people in your life who still need him, and ask God to help them find Jesus as the answer to their search.

DAY 252   Mark 7:1–37

JESUS TEACHES ABOUT BEING CLEAN AND UNCLEAN,
HEALS A DEAF AND MUTE MAN

The Pharisees and some of the teachers of the law who had come from Jerusalem gathered around Jesus and saw some of his disciples eating food with hands that were "unclean," that is, unwashed. (The Pharisees and all the Jews do not eat unless they give their hands a ceremonial washing, holding to the tradition of the elders. When they come from the marketplace they do not eat unless they wash. And they observe many other traditions, such as the washing of cups, pitchers and kettles.)

So the Pharisees and teachers of the law asked Jesus, "Why don't your disciples live according to the tradition of the elders instead of eating their food with 'unclean' hands?"

He replied, "Isaiah was right when he prophesied about you hypocrites; as it is written:

"'These people honor me with their lips,
    but their hearts are far from me.
They worship me in vain;
    their teachings are but rules taught by men.'

You have let go of the commands of God and are holding on to the traditions of men."

And he said to them: "You have a fine way of setting aside the commands of God in order to observe your own traditions! For Moses said, 'Honor your father and your mother,' and, 'Anyone who curses his father or mother must be put to death.' But you say that if a man says to his father or mother: 'Whatever help you might otherwise have received from me is Corban' (that is, a gift devoted to God), then you no longer let him do anything for his father or mother. Thus you nullify the word of God by your tradition that you have handed down. And you do many things like that."

Again Jesus called the crowd to him and said, "Listen to me, everyone, and understand this. Nothing outside a man can make him 'unclean' by going into him. Rather, it is what comes out of a man that makes him 'unclean.'"

After he had left the crowd and entered the house, his disciples asked him about this parable. "Are you so dull?" he asked. "Don't you see that nothing that enters a man from the outside can make him 'unclean'? For it doesn't go into his heart but into his stomach, and then out of his body." (In saying this, Jesus declared all foods "clean.")

He went on: "What comes out of a man is what makes him 'unclean.' For from within, out of men's hearts, come evil thoughts, sexual immorality, theft, murder, adultery, greed, malice, deceit, lewdness, envy, slander, arrogance and folly. All these evils come from inside and make a man 'unclean.'"

Jesus left that place and went to the vicinity of Tyre. He entered a house and did not want anyone to know it; yet he could not keep his presence secret. In fact, as soon as she heard about him, a woman whose little daughter was possessed by an evil spirit came and fell at his feet. The woman was a Greek, born in Syrian Phoenicia. She begged Jesus to drive the demon out of her daughter.

"First let the children eat all they want," he told her, "for it is not right to take the children's bread and toss it to their dogs."

"Yes, Lord," she replied, "but even the dogs under the table eat the children's crumbs."

Then he told her, "For such a reply, you may go; the demon has left your daughter."

She went home and found her child lying on the bed, and the demon gone.

Then Jesus left the vicinity of Tyre and went through Sidon, down to the Sea of Galilee and into the region of the Decapolis. There some people brought to him a man who was deaf and could hardly talk, and they begged him to place his hand on the man.

After he took him aside, away from the crowd, Jesus put his fingers into the man's ears. Then he spit and touched the man's tongue. He looked up to heaven and with a deep sigh said to him, "Ephphatha!" (which means, "Be opened!"). At this, the man's ears were opened, his tongue was loosened and he began to speak plainly.

Jesus commanded them not to tell anyone. But the more he did so, the more they kept talking about it. People were overwhelmed with amazement. "He has done everything well," they said. "He even makes the deaf hear and the mute speak."

Although the crowds sometimes have difficulty swallowing Jesus' message, as long as he keeps healing people they tag along. On the other hand, the religious, political, and intellectual establishments all strongly oppose Jesus but cannot manage to loosen his grip upon the common people. The Pharisees, in particular, keep trying to trap him in a major blunder that might turn the people—or the government—against him.

In many ways, the Pharisees make for an odd set of enemies. They are, in fact, among the most religious people of Jesus' day. More than any other group, they strive to follow the letter of the Old Testament law. But Jesus can see right through the Pharisees' pious behavior. He blasts them for focusing on the "outside" while neglecting the far greater dangers within.

The Pharisees of Jesus' day are strict legalists who proudly embellish Jewish law with their own traditions. For example, they have determined that a person can ride a donkey without breaking the Sabbath rules, but not use a switch to speed up the animal. It is permissible to give to a beggar on the Sabbath only if the beggar sticks his hand inside the home, so the giver needn't reach outside. A woman cannot look in the mirror on the Sabbath—she might see a gray hair and be tempted to pull it out.

Jesus reacts with surprising harshness to such seemingly petty matters. By concentrating on all the rules, the Pharisees risk missing the whole point of the gospel. Such external, showy forms of legalism do not get anyone closer to God; just the opposite, they tend to make people proud and cliquish and self-righteous.

One way Jesus exposes the hypocrisy in the Pharisees' attitude is by publicly healing people on the sacred Sabbath. Fully aware that such acts will scandalize strict Pharisees, he goes ahead anyway, insisting that compassion for needy people must take precedence over any tradition.   —PY

DAILY CONTEMPLATION

In what ways can you try to focus on your own heart and avoid being overly judgmental of the sins of others?

THE PARABLE OF THE UNMERCIFUL SERVANT; TEACHING ON DIVORCE

Then Peter came to Jesus and asked, "Lord, how many times shall I forgive my brother when he sins against me? Up to seven times?"

Jesus answered, "I tell you, not seven times, but seventy-seven times.

"Therefore, the kingdom of heaven is like a king who wanted to settle accounts with his servants. As he began the settlement, a man who owed him ten thousand talents was brought to him. Since he was not able to pay, the master ordered that he and his wife and his children and all that he had be sold to repay the debt.

"The servant fell on his knees before him. 'Be patient with me,' he begged, 'and I will pay back everything.' The servant's master took pity on him, canceled the debt and let him go.

"But when that servant went out, he found one of his fellow servants who owed him a hundred denarii. He grabbed him and began to choke him. 'Pay back what you owe me!' he demanded.

"His fellow servant fell to his knees and begged him, 'Be patient with me, and I will pay you back.'

"But he refused. Instead, he went off and had the man thrown into prison until he could pay the debt. When the other servants saw what had happened, they were greatly distressed and went and told their master everything that had happened.

"Then the master called the servant in. 'You wicked servant,' he said, 'I canceled all that debt of yours because you begged me to. Shouldn't you have had mercy on your fellow servant just as I had on you?' In anger his master turned him over to the jailers to be tortured, until he should pay back all he owed.

"This is how my heavenly Father will treat each of you unless you forgive your brother from your heart."

When Jesus had finished saying these things, he left Galilee and went into the region of Judea to the other side of the Jordan. Large crowds followed him, and he healed them there.

Some Pharisees came to him to test him. They asked, "Is it lawful for a man to divorce his wife for any and every reason?"

"Haven't you read," he replied, "that at the beginning the Creator 'made them male and female,' and said, 'For this reason a man will leave his father and mother and be united to his wife, and the two will become one flesh'? So they are no longer two, but one. Therefore what God has joined together, let man not separate."

"Why then," they asked, "did Moses command that a man give his wife a certificate of divorce and send her away?"

Jesus replied, "Moses permitted you to divorce your wives because your hearts were hard. But it was not this way from the beginning. I tell you that anyone who divorces his wife, except for marital unfaithfulness, and marries another woman commits adultery."

The disciples said to him, "If this is the situation between a husband and wife, it is better not to marry."

Jesus replied, "Not everyone can accept this word, but only those to whom it has been given. For some are eunuchs because they were born that way; others were made that way by men; and others have renounced marriage because of the kingdom of heaven. The one who can accept this should accept it."

Legalists, people who follow strict rules of conduct, at first glance may seem "righteous." But Jesus warns against the subtle dangers of legalism. Oddly, it tends to lower a person's view of God. If I manage to meet all the requirements of a strict rule book, I may begin to feel secure about my own goodness. I may think that I have earned God's approval through my own efforts.

People in the Gospels who question Jesus in person—both his enemies the Pharisees and his friends the disciples—seek a precise list of rules so that they can strive to meet those obligations and thus feel satisfied. To such people, Jesus shouts a loud "No!" We never outgrow our need for God; we never *arrive* in the Christian life. We survive spiritually only if we constantly depend on God.

In the first story in this passage, Peter tries almost ludicrously to reduce forgiveness to a mathematical formula: *Let's see, exactly how many times must I forgive someone? Six? Seven?* Jesus mocks the question and tells a profound story about God's forgiveness, so great and all-encompassing that it defies all mathematics.

Next, the Pharisees try to pin down a formula for divorce. Once again Jesus avoids the answer they want to hear and points instead to the principles that undergird all marriage.

These examples illustrate how Jesus usually handles questions about specific problems. When a pious man asks what neighbors he should go about loving, Jesus tells of the Good Samaritan who shows love even to his enemies. Jesus doesn't tell a rich person to give away 18.5 percent of his belongings; he says give them all away. He doesn't restrict adultery to the act of intercourse; he connects it to lust, adultery of the heart. Murder? In principle, that's no different from anger.

In short, Jesus always refuses to lower the sights. He lashes out at every form of legalism, every human attempt to accumulate a list of credits. The credit goes to God, not us. The chief danger facing legalists is that they risk missing the whole point of the gospel: that it is a gift freely given by God to people who don't deserve it.   —PY

DAILY CONTEMPLATION

When have you had to forgive someone repeatedly?

THE SHEPHERD AND HIS FLOCK; THE UNBELIEF OF THE JEWS

"I tell you the truth, the man who does not enter the sheep pen by the gate, but climbs in by some other way, is a thief and a robber. The man who enters by the gate is the shepherd of his sheep. The watchman opens the gate for him, and the sheep listen to his voice. He calls his own sheep by name and leads them out. When he has brought out all his own, he goes on ahead of them, and his sheep follow him because they know his voice. But they will never follow a stranger; in fact, they will run away from him because they do not recognize a stranger's voice." Jesus used this figure of speech, but they did not understand what he was telling them.

Therefore Jesus said again, "I tell you the truth, I am the gate for the sheep. All who ever came before me were thieves and robbers, but the sheep did not listen to them. I am the gate; whoever enters through me will be saved. He will come in and go out, and find pasture. The thief comes only to steal and kill and destroy; I have come that they may have life, and have it to the full.

"I am the good shepherd. The good shepherd lays down his life for the sheep. The hired hand is not the shepherd who owns the sheep. So when he sees the wolf coming, he abandons the sheep and runs away. Then the wolf attacks the flock and scatters it. The man runs away because he is a hired hand and cares nothing for the sheep.

"I am the good shepherd; I know my sheep and my sheep know me—just as the Father knows me and I know the Father—and I lay down my life for the sheep. I have other sheep that are not of this sheep pen. I must bring them also. They too will listen to my voice, and there shall be one flock and one shepherd. The reason my Father loves me is that I lay down my life—only to take it up again. No one takes it from me, but I lay it down of my own accord. I have authority to lay it down and authority to take it up again. This command I received from my Father."

At these words the Jews were again divided. Many of them said, "He is demon-possessed and raving mad. Why listen to him?"

But others said, "These are not the sayings of a man possessed by a demon. Can a demon open the eyes of the blind?"

Then came the Feast of Dedication at Jerusalem. It was winter, and Jesus was in the temple area walking in Solomon's Colonnade. The Jews gathered around him, saying, "How long will you keep us in suspense? If you are the Christ, tell us plainly."

Jesus answered, "I did tell you, but you do not believe. The miracles I do in my Father's name speak for me, but you do not believe because you are not my sheep. My sheep listen to my voice; I know them, and they follow me. I give them eternal life, and they shall never perish; no one can snatch them out of my hand.

My Father, who has given them to me, is greater than all; no one can snatch them out of my Father's hand. I and the Father are one."

Again the Jews picked up stones to stone him, but Jesus said to them, "I have shown you many great miracles from the Father. For which of these do you stone me?"

"We are not stoning you for any of these," replied the Jews, "but for blasphemy, because you, a mere man, claim to be God."

Jesus answered them, "Is it not written in your Law, 'I have said you are gods'? If he called them 'gods,' to whom the word of God came—and the Scripture cannot be broken—what about the one whom the Father set apart as his very own and sent into the world? Why then do you accuse me of blasphemy because I said, 'I am God's Son'? Do not believe me unless I do what my Father does. But if I do it, even though you do not believe me, believe the miracles, that you may know and understand that the Father is in me, and I in the Father." Again they tried to seize him, but he escaped their grasp.

Then Jesus went back across the Jordan to the place where John had been baptizing in the early days.

Every few years an author or movie director comes out with a new work raising questions about Jesus' identity. Often such portrayals show him wandering around the earth in a daze, trying to figure out why he came and what he is supposed to be doing. Nothing could be further from the account given us by John, Jesus' closest friend. According to him, Jesus was no "man who fell to earth" but God's Son, sent on a mission from the Father. "I know where I came from and where I am going," Jesus said (8:14).

Of the four gospel writers, John dwells most prominently on Jesus' identity as the true Messiah, the Son of God. He states his purpose in writing very clearly: "These are written that you may believe that Jesus is the Christ, the Son of God, and that by believing you may have life in his name" (20:31). His book includes incidents from no more than twenty days in Jesus' life, arranged so as to demonstrate who Jesus is. Significantly, most of these incidents come from the final days of Jesus' life, when he is declaring his mission openly.

"I am the gate," Jesus says in this chapter; "I am the good shepherd." Jews who hear those words undoubtedly think back to Old Testament kings like David, who are known as the shepherds of Israel. When some challenge him bluntly, "If you are the Christ, tell us plainly," Jesus answers with equal bluntness, "I and the Father are one." The pious Jews understand him perfectly: they pick up stones to execute him for blasphemy.

Not even these hostile reactions surprise Jesus. He expects opposition, even execution. As he explains, a truly good shepherd, unlike a hired hand, "lays down his life for the sheep." He is the only person in history who chooses to be born, chooses to die, and chooses to come back again. This chapter explains why he makes those choices. —PY

DAILY CONTEMPLATION

What difference does it make to you that Jesus is God and not just a man?

JESUS FEEDS, TEACHES, AND HEALS

During those days another large crowd gathered. Since they had nothing to eat, Jesus called his disciples to him and said, "I have compassion for these people; they have already been with me three days and have nothing to eat. If I send them home hungry, they will collapse on the way, because some of them have come a long distance."

His disciples answered, "But where in this remote place can anyone get enough bread to feed them?"

"How many loaves do you have?" Jesus asked.

"Seven," they replied.

He told the crowd to sit down on the ground. When he had taken the seven loaves and given thanks, he broke them and gave them to his disciples to set before the people, and they did so. They had a few small fish as well; he gave thanks for them also and told the disciples to distribute them. The people ate and were satisfied. Afterward the disciples picked up seven basketfuls of broken pieces that were left over. About four thousand men were present. And having sent them away, he got into the boat with his disciples and went to the region of Dalmanutha.

The Pharisees came and began to question Jesus. To test him, they asked him for a sign from heaven. He sighed deeply and said, "Why does this generation ask for a miraculous sign? I tell you the truth, no sign will be given to it." Then he left them, got back into the boat and crossed to the other side.

The disciples had forgotten to bring bread, except for one loaf they had with them in the boat. "Be careful," Jesus warned them. "Watch out for the yeast of the Pharisees and that of Herod."

They discussed this with one another and said, "It is because we have no bread."

Aware of their discussion, Jesus asked them: "Why are you talking about having no bread? Do you still not see or understand? Are your hearts hardened? Do you have eyes but fail to see, and ears but fail to hear? And don't you remember? When I broke the five loaves for the five thousand, how many basketfuls of pieces did you pick up?"

"Twelve," they replied.

"And when I broke the seven loaves for the four thousand, how many basketfuls of pieces did you pick up?"

They answered, "Seven."

He said to them, "Do you still not understand?"

They came to Bethsaida, and some people brought a blind man and begged Jesus to touch him. He took the blind man by the hand and led him outside the village. When he had spit on the man's eyes and put his hands on him, Jesus asked, "Do you see anything?"

He looked up and said, "I see people; they look like trees walking around."

Once more Jesus put his hands on the man's eyes. Then his eyes were opened, his sight was restored, and he saw everything clearly. Jesus sent him home, saying, "Don't go into the village."

Jesus and his disciples went on to the villages around Caesarea Philippi. On the way he asked them, "Who do people say I am?"

They replied, "Some say John the Baptist; others say Elijah; and still others, one of the prophets."

"But what about you?" he asked. "Who do you say I am?"

Peter answered, "You are the Christ."

Jesus warned them not to tell anyone about him.

He then began to teach them that the Son of Man must suffer many things and be rejected by the elders, chief priests and teachers of the law, and that he must be killed and after three days rise again. He spoke plainly about this, and Peter took him aside and began to rebuke him.

But when Jesus turned and looked at his disciples, he rebuked Peter. "Get behind me, Satan!" he said. "You do not have in mind the things of God, but the things of men."

Then he called the crowd to him along with his disciples and said: "If anyone would come after me, he must deny himself and take up his cross and follow me. For whoever wants to save his life will lose it, but whoever loses his life for me and for the gospel will save it. What good is it for a man to gain the whole world, yet forfeit his soul? Or what can a man give in exchange for his soul? If anyone is ashamed of me and my words in this adulterous and sinful generation, the Son of Man will be ashamed of him when he comes in his Father's glory with the holy angels."

As this chapter opens, Jesus is exasperated with his disciples. They have seen him feed five thousand people, and then four thousand, and yet still they worry about their next meal. "Do you have eyes but fail to see, and ears but fail to hear?" he asks reproachfully. Still, for all their denseness the disciples have grasped something about Jesus that eludes most others. The crowds see him as a reincarnation of a prophet: Elijah, maybe, or John the Baptist. But in this scene, Peter boldly pronounces Jesus the "Christ," the very Messiah long predicted by the prophets.

It is difficult for us to comprehend the importance of that single word to first-century Jews. Ground down by centuries of foreign domination, they have staked all their hopes on a Messiah who will lead their nation back to glory. Matthew records that Jesus, pleased by Peter's impulsive declaration, lavishes praise on him (16:17–19). Yet Peter's brightest moment is immediately followed by one of his dullest—a few paragraphs later Jesus identifies Peter with Satan. What transpires between those two scenes marks an important turning point in the story of Jesus' life.

To Peter and the other disciples, "Messiah" stands for wealth and fame and political power, the very temptations of an earthly kingdom that Jesus has resisted from Satan. Jesus knows that the true Messiah will first have to endure scorn, humiliation, suffering, and even death. He is the Suffering Servant prophesied by Isaiah. He will take up an executioner's cross, not a worldly position of honor.

Jesus accepts Peter's designation; he is indeed the true Messiah. But from that moment on, Jesus makes a strategic shift. He leaves Galilee and heads toward the capital of Jerusalem. Instead of addressing the crowds, he narrows his scope to the twelve disciples and works to prepare them for the suffering and death to come. Peter may have grasped Jesus' identity, but he has much to learn about his mission. He wants Jesus to avoid pain, not understanding that the pain of the cross will bring salvation to the whole world. —PY

DAILY CONTEMPLATION

If someone were to ask you who Jesus is, what would you say?

DAY 256
Mark 9:1–41

THE TRANSFIGURATION; JESUS HEALS AND TEACHES

[Jesus] said to them, "I tell you the truth, some who are standing here will not taste death before they see the kingdom of God come with power."

After six days Jesus took Peter, James and John with him and led them up a high mountain, where they were all alone. There he was transfigured before them. His clothes became dazzling white, whiter than anyone in the world could bleach them. And there appeared before them Elijah and Moses, who were talking with Jesus.

Peter said to Jesus, "Rabbi, it is good for us to be here. Let us put up three shelters—one for you, one for Moses and one for Elijah." (He did not know what to say, they were so frightened.)

Then a cloud appeared and enveloped them, and a voice came from the cloud: "This is my Son, whom I love. Listen to him!"

Suddenly, when they looked around, they no longer saw anyone with them except Jesus.

As they were coming down the mountain, Jesus gave them orders not to tell anyone what they had seen until the Son of Man had risen from the dead. They kept the matter to themselves, discussing what "rising from the dead" meant.

And they asked him, "Why do the teachers of the law say that Elijah must come first?"

Jesus replied, "To be sure, Elijah does come first, and restores all things. Why then is it written that the Son of Man must suffer much and be rejected? But I tell you, Elijah has come, and they have done to him everything they wished, just as it is written about him."

When they came to the other disciples, they saw a large crowd around them and the teachers of the law arguing with them. As soon as all the people saw Jesus, they were overwhelmed with wonder and ran to greet him.

"What are you arguing with them about?" he asked.

A man in the crowd answered, "Teacher, I brought you my son, who is possessed by a spirit that has robbed him of speech. Whenever it seizes him, it throws him to the ground. He foams at the mouth, gnashes his teeth and becomes rigid. I asked your disciples to drive out the spirit, but they could not."

"O unbelieving generation," Jesus replied, "how long shall I stay with you? How long shall I put up with you? Bring the boy to me."

So they brought him. When the spirit saw Jesus, it immediately threw the boy into a convulsion. He fell to the ground and rolled around, foaming at the mouth.

Jesus asked the boy's father, "How long has he been like this?"

"From childhood," he answered. "It has often thrown him into fire or water to kill him. But if you can do anything, take pity on us and help us."

"'If you can'?" said Jesus. "Everything is possible for him who believes."

Immediately the boy's father exclaimed, "I do believe; help me overcome my unbelief!"

When Jesus saw that a crowd was running to the scene, he rebuked the evil spirit. "You deaf and mute spirit," he said, "I command you, come out of him and never enter him again."

The spirit shrieked, convulsed him violently and came out. The boy looked so much like a corpse that many said, "He's dead." But Jesus took him by the hand and lifted him to his feet, and he stood up.

After Jesus had gone indoors, his disciples asked him privately, "Why couldn't we drive it out?"

He replied, "This kind can come out only by prayer."

They left that place and passed through Galilee. Jesus did not want anyone to know where they were, because he was teaching his disciples. He said to them, "The Son of Man is going to be betrayed into the hands of men. They will kill him, and after three days he will rise." But they did not understand what he meant and were afraid to ask him about it.

They came to Capernaum. When he was in the house, he asked them, "What were you arguing about on the road?" But they kept quiet because on the way they had argued about who was the greatest.

Sitting down, Jesus called the Twelve and said, "If anyone wants to be first, he must be the very last, and the servant of all."

He took a little child and had him stand among them. Taking him in his arms, he said to them, "Whoever welcomes one of these little children in my name welcomes me; and whoever welcomes me does not welcome me but the one who sent me."

"Teacher," said John, "we saw a man driving out demons in your name and we told him to stop, because he was not one of us."

"Do not stop him," Jesus said. "No one who does a miracle in my name can in the next moment say anything bad about me, for whoever is not against us is for us. I tell you the truth, anyone who gives you a cup of water in my name because you belong to Christ will certainly not lose his reward."

Despite the increased attention, Jesus' closest disciples, the Twelve, do not distinguish themselves—to put it mildly. "Are you so dull?" Jesus asks them at one point, and later sighs in exasperation, "How long shall I put up with you?" This chapter alone shows the disciples bungling a work of healing, misunderstanding Jesus' hints about his coming death and resurrection, squabbling about status, and trying to shut down the work of another disciple. Obviously, there is much in Jesus' mission they fail to comprehend.

Three of the disciples observe a dramatic scene that should quell any lingering doubts. "The Transfiguration," reported in vivid detail by Matthew, Mark, and Luke, affords absolute proof of God's approval. Jesus' face shines like the sun and his clothes become dazzling, "whiter than anyone in the world could bleach them." A cloud envelops the disciples and inside that cloud, to their astonishment, they find two long-dead giants of Jewish history: Moses and Elijah. It is too much to take; when God speaks audibly in the cloud, the disciples fall down, terrified. (Most scholars believe Mark got his details from Peter, one of the eyewitnesses. Peter describes the long-term impact of this experience in 2 Peter 1:16–18.)

Yet what impact does such a stupendous event have on the disciples? Does it permanently silence their questions and fill them with solid faith? A few weeks later, each one of the Twelve—including the three eyewitnesses of the Transfiguration—abandon Jesus in his hour of deepest need. Somehow the import of who Jesus is, God in flesh, never really sinks in until after he has left and then comes back.

Actually, the fact of the disciples' abrupt change makes compelling evidence for Jesus' resurrection. The cowering disciples portrayed in Mark hardly resemble the bold, confident figures in the book of Acts. Something incredible had to happen to turn this bunch of bumblers into heroes of the faith.   —PY

DAILY CONTEMPLATION

This chapter includes both highs and lows in the disciples' experience. What would a graph of your spiritual journey look like?

DAY 257   Reflection

STILL TRYING TO FIGURE JESUS OUT

I'm often relieved, when I read the Gospels, that God chose to put me on earth now rather than back in Jesus' day. A part of me envies those who got to see, hear, and touch Jesus in person. This part of me likes to surmise that life would be much easier if he were here before me in the flesh, available to answer my questions in person. But a bigger part of me suspects that would not be true. Would I find more clarity in making decisions after hearing Jesus voice his perspective? Would my life become easier after seeing and touching his physical presence?

I know my suspicious nature. Were I living back then, I'd probably fit right in with the crowds who followed Jesus, astonished by his miracle-working power and touched by his love yet skeptical about his unpretentious claim to be God. I hope that if given the chance, I would discern the truth of who Jesus was, but if many in the crowds didn't, would I?

Worse, would I have been any better than the Pharisees? I too can be self-righteous, convinced I know the mind of God. In reading the many passages in which Jesus chides the Pharisees, I sometimes shudder, feeling his reproach hitting too close to home.

I can also identify with the closest of Jesus' disciples. Even in seeing my master transfigured on the mountain and hearing God audibly commend him, I would likely be gripped with fear, as was Peter, and say something stupid. Or, despite my literary bent, I too might puzzle in ignorance over Jesus' obvious use of metaphor. "'Watch out for the yeast of the Pharisees'? Well of course, Jesus wants us to remember next time to bring more bread."

Yes, I fear that if placed on earth during his day, I would exasperate Jesus in the same way the majority of those who knew him did. Today I have the Bible spread before me. I can see his life from beginning to end and read prophecies about his coming, as well as teaching by the apostles written after he was gone. I have access to countless books and teachers who can open to me the truths Jesus came to reveal. More, I have his Spirit living inside—Jesus in me revealing himself. I can't complain. I have everything I need to know Jesus as he is and love him with my life.

Despite all this knowledge and opportunity, I'm still trying to figure Jesus out. I've walked with him for years yet realize I've hardly scratched the surface in knowing this Savior I call my own. "My sheep know me," Jesus said. I know I couldn't live my life without him. I know he's changed me and everything about me. And I know I need to keep learning to know him better.   —BQ

DAILY CONTEMPLATION

When have you envied those who knew Jesus in person? Come to Jesus with your questions about who he is. The goal of our lives is to walk more closely each day with him. Pray for Jesus to renew that passion in you and draw you more and more deeply into knowledge of himself.

DAY 258   Luke 10:1–24

JESUS SENDS OUT SEVENTY-TWO DISCIPLES

After this the Lord appointed seventy-two others and sent them two by two ahead of him to every town and place where he was about to go. He told them, "The harvest is plentiful, but the workers are few. Ask the Lord of the harvest, therefore, to send out workers into his harvest field. Go! I am sending you out like lambs among wolves. Do not take a purse or bag or sandals; and do not greet anyone on the road.

"When you enter a house, first say, 'Peace to this house.' If a man of peace is there, your peace will rest on him; if not, it will return to you. Stay in that house, eating and drinking whatever they give you, for the worker deserves his wages. Do not move around from house to house.

"When you enter a town and are welcomed, eat what is set before you. Heal the sick who are there and tell them, 'The kingdom of God is near you.' But when you enter a town and are not welcomed, go into its streets and say, 'Even the dust of your town that sticks to our feet we wipe off against you. Yet be sure of this: The kingdom of God is near.' I tell you, it will be more bearable on that day for Sodom than for that town.

"Woe to you, Korazin! Woe to you, Bethsaida! For if the miracles that were performed in you had been performed in Tyre and Sidon, they would have repented long ago, sitting in sackcloth and ashes. But it will be more bearable for Tyre and Sidon at the judgment than for you. And you, Capernaum, will you be lifted up to the skies? No, you will go down to the depths.

"He who listens to you listens to me; he who rejects you rejects me; but he who rejects me rejects him who sent me."

The seventy-two returned with joy and said, "Lord, even the demons submit to us in your name."

He replied, "I saw Satan fall like lightning from heaven. I have given you authority to trample on snakes and scorpions and to overcome all the power of the enemy; nothing will harm you. However, do not rejoice that the spirits submit to you, but rejoice that your names are written in heaven."

At that time Jesus, full of joy through the Holy Spirit, said, "I praise you, Father, Lord of heaven and earth, because you have hidden these things from the wise and learned, and revealed them to little children. Yes, Father, for this was your good pleasure.

"All things have been committed to me by my Father. No one knows who the Son is except the Father, and no one knows who the Father is except the Son and those to whom the Son chooses to reveal him."

Then he turned to his disciples and said privately, "Blessed are the eyes that see what you see. For I tell you that many prophets and kings wanted to see what you see but did not see it, and to hear what you hear but did not hear it."

Jesus' time on earth is running out. Only a few weeks remain for him to prepare others to carry on his work, and he uses that time for a crash training course. The opening scene in this chapter shows a major advance in his plan of "turning over" his work to his followers. This time he commissions not twelve but seventy-two followers in a hazardous assignment.

A seismic change is rumbling. As Jesus describes the mission of the seventy-two, he does not disguise his alarm. "Go! I am sending you out like lambs among wolves," he says. Finally, in a voice that commands attention, he gives this mysterious charge: "He who listens to you listens to me; he who rejects you rejects me."

Luke's next view of Jesus is almost unprecedented in the Gospels. Nowhere else will you find Jesus so happy, so bubbling with joy. The caution in his face has turned to exuberance. It has really worked, the dangerous mission into the hill country, and Jesus celebrates the enormous breakthrough with these seventy-two disciples.

In that triumphant response Jesus reveals the significance of the final phase of his mission. He has come to earth to establish a *church*, a group of people who will carry on his will after his departure. And as these seventy-two disciples plod the dusty roads of Judea, knocking on doors, explaining the Messiah, healing the sick, Jesus watches Satan fall like lightning from heaven. Their actions win a cosmic victory. Jesus' own mission, his own life, is being lived out through seventy-two very ordinary human beings.

—PY

DAILY CONTEMPLATION

When did you last sense Jesus' life being lived out through you?

DAY 259 Luke 10:25–37

THE PARABLE OF THE GOOD SAMARITAN

On one occasion an expert in the law stood up to test Jesus. "Teacher," he asked, "what must I do to inherit eternal life?"

"What is written in the Law?" he replied. "How do you read it?"

He answered: "'Love the Lord your God with all your heart and with all your soul and with all your strength and with all your mind'; and, 'Love your neighbor as yourself.'"

"You have answered correctly," Jesus replied. "Do this and you will live."

But he wanted to justify himself, so he asked Jesus, "And who is my neighbor?"

In reply Jesus said: "A man was going down from Jerusalem to Jericho, when he fell into the hands of robbers. They stripped him of his clothes, beat him and went away, leaving him half dead. A priest happened to be going down the same road, and when he saw the man, he passed by on the other side. So too, a Levite, when he came to the place and saw him, passed by on the other side. But a Samaritan, as he traveled, came where the man was; and when he saw him, he took pity on him. He went to him and bandaged his wounds, pouring on oil and wine. Then he put the man on his own donkey, took him to an inn and took care of him. The next day he took out two silver coins and gave them to the innkeeper. 'Look after him,' he said, 'and when I return, I will reimburse you for any extra expense you may have.'

"Which of these three do you think was a neighbor to the man who fell into the hands of robbers?"

The expert in the law replied, "The one who had mercy on him."

Jesus told him, "Go and do likewise."

esus tells a story about another way in which his followers will live out his life. Jesus, like the Samaritan in the story, has come to care for hurting people who are neglected by the religious leaders of the day, the ones supposed to be their caretakers. Like the priest and Levite, many of these leaders are too busy to interrupt their important agendas and help someone they've unexpectedly encountered. They are too busy working *for* God to care *like* God.

Jesus has another message, another approach. Love for God can't be an ethereal commitment of the head. Rather, it must impact the daily, moment-by-moment decisions a person makes. A heart that looks like Jesus' will fill with compassion upon seeing another person in need. A soul committed to him will resonate with his likeness. A mind surrendered to Jesus will decide like him regardless of feelings or convenience. And a person yielded to him will expend his or her strength in loving God actively. Heart, soul, mind, and strength devoted to God will translate into a real, living love for our neighbors. —BQ

DAILY CONTEMPLATION

When was the last time you went out of your way to help a neighbor in need?

DAY 260   Luke 10:38–42

AT THE HOME OF MARY AND MARTHA

As Jesus and his disciples were on their way, he came to a village where a woman named Martha opened her home to him. She had a sister called Mary, who sat at the Lord's feet listening to what he said. But Martha was distracted by all the preparations that had to be made. She came to him and asked, "Lord, don't you care that my sister has left me to do the work by myself? Tell her to help me!"

"Martha, Martha," the Lord answered, "you are worried and upset about many things, but only one thing is needed. Mary has chosen what is better, and it will not be taken away from her."

esus spends part of his final week on earth in Bethany, located less than two miles from Jerusalem. Here he takes time for two good friends, Mary and Martha, whose brother Lazarus Jesus will raise from the dead.

In this introduction to Mary and Martha, Luke gives a portrait of two personalities, two ways of living life. Though short, the story is packed with meaning. In fact, this scene often disturbs those believers who can identify more easily with Martha than with Mary. Martha is responsible, concerned about meeting the needs of others and preparing properly—certainly respectable qualities. Mary comes off as somewhat lazy and uncaring toward her sister.

If God creates people with individual personalities for his use, why does he commend Mary over Martha? Why does he fault Martha for seeking to be a competent hostess and commend Mary for sitting around doing nothing?

Mary has a deeper sense of priority in this situation. Under other circumstances she might be at fault for not helping her sister. But with Jesus as a guest, time with him takes precedence over all else.

Jesus teaches that ways of loving him won't always look the same. In each situation we should seek the Spirit's guidance in making choices about how best to love him. We will choose wrongly if we insist on always exhibiting our love one way, living inflexibly by our own unchanging standards.   —BQ

DAILY CONTEMPLATION

Do you identify more with Mary or Martha?

DAY 261   John 11:1–44

JESUS RAISES LAZARUS FROM THE DEAD

Now a man named Lazarus was sick. He was from Bethany, the village of Mary and her sister Martha. This Mary, whose brother Lazarus now lay sick, was the same one who poured perfume on the Lord and wiped his feet with her hair. So the sisters sent word to Jesus, "Lord, the one you love is sick."

When he heard this, Jesus said, "This sickness will not end in death. No, it is for God's glory so that God's Son may be glorified through it." Jesus loved Martha and her sister and Lazarus. Yet when he heard that Lazarus was sick, he stayed where he was two more days.

Then he said to his disciples, "Let us go back to Judea."

"But Rabbi," they said, "a short while ago the Jews tried to stone you, and yet you are going back there?"

Jesus answered, "Are there not twelve hours of daylight? A man who walks by day will not stumble, for he sees by this world's light. It is when he walks by night that he stumbles, for he has no light."

After he had said this, he went on to tell them, "Our friend Lazarus has fallen asleep; but I am going there to wake him up."

His disciples replied, "Lord, if he sleeps, he will get better." Jesus had been speaking of his death, but his disciples thought he meant natural sleep.

So then he told them plainly, "Lazarus is dead, and for your sake I am glad I was not there, so that you may believe. But let us go to him."

Then Thomas (called Didymus) said to the rest of the disciples, "Let us also go, that we may die with him."

On his arrival, Jesus found that Lazarus had already been in the tomb for four days. Bethany was less than two miles from Jerusalem, and many Jews had come to Martha and Mary to comfort them in the loss of their brother. When Martha heard that Jesus was coming, she went out to meet him, but Mary stayed at home.

"Lord," Martha said to Jesus, "if you had been here, my brother would not have died. But I know that even now God will give you whatever you ask."

Jesus said to her, "Your brother will rise again."

Martha answered, "I know he will rise again in the resurrection at the last day."

Jesus said to her, "I am the resurrection and the life. He who believes in me will live, even though he dies; and whoever lives and believes in me will never die. Do you believe this?"

"Yes, Lord," she told him, "I believe that you are the Christ, the Son of God, who was to come into the world."

And after she had said this, she went back and called her sister Mary aside. "The Teacher is here," she said, "and is asking for you." When Mary heard this, she got up quickly and went to him. Now Jesus had not yet entered the village, but was still at the place where Martha had met him. When the Jews who had been with Mary in the house, comforting her, noticed how quickly she got up and went out, they followed her, supposing she was going to the tomb to mourn there.

When Mary reached the place where Jesus was and saw him, she fell at his feet and said, "Lord, if you had been here, my brother would not have died."

When Jesus saw her weeping, and the Jews who had come along with her also weeping, he was deeply moved in spirit and troubled. "Where have you laid him?" he asked.

"Come and see, Lord," they replied.

Jesus wept.

Then the Jews said, "See how he loved him!"

But some of them said, "Could not he who opened the eyes of the blind man have kept this man from dying?"

Jesus, once more deeply moved, came to the tomb. It was a cave with a stone laid across the entrance. "Take away the stone," he said.

"But, Lord," said Martha, the sister of the dead man, "by this time there is a bad odor, for he has been there four days."

Then Jesus said, "Did I not tell you that if you believed, you would see the glory of God?"

So they took away the stone. Then Jesus looked up and said, "Father, I thank you that you have heard me. I knew that you always hear me, but I said this for the benefit of the people standing here, that they may believe that you sent me."

When he had said this, Jesus called in a loud voice, "Lazarus, come out!" The dead man came out, his hands and feet wrapped with strips of linen, and a cloth around his face.

Jesus said to them, "Take off the grave clothes and let him go."

Performing his most startling miracle yet, Jesus demonstrates that he is "the resurrection and the life." In doing so, Jesus seals his own death. After this miracle, the Jewish leaders won't risk letting him draw more crowds. Rome might become concerned and clamp down on the Jewish leaders to gain control.

Ironically, though Jesus' greatest exhibition of God's power will endanger his own life, it will ultimately accomplish what God intends. God receives glory both now and in the coming week, when after the death of his Son, a far greater resurrection will take place.

The people don't understand any of this yet. They have simply gathered in good Jewish custom to mourn and support their friends in grief. Many have heard Jesus and seen him do miraculous things, but this time it appears Jesus' help has come too late. Lazarus is long dead, and Jesus doesn't show up till well after the fact.

Imagine being at the tomb when Jesus comes, weeping, and asks to have the stone removed. "Now what?" the people must think aloud. "The guy has some wild ideas, but this time he's really making a spectacle of himself, and of Mary and Martha. Can't he mourn properly, like the rest of us?"

The words are hardly out of their mouths when they wonder if they're seeing a ghost. "How could it be? This is too much! Lazarus can't be alive—he's been dead for four days!"

"You're right," Jesus responds. "This *is* too much. God has much more in store than you could imagine. Now, if you believe, you'll see the glory of God as you've never seen it before."   —BQ

DAILY CONTEMPLATION

When has Jesus astonished you by doing something you'd never have expected?

DAY 262   Mark 10:32–11:11

JESUS PREDICTS HIS DEATH AND HEALS;

THE TRIUMPHAL ENTRY

They were on their way up to Jerusalem, with Jesus leading the way, and the disciples were astonished, while those who followed were afraid. Again he took the Twelve aside and told them what was going to happen to him. "We are going up to Jerusalem," he said, "and the Son of Man will be betrayed to the chief priests and teachers of the law. They will condemn him to death and will hand him over to the Gentiles, who will mock him and spit on him, flog him and kill him. Three days later he will rise."

495

Then James and John, the sons of Zebedee, came to him. "Teacher," they said, "we want you to do for us whatever we ask."

"What do you want me to do for you?" he asked.

They replied, "Let one of us sit at your right and the other at your left in your glory."

"You don't know what you are asking," Jesus said. "Can you drink the cup I drink or be baptized with the baptism I am baptized with?"

"We can," they answered.

Jesus said to them, "You will drink the cup I drink and be baptized with the baptism I am baptized with, but to sit at my right or left is not for me to grant. These places belong to those for whom they have been prepared."

When the ten heard about this, they became indignant with James and John. Jesus called them together and said, "You know that those who are regarded as rulers of the Gentiles lord it over them, and their high officials exercise authority over them. Not so with you. Instead, whoever wants to become great among you must be your servant, and whoever wants to be first must be slave of all. For even the Son of Man did not come to be served, but to serve, and to give his life as a ransom for many."

Then they came to Jericho. As Jesus and his disciples, together with a large crowd, were leaving the city, a blind man, Bartimaeus (that is, the Son of Timaeus), was sitting by the roadside begging. When he heard that it was Jesus of Nazareth, he began to shout, "Jesus, Son of David, have mercy on me!"

Many rebuked him and told him to be quiet, but he shouted all the more, "Son of David, have mercy on me!"

Jesus stopped and said, "Call him."

So they called to the blind man, "Cheer up! On your feet! He's calling you." Throwing his cloak aside, he jumped to his feet and came to Jesus.

"What do you want me to do for you?" Jesus asked him.

The blind man said, "Rabbi, I want to see."

"Go," said Jesus, "your faith has healed you." Immediately he received his sight and followed Jesus along the road.

As they approached Jerusalem and came to Bethphage and Bethany at the Mount of Olives, Jesus sent two of his disciples, saying to them, "Go to the village ahead of you, and just as you enter it, you will find a colt tied there, which no one has ever ridden. Untie it and bring it here. If anyone asks you, 'Why are you doing this?' tell him, 'The Lord needs it and will send it back here shortly.'"

They went and found a colt outside in the street, tied at a doorway. As they untied it, some people standing there asked, "What are you doing, untying that colt?" They answered as Jesus had told them to, and the people let them go. When they brought the colt to Jesus and threw their cloaks over it, he sat on it. Many people spread their cloaks on the road, while others spread branches they had cut in the fields. Those who went ahead and those who followed shouted,

"Hosanna!"

"Blessed is he who comes in the name of the Lord!"

"Blessed is the coming kingdom of our father David!"

"Hosanna in the highest!"

Jesus entered Jerusalem and went to the temple. He looked around at everything, but since it was already late, he went out to Bethany with the Twelve.

This scene opens with yet another prediction of Jesus' death. Showing incredible insensitivity, two of the disciples immediately lapse into a petty dispute about status. They cannot grasp the message Jesus patiently repeats for them: in his kingdom, the greatest is the one who *serves*.

Jesus uses curious techniques to gain recruits for his kingdom. His job descriptions include such words as *cross* and *slave*—rather like a Marine Corps recruiter displaying photos of war amputees and dead soldiers. Not even his closest friends can comprehend how the ugly image of an executioner's cross fits their dreams of a new kingdom. No matter how many times Jesus explains the way of the cross, it never seems to sink in.

As the group reaches Jerusalem, however, Jesus does permit one great display of public adulation. Always before, he has shrunk away from the crowds who try to coronate him. But in the "Triumphal Entry" of Palm Sunday he lets people honor him as the conquering Messiah.

In some ways, the procession is a slapstick affair compared with the lavish processions of the Romans—Jesus rides on a donkey, after all, not a stallion or a gilded chariot. But the event, foretold by the prophets, has deep meaning for the Jews. Jesus is openly declaring himself as Messiah, and the Triumphal Entry sets all Jerusalem astir.

Jewish leaders who oppose Jesus raise an alarm, and even the Romans take note of a man claiming to be a king. The rest of the Gospels, however, demonstrate how tragically short-lived Jesus' public acceptance proves to be. The crowds, like the disciples, are wholly unprepared for Jesus' style of kingdom. Its demands are too hard, its rewards too vague. —PY

DAILY CONTEMPLATION

How can you demonstrate servant leadership today?

DAY 263 Reflection

WAITING ON GOD

Just when I think I know what God is up to in my life, he changes directions and does something I'm not expecting. Although it's disorienting at times, I know God has a bigger and more intricate plan for me than I'll ever foresee. Each change of direction reminds me that I'll always need an attitude of waiting. I'll never arrive spiritually at a place where I can predict God's ways.

Jesus' disciples had to learn this lesson, too. Just a week before his crucifixion, Jesus told them for at least the second time that in Jerusalem he would be betrayed and killed, only to rise again. He was preparing them for difficult days soon to come. However, two of the disciples, James and John, rather than letting Jesus' words soak in and waiting for further guidance from him, impulsively tried to ensure for themselves the best place in heaven. Although two of Jesus' closest friends, they couldn't quiet their own ambitions enough to realize that God was doing something monumental and that they needed to take direction from him rather than proposing their own plan.

Writer Macrina Wiederkehr uses a fitting illustration from her days as a girl helping Mother bake bread. The ritual taught her something important about waiting.

> While she mixed and kneaded the dough we talked of many things, but when she covered the dough and put it in a warm place to rise, it was time to be quiet and wait. For me, it became a sacred, mystery hour, a holy hour, an hour of watching and waiting for the miracle of rising.
>
> During that time of waiting she would always tell me not to frighten the dough. It seems that dough grew best in a silent, peaceful atmosphere. And so if friends came over to play at that time, I would always tell them: *Don't scare the dough!* They would look at me strangely and never quite seem to understand. But I understood.[44]

In the wisdom of Ecclesiastes, there is "a time to be silent and a time to speak" (3:7), and for the disciples this was a time for silence, a time to wait for the miracle of rising. In a while God's greatest act of love would come to pass, and shortly afterward his Spirit would make a home in these men. They didn't understand, but they would see more clearly if only they would continue to watch and wait for the sacred mystery to unfold.

Even in the Old Testament God's followers knew of their need to wait. Job said, "I will wait for my renewal to come" (14:14), and David wrote often about waiting, saying in one psalm, "Be still before the LORD and wait patiently for him" (37:7). The apostles of Christ would sense this continued need for waiting. Paul cautioned Titus to say "'No' to ungodliness and worldly passions . . . while we wait for the blessed hope," Jesus' second coming (2:12–13).

God's work is always in process. Always there will be a warm stove-top place in my life that calls me to be silent and wait on God, a place where his sacred mysteries continue to rise. I am wise to heed David's, and Mother's, caution, "Be still, and don't scare the dough!"   —BQ

DAILY CONTEMPLATION

Is there an area in your life in which you think you know what God is up to? Or maybe one in which you have no idea of God's intentions? Ask God to calm you and help you wait on him.

Jesus Clears the Temple and Teaches

The next day as they were leaving Bethany, Jesus was hungry. Seeing in the distance a fig tree in leaf, he went to find out if it had any fruit. When he reached it, he found nothing but leaves, because it was not the season for figs. Then he said to the tree, "May no one ever eat fruit from you again." And his disciples heard him say it.

On reaching Jerusalem, Jesus entered the temple area and began driving out those who were buying and selling there. He overturned the tables of the money changers and the benches of those selling doves, and would not allow anyone to carry merchandise through the temple courts. And as he taught them, he said, "Is it not written:

"'My house will be called
a house of prayer for all nations'?

But you have made it 'a den of robbers.'"

The chief priests and the teachers of the law heard this and began looking for a way to kill him, for they feared him, because the whole crowd was amazed at his teaching.

When evening came, they went out of the city.

In the morning, as they went along, they saw the fig tree withered from the roots. Peter remembered and said to Jesus, "Rabbi, look! The fig tree you cursed has withered!"

"Have faith in God," Jesus answered. "I tell you the truth, if anyone says to this mountain, 'Go, throw yourself into the sea,' and does not doubt in his heart but believes that what he says will happen, it will be done for him. Therefore I tell you, whatever you ask for in prayer, believe that you have received it, and it will be yours. And when you stand praying, if you hold anything against anyone, forgive him, so that your Father in heaven may forgive you your sins."

They arrived again in Jerusalem, and while Jesus was walking in the temple courts, the chief priests, the teachers of the law and the elders came to him. "By what authority are you doing these things?" they asked. "And who gave you authority to do this?"

Jesus replied, "I will ask you one question. Answer me, and I will tell you by what authority I am doing these things. John's baptism—was it from heaven, or from men? Tell me!"

They discussed it among themselves and said, "If we say, 'From heaven,' he will ask, 'Then why didn't you believe him?' But if we say, 'From men' . . . ." (They feared the people, for everyone held that John really was a prophet.)

So they answered Jesus, "We don't know."

Jesus said, "Neither will I tell you by what authority I am doing these things."

He then began to speak to them in parables: "A man planted a vineyard. He put a wall around it, dug a pit for the winepress and built a watchtower. Then he rented the vineyard to some farmers and went away on a journey. At harvest time he sent a servant to the tenants to collect from them some of the fruit of the vineyard. But they seized him, beat him and sent him away empty-handed. Then he sent another servant to them; they struck this man on the head and treated him shamefully. He sent still another, and that one they killed. He sent many others; some of them they beat, others they killed.

"He had one left to send, a son, whom he loved. He sent him last of all, saying, 'They will respect my son.'

"But the tenants said to one another, 'This is the heir. Come, let's kill him, and the inheritance will be ours.' So they took him and killed him, and threw him out of the vineyard.

"What then will the owner of the vineyard do? He will come and kill those tenants and give the vineyard to others. Haven't you read this scripture:

"'The stone the builders rejected
    has become the capstone;
the Lord has done this,
    and it is marvelous in our eyes'?"

Then they looked for a way to arrest him because they knew he had spoken the parable against them. But they were afraid of the crowd; so they left him and went away.

The last few weeks of Jesus' life show a mounting sense of urgency, as seen in several dramatic confrontations at the temple. That sacred site, supposedly the center for worship of God, has taken on a commercial cast. Merchants, who sell sacrificial animals to pilgrims and foreigners at inflated prices, seem more interested in profit than in true worship. In the spirit of the Old Testament prophets, Jesus brands them "robbers" and forcibly drives them out.

Mark folds that scene into an account of a fig tree cursed by Jesus because of its lack of fruit. He is probably drawing a direct parallel to the religious establishment of the day: it too has "withered," and Jesus plans to take decisive action against it.

Jesus does nothing to temper his harsh message. On the contrary, he tells a parable that seems deliberately provocative. He presents himself as God's last resort, his final attempt to break through stubborn resistance. But he too will be killed, by the same people whose ancestors have mocked and killed the prophets.

Battle lines are drawn. On one side is Jesus, kept safe only by his widespread popularity. On the other are leaders of the religious and political establishments. Threatened by Jesus' radical message of repentance and reform, they determine to find a way to trap Jesus and turn the crowd against him.   —PY

DAILY CONTEMPLATION

In what way can you identify with Jesus' feelings in these stories?

500

JESUS TEACHES ON TAXES AND THE GREATEST
COMMANDMENT; THE WIDOW'S OFFERING

Later they sent some of the Pharisees and Herodians to Jesus to catch him in his words. They came to him and said, "Teacher, we know you are a man of integrity. You aren't swayed by men, because you pay no attention to who they are; but you teach the way of God in accordance with the truth. Is it right to pay taxes to Caesar or not? Should we pay or shouldn't we?"

But Jesus knew their hypocrisy. "Why are you trying to trap me?" he asked. "Bring me a denarius and let me look at it." They brought the coin, and he asked them, "Whose portrait is this? And whose inscription?"

"Caesar's," they replied.

Then Jesus said to them, "Give to Caesar what is Caesar's and to God what is God's."

And they were amazed at him.

Then the Sadducees, who say there is no resurrection, came to him with a question. "Teacher," they said, "Moses wrote for us that if a man's brother dies and leaves a wife but no children, the man must marry the widow and have children for his brother. Now there were seven brothers. The first one married and died without leaving any children. The second one married the widow, but he also died, leaving no child. It was the same with the third. In fact, none of the seven left any children. Last of all, the woman died too. At the resurrection whose wife will she be, since the seven were married to her?"

Jesus replied, "Are you not in error because you do not know the Scriptures or the power of God? When the dead rise, they will neither marry nor be given in marriage; they will be like the angels in heaven. Now about the dead rising—have you not read in the book of Moses, in the account of the bush, how God said to him, 'I am the God of Abraham, the God of Isaac, and the God of Jacob' ? He is not the God of the dead, but of the living. You are badly mistaken!"

One of the teachers of the law came and heard them debating. Noticing that Jesus had given them a good answer, he asked him, "Of all the commandments, which is the most important?"

"The most important one," answered Jesus, "is this: 'Hear, O Israel, the Lord our God, the Lord is one. Love the Lord your God with all your heart and with all your soul and with all your mind and with all your strength.' The second is this: 'Love your neighbor as yourself.' There is no commandment greater than these."

"Well said, teacher," the man replied. "You are right in saying that God is one and there is no other but him. To love him with all your heart, with all your understanding and with all your strength, and to love your neighbor as yourself is more important than all burnt offerings and sacrifices."

When Jesus saw that he had answered wisely, he said to him, "You are not far from the kingdom of God." And from then on no one dared ask him any more questions.

While Jesus was teaching in the temple courts, he asked, "How is it that the teachers of the law say that the Christ is the son of David? David himself, speaking by the Holy Spirit, declared:

> "'The Lord said to my Lord:
>   "Sit at my right hand
> until I put your enemies
>   under your feet."'

David himself calls him 'Lord.' How then can he be his son?"

The large crowd listened to him with delight.

As he taught, Jesus said, "Watch out for the teachers of the law. They like to walk around in flowing robes and be greeted in the marketplaces, and have the most important seats in the synagogues and the places of honor at banquets. They devour widows' houses and for a show make lengthy prayers. Such men will be punished most severely."

Jesus sat down opposite the place where the offerings were put and watched the crowd putting their money into the temple treasury. Many rich people threw in large amounts. But a poor widow came and put in two very small copper coins, worth only a fraction of a penny.

Calling his disciples to him, Jesus said, "I tell you the truth, this poor widow has put more into the treasury than all the others. They all gave out of their wealth; but she, out of her poverty, put in everything—all she had to live on."

Mark 12 records three different skirmishes between Jesus and the groups seeking to trap him.

The Pharisees, allied with a party following Herod, cynically praise Jesus and then spring on him a double-bind question: "Is it right to pay taxes to Caesar or not?" If Jesus says, "Pay the taxes," he will lose popular support, for the independence-minded Jews despise Roman occupation forces. If he says, "Don't pay," he could be turned in to Rome for breaking the law.

Next, a small but powerful religious group tries to stump Jesus with a theological question. The Sadducees, who do not believe in an afterlife, propose a complicated riddle about life after death.

Finally, Jesus' perennial enemies the Pharisees take their turn. Jewish rabbis of the day count 613 commandments in the law, and various splinter groups bicker over which ones are most important. The teacher of the law asks Jesus to select just one as the greatest commandment of all, knowing his choice will offend some of those groups.

Jesus avoids each of the verbal traps, succeeding so brilliantly that Mark concludes, "And from then on no one dared ask him any more questions." In all these skirmishes, Jesus does not try to placate his adversaries. Instead, he uses the occasions of conflict to warn his disciples and the watching crowds against those adversaries, whose fury only increases.

After he has fended off the last critic, Jesus points to a poor widow who has just made a tiny but sacrificial offering for the temple treasury. Her faithfulness, says Jesus, is far more impressive than that of the greedy religious establishment, who "devour widows' houses and for a show make lengthy prayers."
—PY

DAILY CONTEMPLATION

What can you learn from Jesus' style in handling his enemies?

DAY 266   Mark 13:1–37

SIGNS OF THE END OF THE AGE

As he was leaving the temple, one of his disciples said to him, "Look, Teacher! What massive stones! What magnificent buildings!"

"Do you see all these great buildings?" replied Jesus. "Not one stone here will be left on another; every one will be thrown down."

As Jesus was sitting on the Mount of Olives opposite the temple, Peter, James, John and Andrew asked him privately, "Tell us, when will these things happen? And what will be the sign that they are all about to be fulfilled?"

Jesus said to them: "Watch out that no one deceives you. Many will come in my name, claiming, 'I am he,' and will deceive many. When you hear of wars and rumors of wars, do not be alarmed. Such things must happen, but the end is still to come. Nation will rise against nation, and kingdom against kingdom. There will be earthquakes in various places, and famines. These are the beginning of birth pains.

"You must be on your guard. You will be handed over to the local councils and flogged in the synagogues. On account of me you will stand before governors and kings as witnesses to them. And the gospel must first be preached to all nations. Whenever you are arrested and brought to trial, do not worry beforehand about what to say. Just say whatever is given you at the time, for it is not you speaking, but the Holy Spirit.

"Brother will betray brother to death, and a father his child. Children will rebel against their parents and have them put to death. All men will hate you because of me, but he who stands firm to the end will be saved.

"When you see 'the abomination that causes desolation' standing where it does not belong—let the reader understand—then let those who are in Judea flee to the mountains. Let no one on the roof of his house go down or enter the house to take anything out. Let no one in the field go back to get his cloak. How dreadful it will be in those days for pregnant women and nursing mothers! Pray that this will not take place in winter, because those will be days of distress unequaled from the beginning, when God created the world, until now—and never to be equaled again. If the Lord had not cut short those days, no one would survive. But for the sake of the elect, whom he has chosen, he has shortened them. At that time if anyone says to you, 'Look, here is the Christ!' or, 'Look, there he is!' do not believe it. For false Christs and false prophets will appear and perform signs and miracles to deceive the elect—if that were possible. So be on your guard; I have told you everything ahead of time.

"But in those days, following that distress,

"'the sun will be darkened,
    and the moon will not give its light;
the stars will fall from the sky,
    and the heavenly bodies will be shaken.'

"At that time men will see the Son of Man coming in clouds with great power and glory. And he will send his angels and gather his elect from the four winds, from the ends of the earth to the ends of the heavens.

"Now learn this lesson from the fig tree: As soon as its twigs get tender and its leaves come out, you know that summer is near. Even so, when you see these things happening, you know that it is near, right at the door. I tell you the truth, this generation will certainly not pass away until all these things have happened. Heaven and earth will pass away, but my words will never pass away.

"No one knows about that day or hour, not even the angels in heaven, nor the Son, but only the Father. Be on guard! Be alert! You do not know when that time will come. It's like a man going away: He leaves his house and puts his servants in charge, each with his assigned task, and tells the one at the door to keep watch.

"Therefore keep watch because you do not know when the owner of the house will come back—whether in the evening, or at midnight, or when the rooster crows, or at dawn. If he comes suddenly, do not let him find you sleeping. What I say to you, I say to everyone: 'Watch!'"

Move forward a few days, beyond the events of this chapter, as Jesus is prodded by Roman soldiers toward the place of execution. A group of women follows behind, hysterical with grief. Suddenly Jesus turns and silences them with these words, "Daughters of Jerusalem, do not weep for me; weep for yourselves and for your children.... For if men do these things when the tree is green, what will happen when it is dry?" (Luke 23:28, 31).

Even in Jesus' childhood, rumors about him provoked a king's bloody campaign of infanticide. And as this chapter spells out in grim detail, Jesus does not expect the war against God's kingdom to end with his own death. He predicts that evil will only intensify until at last, in one final spasm of rebellion, the earth will give way to God's final restoration.

The words of this chapter echo, and quote from, the Old Testament prophets. "Before we can hear the last word," said Dietrich Bonhoeffer, "we must listen to the next-to-the-last word," and in the Bible that consists of dreadful apocalyptic visions. At the end of time, God will take off all the wraps. And when Jesus returns, he will appear in a new form: not as a helpless babe in a manger, not nailed to a crosspiece of wood, but as "the Son of Man coming in clouds with great power and glory."

Some of Jesus' dire predictions find fulfillment in A.D. 70, when Roman soldiers break through the walls of Jerusalem and demolish Herod's temple—the same temple Jesus' disciples are admiring when Jesus first speaks these words. Other predictions, clearly, have not yet been fulfilled. In this passage, Jesus gives direct clues to events that will precede his second coming. But he ends with a warning that no one can calculate the precise time of his return to earth.

It doesn't take long for doubters to appear on the scene. Just a few decades later scoffers are already mocking the notion of the second coming of Christ. "Where is this 'coming' he promised? Ever since our fathers died, everything goes on as it has since the beginning of creation" (2 Peter 3:4). For all such scoffers, Jesus and the prophets have one ominous word of advice: Just wait. God will not remain silent forever. One day, earth and sky will flee from his presence.   —PY

DAILY CONTEMPLATION

What response does Jesus want from those who hear these words?

DAY 267
Mark 14:1–31

JESUS ANOINTED AT BETHANY; JUDAS AGREES TO BETRAY JESUS; THE LORD'S SUPPER

Now the Passover and the Feast of Unleavened Bread were only two days away, and the chief priests and the teachers of the law were looking for some sly way to arrest Jesus and kill him. "But not during the Feast," they said, "or the people may riot."

While he was in Bethany, reclining at the table in the home of a man known as Simon the Leper, a woman came with an alabaster jar of very expensive perfume, made of pure nard. She broke the jar and poured the perfume on his head.

Some of those present were saying indignantly to one another, "Why this waste of perfume? It could have been sold for more than a year's wages and the money given to the poor." And they rebuked her harshly.

"Leave her alone," said Jesus. "Why are you bothering her? She has done a beautiful thing to me. The poor you will always have with you, and you can help them any time you want. But you will not always have me. She did what she could. She poured perfume on my body beforehand to prepare for my burial. I tell you the truth, wherever the gospel is preached throughout the world, what she has done will also be told, in memory of her."

Then Judas Iscariot, one of the Twelve, went to the chief priests to betray Jesus to them. They were delighted to hear this and promised to give him money. So he watched for an opportunity to hand him over.

On the first day of the Feast of Unleavened Bread, when it was customary to sacrifice the Passover lamb, Jesus' disciples asked him, "Where do you want us to go and make preparations for you to eat the Passover?"

So he sent two of his disciples, telling them, "Go into the city, and a man carrying a jar of water will meet you. Follow him. Say to the owner of the house he enters, 'The Teacher asks: Where is my guest room, where I may eat the Passover with my disciples?' He will show you a large upper room, furnished and ready. Make preparations for us there."

The disciples left, went into the city and found things just as Jesus had told them. So they prepared the Passover.

When evening came, Jesus arrived with the Twelve. While they were reclining at the table eating, he said, "I tell you the truth, one of you will betray me—one who is eating with me."

They were saddened, and one by one they said to him, "Surely not I?"

"It is one of the Twelve," he replied, "one who dips bread into the bowl with me. The Son of Man will go just as it is written about him. But woe to that man who betrays the Son of Man! It would be better for him if he had not been born."

While they were eating, Jesus took bread, gave thanks and broke it, and gave it to his disciples, saying, "Take it; this is my body."

Then he took the cup, gave thanks and offered it to them, and they all drank from it.

"This is my blood of the covenant, which is poured out for many," he said to them. "I tell you the truth, I will not drink again of the fruit of the vine until that day when I drink it anew in the kingdom of God."

When they had sung a hymn, they went out to the Mount of Olives.

"You will all fall away," Jesus told them, "for it is written:

"'I will strike the shepherd,
    and the sheep will be scattered.'

But after I have risen, I will go ahead of you into Galilee."

Peter declared, "Even if all fall away, I will not."

"I tell you the truth," Jesus answered, "today—yes, tonight—before the rooster crows twice you yourself will disown me three times."

But Peter insisted emphatically, "Even if I have to die with you, I will never disown you." And all the others said the same.

The Passover, an annual commemoration of the Israelites' deliverance from Egypt, is one of the high points of the Jewish calendar. In Jesus' day, all males older than twelve travel to Jerusalem for the holiday, filling the city with hundreds of thousands of pilgrims.

Jesus has entered that festive scene in a moment of triumph on Palm Sunday, but very soon a sense of doom steals in. He seems obsessed with death. When a woman splashes him with expensive perfume, he calls it a form of burial preparation.

Passover festivities culminate in a solemn meal, where family and close friends gather to remember the Exodus, the time of liberation. They taste morsels of food, sip wine, and read aloud the stories from the Old Testament. They also select a lamb to take to the temple and offer as a sacrifice to God. Thus the holiday ends on a sad and bloody note.

Outside the room, Jesus' enemies are stalking, waiting for an occasion to seize him. Inside, the disciples swear loyalty to their leader, even as he insists that, to a man, all will soon forsake him. It is at this somber meal that Jesus makes a profound declaration. "This is the blood of the new covenant," he says as he pours the wine. "Take it, this is my body," he says, breaking bread.

What the disciples do not fully understand is that a dream is dying—a dream of a mighty nation, God's covenant nation. Jesus is announcing a new covenant, sealed not with the blood of lambs but with his own blood. The new kingdom, the kingdom of God, will be led not by Jewish generals and kings but rather by the scared band of disciples gathered around the table—the very disciples who will soon betray him.

Today, virtually all Christian churches continue the practice of Communion (Mass, Eucharist, or Lord's Supper) in some form. This solemn ceremony dates back to the original Passover meal when Jesus instituted the new covenant.   —PY

DAILY CONTEMPLATION

What does the celebration of the Lord's Supper mean to you?

DAY 268   Reflection

LOVING JESUS EXTRAVAGANTLY

When I hear the word *extravagance*, I think of beautiful possessions, rich foods, a lavish lifestyle. It's a word we use most often in connection with luxuries.

The Bible, though it does not use the word directly, suggests another use for *extravagance*: to describe ways of loving. The woman who anointed Jesus' feet with perfume, for instance, knew a lot about extravagant loving. John identifies her as Mary, the sister of Martha and Lazarus. Only days earlier Mary had sat at Jesus' feet, absorbed in his company while her sister complained of her laziness. Now Mary takes a valuable jar of perfume and pours it on Jesus' feet out of love for him. Again her actions are misunderstood and criticized. Some protest that she is careless and wasteful, foolishly emptying a valuable flask that could have been sold for the poor.

Jesus observed another woman in a "foolish" act of extravagant love: a widow dropped all the money she had into the temple offering. Another man, in a parable Jesus told, interrupted his journey and "wasted" time and money to help a wounded traveler, one from a group who had oppressed his own people.

A glimpse of a wild, uninhibited King David provides a vivid picture of extravagant love. Leading a procession in bringing the ark of God back to Jerusalem, David "danced before the LORD with all his might" (2 Samuel 6:14), wearing only a skimpy garment, while the others shouted and sounded trumpets. David's wife Michal watched in embarrassment, grimacing. No king should act in such an undignified manner, she felt.

I think of these Bible characters and look at my own life. How extravagantly do I love Jesus? How willing am I to give my most costly possession away? How eager am I to spend stretches of time with God? How apt to offer money I really need? How likely to spend time on someone I don't know and don't particularly care about? How often do I shed my inhibitions to worship God in a physical, demonstrative, even ecstatic way?

Tough questions. Ones I'd rather not look at too honestly. Love for God is good and right, but extravagant love? It feels scary, risky, threatening to take a lot from me and guaranteeing nothing in return. What is more challenging, I need to offer this love spontaneously. Rarely planned or manufactured, extravagant love simply lives out daily God's greatest commandment: to "love the Lord your God with all your heart and with all your soul and with all your mind and with all your strength" (Mark 12:30). Those in the Bible who loved extravagantly displayed an inner love that wouldn't have them do any differently.

With that same love real in my life, I may not look like Mary, the widow, the Good Samaritan, or David. I'll love God extravagantly in ways that flow from the person God made me to be. I'll love God with all my might, no expenses spared, and I'll smile to myself when someday I'm labeled "foolish."   —BQ

DAILY CONTEMPLATION

Does the thought of loving Jesus in an extravagant way scare you? Rather than focusing on what you can do to love Jesus, focus simply on loving him. Ask God to bring you deeper each day into a love relationship with him. Extravagant acts will flow from this life-giving bond.

PART 9

FINAL DAYS

DAY 269 John 13:1–17

Jesus Washes His Disciples' Feet

It was just before the Passover Feast. Jesus knew that the time had come for him to leave this world and go to the Father. Having loved his own who were in the world, he now showed them the full extent of his love.

The evening meal was being served, and the devil had already prompted Judas Iscariot, son of Simon, to betray Jesus. Jesus knew that the Father had put all things under his power, and that he had come from God and was returning to God; so he got up from the meal, took off his outer clothing, and wrapped a towel around his waist. After that, he poured water into a basin and began to wash his disciples' feet, drying them with the towel that was wrapped around him.

He came to Simon Peter, who said to him, "Lord, are you going to wash my feet?"

Jesus replied, "You do not realize now what I am doing, but later you will understand."

"No," said Peter, "you shall never wash my feet."

Jesus answered, "Unless I wash you, you have no part with me."

"Then, Lord," Simon Peter replied, "not just my feet but my hands and my head as well!"

Jesus answered, "A person who has had a bath needs only to wash his feet; his whole body is clean. And you are clean, though not every one of you." For he knew who was going to betray him, and that was why he said not every one was clean.

When he had finished washing their feet, he put on his clothes and returned to his place. "Do you understand what I have done for you?" he asked them. "You call me 'Teacher' and 'Lord,' and rightly so, for that is what I am. Now that I, your Lord and Teacher, have washed your feet, you also should wash one another's feet. I have set you an example that you should do as I have done for you. I tell you the truth, no servant is greater than his master, nor is a messenger greater than the one who sent him. Now that you know these things, you will be blessed if you do them."

Once again Jesus teaches his disciples by doing something that dumbfounds them. Throughout his ministry Jesus has continually resisted the outward status that accompanies leadership. Although clearly a leader, he has refused to pull rank as a leader often does. On this night he demonstrates a humility that will only be exceeded when he goes to the cross.

People in Palestine often traveled dusty roads by foot, wearing sandals on bare feet, which made foot washing a daily necessity. A servant or a woman sometimes washed the feet of guests or family, or more typically people did it themselves. Since people normally washed before meals, Jesus' act in the middle of a meal is especially surprising.

You can easily understand the disciples' chagrin at seeing Jesus, mid-meal, remove some of his clothes and begin to wash the grime of a day's travel from the feet of his friends. On the eve of his death, despite his many clues, they are still hoping for a Messiah to exalt. One who takes the posture of a servant just doesn't fit their image of God's Son.

Jesus' demonstration of love and servanthood lives on as a reminder to believers that nothing we could do for another person is beneath something Jesus would do. No matter what we feel we deserve from others, we can't bend too low in caring for them. Service doesn't demean one's dignity; rather, as Jesus shows, it defines it.—BQ

DAILY CONTEMPLATION

Can you recall a recent time when it was difficult to serve someone else?

DAY 270

John 14:1–31

JESUS THE WAY TO THE FATHER;
JESUS PROMISES THE HOLY SPIRIT

"Do not let your hearts be troubled. Trust in God; trust also in me. In my Father's house are many rooms; if it were not so, I would have told you. I am

510

going there to prepare a place for you. And if I go and prepare a place for you, I will come back and take you to be with me that you also may be where I am. You know the way to the place where I am going."

Thomas said to him, "Lord, we don't know where you are going, so how can we know the way?"

Jesus answered, "I am the way and the truth and the life. No one comes to the Father except through me. If you really knew me, you would know my Father as well. From now on, you do know him and have seen him."

Philip said, "Lord, show us the Father and that will be enough for us."

Jesus answered: "Don't you know me, Philip, even after I have been among you such a long time? Anyone who has seen me has seen the Father. How can you say, 'Show us the Father'? Don't you believe that I am in the Father, and that the Father is in me? The words I say to you are not just my own. Rather, it is the Father, living in me, who is doing his work. Believe me when I say that I am in the Father and the Father is in me; or at least believe on the evidence of the miracles themselves. I tell you the truth, anyone who has faith in me will do what I have been doing. He will do even greater things than these, because I am going to the Father. And I will do whatever you ask in my name, so that the Son may bring glory to the Father. You may ask me for anything in my name, and I will do it.

"If you love me, you will obey what I command. And I will ask the Father, and he will give you another Counselor to be with you forever—the Spirit of truth. The world cannot accept him, because it neither sees him nor knows him. But you know him, for he lives with you and will be in you. I will not leave you as orphans; I will come to you. Before long, the world will not see me anymore, but you will see me. Because I live, you also will live. On that day you will realize that I am in my Father, and you are in me, and I am in you. Whoever has my commands and obeys them, he is the one who loves me. He who loves me will be loved by my Father, and I too will love him and show myself to him."

Then Judas (not Judas Iscariot) said, "But, Lord, why do you intend to show yourself to us and not to the world?"

Jesus replied, "If anyone loves me, he will obey my teaching. My Father will love him, and we will come to him and make our home with him. He who does not love me will not obey my teaching. These words you hear are not my own; they belong to the Father who sent me.

"All this I have spoken while still with you. But the Counselor, the Holy Spirit, whom the Father will send in my name, will teach you all things and will remind you of everything I have said to you. Peace I leave with you; my peace I give you. I do not give to you as the world gives. Do not let your hearts be troubled and do not be afraid.

"You heard me say, 'I am going away and I am coming back to you.' If you loved me, you would be glad that I am going to the Father, for the Father is greater than I. I have told you now before it happens, so that when it does happen you will believe. I will not speak with you much longer, for the prince of this world is coming. He has no hold on me, but the world must learn that I love the Father and that I do exactly what my Father has commanded me.

"Come now; let us leave."

The apostle John devotes one-third of his gospel to the last twenty-four hours of Jesus' life. John stretches the Passover meal out over five chapters (13–17), and nothing like these chapters exists elsewhere in the Bible. Their slow-motion, realistic detail provides an intimate memoir of Jesus' most anguished evening on earth.

Leonardo da Vinci immortalized the setting of the Last Supper in his famous painting, arranging the participants on one side of the table as if they were posing for the artist. John avoids physical details and presents instead the maelstrom of human emotions. He holds a light to the disciples' faces, and you can almost see the awareness flickering in their eyes. All that Jesus has told them over the past three years is setting in.

Never before has Jesus been so direct with them. It is his last chance to communicate to them the significance of his life and his death. He refrains from parables and painstakingly answers the disciples' redundant questions. The world is about to undergo a convulsive trauma, and the eleven fearful men with him are his hope for that world.

"I am going away, and I am coming back to you," Jesus keeps repeating, until at last the disciples show signs of comprehension. God's Son has entered the world to reside in one body. He is now leaving earth to return to the Father. But someone else—the Spirit of truth, the Counselor—will come to take up residence in many bodies, in *their* bodies.

Jesus is planning to die, yes. He is leaving them. But in some mysterious way, he is not leaving. He will not stay dead. This night, Jesus gives them an intimacy with the Father such as they have never known, yet he promises an even greater intimacy to come. He seems aware that much of what they nod their heads at now will not sink in until later.   —PY

DAILY CONTEMPLATION

Which of Jesus' words in this chapter mean the most to you today?

DAY 271   John 15:1–16:4

THE VINE AND THE BRANCHES;

THE WORLD HATES THE DISCIPLES

"I am the true vine, and my Father is the gardener. He cuts off every branch
in me that bears no fruit, while every branch that does bear fruit he prunes

so that it will be even more fruitful. You are already clean because of the word I have spoken to you. Remain in me, and I will remain in you. No branch can bear fruit by itself; it must remain in the vine. Neither can you bear fruit unless you remain in me.

"I am the vine; you are the branches. If a man remains in me and I in him, he will bear much fruit; apart from me you can do nothing. If anyone does not remain in me, he is like a branch that is thrown away and withers; such branches are picked up, thrown into the fire and burned. If you remain in me and my words remain in you, ask whatever you wish, and it will be given you. This is to my Father's glory, that you bear much fruit, showing yourselves to be my disciples.

"As the Father has loved me, so have I loved you. Now remain in my love. If you obey my commands, you will remain in my love, just as I have obeyed my Father's commands and remain in his love. I have told you this so that my joy may be in you and that your joy may be complete. My command is this: Love each other as I have loved you. Greater love has no one than this, that he lay down his life for his friends. You are my friends if you do what I command. I no longer call you servants, because a servant does not know his master's business. Instead, I have called you friends, for everything that I learned from my Father I have made known to you. You did not choose me, but I chose you and appointed you to go and bear fruit—fruit that will last. Then the Father will give you whatever you ask in my name. This is my command: Love each other.

"If the world hates you, keep in mind that it hated me first. If you belonged to the world, it would love you as its own. As it is, you do not belong to the world, but I have chosen you out of the world. That is why the world hates you. Remember the words I spoke to you: 'No servant is greater than his master.' If they persecuted me, they will persecute you also. If they obeyed my teaching, they will obey yours also. They will treat you this way because of my name, for they do not know the One who sent me. If I had not come and spoken to them, they would not be guilty of sin. Now, however, they have no excuse for their sin. He who hates me hates my Father as well. If I had not done among them what no one else did, they would not be guilty of sin. But now they have seen these miracles, and yet they have hated both me and my Father. But this is to fulfill what is written in their Law: 'They hated me without reason.'

"When the Counselor comes, whom I will send to you from the Father, the Spirit of truth who goes out from the Father, he will testify about me. And you also must testify, for you have been with me from the beginning.

"All this I have told you so that you will not go astray. They will put you out of the synagogue; in fact, a time is coming when anyone who kills you will think he is offering a service to God. They will do such things because they have not known the Father or me. I have told you this, so that when the time comes you will remember that I warned you. I did not tell you this at first because I was with you."

The sense of urgency grows inside the stuffy, crowded room. Jesus has just a few more hours to prepare his disciples for the tumult that lies ahead. More, these are his closest friends in all the world, and he is about to leave them.

In this passage, Jesus envisions what will happen to the little band after his departure. He foresees fierce opposition and hatred and beatings and executions. The disciples will face all these trials on his behalf and without his physical presence to protect them.

As he has done so often, Jesus reaches for an allegory, a parable from nature to drive home his point. Just outside Jerusalem, rows of vineyards cover the hills—probably, he and his disciples have walked through them on their way to the city—and Jesus summons up two images from those vineyards.

First, the image of lush, juicy grapes. Not long before, the disciples have drunk the product of those grapes as they listened to Jesus' deeply symbolic words about the blood of the covenant. In order to bear fruit, Jesus says, one thing is essential: they must remain in intimate connection with the vine. Jesus also reminds the Twelve that he has handpicked them for a specific mission: "to go and bear fruit— fruit that will last."

Then Jesus mentions one more image: a pile of dead sticks at the edge of the vineyard. Somehow, these branches have lost their connection with the vine, the source of nourishment. A farmer has snapped them off and thrown them in a heap for burning. They no longer have a useful function.

Most likely, Jesus' disciples do not fully understand his meaning that night. But the symbol, with its abrupt contrast between juicy grapes and withered branches, will stay with them. The spectacular history of the early church gives certain proof that they eventually heed his heartfelt words about "remaining" in him.   —PY

DAILY CONTEMPLATION

In what ways do you work at remaining in Jesus?

DAY 272   John 16:5–33

THE WORK OF THE HOLY SPIRIT;
THE DISCIPLES' GRIEF WILL TURN TO JOY

"Now I am going to him who sent me, yet none of you asks me, 'Where are you going?' Because I have said these things, you are filled with grief. But I tell you the truth: It is for your good that I am going away. Unless I go away, the Counselor will not come to you; but if I go, I will send him to you. When he comes, he will convict the world of guilt in regard to sin and righteousness and judgment: in regard to sin, because men do not believe in me; in regard to righteousness, because I am going to the Father, where you can see me no longer; and in regard to judgment, because the prince of this world now stands condemned.

"I have much more to say to you, more than you can now bear. But when he, the Spirit of truth, comes, he will guide you into all truth. He will not speak on his own; he will speak only what he hears, and he will tell you what is yet to come. He will bring glory to me by taking from what is mine and making it known to you. All that belongs to the Father is mine. That is why I said the Spirit will take from what is mine and make it known to you.

"In a little while you will see me no more, and then after a little while you will see me."

Some of his disciples said to one another, "What does he mean by saying, 'In a little while you will see me no more, and then after a little while you will see me,' and 'Because I am going to the Father'?" They kept asking, "What does he mean by 'a little while'? We don't understand what he is saying."

Jesus saw that they wanted to ask him about this, so he said to them, "Are you asking one another what I meant when I said, 'In a little while you will see me no more, and then after a little while you will see me'? I tell you the truth, you will weep and mourn while the world rejoices. You will grieve, but your grief will turn to joy. A woman giving birth to a child has pain because her time has come; but when her baby is born she forgets the anguish because of her joy that a child is born into the world. So with you: Now is your time of grief, but I will see you again and you will rejoice, and no one will take away your joy. In that day you will no longer ask me anything. I tell you the truth, my Father will give you whatever you ask in my name. Until now you have not asked for anything in my name. Ask and you will receive, and your joy will be complete.

"Though I have been speaking figuratively, a time is coming when I will no longer use this kind of language but will tell you plainly about my Father. In that day you will ask in my name. I am not saying that I will ask the Father on your behalf. No, the Father himself loves you because you have loved me and have believed that I came from God. I came from the Father and entered the world; now I am leaving the world and going back to the Father."

Then Jesus' disciples said, "Now you are speaking clearly and without figures of speech. Now we can see that you know all things and that you do not even need to have anyone ask you questions. This makes us believe that you came from God."

"You believe at last!" Jesus answered. "But a time is coming, and has come, when you will be scattered, each to his own home. You will leave me all alone. Yet I am not alone, for my Father is with me.

"I have told you these things, so that in me you may have peace. In this world you will have trouble. But take heart! I have overcome the world."

After the allegory of the vine and branches, Jesus turns from word pictures and speaks directly about what will happen to the disciples. Never is he more "theological" with them. Some of it they understand, some of it they do not. John shows them whispering to each other, trying to figure out his meaning.

Perhaps the strangest words of all are these: "It is for your good that I am going away." Good? How could it possibly be good for him to abandon them, thus dashing their hopes of a restored kingdom? Jesus tries to explain the advantages to come, when the Spirit will live inside them, but the disciples are too busy discussing what he means by "going away" to comprehend.

Jesus' analogy of childbirth gives a further clue. Although childbirth may involve great pain, the pain is not a dead end, like pain caused by cancer. The effort of giving birth produces something—new life!—and results in joy. In the same way, the great sorrow he and the disciples are about to undergo will not be a dead end. His pain will bring about the salvation of the world; their grief will turn to joy.

Jesus concludes his teaching this fateful evening with a ringing declaration: "Take heart! I have overcome the world." How hollow this statement will seem the next evening when his pale, abused body hangs on an executioner's cross, and the disciples slink away in the darkness. Their emotions, and faith, are to rise and plummet in one unforgettable day—just as Jesus has predicted in his analogy of childbirth. —PY

DAILY CONTEMPLATION

When have you experienced great pain that in the end brought joy?

DAY 273 John 17:1–26

JESUS PRAYS

After Jesus said this, he looked toward heaven and prayed:

"Father, the time has come. Glorify your Son, that your Son may glorify you. For you granted him authority over all people that he might give eternal life to all those you have given him. Now this is eternal life: that they may know you, the only true God, and Jesus Christ, whom you have sent. I have brought you glory on earth by completing the work you gave me to do. And now, Father, glorify me in your presence with the glory I had with you before the world began.

"I have revealed you to those whom you gave me out of the world. They were yours; you gave them to me and they have obeyed your word. Now they know that everything you have given me comes from you. For I gave them the words you gave me and they accepted them. They knew with certainty that I came from you, and they believed that you sent me. I pray for them. I am not praying for the world, but for those you have given me, for they are yours. All I have is yours, and all you have is mine. And glory has come to me through them. I will remain in the world no longer, but they are still in the world, and I am coming to you. Holy Father, protect them by the power of your name—the name you gave me—so that they may be one as we are one. While I was with them, I protected them and kept them safe by that name you gave me. None has been lost except the one doomed to destruction so that Scripture would be fulfilled.

"I am coming to you now, but I say these things while I am still in the world, so that they may have the full measure of my joy within them. I have given them your word and the world has hated them, for they are not of the world any more than I am of the world. My prayer is not that you take them out of the world but that you protect them from the evil one. They are not of the world, even as I am not of it. Sanctify them by the truth; your word is truth. As you sent me into the world, I have sent them into the world. For them I sanctify myself, that they too may be truly sanctified.

"My prayer is not for them alone. I pray also for those who will believe in me through their message, that all of them may be one, Father, just as you are in me and I am in you. May they also be in us so that the world may believe that you have sent me. I have given them the glory that you gave me, that they may be one as we are one: I in them and you in me. May they be brought to complete unity to let the world know that you sent me and have loved them even as you have loved me.

"Father, I want those you have given me to be with me where I am, and to see my glory, the glory you have given me because you loved me before the creation of the world.

"Righteous Father, though the world does not know you, I know you, and they know that you have sent me. I have made you known to them, and will continue to make you known in order that the love you have for me may be in them and that I myself may be in them."

When the disciples respond to Jesus' speech with the bold pronouncement "This makes us believe that you came from God," it seems to settle something in Jesus' mind. "You believe at last!" he says, with obvious relief (John 16:31), and then concludes the intimate get-together with this, his longest recorded prayer. In it, Jesus sums up his feelings and his plans for the tight circle of friends gathered around him.

Their previous missions, the preaching and healing ministries in the countryside, have been mere warm-up exercises. Now he is turning everything over to them. "I confer on you a kingdom, just as my Father conferred one on me," he once said (Luke 22:29). This prayer represents a kind of commissioning or graduation.

Using language full of mystery, Jesus tells them that he must leave the world but they must remain in it to proclaim him. They will now attract the hatred and hostility that have previously been directed against him. And yet, although they live "in the world," they are not quite "of the world." Something sets them apart from the world and binds them together with him in unity with God—a unity so close as to defy all explanation.

Jesus prays too for the other believers who will follow them, stretching in an unbroken chain throughout history. "I pray . . . that all of them may be one, Father, just as you are in me and I am in you. May they also be in us so that the world may believe that you have sent me." And then he leads the frightened little band to his appointment with death. —PY

DAILY CONTEMPLATION

Based on this prayer, how would you sum up Jesus' goals for the church? How well do Christians today fulfill those goals?

DAY 274 Reflection

ABIDING IN JESUS

Remain in me, and I will remain in you. No branch can bear fruit by itself; it must remain in the vine. Neither can you bear fruit unless you remain in me" (John 15:4). When I'm reading the Bible on a regular basis, and especially when I'm reading about Jesus, I feel more connected to him. I feel more in tune with who he is, what he cares about, how he lived, what he means in my life. I come closer to understanding the One who possesses my life. One Christian leader recommends reading something from the Gospels every day, to fill our minds with the words and works of Jesus in daily doses. Now I can see the value.

Yet not only in Bible reading do I come to know Christ. When Jesus left the earth, he gave to believers the Holy Spirit to provide the constant presence of himself. The Holy Spirit reveals Jesus to me day by day as I walk with him; and more, if I'm willing, the Spirit makes me increasingly like Jesus. My mind and actions gradually become one with his.

Oswald Chambers, a teacher and missionary who lived in the early twentieth century, talks about this process, known as *sanctification*. "Sanctification means being made one with Jesus so that the disposition that ruled Him will rule us."[45] The term has largely fallen out of use in the church today, but Jesus himself prayed about it in John 17: "Sanctify them by the truth; your word is truth. As you sent me into the world, I have sent them into the world. For them I sanctify myself, that they too may be truly sanctified" (vv. 17–19). Jesus spoke about setting himself apart for the Father's work so that in turn his disciples could be set apart to do God's work through Christ's Spirit living in them.

There is a big difference between living for Jesus and having Jesus live in us. Attempts to live for him often turn out more Pharisee-like, disciple-like, or crowd-like than Christlike. Only Jesus can produce the life of himself in us. When he inhabits us and his life becomes ours, he acts in all the surprising fullness of himself.

Soaking in the Bible, especially the Gospels, is a way of remaining in Jesus, abiding in the vine so that I can bear his fruit in the world. I need that help. Daily I'm surrounded by much that encourages another way of living—an ultimately destructive way. Keeping the Bible, with its stories of Jesus' life, before me is the link I need to

518

keep drawing sustenance from his roots, growing through his Spirit into the branch that extends from himself.   —BQ

DAILY CONTEMPLATION

Where are you in the process of sanctification? Are you willing to become more and more one with Jesus? Have you already experienced this beginning to happen? Ask God for his Spirit to continue shaping you. Ask Jesus to do his work of sanctification, nourishing you as you abide in him.

DAY 275   Matthew 26:36–75

JESUS IN GETHSEMANE AND BEFORE THE SANHEDRIN; PETER DISOWNS JESUS

Then Jesus went with his disciples to a place called Gethsemane, and he said to them, "Sit here while I go over there and pray." He took Peter and the two sons of Zebedee along with him, and he began to be sorrowful and troubled. Then he said to them, "My soul is overwhelmed with sorrow to the point of death. Stay here and keep watch with me."

Going a little farther, he fell with his face to the ground and prayed, "My Father, if it is possible, may this cup be taken from me. Yet not as I will, but as you will."

Then he returned to his disciples and found them sleeping. "Could you men not keep watch with me for one hour?" he asked Peter. "Watch and pray so that you will not fall into temptation. The spirit is willing, but the body is weak."

He went away a second time and prayed, "My Father, if it is not possible for this cup to be taken away unless I drink it, may your will be done."

When he came back, he again found them sleeping, because their eyes were heavy. So he left them and went away once more and prayed the third time, saying the same thing.

Then he returned to the disciples and said to them, "Are you still sleeping and resting? Look, the hour is near, and the Son of Man is betrayed into the hands of sinners. Rise, let us go! Here comes my betrayer!"

While he was still speaking, Judas, one of the Twelve, arrived. With him was a large crowd armed with swords and clubs, sent from the chief priests and the elders of the people. Now the betrayer had arranged a signal with them: "The one I kiss is the man; arrest him." Going at once to Jesus, Judas said, "Greetings, Rabbi!" and kissed him.

Jesus replied, "Friend, do what you came for."

Then the men stepped forward, seized Jesus and arrested him. With that, one of Jesus' companions reached for his sword, drew it out and struck the servant of the high priest, cutting off his ear.

"Put your sword back in its place," Jesus said to him, "for all who draw the sword will die by the sword. Do you think I cannot call on my Father, and he will at once put at my disposal more than twelve legions of angels? But how then would the Scriptures be fulfilled that say it must happen in this way?"

At that time Jesus said to the crowd, "Am I leading a rebellion, that you have come out with swords and clubs to capture me? Every day I sat in the temple courts teaching, and you did not arrest me. But this has all taken place that the writings of the prophets might be fulfilled." Then all the disciples deserted him and fled.

Those who had arrested Jesus took him to Caiaphas, the high priest, where the teachers of the law and the elders had assembled. But Peter followed him at a distance, right up to the courtyard of the high priest. He entered and sat down with the guards to see the outcome.

The chief priests and the whole Sanhedrin were looking for false evidence against Jesus so that they could put him to death. But they did not find any, though many false witnesses came forward.

Finally two came forward and declared, "This fellow said, 'I am able to destroy the temple of God and rebuild it in three days.'"

Then the high priest stood up and said to Jesus, "Are you not going to answer? What is this testimony that these men are bringing against you?" But Jesus remained silent.

The high priest said to him, "I charge you under oath by the living God: Tell us if you are the Christ, the Son of God."

"Yes, it is as you say," Jesus replied. "But I say to all of you: In the future you will see the Son of Man sitting at the right hand of the Mighty One and coming on the clouds of heaven."

Then the high priest tore his clothes and said, "He has spoken blasphemy! Why do we need any more witnesses? Look, now you have heard the blasphemy. What do you think?"

"He is worthy of death," they answered.

Then they spit in his face and struck him with their fists. Others slapped him and said, "Prophesy to us, Christ. Who hit you?"

Now Peter was sitting out in the courtyard, and a servant girl came to him. "You also were with Jesus of Galilee," she said.

But he denied it before them all. "I don't know what you're talking about," he said.

Then he went out to the gateway, where another girl saw him and said to the people there, "This fellow was with Jesus of Nazareth."

He denied it again, with an oath: "I don't know the man!"

After a little while, those standing there went up to Peter and said, "Surely you are one of them, for your accent gives you away."

Then he began to call down curses on himself and he swore to them, "I don't know the man!"

Immediately a rooster crowed. Then Peter remembered the word Jesus had spoken: "Before the rooster crows, you will disown me three times." And he went outside and wept bitterly.

In a stroke of bitter irony, the intimate scene of the Last Supper butts up against the scene of betrayal in Gethsemane (geth-SEM-uh-nee). The ordeal begins with Jesus praying in a quiet, cool grove of olive trees, with three of his disciples waiting sleepily outside and a large armed mob making its way toward the garden to seize and torture Jesus.

He feels afraid and abandoned. Falling facedown on the ground, he prays for some way out. The future of the human race and of the entire universe comes down to this one weeping figure whose sweat falls to the ground in large drops, like blood.

All the deep ironies of Jesus' life come crashing together this evening in the garden, when the one whom wise men crossed a continent to worship is sold like a slave for thirty pieces of silver. Jesus' disciples still have not come to terms with the kind of "kingdom" Jesus wants to establish. Blustery Peter is prepared to install a kingdom the traditional way—by force. When he hacks off the servant's ear, however, Jesus stops the violence and performs, notably, his last miracle: he heals the servant. Still, Peter later denies knowing Jesus.

With a single prayer, Jesus reminds his friends, he could dispatch squadrons of angels. He has the power to defend himself, but he will not use it. When the disciples realize that they can expect no last-minute rescue operations from the invisible world, they all flee. Their last flicker of hope has been extinguished. If Jesus will not protect himself, how can he protect them?

Matthew's account of what transpires in Gethsemane and before the Sanhedrin shows that, in an odd inversion, the "victim" dominates all that takes place. Jesus, not Judas, not the mob, and not the high priest, acts like one truly in control. "Tell us if you are the Christ [Messiah], the Son of God," they demand. That single admission condemns Jesus to death, for the Sanhedrin have a different expectation of the Messiah. They want a conqueror to set them free by force. Jesus knows that only one thing— his death—will truly set them free. For that reason he has come to earth.   —PY

DAILY CONTEMPLATION

How would you respond if your life were threatened because you were a follower of Christ?

DAY 276   Matthew 27:1–31

JUDAS HANGS HIMSELF; JESUS BEFORE PILATE

Early in the morning, all the chief priests and the elders of the people came to the decision to put Jesus to death. They bound him, led him away and handed him over to Pilate, the governor.

When Judas, who had betrayed him, saw that Jesus was condemned, he was seized with remorse and returned the thirty silver coins to the chief priests and the elders. "I have sinned," he said, "for I have betrayed innocent blood."

"What is that to us?" they replied. "That's your responsibility."

So Judas threw the money into the temple and left. Then he went away and hanged himself.

The chief priests picked up the coins and said, "It is against the law to put this into the treasury, since it is blood money." So they decided to use the money to buy the potter's field as a burial place for foreigners. That is why it has been called the Field of Blood to this day. Then what was spoken by Jeremiah the prophet was fulfilled: "They took the thirty silver coins, the price set on him by the people of Israel, and they used them to buy the potter's field, as the Lord commanded me."

Meanwhile Jesus stood before the governor, and the governor asked him, "Are you the king of the Jews?"

"Yes, it is as you say," Jesus replied.

When he was accused by the chief priests and the elders, he gave no answer. Then Pilate asked him, "Don't you hear the testimony they are bringing against you?" But Jesus made no reply, not even to a single charge—to the great amazement of the governor.

Now it was the governor's custom at the Feast to release a prisoner chosen by the crowd. At that time they had a notorious prisoner, called Barabbas. So when the crowd had gathered, Pilate asked them, "Which one do you want me to release to you: Barabbas, or Jesus who is called Christ?" For he knew it was out of envy that they had handed Jesus over to him.

While Pilate was sitting on the judge's seat, his wife sent him this message: "Don't have anything to do with that innocent man, for I have suffered a great deal today in a dream because of him."

But the chief priests and the elders persuaded the crowd to ask for Barabbas and to have Jesus executed.

"Which of the two do you want me to release to you?" asked the governor.

"Barabbas," they answered.

"What shall I do, then, with Jesus who is called Christ?" Pilate asked.

They all answered, "Crucify him!"

"Why? What crime has he committed?" asked Pilate.

But they shouted all the louder, "Crucify him!"

When Pilate saw that he was getting nowhere, but that instead an uproar was starting, he took water and washed his hands in front of the crowd. "I am innocent of this man's blood," he said. "It is your responsibility!"

All the people answered, "Let his blood be on us and on our children!"

Then he released Barabbas to them. But he had Jesus flogged, and handed him over to be crucified.

Then the governor's soldiers took Jesus into the Praetorium and gathered the whole company of soldiers around him. They stripped him and put a scarlet robe on him, and then twisted together a crown of thorns and set it on his head. They put a staff in his right hand and knelt in front of him and mocked him. "Hail, king of the Jews!" they said. They spit on him, and took the staff and struck him on the head again and again. After they had mocked him, they took off the robe and put his own clothes on him. Then they led him away to crucify him.

The Gospels record a pass-the-buck sequence in Jesus' encounter with "justice." Roman law has granted the Jews many freedoms, including the right to their own court system, the Sanhedrin. When Jesus identifies himself as the Messiah, the Sanhedrin tries and convicts him of the religious charge of blasphemy, a capital offense. However, the Sanhedrin has no authority to carry out a death sentence; that requires the sanction of Roman justice. Thus Jesus' opponents send him to Pilate (PI-luht), the Roman governor of Judea.

Along the way, the accusers change the charge against Jesus from a religious one (which would not have impressed Pilate) to a political one. They portray Jesus as a dangerous revolutionary who has declared himself king of the Jews in defiance of Roman rule. Pilate has grave misgivings about the charge, and his wife's premonitions compound his sense of uneasiness.

Luke records that Pilate at first declares Jesus innocent despite pressure from the crowd. Then he seeks a way out of his dilemma by deferring the case to Herod, who has jurisdiction over Jesus' home region. Herod, disappointed by Jesus' silence and his refusal to perform miracles, ultimately sends him back to Pilate.

As Pilate tries three times to get the Jewish leaders to release their prisoner, the fury of the crowd against Jesus only swells. At last, facing a mob scene, the canny governor yields to their demands, but only after showily washing his hands of innocent blood.

Through all these legal proceedings, Jesus maintains an almost unbroken silence. He is acknowledged king at last—with a crown of thorns jammed onto his head, and a royal robe draped across his bloodied back. Pilate seems to recognize, at some level, the enormity of the injustice he has participated in. He prepares a notice of Jesus' "crime" to be fastened to the cross, which reads, in three languages, "JESUS OF NAZARETH, THE KING OF THE JEWS." When the chief priests protest that it should read only that Jesus *claimed* to be king, Pilate answers, "What I have written, I have written" (John 19:19–22). —PY

DAILY CONTEMPLATION

When have you been punished undeservedly? How did you respond?

DAY 277 Mark 15:21–47

THE CRUCIFIXION, DEATH, AND BURIAL OF JESUS

A certain man from Cyrene, Simon, the father of Alexander and Rufus, was passing by on his way in from the country, and they forced him to carry the cross. They brought Jesus to the place called Golgotha (which means The Place of the Skull). Then they offered him wine mixed with myrrh, but he did not take it. And they crucified him. Dividing up his clothes, they cast lots to see what each would get.

It was the third hour when they crucified him. The written notice of the charge against him read: THE KING OF THE JEWS. They crucified two robbers with him, one on his right and one on his left. Those who passed by hurled insults at him, shaking their heads and saying, "So! You who are going to destroy the temple and build it in three days, come down from the cross and save yourself!"

In the same way the chief priests and the teachers of the law mocked him among themselves. "He saved others," they said, "but he can't save himself! Let this Christ, this King of Israel, come down now from the cross, that we may see and believe." Those crucified with him also heaped insults on him.

At the sixth hour darkness came over the whole land until the ninth hour. And at the ninth hour Jesus cried out in a loud voice, *"Eloi, Eloi, lama sabachthani?"*—which means, "My God, my God, why have you forsaken me?"

When some of those standing near heard this, they said, "Listen, he's calling Elijah."

One man ran, filled a sponge with wine vinegar, put it on a stick, and offered it to Jesus to drink. "Now leave him alone. Let's see if Elijah comes to take him down," he said.

With a loud cry, Jesus breathed his last.

The curtain of the temple was torn in two from top to bottom. And when the centurion, who stood there in front of Jesus, heard his cry and saw how he died, he said, "Surely this man was the Son of God!"

Some women were watching from a distance. Among them were Mary Magdalene, Mary the mother of James the younger and of Joses, and Salome. In Galilee these women had followed him and cared for his needs. Many other women who had come up with him to Jerusalem were also there.

It was Preparation Day (that is, the day before the Sabbath). So as evening approached, Joseph of Arimathea, a prominent member of the Council, who was himself waiting for the kingdom of God, went boldly to Pilate and asked for Jesus' body. Pilate was surprised to hear that he was already dead. Summoning the centurion, he asked him if Jesus had already died. When he learned from the centurion that it was so, he gave the body to Joseph. So Joseph bought some linen cloth, took down the body, wrapped it in the linen, and placed it in a tomb cut out of rock. Then he rolled a stone against the entrance of the tomb. Mary Magdalene and Mary the mother of Joses saw where he was laid.

Long before, at the very beginning of his ministry, Jesus resisted Satan's temptation toward an easier path of safety and physical comfort. Now, as the moment of truth draws near, that temptation must seem more alluring than ever.

On the cross, a criminal at Jesus' left taunts him: "Aren't you the Christ? Save yourself and us!" (Luke 23:39). The crowd milling about the site takes up the cry: "Let him come down now from the cross, and we will believe in him. . . . Let God rescue him now if he wants him" (Matthew 27:42–43).

But there is no rescue, no miracle. There is only silence. The Father has turned his back, or so it seems, letting history take its course, letting everything evil in the world triumph over everything good. For Jesus to save others, quite simply, he cannot save himself.

Why does Jesus have to die? Theologians who ponder such things have debated various theories of "the Atonement" for centuries, with little agreement. Somehow it requires love, sacrificial love, to win what cannot be won by force.

One detail Mark includes may provide a clue. Jesus has just uttered the awful cry, "My God, my God, why have you forsaken me?" He, God's Son, identifies so closely with the human race—taking on their sin!—that God the Father has to turn away. The gulf is that great. But, just as Jesus breathes his last, "the curtain of the temple was torn in two from top to bottom."

That massive curtain serves to seal off the Most Holy Place, where God's presence dwells. No one except the high priest is allowed inside, and he can enter only once a year, on a designated day. As the author of Hebrews will later note (Hebrews 10), the tearing of that curtain shows beyond doubt exactly what is accomplished by Jesus' death on the cross. No more sacrifices will ever be required. Jesus has won for all of us—ordinary people, not just priests—immediate access to God's presence. By taking on the burden of human sin and bearing its punishment, Jesus removes forever the barrier between God and us.   —PY

DAILY CONTEMPLATION

When have you most wanted a miracle in your life and been disappointed? What did you learn from the experience?

DAY 278   Matthew 27:62–28:15

THE RESURRECTION

The next day, the one after Preparation Day, the chief priests and the Pharisees went to Pilate. "Sir," they said, "we remember that while he was still alive that deceiver said, 'After three days I will rise again.' So give the order for the tomb to be made secure until the third day. Otherwise, his disciples may come and steal the body and tell the people that he has been raised from the dead. This last deception will be worse than the first."

"Take a guard," Pilate answered. "Go, make the tomb as secure as you know how." So they went and made the tomb secure by putting a seal on the stone and posting the guard.

After the Sabbath, at dawn on the first day of the week, Mary Magdalene and the other Mary went to look at the tomb.

There was a violent earthquake, for an angel of the Lord came down from heaven and, going to the tomb, rolled back the stone and sat on it. His appearance was like lightning, and his clothes were white as snow. The guards were so afraid of him that they shook and became like dead men.

The angel said to the women, "Do not be afraid, for I know that you are looking for Jesus, who was crucified. He is not here; he has risen, just as he said. Come and see the place where he lay. Then go quickly and tell his disciples: 'He has risen from the dead and is going ahead of you into Galilee. There you will see him.' Now I have told you."

So the women hurried away from the tomb, afraid yet filled with joy, and ran to tell his disciples. Suddenly Jesus met them. "Greetings," he said. They came to him, clasped his feet and worshiped him. Then Jesus said to them, "Do not be afraid. Go and tell my brothers to go to Galilee; there they will see me."

While the women were on their way, some of the guards went into the city and reported to the chief priests everything that had happened. When the chief priests had met with the elders and devised a plan, they gave the soldiers a large sum of money, telling them, "You are to say, 'His disciples came during the night and stole him away while we were asleep.' If this report gets to the governor, we will satisfy him and keep you out of trouble." So the soldiers took the money and did as they were instructed. And this story has been widely circulated among the Jews to this very day.

When the greatest miracle of all history occurs, the only eyewitnesses are soldiers standing guard outside Jesus' tomb. When the earth shakes and an angel appears, bright as lightning, these guards tremble and become like dead men. Then, with an incurably human reflex, they flee to the authorities to report the disturbance.

But here is an astounding fact: Later that afternoon the soldiers, who have seen proof of the Resurrection with their own eyes, change their story. The resurrection of the Son of God does not seem nearly as significant as, say, stacks of freshly minted silver.

A few women, grieving friends of Jesus, are next to learn of the Miracle of Miracles. Matthew reports that when an angel breaks the news of Jesus' resurrection, the women hurry away "afraid yet filled with joy." *Fear*, the reflexive human response to a supernatural encounter—when the women hear from a glowing angel firsthand news of an event beyond comprehension, of course they feel afraid. *Yet filled with joy*—the news they hear is the best news of all, news too good to be true, news so good it has to be true. Jesus is back! He has returned, as promised. The dreams of a Messiah all come surging back as the women run fearfully and joyfully to tell the disciples.

Even as the women run, the soldiers are rehearsing an alibi, their part in an elaborate cover-up scheme. Like everything else in Jesus' life, his resurrection draws forth two contrasting responses. Those who believe are transformed, finding enough hope and courage to go out and change the world. But those who choose not to believe find ways to ignore evidence they have seen with their own eyes.   —PY

DAY 279

John 20:1–31

THE EMPTY TOMB; JESUS APPEARS TO
MARY MAGDALENE AND HIS DISCIPLES

Early on the first day of the week, while it was still dark, Mary Magdalene went to the tomb and saw that the stone had been removed from the entrance. So she came running to Simon Peter and the other disciple, the one Jesus loved, and said, "They have taken the Lord out of the tomb, and we don't know where they have put him!"

So Peter and the other disciple started for the tomb. Both were running, but the other disciple outran Peter and reached the tomb first. He bent over and looked in at the strips of linen lying there but did not go in. Then Simon Peter, who was behind him, arrived and went into the tomb. He saw the strips of linen lying there, as well as the burial cloth that had been around Jesus' head. The cloth was folded up by itself, separate from the linen. Finally the other disciple, who had reached the tomb first, also went inside. He saw and believed. (They still did not understand from Scripture that Jesus had to rise from the dead.)

Then the disciples went back to their homes, but Mary stood outside the tomb crying. As she wept, she bent over to look into the tomb and saw two angels in white, seated where Jesus' body had been, one at the head and the other at the foot.

They asked her, "Woman, why are you crying?"

"They have taken my Lord away," she said, "and I don't know where they have put him." At this, she turned around and saw Jesus standing there, but she did not realize that it was Jesus.

"Woman," he said, "why are you crying? Who is it you are looking for?"

Thinking he was the gardener, she said, "Sir, if you have carried him away, tell me where you have put him, and I will get him."

Jesus said to her, "Mary."

She turned toward him and cried out in Aramaic, "Rabboni!" (which means Teacher).

Jesus said, "Do not hold on to me, for I have not yet returned to the Father. Go instead to my brothers and tell them, 'I am returning to my Father and your Father, to my God and your God.'"

Mary Magdalene went to the disciples with the news: "I have seen the Lord!" And she told them that he had said these things to her.

On the evening of that first day of the week, when the disciples were together, with the doors locked for fear of the Jews, Jesus came and stood among them and said, "Peace be with you!" After he said this, he showed them his hands and side. The disciples were overjoyed when they saw the Lord.

Again Jesus said, "Peace be with you! As the Father has sent me, I am sending you." And with that he breathed on them and said, "Receive the Holy Spirit. If you forgive anyone his sins, they are forgiven; if you do not forgive them, they are not forgiven."

Now Thomas (called Didymus), one of the Twelve, was not with the disciples when Jesus came. So the other disciples told him, "We have seen the Lord!"

But he said to them, "Unless I see the nail marks in his hands and put my finger where the nails were, and put my hand into his side, I will not believe it."

A week later his disciples were in the house again, and Thomas was with them. Though the doors were locked, Jesus came and stood among them and said, "Peace be with you!" Then he said to Thomas, "Put your finger here; see my hands. Reach out your hand and put it into my side. Stop doubting and believe."

Thomas said to him, "My Lord and my God!"

Then Jesus told him, "Because you have seen me, you have believed; blessed are those who have not seen and yet have believed."

Jesus did many other miraculous signs in the presence of his disciples, which are not recorded in this book. But these are written that you may believe that Jesus is the Christ, the Son of God, and that by believing you may have life in his name.

People who discount the resurrection of Christ tend to portray the disciples as gullible country bumpkins with a weakness for ghost stories, or as shrewd conspirators who hatch a Resurrection plot in order to attract popular support for their movement. The Bible presents a radically different picture. It shows Jesus' followers themselves as the ones most skeptical of rumors about a risen Jesus.

Mary Magdalene is still bewildered and afraid even after an angel breaks the news plainly to her. When she meets Jesus himself near the tomb, she doesn't recognize him until he speaks her name.

Reports from the women of an empty tomb fail to convince the disciples, so Peter and another run to the graveyard to see for themselves. That same night all the disciples huddle in a locked room, afraid of the Jewish leaders, apparently still skeptical.

For his part, Jesus goes out of his way to allay the disciples' fears and suspicions. In broad daylight he visits and fishes with them. Once he asks a dubious Thomas to test his scarred skin by touch. Another time he eats a piece of broiled fish in their presence to prove he is not a ghost (Luke 24). This is no mirage, no hallucination; it is Jesus, their master, no one else.

The appearances of the risen Christ recorded in the Bible, fewer than a dozen, show a clear pattern. With one exception (found in 1 Corinthians 15:6), he visits small groups of people closeted indoors or in a remote area. By the garden tomb, in a locked room, on the road to Emmaus (eh-MAY-us), beside the Sea of Galilee, atop the Mount of Olives—such private encounters bolster the faith of people who already believe in Jesus. But as far as we know, not a single unbeliever sees Jesus after his death.

What would happen if Jesus reappeared on Pilate's porch or before the Sanhedrin, this time with a withering blast against those who ordered his death? Surely such a public scene would cause a sensation. But would it kindle faith? Jesus has already answered that question in his story of Lazarus and the rich man: "If they do not listen to Moses and the Prophets, they will not be convinced even if someone rises from the dead" (Luke 16:31). Instead, Jesus chooses another way: to let the disciples themselves spread the word, as his witnesses.   —PY

DAILY CONTEMPLATION

Would you have greeted the news of Jesus' resurrection like Mary? Like Peter? Like Thomas?

DAY 280   Luke 24:13–49

ON THE ROAD TO EMMAUS

Now that same day two of them were going to a village called Emmaus, about seven miles from Jerusalem. They were talking with each other about everything that had happened. As they talked and discussed these things with each other, Jesus himself came up and walked along with them; but they were kept from recognizing him.

He asked them, "What are you discussing together as you walk along?"

They stood still, their faces downcast. One of them, named Cleopas, asked him, "Are you only a visitor to Jerusalem and do not know the things that have happened there in these days?"

"What things?" he asked.

"About Jesus of Nazareth," they replied. "He was a prophet, powerful in word and deed before God and all the people. The chief priests and our rulers handed him over to be sentenced to death, and they crucified him; but we had hoped that he was the one who was going to redeem Israel. And what is more, it is the third day since all this took place. In addition, some of our women amazed us. They went to the tomb early this morning but didn't find his body. They came and told us that they had seen a vision of angels, who said he was alive. Then some of our companions went to the tomb and found it just as the women had said, but him they did not see."

He said to them, "How foolish you are, and how slow of heart to believe all that the prophets have spoken! Did not the Christ have to suffer these things and then enter his glory?" And beginning with Moses and all the Prophets, he explained to them what was said in all the Scriptures concerning himself.

As they approached the village to which they were going, Jesus acted as if he were going farther. But they urged him strongly, "Stay with us, for it is nearly evening; the day is almost over." So he went in to stay with them.

When he was at the table with them, he took bread, gave thanks, broke it and began to give it to them. Then their eyes were opened and they recognized him, and he disappeared from their sight. They asked each other, "Were not our hearts burning within us while he talked with us on the road and opened the Scriptures to us?"

They got up and returned at once to Jerusalem. There they found the Eleven and those with them, assembled together and saying, "It is true! The Lord has risen and has appeared to Simon." Then the two told what had happened on the way, and how Jesus was recognized by them when he broke the bread.

While they were still talking about this, Jesus himself stood among them and said to them, "Peace be with you."

They were startled and frightened, thinking they saw a ghost. He said to them, "Why are you troubled, and why do doubts rise in your minds? Look at my hands and my feet. It is I myself! Touch me and see; a ghost does not have flesh and bones, as you see I have."

When he had said this, he showed them his hands and feet. And while they still did not believe it because of joy and amazement, he asked them, "Do you have anything here to eat?" They gave him a piece of broiled fish, and he took it and ate it in their presence.

He said to them, "This is what I told you while I was still with you: Everything must be fulfilled that is written about me in the Law of Moses, the Prophets and the Psalms."

Then he opened their minds so they could understand the Scriptures. He told them, "This is what is written: The Christ will suffer and rise from the dead on the third day, and repentance and forgiveness of sins will be preached in his name to all nations, beginning at Jerusalem. You are witnesses of these things. I am going to send you what my Father has promised; but stay in the city until you have been clothed with power from on high."

In this scene at the end of Luke's gospel, two followers are walking away from Jerusalem, downhearted and perplexed. Their dream of "the one who was going to redeem Israel" has died along with their leader on the cross. And yet they too have heard the crazy rumors of an empty tomb. What does it all mean?

A stranger appears beside the two forlorn disciples. According to him, the prophets have predicted all along that the Messiah would suffer these things. The stranger fascinates them, so much so that they beg him to stay longer. Then at mealtime, the last link snaps into place. It is Jesus—sitting at their table! Without a doubt, he is alive.

They are two ordinary people, not even counted among the twelve intimates of Jesus. But the encounter with the risen Christ changes them forever. "Were not our hearts burning within us while he talked with us on the road and opened the Scriptures to us?" they recall. They dash to meet the Twelve (now Eleven, with Judas' betrayal), only to learn that Peter too had seen Jesus. Suddenly, in the midst of that chaotic scene of joy and confusion, Jesus himself appears. He explains once and for all that his death and resurrection were not unforeseen but rather lay at the heart of God's plan all along.

Jesus has one last promise to keep: he will depart earth and in his place leave the band of believers to carry out his mission. These people, common people with more than a touch of cowardice, have followed Jesus, listened to him, and watched him die. But seeing Jesus alive changes all that. They return to Jerusalem with great joy, and before long they are out telling the world the good news.   —PY

DAILY CONTEMPLATION

How did the truth about Jesus' resurrection dawn on you?

DAY 281

John 21:1–25

JESUS AND THE MIRACULOUS CATCH OF FISH; JESUS REINSTATES PETER

Afterward Jesus appeared again to his disciples, by the Sea of Tiberias. It happened this way: Simon Peter, Thomas (called Didymus), Nathanael from Cana in Galilee, the sons of Zebedee, and two other disciples were together. "I'm going out to fish," Simon Peter told them, and they said, "We'll go with you." So they went out and got into the boat, but that night they caught nothing.

Early in the morning, Jesus stood on the shore, but the disciples did not realize that it was Jesus.

He called out to them, "Friends, haven't you any fish?"

"No," they answered.

He said, "Throw your net on the right side of the boat and you will find some." When they did, they were unable to haul the net in because of the large number of fish.

Then the disciple whom Jesus loved said to Peter, "It is the Lord!" As soon as Simon Peter heard him say, "It is the Lord," he wrapped his outer garment around him (for he had taken it off) and jumped into the water. The other disciples followed in the boat, towing the net full of fish, for they were not far from shore, about a hundred yards. When they landed, they saw a fire of burning coals there with fish on it, and some bread.

Jesus said to them, "Bring some of the fish you have just caught."

Simon Peter climbed aboard and dragged the net ashore. It was full of large fish, 153, but even with so many the net was not torn. Jesus said to them, "Come and have breakfast." None of the disciples dared ask him, "Who are you?" They knew it was the Lord. Jesus came, took the bread and gave it to them, and did the same with the fish. This was now the third time Jesus appeared to his disciples after he was raised from the dead.

When they had finished eating, Jesus said to Simon Peter, "Simon son of John, do you truly love me more than these?"

"Yes, Lord," he said, "you know that I love you."

Jesus said, "Feed my lambs."

Again Jesus said, "Simon son of John, do you truly love me?"

He answered, "Yes, Lord, you know that I love you."

Jesus said, "Take care of my sheep."

The third time he said to him, "Simon son of John, do you love me?"

Peter was hurt because Jesus asked him the third time, "Do you love me?" He said, "Lord, you know all things; you know that I love you."

Jesus said, "Feed my sheep. I tell you the truth, when you were younger you dressed yourself and went where you wanted; but when you are old you will stretch out your hands, and someone else will dress you and lead you where you do not want to go." Jesus said this to indicate the kind of death by which Peter would glorify God. Then he said to him, "Follow me!"

Peter turned and saw that the disciple whom Jesus loved was following them. (This was the one who had leaned back against Jesus at the supper and had said, "Lord, who is going to betray you?") When Peter saw him, he asked, "Lord, what about him?"

Jesus answered, "If I want him to remain alive until I return, what is that to you? You must follow me." Because of this, the rumor spread among the brothers that this disciple would not die. But Jesus did not say that he would not die; he only said, "If I want him to remain alive until I return, what is that to you?"

This is the disciple who testifies to these things and who wrote them down. We know that his testimony is true.

Jesus did many other things as well. If every one of them were written down, I suppose that even the whole world would not have room for the books that would be written.

Jesus performs a miracle similar to one he performed in his first days with the disciples. He meets them on familiar turf and fills their nets with a great catch of fish. He is the same Lord they came to know then, with the same power, despite dying and being raised again to life. He returns for a short time to finish the message he came to give.

These final scenes will cement for the disciples an understanding of Christ that has begun to deepen. They have struggled all along to understand his true mission, but soon, with the Holy Spirit's help, they finally will know why he came. Buoyed by that knowledge, they will then carry the message to the world.

Peter has recently failed Jesus by denying him three times. Now Jesus gives him another chance, coming to meet with him, share a meal, and express concern three times over their relationship. Jesus' care for Peter sends the message that God's grace extends to believers even when we fail God in a big way. He forgives those who are sorry and genuinely love him.

Jesus twice asks whether Peter "truly loves" him, and another time asks whether he "loves" him. John chose two different Greek forms of the word *love;* some scholars speculate that Jesus was indicating two kinds of love, the first referring to a love of one's whole being, including the will, and the second to a more spontaneous, emotional kind of love.

Whether or not John or Jesus intended this distinction, the Bible teaches that Jesus wants us to love him with a complete love. He wants us to choose to love him with our will, in the good times and bad, when we feel loving toward him and when we don't. And to love him with a love that is free-flowing with emotion—impulsive, affectionate love issuing from the heart. Just as with a lasting romantic love, our love for Jesus should be passionate yet also involve a decision of the mind and will.

Each time Peter replies, Jesus asks him to care for his sheep. In some of his final words on earth, Jesus reminds his disciples that loving him means taking care of the people he places in our lives. Jesus called himself the Shepherd and spent his time on earth caring for many who came across his path and many more whom he sought out. Now all believers will carry on that mission, temporarily keeping watch over God's flock until the Shepherd returns.   —BQ

DAILY CONTEMPLATION

In what ways are you feeding and taking care of Jesus' sheep?

DAY 282   Reflection

REMEMBERING JESUS' DEATH AND VICTORY

This section of the Gospels contains some of my least and most favorite scenes in the Bible. Although central to my faith, these passages about Jesus' torture and crucifixion make me recoil inwardly each time I read them. I want to pass quickly through them to get to his resurrection. Then my spirits soar, relieved once again that God wins in the end, overshadowing all the horrific suffering with his victory.

I once attended a seminar in which the speaker spent hours describing in detail the physical trauma Jesus underwent in his last hours before death. The physical agony Jesus experienced defies understanding. Weighing on him even more heavily was the staggering burden of sin he carried. For him, holy God, the sin of one human being alone would have been a crushing weight to bear. But to carry the sin of all humankind exacted suffering beyond our comprehension.

Our hearts may rightly cringe at the story of Jesus' suffering, yet he hasn't asked us to turn away. Rather, he has instructed us clearly, "This is my body given for you; do this in remembrance of me" (Luke 22:19). We *celebrate* Communion, the Lord's Supper, as a remembrance of Jesus' death. Many observe the season of Lent as another way of remembering his sacrifice.

Without Jesus' death, there could be no resurrection, no final victory over evil in his life or in ours. An observance of Jesus' resurrection without a proper remembrance of his suffering would lead to a cheapening of the victory we celebrate at Easter. Jesus' resurrection is our greatest cause for celebration, yet the ending we relish and love to relive goes hand in hand with his death.

I have a yen for happy endings, which makes the Gospels especially satisfying. God knows how to write—and live—a story. He knows that we yearn for the winners to win and the losers to lose in the end. He has both crafted and starred in a real-life drama that beats any Pulitzer prize winner. God's story carries us along like no other. Each time we engage fully, entering into Jesus' life, death, and resurrection, we take hold once more of the story that has become ours for now and eternity.   —BQ

DAILY CONTEMPLATION

How do you respond to the stories of Jesus' suffering and death? Are you inclined to pass quickly through these passages? Do you do anything on a regular, even yearly, basis to remember his death? Thank Jesus for the pain he endured for you. Ask him to help you better understand the death he died for you and the victory he achieved for you.

PART 10

THE WORD SPREADS

Matthew 28:16–20; Acts 1:1–26

THE GREAT COMMISSION; JESUS TAKEN UP INTO HEAVEN; MATHIAS CHOSEN TO REPLACE JUDAS

Then the eleven disciples went to Galilee, to the mountain where Jesus had told them to go. When they saw him, they worshiped him; but some doubted. Then Jesus came to them and said, "All authority in heaven and on earth has been given to me. Therefore go and make disciples of all nations, baptizing them in the name of the Father and of the Son and of the Holy Spirit, and teaching them to obey everything I have commanded you. And surely I am with you always, to the very end of the age." . . .

In my former book, Theophilus, I wrote about all that Jesus began to do and to teach until the day he was taken up to heaven, after giving instructions through the Holy Spirit to the apostles he had chosen. After his suffering, he showed himself to these men and gave many convincing proofs that he was alive. He appeared to them over a period of forty days and spoke about the kingdom of God. On one occasion, while he was eating with them, he gave them this command: "Do not leave Jerusalem, but wait for the gift my Father promised, which you have heard me speak about. For John baptized with water, but in a few days you will be baptized with the Holy Spirit."

535

So when they met together, they asked him, "Lord, are you at this time going to restore the kingdom to Israel?"

He said to them: "It is not for you to know the times or dates the Father has set by his own authority. But you will receive power when the Holy Spirit comes on you; and you will be my witnesses in Jerusalem, and in all Judea and Samaria, and to the ends of the earth."

After he said this, he was taken up before their very eyes, and a cloud hid him from their sight.

They were looking intently up into the sky as he was going, when suddenly two men dressed in white stood beside them. "Men of Galilee," they said, "why do you stand here looking into the sky? This same Jesus, who has been taken from you into heaven, will come back in the same way you have seen him go into heaven."

Then they returned to Jerusalem from the hill called the Mount of Olives, a Sabbath day's walk from the city. When they arrived, they went upstairs to the room where they were staying. Those present were Peter, John, James and Andrew; Philip and Thomas, Bartholomew and Matthew; James son of Alphaeus and Simon the Zealot, and Judas son of James. They all joined together constantly in prayer, along with the women and Mary the mother of Jesus, and with his brothers.

In those days Peter stood up among the believers (a group numbering about a hundred and twenty) and said, "Brothers, the Scripture had to be fulfilled which the Holy Spirit spoke long ago through the mouth of David concerning Judas, who served as guide for those who arrested Jesus—he was one of our number and shared in this ministry."

(With the reward he got for his wickedness, Judas bought a field; there he fell headlong, his body burst open and all his intestines spilled out. Everyone in Jerusalem heard about this, so they called that field in their language Akeldama, that is, Field of Blood.)

"For," said Peter, "it is written in the book of Psalms,

"'May his place be deserted;
   let there be no one to dwell in it,'

and,

"'May another take his place of leadership.'

Therefore it is necessary to choose one of the men who have been with us the whole time the Lord Jesus went in and out among us, beginning from John's baptism to the time when Jesus was taken up from us. For one of these must become a witness with us of his resurrection."

So they proposed two men: Joseph called Barsabbas (also known as Justus) and Matthias. Then they prayed, "Lord, you know everyone's heart. Show us which of these two you have chosen to take over this apostolic ministry, which Judas left to go where he belongs." Then they cast lots, and the lot fell to Matthias; so he was added to the eleven apostles.

The disciples' obsession with Israel's restored kingdom does not fade even after Jesus dies and comes back to life. For forty days after the Resurrection he appears and disappears seemingly at will. When he comes, his followers listen eagerly to his explanations from Scripture of all that has happened. When he leaves, they plot the structure of the new kingdom that he will surely inaugurate. Think of it: Jerusalem free at last from Roman domination.

Jesus gives some mystifying orders, however. He tells his followers to return to Jerusalem and simply wait. Something more is needed. Do not leave the city, he says, until the Holy Spirit comes. At last, one of the disciples puts to Jesus the question they have all been debating together: "Lord, are you at this time going to restore the kingdom to Israel?"

No one is prepared for Jesus' reaction. He seems to brush the question aside, deflecting attention away from Israel toward neighboring countries, all the way to the ends of the earth. He mentions the Holy Spirit again, and then, to everyone's utter amazement, his body lifts off the ground, suspends there for a moment, then disappears into a cloud. And they never see him again.

Christians believe that all of history revolves around the life of Jesus the Christ. But the plain fact is that Jesus left earth after thirty-three years. Furthermore, he declared it a good thing: "You are filled with grief. But I tell you the truth: It is for your good that I am going away. Unless I go away, the Counselor will not come to you" (John 16:6–7).

The book of Acts, written by the same author as the gospel of Luke, tells what happens after Jesus' departure when the Counselor comes at last. First, though, the disciples begin adjusting to new realities: they select a replacement for Judas, make plans to follow Jesus' final instructions, and return to Jerusalem to await the Holy Spirit. —PY

DAILY CONTEMPLATION

When have you realized that Jesus' plans in your life were different from what you'd assumed they were?

DAY 284   Acts 2:1–41

THE HOLY SPIRIT COMES AT PENTECOST

When the day of Pentecost came, they were all together in one place. Suddenly a sound like the blowing of a violent wind came from heaven and filled the whole house where they were sitting. They saw what seemed to be tongues of fire that separated and came to rest on each of them. All of them were filled with the Holy Spirit and began to speak in other tongues as the Spirit enabled them.

Now there were staying in Jerusalem God-fearing Jews from every nation under heaven. When they heard this sound, a crowd came together in bewilderment, because each one heard them speaking in his own language. Utterly amazed, they asked: "Are not all these men who are speaking Galileans? Then how is it that each of us hears them in his own native language? Parthians, Medes and Elamites; residents of Mesopotamia, Judea and Cappadocia, Pontus and Asia, Phrygia and Pamphylia, Egypt and the parts of Libya near Cyrene; visitors from Rome (both Jews and converts to Judaism); Cretans and Arabs—we hear them declaring the wonders of God in our own tongues!" Amazed and perplexed, they asked one another, "What does this mean?"

Some, however, made fun of them and said, "They have had too much wine."

Then Peter stood up with the Eleven, raised his voice and addressed the crowd: "Fellow Jews and all of you who live in Jerusalem, let me explain this to you; listen carefully to what I say. These men are not drunk, as you suppose. It's only nine in the morning! No, this is what was spoken by the prophet Joel:

"'In the last days, God says,
   I will pour out my Spirit on all people.
Your sons and daughters will prophesy,
   your young men will see visions,
   your old men will dream dreams.
Even on my servants, both men and women,
   I will pour out my Spirit in those days,
   and they will prophesy.
I will show wonders in the heaven above
   and signs on the earth below,
   blood and fire and billows of smoke.
The sun will be turned to darkness
   and the moon to blood
   before the coming of the great and glorious day of the Lord.
And everyone who calls
   on the name of the Lord will be saved.'

"Men of Israel, listen to this: Jesus of Nazareth was a man accredited by God to you by miracles, wonders and signs, which God did among you through him, as you yourselves know. This man was handed over to you by God's set purpose and foreknowledge; and you, with the help of wicked men, put him to death by nailing him to the cross. But God raised him from the dead, freeing him from the agony of death, because it was impossible for death to keep its hold on him. David said about him:

"'I saw the Lord always before me.
   Because he is at my right hand,
   I will not be shaken.
Therefore my heart is glad and my tongue rejoices;
   my body also will live in hope,
because you will not abandon me to the grave,
   nor will you let your Holy One see decay.

You have made known to me the paths of life;
  you will fill me with joy in your presence.'

"Brothers, I can tell you confidently that the patriarch David died and was buried, and his tomb is here to this day. But he was a prophet and knew that God had promised him on oath that he would place one of his descendants on his throne. Seeing what was ahead, he spoke of the resurrection of the Christ, that he was not abandoned to the grave, nor did his body see decay. God has raised this Jesus to life, and we are all witnesses of the fact. Exalted to the right hand of God, he has received from the Father the promised Holy Spirit and has poured out what you now see and hear. For David did not ascend to heaven, and yet he said,

"'The Lord said to my Lord:
  "Sit at my right hand
until I make your enemies
  a footstool for your feet."'

"Therefore let all Israel be assured of this: God has made this Jesus, whom you crucified, both Lord and Christ."

When the people heard this, they were cut to the heart and said to Peter and the other apostles, "Brothers, what shall we do?"

Peter replied, "Repent and be baptized, every one of you, in the name of Jesus Christ for the forgiveness of your sins. And you will receive the gift of the Holy Spirit. The promise is for you and your children and for all who are far off—for all whom the Lord our God will call."

With many other words he warned them; and he pleaded with them, "Save yourselves from this corrupt generation." Those who accepted his message were baptized, and about three thousand were added to their number that day.

On the Jewish feast day of Pentecost, the disciples get what they have been waiting for. The Holy Spirit, the presence of God himself, takes up residence inside ordinary bodies—their bodies. The disciples hit the streets with a bold new style that the world has never recovered from. Soon everyone in Jerusalem is talking about the Jesus followers. Clearly, something is afoot. To their amazement, pilgrims from all over the world hear the Galileans' message in their own native languages.

Peter, coward apostle who denied Christ three times to save his own neck, brazenly takes on both Jewish and Roman authorities. Quoting from King David and the prophet Joel, he proclaims that his audience has just lived through the most important event of all history. "God has raised this Jesus to life, and we are all witnesses of the fact," he says and goes on to declare Jesus as the very Messiah, the fulfillment of the Jews' long-awaited dream. Three thousand people respond to Peter's powerful message on that first day. And thus the Christian church is born.

Beginning with this boisterous scene in Jerusalem, Luke weaves a historical adventure tale. The group of new believers, at first a mere annoyance to the Jews and the Romans, will not stop growing. Just as Jesus has predicted, the message spreads throughout Judea and Samaria and in less than one generation penetrates into Rome, the center of civilization. In an era when new religions are a dime a dozen, the Christian faith becomes a worldwide phenomenon. It all begins with this scene on the day of Pentecost. —PY

DAILY CONTEMPLATION

When have you been in a place where God moved in many people at one time? Did you sense the Holy Spirit's presence?

DAY 285

Acts 3:1–26

PETER HEALS THE CRIPPLED BEGGAR

One day Peter and John were going up to the temple at the time of prayer—at three in the afternoon. Now a man crippled from birth was being carried to the temple gate called Beautiful, where he was put every day to beg from those going into the temple courts. When he saw Peter and John about to enter, he asked them for money. Peter looked straight at him, as did John. Then Peter said, "Look at us!" So the man gave them his attention, expecting to get something from them.

Then Peter said, "Silver or gold I do not have, but what I have I give you. In the name of Jesus Christ of Nazareth, walk." Taking him by the right hand, he helped him up, and instantly the man's feet and ankles became strong. He jumped to his feet and began to walk. Then he went with them into the temple courts, walking and jumping, and praising God. When all the people saw him walking and praising God, they recognized him as the same man who used to sit begging at the temple gate called Beautiful, and they were filled with wonder and amazement at what had happened to him.

While the beggar held on to Peter and John, all the people were astonished and came running to them in the place called Solomon's Colonnade. When Peter saw this, he said to them: "Men of Israel, why does this surprise you? Why do you stare at us as if by our own power or godliness we had made this man walk? The God of Abraham, Isaac and Jacob, the God of our fathers, has glorified his servant Jesus. You handed him over to be killed, and you disowned him before Pilate, though he had decided to let him go. You disowned the Holy and Righteous One and asked that a murderer be released to you. You killed the author of life, but God raised him from the dead. We are witnesses of this. By faith in the name of Jesus, this man whom you see and know was made strong. It is Jesus' name and the faith that comes through him that has given this complete healing to him, as you can all see.

"Now, brothers, I know that you acted in ignorance, as did your leaders. But this is how God fulfilled what he had foretold through all the prophets, saying that his Christ would suffer. Repent, then, and turn to God, so that your sins may be wiped out, that times of refreshing may come from the Lord, and that he may send the Christ, who has been appointed for you—even Jesus. He must remain in heaven until the time comes for God to restore everything, as he promised long ago through his holy prophets. For Moses said, 'The Lord your God will raise up for you a prophet like me from among your own people; you must listen to everything he tells you. Anyone who does not listen to him will be completely cut off from among his people.'

"Indeed, all the prophets from Samuel on, as many as have spoken, have foretold these days. And you are heirs of the prophets and of the covenant God made with your fathers. He said to Abraham, 'Through your offspring all peoples on earth will be blessed.' When God raised up his servant, he sent him first to you to bless you by turning each of you from your wicked ways."

The change produced by the Holy Spirit becomes evident right away in the disciples, now called apostles. As Peter and John are headed into the temple to pray, a beggar asks for money. These men, who—like many of us today—are accustomed to encountering "down and out" individuals, would normally pass by these seeming fixtures in society to get on to more important business. Instead, they stop and make eye contact with the beggar. They don't simply throw a few coins and hurriedly move on. Both men stop and look at him as a person worthy of respect, waiting for him to return their attention.

Then they do what they have had trouble doing in the past. They heal the man in an instant, through the name and power of Christ. Just as Jesus' miracles did, this one draws a crowd, and Peter takes the opportunity to teach about the meaning of Jesus' life, death, and resurrection.

"Repent, then," Peter urges, "and turn to God, so that your sins may be wiped out, that times of refreshing may come from the Lord." Peter knows that the only hope for individuals lies in coming to God for relief from the guilt of sin. Life without Jesus proves burdensome, draining. But when we come to God, we find refreshment at last. —BQ

DAILY CONTEMPLATION

In what ways have you felt refreshed since coming to God?

DAY 286
Acts 4:1–31

PETER AND JOHN BEFORE THE SANHEDRIN

The priests and the captain of the temple guard and the Sadducees came up to Peter and John while they were speaking to the people. They were greatly disturbed because the apostles were teaching the people and proclaiming in Jesus the resurrection of the dead. They seized Peter and John, and because it was evening, they put them in jail until the next day. But many who heard the message believed, and the number of men grew to about five thousand.

The next day the rulers, elders and teachers of the law met in Jerusalem. Annas the high priest was there, and so were Caiaphas, John, Alexander and the other men of the high priest's family. They had Peter and John brought before them and began to question them: "By what power or what name did you do this?"

Then Peter, filled with the Holy Spirit, said to them: "Rulers and elders of the people! If we are being called to account today for an act of kindness shown to a cripple and are asked how he was healed, then know this, you and all the people of Israel: It is by the name of Jesus Christ of Nazareth, whom you crucified but whom God raised from the dead, that this man stands before you healed. He is

> "'the stone you builders rejected,
>   which has become the capstone.'

Salvation is found in no one else, for there is no other name under heaven given to men by which we must be saved."

When they saw the courage of Peter and John and realized that they were unschooled, ordinary men, they were astonished and they took note that these men had been with Jesus. But since they could see the man who had been healed standing there with them, there was nothing they could say. So they ordered them to withdraw from the Sanhedrin and then conferred together. "What are we going to do with these men?" they asked. "Everybody living in Jerusalem knows they have done an outstanding miracle, and we cannot deny it. But to stop this thing from spreading any further among the people, we must warn these men to speak no longer to anyone in this name."

Then they called them in again and commanded them not to speak or teach at all in the name of Jesus. But Peter and John replied, "Judge for yourselves whether it is right in God's sight to obey you rather than God. For we cannot help speaking about what we have seen and heard."

After further threats they let them go. They could not decide how to punish them, because all the people were praising God for what had happened. For the man who was miraculously healed was over forty years old.

On their release, Peter and John went back to their own people and reported all that the chief priests and elders had said to them. When they heard this, they raised their voices together in prayer to God. "Sovereign Lord," they said, "you made the heaven and the earth and the sea, and everything in them. You spoke by the Holy Spirit through the mouth of your servant, our father David:

> "'Why do the nations rage
>   and the peoples plot in vain?

The kings of the earth take their stand
and the rulers gather together
against the Lord
and against his Anointed One.'

Indeed Herod and Pontius Pilate met together with the Gentiles and the people of Israel in this city to conspire against your holy servant Jesus, whom you anointed. They did what your power and will had decided beforehand should happen. Now, Lord, consider their threats and enable your servants to speak your word with great boldness. Stretch out your hand to heal and perform miraculous signs and wonders through the name of your holy servant Jesus."

After they prayed, the place where they were meeting was shaken. And they were all filled with the Holy Spirit and spoke the word of God boldly.

The Jewish religious leaders continue in the same disbelief they held when Jesus was on earth. Here we see the first of many imprisonments the apostles will endure throughout the book of Acts. Just as the Pharisees and Sadducees tried repeatedly to silence Jesus, they will try to restrain the apostles. Yet the news about the resurrected Messiah, Jesus, continues to spread.

Despite jailing and persecution, the apostles speak out more boldly than ever, empowered by the Holy Spirit. People respond, with God's Spirit drawing new Christians from all parts of the known world.

Acts records the beginnings of the Christian church. Despite periods of ongoing persecution, the church has continued to grow and spread even to the most remote areas of the world in the two thousand years since Jesus came to earth.   —BQ

DAILY CONTEMPLATION

Do you have a desire, as did Peter and John, to talk to the people in your life about the things Jesus has done for you?

DAY 287   Reflection

THE GIFT OF THE HOLY SPIRIT

Who is the Holy Spirit, anyway?

Talk of this Spirit began when Jesus promised to send a Counselor to take his place when he left the earth. Pentecost followed soon after, in which Jesus' disciples, long confused, afraid, and immature, changed nearly overnight into passionate, fearless believers who knew exactly why they were alive. The Spirit made a sudden, dramatic impact on Jesus' followers.

Jesus called the Holy Spirit the Paraclete, *parakletos* in Greek, which means "Comforter, Counselor, Helper, Advocate, Strengthener, Supporter." Jesus and God the Father fill all of these roles, and the Spirit fills them in a way immediately present to us. This is a function of the Trinity—God in three forms, all alive and present but most accessible to us through the Spirit.

J. I. Packer, a respected theologian, professor, and author, explains that through the Holy Spirit we have a personal relationship with Jesus, we are transformed to be more and more like him (sanctification), and we are given confidence that God loves us, has redeemed us, and has made us part of his family through Jesus.[46]

When the Bible talks about the Holy Spirit, it often uses the word *power* in the same sentence. The Spirit gives us the power we need each day to overcome temptation and live in God's strength rather than in our own weakness. He also reveals God's truth to unbelievers. John Stott, another theologian, stresses that the Holy Spirit acts primarily as a "missionary Spirit."[47] The entire book of Acts, he explains, tells the story of God, through his Spirit, making his plan of salvation known far and wide. Still today the Spirit enables us to share about Jesus with others.

These definitions of the Holy Spirit apply to all believers, for we all have the Holy Spirit living in us. Do all of us, then, experience the same presence of the Spirit in our lives? Christians have disagreed as to what role God has given the Holy Spirit today. Some believe God granted certain gifts of the Spirit to believers in Acts exclusively for that time of early church growth. Gifts such as speaking in tongues, healing, and prophecy are not God's will for believers today, they claim. Others believe that the Holy Spirit can and does give the same gifts to many believers in our day.

Whether or not all of us experience these more "charismatic" or "sign" gifts, the Bible teaches that the Holy Spirit was alive at the creation of the world, spoke through the prophets in the Old Testament, and is alive still today. We have the challenge, then, to give the Holy Spirit the freedom to be whatever God intends him to be in our lives.

Catherine Marshall writes, "For years (sometimes a lifetime) a Christian can keep the Spirit at a sub-basement level by the insistence on running one's own life. Then . . . the person consciously recognizes his divine Guest's presence, opens the hitherto closed doors into certain rooms in his being so that the Spirit can enter there too." She quotes Hannah Whitall Smith, who says that when the Spirit influences every part of us, "the real evidence . . . is neither emotion nor any single gift such as tongues, rather . . . there *must* be Christ-likeness in life and character: by fruits in the life we shall know whether or not we have the Spirit."[48]

Unfortunately, the Christian world has sometimes attached an inappropriate measure of mystery to its teaching on the Holy Spirit. Believers may be taught to seek extreme behavior as proof of the Spirit's presence. As a result, many are afraid of giving God complete control. Some fear the Holy Spirit will make them too emotional or force them to do things they don't want to do. Some fear the unknown or feel reluctant to open themselves to something that could be controversial. Yet if we know God at all, we can believe that he intends only good for us. The Holy Spirit is simply a present, accessible part of himself, meant to bring not fear but comfort and help.   —BQ

DAY 288
Acts 2:42–47; 4:32–37

THE FELLOWSHIP OF THE BELIEVERS

They devoted themselves to the apostles' teaching and to the fellowship, to the breaking of bread and to prayer. Everyone was filled with awe, and many wonders and miraculous signs were done by the apostles. All the believers were together and had everything in common. Selling their possessions and goods, they gave to anyone as he had need. Every day they continued to meet together in the temple courts. They broke bread in their homes and ate together with glad and sincere hearts, praising God and enjoying the favor of all the people. And the Lord added to their number daily those who were being saved. . . .

All the believers were one in heart and mind. No one claimed that any of his possessions was his own, but they shared everything they had. With great power the apostles continued to testify to the resurrection of the Lord Jesus, and much grace was upon them all. There were no needy persons among them. For from time to time those who owned lands or houses sold them, brought the money from the sales and put it at the apostles' feet, and it was distributed to anyone as he had need.

Joseph, a Levite from Cyprus, whom the apostles called Barnabas (which means Son of Encouragement), sold a field he owned and brought the money and put it at the apostles' feet.

Just a few months after Jesus prayed, on the eve of his death, that believers would live in complete unity so the world would believe in him, his prayer is answered. The earliest Christians live and worship together in unity and purity of love for each other. They are unselfish, helping any among them who have a need, even selling land or houses to give to others and support the ministry of the apostles.

These early Christians achieve the delicate balance of becoming a supportive, life-giving community while staying focused on spreading the word about Jesus to those who don't know him. They neither get stuck in their inner circles nor exalt evangelism to the exclusion of caring deeply for one another. This was Jesus' desire—that believers would be one, loving and caring for each other just as he cares for them, and in so doing, reach out to the rest of the world, drawing in those who hunger for the same fellowship with Christ and his people.

In their time together, believers of the early church hold to a fourfold focus. They are committed to the apostles' teaching; to fellowship, or worship; to the breaking of bread, or the Lord's Supper; and to prayer. These elements in their spiritual life together carry equal weight. None is neglected or reduced for the sake of the other. The early Christians share meals together in their homes and make a habit of living in gladness and praise to God.

We live in a different time and situation than did the believers of Acts, but we find here a picture of the ideal realization of one of Jesus' last hopes while on earth. A picture still possible for believers today, it remains the highest desire of Jesus' heart.

What, then, keeps us from displaying such unity with each other? What keeps us from readily sharing all that we have, to help others who will live with us for eternity? What keeps us from desiring to meet together often and joyfully worship God and enjoy each other? Too often human fear, pride, and self-absorption get in the way. When they do, we fall short of having the same powerful witness the first Christians had in their society. —BQ

DAILY CONTEMPLATION

Have you observed a group of believers who resemble the first Christians in Acts?

DAY 289   Acts 5:1–42

ANANIAS AND SAPPHIRA;

THE APOSTLES PERSECUTED

Now a man named Ananias, together with his wife Sapphira, also sold a piece of property. With his wife's full knowledge he kept back part of the money for himself, but brought the rest and put it at the apostles' feet.

Then Peter said, "Ananias, how is it that Satan has so filled your heart that you have lied to the Holy Spirit and have kept for yourself some of the money you received for the land? Didn't it belong to you before it was sold? And after it was sold, wasn't the money at your disposal? What made you think of doing such a thing? You have not lied to men but to God."

When Ananias heard this, he fell down and died. And great fear seized all who heard what had happened. Then the young men came forward, wrapped up his body, and carried him out and buried him.

About three hours later his wife came in, not knowing what had happened. Peter asked her, "Tell me, is this the price you and Ananias got for the land?"

"Yes," she said, "that is the price."

Peter said to her, "How could you agree to test the Spirit of the Lord? Look! The feet of the men who buried your husband are at the door, and they will carry you out also."

At that moment she fell down at his feet and died. Then the young men came in and, finding her dead, carried her out and buried her beside her husband. Great fear seized the whole church and all who heard about these events.

The apostles performed many miraculous signs and wonders among the people. And all the believers used to meet together in Solomon's Colonnade. No one else dared join them, even though they were highly regarded by the people. Nevertheless, more and more men and women believed in the Lord and were added to their number. As a result, people brought the sick into the streets and laid them on beds and mats so that at least Peter's shadow might fall on some of them as he passed by. Crowds gathered also from the towns around Jerusalem, bringing their sick and those tormented by evil spirits, and all of them were healed.

Then the high priest and all his associates, who were members of the party of the Sadducees, were filled with jealousy. They arrested the apostles and put them in the public jail. But during the night an angel of the Lord opened the doors of the jail and brought them out. "Go, stand in the temple courts," he said, "and tell the people the full message of this new life."

At daybreak they entered the temple courts, as they had been told, and began to teach the people.

When the high priest and his associates arrived, they called together the Sanhedrin—the full assembly of the elders of Israel—and sent to the jail for the apostles. But on arriving at the jail, the officers did not find them there. So they went back and reported, "We found the jail securely locked, with the guards standing at the doors; but when we opened them, we found no one inside." On hearing this report, the captain of the temple guard and the chief priests were puzzled, wondering what would come of this.

Then someone came and said, "Look! The men you put in jail are standing in the temple courts teaching the people." At that, the captain went with his officers and brought the apostles. They did not use force, because they feared that the people would stone them.

Having brought the apostles, they made them appear before the Sanhedrin to be questioned by the high priest. "We gave you strict orders not to teach in this name," he said. "Yet you have filled Jerusalem with your teaching and are determined to make us guilty of this man's blood."

Peter and the other apostles replied: "We must obey God rather than men! The God of our fathers raised Jesus from the dead—whom you had killed by hanging him on a tree. God exalted him to his own right hand as Prince and Savior that he might give repentance and forgiveness of sins to Israel. We are witnesses of these things, and so is the Holy Spirit, whom God has given to those who obey him."

When they heard this, they were furious and wanted to put them to death. But a Pharisee named Gamaliel, a teacher of the law, who was honored by all the people, stood up in the Sanhedrin and ordered that the men be put outside for a little while. Then he addressed them: "Men of Israel, consider carefully what you intend to do to these men. Some time ago Theudas appeared, claiming to be somebody, and about four hundred men rallied to him. He was killed, all his followers were dispersed, and it all came to nothing. After him, Judas the Galilean appeared in the days of the census and led a band of people in revolt. He too was killed, and all his followers were scattered. Therefore, in the present case I advise you: Leave these men alone! Let them go! For if their purpose or activity is of human origin, it will fail. But if it is from God, you will not be able to stop these men; you will only find yourselves fighting against God."

His speech persuaded them. They called the apostles in and had them flogged. Then they ordered them not to speak in the name of Jesus, and let them go.

The apostles left the Sanhedrin, rejoicing because they had been counted worthy of suffering disgrace for the Name. Day after day, in the temple courts and from house to house, they never stopped teaching and proclaiming the good news that Jesus is the Christ.

The disciples, newly empowered with the Holy Spirit, start acting a lot like Jesus. They go to the temple and preach sermons; they heal the sick; they meet the needs of the poor. To many bystanders, the message of new life in Jesus sounds wonderful, like the first note of music to people born deaf. Five thousand men believe, including some priests. The followers are soon organizing and electing officers to handle the demands of a growing church.

But problems spring up alongside the successes. The church becomes popular, an "in" place to belong. Sorcerers and magicians drop in, drawn by the reports of healings and other wonders. Wealthy people, such as Ananias (AN-uh-NI-uhs) and Sapphira (suh-FI-ruh), see the church as a place to gain applause for their benevolence. Such opportunists learn that the apostles, not to mention God, will not tolerate corruption in the fledgling church.

Before long, the focus of concern shifts away from internal problems to outside opposition. The same forces that conspired against Jesus—temple officers, the Sadducees, the high priest, the Sanhedrin, Roman guards—align themselves against the new phenomenon of the church. Every so often they haul in the leaders, but for what can they prosecute them—healing the sick? Inciting people to praise God? The Christians hardly resemble dangerous conspirators: they usually meet openly on the temple porch.

Even so, religious leaders beat and jail the apostles on trumped-up charges. What happens next should give the establishment a clue into exactly what they are up against: the apostles respond to the beatings with praise to God for the privilege of suffering in his name, and an angel of the Lord springs them free from jail.

Gamaliel (guh-MAY-lee-uhl), a wise old Pharisee, has perhaps the best advice of all (vv. 38–39): "Let them go! For if their purpose or activity is of human origin, it will fail. But if it is from God, you will not be able to stop these men." He could not have been more prophetic.   —PY

DAY 290   Acts 6:8–7:5; 7:51–8:3

THE STONING OF STEPHEN

Now Stephen, a man full of God's grace and power, did great wonders and miraculous signs among the people. Opposition arose, however, from members of the Synagogue of the Freedmen (as it was called)—Jews of Cyrene and Alexandria as well as the provinces of Cilicia and Asia. These men began to argue with Stephen, but they could not stand up against his wisdom or the Spirit by whom he spoke.

Then they secretly persuaded some men to say, "We have heard Stephen speak words of blasphemy against Moses and against God."

So they stirred up the people and the elders and the teachers of the law. They seized Stephen and brought him before the Sanhedrin. They produced false witnesses, who testified, "This fellow never stops speaking against this holy place and against the law. For we have heard him say that this Jesus of Nazareth will destroy this place and change the customs Moses handed down to us."

All who were sitting in the Sanhedrin looked intently at Stephen, and they saw that his face was like the face of an angel.

Then the high priest asked him, "Are these charges true?"

To this he replied: "Brothers and fathers, listen to me! The God of glory appeared to our father Abraham while he was still in Mesopotamia, before he lived in Haran. 'Leave your country and your people,' God said, 'and go to the land I will show you.'

"So he left the land of the Chaldeans and settled in Haran. After the death of his father, God sent him to this land where you are now living. He gave him no inheritance here, not even a foot of ground. But God promised him that he and his descendants after him would possess the land, even though at that time Abraham had no child. . . .

"You stiff-necked people, with uncircumcised hearts and ears! You are just like your fathers: You always resist the Holy Spirit! Was there ever a prophet your fathers did not persecute? They even killed those who predicted the coming of the Righteous One. And now you have betrayed and murdered him—you who have received the law that was put into effect through angels but have not obeyed it."

When they heard this, they were furious and gnashed their teeth at him. But Stephen, full of the Holy Spirit, looked up to heaven and saw the glory of

God, and Jesus standing at the right hand of God. "Look," he said, "I see heaven open and the Son of Man standing at the right hand of God."

At this they covered their ears and, yelling at the top of their voices, they all rushed at him, dragged him out of the city and began to stone him. Meanwhile, the witnesses laid their clothes at the feet of a young man named Saul.

While they were stoning him, Stephen prayed, "Lord Jesus, receive my spirit." Then he fell on his knees and cried out, "Lord, do not hold this sin against them." When he had said this, he fell asleep.

And Saul was there, giving approval to his death.

On that day a great persecution broke out against the church at Jerusalem, and all except the apostles were scattered throughout Judea and Samaria. Godly men buried Stephen and mourned deeply for him. But Saul began to destroy the church. Going from house to house, he dragged off men and women and put them in prison.

Opposition to the early Christians gets worse. Not only are the apostles working miracles, but now other believers are doing the same, threatening the Jewish religious establishment. The Jews can't win arguments against one of these believers, Stephen, so they resort to lying about him before the Sanhedrin. Stephen's speech so incenses those listening that they drag him outside the city and stone him, making him the first recorded martyr of the early church.

Stephen's speech to the Jewish court, only partially printed here, reviews the history of the Israelite people from Abraham through Isaac, Jacob, Joseph, Moses, Joshua, David, and Solomon (7:6–50). Stephen notes God's promises to his people throughout the generations, and the people's repeated unfaithfulness. Charged with speaking against the synagogue, Stephen reminds the Jewish leaders of God's words through Isaiah (7:49–50). All creation is God's temple, and further, Christ replaced the temple by becoming the way for all people to come to God.

Stephen's accusations bear themselves out even in his own life. The Israelite people have a history of persecuting God's prophets. Insistent on their agendas for God, they have often closed themselves to the new things God was accomplishing. They even killed God's Son, their Messiah. Now they follow suit by stoning Stephen. Like the prophets before him, and like Jesus himself, Stephen remains fixed on God to the end, praying for those who take his life.

Now the church must go underground. Believers are forced to scatter, and in this way they bring the gospel to new places. The church continues to grow rapidly. As it does, we meet one of its most vengeful opponents, Saul. With the same fervency that new believers show toward Christ, Saul seeks to imprison them and squelch the burgeoning threat to Judaism. He is intent on his mission, but God has other plans.

—BQ

DAILY CONTEMPLATION

Where, other than in a church, have you been especially focused on God?

PHILIP AND THE ETHIOPIAN

Now an angel of the Lord said to Philip, "Go south to the road—the desert road—that goes down from Jerusalem to Gaza." So he started out, and on his way he met an Ethiopian eunuch, an important official in charge of all the treasury of Candace, queen of the Ethiopians. This man had gone to Jerusalem to worship, and on his way home was sitting in his chariot reading the book of Isaiah the prophet. The Spirit told Philip, "Go to that chariot and stay near it."

Then Philip ran up to the chariot and heard the man reading Isaiah the prophet. "Do you understand what you are reading?" Philip asked.

"How can I," he said, "unless someone explains it to me?" So he invited Philip to come up and sit with him.

The eunuch was reading this passage of Scripture:

"He was led like a sheep to the slaughter,
and as a lamb before the shearer is silent,
so he did not open his mouth.
In his humiliation he was deprived of justice.
Who can speak of his descendants?
For his life was taken from the earth."

The eunuch asked Philip, "Tell me, please, who is the prophet talking about, himself or someone else?" Then Philip began with that very passage of Scripture and told him the good news about Jesus.

As they traveled along the road, they came to some water and the eunuch said, "Look, here is water. Why shouldn't I be baptized?" And he gave orders to stop the chariot. Then both Philip and the eunuch went down into the water and Philip baptized him. When they came up out of the water, the Spirit of the Lord suddenly took Philip away, and the eunuch did not see him again, but went on his way rejoicing. Philip, however, appeared at Azotus and traveled about, preaching the gospel in all the towns until he reached Caesarea.

The early church looked after minorities. Philip and Stephen were part of a group of seven men chosen to help the apostles by caring especially for Greek believers in need. Like Stephen, Philip performed miracles of healing and exorcism of demons. He left Jerusalem, along with many other believers, after Stephen's death and first went to Samaria, where he continued to preach about Christ among another minority group.

From there an angel directs Philip to head south again and journey on a desolate road leading from Jerusalem to Gaza. The Holy Spirit guides him to an Ethiopian official, and Philip helps him understand a passage from Isaiah 53, which speaks of Jesus. This man, a castrated African bureaucrat, may have seemed an unlikely candidate for Christianity, but God had been working in him even before he and Philip met. God provides water, and the man himself suggests that Philip baptize him.

As these stories show, God has a plan for drawing individuals to himself, and he uses believers in specific ways to carry out his plan. As Philip was used and directed by the Holy Spirit, so believers today are used and directed by God to carry out his will for those who need him. We'll find, as Philip did, that God often surprises us with his timing and circumstances. If we are willing to venture out and be used, God will speak through us in similarly powerful ways.   —BQ

DAILY CONTEMPLATION

When have you had the opportunity to share with someone the good news about Jesus, only to find out that God had previously prepared that person for this moment?

DAY 292   Reflection

LIVING BY THE SPIRIT

The book of Acts illustrates that life with the Holy Spirit adds another dimension to our faith. Our days can become unpredictably exciting, and our lives may take unexpected and miraculous turns. But life with the Spirit doesn't mean we become perfect. We will still fail, and we will not always make the right decisions.

The apostles experienced drastic change, but they did not become perfect. Ananias and Sapphira proved that people in Spirit-filled communities go their own way sometimes. Living in the Spirit is a growth process of continually giving over control to him.

Hannah Whitall Smith, author of *The Christian's Secret of a Happy Life*, found this to be poignantly true. Catherine Marshall tells Smith's story. Born in Philadelphia in 1832 to a Quaker family, Smith felt from a young age a great zeal for spiritual things. Her Quaker upbringing gave her a thorough knowledge of the Bible, and she began to believe early that Christians must know God primarily through what he says in his Word rather than through their emotions toward him. Emotions, she found, can be unreliable and deceptive.

Hannah and her husband, Robert, became part of a lively church and one summer attended a camp meeting at a woodland campsite. Here, in the woods, Robert had an emotional experience with the Holy Spirit. He felt the Spirit enter him in a way that brought joy and connection to God such as he'd never known. Soon after, he became a powerful evangelistic teacher, drawing crowds wherever he spoke. Hannah meanwhile tried repeatedly to prompt a similar experience with the Holy Spirit, but to no avail. She realized in time that her experience with God was as real as her husband's but simply different. Marshall writes, "She wanted emotions and was given conviction. She 'wanted a vision and got a fact.'"[49]

Robert's success in preaching flourished but then was suddenly cut short. Gossip began circulating about improper conduct with females, causing him to lose the respect of audiences and the support of sponsors. We don't know how much truth the gossip contained, but it seems that at some level Robert let his emotions carry him to actions the Spirit wouldn't have prompted. He never regained his passion for living or sharing Christ. Hannah meanwhile kept on in a steady faith that strengthened her and enabled her to continue being used by God.

We learn from the Smiths' story that if we let our emotions become our primary means of connection with God, we risk moving outside of the Spirit's control. We become prone to following our own urges. Marshall sees this emotionalism as a real danger for the church today. It can happen if we allow "too great a love affair with emotion, too little grounding in Scripture, too [much] wanting in garden-variety discipline, too small an emphasis on purity, strict honesty, morality—Christ's own life living in us. What is needed, of course, is a balance: plenty of solid teaching—but plenty of joy as well."[50]

More, we need to open our lives to other believers who can see when we're moving in a dangerous direction. "We must deliberately make ourselves subject one to the other," Marshall urges, "be willing to be checked and corrected as well as encouraged and strengthened."[51]

We don't need to fear letting the Holy Spirit control our lives. He is God and we can fully trust him. When we continue to live in God's Word and walk each day in humility with him, we can trust that the Spirit will protect us and lead us into a richer, more mature life with himself.   —BQ

DAILY CONTEMPLATION

What has been your experience with the Holy Spirit? Do you need to guard against over-emotionalism? Are you resistant to letting the Spirit take control? Ask God to help you stay balanced, open, and committed to all he desires you to be through his Spirit.

DAY 293
Acts 9:1–31

SAUL'S CONVERSION

Meanwhile, Saul was still breathing out murderous threats against the Lord's disciples. He went to the high priest and asked him for letters to the synagogues in Damascus, so that if he found any there who belonged to the Way, whether men or women, he might take them as prisoners to Jerusalem. As he neared Damascus on his journey, suddenly a light from heaven flashed around him. He fell to the ground and heard a voice say to him, "Saul, Saul, why do you persecute me?"

"Who are you, Lord?" Saul asked.

"I am Jesus, whom you are persecuting," he replied. "Now get up and go into the city, and you will be told what you must do."

The men traveling with Saul stood there speechless; they heard the sound but did not see anyone. Saul got up from the ground, but when he opened his eyes he could see nothing. So they led him by the hand into Damascus. For three days he was blind, and did not eat or drink anything.

In Damascus there was a disciple named Ananias. The Lord called to him in a vision, "Ananias!"

"Yes, Lord," he answered.

The Lord told him, "Go to the house of Judas on Straight Street and ask for a man from Tarsus named Saul, for he is praying. In a vision he has seen a man named Ananias come and place his hands on him to restore his sight."

"Lord," Ananias answered, "I have heard many reports about this man and all the harm he has done to your saints in Jerusalem. And he has come here with authority from the chief priests to arrest all who call on your name."

But the Lord said to Ananias, "Go! This man is my chosen instrument to carry my name before the Gentiles and their kings and before the people of Israel. I will show him how much he must suffer for my name."

Then Ananias went to the house and entered it. Placing his hands on Saul, he said, "Brother Saul, the Lord—Jesus, who appeared to you on the road as you were coming here—has sent me so that you may see again and be filled with the Holy Spirit." Immediately, something like scales fell from Saul's eyes, and he could see again. He got up and was baptized, and after taking some food, he regained his strength.

Saul spent several days with the disciples in Damascus. At once he began to preach in the synagogues that Jesus is the Son of God. All those who heard him were astonished and asked, "Isn't he the man who raised havoc in Jerusalem among those who call on this name? And hasn't he come here to take them as prisoners to the chief priests?" Yet Saul grew more and more powerful and baffled the Jews living in Damascus by proving that Jesus is the Christ.

After many days had gone by, the Jews conspired to kill him, but Saul learned of their plan. Day and night they kept close watch on the city gates in order to kill him. But his followers took him by night and lowered him in a basket through an opening in the wall.

When he came to Jerusalem, he tried to join the disciples, but they were all afraid of him, not believing that he really was a disciple. But Barnabas took him and brought him to the apostles. He told them how Saul on his journey had seen the Lord and that the Lord had spoken to him, and how in Damascus he had preached fearlessly in the name of Jesus. So Saul stayed with them and moved about freely in Jerusalem, speaking boldly in the name of the Lord. He talked and debated with the Grecian Jews, but they tried to kill him. When the brothers learned of this, they took him down to Caesarea and sent him off to Tarsus.

Then the church throughout Judea, Galilee and Samaria enjoyed a time of peace. It was strengthened; and encouraged by the Holy Spirit, it grew in numbers, living in the fear of the Lord.

The most surprising converts often make the best crusaders. Former alcoholics can convince others of drinking's dangers; former drug addicts give the most forceful warnings against drugs. And when the book of Acts introduces the most effective Christian missionary of all time, he turns out to be a former bounty hunter of Christians.

Acts 9 shows a glimpse of the early church even before it has a name; people call its followers "the Way" or "the brothers" or "the Nazarene sect." Its members live in constant fear of arrest and persecution—if not from the Romans, then from the Jews. Already a leader named Stephen has been publicly stoned. And no one inspires more fear in the hearts of the early Christians than a man named Saul, who participated in Stephen's execution.

But then comes a miraculous turnabout on the road to Damascus. In a dramatic move, God steps in and, against all odds, selects the bounty hunter Saul to lead the young church. It doesn't take much to convince Saul: a blinding light and a voice from heaven knock him out of commission for three days and change his whole attitude toward Jesus. Such is Saul's murderous reputation, however, that the Christians in Damascus and Jerusalem accept him only gradually.

Soon Saul (renamed Paul) is on the other side of the persecutors' whips; his former colleagues are now trying to kill *him*. He proves to be as fearless in preaching Christ as he has been in working against him. In four great missionary journeys, Paul will take the news of the gospel around the shores of the Mediterranean. During those journeys he finds time to write half the books of the New Testament, and in so doing lays the groundwork for Christian theology. Paul is perhaps the most thoroughly converted man who has ever lived. —PY

DAILY CONTEMPLATION

Have you ever had an abrupt about-face?

DAY 294   Acts 10:1–48

PETER'S VISION; PETER AT CORNELIUS' HOUSE

At Caesarea there was a man named Cornelius, a centurion in what was known as the Italian Regiment. He and all his family were devout and God-fearing; he gave generously to those in need and prayed to God regularly. One day at about three in the afternoon he had a vision. He distinctly saw an angel of God, who came to him and said, "Cornelius!"

Cornelius stared at him in fear. "What is it, Lord?" he asked.

The angel answered, "Your prayers and gifts to the poor have come up as a memorial offering before God. Now send men to Joppa to bring back a man named Simon who is called Peter. He is staying with Simon the tanner, whose house is by the sea."

When the angel who spoke to him had gone, Cornelius called two of his servants and a devout soldier who was one of his attendants. He told them everything that had happened and sent them to Joppa.

About noon the following day as they were on their journey and approaching the city, Peter went up on the roof to pray. He became hungry and wanted something to eat, and while the meal was being prepared, he fell into a trance. He saw heaven opened and something like a large sheet being let down to earth by its four corners. It contained all kinds of four-footed animals, as well as reptiles of the earth and birds of the air. Then a voice told him, "Get up, Peter. Kill and eat."

"Surely not, Lord!" Peter replied. "I have never eaten anything impure or unclean."

The voice spoke to him a second time, "Do not call anything impure that God has made clean."

This happened three times, and immediately the sheet was taken back to heaven.

While Peter was wondering about the meaning of the vision, the men sent by Cornelius found out where Simon's house was and stopped at the gate. They called out, asking if Simon who was known as Peter was staying there.

While Peter was still thinking about the vision, the Spirit said to him, "Simon, three men are looking for you. So get up and go downstairs. Do not hesitate to go with them, for I have sent them."

Peter went down and said to the men, "I'm the one you're looking for. Why have you come?"

The men replied, "We have come from Cornelius the centurion. He is a righteous and God-fearing man, who is respected by all the Jewish people. A holy angel told him to have you come to his house so that he could hear what you have to say." Then Peter invited the men into the house to be his guests.

The next day Peter started out with them, and some of the brothers from Joppa went along. The following day he arrived in Caesarea. Cornelius was expecting them and had called together his relatives and close friends. As Peter entered the house, Cornelius met him and fell at his feet in reverence. But Peter made him get up. "Stand up," he said, "I am only a man myself."

Talking with him, Peter went inside and found a large gathering of people. He said to them: "You are well aware that it is against our law for a Jew to associate with a Gentile or visit him. But God has shown me that I should not call any man impure or unclean. So when I was sent for, I came without raising any objection. May I ask why you sent for me?"

Cornelius answered: "Four days ago I was in my house praying at this hour, at three in the afternoon. Suddenly a man in shining clothes stood before me and said, 'Cornelius, God has heard your prayer and remembered your gifts to the poor. Send to Joppa for Simon who is called Peter. He is a guest in the home of Simon the tanner, who lives by the sea.' So I sent for you immediately, and it was good of you to come. Now we are all here in the presence of God to listen to everything the Lord has commanded you to tell us."

Then Peter began to speak: "I now realize how true it is that God does not show favoritism but accepts men from every nation who fear him and do what is right. You know the message God sent to the people of Israel, telling the good news of peace through Jesus Christ, who is Lord of all. You know what has happened throughout Judea, beginning in Galilee after the baptism that John preached—how God anointed Jesus of Nazareth with the Holy Spirit and power, and how he went around doing good and healing all who were under the power of the devil, because God was with him.

"We are witnesses of everything he did in the country of the Jews and in Jerusalem. They killed him by hanging him on a tree, but God raised him from the dead on the third day and caused him to be seen. He was not seen by all the people, but by witnesses whom God had already chosen—by us who ate and drank with him after he rose from the dead. He commanded us to preach to the people and to testify that he is the one whom God appointed as judge of the living and the dead. All the prophets testify about him that everyone who believes in him receives forgiveness of sins through his name."

While Peter was still speaking these words, the Holy Spirit came on all who heard the message. The circumcised believers who had come with Peter were astonished that the gift of the Holy Spirit had been poured out even on the Gentiles. For they heard them speaking in tongues and praising God.

Then Peter said, "Can anyone keep these people from being baptized with water? They have received the Holy Spirit just as we have." So he ordered that they be baptized in the name of Jesus Christ. Then they asked Peter to stay with them for a few days.

An important step in the spread of the gospel has taken place. During his time on earth, Jesus ministered primarily to the Jewish people. Yet throughout his ministry he proclaimed salvation not only for the Jews but for all people. His last words on earth spoke of the spreading of his name to all the world.

Although his disciples accepted these words, in the first days of the early church they still do not change their long-held practice of associating and worshiping with other Jews exclusively. Now this practice must end. God comes to Peter when he's hungry, and uses a vision of food to reveal one more characteristic of Christ's new church. God's old covenant declared certain foods—and people—unclean and commanded God's people to stay separate from them. His new covenant, heralded by Jesus Christ, does away with distinctions of clean and unclean. Now all are clean through salvation in Jesus.

Overnight Peter must give up a way of life he has followed since birth and then instruct believers everywhere to accept God's new command. Now Peter and the other apostles will preach to Gentiles as well as Jews. They will all worship together as one family.   —BQ

DAILY CONTEMPLATION

What old ways of thinking did you have to give up when you became a believer?

PETER'S MIRACULOUS ESCAPE FROM PRISON

It was about this time that King Herod arrested some who belonged to the church, intending to persecute them. He had James, the brother of John, put to death with the sword. When he saw that this pleased the Jews, he proceeded to seize Peter also. This happened during the Feast of Unleavened Bread. After arresting him, he put him in prison, handing him over to be guarded by four squads of four soldiers each. Herod intended to bring him out for public trial after the Passover.

So Peter was kept in prison, but the church was earnestly praying to God for him.

The night before Herod was to bring him to trial, Peter was sleeping between two soldiers, bound with two chains, and sentries stood guard at the entrance. Suddenly an angel of the Lord appeared and a light shone in the cell. He struck Peter on the side and woke him up. "Quick, get up!" he said, and the chains fell off Peter's wrists.

Then the angel said to him, "Put on your clothes and sandals." And Peter did so. "Wrap your cloak around you and follow me," the angel told him. Peter followed him out of the prison, but he had no idea that what the angel was doing was really happening; he thought he was seeing a vision. They passed the first and second guards and came to the iron gate leading to the city. It opened for them by itself, and they went through it. When they had walked the length of one street, suddenly the angel left him.

Then Peter came to himself and said, "Now I know without a doubt that the Lord sent his angel and rescued me from Herod's clutches and from everything the Jewish people were anticipating."

When this had dawned on him, he went to the house of Mary the mother of John, also called Mark, where many people had gathered and were praying. Peter knocked at the outer entrance, and a servant girl named Rhoda came to answer the door. When she recognized Peter's voice, she was so overjoyed she ran back without opening it and exclaimed, "Peter is at the door!"

"You're out of your mind," they told her. When she kept insisting that it was so, they said, "It must be his angel."

But Peter kept on knocking, and when they opened the door and saw him, they were astonished. Peter motioned with his hand for them to be quiet and described how the Lord had brought him out of prison. "Tell James and the brothers about this," he said, and then he left for another place.

In the morning, there was no small commotion among the soldiers as to what had become of Peter. After Herod had a thorough search made for him and did not find him, he cross-examined the guards and ordered that they be executed.

Then Herod went from Judea to Caesarea and stayed there a while.

Although Christians are being persecuted and some killed, still God's plan prevails. With further work for Peter to do, God easily removes him from a situation of danger that is not part of this plan. God is capable of such miraculous acts as making chains fall from a prisoner, restraining guards, and opening iron gates. His power controls humans as well as the things they build to empower themselves.

In this second prison escape, the prayers of the church play a big part in accomplishing Peter's release. Many believers have gathered in a home to pray for Peter's safety. Even they don't realize the power their prayers carry—when Peter appears at the door, they don't believe it's him. In answer to the earnest prayers of the church, God spares Peter from further suffering and releases him to continue his work. —BQ

DAILY CONTEMPLATION

Are you praying for anything you inwardly doubt God can provide?

DAY 296   Galatians 3:1–4:7

FAITH OR OBSERVANCE OF THE LAW

You foolish Galatians! Who has bewitched you? Before your very eyes Jesus Christ was clearly portrayed as crucified. I would like to learn just one thing from you: Did you receive the Spirit by observing the law, or by believing what you heard? Are you so foolish? After beginning with the Spirit, are you now trying to attain your goal by human effort? Have you suffered so much for nothing—if it really was for nothing? Does God give you his Spirit and work miracles among you because you observe the law, or because you believe what you heard?

Consider Abraham: "He believed God, and it was credited to him as righteousness." Understand, then, that those who believe are children of Abraham. The Scripture foresaw that God would justify the Gentiles by faith, and announced the gospel in advance to Abraham: "All nations will be blessed through you." So those who have faith are blessed along with Abraham, the man of faith.

All who rely on observing the law are under a curse, for it is written: "Cursed is everyone who does not continue to do everything written in the Book of the Law." Clearly no one is justified before God by the law, because, "The righteous will live by faith." The law is not based on faith; on the contrary, "The man who does these things will live by them." Christ redeemed us from the curse of the law by becoming a curse for us, for it is written: "Cursed is everyone who is hung on a tree." He redeemed us in order that the blessing given to Abraham might come to the Gentiles through Christ Jesus, so that by faith we might receive the promise of the Spirit.

Brothers, let me take an example from everyday life. Just as no one can set aside or add to a human covenant that has been duly established, so it is in this case. The promises were spoken to Abraham and to his seed. The Scripture does not say "and to seeds," meaning many people, but "and to your seed," meaning one person, who is Christ. What I mean is this: The law, introduced 430 years later, does not set aside the covenant previously established by God and thus do away with the promise. For if the inheritance depends on the law, then it no longer depends on a promise; but God in his grace gave it to Abraham through a promise.

What, then, was the purpose of the law? It was added because of transgressions until the Seed to whom the promise referred had come. The law was put into effect through angels by a mediator. A mediator, however, does not represent just one party; but God is one.

Is the law, therefore, opposed to the promises of God? Absolutely not! For if a law had been given that could impart life, then righteousness would certainly have come by the law. But the Scripture declares that the whole world is a prisoner of sin, so that what was promised, being given through faith in Jesus Christ, might be given to those who believe.

Before this faith came, we were held prisoners by the law, locked up until faith should be revealed. So the law was put in charge to lead us to Christ that we might be justified by faith. Now that faith has come, we are no longer under the supervision of the law.

You are all sons of God through faith in Christ Jesus, for all of you who were baptized into Christ have clothed yourselves with Christ. There is neither Jew nor Greek, slave nor free, male nor female, for you are all one in Christ Jesus. If you belong to Christ, then you are Abraham's seed, and heirs according to the promise.

What I am saying is that as long as the heir is a child, he is no different from a slave, although he owns the whole estate. He is subject to guardians and trustees until the time set by his father. So also, when we were children, we were in slavery under the basic principles of the world. But when the time had fully come, God sent his Son, born of a woman, born under law, to redeem those under law, that we might receive the full rights of sons. Because you are sons, God sent the Spirit of his Son into our hearts, the Spirit who calls out, "Abba, Father." So you are no longer a slave, but a son; and since you are a son, God has made you also an heir.

All Jesus' disciples were Jewish, as were most of the converts from the day of Pentecost. On his first missionary journey, however, Paul learns to his surprise that non-Jews are more receptive to the news about Jesus. He begins a policy that he will follow throughout his career: he goes first to the synagogue and preaches among Jews; if they reject him, he turns immediately to the Gentiles.

In a twist of history, Paul gains a reputation as "the Apostle to the Gentiles." Before conversion he has been a Pharisee, a strict Jewish legalist. But as he sees God work among non-Jews, he becomes their champion. This letter to the churches in

Galatia (guh-LAY-shuh) dates from the time of the early Jew-Gentile controversy. Paul is emotionally worked up. In fact, he is downright furious at misguided attempts to shackle the church with legalism. In the first paragraph, Paul explodes with full force; he then proceeds to give a "Christian," rather than Jewish, interpretation of the Old Testament covenants with Abraham and Moses.

Legalism may seem like a rather harmless quirk of the church, but Paul can foresee the outcome of the Galatians' thinking. They will start trusting in their own human effort (keeping the law) to gain acceptance with God. Faith in Christ will become just one of many steps in salvation, not the only one. The bedrock of the gospel will crumble as they, in effect, devalue what Christ has done.

Paul's letter to the Galatians stands, then, as a protest against treason. Paul insists that faith in Christ alone, not anyone's set of laws, opens the door to acceptance by God. If a person could reach God by obeying the law, then he, the strict Pharisee, would have done it. Galatians teaches that there is nothing we can do to make God love us more or love us less. We can't "earn" God's love by slavishly following rules.

—PY

DAILY CONTEMPLATION

The Galatians became obsessed with legalism. Others refused to follow anyone's rules. Which are you more prone to do?

DAY 297   Reflection

FAITH, THE ONLY WAY

Belonging to a Christian community can be nerve-racking. Believing, it seems, opens up a whole new world of voices telling us what to do, how to act, who to vote for, how to worship, what to buy or not buy, and more. Gaining a grasp of the Bible and getting to know God are merely the beginning, we're often led to believe. Then comes the indoctrination into what a "Christian" must look like.

These pressures are hardly new. Since the days of the early church God has had to remind believers that only one thing matters for salvation: faith in Christ. In the apostle Paul's day, Jewish Christians, accustomed to following the letter of the law, pressured the Gentile people of Galatia to keep particular parts of the Old Testament law to retain their salvation. The Jews knew the Scriptures and appeared to be several notches higher on the religious ladder, so the Galatians followed their teaching.

The Jews could not grasp that when Jesus came, he changed all the requirements, replacing the law and making belief in himself the one and final way to be saved. Emphatic about this point in his letter to the Galatians, Paul warned they were allowing themselves to be "bewitched" by wrong teaching. In so doing, they had accepted an unnecessary burden and were misleading others. One who believes in Jesus, Paul declared, is saved from sin. Period. Nothing else factors into the equation.

Paul's letter could not have been clearer. Still, each ensuing generation of believers has lost sight of his words and struggled with its own contingent of Christians who require specific actions or behaviors, outside of faith, for ultimate salvation. Martin Luther, father of the Reformation, rediscovered the burning message of Galatians and helped direct many to a more grace-filled theology. He spoke to a church requiring religious routines and penance to achieve salvation. Luther's teaching made Galatians the "cornerstone of the Protestant Reformation," and he was so indebted to the book, he even referred to it on occasion as his "wife."

Despite the insistence of Paul, Luther, and others who have striven to keep believers on guard, the burden of legalism (following rules prescribed by people, not God) still exists today, with believers imposing wrong theology on one another. J. B. Phillips, a British pastor and scholar of the Anglican Church, wrote about various false gods that believers often mix with the true God. One, the god of "one hundred per cent," expects perfection. This god "has led quite a number of sensitive conscientious people to what is popularly called a 'nervous breakdown.' And it has taken the joy and spontaneity out of the Christian lives of many more who dimly realize that what was meant to be a life of 'perfect freedom' has become an anxious slavery."[52]

Phillips continues: "Some of our modern enthusiastic Christians of the hearty type tend to regard Christianity as a performance. But it still is, as it was originally, a way of living, and in no sense a performance acted for the benefit of the surrounding world. . . . The modern high-pressure Christian of certain circles would like to impose perfection of one hundred per cent as a set of rules to be immediately enforced, instead of as a shining ideal to be faithfully pursued."[53]

God gives guidance in the Bible about how to live. He doesn't, however, hold these standards over our heads as a prerequisite for salvation. Jesus and the rest of the Bible teach us God's true ideal. This ideal, when taken as God intended, doesn't threaten us but rather "stimulates, encourages, and produces likeness to itself," Phillips writes.[54]

As we hear the voices that would lead us in how to live as believers, no voice should be stronger than God's Word: "Clearly no one is justified before God by the law, because, 'The righteous will live by faith'" (Galatians 3:11).   —BQ

DAILY CONTEMPLATION

Do you worry about whether or not you measure up as a Christian? Do you get confused or frustrated by what the voices around you are telling you to do? Ask God to help you remain grounded in the message of Galatians, trusting that already and always you are saved by your faith in Jesus.

LYDIA'S CONVERSION IN PHILIPPI;
PAUL AND SILAS IN PRISON

Paul and his companions traveled throughout the region of Phrygia and Galatia, having been kept by the Holy Spirit from preaching the word in the province of Asia. When they came to the border of Mysia, they tried to enter Bithynia, but the Spirit of Jesus would not allow them to. So they passed by Mysia and went down to Troas. During the night Paul had a vision of a man of Macedonia standing and begging him, "Come over to Macedonia and help us." After Paul had seen the vision, we got ready at once to leave for Macedonia, concluding that God had called us to preach the gospel to them.

From Troas we put out to sea and sailed straight for Samothrace, and the next day on to Neapolis. From there we traveled to Philippi, a Roman colony and the leading city of that district of Macedonia. And we stayed there several days.

On the Sabbath we went outside the city gate to the river, where we expected to find a place of prayer. We sat down and began to speak to the women who had gathered there. One of those listening was a woman named Lydia, a dealer in purple cloth from the city of Thyatira, who was a worshiper of God. The Lord opened her heart to respond to Paul's message. When she and the members of her household were baptized, she invited us to her home. "If you consider me a believer in the Lord," she said, "come and stay at my house." And she persuaded us.

Once when we were going to the place of prayer, we were met by a slave girl who had a spirit by which she predicted the future. She earned a great deal of money for her owners by fortune-telling. This girl followed Paul and the rest of us, shouting, "These men are servants of the Most High God, who are telling you the way to be saved." She kept this up for many days. Finally Paul became so troubled that he turned around and said to the spirit, "In the name of Jesus Christ I command you to come out of her!" At that moment the spirit left her.

When the owners of the slave girl realized that their hope of making money was gone, they seized Paul and Silas and dragged them into the marketplace to face the authorities. They brought them before the magistrates and said, "These men are Jews, and are throwing our city into an uproar by advocating customs unlawful for us Romans to accept or practice."

The crowd joined in the attack against Paul and Silas, and the magistrates ordered them to be stripped and beaten. After they had been severely flogged, they were thrown into prison, and the jailer was commanded to guard them carefully. Upon receiving such orders, he put them in the inner cell and fastened their feet in the stocks.

About midnight Paul and Silas were praying and singing hymns to God, and the other prisoners were listening to them. Suddenly there was such a violent earthquake that the foundations of the prison were shaken. At once all the prison doors flew open, and everybody's chains came loose. The jailer woke up, and when he saw the prison doors open, he drew his sword and was about to kill himself because he thought the prisoners had escaped. But Paul shouted, "Don't harm yourself! We are all here!"

The jailer called for lights, rushed in and fell trembling before Paul and Silas. He then brought them out and asked, "Sirs, what must I do to be saved?"

They replied, "Believe in the Lord Jesus, and you will be saved—you and your household." Then they spoke the word of the Lord to him and to all the others in his house. At that hour of the night the jailer took them and washed their wounds; then immediately he and all his family were baptized. The jailer brought them into his house and set a meal before them; he was filled with joy because he had come to believe in God—he and his whole family.

When it was daylight, the magistrates sent their officers to the jailer with the order: "Release those men." The jailer told Paul, "The magistrates have ordered that you and Silas be released. Now you can leave. Go in peace."

But Paul said to the officers: "They beat us publicly without a trial, even though we are Roman citizens, and threw us into prison. And now do they want to get rid of us quietly? No! Let them come themselves and escort us out."

The officers reported this to the magistrates, and when they heard that Paul and Silas were Roman citizens, they were alarmed. They came to appease them and escorted them from the prison, requesting them to leave the city. After Paul and Silas came out of the prison, they went to Lydia's house, where they met with the brothers and encouraged them. Then they left.

The book of Acts follows Paul on three distinct missionary journeys. All in all, it is a good time to travel, for by Paul's lifetime Rome has established absolute mastery over a vast territory. Language is unified, and a rare empire-wide peace, the Pax Romana, prevails. Moreover, Roman engineers have crisscrossed the empire with a network of roads (built so well that many still survive), and as a Roman citizen Paul holds a passport valid anywhere.

In his travels, Paul concentrates on the chief trade towns and capital cities of Roman colonies. From them, the gospel message can radiate out across the globe. If a young church shows promise, Paul will stay on, sometimes as long as three years, to direct its spiritual growth. His letters glow with affection for the friends he develops in this way. On his second and third journeys Paul revisits many of the churches he has founded.

This chapter shows how one of Paul's favorite churches comes into existence. Philippi (FIL-ih-pie) is a leading city in the region of Macedonia, where the vision has directed him. A casual conversation with a woman by a river opens the way for Paul (women play a crucial role in many of the early churches). What takes place in Philippi stands almost as a pattern for Paul's never-dull missionary visits: early acceptance, violent opposition, and providential deliverance from danger.

As this account reveals, Paul does not hesitate to use the prestige and status that come with his Roman citizenship. He is escorted from the city with proper respect, but he leaves behind two transformed households: one led by a woman cloth merchant, one by a city jailer. From that unlikely combination will grow the lively church at Philippi.   —PY

DAY 299

Philippians 2:1–30

IMITATING CHRIST'S HUMILITY

If you have any encouragement from being united with Christ, if any comfort from his love, if any fellowship with the Spirit, if any tenderness and compassion, then make my joy complete by being like-minded, having the same love, being one in spirit and purpose. Do nothing out of selfish ambition or vain conceit, but in humility consider others better than yourselves. Each of you should look not only to your own interests, but also to the interests of others.

Your attitude should be the same as that of Christ Jesus:

Who, being in very nature God,
    did not consider equality with God something to be grasped,
but made himself nothing,
    taking the very nature of a servant,
    being made in human likeness.
And being found in appearance as a man,
    he humbled himself
    and became obedient to death—
    even death on a cross!
Therefore God exalted him to the highest place
    and gave him the name that is above every name,
that at the name of Jesus every knee should bow,
    in heaven and on earth and under the earth,
and every tongue confess that Jesus Christ is Lord,
    to the glory of God the Father.

Therefore, my dear friends, as you have always obeyed—not only in my presence, but now much more in my absence—continue to work out your salvation with fear and trembling, for it is God who works in you to will and to act according to his good purpose.

Do everything without complaining or arguing, so that you may become blameless and pure, children of God without fault in a crooked and depraved generation, in which you shine like stars in the universe as you hold out the word of life—in order that I may boast on the day of Christ that I did not run or labor for nothing. But even if I am being poured out like a drink offering on the sacrifice and service coming from your faith, I am glad and rejoice with all of you. So you too should be glad and rejoice with me.

I hope in the Lord Jesus to send Timothy to you soon, that I also may be cheered when I receive news about you. I have no one else like him, who takes a genuine interest in your welfare. For everyone looks out for his own interests, not those of Jesus Christ. But you know that Timothy has proved himself, because as a son with his father he has served with me in the work of the gospel. I hope, therefore, to send him as soon as I see how things go with me. And I am confident in the Lord that I myself will come soon.

But I think it is necessary to send back to you Epaphroditus, my brother, fellow worker and fellow soldier, who is also your messenger, whom you sent to take care of my needs. For he longs for all of you and is distressed because you heard he was ill. Indeed he was ill, and almost died. But God had mercy on him, and not on him only but also on me, to spare me sorrow upon sorrow. Therefore I am all the more eager to send him, so that when you see him again you may be glad and I may have less anxiety. Welcome him in the Lord with great joy, and honor men like him, because he almost died for the work of Christ, risking his life to make up for the help you could not give me.

Fully a decade after founding the church, Paul writes his Philippian friends a personal letter. He has suffered much in the intervening years: beatings, imprisonment, shipwreck, hostility from jealous competitors. Surely he must have sometimes wondered, *Is it worth all this pain?* Even as he writes this letter, he is under arrest, "in chains for Christ" (1:13). But whenever Paul's thoughts turn to Philippi, the old apostle's spirits lift.

Paul declines gifts from most churches, out of fear that his enemies might twist the facts and accuse him of being a crook. But he trusts the Philippians. At least four separate times they sacrifice to meet his needs. Just recently, they have sent Epaphroditus (eh-paf-roh-DI-tuhs) on an arduous journey to care for Paul in prison. Paul writes the book of Philippians, in fact, mainly as a thank-you for all that his friends have done.

If someone bluntly asked the apostle, "Paul, tell me, what keeps you going through hard times?" he likely would answer with words straight out of this chapter. In Philippians 2, Paul reveals the source of his irrepressible drive. First, Paul gives the example of Jesus. In a stately, hymn-like paragraph, he marvels that Jesus gave up all the glory of heaven to take on the form of a man—and not just a man but a servant, one who pours out his life for others. Paul takes on that pattern for himself.

Then, in a seeming paradox, Paul describes a kind of "teamwork" with God: while God is working within, we must "work out" salvation with fear and trembling. A later spiritual giant, Saint Teresa of Avila, expressed the paradox this way: "I pray as if all depends on God; I work as if all depends on me." Her formula aptly summarizes Paul's spiritual style.

Philippians gives an occasional glimpse of the apostle Paul's fatigue. But it also shows flashes of what keeps him from "burnout." To him, the converts in Philippi shine "like stars in the universe." That kind of reward, and joy in their progress, keeps Paul going.   —PY

DAILY CONTEMPLATION

How can you "consider others better than yourself" without developing a bad self-image?

Paul in Thessalonica, Berea, and Athens

When they had passed through Amphipolis and Apollonia, they came to Thessalonica, where there was a Jewish synagogue. As his custom was, Paul went into the synagogue, and on three Sabbath days he reasoned with them from the Scriptures, explaining and proving that the Christ had to suffer and rise from the dead. "This Jesus I am proclaiming to you is the Christ," he said. Some of the Jews were persuaded and joined Paul and Silas, as did a large number of God-fearing Greeks and not a few prominent women.

But the Jews were jealous; so they rounded up some bad characters from the marketplace, formed a mob and started a riot in the city. They rushed to Jason's house in search of Paul and Silas in order to bring them out to the crowd. But when they did not find them, they dragged Jason and some other brothers before the city officials, shouting: "These men who have caused trouble all over the world have now come here, and Jason has welcomed them into his house. They are all defying Caesar's decrees, saying that there is another king, one called Jesus." When they heard this, the crowd and the city officials were thrown into turmoil. Then they made Jason and the others post bond and let them go.

As soon as it was night, the brothers sent Paul and Silas away to Berea. On arriving there, they went to the Jewish synagogue. Now the Bereans were of more noble character than the Thessalonians, for they received the message with great eagerness and examined the Scriptures every day to see if what Paul said was true. Many of the Jews believed, as did also a number of prominent Greek women and many Greek men.

When the Jews in Thessalonica learned that Paul was preaching the word of God at Berea, they went there too, agitating the crowds and stirring them up. The brothers immediately sent Paul to the coast, but Silas and Timothy stayed at Berea. The men who escorted Paul brought him to Athens and then left with instructions for Silas and Timothy to join him as soon as possible.

While Paul was waiting for them in Athens, he was greatly distressed to see that the city was full of idols. So he reasoned in the synagogue with the Jews and the God-fearing Greeks, as well as in the marketplace day by day with those who happened to be there. A group of Epicurean and Stoic philosophers began to dispute with him. Some of them asked, "What is this babbler trying to say?" Others remarked, "He seems to be advocating foreign gods." They said this because Paul was preaching the good news about Jesus and the resurrection. Then they took him and brought him to a meeting of the Areopagus, where they said to him, "May we know what this new teaching is that you are presenting? You are bringing some strange ideas to our ears, and we want to know what they mean." (All the Athenians and the foreigners who lived there spent their time doing nothing but talking about and listening to the latest ideas.)

Paul then stood up in the meeting of the Areopagus and said: "Men of Athens! I see that in every way you are very religious. For as I walked around and looked carefully at your objects of worship, I even found an altar with this inscription: TO AN UNKNOWN GOD. Now what you worship as something unknown I am going to proclaim to you.

"The God who made the world and everything in it is the Lord of heaven and earth and does not live in temples built by hands. And he is not served by human hands, as if he needed anything, because he himself gives all men life and breath and everything else. From one man he made every nation of men, that they should inhabit the whole earth; and he determined the times set for them and the exact places where they should live. God did this so that men would seek him and perhaps reach out for him and find him, though he is not far from each one of us. 'For in him we live and move and have our being.' As some of your own poets have said, 'We are his offspring.'

"Therefore since we are God's offspring, we should not think that the divine being is like gold or silver or stone—an image made by man's design and skill. In the past God overlooked such ignorance, but now he commands all people everywhere to repent. For he has set a day when he will judge the world with justice by the man he has appointed. He has given proof of this to all men by raising him from the dead."

When they heard about the resurrection of the dead, some of them sneered, but others said, "We want to hear you again on this subject." At that, Paul left the Council. A few men became followers of Paul and believed. Among them was Dionysius, a member of the Areopagus, also a woman named Damaris, and a number of others.

Jesus told a parable about a farmer sowing seed, some of which fell on rocky places, some among thorns, and some on fertile ground. This chapter, which reviews events from Paul's second journey, proves that he, the first foreign missionary, encountered all those responses in quick succession.

In Thessalonica (THES-uh-lah-NIE-kuh), Paul's visit sparks a riot. An angry mob chases the apostle out of town, accusing him of causing "trouble all over the world." The next town, Berea, proves far more receptive. After studying the Scriptures to test out Paul's message, many believe, both Jews and non-Jews. Yet agitators from Thessalonica soon stir up trouble there as well. (Paul is often trailed by hostile opponents who seek to confute his work.)

In Athens, Paul faces perhaps his most daunting missionary challenge. That renowned city of philosophers subjects each new thinker to a grueling intellectual ordeal. Local philosophers, full of scorn for Paul ("this babbler"), haul him before the council of Aeropagus that oversees religion and morals.

Confident that the new faith can compete in the marketplace of ideas, Paul stands before the skeptical audience and, in a burst of eloquence, delivers the extraordinary speech contained in this chapter. Paul gains few converts among the elite Athenians, but he will next travel to the melting pot city of Corinth (KOR-inth) and found a church remarkable for its ethnic diversity.

A modern-day evangelist assessing Paul's career said with a sigh, "Whenever the apostle Paul visited a city, the residents started a riot; when I visit one, they serve tea." —PY

DAY 301   Reflection

FINDING COMMON GROUND FOR THE GOSPEL

Charles Colson tells the story of an encounter with a well-known media figure who invited him to dinner to "talk to me about God." This man—Colson calls him Tom—set the record straight from the start. He didn't believe in God but wanted to hear Colson's opinions nonetheless.

A former member of Richard Nixon's presidential staff who was sentenced for his Watergate crimes, Colson came to belief in Christ during time in prison. He began to tell Tom his story but was soon cut off. Tom knew the story and accepted that Jesus had "worked" for Colson. Nice but unconvincing, as New Age spirituality had also "worked" for another of Tom's friends.

Colson proceeded to speak of Jesus as a historical person, of the assurance of heaven, and of an afterlife for those who believe in Christ. He discussed Scripture and the Bible's historical validity. Yet none of these made an impression on Tom. He had reasons for dismissing each argument supporting Christianity.

Straining for a new tack, Colson threw out a question. "Have you seen Woody Allen's movie *Crimes and Misdemeanors?*" Then showing in theaters, the movie depicts a doctor who hires a killer to murder his mistress. Haunted by guilt, the doctor ponders the meaning of justice and God's punishment. Never caught, he eases his conscience by concluding that justice does not happen in the real world. Rather, as Darwin proposed, the powerful come out on top.

"When we do wrong, is that the only choice?" Colson asked Tom. "Either live tormented by guilt—or kill our conscience and live like beasts?" At last Tom remained silent for a few moments. Colson went on to discuss Leo Tolstoy's *War and Peace,* another story of a man who wrestled with his conscience, decrying his own inability to do what he knew to be right. Then Colson spoke of writer C. S. Lewis's argument for natural law, and of the teachings of the book of Romans in the Bible on sin and conscience. Christ, he explained, is the only one who can rightfully remove the guilt of sin.[55]

Though Tom didn't come to belief in Christ that evening, Colson learned something. Apart from Woody Allen, Tolstoy, and Lewis, he would not have found a connection with Tom to discuss spiritual matters. Like the Greeks of Athens in Paul's day, unbelievers in our society need conversation that challenges them on a level at which they are already thinking. Just as Paul began his speech by talking of the "unknown god" familiar to all Athenians, we must use familiar ideas and needs when speaking about the gospel to unbelievers of our society. Meaningful discussion comes when we find common ground and then explain how Jesus and the Bible speak to these important parts of our lives.[55]

In the spiritually thirsty culture of today, we may find the invitation "Talk to me about God" coming more frequently than we expect or feel prepared to handle. When it comes, we can look at the world around us and start a conversation there. God will help us to weave biblical truth into this real world so familiar to those who listen. He knows their needs and is the one answer that works. —BQ

DAILY CONTEMPLATION

What were the personal needs that first drew you to Jesus? What made the message of the Bible relevant to your life? Ask God to help you find common ground in discussing him with those around you who don't know him.

DAY 302   1 Thessalonians 2:17–4:12

LIVING TO PLEASE GOD

Brothers, when we were torn away from you for a short time (in person, not in thought), out of our intense longing we made every effort to see you. For we wanted to come to you—certainly I, Paul, did, again and again—but Satan stopped us. For what is our hope, our joy, or the crown in which we will glory in the presence of our Lord Jesus when he comes? Is it not you? Indeed, you are our glory and joy.

So when we could stand it no longer, we thought it best to be left by ourselves in Athens. We sent Timothy, who is our brother and God's fellow worker in spreading the gospel of Christ, to strengthen and encourage you in your faith, so that no one would be unsettled by these trials. You know quite well that we were destined for them. In fact, when we were with you, we kept telling you that we would be persecuted. And it turned out that way, as you well know. For this reason, when I could stand it no longer, I sent to find out about your faith. I was afraid that in some way the tempter might have tempted you and our efforts might have been useless.

But Timothy has just now come to us from you and has brought good news about your faith and love. He has told us that you always have pleasant memories of us and that you long to see us, just as we also long to see you. Therefore, brothers, in all our distress and persecution we were encouraged about you because of your faith. For now we really live, since you are standing firm in the Lord. How can we thank God enough for you in return for all the joy we have in the presence of our God because of you? Night and day we pray most earnestly that we may see you again and supply what is lacking in your faith.

Now may our God and Father himself and our Lord Jesus clear the way for us to come to you. May the Lord make your love increase and overflow for each other and for everyone else, just as ours does for you. May he strengthen your hearts so that you will be blameless and holy in the presence of our God and Father when our Lord Jesus comes with all his holy ones.

Finally, brothers, we instructed you how to live in order to please God, as in fact you are living. Now we ask you and urge you in the Lord Jesus to do this more and more. For you know what instructions we gave you by the authority of the Lord Jesus.

It is God's will that you should be sanctified: that you should avoid sexual immorality; that each of you should learn to control his own body in a way that is holy and honorable, not in passionate lust like the heathen, who do not know God; and that in this matter no one should wrong his brother or take advantage of him. The Lord will punish men for all such sins, as we have already told you and warned you. For God did not call us to be impure, but to live a holy life. Therefore, he who rejects this instruction does not reject man but God, who gives you his Holy Spirit.

Now about brotherly love we do not need to write to you, for you yourselves have been taught by God to love each other. And in fact, you do love all the brothers throughout Macedonia. Yet we urge you, brothers, to do so more and more.

Make it your ambition to lead a quiet life, to mind your own business and to work with your hands, just as we told you, so that your daily life may win the respect of outsiders and so that you will not be dependent on anybody.

Born in the midst of strife, the church at Thessalonica continues to meet hostility long after Paul has been chased out of town. When he hears of their troubles, the apostle writes this intimate letter, which provides important clues into what makes him so effective as a "pastor." First Thessalonians, dating probably from A.D. 50 or 51, is our earliest record of the life of a Christian community. As such, it provides a firsthand account of Paul's relationship with a missionary church barely twenty years after Jesus' departure.

Paul reviews his pastoral style with the Thessalonians, reminding them that while among them he was gentle and loving, "like a mother caring for her little children" (2:7). He writes as if he has only them on his mind all day. He praises their strengths, fusses over their weaknesses, and continually thanks God for their spiritual progress. A recent report from Timothy has indicated they are heading down the right path, but Paul urges them to live for God and to love each other "more and more."

In this letter, Paul also answers criticisms that have been leveled against him. Is he in it for the money? Paul claims that during his sojourn with the Thessalonians he worked night and day (he supported himself as a tentmaker) to avoid becoming a financial burden. Has he abandoned them? Paul takes pains to explain the reasons behind his unavoidable absence.

Unlike some of Paul's other letters, 1 Thessalonians does not major in theology. Rather, it reveals the gratitude, disappointment, and joy of a beloved missionary who can't stop thinking about the church he left behind. Surely one reason for Paul's success centers on his churches' having made as big an impression on Paul as he made on them.

—PY

DAILY CONTEMPLATION

Who has been like a parent to you in your spiritual life?

DAY 303   2 Thessalonians 2:1–3:13

STAND FIRM

Concerning the coming of our Lord Jesus Christ and our being gathered to him, we ask you, brothers, not to become easily unsettled or alarmed by some prophecy, report or letter supposed to have come from us, saying that the day of the Lord has already come. Don't let anyone deceive you in any way, for that day will not come until the rebellion occurs and the man of lawlessness is revealed, the man doomed to destruction. He will oppose and will exalt himself over everything that is called God or is worshiped, so that he sets himself up in God's temple, proclaiming himself to be God.

Don't you remember that when I was with you I used to tell you these things? And now you know what is holding him back, so that he may be revealed at the proper time. For the secret power of lawlessness is already at work; but the one who now holds it back will continue to do so till he is taken out of the way. And then the lawless one will be revealed, whom the Lord Jesus will overthrow with the breath of his mouth and destroy by the splendor of his coming. The coming of the lawless one will be in accordance with the work of Satan displayed in all kinds of counterfeit miracles, signs and wonders, and in every sort of evil that deceives those who are perishing. They perish because they refused to love the truth and so be saved. For this reason God sends them a powerful delusion so that they will believe the lie and so that all will be condemned who have not believed the truth but have delighted in wickedness.

But we ought always to thank God for you, brothers loved by the Lord, because from the beginning God chose you to be saved through the sanctifying work of the Spirit and through belief in the truth. He called you to this through our gospel, that you might share in the glory of our Lord Jesus Christ. So then, brothers, stand firm and hold to the teachings we passed on to you, whether by word of mouth or by letter.

May our Lord Jesus Christ himself and God our Father, who loved us and by his grace gave us eternal encouragement and good hope, encourage your hearts and strengthen you in every good deed and word.

Finally, brothers, pray for us that the message of the Lord may spread rapidly and be honored, just as it was with you. And pray that we may be delivered from wicked and evil men, for not everyone has faith. But the Lord is faithful, and he will strengthen and protect you from the evil one. We have confidence in the Lord that you are doing and will continue to do the things we command. May the Lord direct your hearts into God's love and Christ's perseverance.

In the name of the Lord Jesus Christ, we command you, brothers, to keep away from every brother who is idle and does not live according to the teaching you received from us. For you yourselves know how you ought to follow our example. We were not idle when we were with you, nor did we eat anyone's food without paying for it. On the contrary, we worked night and day, laboring and toiling so that we would not be a burden to any of you. We did this, not because we do not have the right to such help, but in order to make ourselves a model for you to follow. For even when we were with you, we gave you this rule: "If a man will not work, he shall not eat."

We hear that some among you are idle. They are not busy; they are busybodies. Such people we command and urge in the Lord Jesus Christ to settle down and earn the bread they eat. And as for you, brothers, never tire of doing what is right.

One topic dominates 2 Thessalonians more than any other: Jesus' return to earth. Church members are disturbed by a rumor, allegedly from Paul, that the last days have already arrived. In this letter, Paul denies the report and outlines what must occur before the Day of the Lord arrives.

The controversy actually traces back to a portion of Paul's first letter. Toward the end of 1 Thessalonians, he gave direct answers to questions about the afterlife. Would people who had already died miss out on resurrection from the dead? It is more than an idle question for the Thessalonians, who live with the constant danger of persecution. On any night a knock on the door could mean imprisonment or death.

Paul initially allayed the Christians' fears by assuring them that people still living when Jesus returns to earth will rejoin those who have died before them. In the meantime, however, the Thessalonians have gone several steps beyond Paul's advice. Their speculation about the impending Day of the Lord, fueled by the recent rumors, has become an obsession. Some of them have quit their jobs and simply sit around in anticipation of that day. They are becoming, in Paul's words, "idle" and "busybodies."

Paul writes 2 Thessalonians mainly to correct the imbalance. In the second chapter he tells of certain obscure events that must precede the second coming of Jesus. (No one is sure of Paul's exact meaning in every detail because he is building on teaching he has given the Thessalonians in private.)

Here, as elsewhere, the Bible does not focus on the last days in an abstract, theoretical way. Rather, it makes a practical application to how we should live. Paul counsels patience and steadiness. He asks his readers to trust that Jesus' return will finally bring justice to the earth, urges them to live worthily for that day, and commands them not to tolerate idleness—a good prescription for an obsession with the future in any time period. —PY

DAY 304

Acts 18:1–28

PAUL IN CORINTH

After this, Paul left Athens and went to Corinth. There he met a Jew named Aquila, a native of Pontus, who had recently come from Italy with his wife Priscilla, because Claudius had ordered all the Jews to leave Rome. Paul went to see them, and because he was a tentmaker as they were, he stayed and worked with them. Every Sabbath he reasoned in the synagogue, trying to persuade Jews and Greeks.

When Silas and Timothy came from Macedonia, Paul devoted himself exclusively to preaching, testifying to the Jews that Jesus was the Christ. But when the Jews opposed Paul and became abusive, he shook out his clothes in protest and said to them, "Your blood be on your own heads! I am clear of my responsibility. From now on I will go to the Gentiles."

Then Paul left the synagogue and went next door to the house of Titius Justus, a worshiper of God. Crispus, the synagogue ruler, and his entire household believed in the Lord; and many of the Corinthians who heard him believed and were baptized.

One night the Lord spoke to Paul in a vision: "Do not be afraid; keep on speaking, do not be silent. For I am with you, and no one is going to attack and harm you, because I have many people in this city." So Paul stayed for a year and a half, teaching them the word of God.

While Gallio was proconsul of Achaia, the Jews made a united attack on Paul and brought him into court. "This man," they charged, "is persuading the people to worship God in ways contrary to the law."

Just as Paul was about to speak, Gallio said to the Jews, "If you Jews were making a complaint about some misdemeanor or serious crime, it would be reasonable for me to listen to you. But since it involves questions about words and names and your own law—settle the matter yourselves. I will not be a judge of such things." So he had them ejected from the court. Then they all turned on Sosthenes the synagogue ruler and beat him in front of the court. But Gallio showed no concern whatever.

Paul stayed on in Corinth for some time. Then he left the brothers and sailed for Syria, accompanied by Priscilla and Aquila. Before he sailed, he had his hair cut off at Cenchrea because of a vow he had taken. They arrived at Ephesus, where Paul left Priscilla and Aquila. He himself went into the synagogue and reasoned with the Jews. When they asked him to spend more time with them, he declined. But as he left, he promised, "I will come back if it is God's will." Then he set sail from Ephesus. When he landed at Caesarea, he went up and greeted the church and then went down to Antioch.

After spending some time in Antioch, Paul set out from there and traveled from place to place throughout the region of Galatia and Phrygia, strengthening all the disciples.

Meanwhile a Jew named Apollos, a native of Alexandria, came to Ephesus. He was a learned man, with a thorough knowledge of the Scriptures. He had been instructed in the way of the Lord, and he spoke with great fervor and taught about Jesus accurately, though he knew only the baptism of John. He began to speak boldly in the synagogue. When Priscilla and Aquila heard him, they invited him to their home and explained to him the way of God more adequately.

When Apollos wanted to go to Achaia, the brothers encouraged him and wrote to the disciples there to welcome him. On arriving, he was a great help to those who by grace had believed. For he vigorously refuted the Jews in public debate, proving from the Scriptures that Jesus was the Christ.

As a strategic center for land and sea trade, the city of Corinth attracts people as well as goods from surrounding regions, making it a place of ethnic and cultural diversity. In Paul's day Corinth is known for immoral living and the worship of Aphrodite, or Venus, the goddess of love. Woven even into its religious fabric, the practice of free love is widely accepted and even encouraged. No wonder Paul enters the city in weakness, fear, and much trembling (1 Corinthians 2:1–5).

While in Corinth, Paul meets Aquila and Priscilla, a husband and wife who become strong partners in ministry. They establish a church in their home and ultimately risk their lives for Paul. In his absence they take an Egyptian named Apollos into their home and teach him about God's work through Jesus. Apollos needs a more complete understanding of salvation, and through the help of Priscilla and Aquila he too becomes an active partner in ministry, helping to continue the spread of the gospel to Jews and Gentiles.

The ministry of Priscilla and Aquila displays the importance of both men and women to the work of the early church. Paul calls Priscilla his "fellow worker" (Romans 16:3), a term he also uses to describe key male partners in ministry. Called by God and gifted to draw others to the truths of Christ, Priscilla responds faithfully to the opportunities before her.　　　　　　　　　　　　　　　　　　—BQ

DAILY CONTEMPLATION

Whom would you identify as your partners, or fellow workers, in your life with God?

ONE BODY, MANY PARTS; LOVE

Now about spiritual gifts, brothers, I do not want you to be ignorant. You know that when you were pagans, somehow or other you were influenced and led astray to mute idols. Therefore I tell you that no one who is speaking by the Spirit of God says, "Jesus be cursed," and no one can say, "Jesus is Lord," except by the Holy Spirit.

There are different kinds of gifts, but the same Spirit. There are different kinds of service, but the same Lord. There are different kinds of working, but the same God works all of them in all men.

Now to each one the manifestation of the Spirit is given for the common good. To one there is given through the Spirit the message of wisdom, to another the message of knowledge by means of the same Spirit, to another faith by the same Spirit, to another gifts of healing by that one Spirit, to another miraculous powers, to another prophecy, to another distinguishing between spirits, to another speaking in different kinds of tongues, and to still another the interpretation of tongues. All these are the work of one and the same Spirit, and he gives them to each one, just as he determines.

The body is a unit, though it is made up of many parts; and though all its parts are many, they form one body. So it is with Christ. For we were all baptized by one Spirit into one body—whether Jews or Greeks, slave or free—and we were all given the one Spirit to drink.

Now the body is not made up of one part but of many. If the foot should say, "Because I am not a hand, I do not belong to the body," it would not for that reason cease to be part of the body. And if the ear should say, "Because I am not an eye, I do not belong to the body," it would not for that reason cease to be part of the body. If the whole body were an eye, where would the sense of hearing be? If the whole body were an ear, where would the sense of smell be? But in fact God has arranged the parts in the body, every one of them, just as he wanted them to be. If they were all one part, where would the body be? As it is, there are many parts, but one body.

The eye cannot say to the hand, "I don't need you!" And the head cannot say to the feet, "I don't need you!" On the contrary, those parts of the body that seem to be weaker are indispensable, and the parts that we think are less honorable we treat with special honor. And the parts that are unpresentable are treated with special modesty, while our presentable parts need no special treatment. But God has combined the members of the body and has given greater honor to the parts that lacked it, so that there should be no division in the body, but that its parts should have equal concern for each other. If one part suffers, every part suffers with it; if one part is honored, every part rejoices with it.

Now you are the body of Christ, and each one of you is a part of it. And in the church God has appointed first of all apostles, second prophets, third teachers, then workers of miracles, also those having gifts of healing, those able to help others, those with gifts of administration, and those speaking in different kinds of tongues. Are all apostles? Are all prophets? Are all teachers? Do all work miracles? Do all have gifts of healing? Do all speak in tongues? Do all interpret? But eagerly desire the greater gifts.

And now I will show you the most excellent way.

If I speak in the tongues of men and of angels, but have not love, I am only a resounding gong or a clanging cymbal. If I have the gift of prophecy and can fathom all mysteries and all knowledge, and if I have a faith that can move mountains, but have not love, I am nothing. If I give all I possess to the poor and surrender my body to the flames, but have not love, I gain nothing.

Love is patient, love is kind. It does not envy, it does not boast, it is not proud. It is not rude, it is not self-seeking, it is not easily angered, it keeps no record of wrongs. Love does not delight in evil but rejoices with the truth. It always protects, always trusts, always hopes, always perseveres.

Love never fails. But where there are prophecies, they will cease; where there are tongues, they will be stilled; where there is knowledge, it will pass away. For we know in part and we prophesy in part, but when perfection comes, the imperfect disappears. When I was a child, I talked like a child, I thought like a child, I reasoned like a child. When I became a man, I put childish ways behind me. Now we see but a poor reflection as in a mirror; then we shall see face to face. Now I know in part; then I shall know fully, even as I am fully known.

And now these three remain: faith, hope and love. But the greatest of these is love.

Paul's first visit to the Grecian city of Corinth occurs during one of the most stressful times of his career. Lynch mobs chased him out of Thessalonica and Berea. The next stop, Athens, brought on confrontation with intellectual scoffers, and by the time Paul arrives at Corinth he is in a fragile emotional state.

Shortly, opposition springs up in Corinth, and Jewish leaders haul Paul into court. But in the midst of this crisis, God visits Paul with a special message of comfort: "I am with you, and no one is going to attack and harm you, because I have many people in this city" (Acts 18:10).

These last words must be startling to Paul, for in his day Corinth is known mainly for its lewdness and drunken brawling. The Corinthians worship the goddess of love, after all, and a temple built in her honor employs more than a thousand prostitutes. Thus Corinth seems the last place on earth to expect a church to take root. Yet that's exactly what happens. A Jewish couple has opened their home to Paul, and for the next eighteen months he stays in Corinth to nurture an eager band of converts.

Corinth is filled with Orientals, Jews, Greeks, Egyptians, slaves, sailors, athletes, gamblers, and charioteers. And the Corinthian church reflects that same crazy-quilt pattern of diversity. When Paul writes them this letter, he searches for a way to drive home the importance of Christian unity. At last he settles on a striking analogy from the human body. By comparing members of the church of Christ to individual parts of a human body, he can neatly illustrate how *diverse* members can indeed work together in *unity*.

This analogy fits so well that it becomes Paul's favorite way of portraying the church. He will refer to "the body of Christ" more than thirty times in his various letters. Having also raised the question of how diverse people can work together in a spiritual body, he answers that question with a lyrical description of love, the greatest of all spiritual gifts. —PY

DAILY CONTEMPLATION

First Corinthians 13 describes ideal love. Which of these characteristics do you need to work on?

DAY 306
Reflection

WHAT IS A CHURCH?

The first few chapters of 1 Corinthians show the apostle Paul struggling with a basic question: Just what is this thing called a "church"? Paul had never asked such questions about Judaism; culture, religious tradition, race, and even the physical characteristics of worshipers clearly established the identity of that religion. But what is a Christian church? What does God have in mind? The answer must have seemed elusive indeed in the unruly context of Corinth. Almost twenty centuries later, the answer still seems elusive.

Paul's letter to Corinth betrays his hesitation, mainly in the way he gropes for words. You are God's field, he says in chapter 3 and explores that metaphor for a while. On the other hand, you are more like God's building. Yes, exactly. I lay the foundation, and someone else adds the next layer. Better yet, you're a temple, a building designed to house God. Yes, indeed! Think about that: God living in you, his sacred building.

He continues in such a vein throughout the book until finally, in chapter 12, he seizes upon a metaphor that fits best: the church as God's body. The book changes tone at that point, its style elevating from that of personal correspondence to the magnificent prose of chapter 13.

What would Paul, the master of metaphor, say if he were to write 1 Corinthians today—if he were writing, say, to the First Presbyterian Church of Spokane, Washington, or to St. Mark's Episcopal Church in Atlanta, Georgia, or LaSalle Street Church in downtown Chicago? What word pictures would best communicate to us moderns what God has in mind for the church?

I feel secure using the image of family for the church, for it is one used within the Bible. I believe, though, that the vision of the church as a family has even more meaning today than in biblical times because of changes in society.

In an institution, status derives from performance. The business world has learned that human beings respond well to rewards of status; they can be powerful motivators.

In families, however, status works differently. How does one earn status in a family? A child "earns" the family's rights solely by virtue of birth. An underachieving child is not kicked out of the family. Indeed, a sickly child, who "produces" very little, may actually receive more attention than her healthy siblings. As novelist John Updike once wrote, "Families teach us how love exists in a realm beyond liking or disliking, coexisting with indifference, rivalry, and even antipathy."

Similarly in God's family, we are plainly told, "there is neither Jew nor Greek, slave nor free, male nor female" (Galatians 3:28). All such artificial distinctions have melted under the sun of God's grace. As God's adopted children we gain the same rights, clearly undeserved, as those enjoyed by the firstborn, Jesus Christ himself—a book like Ephesians underscores that astonishing truth again and again.

For this reason, it grieves me to see local churches that run more like a business institution than a family. In his discussion of spiritual gifts, the apostle Paul warns sternly against valuing one member more highly than another (1 Corinthians 12:21–26).

In this passage Paul is drawing on his favorite metaphor for the church: the human body. And yet the best way I can visualize how these truths might play themselves out in an actual group of people is to go back to a scene of a human family gathered around a table for a holiday meal.

Every family contains some successful individuals and some miserable failures. At Thanksgiving, corporate vice-president Aunt Mary sits next to Uncle Charles, who drinks too much and has never held a job. Although some of the folks gathered around the table are clever and some stupid, some are ugly and some attractive, some healthy and some disabled, in a family these differences become insignificant.

I sometimes think that God invented the human institution of the family as a training ground to prepare us for how we should relate within other institutions. Families work best not by papering over their differences but rather by celebrating them. A healthy family builds up the weakest members while not tearing down the strong. As John Wesley's mother put it, "Which child of mine do I love best? I love the sick one until he's well, the one away from home until she's back."

Family is the one human institution we have no choice over. We get in simply by being born, and as a result we are involuntarily thrown together with a menagerie of strange and unlike people. Church calls for another step: to voluntarily choose to band together with a strange menagerie because of a common bond in Jesus Christ. I have found that such a community more resembles a family than any other human institution. Henri Nouwen once defined a community as "a place where the person you least want to live with always lives." His definition applies equally to the group that gathers each Thanksgiving and the group that congregates each Sunday morning.[56]   —PY

DAILY CONTEMPLATION

What challenges have you encountered in attending a church? What benefits have you realized? Thank God for the ways in which the church has helped you meet him and sense his love. Ask God to help you accept the less-than-perfect aspects as just a part of the larger blessing he intends the church to be.

THE RESURRECTION OF CHRIST AND THE DEAD

What I received I passed on to you as of first importance: that Christ died for our sins according to the Scriptures, that he was buried, that he was raised on the third day according to the Scriptures, and that he appeared to Peter, and then to the Twelve. After that, he appeared to more than five hundred of the brothers at the same time, most of whom are still living, though some have fallen asleep. Then he appeared to James, then to all the apostles, and last of all he appeared to me also, as to one abnormally born.

For I am the least of the apostles and do not even deserve to be called an apostle, because I persecuted the church of God. But by the grace of God I am what I am, and his grace to me was not without effect. No, I worked harder than all of them—yet not I, but the grace of God that was with me. Whether, then, it was I or they, this is what we preach, and this is what you believed.

But if it is preached that Christ has been raised from the dead, how can some of you say that there is no resurrection of the dead? If there is no resurrection of the dead, then not even Christ has been raised. And if Christ has not been raised, our preaching is useless and so is your faith. More than that, we are then found to be false witnesses about God, for we have testified about God that he raised Christ from the dead. But he did not raise him if in fact the dead are not raised. For if the dead are not raised, then Christ has not been raised either. And if Christ has not been raised, your faith is futile; you are still in your sins. Then those also who have fallen asleep in Christ are lost. If only for this life we have hope in Christ, we are to be pitied more than all men.

But Christ has indeed been raised from the dead, the firstfruits of those who have fallen asleep. For since death came through a man, the resurrection of the dead comes also through a man. For as in Adam all die, so in Christ all will be made alive. But each in his own turn: Christ, the firstfruits; then, when he comes, those who belong to him. Then the end will come, when he hands over the kingdom to God the Father after he has destroyed all dominion, authority and power. For he must reign until he has put all his enemies under his feet. The last enemy to be destroyed is death. For he "has put everything under his feet." Now when it says that "everything" has been put under him, it is clear that this does not include God himself, who put everything under Christ. When he has done this, then the Son himself will be made subject to him who put everything under him, so that God may be all in all.

Now if there is no resurrection, what will those do who are baptized for the dead? If the dead are not raised at all, why are people baptized for them? And as for us, why do we endanger ourselves every hour? I die every day—I mean that, brothers—just as surely as I glory over you in Christ Jesus our Lord. If I fought wild beasts in Ephesus for merely human reasons, what have I gained? If the dead are not raised,

"Let us eat and drink,
   for tomorrow we die."

Do not be misled:"Bad company corrupts good character." Come back to your senses as you ought, and stop sinning; for there are some who are ignorant of God—I say this to your shame.

But someone may ask,"How are the dead raised? With what kind of body will they come?" How foolish! What you sow does not come to life unless it dies. When you sow, you do not plant the body that will be, but just a seed, perhaps of wheat or of something else. But God gives it a body as he has determined, and to each kind of seed he gives its own body. All flesh is not the same: Men have one kind of flesh, animals have another, birds another and fish another. There are also heavenly bodies and there are earthly bodies; but the splendor of the heavenly bodies is one kind, and the splendor of the earthly bodies is another. The sun has one kind of splendor, the moon another and the stars another; and star differs from star in splendor.

So will it be with the resurrection of the dead. The body that is sown is perishable, it is raised imperishable; it is sown in dishonor, it is raised in glory; it is sown in weakness, it is raised in power; it is sown a natural body, it is raised a spiritual body.

If there is a natural body, there is also a spiritual body. So it is written:"The first man Adam became a living being"; the last Adam, a life-giving spirit. The spiritual did not come first, but the natural, and after that the spiritual. The first man was of the dust of the earth, the second man from heaven. As was the earthly man, so are those who are of the earth; and as is the man from heaven, so also are those who are of heaven. And just as we have borne the likeness of the earthly man, so shall we bear the likeness of the man from heaven.

I declare to you, brothers, that flesh and blood cannot inherit the kingdom of God, nor does the perishable inherit the imperishable. Listen, I tell you a mystery: We will not all sleep, but we will all be changed—in a flash, in the twinkling of an eye, at the last trumpet. For the trumpet will sound, the dead will be raised imperishable, and we will be changed. For the perishable must clothe itself with the imperishable, and the mortal with immortality. When the perishable has been clothed with the imperishable, and the mortal with immortality, then the saying that is written will come true:"Death has been swallowed up in victory."

"Where, O death, is your victory?
   Where, O death, is your sting?"

The sting of death is sin, and the power of sin is the law. But thanks be to God! He gives us the victory through our Lord Jesus Christ.

Some people in Paul's day are challenging the Christian belief in an afterlife. Death, they say, is the end. Throughout history, many people have taken such a position. In Jesus' day, a Jewish sect called Sadducees denied the resurrection from the dead.

Doubters persist today: among them are Black Muslims, Buddhists, Marxists, and most atheists. Some New Age advocates present death as a natural part of the cycle of life. Why consider it bad at all?

The Corinthian church soon learns not to voice such an attitude around the apostle Paul. Belief in an afterlife to him is no fairy tale; it is the fulcrum of his entire faith. If there's no future life, he thunders, the Christian message would be a lie. He, Paul, would have no reason to continue as a minister, Christ's death would have merely wasted blood, and Christians would be the most pitiable of all people on earth.

The Bible presents a gradually developing emphasis on the afterlife. Old Testament Jews had only the vaguest conception of life after death. But as Paul points out, Jesus' resurrection from the dead changed all that. Suddenly the world had primary proof that God had the power and the will to overcome death. Chapter 15 weaves together the threads of Christian belief about death. With no hesitation, Paul brands death "the enemy," the last enemy to be destroyed.

This chapter often gets read at funerals, and with good reason. As people gather around a casket, they sense as if by instinct the *unnaturalness*, the horror, of death. To such people, to all of us, this passage offers soaring words of hope. Death is not an end but a beginning. —PY

DAILY CONTEMPLATION

How does a belief in the afterlife affect your life now?

DAY 308   2 Corinthians 4:1–5:10

TREASURES IN JARS OF CLAY

Therefore, since through God's mercy we have this ministry, we do not lose heart. Rather, we have renounced secret and shameful ways; we do not use deception, nor do we distort the word of God. On the contrary, by setting forth the truth plainly we commend ourselves to every man's conscience in the sight of God. And even if our gospel is veiled, it is veiled to those who are perishing. The god of this age has blinded the minds of unbelievers, so that they cannot see the light of the gospel of the glory of Christ, who is the image of God. For we do not preach ourselves, but Jesus Christ as Lord, and ourselves as your servants for Jesus' sake. For God, who said, "Let light shine out of darkness," made his light shine in our hearts to give us the light of the knowledge of the glory of God in the face of Christ.

But we have this treasure in jars of clay to show that this all-surpassing power is from God and not from us. We are hard pressed on every side, but not crushed; perplexed, but not in despair; persecuted, but not abandoned; struck down, but not destroyed. We always carry around in our body the death of Jesus, so that the life of Jesus may also be revealed in our body. For we who are alive are always being given over to death for Jesus' sake, so that his life may be revealed in our mortal body. So then, death is at work in us, but life is at work in you.

It is written: "I believed; therefore I have spoken." With that same spirit of faith we also believe and therefore speak, because we know that the one who raised the Lord Jesus from the dead will also raise us with Jesus and present us with you in his presence. All this is for your benefit, so that the grace that is reaching more and more people may cause thanksgiving to overflow to the glory of God.

Therefore we do not lose heart. Though outwardly we are wasting away, yet inwardly we are being renewed day by day. For our light and momentary troubles are achieving for us an eternal glory that far outweighs them all. So we fix our eyes not on what is seen, but on what is unseen. For what is seen is temporary, but what is unseen is eternal.

Now we know that if the earthly tent we live in is destroyed, we have a building from God, an eternal house in heaven, not built by human hands. Meanwhile we groan, longing to be clothed with our heavenly dwelling, because when we are clothed, we will not be found naked. For while we are in this tent, we groan and are burdened, because we do not wish to be unclothed but to be clothed with our heavenly dwelling, so that what is mortal may be swallowed up by life. Now it is God who has made us for this very purpose and has given us the Spirit as a deposit, guaranteeing what is to come.

Therefore we are always confident and know that as long as we are at home in the body we are away from the Lord. We live by faith, not by sight. We are confident, I say, and would prefer to be away from the body and at home with the Lord. So we make it our goal to please him, whether we are at home in the body or away from it. For we must all appear before the judgment seat of Christ, that each one may receive what is due him for the things done while in the body, whether good or bad.

Paul blasts anyone who, as the phrase goes, "is too heavenly minded to be of any earthly good." He does *not* prepare for the next life by sitting around all day waiting for it to happen. Paul works as hard as anyone has ever worked, but with a new purpose: "We make it our goal to please him, whether we are at home in the body or away from it." He seeks to do God's will on earth just as it is done in heaven.

This passage shows that Paul's hope for the future keeps him motivated when the crush of life tempts him to "lose heart." He writes this letter just as an intense struggle with the Corinthian church is coming to a head, and as a result it reveals the apostle in one of his lowest, most vulnerable moments. He has, barely, survived hardships "far beyond our ability to endure, so that we despaired even of life" (1:8). He describes his present state as "hard pressed on every side, but not crushed; perplexed, but not in despair; persecuted, but not abandoned; struck down, but not destroyed."

In typical style, Paul uses a word picture to express his inner thoughts: "treasure in jars of clay." In his day, jars of clay are nearly as common—and as disposable—as cardboard boxes are today. Beset by difficulties, Paul feels as durable as one of those fragile jars. Yet he recognizes that God has chosen to entrust the gospel, and its good news of forgiveness and eternal life, to such ordinary people as himself.

That insight seems to give Paul renewed hope. He offers a stirring example of how a future life with God can affect a person on earth: "Therefore we do not lose heart. Though outwardly we are wasting away, yet inwardly we are being renewed day by day. For our light and momentary troubles are achieving for us an eternal glory that far outweighs them all. So we fix our eyes not on what is seen, but on what is unseen. For what is seen is temporary, but what is unseen is eternal."   —PY

DAILY CONTEMPLATION

When you feel the way Paul feels in this passage, how likely are you to fix your eyes "not on what is seen, but on what is unseen"?

DAY 309   2 Corinthians 5:11–6:2; 6:14–7:1

THE MINISTRY OF RECONCILIATION; DO NOT BE YOKED WITH UNBELIEVERS

Since, then, we know what it is to fear the Lord, we try to persuade men. What we are is plain to God, and I hope it is also plain to your conscience. We are not trying to commend ourselves to you again, but are giving you an opportunity to take pride in us, so that you can answer those who take pride in what is seen rather than in what is in the heart. If we are out of our mind, it is for the sake of God; if we are in our right mind, it is for you. For Christ's love compels us, because we are convinced that one died for all, and therefore all died. And he died for all, that those who live should no longer live for themselves but for him who died for them and was raised again.

So from now on we regard no one from a worldly point of view. Though we once regarded Christ in this way, we do so no longer. Therefore, if anyone is in Christ, he is a new creation; the old has gone, the new has come! All this is from God, who reconciled us to himself through Christ and gave us the ministry of reconciliation: that God was reconciling the world to himself in Christ, not counting men's sins against them. And he has committed to us the message of reconciliation. We are therefore Christ's ambassadors, as though God were making his appeal through us. We implore you on Christ's behalf: Be reconciled to God. God made him who had no sin to be sin for us, so that in him we might become the righteousness of God.

As God's fellow workers we urge you not to receive God's grace in vain. For he says,

"In the time of my favor I heard you,
and in the day of salvation I helped you."

I tell you, now is the time of God's favor, now is the day of salvation....

Do not be yoked together with unbelievers. For what do righteousness and wickedness have in common? Or what fellowship can light have with darkness? What harmony is there between Christ and Belial? What does a believer have in common with an unbeliever? What agreement is there between the temple of God and idols? For we are the temple of the living God. As God has said: "I will live with them and walk among them, and I will be their God, and they will be my people."

"Therefore come out from them
and be separate,
says the Lord.
Touch no unclean thing,
and I will receive you."
"I will be a Father to you,
and you will be my sons and daughters,
says the Lord Almighty."

Since we have these promises, dear friends, let us purify ourselves from everything that contaminates body and spirit, perfecting holiness out of reverence for God.

These passages may seem to contradict each other, with one encouraging a coming together of all people through Christ, and the other warning believers to join themselves only with other followers of Christ. Which way does Paul want it?

He is passionate about both, with good reason. The message Paul preaches everywhere is one of salvation through Jesus' death and resurrection. No longer does belonging to a special group of people or adhering to a particular set of laws define acceptance by God. Now faith in Christ puts all who believe on equal footing. We can all become right before God through belief in Christ.

But some people, denying Christ as the only way to salvation, are influencing others in Corinth with their wrong views. Rather than being influenced by the believers, these false teachers are enticing others away from God's truth. They are dangerous, and Paul warns that nothing good will come of such relationships.

The false teachers have heard the true gospel. They have had a chance to come to Christ but have chosen another way. At this point believers must be cautious in remaining in close association. The teachers have veered from God's truth and pose too great a threat. When an unbeliever becomes influential over believers, God no longer asks his people to reach out. Rather, to protect their faithfulness, he asks them to separate themselves and live in reverence for him.   —BQ

DAILY CONTEMPLATION

Have you become yoked in a relationship that is drawing you away from Jesus rather than toward him?

SOWING GENEROUSLY

Remember this: Whoever sows sparingly will also reap sparingly, and whoever sows generously will also reap generously. Each man should give what he has decided in his heart to give, not reluctantly or under compulsion, for God loves a cheerful giver. And God is able to make all grace abound to you, so that in all things at all times, having all that you need, you will abound in every good work. As it is written:

"He has scattered abroad his gifts to the poor;
    his righteousness endures forever."

Now he who supplies seed to the sower and bread for food will also supply and increase your store of seed and will enlarge the harvest of your righteousness. You will be made rich in every way so that you can be generous on every occasion, and through us your generosity will result in thanksgiving to God.

This service that you perform is not only supplying the needs of God's people but is also overflowing in many expressions of thanks to God. Because of the service by which you have proved yourselves, men will praise God for the obedience that accompanies your confession of the gospel of Christ, and for your generosity in sharing with them and with everyone else. And in their prayers for you their hearts will go out to you, because of the surpassing grace God has given you. Thanks be to God for his indescribable gift!

The Corinthian church has collected money for believers living in poverty in Jerusalem. Some of the Corinthians worry that the money isn't all going to Jerusalem and accuse Paul of taking some for himself.

Earlier Paul has defended his integrity, stating that he is "taking pains to do what is right, not only in the eyes of the Lord but also in the eyes of men" (8:21). Now he takes a spiritual view of the matter, reminding the people that God is the giver. All we have comes from God; whatever we give out of a willingness of heart, God is able to give back to us in even greater measure. Paul encourages believers to give generously and cheerfully. When we give, we'll find that we are blessed in return, both by God and by those who receive.   —BQ

DAILY CONTEMPLATION

What goes through your mind when you are given an opportunity to help someone in need?

Paul Boasts about His Sufferings

and His Thorn

I repeat: Let no one take me for a fool. But if you do, then receive me just as you would a fool, so that I may do a little boasting. In this self-confident boasting I am not talking as the Lord would, but as a fool. Since many are boasting in the way the world does, I too will boast. You gladly put up with fools since you are so wise! In fact, you even put up with anyone who enslaves you or exploits you or takes advantage of you or pushes himself forward or slaps you in the face. To my shame I admit that we were too weak for that!

What anyone else dares to boast about—I am speaking as a fool—I also dare to boast about. Are they Hebrews? So am I. Are they Israelites? So am I. Are they Abraham's descendants? So am I. Are they servants of Christ? (I am out of my mind to talk like this.) I am more. I have worked much harder, been in prison more frequently, been flogged more severely, and been exposed to death again and again. Five times I received from the Jews the forty lashes minus one. Three times I was beaten with rods, once I was stoned, three times I was shipwrecked, I spent a night and a day in the open sea, I have been constantly on the move. I have been in danger from rivers, in danger from bandits, in danger from my own countrymen, in danger from Gentiles; in danger in the city, in danger in the country, in danger at sea; and in danger from false brothers. I have labored and toiled and have often gone without sleep; I have known hunger and thirst and have often gone without food; I have been cold and naked. Besides everything else, I face daily the pressure of my concern for all the churches. Who is weak, and I do not feel weak? Who is led into sin, and I do not inwardly burn?

If I must boast, I will boast of the things that show my weakness. The God and Father of the Lord Jesus, who is to be praised forever, knows that I am not lying. In Damascus the governor under King Aretas had the city of the Damascenes guarded in order to arrest me. But I was lowered in a basket from a window in the wall and slipped through his hands.

I must go on boasting. Although there is nothing to be gained, I will go on to visions and revelations from the Lord. I know a man in Christ who fourteen years ago was caught up to the third heaven. Whether it was in the body or out of the body I do not know—God knows. And I know that this man—whether in the body or apart from the body I do not know, but God knows—was caught up to paradise. He heard inexpressible things, things that man is not permitted to tell. I will boast about a man like that, but I will not boast about myself, except about my weaknesses. Even if I should choose to boast, I would not be a fool, because I would be speaking the truth. But I refrain, so no one will think more of me than is warranted by what I do or say.

To keep me from becoming conceited because of these surpassingly great revelations, there was given me a thorn in my flesh, a messenger of Satan, to torment me. Three times I pleaded with the Lord to take it away from me. But he said to me, "My grace is sufficient for you, for my power is made perfect in weakness." Therefore I will boast all the more gladly about my weaknesses, so that Christ's power may rest on me. That is why, for Christ's sake, I delight in weaknesses, in insults, in hardships, in persecutions, in difficulties. For when I am weak, then I am strong.

Although Jewish and Roman establishments treat Paul as a major threat, Paul expects their opposition. Antagonism from fellow Christians bothers him far more. Jealous competitors have infiltrated the Corinthian church, spreading rumors to undercut Paul's reputation. He isn't fully Jewish, they charge. He doesn't deserve the title "apostle" since he has not followed Jesus on earth. And, like other false teachers, he is in it for the money.

In his letters to the Corinthians, Paul confesses a reluctance to defend himself— "I am out of my mind to talk like this"—but their criticisms have gotten out of hand. Jewish? Paul is a strict Pharisee who has studied with the famous teacher Gamaliel. Apostle? True, Paul did not serve as one of the twelve disciples. But he met the risen Jesus on the road to Damascus and was later granted a special revelation of "inexpressible things, things that man is not permitted to tell." Exploiter? Paul has supported himself financially to avoid taking money from the church.

Paul then begins to "boast" about his weaknesses. He runs through the amazing list of beatings, imprisonments, insults, and hardships that have marked his career. And he balances his veiled reference to the special vision with a frank account of one urgent prayer that has never been answered.

Three times Paul has asked God to remove a mysterious "thorn in the flesh." Bible scholars don't agree on the precise nature of the "thorn." Some suggest a physical ailment, such as an eye disease, malaria, or epilepsy. Others interpret it as a spiritual temptation or a series of failures in his ministry. Whatever the ailment, Paul stresses that God declined to remove the thorn, despite all his prayers for relief, in order to teach him an important lesson about humility, grace, and dependence.

Paul never seems to get over the wonder of the fact that God has chosen him, a former enemy, to bear the good news. He feels humbled and honored that even his weaknesses—*especially* his weaknesses—could be used to advance the kingdom.   —PY

DAILY CONTEMPLATION

How has God spoken to you through your weaknesses?

LIVING WITH THORNS

Paul's imagery is to the point—literally—when he describes the "thorn in my flesh" that was given to torment him. Although we don't know the specifics of the thorn, the metaphor makes us squirm with understanding. Whatever plagued him was a painful, ongoing trial.

When I'm worrying over some frustration with myself or my circumstances, I imagine my misfortune as a brier and seek comfort in Paul's, and God's, words. "'My grace is sufficient for you, for my power is made perfect in weakness.' Therefore I will boast all the more gladly about my weaknesses, so that Christ's power may rest on me. That is why, for Christ's sake, I delight in weaknesses, in insults, in hardships, in persecutions, in difficulties. For when I am weak, then I am strong."

As one person put it, "Grace, like water, flows to the lowest place." When I am the weakest and most desperately in need of help, God is most free to give it. When I let him, God works my circumstances or my self into something good.

Paul is describing one of the paradoxes of life: A painful thorn bringing good? How could a weakness in me, or a painful circumstance over which I'm powerless, bring me delight? It seems a nice, churchy idea that would never survive outside sanctuary doors.

Author and speaker Brennan Manning found the truth of this principle after becoming an alcoholic, losing his home and job, and finally landing on the street. "Probably the moment in my own life when I was closest to the Truth who is Jesus Christ was the experience of being a hopeless derelict in the gutter in Fort Lauderdale, Florida. In his novel *The Moviegoer*, Walker Percy says: 'Only once in my life was the grip of everydayness broken: when I lay bleeding in the ditch.' Paradoxically, such an experience of powerlessness does not make one sad. It is a great relief because it makes us rely not on our own strength but on the limitless power of God. The realization that God is the main agent makes the yoke easy, the burden light, and the heart still."[57]

Each of us struggles with our own personal thorn. We can shut God out and continue to fail, or we can let his power fill the thorn-shaped wound within. When God fills our wound, he engages us in a profoundly loving and satisfying relationship with himself. Delight becomes possible. The wound will still bring pain, yet if it takes a thorn to throw me into the arms of a lifetime Lover, maybe I can learn to see the thorn as a harbinger of hope.

Psychologist Larry Crabb describes it this way: "We rarely learn to meaningfully depend on God when our lives are comfortable. . . . The entire fabric of Scripture is woven with the thread of relationship. God longs for us to give our heart to Him. He loves us. To the degree that we embrace our thirst and realize who He is, we long for Him. There is nothing dull about the romance between our heavenly Bridegroom and His hurting but fickle bride. The more honestly we face whatever may be locked inside, the more passionately we can be drawn to the beauty of a Lover who responds consistently with all the tender strength our heart desires."[58]　　　　　—BQ

DAILY CONTEMPLATION

What thorn is causing you pain? Have you asked God to remove it? Have you asked him to fill your wound with his power, to replace your weakness with his strength? Talk to him about your struggle. Ask for his help in letting go so you can let him take over.

PART 11

PAUL'S LEGACY

NO ONE IS RIGHTEOUS

As it is written:

"There is no one righteous, not even one;
 there is no one who understands,
 no one who seeks God.
All have turned away,
 they have together become worthless;
there is no one who does good,
 not even one."
"Their throats are open graves;
 their tongues practice deceit."
"The poison of vipers is on their lips."
 "Their mouths are full of cursing and bitterness."
"Their feet are swift to shed blood;
 ruin and misery mark their ways,
and the way of peace they do not know."
 "There is no fear of God before their eyes."

Now we know that whatever the law says, it says to those who are under
the law, so that every mouth may be silenced and the whole world held

591

accountable to God. Therefore no one will be declared righteous in his sight by observing the law; rather, through the law we become conscious of sin.

But now a righteousness from God, apart from law, has been made known, to which the Law and the Prophets testify. This righteousness from God comes through faith in Jesus Christ to all who believe. There is no difference, for all have sinned and fall short of the glory of God, and are justified freely by his grace through the redemption that came by Christ Jesus. God presented him as a sacrifice of atonement, through faith in his blood. He did this to demonstrate his justice, because in his forbearance he had left the sins committed beforehand unpunished—he did it to demonstrate his justice at the present time, so as to be just and the one who justifies those who have faith in Jesus.

Where, then, is boasting? It is excluded. On what principle? On that of observing the law? No, but on that of faith. For we maintain that a man is justified by faith apart from observing the law. Is God the God of Jews only? Is he not the God of Gentiles too? Yes, of Gentiles too, since there is only one God, who will justify the circumcised by faith and the uncircumcised through that same faith. Do we, then, nullify the law by this faith? Not at all! Rather, we uphold the law.

Throughout his arduous and adventurous life, the apostle Paul keeps one career goal constantly before him: a visit to Rome. In his day, Rome stands alone, the center in every way—law, culture, power, and learning. From that capital, a powerful empire rules over the entire Western world.

A tiny new church has formed there, causing great excitement among other Christians. They know that in some ways the future of the church rests on what happens in Rome. If they ever expect to make a dent in the larger world, they will have to penetrate Rome.

Paul prays for the Roman church constantly and makes many plans to visit there. Since none of those plans have yet materialized, Paul writes this letter in preparation for his long-awaited visit.

Unlike the letters to the Corinthians, Romans contains few personal asides or emotional outbursts. Paul is addressing sophisticated, demanding readers, most of whom he has never met. In the letter he seeks to set forth the whole scope of Christian doctrine, which is still being passed along orally from town to town. The resulting book has no equal as a concise yet all-encompassing summation of the Christian faith.

Romans is a book to savor slowly and carefully. The logic of Paul's argument unfolds thought by thought from the first chapter. He is presenting the good news about God's amazing grace: a complete cure is available to all. But people won't seek a cure until they know they are ill. Thus Romans begins with one of the darkest summaries in the Bible. "There is no one righteous, not even one," Paul concludes. The entire world is doomed to spiritual death unless a cure can be found.

Out of the mournful notes, however, comes a bright sound of wonderful news, expressed in what some have called the central theological passage in the Bible. Paul expresses the core message of the gospel in these verses (21–31).   —PY

DAY 314

Romans 7:1–25

STRUGGLING WITH SIN

Do you not know, brothers—for I am speaking to men who know the law—that the law has authority over a man only as long as he lives? For example, by law a married woman is bound to her husband as long as he is alive, but if her husband dies, she is released from the law of marriage. So then, if she marries another man while her husband is still alive, she is called an adulteress. But if her husband dies, she is released from that law and is not an adulteress, even though she marries another man.

So, my brothers, you also died to the law through the body of Christ, that you might belong to another, to him who was raised from the dead, in order that we might bear fruit to God. For when we were controlled by the sinful nature, the sinful passions aroused by the law were at work in our bodies, so that we bore fruit for death. But now, by dying to what once bound us, we have been released from the law so that we serve in the new way of the Spirit, and not in the old way of the written code.

What shall we say, then? Is the law sin? Certainly not! Indeed I would not have known what sin was except through the law. For I would not have known what coveting really was if the law had not said, "Do not covet." But sin, seizing the opportunity afforded by the commandment, produced in me every kind of covetous desire. For apart from law, sin is dead. Once I was alive apart from law; but when the commandment came, sin sprang to life and I died. I found that the very commandment that was intended to bring life actually brought death. For sin, seizing the opportunity afforded by the commandment, deceived me, and through the commandment put me to death. So then, the law is holy, and the commandment is holy, righteous and good.

Did that which is good, then, become death to me? By no means! But in order that sin might be recognized as sin, it produced death in me through what was good, so that through the commandment sin might become utterly sinful.

We know that the law is spiritual; but I am unspiritual, sold as a slave to sin. I do not understand what I do. For what I want to do I do not do, but what I hate I do. And if I do what I do not want to do, I agree that the law is good. As it is, it is no longer I myself who do it, but it is sin living in me. I know that nothing good lives in me, that is, in my sinful nature. For I have the desire to do what is good, but I cannot carry it out. For what I do is not the good I want to do; no, the evil I do not want to do—this I keep on doing. Now if I do what I do not want to do, it is no longer I who do it, but it is sin living in me that does it.

So I find this law at work: When I want to do good, evil is right there with me. For in my inner being I delight in God's law; but I see another law at work in the members of my body, waging war against the law of my mind and making me a prisoner of the law of sin at work within my members. What a wretched man I am! Who will rescue me from this body of death? Thanks be to God—through Jesus Christ our Lord!

So then, I myself in my mind am a slave to God's law, but in the sinful nature a slave to the law of sin.

One issue comes up in virtually every one of Paul's letters: What good is the law? To most of Paul's readers, the word *law* stands for the huge collection of rules and rituals codified from the Old Testament. Thanks to his earlier days as a Pharisee, Paul knows those rules well. And whenever he starts talking about "the new covenant" or "freedom in Christ," the Jews want to know what he now thinks about that law.

This chapter, the most personal and autobiographical in Romans, discloses exactly what Paul thinks.

Paul never recommends throwing out the law entirely. He sees that it reveals a basic code of morality, an ideal of the kind of behavior that pleases God. The law is good for one thing: it exposes sin. "Indeed I would not have known what sin was except through the law." To Paul, such rules as the Ten Commandments are helpful, righteous, and good.

The law has one major problem, however: although it proves how bad you are, it doesn't make you any better. As a heritage of his days of legalism, Paul has developed a very sensitive conscience, but, as he poignantly recounts, it mainly makes him feel guilty all the time. "What a wretched man I am!" he confesses. The law bares his weaknesses but cannot provide the power needed to overcome them. The law—or *any* set of rules—leads ultimately to a dead end.

Romans 7 gives a striking illustration of the struggle that ensues when an imperfect person commits himself to a perfect God. Any Christian who wonders, *How can I ever get rid of my nagging sins?* will find comfort in Paul's frank confession. In the face of God's standards, every one of us feels helpless, and that is Paul's point precisely. No set of rules can break the terrible cycle of guilt and failure. We need outside help to "serve in the new way of the Spirit, and not in the old way of the written code." Paul celebrates that help in the next chapter.   —PY

DAILY CONTEMPLATION

What personal struggle makes you feel most helpless? Where do you turn?

LIFE THROUGH THE SPIRIT

Therefore, there is now no condemnation for those who are in Christ Jesus, because through Christ Jesus the law of the Spirit of life set me free from the law of sin and death. For what the law was powerless to do in that it was weakened by the sinful nature, God did by sending his own Son in the likeness of sinful man to be a sin offering. And so he condemned sin in sinful man, in order that the righteous requirements of the law might be fully met in us, who do not live according to the sinful nature but according to the Spirit.

Those who live according to the sinful nature have their minds set on what that nature desires; but those who live in accordance with the Spirit have their minds set on what the Spirit desires. The mind of sinful man is death, but the mind controlled by the Spirit is life and peace; the sinful mind is hostile to God. It does not submit to God's law, nor can it do so. Those controlled by the sinful nature cannot please God.

You, however, are controlled not by the sinful nature but by the Spirit, if the Spirit of God lives in you. And if anyone does not have the Spirit of Christ, he does not belong to Christ. But if Christ is in you, your body is dead because of sin, yet your spirit is alive because of righteousness. And if the Spirit of him who raised Jesus from the dead is living in you, he who raised Christ from the dead will also give life to your mortal bodies through his Spirit, who lives in you.

Therefore, brothers, we have an obligation—but it is not to the sinful nature, to live according to it. For if you live according to the sinful nature, you will die; but if by the Spirit you put to death the misdeeds of the body, you will live, because those who are led by the Spirit of God are sons of God. For you did not receive a spirit that makes you a slave again to fear, but you received the Spirit of sonship. And by him we cry, "Abba, Father." The Spirit himself testifies with our spirit that we are God's children. Now if we are children, then we are heirs—heirs of God and co-heirs with Christ, if indeed we share in his sufferings in order that we may also share in his glory.

I consider that our present sufferings are not worth comparing with the glory that will be revealed in us. The creation waits in eager expectation for the sons of God to be revealed. For the creation was subjected to frustration, not by its own choice, but by the will of the one who subjected it, in hope that the creation itself will be liberated from its bondage to decay and brought into the glorious freedom of the children of God.

We know that the whole creation has been groaning as in the pains of childbirth right up to the present time. Not only so, but we ourselves, who have the firstfruits of the Spirit, groan inwardly as we wait eagerly for our adoption as sons, the redemption of our bodies. For in this hope we were saved. But hope that is seen is no hope at all. Who hopes for what he already has? But if we hope for what we do not yet have, we wait for it patiently.

In the same way, the Spirit helps us in our weakness. We do not know what we ought to pray for, but the Spirit himself intercedes for us with groans that words cannot express. And he who searches our hearts knows the mind of the Spirit, because the Spirit intercedes for the saints in accordance with God's will.

The Holy Spirit is the theme of Romans 8, and in this chapter Paul gives a panoramic survey of how the Spirit can make a difference in a person's life.

First, Paul sets to rest the nagging problem of sin he has just raised so forcefully. "There is now no condemnation . . . ," he announces. Jesus Christ, through his life and death, took care of "the sin problem" for all time.

Elsewhere (ch. 4), Paul borrows a word from banking to explain the process. God "credits" Jesus' own perfection to our accounts, so that we are judged not by our behavior but by his. Similarly, God has transferred all the punishment we deserve onto Jesus, through his death on the cross. In this transaction, human beings come out the clear winners, set free at last from the curse of sin.

And, as always, Paul insists on the best news of all: that Jesus Christ did not stay dead. Paul marvels that the very same power that raised Christ from the dead can also "enliven" us. The Spirit is a life-giver who alone can break the gloomy, deathlike pattern described in Romans 7.

To be sure, the Spirit does not remove all problems. The very titles the Bible applies to him—Intercessor, Helper, Counselor, Comforter—assume there will be problems. But "the God within" can do for us what we could never do for ourselves. The Spirit works alongside us as we relate to God, helping us in our weakness, even praying for us when we don't know what to ask.

The way Paul tells it, what happens inside individual believers is the central drama of history: "The creation waits in eager expectation for the sons of God to be revealed." Somehow, spiritual victories within us will help bring about the liberation and healing of a "groaning" creation. The apostle can hardly contain himself as he contemplates these matters. Romans 8 ends with a ringing declaration that nothing—*absolutely, positively nothing*—can ever separate us from God's love. For Paul, that is a fact worth shouting about.   —PY

DAILY CONTEMPLATION

According to this passage, how can the Holy Spirit make a difference in your daily life?

DAY 316   Reflection

HELP FOR STRUGGLES WITH SIN

After we give our lives to Jesus, our thinking about ourselves changes. The self we once viewed as basically good begins to look hopelessly flawed. Bad behavior, wrong thoughts, unnecessary words happen all too frequently, and the mind can work like a tape player, constantly replaying all our mistakes and regrets.

Maybe your tape plays words of inner frustration like these: "I do not understand what I do. For what I want to do I do not do, but what I hate I do.... I have the desire to do what is good, but I cannot carry it out" (Romans 7:15, 18). Even Paul, writer of much of the New Testament, struggled with his own inability to master himself. If your thinking runs like Paul's, you have probably begun to grasp at a deeper level the holy character of God, which we on this earth still come so far from resembling.

When I was a young teenager trying to live more closely with Jesus, my sin presented itself most clearly in the form of gossip. My friends and I were daily aware of the temptation, and almost daily I succumbed. For the first time I learned about working with God on a habit that with each fresh failure seemed beyond repair. I smile now at the frustrations of those years, yet I must admit that the failures of the tongue haven't proved less challenging as I've aged. Still I find myself confessing, and confounded by, a slip of my tongue.

Is this the way God intends us to live, ever aware of our failure?

God aims not to torture but to soften us in revealing our ongoing need for him. This side of heaven, we will continue to act in ways that don't match up to his holiness. Yet, astonishingly, he isn't keeping score anymore. In God's eyes our sin is forgiven.

Paul's powerful message in Romans does not stop with sin. It follows with the emphatic reminder that "thanks be to God—through Jesus Christ our Lord" (7:25) we are saved. We are good in God's eyes because of Jesus, and though we fail, we have his Spirit inside doing wonderful, life-giving acts through us. We're God's people, his children, just like Christ. His Spirit prays for us, and in him we are more than conquerors.

These are the words Paul places alongside his confession of personal failure, words that deserve replaying as often as our own messages of defeat. Yes, we're flawed. Yes, we seem never to learn some things. Yet Jesus is the final word on failure. His Spirit lives alongside our regrets, bringing life where we find stagnancy, hope where we feel despair.   —BQ

DAILY CONTEMPLATION

How often do you get caught up in regret because of your sin? Have you felt more despair or more hope since becoming a believer? Ask God for help in gaining a right perspective on your sin and on the new life he has given you.

DAY 317   Romans 5:1–11; 8:28–39

PEACE AND JOY; MORE THAN CONQUERORS

Therefore, since we have been justified through faith, we have peace with
God through our Lord Jesus Christ, through whom we have gained access

by faith into this grace in which we now stand. And we rejoice in the hope of the glory of God. Not only so, but we also rejoice in our sufferings, because we know that suffering produces perseverance; perseverance, character; and character, hope. And hope does not disappoint us, because God has poured out his love into our hearts by the Holy Spirit, whom he has given us.

You see, at just the right time, when we were still powerless, Christ died for the ungodly. Very rarely will anyone die for a righteous man, though for a good man someone might possibly dare to die. But God demonstrates his own love for us in this: While we were still sinners, Christ died for us.

Since we have now been justified by his blood, how much more shall we be saved from God's wrath through him! For if, when we were God's enemies, we were reconciled to him through the death of his Son, how much more, having been reconciled, shall we be saved through his life! Not only is this so, but we also rejoice in God through our Lord Jesus Christ, through whom we have now received reconciliation....

And we know that in all things God works for the good of those who love him, who have been called according to his purpose. For those God foreknew he also predestined to be conformed to the likeness of his Son, that he might be the firstborn among many brothers. And those he predestined, he also called; those he called, he also justified; those he justified, he also glorified.

What, then, shall we say in response to this? If God is for us, who can be against us? He who did not spare his own Son, but gave him up for us all—how will he not also, along with him, graciously give us all things? Who will bring any charge against those whom God has chosen? It is God who justifies. Who is he that condemns? Christ Jesus, who died—more than that, who was raised to life—is at the right hand of God and is also interceding for us. Who shall separate us from the love of Christ? Shall trouble or hardship or persecution or famine or nakedness or danger or sword? As it is written:

"For your sake we face death all day long;
    we are considered as sheep to be slaughtered."

No, in all these things we are more than conquerors through him who loved us. For I am convinced that neither death nor life, neither angels nor demons, neither the present nor the future, nor any powers, neither height nor depth, nor anything else in all creation, will be able to separate us from the love of God that is in Christ Jesus our Lord.

These passages focus on a part of life familiar to all of us: suffering. The moment sin came into the world with Adam and Eve, suffering became an inescapable reality. Sin brought a separation from God that causes pain of many kinds. Sin also gave evil a place in the world, which won't fully be eliminated until Jesus comes again.

Until then we have these passages in Romans to remind us that in the midst of our suffering, even now God is more powerful. We may suffer, but God will turn the harm that sin intends us into our good. In moments when we're hurting, this seems hard to believe—these words may be the last we want to hear. Yet in time, as we look back on difficulty and as we grow nearer to God, we begin to see that God is right. The verses hold true.

Suffering produces perseverance, character, and hope in us. It can bring us closer to God and make us better, more mature people. Mysteriously, God brings lasting good from what at first seems utter despair. Regardless of where we go or what we encounter, his love looms greater, letting nothing come between us. And in the midst of our pain, Jesus prays continually, holding us in the center of God's presence.   —BQ

DAILY CONTEMPLATION

What time of suffering can you look back on and see that God brought good out of a lot of pain?

DAY 318   Romans 12:1–21

LIVING SACRIFICES; LOVE

Therefore, I urge you, brothers, in view of God's mercy, to offer your bodies as living sacrifices, holy and pleasing to God—this is your spiritual act of worship. Do not conform any longer to the pattern of this world, but be transformed by the renewing of your mind. Then you will be able to test and approve what God's will is—his good, pleasing and perfect will.

For by the grace given me I say to every one of you: Do not think of yourself more highly than you ought, but rather think of yourself with sober judgment, in accordance with the measure of faith God has given you. Just as each of us has one body with many members, and these members do not all have the same function, so in Christ we who are many form one body, and each member belongs to all the others. We have different gifts, according to the grace given us. If a man's gift is prophesying, let him use it in proportion to his faith. If it is serving, let him serve; if it is teaching, let him teach; if it is encouraging, let him encourage; if it is contributing to the needs of others, let him give generously; if it is leadership, let him govern diligently; if it is showing mercy, let him do it cheerfully.

Love must be sincere. Hate what is evil; cling to what is good. Be devoted to one another in brotherly love. Honor one another above yourselves. Never be lacking in zeal, but keep your spiritual fervor, serving the Lord. Be joyful in hope, patient in affliction, faithful in prayer. Share with God's people who are in need. Practice hospitality.

Bless those who persecute you; bless and do not curse. Rejoice with those who rejoice; mourn with those who mourn. Live in harmony with one another. Do not be proud, but be willing to associate with people of low position. Do not be conceited.

Do not repay anyone evil for evil. Be careful to do what is right in the eyes of everybody. If it is possible, as far as it depends on you, live at peace with everyone. Do not take revenge, my friends, but leave room for God's wrath, for it is written: "It is mine to avenge; I will repay," says the Lord. On the contrary:

"If your enemy is hungry, feed him;
    if he is thirsty, give him something to drink.
In doing this, you will heap burning coals on his head."

Do not be overcome by evil, but overcome evil with good.

Too often people view theology as stuff for hermits to think about. When there's nothing else to do, *then* is the time to ask abstract questions about God. Such a notion would have exasperated the apostle Paul. To him, theology is worthless unless it makes a difference in how people live. Thus, after laying out the most thorough, concise summary of Christian theology in the Bible, he turns his attention at the end of Romans to a down-to-earth discussion of everyday problems.

Paul's own life offers a good example of how to make theology practical. In fact, he writes the lofty book of Romans while traveling to raise funds for Jewish famine relief. By collecting offerings from Gentile Christians for the sake of Jews in Jerusalem, Paul models the kind of unity sorely needed by both groups. (See 2 Corinthians 8 for more details of this mercy mission.)

Romans 12 needs no special commentary or study aids. The problem lies not in understanding these words but in obeying them. Paul is describing what love in action should look like. Once more he uses the analogy of the human body to illustrate how diverse parts can work together in unity.

"Offer your bodies as living sacrifices," Paul urges his readers. The Romans of his day, both Jews and Gentiles, associate the word *sacrifices* with the lambs and other animals they bring to the temple for priests to kill on an altar. But Paul makes clear that God wants *living* human beings, not dead animals. A person committed to God's will is the kind of offering most pleasing to God.   —PY

DAILY CONTEMPLATION

Use the second half of this passage as a kind of checklist. Which commands do you have the most trouble with? Which are the easiest?

DAY 319   Romans 13:1–14

SUBMISSION TO AUTHORITIES;
LOVE, FOR THE DAY IS NEAR

Everyone must submit himself to the governing authorities, for there is no authority except that which God has established. The authorities that exist have been established by God. Consequently, he who rebels against the authority is rebelling against what God has instituted, and those who do so will bring judgment on themselves. For rulers hold no terror for those who do right, but for those who do wrong. Do you want to be free from fear of the one in authority? Then do what is right and he will commend you. For he is God's servant to do you good. But if you do wrong, be afraid, for he does not bear the sword for nothing. He is God's servant, an agent of wrath to bring punishment on the wrongdoer. Therefore, it is necessary to submit to the authorities, not only because of possible punishment but also because of conscience.

This is also why you pay taxes, for the authorities are God's servants, who give their full time to governing. Give everyone what you owe him: If you owe taxes, pay taxes; if revenue, then revenue; if respect, then respect; if honor, then honor.

Let no debt remain outstanding, except the continuing debt to love one another, for he who loves his fellowman has fulfilled the law. The commandments, "Do not commit adultery," "Do not murder," "Do not steal," "Do not covet," and whatever other commandment there may be, are summed up in this one rule: "Love your neighbor as yourself." Love does no harm to its neighbor. Therefore love is the fulfillment of the law.

And do this, understanding the present time. The hour has come for you to wake up from your slumber, because our salvation is nearer now than when we first believed. The night is nearly over; the day is almost here. So let us put aside the deeds of darkness and put on the armor of light. Let us behave decently, as in the daytime, not in orgies and drunkenness, not in sexual immorality and debauchery, not in dissension and jealousy. Rather, clothe yourselves with the Lord Jesus Christ, and do not think about how to gratify the desires of the sinful nature.

Once more Paul encourages believers to keep one thing at the top of the list: love. The second half of the chapter is clear: Love others and you will be following all of God's commandments. Live like followers of Jesus and stop trying to find satisfaction in things that will never satisfy.

The first half of the chapter raises some questions, however. The way Paul writes, you may conclude that the authorities he is discussing are good, moral leaders deserving of God's appointment. In reality, the leaders of Paul's day are pagans involved in immoral practices who regularly and openly persecute Christians. Paul knows this well, yet he tells his readers—other believers—to submit anyway. He stresses that regardless of their actions, governing authorities are established by God.

In Acts, Peter and the apostles demonstrate that a time comes when "we must obey God rather than men" (Acts 5:29; see also 4:19). When a believer faces a choice between following God or following a human authority, he or she must obey God. Submission to authority never extends to disobedience toward God. Yet outside of that occasion, Paul advises us to submit, honor, respect, and give what we owe to those in authority. In the gray areas, where we're unsure how far we should rightfully go in being obedient, we can prayerfully ask for God's direction.   —BQ

DAY 320   Romans 14:1–15:13

THE WEAK AND THE STRONG

Accept him whose faith is weak, without passing judgment on disputable matters. One man's faith allows him to eat everything, but another man, whose faith is weak, eats only vegetables. The man who eats everything must not look down on him who does not, and the man who does not eat everything must not condemn the man who does, for God has accepted him. Who are you to judge someone else's servant? To his own master he stands or falls. And he will stand, for the Lord is able to make him stand.

One man considers one day more sacred than another; another man considers every day alike. Each one should be fully convinced in his own mind. He who regards one day as special, does so to the Lord. He who eats meat, eats to the Lord, for he gives thanks to God; and he who abstains, does so to the Lord and gives thanks to God. For none of us lives to himself alone and none of us dies to himself alone. If we live, we live to the Lord; and if we die, we die to the Lord. So, whether we live or die, we belong to the Lord.

For this very reason, Christ died and returned to life so that he might be the Lord of both the dead and the living. You, then, why do you judge your brother? Or why do you look down on your brother? For we will all stand before God's judgment seat. It is written:

"'As surely as I live,' says the Lord,
'every knee will bow before me;
    every tongue will confess to God.'"

So then, each of us will give an account of himself to God.

Therefore let us stop passing judgment on one another. Instead, make up your mind not to put any stumbling block or obstacle in your brother's way. As one who is in the Lord Jesus, I am fully convinced that no food is unclean in itself. But if anyone regards something as unclean, then for him it is unclean. If your brother is distressed because of what you eat, you are no longer acting in love. Do not by your eating destroy your brother for whom Christ died. Do not allow what you consider good to be spoken of as evil. For the kingdom of God is not a matter of eating and drinking, but of righteousness, peace and joy in the Holy Spirit, because anyone who serves Christ in this way is pleasing to God and approved by men.

Let us therefore make every effort to do what leads to peace and to mutual edification. Do not destroy the work of God for the sake of food. All food is clean, but it is wrong for a man to eat anything that causes someone else to stumble. It is better not to eat meat or drink wine or to do anything else that will cause your brother to fall.

So whatever you believe about these things keep between yourself and God. Blessed is the man who does not condemn himself by what he approves. But the man who has doubts is condemned if he eats, because his eating is not from faith; and everything that does not come from faith is sin.

We who are strong ought to bear with the failings of the weak and not to please ourselves. Each of us should please his neighbor for his good, to build him up. For even Christ did not please himself but, as it is written: "The insults of those who insult you have fallen on me." For everything that was written in the past was written to teach us, so that through endurance and the encouragement of the Scriptures we might have hope.

May the God who gives endurance and encouragement give you a spirit of unity among yourselves as you follow Christ Jesus, so that with one heart and mouth you may glorify the God and Father of our Lord Jesus Christ.

Accept one another, then, just as Christ accepted you, in order to bring praise to God. For I tell you that Christ has become a servant of the Jews on behalf of God's truth, to confirm the promises made to the patriarchs so that the Gentiles may glorify God for his mercy, as it is written:

"Therefore I will praise you among the Gentiles;
    I will sing hymns to your name."

Again, it says,

"Rejoice, O Gentiles, with his people."
And again,

"Praise the Lord, all you Gentiles,
    and sing praises to him, all you peoples."

And again, Isaiah says,

"The Root of Jesse will spring up,
    one who will arise to rule over the nations;
the Gentiles will hope in him."

May the God of hope fill you with all joy and peace as you trust in him, so that you may overflow with hope by the power of the Holy Spirit.

Part of loving others, Paul teaches, involves accepting that we will live differently from each other. Some are weaker or less mature in their faith, and some are stronger. God may lead some to live one way, within the realm of his overall guidelines, and others to live another way. As long as all are living within God's basic commands in the Bible, we shouldn't insist that one way is right for all. Love calls us to let God guide each believer, keeping our focus on our own relationship with him and how he calls us to live as individuals.

In this way, we allow each other the freedom to hear God's voice and follow him, letting God correct us if need be. Then we can most freely and genuinely love each other. —BQ

DAILY CONTEMPLATION

What kinds of differences do you have with other believers that fit what Paul is talking about here? How well do you succeed at not passing judgment?

DAY 321 Reflection

SPENDING MYSELF ON GOD

How are you spending your life?

The word *spend* may first bring to mind questions related to money—how we choose to use what we have. *Spend* also speaks of time—how we use the time we have. Both issues are important to Paul as he writes to the Romans about becoming "living sacrifices" (Romans 12:1–8). In the last several chapters of his letter, Paul encourages the Christians to let their beliefs influence all they do. Their daily lives need to reflect their love for God.

Animal sacrifices are a thing of the past, merely token gifts. Now God wants people themselves, living sacrifices! And if we give ourselves, we'll begin making new choices about how we spend time, money, and everything else. "Do not conform any longer to the pattern of this world," Paul explains (Romans 12:2). God's business is more important. Conforming to God brings God joy and in turn brings us deeper joy than did our former ways of spending ourselves.

Popular business leader and author Stephen Covey writes about managing one's time and personal life. "The way you spend your time is a result of the way you see your time and the way you really see your priorities," he says.[59] Although he is not speaking from a strictly spiritual perspective, Covey is in essence echoing Paul's teaching. The things most important to us will impact the choices we make in using our time, our money, our very selves. If God is most important, we'll want to spend ourselves on him.

How, then, does God want us to go about doing this?

Paul is quick to explain. The way we spend ourselves will look different for each of us. Together we constitute a body of believers, and like the parts of the human body, we all have a unique function. God has made us with different strengths, or gifts. Paul's examples include gifts of prophecy, serving, teaching, encouraging, contributing to the needs of others, leadership, and mercy. These are just a few. His point: God gave us a particular function within the world and the Christian community. We each have strength in at least one area, and this strength should bring into focus the way in which he means us to spend ourselves.

What are your strengths? What compliments have you received from others concerning your abilities? What are the ways in which you feel most comfortable and energized in giving to God and other people? Most likely these strengths relate directly to your gifts, and this should guide your choices. Are you gifted at encouraging? Then why spend time watching a television soap opera when you could be making a phone call to a hurting friend or visiting someone lonely? Are you gifted at contributing to others' needs? Then why focus your dollars and your energy on accumulating things for yourself when you could help relieve the real needs of other people?

Neither Paul nor God is asking us to give to others every minute. Rather, overall, in the life we live day to day, hour by hour, our love for God should impact all we do—even the way we play and rest.

Stephen Covey explains that if we're to change the way we spend our time, holding to our priorities rather than doing the things we've always done, we must have a "bigger 'yes' burning inside."[60] That yes in a believer's mind is a yes to living for God. It's a yes to worshiping him with our daily lives. It's a yes to spending what we have and who we are on him. —BQ

DAILY CONTEMPLATION

Do you know what your personal gifts are? If not, ask God to help you better understand who he has made you to be. If you know your gifts, are you focused on spending yourself accordingly? Ask God to show you how he wants you to worship him by using your gifts.

DAY 322

PAUL BEFORE AGRIPPA

The next day Agrippa and Bernice came with great pomp and entered the audience room with the high ranking officers and the leading men of the city. At the command of Festus, Paul was brought in. Festus said: "King Agrippa, and all who are present with us, you see this man! The whole Jewish community has petitioned me about him in Jerusalem and here in Caesarea, shouting that he ought not to live any longer. I found he had done nothing deserving of death, but because he made his appeal to the Emperor I decided to send him to Rome. But I have nothing definite to write to His Majesty about him. Therefore I have brought him before all of you, and especially before you, King Agrippa, so that as a result of this investigation I may have something to write. For I think it is unreasonable to send on a prisoner without specifying the charges against him."

Then Agrippa said to Paul, "You have permission to speak for yourself."

So Paul motioned with his hand and began his defense: "King Agrippa, I consider myself fortunate to stand before you today as I make my defense against all the accusations of the Jews, and especially so because you are well acquainted with all the Jewish customs and controversies. Therefore, I beg you to listen to me patiently.

"The Jews all know the way I have lived ever since I was a child, from the beginning of my life in my own country, and also in Jerusalem. They have known me for a long time and can testify, if they are willing, that according to the strictest sect of our religion, I lived as a Pharisee. And now it is because of my hope in what God has promised our fathers that I am on trial today. This is the promise our twelve tribes are hoping to see fulfilled as they earnestly serve God day and night. O king, it is because of this hope that the Jews are accusing me. Why should any of you consider it incredible that God raises the dead?

"I too was convinced that I ought to do all that was possible to oppose the name of Jesus of Nazareth. And that is just what I did in Jerusalem. On the authority of the chief priests I put many of the saints in prison, and when they were put to death, I cast my vote against them. Many a time I went from one synagogue to another to have them punished, and I tried to force them to blaspheme. In my obsession against them, I even went to foreign cities to persecute them.

"On one of these journeys I was going to Damascus with the authority and commission of the chief priests. About noon, O king, as I was on the road, I saw a light from heaven, brighter than the sun, blazing around me and my companions. We all fell to the ground, and I heard a voice saying to me in Aramaic, 'Saul, Saul, why do you persecute me? It is hard for you to kick against the goads.'

"Then I asked, 'Who are you, Lord?'

"'I am Jesus, whom you are persecuting,' the Lord replied. 'Now get up and stand on your feet. I have appeared to you to appoint you as a servant and as a witness of what you have seen of me and what I will show you. I will rescue you from your own people and from the Gentiles. I am sending you to them to open their eyes and turn them from darkness to light, and from the power of Satan to God, so that they may receive forgiveness of sins and a place among those who are sanctified by faith in me.'

"So then, King Agrippa, I was not disobedient to the vision from heaven. First to those in Damascus, then to those in Jerusalem and in all Judea, and to the Gentiles also, I preached that they should repent and turn to God and prove their repentance by their deeds. That is why the Jews seized me in the temple courts and tried to kill me. But I have had God's help to this very day, and so I stand here and testify to small and great alike. I am saying nothing beyond what the prophets and Moses said would happen—that the Christ would suffer and, as the first to rise from the dead, would proclaim light to his own people and to the Gentiles."

At this point Festus interrupted Paul's defense. "You are out of your mind, Paul!" he shouted. "Your great learning is driving you insane."

"I am not insane, most excellent Festus," Paul replied. "What I am saying is true and reasonable. The king is familiar with these things, and I can speak freely to him. I am convinced that none of this has escaped his notice, because it was not done in a corner. King Agrippa, do you believe the prophets? I know you do."

Then Agrippa said to Paul, "Do you think that in such a short time you can persuade me to be a Christian?"

Paul replied, "Short time or long—I pray God that not only you but all who are listening to me today may become what I am, except for these chains."

The king rose, and with him the governor and Bernice and those sitting with them. They left the room, and while talking with one another, they said, "This man is not doing anything that deserves death or imprisonment."

Agrippa said to Festus, "This man could have been set free if he had not appealed to Caesar."

Paul determines to deliver in person the relief money he has collected. Friends beg him not to go to Jerusalem, still a hotbed of persecution against the Christians. But Paul, "compelled by the Spirit" (20:22), persists. He knows that God wants him to carry his word to Rome, and no disaster in Jerusalem can interfere with that plan.

When Paul reaches Jerusalem, the worst happens: he is arrested on trumped-up charges. Forty Jewish fanatics vow not to eat or drink until they have killed Paul. His reputation as a Christian missionary has so aroused the conspirators that it takes a brigade of 470 Roman soldiers to protect him.

The last few chapters of Acts show Paul at his most fearless. He boldly confronts a lynch mob until Roman soldiers have to drag him into barracks for his own protection. The next day, he takes on the Jewish ruling body, the Sanhedrin, causing such a ruckus that the Roman commander fears they will tear Paul in pieces. In the midst of all this turmoil, Paul gets a comforting vision from the Lord, who says, "Take courage! As you have testified about me in Jerusalem, so you must also testify in Rome" (23:11). That is all the encouragement Paul needs.

Smuggled out of town under heavy guard and the cover of darkness, Paul arrives at last in the palace of the Roman governor. His troubles are far from over. After hearing Paul's defense, Felix sends him to prison for two years, as a political favor to the Jews. Even that does not quiet the furor. The moment the new governor Festus arrives, Jewish leaders hatch yet another death plot against Paul.

Acts preserves three of the speeches delivered by Paul on trial. Roman officials, intrigued by the most talked-about prisoner in their corner of the empire, bring him out to perform, like a circus sideshow. As always, Paul makes the best of his opportunities. This chapter records the impression he makes on the most distinguished judge of all, King Herod Agrippa.

As a result of the Romans' inquisitions, Paul gets his long-awaited trip to Rome—not via a missionary journey but in a Roman ship, as a prisoner of the empire.—PY

DAY 323
Acts 27:1–44

PAUL SAILS FOR ROME; SHIPWRECK

When it was decided that we would sail for Italy, Paul and some other prisoners were handed over to a centurion named Julius, who belonged to the Imperial Regiment. We boarded a ship from Adramyttium about to sail for ports along the coast of the province of Asia, and we put out to sea. Aristarchus, a Macedonian from Thessalonica, was with us.

The next day we landed at Sidon; and Julius, in kindness to Paul, allowed him to go to his friends so they might provide for his needs. From there we put out to sea again and passed to the lee of Cyprus because the winds were against us. When we had sailed across the open sea off the coast of Cilicia and Pamphylia, we landed at Myra in Lycia. There the centurion found an Alexandrian ship sailing for Italy and put us on board. We made slow headway for many days and had difficulty arriving off Cnidus. When the wind did not allow us to hold our course, we sailed to the lee of Crete, opposite Salmone. We moved along the coast with difficulty and came to a place called Fair Havens, near the town of Lasea.

Much time had been lost, and sailing had already become dangerous because by now it was after the Fast. So Paul warned them, "Men, I can see that our voyage is going to be disastrous and bring great loss to ship and cargo, and to our own lives also." But the centurion, instead of listening to what Paul said, followed the advice of the pilot and of the owner of the ship. Since the harbor was unsuitable to winter in, the majority decided that we should sail on, hoping to reach Phoenix and winter there. This was a harbor in Crete, facing both southwest and northwest.

When a gentle south wind began to blow, they thought they had obtained what they wanted; so they weighed anchor and sailed along the shore of Crete. Before very long, a wind of hurricane force, called the "northeaster," swept down from the island. The ship was caught by the storm and could not head into the wind; so we gave way to it and were driven along. As we passed to the lee of a small island called Cauda, we were hardly able to make the lifeboat secure. When the men had hoisted it aboard, they passed ropes under the ship itself to hold it together. Fearing that they would run aground on the sandbars of Syrtis, they lowered the sea anchor and let the ship be driven along. We took such a violent battering from the storm that the next day they began to throw the cargo overboard. On the third day, they threw the ship's tackle overboard with their own hands. When neither sun nor stars appeared for many days and the storm continued raging, we finally gave up all hope of being saved.

After the men had gone a long time without food, Paul stood up before them and said: "Men, you should have taken my advice not to sail from Crete; then you would have spared yourselves this damage and loss. But now I urge you to keep up your courage, because not one of you will be lost; only the ship will be destroyed. Last night an angel of the God whose I am and whom I serve stood beside me and said, 'Do not be afraid, Paul. You must stand trial before Caesar; and God has graciously given you the lives of all who sail with you.' So keep up your courage, men, for I have faith in God that it will happen just as he told me. Nevertheless, we must run aground on some island."

On the fourteenth night we were still being driven across the Adriatic Sea, when about midnight the sailors sensed they were approaching land. They took soundings and found that the water was a hundred and twenty feet deep. A short time later they took soundings again and found it was ninety feet deep. Fearing that we would be dashed against the rocks, they dropped four anchors from the stern and prayed for daylight. In an attempt to escape from the ship, the sailors let the lifeboat down into the sea, pretending they were going to lower some anchors from the bow. Then Paul said to the centurion and the soldiers, "Unless these men stay with the ship, you cannot be saved." So the soldiers cut the ropes that held the lifeboat and let it fall away.

Just before dawn Paul urged them all to eat. "For the last fourteen days," he said, "you have been in constant suspense and have gone without food—you haven't eaten anything. Now I urge you to take some food. You need it to survive. Not one of you will lose a single hair from his head." After he said this, he took some bread and gave thanks to God in front of them all. Then he broke it and began to eat. They were all encouraged and ate some food themselves. Altogether there were 276 of us on board. When they had eaten as much as they wanted, they lightened the ship by throwing the grain into the sea.

When daylight came, they did not recognize the land, but they saw a bay with a sandy beach, where they decided to run the ship aground if they could. Cutting loose the anchors, they left them in the sea and at the same time untied the ropes that held the rudders. Then they hoisted the foresail to the wind and made for the beach. But the ship struck a sandbar and ran aground. The bow stuck fast and would not move, and the stern was broken to pieces by the pounding of the surf.

The soldiers planned to kill the prisoners to prevent any of them from swimming away and escaping. But the centurion wanted to spare Paul's life and kept them from carrying out their plan. He ordered those who could swim to jump overboard first and get to land. The rest were to get there on planks or on pieces of the ship. In this way everyone reached land in safety.

After surviving assassination plots, riots, imprisonment, and a corrupt judicial system, Paul encounters a new set of obstacles on his voyage to Rome. This chapter gives an eyewitness account of an ocean storm, the once-in-a-decade kind of storm that survivors would never forget.

Luke, a passenger accompanying Paul (note the prominent "we"), recounts the experience in vivid detail. He depicts the frenzy onboard: sailors lashing ropes around their groaning ship, the crew heaving precious food supplies and even the ship's tackle overboard, Roman soldiers with drawn swords halting the sailors' save-our-own-necks escape attempts and preparing to slash their prisoners' throats. In the midst of all this hysteria stands the apostle Paul, perfectly calm, foretelling what will happen next. God has promised he will visit Rome, a vision confirmed it, and Paul never doubts it, even when the boat breaks in pieces around him.

Once more Paul reveals himself as a man of unassailable courage. The Roman centurion surely recognizes it: he grants Paul extraordinary privileges and protection. By the end of the storm, everyone on the ship is following the advice of the strange, unflappable prisoner from Tarsus. —PY

DAILY CONTEMPLATION

How do you normally react in a crisis?

DAY 324
Acts 28:1–31

ASHORE ON MALTA; ARRIVAL AT ROME

Once safely on shore, we found out that the island was called Malta. The islanders showed us unusual kindness. They built a fire and welcomed us all because it was raining and cold. Paul gathered a pile of brushwood and, as he put it on the fire, a viper, driven out by the heat, fastened itself on his hand. When the islanders saw the snake hanging from his hand, they said to each other, "This man must be a murderer; for though he escaped from the sea, Justice has not allowed him to live." But Paul shook the snake off into the fire and suffered no ill effects. The people expected him to swell up or suddenly fall dead, but after waiting a long time and seeing nothing unusual happen to him, they changed their minds and said he was a god.

There was an estate nearby that belonged to Publius, the chief official of the island. He welcomed us to his home and for three days entertained us hospitably. His father was sick in bed, suffering from fever and dysentery. Paul went in to see him and, after prayer, placed his hands on him and healed him. When this had happened, the rest of the sick on the island came and were cured. They honored us in many ways and when we were ready to sail, they furnished us with the supplies we needed.

After three months we put out to sea in a ship that had wintered in the island. It was an Alexandrian ship with the figurehead of the twin gods Castor and Pollux. We put in at Syracuse and stayed there three days. From there we set sail and arrived at Rhegium. The next day the south wind came up, and on the following day we reached Puteoli. There we found some brothers who invited us to spend a week with them. And so we came to Rome. The brothers there had heard that we were coming, and they traveled as far as the Forum of Appius and the Three Taverns to meet us. At the sight of these men Paul thanked God and was encouraged. When we got to Rome, Paul was allowed to live by himself, with a soldier to guard him.

Three days later he called together the leaders of the Jews. When they had assembled, Paul said to them: "My brothers, although I have done nothing against our people or against the customs of our ancestors, I was arrested in Jerusalem and handed over to the Romans. They examined me and wanted to release me, because I was not guilty of any crime deserving death. But when the Jews objected, I was compelled to appeal to Caesar—not that I had any charge to bring against my own people. For this reason I have asked to see you and talk with you. It is because of the hope of Israel that I am bound with this chain."

They replied, "We have not received any letters from Judea concerning you, and none of the brothers who have come from there has reported or said anything bad about you. But we want to hear what your views are, for we know that people everywhere are talking against this sect."

They arranged to meet Paul on a certain day, and came in even larger numbers to the place where he was staying. From morning till evening he explained and declared to them the kingdom of God and tried to convince them about Jesus from the Law of Moses and from the Prophets. Some were convinced by what he said, but others would not believe. They disagreed among themselves and began to leave after Paul had made this final statement: "The Holy Spirit spoke the truth to your forefathers when he said through Isaiah the prophet:

"'Go to this people and say,
"You will be ever hearing but never understanding;
    you will be ever seeing but never perceiving."
For this people's heart has become calloused;
    they hardly hear with their ears,
    and they have closed their eyes.
Otherwise they might see with their eyes,
    hear with their ears,
    understand with their hearts
and turn, and I would heal them.'

"Therefore I want you to know that God's salvation has been sent to the Gentiles, and they will listen!"

For two whole years Paul stayed there in his own rented house and welcomed all who came to see him. Boldly and without hindrance he preached the kingdom of God and taught about the Lord Jesus Christ.

The future of the Gentile church depends in large measure on what happens to Paul, God's chosen apostle to the Gentiles. Thus the last few chapters of Acts portray a kind of spiritual warfare in which God turns apparent tragedy into good. Paul gets arrested; he's sent at last to Rome. The ship wrecks; they all survive. A poisonous snake bites Paul; he shakes it off and starts a healing ministry.

Paul arrives in Rome, his ultimate destination, under guard. Undoubtedly the reputation he has gained on the voyage helps convince authorities to treat him leniently. He lives by himself under a kind of "house arrest," with a soldier always present, possibly chained to the apostle. In typical fashion, Paul puts his time to good use. The very first week he calls in Jewish leaders to explain to them the Christian "sect" everyone is talking about. Over the next months and years Paul gets hours of quiet solitude to work on fond letters to the churches he has left behind.

Luke details the process of Roman justice so thoroughly that some have speculated he wrote Acts as a legal brief for Paul's defense. Is Paul intent on inciting revolt? Luke meticulously records that, no, Paul has no political ambitions and consistently works within Roman law.

Luke breaks off the story with Paul's fate still undecided. Most scholars believe that Paul, released from this imprisonment, goes on to take his message to new frontiers. Luke records nothing of these journeys and nothing about Paul's trial or sentencing. He ends with a single memory, frozen in time: Paul, confined to his house, preaching to all his visitors. Paul can no longer choose his audience; they have to seek him. But boldly, in the heart of mighty Rome, he proclaims a new kingdom and a new king. Before long, some of Caesar's own household staff are converting to the new faith. Christianity has made the journey, and the transition, from Jerusalem to Rome.

Tradition records that a few years later the Emperor Nero has Paul executed. The final verse of Acts serves as a fitting epitaph of the apostle's remarkable career.   —PY

DAILY CONTEMPLATION

Do you, like Paul, strive to make the best of bad situations?

DAY 325   Ephesians 1:15–2:13

THANKSGIVING AND PRAYER;

MADE ALIVE IN CHRIST

For this reason, ever since I heard about your faith in the Lord Jesus and your love for all the saints, I have not stopped giving thanks for you, remembering you in my prayers. I keep asking that the God of our Lord Jesus Christ, the glorious Father, may give you the Spirit of wisdom and revelation, so that you may know him better. I pray also that the eyes of your heart may be enlightened in order that you may know the hope to which he has called you, the riches of his glorious inheritance in the saints, and his incomparably great power for us who believe. That power is like the working of his mighty strength, which he exerted in Christ when he raised him from the dead and seated him at his right hand in the heavenly realms, far above all rule and authority, power and dominion, and every title that can be given, not only in the present age but also in the one to come. And God placed all things under his feet and appointed him to be head over everything for the church, which is his body, the fullness of him who fills everything in every way.

As for you, you were dead in your transgressions and sins, in which you used to live when you followed the ways of this world and of the ruler of the kingdom of the air, the spirit who is now at work in those who are disobedient. All of us also lived among them at one time, gratifying the cravings of our sinful nature and following its desires and thoughts. Like the rest, we were by nature objects of wrath. But because of his great love for us, God, who is rich in mercy, made us alive with Christ even when we were dead in transgressions—it is by grace you have been saved. And God raised us up with Christ and seated us with him in the heavenly realms in Christ Jesus, in order that in the coming ages he might show the incomparable riches of his grace, expressed in his kindness to us in Christ Jesus. For it is by grace you have been saved, through faith—and this not from yourselves, it is the gift of God—not by works, so that no one can boast. For we are God's workmanship, created in Christ Jesus to do good works, which God prepared in advance for us to do.

Therefore, remember that formerly you who are Gentiles by birth and called "uncircumcised" by those who call themselves "the circumcision" (that done in the body by the hands of men)—remember that at that time you were separate from Christ, excluded from citizenship in Israel and foreigners to the covenants of the promise, without hope and without God in the world. But now in Christ Jesus you who once were far away have been brought near through the blood of Christ.

Ironically, some of the brightest, most hopeful books of the Bible—the letters to the Philippians, Colossians, and Ephesians—come out of Paul's term of house arrest in Rome. There's a good reason: Prison offers him the precious commodity of time. Paul is no longer journeying from town to town, stamping out fires set by his enemies. Settled into passably comfortable surroundings, he can devote attention to lofty thoughts about the meaning of life.

A prisoner who survived fourteen years in a Cuban jail told how he kept his spirits up: "The worst part was the monotony. I had no window in my cell, and so I mentally constructed one on the door. I 'saw' in my mind a beautiful scene from the mountains, with water tumbling down a ravine over rocks. It became so real to me that I would visualize it without effort every time I looked at the cell door."

The letter to Ephesians gives a hint as to what the apostle Paul "sees" when he lets his mind wander beyond the monotony of his place of confinement. First he visualizes the spiritual growth in the churches he has left behind. This passage opens with a burst of thanksgiving for the vitality of the Ephesian church. Then he seeks to open "the eyes of their hearts" to even more exalted sights: the "incomparable riches" of God's grace.

Ephesians is full of staggering good news. In it, Paul asks the grandest question of all: What is God's overall purpose for this world? He raises the sights far above his own circumstances to bigger issues, cosmic issues. And when he cranks up the volume to express God's plan of love, not one low, mournful note sneaks in.

If you feel discouraged, or wonder if God really cares, or question whether the Christian life is worth the effort, Ephesians provides a great tonic. It prescribes the "riches in Christ" available to all.   —PY

DAILY CONTEMPLATION

What do you find most encouraging about Paul's good-news message?

DAY 326   Ephesians 2:14–3:21

PAUL THE PREACHER TO THE GENTILES; A PRAYER

He himself is our peace, who has made the two one and has destroyed the barrier, the dividing wall of hostility, by abolishing in his flesh the law with its commandments and regulations. His purpose was to create in himself one new man out of the two, thus making peace, and in this one body to reconcile both of them to God through the cross, by which he put to death their hostility. He came and preached peace to you who were far away and peace to those who were near. For through him we both have access to the Father by one Spirit.

Consequently, you are no longer foreigners and aliens, but fellow citizens with God's people and members of God's household, built on the foundation of the apostles and prophets, with Christ Jesus himself as the chief cornerstone. In him the whole building is joined together and rises to become a holy temple in the Lord. And in him you too are being built together to become a dwelling in which God lives by his Spirit.

For this reason I, Paul, the prisoner of Christ Jesus for the sake of you Gentiles—

Surely you have heard about the administration of God's grace that was given to me for you, that is, the mystery made known to me by revelation, as I have already written briefly. In reading this, then, you will be able to understand my insight into the mystery of Christ, which was not made known to men in other generations as it has now been revealed by the Spirit to God's holy apostles and prophets. This mystery is that through the gospel the Gentiles are heirs together with Israel, members together of one body, and sharers together in the promise in Christ Jesus.

I became a servant of this gospel by the gift of God's grace given me through the working of his power. Although I am less than the least of all God's people, this grace was given me: to preach to the Gentiles the unsearchable riches of

Christ, and to make plain to everyone the administration of this mystery, which for ages past was kept hidden in God, who created all things. His intent was that now, through the church, the manifold wisdom of God should be made known to the rulers and authorities in the heavenly realms, according to his eternal purpose which he accomplished in Christ Jesus our Lord. In him and through faith in him we may approach God with freedom and confidence. I ask you, therefore, not to be discouraged because of my sufferings for you, which are your glory.

For this reason I kneel before the Father, from whom his whole family in heaven and on earth derives its name. I pray that out of his glorious riches he may strengthen you with power through his Spirit in your inner being, so that Christ may dwell in your hearts through faith. And I pray that you, being rooted and established in love, may have power, together with all the saints, to grasp how wide and long and high and deep is the love of Christ, and to know this love that surpasses knowledge—that you may be filled to the measure of all the fullness of God.

Now to him who is able to do immeasurably more than all we ask or imagine, according to his power that is at work within us, to him be glory in the church and in Christ Jesus throughout all generations, for ever and ever! Amen.

The missionary church at Ephesus (EF-eh-sus) is one of Paul's success stories. He first visits this most important city in western Asia Minor (now Turkey) on his third missionary journey. The Ephesus of his day is renowned for its religion—but not the kind of religion Paul represents. Worship of the Roman goddess Diana centers in Ephesus, and its residents take great pride in the temple devoted to her. The temple building ranks among the seven wonders of the ancient world, and inside it hundreds of professional prostitute-priestesses assist the "worshipers."

In this unlikely place, Paul discovers a tiny Christian community already in existence. They know something about John the Baptist, not much about Jesus, and they have never even heard of the Holy Spirit. For the next two years Paul preaches to the Jews and to the Gentiles. A burgeoning church takes root, and soon word spreads throughout the entire province of Asia.

Miraculous signs and wonders mark Paul's ministry in Ephesus, so impressing local sorcerers and magicians that they spontaneously hold a public burning of their valuable scrolls. In the face of such religious enthusiasm, the Ephesian merchants, who make their living on profitable sales of idols, finally chase Paul out of town. (See Acts 19 for background.)

Like most early churches, the one at Ephesus struggles with Jew-Gentile differences. Believers from a Jewish background, raised on a steady diet of anti-idolatry, have huge obstacles to overcome in accepting former idol worshipers into their church. This section of Ephesians addresses the unity issues head-on.

In keeping with the spirit of this letter, and the healthy state of the church, Paul maintains an upbeat tone. He presents Christ as the great destroyer of barriers, the one who demolishes walls of division. (The Jewish temple in Jerusalem had an actual wall that no Gentile could go beyond.) No early church demonstrates the miracle of new community better than the one at Ephesus. There, idol worshipers—as far from God as anyone on earth—have been "brought near," joining Jews, the chosen people, as full members of God's household.

To Paul, the new community formed of both Jews and Gentiles is one of the great mysteries of the ages, a culmination of God's original plan, kept secret for many centuries but now made known. He can hardly contain his soaring language as he marvels at God's plan being fulfilled at that moment. —PY

DAILY CONTEMPLATION

In Paul's time, Jews and Gentiles were the two factions most given to quarreling and division. From your perspective, what groups divide Christians today?

DAY 327   Ephesians 4:1–5:20

UNITY IN THE BODY OF CHRIST;
LIVING AS CHILDREN OF THE LIGHT

As a prisoner for the Lord, then, I urge you to live a life worthy of the calling you have received. Be completely humble and gentle; be patient, bearing with one another in love. Make every effort to keep the unity of the Spirit through the bond of peace. There is one body and one Spirit—just as you were called to one hope when you were called—one Lord, one faith, one baptism; one God and Father of all, who is over all and through all and in all.

But to each one of us grace has been given as Christ apportioned it. This is why it says:

"When he ascended on high,
   he led captives in his train
   and gave gifts to men."

(What does "he ascended" mean except that he also descended to the lower, earthly regions? He who descended is the very one who ascended higher than all the heavens, in order to fill the whole universe.) It was he who gave some to be apostles, some to be prophets, some to be evangelists, and some to be pastors and teachers, to prepare God's people for works of service, so that the body of Christ may be built up until we all reach unity in the faith and in the knowledge of the Son of God and become mature, attaining to the whole measure of the fullness of Christ.

Then we will no longer be infants, tossed back and forth by the waves, and blown here and there by every wind of teaching and by the cunning and craftiness of men in their deceitful scheming. Instead, speaking the truth in love, we will in all things grow up into him who is the Head, that is, Christ. From him the whole body, joined and held together by every supporting ligament, grows and builds itself up in love, as each part does its work.

So I tell you this, and insist on it in the Lord, that you must no longer live as the Gentiles do, in the futility of their thinking. They are darkened in their understanding and separated from the life of God because of the ignorance that is in them due to the hardening of their hearts. Having lost all sensitivity, they have given themselves over to sensuality so as to indulge in every kind of impurity, with a continual lust for more.

You, however, did not come to know Christ that way. Surely you heard of him and were taught in him in accordance with the truth that is in Jesus. You were taught, with regard to your former way of life, to put off your old self, which is being corrupted by its deceitful desires; to be made new in the attitude of your minds; and to put on the new self, created to be like God in true righteousness and holiness.

Therefore each of you must put off falsehood and speak truthfully to his neighbor, for we are all members of one body. "In your anger do not sin": Do not let the sun go down while you are still angry, and do not give the devil a foothold. He who has been stealing must steal no longer, but must work, doing something useful with his own hands, that he may have something to share with those in need.

Do not let any unwholesome talk come out of your mouths, but only what is helpful for building others up according to their needs, that it may benefit those who listen. And do not grieve the Holy Spirit of God, with whom you were sealed for the day of redemption. Get rid of all bitterness, rage and anger, brawling and slander, along with every form of malice. Be kind and compassionate to one another, forgiving each other, just as in Christ God forgave you.

Be imitators of God, therefore, as dearly loved children and live a life of love, just as Christ loved us and gave himself up for us as a fragrant offering and sacrifice to God.

But among you there must not be even a hint of sexual immorality, or of any kind of impurity, or of greed, because these are improper for God's holy people. Nor should there be obscenity, foolish talk or coarse joking, which are out of place, but rather thanksgiving. For of this you can be sure: No immoral, impure or greedy person—such a man is an idolater—has any inheritance in the kingdom of Christ and of God. Let no one deceive you with empty words, for because of such things God's wrath comes on those who are disobedient. Therefore do not be partners with them.

For you were once darkness, but now you are light in the Lord. Live as children of light (for the fruit of the light consists in all goodness, righteousness and truth) and find out what pleases the Lord. Have nothing to do with the fruitless deeds of darkness, but rather expose them. For it is shameful even to mention what the disobedient do in secret. But everything exposed by the light becomes visible, for it is light that makes everything visible. This is why it is said:

> "Wake up, O sleeper,
>   rise from the dead,
> and Christ will shine on you."

Be very careful, then, how you live—not as unwise but as wise, making the most of every opportunity, because the days are evil. Therefore do not be foolish, but understand what the Lord's will is. Do not get drunk on wine, which leads to debauchery. Instead, be filled with the Spirit. Speak to one another with psalms, hymns and spiritual songs. Sing and make music in your heart to the Lord, always giving thanks to God the Father for everything, in the name of our Lord Jesus Christ.

It is a passage we would do well to read every day. Paul continues to stress the importance of unity among believers and explains why unity is important and what we will look like as believers who are maturing together.

God gives believers different gifts so each can serve the others in a unique way, to help all become mature in their union with Jesus. This maturing process will show in the way we live, day to day and minute by minute. "Be very careful, then, how you live," Paul implores. We are children of the light, and this shines through in our behavior.

The things we talk about, the way we joke together, the way we handle sexual desires, the place we give to greed, the people we choose for close companions, the way we handle anger, the things with which we fill our minds—all these matter because they reflect who we are. If we belong to Jesus, we long to live for him, seeking sanctification—a growing likeness to him—every day. This won't happen if we take lightly the choices we make about how to live.

As believers, we "put off [our] old self" and "put on the new self, created to be like God." When this is our prayer, God gives us the help we need to care about the way we live, and then to live as if we care. —BQ

DAILY CONTEMPLATION

How often, in the course of a day, do you consider whether your behavior is pleasing to God? Pray that with each day you would more closely resemble Jesus.

DAY 328 Reflection

FIXING BROKEN LOVE

In a day of broken families, broken relationships, and broken concepts of love, Paul's prayer for the Ephesians is one most of us today need to pray for ourselves and each other. He says in 3:14–21:

For this reason I kneel before the Father, from whom his whole family in heaven and on earth derives its name. I pray that out of his glorious riches he may strengthen you with power through his Spirit in your inner being, so that Christ may dwell in your hearts through faith. And I pray that you, being rooted and established in love, may have power, together with all the saints, to grasp how wide and long and high and deep is the love of Christ, and to know this love that surpasses knowledge—that you may be filled to the measure of all the fullness of God.

Now to him who is able to do immeasurably more than all we ask or imagine, according to his power that is at work within us, to him be glory in the church and in Christ Jesus throughout all generations, for ever and ever! Amen.

English poet Samuel Taylor Coleridge called the book of Ephesians "the divinest composition of man." Paul's language is so divine, in fact, that in places it can be hard to understand. One thing rings clear, though: his message is about love.

Paul talks about being rooted and established in love, a precursor to understanding Jesus' love for us. Pediatrician Dr. Frederic Burke speaks of the importance of love from an early age in enabling people to love later. "I firmly believe that early physical experience with parents' loving hands and arms is imprinted in the child's mind; and while apparently forgotten, it has a tremendous influence on the child's ego and the kind of adolescent he or she becomes."[61]

Maybe you didn't receive a lot of physical love as a child, or maybe the problem was not just physical but emotional. Maybe love was spoken to you yet was not reliable and available. Maybe you were wounded by love later in life. For love-starved people especially, a "rooted and established" love needs to come from somewhere else. Those who feel that the foundation of love has never been solid can find dependable love in community with other believers. Yet ultimately only in Jesus will we find the fullness of love we need. Paul describes the love of Jesus as "wide and long and high and deep," a love that "surpasses knowledge." When we understand the immense love of Jesus, we experience the fullness of God, and life finally satisfies.

Paul ends his prayer as he began it, referring to God's power. All hope for change may seem unlikely, even impossible, when we look at the brokenness imperfect love has caused our lives. But God's power can't be underestimated. One of the best promises of the Bible lies in Paul's closing words: "To him who is able to do immeasurably more than all we ask or imagine ..." God truly is able to fill us full of love so we don't feel hungry, hurting, angry. He is able to mend the wounds of a broken past and work out for us a new future. We don't need to live in cynicism or resignation. Satisfying, life-giving love can be a reality. God's power works within us to make it happen.   —BQ

DAILY CONTEMPLATION

What brokenness have you known in the relationships of your life? Do you have doubts as to whether love—God's or people's—can be trusted? Pray Paul's prayer slowly and talk to God about the pain you feel over failed love. Ask him to help you experience the love of Christ.

SUBMIT TO ONE ANOTHER; THE ARMOR OF GOD

Submit to one another out of reverence for Christ.

Wives, submit to your husbands as to the Lord. For the husband is the head of the wife as Christ is the head of the church, his body, of which he is the Savior. Now as the church submits to Christ, so also wives should submit to their husbands in everything.

Husbands, love your wives, just as Christ loved the church and gave himself up for her to make her holy, cleansing her by the washing with water through the word, and to present her to himself as a radiant church, without stain or wrinkle or any other blemish, but holy and blameless. In this same way, husbands ought to love their wives as their own bodies. He who loves his wife loves himself. After all, no one ever hated his own body, but he feeds and cares for it, just as Christ does the church—for we are members of his body. "For this reason a man will leave his father and mother and be united to his wife, and the two will become one flesh." This is a profound mystery—but I am talking about Christ and the church. However, each one of you also must love his wife as he loves himself, and the wife must respect her husband.

Children, obey your parents in the Lord, for this is right. "Honor your father and mother"—which is the first commandment with a promise—"that it may go well with you and that you may enjoy long life on the earth."

Fathers, do not exasperate your children; instead, bring them up in the training and instruction of the Lord.

Slaves, obey your earthly masters with respect and fear, and with sincerity of heart, just as you would obey Christ. Obey them not only to win their favor when their eye is on you, but like slaves of Christ, doing the will of God from your heart. Serve wholeheartedly, as if you were serving the Lord, not men, because you know that the Lord will reward everyone for whatever good he does, whether he is slave or free.

And masters, treat your slaves in the same way. Do not threaten them, since you know that he who is both their Master and yours is in heaven, and there is no favoritism with him.

Finally, be strong in the Lord and in his mighty power. Put on the full armor of God so that you can take your stand against the devil's schemes. For our struggle is not against flesh and blood, but against the rulers, against the authorities, against the powers of this dark world and against the spiritual forces of evil in the heavenly realms. Therefore put on the full armor of God, so that when the day of evil comes, you may be able to stand your ground, and after you have done everything, to stand. Stand firm then, with the belt of truth buckled around your waist, with the breastplate of righteousness in place, and with your feet fitted with the readiness that comes from the gospel of peace. In addition to all this, take up the shield of faith, with which you can extinguish all the flaming arrows of the evil one. Take the helmet of salvation and the sword of the Spirit, which is the word of God. And pray in the Spirit on all occasions with all kinds of prayers and requests. With this in mind, be alert and always keep on praying for all the saints.

Pray also for me, that whenever I open my mouth, words may be given me so that I will fearlessly make known the mystery of the gospel, for which I am an ambassador in chains. Pray that I may declare it fearlessly, as I should.

After setting down the theory, Paul gives specifics on what some relationships will look like among believers who are living together in unity. Overall, he begins, believers will "submit to one another out of reverence for Christ." Jesus lived his life on earth in an attitude of voluntary submission—service—to others. In the same way we should submit to others, serving them as we allow Christ to live through us.

Paul looks first at marriage. These verses have been a source of confusion, and even resentment, for many women and men since they were written, but when we understand them as God intends, they only reflect what Jesus taught throughout his life on earth. Paul asks both husband and wife to sacrificially love one another. This mutual submission does not imply that one partner is subservient to the other; it means that both choose to serve the other, putting the other's needs first.

Wives are asked to submit in the way that all believers voluntarily submit to Christ. The comparison to Christ implies a voluntary servanthood springing from a love relationship; it does not indicate a "doormat" submission. Husbands, as well, are asked to love in the way Christ himself loved believers, submitting his very life to redeem them. He could not have loved more deeply or served more humbly, and this is the character Paul asks husbands to reflect.

Paul tells children to obey and honor their parents, and fathers to raise their children to know God. Then he speaks to the slaves of his day, instructing that even for them the rule of love, submission, and respect applies. Paul isn't condoning slavery; rather, he gives practical advice for believers living with the reality of their enslavement.

Paul concludes his letter to the Ephesians by reminding them of the spiritual battle they can expect. We aren't merely fighting against ourselves to live the life of Jesus. We are fighting Satan's forces, who want to separate us from each other and from God's ways. It's a battle we can win, however, and Paul tells us how to fight.   —BQ

DAILY CONTEMPLATION

What makes submitting to or serving the people in your life difficult?

THANKSGIVING AND PRAYER;

THE SUPREMACY OF CHRIST

Paul, an apostle of Christ Jesus by the will of God, and Timothy our brother,

To the holy and faithful brothers in Christ at Colosse:

Grace and peace to you from God our Father.

We always thank God, the Father of our Lord Jesus Christ, when we pray for you, because we have heard of your faith in Christ Jesus and of the love you have for all the saints—the faith and love that spring from the hope that is stored up for you in heaven and that you have already heard about in the word of truth, the gospel that has come to you. All over the world this gospel is bearing fruit and growing, just as it has been doing among you since the day you heard it and understood God's grace in all its truth. You learned it from Epaphras, our dear fellow servant, who is a faithful minister of Christ on our behalf, and who also told us of your love in the Spirit.

For this reason, since the day we heard about you, we have not stopped praying for you and asking God to fill you with the knowledge of his will through all spiritual wisdom and understanding. And we pray this in order that you may live a life worthy of the Lord and may please him in every way: bearing fruit in every good work, growing in the knowledge of God, being strengthened with all power according to his glorious might so that you may have great endurance and patience, and joyfully giving thanks to the Father, who has qualified you to share in the inheritance of the saints in the kingdom of light. For he has rescued us from the dominion of darkness and brought us into the kingdom of the Son he loves, in whom we have redemption, the forgiveness of sins.

He is the image of the invisible God, the firstborn over all creation. For by him all things were created: things in heaven and on earth, visible and invisible, whether thrones or powers or rulers or authorities; all things were created by him and for him. He is before all things, and in him all things hold together. And he is the head of the body, the church; he is the beginning and the firstborn from among the dead, so that in everything he might have the supremacy. For God was pleased to have all his fullness dwell in him, and through him to reconcile to himself all things, whether things on earth or things in heaven, by making peace through his blood, shed on the cross.

Once you were alienated from God and were enemies in your minds because of your evil behavior. But now he has reconciled you by Christ's physical body through death to present you holy in his sight, without blemish and free from accusation—if you continue in your faith, established and firm, not moved from the hope held out in the gospel. This is the gospel that you heard and that has been proclaimed to every creature under heaven, and of which I, Paul, have become a servant.

Now I rejoice in what was suffered for you, and I fill up in my flesh what is still lacking in regard to Christ's afflictions, for the sake of his body, which is the church. I have become its servant by the commission God gave me to present to you the word of God in its fullness—the mystery that has been kept hidden for ages and generations, but is now disclosed to the saints. To them God has chosen to make known among the Gentiles the glorious riches of this mystery, which is Christ in you, the hope of glory.

We proclaim him, admonishing and teaching everyone with all wisdom, so that we may present everyone perfect in Christ. To this end I labor, struggling with all his energy, which so powerfully works in me.

I want you to know how much I am struggling for you and for those at Laodicea, and for all who have not met me personally. My purpose is that they may be encouraged in heart and united in love, so that they may have the full riches of complete understanding, in order that they may know the mystery of God, namely, Christ, in whom are hidden all the treasures of wisdom and knowledge. I tell you this so that no one may deceive you by fine-sounding arguments. For though I am absent from you in body, I am present with you in spirit and delight to see how orderly you are and how firm your faith in Christ is.

The book of Colossians may sound like Ephesians, and with good reason—fully half the verses in Ephesians appear in some form in Colossians. The two cities are neighbors in Paul's day, and one of the converts from Paul's stay in Ephesus has taken the gospel over to Colosse (kuh-LAH-see). Paul himself has never visited Colosse and thus writes this book to people who know him by reputation only.

The letter opens on an optimistic note, with Paul thanking God for the Colossians' spiritual progress. Yet he also brings up for discussion a doctrinal flaw that has crept into their church. The best modern equivalent would be a "cult," one that includes some Christian principles overlaid with many other mysterious beliefs.

First-century Colosse, situated on a major trade route from the East, is a perfect breeding ground for cults. Even Jews in this area worship angels and river spirits. Often these cults (like many now) do not reject Jesus Christ outright; they merely work him into a more elaborate scheme. Christ and simple forms of worship, they teach, are fine for beginners, but the "deep things of God" require some further steps.

Rather than attacking each peculiar belief point by point, Paul counters with a positive theology. "Christ is enough," he declares in this first chapter. He is God, the fullness of God, the one who made the world, the reason that everything exists. All the "mystery" and treasure and wisdom you could ask for are found in the person of Jesus Christ; there is no need to look elsewhere. The masterful summation paragraph that begins at verse 15 may have been adapted for use as a hymn by the early church.

Paul tells the Colossians just what he has told the Ephesians: Before Christ, a mystery was kept hidden for many centuries. But when Christ came, everything broke out into the open. The fullness of God lived, died, and then reappeared after death, all in broad daylight. Why settle for counterfeits? —PY

DAY 331   Colossians 3:1–25

RULES FOR HOLY LIVING

Since, then, you have been raised with Christ, set your hearts on things above, where Christ is seated at the right hand of God. Set your minds on things above, not on earthly things. For you died, and your life is now hidden with Christ in God. When Christ, who is your life, appears, then you also will appear with him in glory.

Put to death, therefore, whatever belongs to your earthly nature: sexual immorality, impurity, lust, evil desires and greed, which is idolatry. Because of these, the wrath of God is coming. You used to walk in these ways, in the life you once lived. But now you must rid yourselves of all such things as these: anger, rage, malice, slander, and filthy language from your lips. Do not lie to each other, since you have taken off your old self with its practices and have put on the new self, which is being renewed in knowledge in the image of its Creator. Here there is no Greek or Jew, circumcised or uncircumcised, barbarian, Scythian, slave or free, but Christ is all, and is in all.

Therefore, as God's chosen people, holy and dearly loved, clothe yourselves with compassion, kindness, humility, gentleness and patience. Bear with each other and forgive whatever grievances you may have against one another. Forgive as the Lord forgave you. And over all these virtues put on love, which binds them all together in perfect unity.

Let the peace of Christ rule in your hearts, since as members of one body you were called to peace. And be thankful. Let the word of Christ dwell in you richly as you teach and admonish one another with all wisdom, and as you sing psalms, hymns and spiritual songs with gratitude in your hearts to God. And whatever you do, whether in word or deed, do it all in the name of the Lord Jesus, giving thanks to God the Father through him.

Wives, submit to your husbands, as is fitting in the Lord.

Husbands, love your wives and do not be harsh with them.

Children, obey your parents in everything, for this pleases the Lord.

Fathers, do not embitter your children, or they will become discouraged.

Slaves, obey your earthly masters in everything; and do it, not only when their eye is on you and to win their favor, but with sincerity of heart and reverence for the Lord. Whatever you do, work at it with all your heart, as working for the Lord, not for men, since you know that you will receive an inheritance from the Lord as a reward. It is the Lord Christ you are serving.

Anyone who does wrong will be repaid for his wrong, and there is no favoritism.

Once more Paul writes a message to the Colossians that resembles the one he gave the Ephesians. He tells them how to live holy lives, as people who belong to Christ. He shortens some of his instructions and then summarizes for slaves, as well as for all believers, the attitude we should have toward daily life as we work and as we strive to live the way God calls us to live: "Whatever you do, work at it with all your heart, as working for the Lord, not for men, since you know that you will receive an inheritance from the Lord as a reward. It is the Lord Christ you are serving."　　　—BQ

DAILY CONTEMPLATION

In what area of your work do you especially need to remember that you are working for the Lord, not for men or women?

DAY 332　　　　　　　　　　　　　　Reflection

FIGHTING A SPIRITUAL WAR

As I was growing up, I often sang in Sunday school a popular hymn titled "Onward Christian Soldiers." The first verse goes,

> Onward Christian soldiers, Marching as to war,
> With the cross of Jesus, Going on before;
> Christ, the royal Master, Leads against the foe;
> Forward into battle See His banners go.

As a child, I had fun with the song. Sometimes we would march around the room, maybe carrying a Christian flag, envisioning ourselves in Jesus' army. That was before I knew anything of the realities of war. Back then war was an otherworldly prospect, a nebulous vision that revolved around the words of a song.

My feelings have changed toward that childhood hymn. I've become too peace-loving to sing the song with the relish I once did. Now I'd rather sing about love. I'd rather look at life through eyes that see the good, the potential, even in those with whom I disagree.

I've also come to realize, however, that a proper understanding of the hymn, and many biblical references to warfare, point to a war not so much against people as against the evil that rages out of sight in a realm beyond our world. Such evil, directed by Satan, focuses on the undoing of the people and things of God.

Paul never lost sight of this battle. In his letter to the Ephesians he wrote, "Put on the full armor of God so that you can take your stand against the devil's schemes. For our struggle is not against flesh and blood, but against the rulers, against the authorities, against the powers of this dark world and against the spiritual forces of evil in the heavenly realms" (Ephesians 6:11–12). Many times we feel that the hardships we encounter, and temptations we face, stem from sin and our own weakness. We assume that only a determined outlook and strong will can help us overcome. Paul reminds us that we may have forgotten one component in the equation: the very real presence of spiritual forces opposing us. We're not merely fighting ourselves; we are fighting Satan and his agents.

After discussing the armor believers need to do battle—truth, righteousness, peace, faith, salvation, the Spirit, and the Word of God—Paul speaks of prayer, both for ourselves and for one another. When the battle rages, we need frequent contact with the One on our side. We need him fighting every struggle we enter, and we need the prayers of those around us to give further strength.

Paul mentions one believer who prayed like this for the church he loved. Paul writes in his letter to the Colossians that Epaphras (eh-PAF-ruhs), though a prisoner, was "always wrestling in prayer" for them (4:12). Epaphras and Paul both faced their own enemies, on earth and in spiritual realms, yet they recognized and helped fight the battles of the ones they loved.

Those who still sing "Onward Christian Soldiers" would do well to approach it again from a child's perspective, envisioning a battle fought not here on earth but in another realm. We should sing both for ourselves and for others, with all the fervor a child can muster. The battle is real. It is God's. And in the words of a hymn by Martin Luther, "He must win the battle."   —BQ

DAILY CONTEMPLATION

Do you feel ready to face the reality of spiritual warfare? Talk to God about your need for his help. Take a moment to pray for a friend or family member who may be facing a spiritual battle right now. Thank God that he is more powerful than anything that can come against us.

DAY 333   Philemon 1–25

PAUL'S PLEA FOR ONESIMUS

Paul, a prisoner of Christ Jesus, and Timothy our brother,

To Philemon our dear friend and fellow worker, to Apphia our sister, to Archippus our fellow soldier and to the church that meets in your home:

Grace to you and peace from God our Father and the Lord Jesus Christ.

I always thank my God as I remember you in my prayers, because I hear about your faith in the Lord Jesus and your love for all the saints. I pray that you may be active in sharing your faith, so that you will have a full understanding of every good thing we have in Christ. Your love has given me great joy and encouragement, because you, brother, have refreshed the hearts of the saints.

Therefore, although in Christ I could be bold and order you to do what you ought to do, yet I appeal to you on the basis of love. I then, as Paul—an old man and now also a prisoner of Christ Jesus—I appeal to you for my son Onesimus, who became my son while I was in chains. Formerly he was useless to you, but now he has become useful both to you and to me.

I am sending him—who is my very heart—back to you. I would have liked to keep him with me so that he could take your place in helping me while I am in chains for the gospel. But I did not want to do anything without your consent, so that any favor you do will be spontaneous and not forced. Perhaps the reason he was separated from you for a little while was that you might have him back for good—no longer as a slave, but better than a slave, as a dear brother. He is very dear to me but even dearer to you, both as a man and as a brother in the Lord.

So if you consider me a partner, welcome him as you would welcome me. If he has done you any wrong or owes you anything, charge it to me. I, Paul, am writing this with my own hand. I will pay it back—not to mention that you owe me your very self. I do wish, brother, that I may have some benefit from you in the Lord; refresh my heart in Christ. Confident of your obedience, I write to you, knowing that you will do even more than I ask.

And one thing more: Prepare a guest room for me, because I hope to be restored to you in answer to your prayers.

Epaphras, my fellow prisoner in Christ Jesus, sends you greetings. And so do Mark, Aristarchus, Demas and Luke, my fellow workers.

The grace of the Lord Jesus Christ be with your spirit.

The New Testament includes four of the apostle Paul's letters to individuals (Philemon [fi-LEE-muhn], Titus, 1 and 2 Timothy). Of these, Philemon is the briefest and also the most personal. Paul is writing a friend to ask a favor—a *big* favor, for a person's life hangs in the balance.

Like most respectable citizens of his day, Philemon owns slaves (historians estimate as many as sixty million slaves served the Roman Empire). One of these, Onesimus (oh-NES-ih-muhs), has stolen from his master and run away to Rome. There he has met Paul and become a Christian.

As a Christian, the slave Onesimus feels the need to make restitution to his master, whom he has wronged. But the laws of the empire are merciless to runaway slaves. If Onesimus returns, his master Philemon has the legal power to sentence him to immediate execution. Or he can brand the letter F (for *Fugitivus*) on his forehead with a hot iron, marking him for life.

The apostle Paul agrees to use his full influence on Philemon, and this brief letter, a masterpiece of persuasion and diplomacy, is the result. Every phrase in Philemon seems crafted to produce the best possible effect. Paul appeals to Philemon's friendship, his status as a Christian leader, his sense of love and compassion. He applies blatant pressure, reminding Philemon that "you owe me your very self." He even offers to pay back Onesimus's debts.

Paul does not call for the outright abolition of slavery in this letter. Such a call would threaten the economic base of the empire and bring the crushing weight of Rome down on the fledgling church. In fact, slavery will endure for another eighteen hundred years after this letter is written. The tiny book of Philemon, however, shows that faith has a profound impact on slavery long before its abolition.

Onesimus, his Christian conscience pricked, is assuming a grave risk by turning himself in. In Philemon, Paul asks for a second miracle, pleading with the slave's owner to "welcome him as you would welcome me." Onesimus is no longer "property" but rather a Christian brother. Such an attitude, in this culture, is social dynamite.   —PY

DAILY CONTEMPLATION

Do you know of any situations in which you could be a reconciler between two estranged parties?

DAY 334

Titus 2:1–3:8

WHAT MUST BE TAUGHT TO VARIOUS GROUPS;
DOING WHAT IS GOOD

You must teach what is in accord with sound doctrine. Teach the older men to be temperate, worthy of respect, self-controlled, and sound in faith, in love and in endurance.

Likewise, teach the older women to be reverent in the way they live, not to be slanderers or addicted to much wine, but to teach what is good. Then they can train the younger women to love their husbands and children, to be self-controlled and pure, to be busy at home, to be kind, and to be subject to their husbands, so that no one will malign the word of God.

Similarly, encourage the young men to be self-controlled. In everything set them an example by doing what is good. In your teaching show integrity, seriousness and soundness of speech that cannot be condemned, so that those who oppose you may be ashamed because they have nothing bad to say about us.

Teach slaves to be subject to their masters in everything, to try to please them, not to talk back to them, and not to steal from them, but to show that they can be fully trusted, so that in every way they will make the teaching about God our Savior attractive.

For the grace of God that brings salvation has appeared to all men. It teaches us to say "No" to ungodliness and worldly passions, and to live self-controlled, upright and godly lives in this present age, while we wait for the blessed hope—the glorious appearing of our great God and Savior, Jesus

Christ, who gave himself for us to redeem us from all wickedness and to purify for himself a people that are his very own, eager to do what is good.

These, then, are the things you should teach. Encourage and rebuke with all authority. Do not let anyone despise you.

Remind the people to be subject to rulers and authorities, to be obedient, to be ready to do whatever is good, to slander no one, to be peaceable and considerate, and to show true humility toward all men.

At one time we too were foolish, disobedient, deceived and enslaved by all kinds of passions and pleasures. We lived in malice and envy, being hated and hating one another. But when the kindness and love of God our Savior appeared, he saved us, not because of righteous things we had done, but because of his mercy. He saved us through the washing of rebirth and renewal by the Holy Spirit, whom he poured out on us generously through Jesus Christ our Savior, so that, having been justified by his grace, we might become heirs having the hope of eternal life. This is a trustworthy saying. And I want you to stress these things, so that those who have trusted in God may be careful to devote themselves to doing what is good. These things are excellent and profitable for everyone.

In his early years Paul, in a whirlwind of energy, personally carried the message of the gospel to the far corners of the Near East. But age and poor health gradually have slowed him down, and he spends many of his later years locked away in prison. Increasingly he turns to loyal helpers to carry on his work.

The name Titus appears fourteen times in Paul's letters. The book of Galatians (2:1–5) introduces him as Paul's "exhibit A" proving that a Gentile can become a fully acceptable Christian. For more than a decade Paul relies on his trusted associate, who seems to specialize in crisis churches. Twice Titus is dispatched on a diplomatic mission to the rowdy church at Corinth. This letter indicates he faces an equally challenging task on Crete. Paul is writing him a set of personal instructions on how to handle a difficult assignment.

Crete, an island in the Mediterranean, has an ethnically divided population. Its main knowledge of the outside world comes through pirates and coarse sailors. You can get an idea of the challenges Titus faces there by reading between the lines of Paul's advice. For example, Paul's advice to the older men to "be temperate, worthy of respect, self-controlled" reveals something about their normal patterns; likewise, his charge to the women "not to be slanderers or addicted to much wine." One of the island's own poets described Cretans as "liars, evil brutes, lazy gluttons."

Paul always keeps in mind that the Christian church, as a new phenomenon, will attract close scrutiny from the outside world. In Titus, he gives advice on how each of the diverse groups in the church—older men, older women, younger women, young men, slaves—can provide the best example for that watching world. The goal: "so that those who oppose you may be ashamed because they have nothing bad to say about us."

—PY

DAILY CONTEMPLATION

Of the advice Paul gives to the various groups, which applies most directly to you?

629

WARNING AGAINST FALSE TEACHERS;

GOD'S GRACE TO PAUL; INSTRUCTIONS ON

WORSHIP; OVERSEERS AND DEACONS

Paul, an apostle of Christ Jesus by the command of God our Savior and of Christ Jesus our hope,

To Timothy my true son in the faith:

Grace, mercy and peace from God the Father and Christ Jesus our Lord.

As I urged you when I went into Macedonia, stay there in Ephesus so that you may command certain men not to teach false doctrines any longer nor to devote themselves to myths and endless genealogies. These promote controversies rather than God's work—which is by faith. The goal of this command is love, which comes from a pure heart and a good conscience and a sincere faith. Some have wandered away from these and turned to meaningless talk. They want to be teachers of the law, but they do not know what they are talking about or what they so confidently affirm.

We know that the law is good if one uses it properly. We also know that law is made not for the righteous but for lawbreakers and rebels, the ungodly and sinful, the unholy and irreligious; for those who kill their fathers or mothers, for murderers, for adulterers and perverts, for slave traders and liars and perjurers—and for whatever else is contrary to the sound doctrine that conforms to the glorious gospel of the blessed God, which he entrusted to me.

I thank Christ Jesus our Lord, who has given me strength, that he considered me faithful, appointing me to his service. Even though I was once a blasphemer and a persecutor and a violent man, I was shown mercy because I acted in ignorance and unbelief. The grace of our Lord was poured out on me abundantly, along with the faith and love that are in Christ Jesus.

Here is a trustworthy saying that deserves full acceptance: Christ Jesus came into the world to save sinners—of whom I am the worst. But for that very reason I was shown mercy so that in me, the worst of sinners, Christ Jesus might display his unlimited patience as an example for those who would believe on him and receive eternal life. Now to the King eternal, immortal, invisible, the only God, be honor and glory for ever and ever. Amen.

Timothy, my son, I give you this instruction in keeping with the prophecies once made about you, so that by following them you may fight the good fight, holding on to faith and a good conscience. Some have rejected these and so have shipwrecked their faith. Among them are Hymenaeus and Alexander, whom I have handed over to Satan to be taught not to blaspheme.

I urge, then, first of all, that requests, prayers, intercession and thanksgiving be made for everyone—for kings and all those in authority, that we may live peaceful and quiet lives in all godliness and holiness. This is good, and pleases God our Savior, who wants all men to be saved and to come to a knowledge of the truth. For there is one God and one mediator between God and men, the man Christ Jesus, who gave himself as a ransom for all men— the testimony given in its proper time. And for this purpose I was appointed a herald and an apostle—I am telling the truth, I am not lying—and a teacher of the true faith to the Gentiles.

I want men everywhere to lift up holy hands in prayer, without anger or disputing.

I also want women to dress modestly, with decency and propriety, not with braided hair or gold or pearls or expensive clothes, but with good deeds, appropriate for women who profess to worship God.

A woman should learn in quietness and full submission. I do not permit a woman to teach or to have authority over a man; she must be silent. For Adam was formed first, then Eve. And Adam was not the one deceived; it was the woman who was deceived and became a sinner. But women will be saved through childbearing—if they continue in faith, love and holiness with propriety.

Here is a trustworthy saying: If anyone sets his heart on being an overseer, he desires a noble task. Now the overseer must be above reproach, the husband of but one wife, temperate, self-controlled, respectable, hospitable, able to teach, not given to drunkenness, not violent but gentle, not quarrelsome, not a lover of money. He must manage his own family well and see that his children obey him with proper respect. (If anyone does not know how to manage his own family, how can he take care of God's church?) He must not be a recent convert, or he may become conceited and fall under the same judgment as the devil. He must also have a good reputation with outsiders, so that he will not fall into disgrace and into the devil's trap.

Deacons, likewise, are to be men worthy of respect, sincere, not indulging in much wine, and not pursuing dishonest gain.

The role of women in the church, social welfare programs, fund-raising techniques, a Christian's relationship to society, materialism, order of worship—the list could describe the agenda for a modern-day denominational convention. But the apostle Paul is already addressing these issues in the first century, just a few decades after Jesus' life on earth.

Actually, the problems discussed in 1 Timothy represent growth pains. For example, out of Christian compassion believers have extended help to needy widows. But before long some members with a "welfare mentality" see the widows' list as an easy way to avoid financial responsibility for their families. In 1 Timothy, Paul outlines a form of "enrollment" to establish who is truly needy.

These and other problems are afflicting the church at Ephesus, where Timothy now serves as pastor. The church has grown and thrived despite intense opposition from within this secular city. The letter to the Ephesians was one of Paul's happiest, but now, almost ten years after his visit to Ephesus, Paul has learned of the major troubles brewing. The time has come for older churches to get organized and to bring some order to their worship and outreach programs. Otherwise they will drift toward endless division and disagreement.

For that thankless job, Paul turns to his trusted companion Timothy. Converted during Paul's first missionary journey, Timothy has over time gained the apostle's complete trust, despite some major differences in personality. Timothy has a reserved, timid disposition, which may contribute to his chronic stomach trouble. Given his shyness and his half-Jewish, half-Gentile ancestry, Timothy does not seem the ideal choice for a heresy fighter in a turbulent church. But Paul is convinced he can do the job.

"I have no one else like him," Paul once wrote of Timothy. "As a son with his father he has served with me in the work of the gospel" (Philippians 2:20, 22). Through disturbances, riots, and even into prison, Timothy has loyally accompanied the apostle. Six of Paul's letters begin with the news that Timothy is at his side. Despite a weak stomach and timid disposition, Timothy has proved his mettle to Paul in many ways, and Paul writes this letter to encourage him in a difficult task.   —PY

DAILY CONTEMPLATION

Do you have any personality traits that make Christian service seem difficult?

DAY 336   Reflection

FINDING A FAMILY THAT WORKS

Many believers today look upon church involvement as optional. Maybe they're content with a small group of Christian friends and reluctant to reach further into the church to develop more relationships. Maybe church isn't even a part of their life right now. To Paul, the question for believers is not whether to be part of a church but *how* to be involved, how to make church life work. Paul speaks to the important role we should have in one another's lives.

Today's culture presents special challenges when it comes to joining together as the body, or family, of Christ. Connecting with other Christians becomes a discomfiting proposal when we look around and see the vast differences that exist among us. We also tend to live with greater isolation than did past generations. Commonly we keep small circles of friends who are quite alike, yet time and energy constraints keep us from spending much time even with them.

The church Titus pastored on the island of Crete also faced challenges. Its members knew little about conventional ways of "being the church" to one another. For them, a personal spiritual life was challenge enough. In the book of Titus Paul tells believers that we have something to give one another that will help us, not burden us. Joining with those "different" believers in the church holds the potential of completing our lives and making them more meaningful and satisfying, not less.

Paul mentions "sound doctrine" as the first step needed in coming together (Titus 2:1). Beyond that, all believers need to be self-controlled, reverent, kind, and full of integrity. Some differences add diversity to the body, but in areas of character all must pursue the same goals.

Furthermore, we must realize that we need each other across generations. Younger women need older women. Younger men need older men. Older believers are responsible to act as role models and encouragers to younger believers. If not, the church will muddle along with the younger generation trying to discern on their own how best to live, and the older generation feeling past their prime and unneeded.

"But they don't understand me," we may protest about others in the church. "I can't relate to them. We can't come together."

Dietrich Bonhoeffer, German pastor of an underground seminary during the Nazi years, writes about the changes Jesus brings to relationships. "Christ became the Mediator and made peace with God and among men. Without Christ we should not know God, we could not call upon Him, nor come to Him. But without Christ we also would not know our brother, nor could we come to him. The way is blocked by our own ego. Christ opened up the way to God and to our brother. Now Christians can live with one another in peace; they can love and serve one another; they can become one. But they can continue to do so only by way of Jesus Christ."[62]

In the natural world, we may be unable to connect with other age groups and diverse people. Jesus changes that. Although challenges may still exist, he connects us in unexpected and soul-filling ways. Through these unlikely others we meet him and find our lives fuller, our perspectives healthier. Jesus makes us one family.   —BQ

DAILY CONTEMPLATION

How big a role does the church play in your life? Do you regularly interact with Christians of other generations or of other social, economic, or ethnic backgrounds? Pray about the struggles you may be having with your church or in getting involved in a church. Ask God to help you understand your needs and find ways to meet those needs through other believers.

DAY 337
1 Timothy 6:3–21

LOVE OF MONEY

If anyone teaches false doctrines and does not agree to the sound instruction of our Lord Jesus Christ and to godly teaching, he is conceited and understands nothing. He has an unhealthy interest in controversies and quarrels about words that result in envy, strife, malicious talk, evil suspicions and constant friction between men of corrupt mind, who have been robbed of the truth and who think that godliness is a means to financial gain.

But godliness with contentment is great gain. For we brought nothing into the world, and we can take nothing out of it. But if we have food and clothing, we will be content with that. People who want to get rich fall into temptation and a trap and into many foolish and harmful desires that plunge men into ruin and destruction. For the love of money is a root of all kinds of evil. Some people, eager for money, have wandered from the faith and pierced themselves with many griefs.

But you, man of God, flee from all this, and pursue righteousness, godliness, faith, love, endurance and gentleness. Fight the good fight of the faith. Take hold of the eternal life to which you were called when you made your good confession in the presence of many witnesses. In the sight of God, who gives life to everything, and of Christ Jesus, who while testifying before Pontius Pilate made the good confession, I charge you to keep this command without spot or blame until the appearing of our Lord Jesus Christ, which God will bring about in his own time—God, the blessed and only Ruler, the King of kings and Lord of lords, who alone is immortal and who lives in unapproachable light, whom no one has seen or can see. To him be honor and might forever. Amen.

Command those who are rich in this present world not to be arrogant nor to put their hope in wealth, which is so uncertain, but to put their hope in God, who richly provides us with everything for our enjoyment. Command them to do good, to be rich in good deeds, and to be generous and willing to share. In this way they will lay up treasure for themselves as a firm foundation for the coming age, so that they may take hold of the life that is truly life.

Timothy, guard what has been entrusted to your care. Turn away from godless chatter and the opposing ideas of what is falsely called knowledge, which some have professed and in so doing have wandered from the faith.

Grace be with you.

Money represents a dangerous attraction for all believers, Paul warns. Money isn't inherently evil—all need it to survive. But, similar to a love for food, the love of money can get out of hand. The distraction it poses can turn a person from pursuing God to pursuing what seems attractive on the surface but has no real or lasting value. Satan uses money to draw us away from God and consume our thoughts, time, and energy in things that aren't important to God's kingdom.

Jesus spoke often about money, warning that "it is hard for a rich man to enter the kingdom of heaven" (Matthew 19:23) and "you cannot serve both God and Money" (Matthew 6:24). More concerned about a person's heart than about the size of his or her bank account, Jesus knew that money has a way of stealing away the love that should belong to God. And it can bankrupt a person's soul, promising to make one feel secure, satisfied, and respected but in the end leaving emptiness. No matter how much or how little money a person has, God cares about the heart. Only a heart centered on God and generous with all things can experience the fullness of a relationship with him.

"A man's life does not consist in the abundance of his possessions," Jesus said (Luke 12:15). His words, and Paul's, offer loving insight we as believers can take to heart. What we *have* has nothing to do with who we *are*. Solomon, the wisest man of all time (and one of the wealthiest), said, "Whoever loves wealth is never satisfied" (Ecclesiastes 5:10). God has made it clear: Money won't give us what we truly need. Only he can do that. —BQ

DAY 338   2 Timothy 1:1–18

ENCOURAGEMENT TO BE FAITHFUL

Paul, an apostle of Christ Jesus by the will of God, according to the promise of life that is in Christ Jesus,

To Timothy, my dear son:

Grace, mercy and peace from God the Father and Christ Jesus our Lord.

I thank God, whom I serve, as my forefathers did, with a clear conscience, as night and day I constantly remember you in my prayers. Recalling your tears, I long to see you, so that I may be filled with joy. I have been reminded of your sincere faith, which first lived in your grandmother Lois and in your mother Eunice and, I am persuaded, now lives in you also. For this reason I remind you to fan into flame the gift of God, which is in you through the laying on of my hands. For God did not give us a spirit of timidity, but a spirit of power, of love and of self-discipline.

So do not be ashamed to testify about our Lord, or ashamed of me his prisoner. But join with me in suffering for the gospel, by the power of God, who has saved us and called us to a holy life—not because of anything we have done but because of his own purpose and grace. This grace was given us in Christ Jesus before the beginning of time, but it has now been revealed through the appearing of our Savior, Christ Jesus, who has destroyed death and has brought life and immortality to light through the gospel. And of this gospel I was appointed a herald and an apostle and a teacher. That is why I am suffering as I am. Yet I am not ashamed, because I know whom I have believed, and am convinced that he is able to guard what I have entrusted to him for that day.

What you heard from me, keep as the pattern of sound teaching, with faith and love in Christ Jesus. Guard the good deposit that was entrusted to you—guard it with the help of the Holy Spirit who lives in us.

You know that everyone in the province of Asia has deserted me, including Phygelus and Hermogenes.

May the Lord show mercy to the household of Onesiphorus, because he often refreshed me and was not ashamed of my chains. On the contrary, when he was in Rome, he searched hard for me until he found me. May the Lord grant that he will find mercy from the Lord on that day! You know very well in how many ways he helped me in Ephesus.

Paul, now imprisoned for the second time in Rome, has little time left on earth. He writes to Timothy, reassuring him of the hope and conviction that yet fill him: "I know whom I have believed, and am convinced that he is able to guard what I have entrusted to him for that day" (1:12). Paul is able to look ahead with such confidence because of his bedrock belief in the God who has walked with him and shown himself real in so many ways.

Despite the beatings, stonings, imprisonments, shipwrecks, and times without food, water, or clothing, Paul knows he can trust God. Something wonderful awaits him, and his present suffering will be redeemed and will one day seem as nothing. Paul knows God and the love of Jesus, through the Holy Spirit. This relationship gives him strength no matter what he experiences.   —BQ

DAILY CONTEMPLATION

How does your relationship with God affect how you handle suffering?

DAY 339   2 Timothy 2:1–26

A WORKMAN APPROVED BY GOD

You then, my son, be strong in the grace that is in Christ Jesus. And the things you have heard me say in the presence of many witnesses entrust to reliable men who will also be qualified to teach others. Endure hardship with us like a good soldier of Christ Jesus. No one serving as a soldier gets involved in civilian affairs—he wants to please his commanding officer. Similarly, if anyone competes as an athlete, he does not receive the victor's crown unless he competes according to the rules. The hardworking farmer should be the first to receive a share of the crops. Reflect on what I am saying, for the Lord will give you insight into all this.

Remember Jesus Christ, raised from the dead, descended from David. This is my gospel, for which I am suffering even to the point of being chained like a criminal. But God's word is not chained. Therefore I endure everything for the sake of the elect, that they too may obtain the salvation that is in Christ Jesus, with eternal glory.

Here is a trustworthy saying:

If we died with him,
   we will also live with him;
if we endure,
   we will also reign with him.
If we disown him,
   he will also disown us;
if we are faithless,
   he will remain faithful,
   for he cannot disown himself.

Keep reminding them of these things. Warn them before God against quarreling about words; it is of no value, and only ruins those who listen. Do your best to present yourself to God as one approved, a workman who does not need to be ashamed and who correctly handles the word of truth. Avoid godless chatter, because those who indulge in it will become more and more ungodly. Their teaching will spread like gangrene. Among them are Hymenaeus and Philetus, who have wandered away from the truth. They say that the resurrection has already taken place, and they destroy the faith of some. Nevertheless, God's solid foundation stands firm, sealed with this inscription: "The Lord knows those who are his," and, "Everyone who confesses the name of the Lord must turn away from wickedness."

In a large house there are articles not only of gold and silver, but also of wood and clay; some are for noble purposes and some for ignoble. If a man cleanses himself from the latter, he will be an instrument for noble purposes, made holy, useful to the Master and prepared to do any good work.

Flee the evil desires of youth, and pursue righteousness, faith, love and peace, along with those who call on the Lord out of a pure heart. Don't have anything to do with foolish and stupid arguments, because you know they produce quarrels. And the Lord's servant must not quarrel; instead, he must be kind to everyone, able to teach, not resentful. Those who oppose him he must gently instruct, in the hope that God will grant them repentance leading them to a knowledge of the truth, and that they will come to their senses and escape from the trap of the devil, who has taken them captive to do his will.

I am suffering even to the point of being chained like a criminal. But God's word is not chained." These words from Paul to Timothy sum up both Paul's personal plight and his burning desire to see his life's work continue after his death.

The second letter to Timothy contains many clues about Paul's circumstances. This time the treatment seems far harsher than the previous house arrest in Rome. Now he is being kept in chains, in a cold dungeon that his friends can barely locate. Paul's spirits are sagging. He feels abandoned by "everyone in the province of Asia" (1:15).

This letter almost certainly dates from the time of Emperor Nero, around A.D. 66–67. By now Christianity has grown from a splinter sect of Judaism into a major force with many thousands of converts, and Nero seizes upon it as a scapegoat for the ills of the empire. He burns Rome to the ground and promptly blames the Christians for the fire. Soon the crazed emperor is torturing believers by crucifying them, by wrapping them in animal skins and turning his hunting dogs loose on them, and by burning them alive as human torches to illuminate the games in his garden.

Little wonder that Paul, imprisoned during this era, exhorts Timothy on the need for boldness in the face of suffering. Paul's own life is nearing an end, and he writes these, his last recorded words, as a legacy to pass on to Timothy and other "reliable men who will also be qualified to teach others."

Second Timothy is a moody book. Sometimes Paul makes himself vulnerable, exposing his fears and his loneliness. Other times, as in this chapter, he gives a rousing "pep talk" meant to cheer Timothy's spirits—and perhaps his own. Life is closing in on the apostle, and he strings together last-minute reminders: advice on pure living, essential nuggets of theology, inspiring analogies, one-line proverbs, warnings, common sayings. There is no particular order to this book; Paul has no time for that. He is setting down a kind of spiritual "last will and testament" for his son in Christ.

Tradition teaches that in the end Rome executed Paul for his faith. But thanks to his life and the legacy he passed on to converts like Timothy, the world changed forever. —PY

DAILY CONTEMPLATION

What issues would concern you if you were facing death?

DAY 340

Reflection

CHOOSING TO RUN OR REMAIN

How do we live in the midst of people who don't know Jesus, who aren't following God's Word?

I used to reason that in most cases I should stick with people who were taking part in behavior I didn't condone as a Christian. Better to stay and be a light, a person living God's way in their midst, than to leave and perhaps create the impression that I thought myself too good for them. If I gave in to sin or somehow suffered, the fault was mine, I felt. I had not relied enough on God's strength.

I've since come to know and better understand Paul's admonitions to Timothy. Paul wrote, "Flee the evil desires of youth, and pursue righteousness, faith, love and peace, along with those who call on the Lord out of a pure heart" (2 Timothy 2:22). Paul didn't counsel Timothy to stick it out and remain strong in the midst of sin. He told him to run the other way.

Probably in his mid-thirties at the time, Timothy had likely come to Christ after meeting Paul and still knew well the "evil desires of youth," or "youthful passions," as another translation words it (NRSV). Paul taught Timothy and us that in some cases, believers should remove themselves from risky situations. Sometimes God clearly prefers us to surround ourselves with others "who call on the Lord."

C. S. Lewis helps explain. "What makes [the] contact with wicked people so difficult is that to handle the situation successfully requires not merely good intentions, even with humility and courage thrown in; it may call for social and even intellectual talents which God has not given us. It is therefore not self-righteousness but mere prudence to avoid it when we can."[63]

Lewis and Paul understood that believers are still human. We have God's Spirit and his power, yet we fail at times. God asks that when obvious temptations loom, we flee rather than expose ourselves to what we may not be able to handle.

We need a balance, of course. Jesus modeled that balance for us, spending time with the most common of sinners. Even Paul explains to Timothy that with those who oppose him, Timothy must "gently instruct, in the hope that God will grant them repentance leading them to a knowledge of the truth, and that they will come to their senses" (2 Timothy 2:25–26).

Like Timothy, we can expect to associate often with people who live or believe differently than we do. God asks us to be faithful and kind, to avoid quarrels yet be honest (2 Timothy 2:24). Sometimes we need to flee, and sometimes we must remain to gently but firmly tell another about God's standards. With God's help, we must decide which action to take in each situation. First and foremost we seek to preserve our faithfulness to God. Then, when God gives us strength and boldness, we can enter the lives of those who need help following him.   —BQ

DAILY CONTEMPLATION

In what situations are you likely to be pulled away from God? Are you able to flee when faced with such situations? Where in your life is God asking you to stay and, in kindness and gentleness, speak the truth? Ask God to give you wisdom in knowing when to run and when to remain.

PART 12

VITAL LETTERS

Hebrews 2:1–3:6

THE SON SUPERIOR TO ANGELS;

JESUS MADE LIKE HIS BROTHERS

We must pay more careful attention, therefore, to what we have heard, so that we do not drift away. For if the message spoken by angels was binding, and every violation and disobedience received its just punishment, how shall we escape if we ignore such a great salvation? This salvation, which was first announced by the Lord, was confirmed to us by those who heard him. God also testified to it by signs, wonders and various miracles, and gifts of the Holy Spirit distributed according to his will.

It is not to angels that he has subjected the world to come, about which we are speaking. But there is a place where someone has testified:

"What is man that you are mindful of him,
    the son of man that you care for him?
You made him a little lower than the angels;
    you crowned him with glory and honor
    and put everything under his feet."

In putting everything under him, God left nothing that is not subject to him. Yet at present we do not see everything subject to him. But we see Jesus, who was made a little lower than the angels, now crowned with glory and honor because he suffered death, so that by the grace of God he might taste death for everyone.

In bringing many sons to glory, it was fitting that God, for whom and through whom everything exists, should make the author of their salvation perfect through suffering. Both the one who makes men holy and those who are made holy are of the same family. So Jesus is not ashamed to call them brothers. He says,

"I will declare your name to my brothers;
  in the presence of the congregation I will sing your praises."

And again,

"I will put my trust in him."

And again he says,

"Here am I, and the children God has given me."

Since the children have flesh and blood, he too shared in their humanity so that by his death he might destroy him who holds the power of death—that is, the devil—and free those who all their lives were held in slavery by their fear of death. For surely it is not angels he helps, but Abraham's descendants. For this reason he had to be made like his brothers in every way, in order that he might become a merciful and faithful high priest in service to God, and that he might make atonement for the sins of the people. Because he himself suffered when he was tempted, he is able to help those who are being tempted.

Therefore, holy brothers, who share in the heavenly calling, fix your thoughts on Jesus, the apostle and high priest whom we confess. He was faithful to the one who appointed him, just as Moses was faithful in all God's house. Jesus has been found worthy of greater honor than Moses, just as the builder of a house has greater honor than the house itself. For every house is built by someone, but God is the builder of everything. Moses was faithful as a servant in all God's house, testifying to what would be said in the future. But Christ is faithful as a son over God's house. And we are his house, if we hold on to our courage and the hope of which we boast.

Are religions all that different?" skeptics ask. "Isn't the most important thing to be sincere in whatever you believe?" Such "modern" questions have in fact been debated for thousands of years. The book of Hebrews is written in response to people of the early church torn between the Jewish religion and the new faith of Christianity.

Some favor sticking with the familiar routine of Judaism, which has centuries-old traditions behind it. Another advantage: The Jews of the day enjoy Rome's official protection, while Christians are subject to persecution. Is faith in Christ worth the risk?

Hebrews insists there are decisive reasons to choose Christ. The whole book revolves around the word *better*. Jesus is better than the angels or Moses or the Old Testament way—better than anything the world has to offer.

Even so, after recording a gust of grand theology from the Psalms, the author of Hebrews (whose identity we don't know) seems to pause and reconsider. "At present we do not see everything subject to him." Could a world in which Christians are being arrested, tortured, and tossed into jail really be subject to Christ?

From there, the author explains why it matters that God descended to the world and became a human being. He did not magically remove all human problems but rather *subjected himself* to the same hardships that any of us face. Hebrews goes further than any other New Testament book in explaining Jesus' human nature.

This chapter gives two powerful reasons why Jesus came to earth. First, by dying, he freed us from the power of death and won for us eternal life. And second, by experiencing normal human temptations, he can better help us with our own temptations.

No angel, and no God in distant heaven, could have accomplished those things. Jesus came, in effect, on a rescue mission, to free humanity from slavery. Apart from Christ, we live in constant fear of death and in constant bondage to our failures, or sins. Only Jesus can set us free. That's why he's worth the risk.   —PY

DAILY CONTEMPLATION

From what fears or bondage has Jesus set you free?

DAY 342   Hebrews 10:5–10, 19–39

A CALL TO PERSEVERE

When Christ came into the world, he said:

"Sacrifice and offering you did not desire,
    but a body you prepared for me;
with burnt offerings and sin offerings
    you were not pleased.
Then I said, 'Here I am—it is written about me in the scroll—
    I have come to do your will, O God.'"

First he said, "Sacrifices and offerings, burnt offerings and sin offerings you did not desire, nor were you pleased with them" (although the law required them to be made). Then he said, "Here I am, I have come to do your will." He sets aside the first to establish the second. And by that will, we have been made holy through the sacrifice of the body of Jesus Christ once for all. . . .

Therefore, brothers, since we have confidence to enter the Most Holy Place by the blood of Jesus, by a new and living way opened for us through the curtain, that is, his body, and since we have a great priest over the house of God, let us draw near to God with a sincere heart in full assurance of faith, having our hearts sprinkled to cleanse us from a guilty conscience and having our bodies washed with pure water. Let us hold unswervingly to the hope we profess,

643

for he who promised is faithful. And let us consider how we may spur one another on toward love and good deeds. Let us not give up meeting together, as some are in the habit of doing, but let us encourage one another—and all the more as you see the Day approaching.

If we deliberately keep on sinning after we have received the knowledge of the truth, no sacrifice for sins is left, but only a fearful expectation of judgment and of raging fire that will consume the enemies of God. Anyone who rejected the law of Moses died without mercy on the testimony of two or three witnesses. How much more severely do you think a man deserves to be punished who has trampled the Son of God under foot, who has treated as an unholy thing the blood of the covenant that sanctified him, and who has insulted the Spirit of grace? For we know him who said, "It is mine to avenge; I will repay," and again, "The Lord will judge his people." It is a dreadful thing to fall into the hands of the living God.

Remember those earlier days after you had received the light, when you stood your ground in a great contest in the face of suffering. Sometimes you were publicly exposed to insult and persecution; at other times you stood side by side with those who were so treated. You sympathized with those in prison and joyfully accepted the confiscation of your property, because you knew that you yourselves had better and lasting possessions.

So do not throw away your confidence; it will be richly rewarded. You need to persevere so that when you have done the will of God, you will receive what he has promised. For in just a very little while,

"He who is coming will come and will not delay.
    But my righteous one will live by faith.
And if he shrinks back,
    I will not be pleased with him."

But we are not of those who shrink back and are destroyed, but of those who believe and are saved.

The author of Hebrews reminds believers that because of what Jesus has done for us, we can approach God with confidence. We have no need to feel afraid, unworthy, or unloved. We can come to God freely, without a guilty conscience, because of the forgiveness we've accepted. As we draw near to God, we can hold tightly to the hope he gives us in the Bible. God means for us to count on his promises.

The writer also encourages believers to keep gathering together, even in difficult, dangerous times. We need each other. God never intended his people to walk alone with him. He wants us to find support and encouragement in each other.

Finally, the writer answers the question of why a loving God would punish those who aren't committed to him. God gave his entire self, through Jesus, for all people. If some do not accept his gift, they are choosing to remain separate from God. If they do not respond to the Spirit of grace, they thus cut themselves off from God. Those following Jesus, however, have every reason for confidence. God is faithful, and no matter how things look in difficult times, his promises will come true.   —BQ

DAY 343   Hebrews 11:1–40

BY FAITH

Now faith is being sure of what we hope for and certain of what we do not see. This is what the ancients were commended for.

By faith we understand that the universe was formed at God's command, so that what is seen was not made out of what was visible.

By faith Abel offered God a better sacrifice than Cain did. By faith he was commended as a righteous man, when God spoke well of his offerings. And by faith he still speaks, even though he is dead.

By faith Enoch was taken from this life, so that he did not experience death; he could not be found, because God had taken him away. For before he was taken, he was commended as one who pleased God. And without faith it is impossible to please God, because anyone who comes to him must believe that he exists and that he rewards those who earnestly seek him.

By faith Noah, when warned about things not yet seen, in holy fear built an ark to save his family. By his faith he condemned the world and became heir of the righteousness that comes by faith.

By faith Abraham, when called to go to a place he would later receive as his inheritance, obeyed and went, even though he did not know where he was going. By faith he made his home in the promised land like a stranger in a foreign country; he lived in tents, as did Isaac and Jacob, who were heirs with him of the same promise. For he was looking forward to the city with foundations, whose architect and builder is God.

By faith Abraham, even though he was past age—and Sarah herself was barren—was enabled to become a father because he considered him faithful who had made the promise. And so from this one man, and he as good as dead, came descendants as numerous as the stars in the sky and as countless as the sand on the seashore.

All these people were still living by faith when they died. They did not receive the things promised; they only saw them and welcomed them from a distance. And they admitted that they were aliens and strangers on earth. People who say such things show that they are looking for a country of their own. If they had been thinking of the country they had left, they would have had opportunity to return. Instead, they were longing for a better country—a heavenly one. Therefore God is not ashamed to be called their God, for he has prepared a city for them.

By faith Abraham, when God tested him, offered Isaac as a sacrifice. He who had received the promises was about to sacrifice his one and only son, even though God had said to him, "It is through Isaac that your offspring will be reckoned." Abraham reasoned that God could raise the dead, and figuratively speaking, he did receive Isaac back from death.

By faith Isaac blessed Jacob and Esau in regard to their future.

By faith Jacob, when he was dying, blessed each of Joseph's sons, and worshiped as he leaned on the top of his staff.

By faith Joseph, when his end was near, spoke about the exodus of the Israelites from Egypt and gave instructions about his bones.

By faith Moses' parents hid him for three months after he was born, because they saw he was no ordinary child, and they were not afraid of the king's edict.

By faith Moses, when he had grown up, refused to be known as the son of Pharaoh's daughter. He chose to be mistreated along with the people of God rather than to enjoy the pleasures of sin for a short time. He regarded disgrace for the sake of Christ as of greater value than the treasures of Egypt, because he was looking ahead to his reward. By faith he left Egypt, not fearing the king's anger; he persevered because he saw him who is invisible. By faith he kept the Passover and the sprinkling of blood, so that the destroyer of the firstborn would not touch the firstborn of Israel.

By faith the people passed through the Red Sea as on dry land; but when the Egyptians tried to do so, they were drowned.

By faith the walls of Jericho fell, after the people had marched around them for seven days.

By faith the prostitute Rahab, because she welcomed the spies, was not killed with those who were disobedient.

And what more shall I say? I do not have time to tell about Gideon, Barak, Samson, Jephthah, David, Samuel and the prophets, who through faith conquered kingdoms, administered justice, and gained what was promised; who shut the mouths of lions, quenched the fury of the flames, and escaped the edge of the sword; whose weakness was turned to strength; and who became powerful in battle and routed foreign armies. Women received back their dead, raised to life again. Others were tortured and refused to be released, so that they might gain a better resurrection. Some faced jeers and flogging, while still others were chained and put in prison. They were stoned; they were sawed in two; they were put to death by the sword. They went about in sheepskins and goatskins, destitute, persecuted and mistreated—the world was not worthy of them. They wandered in deserts and mountains, and in caves and holes in the ground.

These were all commended for their faith, yet none of them received what had been promised. God had planned something better for us so that only together with us would they be made perfect.

The last few paragraphs of chapter 10 reveal much about the original readers of Hebrews. Converting to Christ has brought them abuse: confiscation of property, public insult, and even imprisonment. In the early days they accepted such persecution gladly, even joyfully. But as time has gone on, and the trials continue, some are beginning to lose heart.

To these discouraged people, Hebrews 11 presents a stirring reminder of what constitutes "true faith." It's tempting to think of faith as a kind of magic formula: if you muster up enough of it, you'll get rich, stay healthy, and live a contented life, with automatic answers to all your prayers. But the readers of Hebrews are discovering that life does not work according to such neat formulas. As proof, the author painstakingly reviews the lives of some Old Testament giants of faith. (Some have dubbed Hebrews 11 the "Faith Hall of Fame.")

"Without faith," Hebrews says bluntly, "it is impossible to please God." But the author uses rather pointed words in describing that faith: "persevere," "endure," "don't lose heart." As a result of their faith, some heroes triumphed: they routed armies, escaped the sword, survived lions. But others met less happy ends: they were flogged, chained, stoned, sawed in two. The chapter concludes, "These were all commended for their faith, yet none of them received what had been promised."

The picture of faith that emerges from this chapter does not fit into an easy formula. Sometimes faith leads to victory and triumph. Sometimes it requires a gritty determination to "hang on at any cost." Hebrews 11 does not hold up one kind of faith as superior to the other. Both rest on the belief that God is in ultimate control and will indeed keep his promises—whether that happens in this life or in the next. Of such people, Hebrews says, "God is not ashamed to be called their God, for he has prepared a city for them."
—PY

DAILY CONTEMPLATION

As a believer, do you more closely identify with the victorious heroes of faith or with those who hung on at any cost?

DAY 344
Hebrews 12:1–28

GOD DISCIPLINES HIS SONS

Therefore, since we are surrounded by such a great cloud of witnesses, let us throw off everything that hinders and the sin that so easily entangles, and let us run with perseverance the race marked out for us. Let us fix our eyes on Jesus, the author and perfecter of our faith, who for the joy set before him endured the cross, scorning its shame, and sat down at the right hand of the throne of God. Consider him who endured such opposition from sinful men, so that you will not grow weary and lose heart.

In your struggle against sin, you have not yet resisted to the point of shedding your blood. And you have forgotten that word of encouragement that addresses you as sons:

"My son, do not make light of the Lord's discipline,
   and do not lose heart when he rebukes you,
because the Lord disciplines those he loves,
   and he punishes everyone he accepts as a son."

Endure hardship as discipline; God is treating you as sons. For what son is not disciplined by his father? If you are not disciplined (and everyone undergoes discipline), then you are illegitimate children and not true sons. Moreover, we have all had human fathers who disciplined us and we respected them for it. How much more should we submit to the Father of our spirits and live! Our fathers disciplined us for a little while as they thought best; but God disciplines us for our good, that we may share in his holiness. No discipline seems pleasant at the time, but painful. Later on, however, it produces a harvest of righteousness and peace for those who have been trained by it.

Therefore, strengthen your feeble arms and weak knees. "Make level paths for your feet," so that the lame may not be disabled, but rather healed.

Make every effort to live in peace with all men and to be holy; without holiness no one will see the Lord. See to it that no one misses the grace of God and that no bitter root grows up to cause trouble and defile many. See that no one is sexually immoral, or is godless like Esau, who for a single meal sold his inheritance rights as the oldest son. Afterward, as you know, when he wanted to inherit this blessing, he was rejected. He could bring about no change of mind, though he sought the blessing with tears.

You have not come to a mountain that can be touched and that is burning with fire; to darkness, gloom and storm; to a trumpet blast or to such a voice speaking words that those who heard it begged that no further word be spoken to them, because they could not bear what was commanded: "If even an animal touches the mountain, it must be stoned." The sight was so terrifying that Moses said, "I am trembling with fear."

But you have come to Mount Zion, to the heavenly Jerusalem, the city of the living God. You have come to thousands upon thousands of angels in joyful assembly, to the church of the firstborn, whose names are written in heaven. You have come to God, the judge of all men, to the spirits of righteous men made perfect, to Jesus the mediator of a new covenant, and to the sprinkled blood that speaks a better word than the blood of Abel.

See to it that you do not refuse him who speaks. If they did not escape when they refused him who warned them on earth, how much less will we, if we turn away from him who warns us from heaven? At that time his voice shook the earth, but now he has promised, "Once more I will shake not only the earth but also the heavens." The words "once more" indicate the removing of what can be shaken—that is, created things—so that what cannot be shaken may remain.

Therefore, since we are receiving a kingdom that cannot be shaken, let us be thankful, and so worship God acceptably with reverence and awe.

Hebrews 12 takes up right where the previous chapter left off, only the author moves the spotlight from Old Testament history to the readers themselves. He likens faith to an athletic contest in a stadium. Those who have gone before—the giants of faith from chapter 11—are like "a great cloud of witnesses" watching the rest of us run the race of faith. Therefore, "throw off everything that hinders," Hebrews coaches, and again, "strengthen your feeble arms and weak knees."

Evidently, the original readers of Hebrews have expected a short sprint, not a grueling marathon run. They need extra encouragement and discipline to survive a long-distance spiritual contest.

The analogy of a marathon race provides a convenient way to think about the Christian life. Why do people punish their bodies through a twenty-six-mile course? Most runners mention a sense of personal accomplishment, combined with the physical benefits of exercise. There are parallel benefits in a "spiritual marathon." Applying the discipline needed to resist temptation and to endure hardship leads to certain good results: namely, strong character and a clean conscience. Not to mention the eternal rewards that await all who finish the race.

True competitors set their sights on the lead runner, and, as might be expected, Hebrews holds up Jesus as the ultimate standard for our faith. He endured the terrible suffering of the cross for the sake of "the joy set before him." Because of Jesus, no one can complain, "God doesn't know what it's like down here." He does know, for he too has been here. And for anyone tempted to grow weary and lose heart, the very best cure is to "fix our eyes on Jesus, the author and perfecter of our faith."

The chapter ends with a soaring passage that celebrates how much better is Christ's new covenant than the old one between God and the Israelites. The new covenant will culminate in a new creation and a new kingdom—one that can never be shaken.   —PY

DAILY CONTEMPLATION

If maturing spiritually is like a marathon race, how far along are you?

DAY 345   Reflection

THE RADICAL SIDE OF FAITH

The book of Hebrews devotes a whole chapter to faith, first giving a memorable definition—"Faith is being sure of what we hope for and certain of what we do not see" (11:1)—and then detailing the many ways in which people of the Old Testament demonstrated their faith.

Some, such as Abel, exhibited faith through a simple love for God, giving him a gift that came from the heart. Others took more extreme measures, such as Isaac, Jacob, and Joseph, who believed God's promises about the future even as death seemed certain. Abraham and Moses left their homes to move to a foreign land. Noah built an ark, Abraham offered his son on an altar to God, and others accepted prison, torture, and death. This group sacrificed themselves and their plans to let God have his way. Only radical faith could have enabled these people to make the choices they did.

Former seminary president and writer Vernon Grounds tells the modern-day stories of three people who had such faith. Mildred Cable grew up in Great Britain and believed God had called her to a ministry in China. Before going, she fell in love with another believer and the two desired to marry. He, however, felt a strong call to remain in ministry in England. After much prayer and many tears, the two parted, convinced of God's will for them to carry on with separate purposes. Mildred went on to establish a long and fruitful ministry in China.

George Müller, a poor man with a rich love for God, cared for more than ten thousand orphans in England by building five orphanages. He established Sunday schools worldwide, published two million Bibles and Scripture resources and three million books and tracts, and liberally supported missionaries in many countries. His faith enabled him to do, humanly speaking, the impossible.

Frank Laubach, in his early ministry, worked in the Philippines with people he literally despised. He felt unhappy and unproductive. One afternoon he sat alone on a hill and wept, wishing to die rather than continue with life as he knew it. Instead, his attitudes died, along with his self-pity and pride. He became a different man and went on to serve Jesus in a global ministry that helped millions learn to read God's Word in their own language.[64]

Mildred Cable, George Müller, and Frank Laubach died to themselves. They died to their desires and their human limitations. In exchange they took on Christ's life and, in believing what they could not see, gave God the chance to accomplish much both seen and unseen. Müller explained, "There was a day when I died, utterly died, to George Müller, his opinions, preferences, tastes, and will—died to the world, its approval or censure; died to the approval or blame even of my brethren and friends—and since then I have studied only to show myself approved to God."[65]

We are now surrounded by this cloud of witnesses—Cable, Müller, Laubach, Noah, Abraham, and countless others who gave their lives in radical faith. And we pray that we too may have the courage and abandon to take the steps of faith God asks of us, to give him ourselves. —BQ

DAILY CONTEMPLATION

Do you desire to live out a radical faith in God if he asks you to? How do you feel about giving up your plans for God's plans? Pray about this, asking God to continue developing in you a greater longing for his way for you.

TRIALS AND TEMPTATIONS;

LISTENING AND DOING; FAVORITISM FORBIDDEN

James, a servant of God and of the Lord Jesus Christ,

To the twelve tribes scattered among the nations:

Greetings.

Consider it pure joy, my brothers, whenever you face trials of many kinds, because you know that the testing of your faith develops perseverance. Perseverance must finish its work so that you may be mature and complete, not lacking anything. If any of you lacks wisdom, he should ask God, who gives generously to all without finding fault, and it will be given to him. But when he asks, he must believe and not doubt, because he who doubts is like a wave of the sea, blown and tossed by the wind. That man should not think he will receive anything from the Lord; he is a double-minded man, unstable in all he does.

The brother in humble circumstances ought to take pride in his high position. But the one who is rich should take pride in his low position, because he will pass away like a wild flower. For the sun rises with scorching heat and withers the plant; its blossom falls and its beauty is destroyed. In the same way, the rich man will fade away even while he goes about his business.

Blessed is the man who perseveres under trial, because when he has stood the test, he will receive the crown of life that God has promised to those who love him.

When tempted, no one should say, "God is tempting me." For God cannot be tempted by evil, nor does he tempt anyone; but each one is tempted when, by his own evil desire, he is dragged away and enticed. Then, after desire has conceived, it gives birth to sin; and sin, when it is full-grown, gives birth to death.

Don't be deceived, my dear brothers. Every good and perfect gift is from above, coming down from the Father of the heavenly lights, who does not change like shifting shadows. He chose to give us birth through the word of truth, that we might be a kind of firstfruits of all he created.

My dear brothers, take note of this: Everyone should be quick to listen, slow to speak and slow to become angry, for man's anger does not bring about the righteous life that God desires. Therefore, get rid of all moral filth and the evil that is so prevalent and humbly accept the word planted in you, which can save you.

Do not merely listen to the word, and so deceive yourselves. Do what it says. Anyone who listens to the word but does not do what it says is like a man who looks at his face in a mirror and, after looking at himself, goes away and immediately forgets what he looks like. But the man who looks intently into the perfect law that gives freedom, and continues to do this, not forgetting what he has heard, but doing it—he will be blessed in what he does.

If anyone considers himself religious and yet does not keep a tight rein on his tongue, he deceives himself and his religion is worthless. Religion that God our Father accepts as pure and faultless is this: to look after orphans and widows in their distress and to keep oneself from being polluted by the world.

My brothers, as believers in our glorious Lord Jesus Christ, don't show favoritism. Suppose a man comes into your meeting wearing a gold ring and fine clothes, and a poor man in shabby clothes also comes in. If you show special attention to the man wearing fine clothes and say, "Here's a good seat for you," but say to the poor man, "You stand there" or "Sit on the floor by my feet," have you not discriminated among yourselves and become judges with evil thoughts?

Listen, my dear brothers: Has not God chosen those who are poor in the eyes of the world to be rich in faith and to inherit the kingdom he promised those who love him? But you have insulted the poor. Is it not the rich who are exploiting you? Are they not the ones who are dragging you into court? Are they not the ones who are slandering the noble name of him to whom you belong?

If you really keep the royal law found in Scripture, "Love your neighbor as yourself," you are doing right. But if you show favoritism, you sin and are convicted by the law as lawbreakers. For whoever keeps the whole law and yet stumbles at just one point is guilty of breaking all of it.

You get a sense of James's style in the first two sentences of his letter. After the sparsest greeting, he dives directly into the topic at hand and starts dishing out advice. James lacks the education and sophistication of the apostle Paul; you won't find his letter wandering off into abstract theology. He is a simple man, a man of the soil. He draws analogies from nature—ocean waves, wilted flowers, a forest fire, spring rains—and expresses his thoughts in pithy sayings almost like proverbs.

Since James's church in Jerusalem is attracting persecution in his day, his letter understandably begins with encouragement for people undergoing trials. But it quickly moves on to a variety of topics, in each case exhorting readers to live out their beliefs. *Be humble!* James orders. *Control your tongue! Stop sinning!* James is as forthright as an Old Testament prophet. His point is hard to miss.

One verse in the first chapter neatly summarizes the pervasive message of this book: "Do not merely listen to the word, and so deceive yourselves. Do what it says." James offers up a very pointed illustration of exactly the kind of hypocrisy he is talking about: church members who defer to the wealthy and powerful. The message hits close to home and leaves no room for ambiguity.

The illustration of preferential treatment seems as relevant today as when James first wrote it nineteen hundred years ago. Modern readers face the same dilemma as the first recipients of this unsettling letter. His words are easy enough to understand, but are we doing what he says? —PY

DAILY CONTEMPLATION

To whom do you tend to show favoritism? The rich? People of your race? Those who are like you? Whom do you tend to look down upon?

FAITH AND DEEDS; TAMING THE TONGUE;

TWO KINDS OF WISDOM

What good is it, my brothers, if a man claims to have faith but has no deeds? Can such faith save him? Suppose a brother or sister is without clothes and daily food. If one of you says to him, "Go, I wish you well; keep warm and well fed," but does nothing about his physical needs, what good is it? In the same way, faith by itself, if it is not accompanied by action, is dead.

But someone will say, "You have faith; I have deeds."

Show me your faith without deeds, and I will show you my faith by what I do. You believe that there is one God. Good! Even the demons believe that— and shudder.

You foolish man, do you want evidence that faith without deeds is useless? Was not our ancestor Abraham considered righteous for what he did when he offered his son Isaac on the altar? You see that his faith and his actions were working together, and his faith was made complete by what he did. And the scripture was fulfilled that says, "Abraham believed God, and it was credited to him as righteousness," and he was called God's friend. You see that a person is justified by what he does and not by faith alone.

In the same way, was not even Rahab the prostitute considered righteous for what she did when she gave lodging to the spies and sent them off in a different direction? As the body without the spirit is dead, so faith without deeds is dead.

Not many of you should presume to be teachers, my brothers, because you know that we who teach will be judged more strictly. We all stumble in many ways. If anyone is never at fault in what he says, he is a perfect man, able to keep his whole body in check.

When we put bits into the mouths of horses to make them obey us, we can turn the whole animal. Or take ships as an example. Although they are so large and are driven by strong winds, they are steered by a very small rudder wherever the pilot wants to go. Likewise the tongue is a small part of the body, but it makes great boasts. Consider what a great forest is set on fire by a small spark. The tongue also is a fire, a world of evil among the parts of the body. It corrupts the whole person, sets the whole course of his life on fire, and is itself set on fire by hell.

All kinds of animals, birds, reptiles and creatures of the sea are being tamed and have been tamed by man, but no man can tame the tongue. It is a restless evil, full of deadly poison.

With the tongue we praise our Lord and Father, and with it we curse men, who have been made in God's likeness. Out of the same mouth come praise and cursing. My brothers, this should not be. Can both fresh water and salt water flow from the same spring? My brothers, can a fig tree bear olives, or a grapevine bear figs? Neither can a salt spring produce fresh water.

Who is wise and understanding among you? Let him show it by his good life, by deeds done in the humility that comes from wisdom. But if you harbor bitter envy and selfish ambition in your hearts, do not boast about it or deny the truth. Such "wisdom" does not come down from heaven but is earthly, unspiritual, of the devil. For where you have envy and selfish ambition, there you find disorder and every evil practice.

But the wisdom that comes from heaven is first of all pure; then peace-loving, considerate, submissive, full of mercy and good fruit, impartial and sincere. Peacemakers who sow in peace raise a harvest of righteousness.

James, the author of this letter, was probably one of Jesus' brothers—the oldest and a prominent leader in the early church. He teaches, as Jesus did, that how we live reveals the sincerity of our faith. Certainly good works do not bring us salvation, but if our salvation has not changed who we are and how we live, we might question whether we've really given our life to Christ. "Faith without deeds is dead," writes James.

One great danger we face in living an authentic faith involves one of the smallest parts of the body—the tongue. It is "a restless evil, full of deadly poison," capable of causing great harm and damage. However, the tongue can also be a source of healing and life. Believers face an ongoing challenge to control their tongues by speaking wisely. Words, both spoken and unspoken, matter.

May God's Spirit prompt and enable us to speak the words that give life and leave unspoken the words that destroy. —BQ

DAILY CONTEMPLATION

When have you most recently spoken life-giving words? When have you lost control and spoken destructive words?

DAY 348
James 4:1–17

SUBMIT YOURSELVES TO GOD

What causes fights and quarrels among you? Don't they come from your desires that battle within you? You want something but don't get it. You kill and covet, but you cannot have what you want. You quarrel and fight. You do not have, because you do not ask God. When you ask, you do not receive, because you ask with wrong motives, that you may spend what you get on your pleasures.

You adulterous people, don't you know that friendship with the world is hatred toward God? Anyone who chooses to be a friend of the world becomes an enemy of God. Or do you think Scripture says without reason that the spirit he caused to live in us envies intensely? But he gives us more grace. That is why Scripture says:

"God opposes the proud
but gives grace to the humble."

Submit yourselves, then, to God. Resist the devil, and he will flee from you. Come near to God and he will come near to you. Wash your hands, you sinners, and purify your hearts, you double-minded. Grieve, mourn and wail. Change your laughter to mourning and your joy to gloom. Humble yourselves before the Lord, and he will lift you up.

Brothers, do not slander one another. Anyone who speaks against his brother or judges him speaks against the law and judges it. When you judge the law, you are not keeping it, but sitting in judgment on it. There is only one Lawgiver and Judge, the one who is able to save and destroy. But you—who are you to judge your neighbor?

Now listen, you who say, "Today or tomorrow we will go to this or that city, spend a year there, carry on business and make money." Why, you do not even know what will happen tomorrow. What is your life? You are a mist that appears for a little while and then vanishes. Instead, you ought to say, "If it is the Lord's will, we will live and do this or that." As it is, you boast and brag. All such boasting is evil. Anyone, then, who knows the good he ought to do and doesn't do it, sins.

A relationship with God, like any relationship, works in two ways. The Bible assures us of God's love, reminds us of his forgiveness, and pictures his grace. We have no reason to doubt that God longs to be in relationship with us. The book of James turns the focus back on believers, reminding that there is a right way and a wrong way to treat God. Just as in any friendship, business partnership, or marriage, relationship with God requires that we act in specific ways to make it work.

James sternly reminds us in this passage that God needs our total commitment. New or stagnant believers may be tempted to try to keep one foot in the world and the other foot in the path of God. Yet we can't have life both ways. James compares this attempt to unfaithfulness in marriage—we are adulterers toward God when we cheat on the covenant we've made with him.

All believers find themselves drawn back into the world at times, pulled by material things, desires for sex or prestige, tendencies to live with self-centered priorities. All of us, then, need to live with an attitude of continual submission and humility toward God. No one is so spiritual as to never slip back into the world. No one is so mature as to no longer need fresh cleansing from God.   —BQ

DAILY CONTEMPLATION

For what reasons do you need to come near to God today and receive cleansing?

WARNING TO RICH OPPRESSORS;

PATIENCE IN SUFFERING; THE PRAYER OF FAITH

Now listen, you rich people, weep and wail because of the misery that is coming upon you. Your wealth has rotted, and moths have eaten your clothes. Your gold and silver are corroded. Their corrosion will testify against you and eat your flesh like fire. You have hoarded wealth in the last days. Look! The wages you failed to pay the workmen who mowed your fields are crying out against you. The cries of the harvesters have reached the ears of the Lord Almighty. You have lived on earth in luxury and self-indulgence. You have fattened yourselves in the day of slaughter. You have condemned and murdered innocent men, who were not opposing you.

Be patient, then, brothers, until the Lord's coming. See how the farmer waits for the land to yield its valuable crop and how patient he is for the autumn and spring rains. You too, be patient and stand firm, because the Lord's coming is near. Don't grumble against each other, brothers, or you will be judged. The Judge is standing at the door!

Brothers, as an example of patience in the face of suffering, take the prophets who spoke in the name of the Lord. As you know, we consider blessed those who have persevered. You have heard of Job's perseverance and have seen what the Lord finally brought about. The Lord is full of compassion and mercy.

Above all, my brothers, do not swear—not by heaven or by earth or by anything else. Let your "Yes" be yes, and your "No," no, or you will be condemned.

Is any one of you in trouble? He should pray. Is anyone happy? Let him sing songs of praise. Is any one of you sick? He should call the elders of the church to pray over him and anoint him with oil in the name of the Lord. And the prayer offered in faith will make the sick person well; the Lord will raise him up. If he has sinned, he will be forgiven. Therefore confess your sins to each other and pray for each other so that you may be healed. The prayer of a righteous man is powerful and effective.

Elijah was a man just like us. He prayed earnestly that it would not rain, and it did not rain on the land for three and a half years. Again he prayed, and the heavens gave rain, and the earth produced its crops.

My brothers, if one of you should wander from the truth and someone should bring him back, remember this: Whoever turns a sinner from the error of his way will save him from death and cover over a multitude of sins.

James finishes his letter with practical reminders about what spiritual maturity looks like in believers. They should not hoard wealth or fail to pay what they owe their workers. Ideally they are patient in suffering, remembering all those in the past who have persevered and seen God bring victory. They should be trustworthy in what they say, following through with a yes or no. And they should pray faithfully about everything—troubles, joys, and sickness. God hears and answers prayer. We must never underestimate the power he unleashes when we pray.

Finally, believers should remember the power they have over one another. James's words offer an important corrective today, in a culture in which social etiquette prescribes for us a hands-off approach to each other's lives. We tend to mind our own business and let others live as they choose. This attitude may be preferable to an environment of judgment and legalism, yet taken to the extreme, it's not fully biblical. In the community of believers, James stresses, we are committed to one another's spiritual lives. By caring enough to confront, we can help turn a brother or sister back to God.   —BQ

DAILY CONTEMPLATION

When have you, in conviction and love, challenged another believer to hold to his or her commitment to God?

DAY 350   Reflection

GRACE AND WORKS

A few years ago I attended a conference at a place called New Harmony, the restored site of a century-old Utopian community. As I ran my fingers over the fine workmanship of the buildings and read the plaques describing the daily lives of the true believers, I marveled at the energy that drove this movement, one of the dozens spawned by American idealism and religious fervor.

Many varieties of perfectionism have grown on American soil: the offshoots of the Second Great Awakening, the Victorious Life movement, the communes of the Jesus movement. It struck me, though, that in recent times the urge to achieve perfection has nearly disappeared. Nowadays we tilt in the opposite direction, toward a kind of anti-Utopianism. The recovery movement, for example, hinges on a person's self-confessed *inability* to be perfect.

I prefer this modern trend. I find it much easier to believe in human fallibility than perfectibility, and I have cast my lot with a gospel based on grace. Yet in New Harmony, Indiana, I felt an unaccountable nostalgia for the Utopians: all those solemn figures in black clothes breaking rocks in the fields, devising ever-stricter rules in an attempt to rein in lust and greed, striving to fulfill the lofty commands of the New Testament. The names they left behind tug at the heart: New Harmony, Peace Dale, New Hope, New Haven.

Yet most Utopian communities—like the one I was standing in—survive only as museums. Perfectionism keeps running aground on the barrier reef of original sin.

High ideals paradoxically lead to despair and defeatism. Despite all good efforts, human beings don't achieve a state of sinlessness, and in the end they often blame themselves (a blame encouraged by their leaders: "If it is not working, there must be something wrong with you").

Still, I admit that I sometimes feel a nostalgia, even longing, for the quest itself. How can we uphold the ideal of holiness, the proper striving for life on the highest plane, while avoiding the consequences of disillusionment, pettiness, abuse of authority, spiritual pride, and exclusivism?

Or, to ask the opposite question, how can we moderns who emphasize community support (never judgment), honesty, and introspection keep from aiming too low? An individualistic society, America stands in constant danger of freedom abuse; its churches are in danger of grace abuse.

It was with these questions in mind that I read through the Epistles, charting the motives they appealed to. I read them in a different order than usual. First I read Galatians, with its magnificent charter of Christian liberty and its fiery pronouncements against petty legalism. Next I turned to James, that "right strawy epistle" that stuck in Martin Luther's throat. I read Ephesians and then 1 Corinthians, Romans and then 1 Timothy, Colossians and then 1 Peter. In every epistle without exception I found both messages: the high ideals of holiness and also the safety net of grace reminding us that salvation does not depend on our meeting those ideals. I will not attempt to resolve the tension between grace and works because the New Testament does not. We must not try to solve the contradiction by reducing the force of either grace or morality. Grace presents a "Yes and," not a "Yes but."

Ephesians pulls the two strands neatly together: "For it is by *grace you have been saved,* through faith—and this not from yourselves, it is the gift of God—not by works, so that no one can boast. For we are God's workmanship, created in Christ Jesus *to do good works,* which God prepared in advance for us to do" (2:8–10, emphasis added). Philippians expresses the same dialectic: "... *work out your salvation* with fear and trembling, for it is God *who works in you* to will and to act according to his good purpose" (2:12–13, emphasis added). First Peter adds, "Live as free men, but do not use your freedom as a cover-up for evil; live as servants of God" (2:16).

I take some comfort in the fact that the church in the first century was already on a seesaw, tilting now toward perfectionist legalism and now toward raucous freedom. James wrote to one extreme; Paul often addressed the other. Each letter has a strong correcting emphasis, but all stress the dual message of the gospel. The church should be both: a people who strive toward holiness and yet relax in grace, a people who condemn themselves but not others, a people who depend on God and not themselves.[66] —PY

DAILY CONTEMPLATION

Do you lean more toward perfectionistic legalism or raucous freedom? Talk with God about the way you usually approach your spiritual life. Ask him to help you find the balance you need.

PRAISE TO GOD FOR A LIVING HOPE;

BE HOLY

Peter, an apostle of Jesus Christ,

To God's elect, strangers in the world, scattered throughout Pontus, Galatia, Cappadocia, Asia and Bithynia, who have been chosen according to the foreknowledge of God the Father, through the sanctifying work of the Spirit, for obedience to Jesus Christ and sprinkling by his blood:

Grace and peace be yours in abundance.

Praise be to the God and Father of our Lord Jesus Christ! In his great mercy he has given us new birth into a living hope through the resurrection of Jesus Christ from the dead, and into an inheritance that can never perish, spoil or fade—kept in heaven for you, who through faith are shielded by God's power until the coming of the salvation that is ready to be revealed in the last time. In this you greatly rejoice, though now for a little while you may have had to suffer grief in all kinds of trials. These have come so that your faith—of greater worth than gold, which perishes even though refined by fire—may be proved genuine and may result in praise, glory and honor when Jesus Christ is revealed. Though you have not seen him, you love him; and even though you do not see him now, you believe in him and are filled with an inexpressible and glorious joy, for you are receiving the goal of your faith, the salvation of your souls.

Concerning this salvation, the prophets, who spoke of the grace that was to come to you, searched intently and with the greatest care, trying to find out the time and circumstances to which the Spirit of Christ in them was pointing when he predicted the sufferings of Christ and the glories that would follow. It was revealed to them that they were not serving themselves but you, when they spoke of the things that have now been told you by those who have preached the gospel to you by the Holy Spirit sent from heaven. Even angels long to look into these things.

Therefore, prepare your minds for action; be self-controlled; set your hope fully on the grace to be given you when Jesus Christ is revealed. As obedient children, do not conform to the evil desires you had when you lived in ignorance. But just as he who called you is holy, so be holy in all you do; for it is written: "Be holy, because I am holy."

Since you call on a Father who judges each man's work impartially, live your lives as strangers here in reverent fear. For you know that it was not with perishable things such as silver or gold that you were redeemed from the empty way of life handed down to you from your forefathers, but with the precious blood of Christ, a lamb without blemish or defect. He was chosen before the creation of the world, but was revealed in these last times for your sake.

Through him you believe in God, who raised him from the dead and glorified him, and so your faith and hope are in God.

Now that you have purified yourselves by obeying the truth so that you have sincere love for your brothers, love one another deeply, from the heart. For you have been born again, not of perishable seed, but of imperishable, through the living and enduring word of God. For,

"All men are like grass,
  and all their glory is like the flowers of the field;
the grass withers and the flowers fall,
  but the word of the Lord stands forever."

And this is the word that was preached to you.

Therefore, rid yourselves of all malice and all deceit, hypocrisy, envy, and slander of every kind. Like newborn babies, crave pure spiritual milk, so that by it you may grow up in your salvation, now that you have tasted that the Lord is good.

The Gospels portray Peter cowering in the darkness the night of Jesus' trial and execution, and denying with an oath that he had ever known the man he had followed for three years. But in this letter Peter welcomes suffering as a badge of honor, proof of his commitment to Christ at any cost. Seeing the resurrected Jesus—especially in the poignant scene by a lake when Jesus reinstated him (John 21)—changed Peter forever.

Most likely, Peter is writing this letter during an outbreak of persecution under Nero. Urgent questions stir up within the embattled Christian community. Should they flee or resist? Should they tone down their outward signs of faith? Peter's readers, their lives in danger, need clear advice. Beyond that, they also want some explanation of the meaning of suffering. Why does God allow it? Does God care?

As this chapter shows, Peter's response focuses not on the *cause* of suffering—the "Why?"—but rather on the *results*. He answers that suffering can "refine" faith, much as a furnace refines impure metals. Suffering shifts attention from the rewards of this world—wealth, status, power—to more permanent, "imperishable" rewards in the life to come. And if Christians maintain their faith through persecution, a watching world will have to acknowledge the source of that faith, God himself.

Evidently, the early Christians heed Peter's advice. More often than not, intense persecution has led to a spurt of growth in the church. An ancient saying expresses this phenomenon: "The blood of martyrs is the seed of the church." According to tradition, Peter himself dies a martyr's death, crucified head downward on a Roman cross because he thinks himself unworthy to die right side up like Jesus.

In this first chapter, Peter turns what could be a reason for despair into a reason for great hope. He sees the church, in all its birth pangs, as the long-awaited goal of the Old Testament prophets—indeed, the goal of all history.   —PY

DAILY CONTEMPLATION

When have you most recently questioned the reason for suffering in your life?

SUFFERING FOR DOING GOOD; LIVING FOR GOD

Finally, all of you, live in harmony with one another; be sympathetic, love as brothers, be compassionate and humble. Do not repay evil with evil or insult with insult, but with blessing, because to this you were called so that you may inherit a blessing. For,

"Whoever would love life
　　and see good days
must keep his tongue from evil
　　and his lips from deceitful speech.
He must turn from evil and do good;
　　he must seek peace and pursue it.
For the eyes of the Lord are on the righteous
　　and his ears are attentive to their prayer,
but the face of the Lord is against those who do evil."

Who is going to harm you if you are eager to do good? But even if you should suffer for what is right, you are blessed. "Do not fear what they fear; do not be frightened." But in your hearts set apart Christ as Lord. Always be prepared to give an answer to everyone who asks you to give the reason for the hope that you have. But do this with gentleness and respect, keeping a clear conscience, so that those who speak maliciously against your good behavior in Christ may be ashamed of their slander. It is better, if it is God's will, to suffer for doing good than for doing evil. For Christ died for sins once for all, the righteous for the unrighteous, to bring you to God. He was put to death in the body but made alive by the Spirit, through whom also he went and preached to the spirits in prison who disobeyed long ago when God waited patiently in the days of Noah while the ark was being built. In it only a few people, eight in all, were saved through water, and this water symbolizes baptism that now saves you also—not the removal of dirt from the body but the pledge of a good conscience toward God. It saves you by the resurrection of Jesus Christ, who has gone into heaven and is at God's right hand—with angels, authorities and powers in submission to him.

Therefore, since Christ suffered in his body, arm yourselves also with the same attitude, because he who has suffered in his body is done with sin. As a result, he does not live the rest of his earthly life for evil human desires, but rather for the will of God. For you have spent enough time in the past doing what pagans choose to do—living in debauchery, lust, drunkenness, orgies, carousing and detestable idolatry. They think it strange that you do not plunge with them into the same flood of dissipation, and they heap abuse on you. But they will have to give account to him who is ready to judge the living and the dead. For this is the reason the gospel was preached even to those who are now dead, so that they might be judged according to men in regard to the body, but live according to God in regard to the spirit.

The end of all things is near. Therefore be clear minded and self-controlled so that you can pray. Above all, love each other deeply, because love covers over a multitude of sins. Offer hospitality to one another without grumbling. Each one should use whatever gift he has received to serve others, faithfully administering God's grace in its various forms. If anyone speaks, he should do it as one speaking the very words of God. If anyone serves, he should do it with the strength God provides, so that in all things God may be praised through Jesus Christ. To him be the glory and the power for ever and ever. Amen.

Dear friends, do not be surprised at the painful trial you are suffering, as though something strange were happening to you. But rejoice that you participate in the sufferings of Christ, so that you may be overjoyed when his glory is revealed. If you are insulted because of the name of Christ, you are blessed, for the Spirit of glory and of God rests on you. If you suffer, it should not be as a murderer or thief or any other kind of criminal, or even as a meddler. However, if you suffer as a Christian, do not be ashamed, but praise God that you bear that name. For it is time for judgment to begin with the family of God; and if it begins with us, what will the outcome be for those who do not obey the gospel of God? And,

"If it is hard for the righteous to be saved,
    what will become of the ungodly and the sinner?"

So then, those who suffer according to God's will should commit themselves to their faithful Creator and continue to do good.

Peter teaches that believers may have to suffer for doing good, and they may even suffer for being Christians. His teaching remains foreign to many of us who, in the Western world, don't see blatant physical persecution occurring. But it is a reality in other parts of the world, such as China or strict Muslim countries. There Christians are forbidden to practice their faith. If caught they are often beaten, imprisoned, or killed.

Even in our own culture, however, Christians may suffer a bad name. For example, we may be classed as fanatics who care only about politics and protecting ourselves and our agendas. The media sometimes lump together all Christians as fundamentalists: poor, uneducated zealots. As a result, new believers may feel hesitant identifying themselves as Christians, because of the assumptions others may make.

"Do not be surprised," Peter says, "as though something strange were happening to you" (1 Peter 4:12). And "do not be ashamed, but praise God that you bear that name" (4:16). Be open about your faith, no matter what others think, and always be ready to "give the reason for the hope that you have" (3:15). "Do this with gentleness and respect," Peter adds (3:15). This attitude holds the key to sharing the true identity of a Christian.

Sandwiched between his verses about suffering, Peter tells more about living as a Christian. We live for God's will, not ours. The end is near, and when it comes everyone will answer to God, even those who now condemn us. In the meantime love should characterize our lives. With love, we can hope to change the hearts of those who misunderstand. —BQ

> ## DAILY CONTEMPLATION
> *When have you been hesitant to admit you are a Christian?*

DAY 353   2 Peter 1:1–2:3

MAKING ONE'S CALLING AND ELECTION SURE

Simon Peter, a servant and apostle of Jesus Christ,

To those who through the righteousness of our God and Savior Jesus Christ have received a faith as precious as ours:

Grace and peace be yours in abundance through the knowledge of God and of Jesus our Lord.

His divine power has given us everything we need for life and godliness through our knowledge of him who called us by his own glory and goodness. Through these he has given us his very great and precious promises, so that through them you may participate in the divine nature and escape the corruption in the world caused by evil desires.

For this very reason, make every effort to add to your faith goodness; and to goodness, knowledge; and to knowledge, self-control; and to self-control, perseverance; and to perseverance, godliness; and to godliness, brotherly kindness; and to brotherly kindness, love. For if you possess these qualities in increasing measure, they will keep you from being ineffective and unproductive in your knowledge of our Lord Jesus Christ. But if anyone does not have them, he is nearsighted and blind, and has forgotten that he has been cleansed from his past sins.

Therefore, my brothers, be all the more eager to make your calling and election sure. For if you do these things, you will never fall, and you will receive a rich welcome into the eternal kingdom of our Lord and Savior Jesus Christ.

So I will always remind you of these things, even though you know them and are firmly established in the truth you now have. I think it is right to refresh your memory as long as I live in the tent of this body, because I know that I will soon put it aside, as our Lord Jesus Christ has made clear to me. And I will make every effort to see that after my departure you will always be able to remember these things.

We did not follow cleverly invented stories when we told you about the power and coming of our Lord Jesus Christ, but we were eyewitnesses of his majesty. For he received honor and glory from God the Father when the voice came to him from the Majestic Glory, saying, "This is my Son, whom I love; with him I am well pleased." We ourselves heard this voice that came from heaven when we were with him on the sacred mountain.

And we have the word of the prophets made more certain, and you will do well to pay attention to it, as to a light shining in a dark place, until the day dawns and the morning star rises in your hearts. Above all, you must understand that no prophecy of Scripture came about by the prophet's own interpretation. For prophecy never had its origin in the will of man, but men spoke from God as they were carried along by the Holy Spirit.

But there were also false prophets among the people, just as there will be false teachers among you. They will secretly introduce destructive heresies, even denying the sovereign Lord who bought them—bringing swift destruction on themselves. Many will follow their shameful ways and will bring the way of truth into disrepute. In their greed these teachers will exploit you with stories they have made up. Their condemnation has long been hanging over them, and their destruction has not been sleeping.

As 1 Peter demonstrates, leaders of the New Testament church do not consider persecution a grave threat. To the contrary, such trials purify and strengthen the church by forcing true believers to come forward and exhibit their courage and faith.

The real dangers to the church come from within. Take the matter of unity. At the Last Supper with the disciples, Jesus prayed that believers "may be one as we are one" (John 17:11). But within a generation the church has splintered into followers of Paul or his rivals, legalists, freewheelers, Judaizers, doomsdayers, and dozens of different groups.

Typically, these groups focus on a minor doctrinal issue and waste energy on meaningless debates. This letter, for example, seems directed toward Christians obsessed with the last days. Some, impatient over unfulfilled predictions of Christ's second coming, are already beginning to scoff at the whole idea.

The author of 2 Peter has strong words of correction for such splinter groups. He reminds them that the gospel is no fairy tale, no collection of "cleverly invented stories." As an eyewitness on the Mount of Transfiguration, he has heard God give resounding approval to his Son Jesus. If that God has promised a second coming, then rest assured it will take place.

As in many New Testament letters, the emphasis in 2 Peter strays back and forth between what to believe and what kind of person to be. The author lays out a progressive list of qualities—faith, goodness, knowledge, self-control, perseverance, godliness, brotherly kindness, love—that will strengthen against any temptations toward disunity.

The author of this letter is an old man, soon to face death. As a final swan song, he can do no better than remind his readers of the most basic truths of the Christian life. The answer to false knowledge is true knowledge; the answer to immoral living is moral living. As he prepares to die, the author of 2 Peter gets in one last appeal for truth.   —PY

DAILY CONTEMPLATION

Of the seven qualities mentioned in 1:5–7, which describe your life now? Which need work?

REFINED BY FIRE

Occasionally I hear a Christian song that praises suffering. The singer seems nearly to welcome the onset of hard times because of the benefits to be reaped. I often recoil at this music. It's too agreeable, too catchy for the message it delivers. Has this artist ever suffered, I wonder? Does anyone, no matter how spiritual, really welcome struggle?

I think of James's words, "Consider it pure joy, my brothers, whenever you face trials of many kinds" (1:9) and Paul's words in Romans, "We also rejoice in our sufferings" (5:3). They offer a similar message: believers can and should see the positive side of suffering. Both link suffering with the development of perseverance, and Paul adds character and hope to the list of benefits. Hard times make us stronger. They also give us new eyes to see that heaven awaits us. This life and its troubles are only momentary in relation to the new world that lies ahead for us in eternity.

Peter emphasizes this future hope. God has "an inheritance that can never perish, spoil or fade—kept in heaven for you" (1 Peter 1:4). As if writing a promise in a will, God reminds us of what he has in store. I do need that reminder, and suffering can help. It's far too easy in the good times to get comfortable with the here and now. My vision slips into a shortsightedness, with my goals focusing on short-term pleasures of life at the moment. I forget about heaven, rarely thinking of the inheritance awaiting me.

Suffering changes my awareness. As Peter says, it *refines* my faith, burning away all the distractions that have built up and kept me from seeing the truth about my life with Jesus. Suffering puts me in touch—as probably nothing else can—with what matters. This gives cause for rejoicing, a reason for joy. As C. S. Lewis says, "God whispers to us in our pleasures, speaks in our conscience, but shouts in our pains."[67] During that process of refining, I can hear God more clearly. His voice sounds stronger and more direct. The dross that used to block my ears has now melted away.

One song on suffering I *can* sing with heart: "Refiner's fire, my heart's one desire is to be holy. . . ." I look at times of past or present suffering and still can't say I hope for more of it. I can't say I'm ready for the next onslaught. Yet I can sing of a desire for God to do his good work in me when that suffering comes. He has done it in the past, and I trust him to take care of me. While being refined by God may be painful, it also points ahead toward a better life that awaits me—a life with no need for songs about suffering. —BQ

DAILY CONTEMPLATION

Can you look back on a hard time and see how God refined you, making you stronger, building your character, setting your sights on heaven? Consider any struggles you are facing now. Ask God to bring good from the pain, making you more of the person he created you to be.

THE SIN AND DOOM OF GODLESS MEN;

A CALL TO PERSEVERE

Jude, a servant of Jesus Christ and a brother of James,

To those who have been called, who are loved by God the Father and kept by Jesus Christ:

Mercy, peace and love be yours in abundance.

Dear friends, although I was very eager to write to you about the salvation we share, I felt I had to write and urge you to contend for the faith that was once for all entrusted to the saints. For certain men whose condemnation was written about long ago have secretly slipped in among you. They are godless men, who change the grace of our God into a license for immorality and deny Jesus Christ our only Sovereign and Lord.

Though you already know all this, I want to remind you that the Lord delivered his people out of Egypt, but later destroyed those who did not believe. And the angels who did not keep their positions of authority but abandoned their own home—these he has kept in darkness, bound with everlasting chains for judgment on the great Day. In a similar way, Sodom and Gomorrah and the surrounding towns gave themselves up to sexual immorality and perversion. They serve as an example of those who suffer the punishment of eternal fire.

In the very same way, these dreamers pollute their own bodies, reject authority and slander celestial beings. But even the archangel Michael, when he was disputing with the devil about the body of Moses, did not dare to bring a slanderous accusation against him, but said, "The Lord rebuke you!" Yet these men speak abusively against whatever they do not understand; and what things they do understand by instinct, like unreasoning animals—these are the very things that destroy them.

Woe to them! They have taken the way of Cain; they have rushed for profit into Balaam's error; they have been destroyed in Korah's rebellion.

These men are blemishes at your love feasts, eating with you without the slightest qualm—shepherds who feed only themselves. They are clouds without rain, blown along by the wind; autumn trees, without fruit and uprooted—twice dead. They are wild waves of the sea, foaming up their shame; wandering stars, for whom blackest darkness has been reserved forever.

Enoch, the seventh from Adam, prophesied about these men: "See, the Lord is coming with thousands upon thousands of his holy ones to judge everyone, and to convict all the ungodly of all the ungodly acts they have done in the ungodly way, and of all the harsh words ungodly sinners have spoken against him." These men are grumblers and faultfinders; they follow their own evil desires; they boast about themselves and flatter others for their own advantage.

But, dear friends, remember what the apostles of our Lord Jesus Christ foretold. They said to you, "In the last times there will be scoffers who will follow their own ungodly desires." These are the men who divide you, who follow mere natural instincts and do not have the Spirit.

But you, dear friends, build yourselves up in your most holy faith and pray in the Holy Spirit. Keep yourselves in God's love as you wait for the mercy of our Lord Jesus Christ to bring you to eternal life.

Be merciful to those who doubt; snatch others from the fire and save them; to others show mercy, mixed with fear—hating even the clothing stained by corrupted flesh.

To him who is able to keep you from falling and to present you before his glorious presence without fault and with great joy—to the only God our Savior be glory, majesty, power and authority, through Jesus Christ our Lord, before all ages, now and forevermore! Amen.

The brief letter from Jude (possibly the brother of Jesus) has much in common with 2 Peter. Both of them concern danger signs in the church, and the actual wording in Jude closely parallels that of 2 Peter 2. But Jude speaks with an even shriller tone. The disease has spread. If not arrested, it will infect the entire body.

In its approach, Jude resembles the scary movies against drugs and drunk driving that high schools sometimes show their students. They make viewers uncomfortable—which is precisely their purpose. Jude confesses that although he would prefer to write a more joyful letter about salvation, first he must alert them to the serious threat posed by certain troublemakers.

Jude doesn't elaborate on what the troublemakers are saying, but the early church is plagued by roving teachers who claim some special "word from the Lord." Often these false teachers, seeking a profit, tell audiences exactly what they want to hear: God's grace is so great that you can live however you want, with no penalty. Jude makes devastatingly clear what he thinks of such ideas. He calls the impostors spies and urges believers to fight for the true faith.

Ironically, only one portion of Jude gets much attention today: the beautiful doxology at the end. Evidently, Jude's strong words are no easier to take today than when they were first given.   —PY

DAILY CONTEMPLATION

When have you been influenced by a "spiritual" book or teacher who strayed from the central teachings of the Bible? Did you sense any danger?

CHILDREN OF GOD; LOVE ONE ANOTHER

How great is the love the Father has lavished on us, that we should be called children of God! And that is what we are! The reason the world does not know us is that it did not know him. Dear friends, now we are children of God, and what we will be has not yet been made known. But we know that when he appears, we shall be like him, for we shall see him as he is. Everyone who has this hope in him purifies himself, just as he is pure.

Everyone who sins breaks the law; in fact, sin is lawlessness. But you know that he appeared so that he might take away our sins. And in him is no sin. No one who lives in him keeps on sinning. No one who continues to sin has either seen him or known him.

Dear children, do not let anyone lead you astray. He who does what is right is righteous, just as he is righteous. He who does what is sinful is of the devil, because the devil has been sinning from the beginning. The reason the Son of God appeared was to destroy the devil's work. No one who is born of God will continue to sin, because God's seed remains in him; he cannot go on sinning, because he has been born of God. This is how we know who the children of God are and who the children of the devil are: Anyone who does not do what is right is not a child of God; nor is anyone who does not love his brother.

This is the message you heard from the beginning: We should love one another. Do not be like Cain, who belonged to the evil one and murdered his brother. And why did he murder him? Because his own actions were evil and his brother's were righteous. Do not be surprised, my brothers, if the world hates you. We know that we have passed from death to life, because we love our brothers. Anyone who does not love remains in death. Anyone who hates his brother is a murderer, and you know that no murderer has eternal life in him.

This is how we know what love is: Jesus Christ laid down his life for us. And we ought to lay down our lives for our brothers. If anyone has material possessions and sees his brother in need but has no pity on him, how can the love of God be in him? Dear children, let us not love with words or tongue but with actions and in truth. This then is how we know that we belong to the truth, and how we set our hearts at rest in his presence whenever our hearts condemn us. For God is greater than our hearts, and he knows everything.

Dear friends, if our hearts do not condemn us, we have confidence before God and receive from him anything we ask, because we obey his commands and do what pleases him. And this is his command: to believe in the name of his Son, Jesus Christ, and to love one another as he commanded us. Those who obey his commands live in him, and he in them. And this is how we know that he lives in us: We know it by the Spirit he gave us.

Shortly after World War II, the brilliant Christian thinker C. S. Lewis communicated his beliefs about the faith in a series of British radio broadcasts that were then edited into the book *Mere Christianity*. He covered the basics, the bare essentials of Christian belief. Yet even that slim book would seem overly long and complex to the apostle John, author of this letter. John uses the simplest language of any New Testament writer—his three letters together employ barely three hundred different Greek words—to express the gospel in its most distilled form.

An early Christian writer named Jerome tells the story of John as a very old man being carried into the church at Ephesus. The people had gathered to hear a message from the famous apostle, but he would only repeat, "Little children, love one another." When asked why, he replied, "Because it is the Lord's command, and if this is done, it is enough."

That kind of single-mindedness shines through John's letters. This passage begins with wonder, astonishment even, that God has lavished his love on us. We are his children! But then John asks the obvious question: If we are God's children, why don't we act like it? Don't children of good parents naturally want to emulate them?

John is the last surviving apostle. He lives almost to the end of the first century and may be in his eighties when he writes this book. Already, elite cults such as the Gnostics have sprung up within the church, and Christians are hotly debating esoteric matters of theology and ethics. John dismisses these with a wave of his hand. To him, the proof of a person's faith is perfectly obvious: "If anyone has material possessions and sees his brother in need but has no pity on him, how can the love of God be in him?" His words are as piercingly direct as the words of the Sermon on the Mount. A person who loves God acts like it—it's that simple.   —PY

DAILY CONTEMPLATION

If you could condense the code you live by into one sentence, what would it be?

DAY 357
1 John 4:1–21

TEST THE SPIRITS; GOD'S LOVE AND OURS

Dear friends, do not believe every spirit, but test the spirits to see whether they are from God, because many false prophets have gone out into the world. This is how you can recognize the Spirit of God: Every spirit that acknowledges that Jesus Christ has come in the flesh is from God, but every spirit that does not acknowledge Jesus is not from God. This is the spirit of the antichrist, which you have heard is coming and even now is already in the world.

You, dear children, are from God and have overcome them, because the one who is in you is greater than the one who is in the world. They are from the world and therefore speak from the viewpoint of the world, and the world listens to them. We are from God, and whoever knows God listens to us; but whoever is not from God does not listen to us. This is how we recognize the Spirit of truth and the spirit of falsehood.

Dear friends, let us love one another, for love comes from God. Everyone who loves has been born of God and knows God. Whoever does not love does not know God, because God is love. This is how God showed his love among us: He sent his one and only Son into the world that we might live through him. This is love: not that we loved God, but that he loved us and sent his Son as an atoning sacrifice for our sins. Dear friends, since God so loved us, we also ought to love one another. No one has ever seen God; but if we love one another, God lives in us and his love is made complete in us.

We know that we live in him and he in us, because he has given us of his Spirit. And we have seen and testify that the Father has sent his Son to be the Savior of the world. If anyone acknowledges that Jesus is the Son of God, God lives in him and he in God. And so we know and rely on the love God has for us.

God is love. Whoever lives in love lives in God, and God in him. In this way, love is made complete among us so that we will have confidence on the day of judgment, because in this world we are like him. There is no fear in love. But perfect love drives out fear, because fear has to do with punishment. The one who fears is not made perfect in love.

We love because he first loved us. If anyone says, "I love God," yet hates his brother, he is a liar. For anyone who does not love his brother, whom he has seen, cannot love God, whom he has not seen. And he has given us this command: Whoever loves God must also love his brother.

John begins this part of his letter with a caution that applies as much today as it does in John's day. The early church is being exposed to a variety of spiritual voices, some of which sound interesting, helpful, even authoritative. But believers need to realize that not all seemingly spiritual teaching is from God. Those who don't acknowledge Jesus Christ as God's Son are not teachers filled by God and inspired by him.

Frank Gaebelein, a respected Bible scholar, once wrote, "All truth is God's truth." He makes the point that truth may be revealed even through those who aren't committed to God. We need to be careful, however. False teachers may present pieces of God's truth, but mixed in with untruth. John stresses that believers must maturely discern what is of God and what is not.

John returns in this passage to his favorite theme of love, emphasizing two aspects of God's love for us: it came first, preceding our love for him, and it carries no fear. All the love we feel for God and others is a reflection of God's initial and lasting love for us. If we're having trouble loving, we haven't really come to know God's love for us. And when we see God's love as it is, fear dissolves. Fear has no place alongside love. —BQ

DAILY CONTEMPLATION

When have you experienced for or from someone a love that involved fear?

Faith in the Son of God

Everyone who believes that Jesus is the Christ is born of God, and everyone who loves the father loves his child as well. This is how we know that we love the children of God: by loving God and carrying out his commands. This is love for God: to obey his commands. And his commands are not burdensome, for everyone born of God overcomes the world. This is the victory that has overcome the world, even our faith. Who is it that overcomes the world? Only he who believes that Jesus is the Son of God.

This is the one who came by water and blood—Jesus Christ. He did not come by water only, but by water and blood. And it is the Spirit who testifies, because the Spirit is the truth. For there are three that testify: the Spirit, the water and the blood; and the three are in agreement. We accept man's testimony, but God's testimony is greater because it is the testimony of God, which he has given about his Son. Anyone who believes in the Son of God has this testimony in his heart. Anyone who does not believe God has made him out to be a liar, because he has not believed the testimony God has given about his Son. And this is the testimony: God has given us eternal life, and this life is in his Son. He who has the Son has life; he who does not have the Son of God does not have life.

I write these things to you who believe in the name of the Son of God so that you may know that you have eternal life. This is the confidence we have in approaching God: that if we ask anything according to his will, he hears us. And if we know that he hears us—whatever we ask—we know that we have what we asked of him.

John concludes his letter by finishing his discussion on love. If we know God's love for us, we'll love him and his Son Jesus in return. This love will compel us to follow God's commands, trusting what he tells us to do. Out of our growing love we'll want to please him, and following his way won't feel like a burden. We may not obey him perfectly, but any burden we sense will come only from ourselves or from a source at odds with God.

Christians have the victory in this world, John proclaims. Jesus won the victory for us: as God, he died a physical death and rose again. A popular teacher of John's day taught Christ as essentially human, with only a short period of divinity coming on at his baptism and leaving him before his crucifixion. John refutes this belief and affirms rather that Jesus was proved fully God by "the Spirit, the water and the blood."

The love of God and the victory we're promised will become evident in our prayers. As we try to follow his ways, God promises to help. He'll answer any prayer, meeting our needs and giving us strength. When it seems God hasn't answered a prayer, we need to reconsider whether our desire was in line with his will. True to his love, he'll never fail in his promise. Unless we insist, he won't let us stray outside what is his best for us.

—BQ

DAILY CONTEMPLATION

What are you praying for today? Are you asking for God's will to shape your desires and even your prayers?

DAY 359   2 John 1–13; 3 John 1–14

WHEN TO BE HOSPITABLE

The elder,

To the chosen lady and her children, whom I love in the truth—and not I only, but also all who know the truth—because of the truth, which lives in us and will be with us forever:

Grace, mercy and peace from God the Father and from Jesus Christ, the Father's Son, will be with us in truth and love.

It has given me great joy to find some of your children walking in the truth, just as the Father commanded us. And now, dear lady, I am not writing you a new command but one we have had from the beginning. I ask that we love one another. And this is love: that we walk in obedience to his commands. As you have heard from the beginning, his command is that you walk in love.

Many deceivers, who do not acknowledge Jesus Christ as coming in the flesh, have gone out into the world. Any such person is the deceiver and the antichrist. Watch out that you do not lose what you have worked for, but that you may be rewarded fully. Anyone who runs ahead and does not continue in the teaching of Christ does not have God; whoever continues in the teaching has both the Father and the Son. If anyone comes to you and does not bring this teaching, do not take him into your house or welcome him. Anyone who welcomes him shares in his wicked work.

I have much to write to you, but I do not want to use paper and ink. Instead, I hope to visit you and talk with you face to face, so that our joy may be complete.

The children of your chosen sister send their greetings. . . .

The elder,

To my dear friend Gaius, whom I love in the truth.

Dear friend, I pray that you may enjoy good health and that all may go well with you, even as your soul is getting along well. It gave me great joy to have some brothers come and tell about your faithfulness to the truth and how you continue to walk in the truth. I have no greater joy than to hear that my children are walking in the truth.

Dear friend, you are faithful in what you are doing for the brothers, even though they are strangers to you. They have told the church about your love. You will do well to send them on their way in a manner worthy of God. It was for the sake of the Name that they went out, receiving no help from the pagans. We ought therefore to show hospitality to such men so that we may work together for the truth.

I wrote to the church, but Diotrephes, who loves to be first, will have nothing to do with us. So if I come, I will call attention to what he is doing, gossiping maliciously about us. Not satisfied with that, he refuses to welcome the brothers. He also stops those who want to do so and puts them out of the church.

Dear friend, do not imitate what is evil but what is good. Anyone who does what is good is from God. Anyone who does what is evil has not seen God. Demetrius is well spoken of by everyone—and even by the truth itself. We also speak well of him, and you know that our testimony is true.

I have much to write you, but I do not want to do so with pen and ink. I hope to see you soon, and we will talk face to face.

Peace to you. The friends here send their greetings. Greet the friends there by name.

Most early churches founded by missionaries like the apostle Paul meet in private homes. Later on, Paul begins sending out emissaries, such as Timothy and Titus, who join the original apostles in making "the circuit" from church to church. Christians begin the practice of hosting traveling teachers in their homes, rather than making them stay in the notoriously unsafe Roman inns.

Before long, however, "false teachers" follow suit, bringing distortions of the original gospel and sowing confusion and discord. Soon religious racketeers join in, seeking free food and lodging. The issue arises of what to do with the new breed of pseudo-evangelists. Should Christians offer hospitality to them too? The letters of 2 and 3 John, the shortest letters in the New Testament, deal with this very problem.

These two letters are best read together, since each gives one side of a problem facing a young church. The book of 2 John urges Christians to use discretion in testing a visitor's message and motive. It cautions against hosting visitors who do not teach the truth about Christ. True to his nickname, the Apostle of Love repeats his motto, "Love one another," even in this letter of warning.

On the other hand, 3 John praises a man named Gaius (GAY-yuhs) for warmly welcoming genuine Christian teachers. Gaius's church is dominated by a gossipy dictator who excludes all outsiders.

In a very condensed form, John's two letters deal with heresy and church splits, two problems that have plagued the church in every age, in every place. To defend against those dangers, John stresses the need for love and discernment. Believers must know whom to accept and support, and whom to resist.   —PY

DAILY CONTEMPLATION

When have you encountered a modern deceiver or false teacher?

THE SONG OF THE BIBLE

It's appropriate that John's letters on love fall at the end of the Bible. From the first pages of Genesis, the Bible tells a long story of God's love for humanity, and his desire for us to love him and each other. Early in the story Moses and the Israelites sang, "In your unfailing love you will lead the people you have redeemed. In your strength you will guide them to your holy dwelling" (Exodus 15:13). Without knowing it, they were singing a summary song of the entire Bible. From creation to eternity God would lead and redeem his people, bringing them finally to their true home.

Unlike Moses and the people, God knew very well what lay ahead. He described himself to Moses, proclaiming, "The LORD, the LORD, the compassionate and gracious God, slow to anger, abounding in love and faithfulness, maintaining love to thousands, and forgiving wickedness, rebellion and sin" (Exodus 34:6–7). Many of those he loved in the centuries to come would rebel, living for themselves rather than for him, and God would forgive again and again, never losing his love for those he'd created.

The Israelites would rebel many times in the desert with Moses, despite the miracles they saw with their own eyes. David later murdered and committed adultery despite God's clear hand in sparing his life and making him king. Solomon, in all his wisdom, ended his life reveling in wealth and women rather than in God. After Israel split into two kingdoms, both fell prey to an attraction for other nations' gods and riches. God expressed through Hosea his grief and his love for his wayward children. Eventually they did return to him, yet the pattern of waywardness would continue to the time of Christ.

Finally, God's Son came to earth to stop the cycle of sin and punishment. Living a life of love and then dying to end the power of sin, Jesus redeemed the people God so dearly loves. Christ rose again to live his life in believers through his Spirit.

Now, after many letters of instruction to those believers who have followed Christ, John returns us again to the theme of love. "We know and rely on the love God has for us," John says. "Perfect love drives out fear" (1 John 4:16, 18). He knew that love and fear are two of the greatest motivators of the human spirit. They drove the lives of many in the Old Testament and are at the root of humanity's fickle relationship with God. Fear often causes rebellion, but God's love has the power to conquer fear.

Henri Nouwen, writer and scholar, declared that all people live either in the "house of fear" or in the "house of love." He explained, "When St. John says that fear is driven out by perfect love, he points to a love that comes from God, a divine love.... The home, the intimate place, the place of true belonging, is therefore not a place made by human hands. It is fashioned for us by God, who came to pitch his tent among us, invite us to his place, and prepare a room for us in his own house."[68]

We can rely on the love God has for us. He desires that we live in his love, making our homes there and acting with others out of the comfort of his love. To guide us we have the Bible, God's storybook about life lived both in his house of love and in the house of fear. The choice is ours. Each time we waver, we need only open the Bible and listen to its song—a love song, one the Israelites heard thousands of years ago—calling us to our true home. —BQ

DAILY CONTEMPLATION

Do you act more often out of fear or out of love? Is your relationship with God filled more with fear or with love? Ask God to help you move out of the house of fear and into his house of love, confidently believing the message he has given you throughout the Bible.

DAY 361

Revelation 1:1–20

ONE LIKE A SON OF MAN

The revelation of Jesus Christ, which God gave him to show his servants what must soon take place. He made it known by sending his angel to his servant John, who testifies to everything he saw—that is, the word of God and the testimony of Jesus Christ. Blessed is the one who reads the words of this prophecy, and blessed are those who hear it and take to heart what is written in it, because the time is near.

John,

To the seven churches in the province of Asia:

Grace and peace to you from him who is, and who was, and who is to come, and from the seven spirits before his throne, and from Jesus Christ, who is the faithful witness, the firstborn from the dead, and the ruler of the kings of the earth.

To him who loves us and has freed us from our sins by his blood, and has made us to be a kingdom and priests to serve his God and Father—to him be glory and power for ever and ever! Amen.

Look, he is coming with the clouds,
    and every eye will see him,
even those who pierced him;
    and all the peoples of the earth will mourn because of him.
        So shall it be! Amen.

"I am the Alpha and the Omega," says the Lord God, "who is, and who was, and who is to come, the Almighty."

I, John, your brother and companion in the suffering and kingdom and patient endurance that are ours in Jesus, was on the island of Patmos because of the word of God and the testimony of Jesus. On the Lord's Day I was in the Spirit, and I heard behind me a loud voice like a trumpet, which said: "Write on a scroll what you see and send it to the seven churches: to Ephesus, Smyrna, Pergamum, Thyatira, Sardis, Philadelphia and Laodicea."

I turned around to see the voice that was speaking to me. And when I turned I saw seven golden lampstands, and among the lampstands was someone "like a son of man," dressed in a robe reaching down to his feet and with a golden sash around his chest. His head and hair were white like wool, as white as snow, and his eyes were like blazing fire. His feet were like bronze glowing in a furnace, and his voice was like the sound of rushing waters. In his right hand he held seven stars, and out of his mouth came a sharp double-edged sword. His face was like the sun shining in all its brilliance.

When I saw him, I fell at his feet as though dead. Then he placed his right hand on me and said: "Do not be afraid. I am the First and the Last. I am the Living One; I was dead, and behold I am alive for ever and ever! And I hold the keys of death and Hades.

"Write, therefore, what you have seen, what is now and what will take place later. The mystery of the seven stars that you saw in my right hand and of the seven golden lampstands is this: The seven stars are the angels of the seven churches, and the seven lampstands are the seven churches."

Imagine the Bible without the book of Revelation. After the Old Testament come the four gospels, which then lead into Acts and its account of missionary ventures, followed by the letters to the resulting churches. All fine so far, but one thing is missing: Where is history going? Where will it end up?

Jesus' disciples, all Jewish, grew up hearing about a Messiah who would overturn injustice and unrighteousness and usher in a new kingdom of peace and love and justice. Such long-awaited dreams disappeared as they watched Jesus die between two thieves, but the dreams came surging back a few days later when Jesus reappeared. "Lord, are you at this time going to restore the kingdom to Israel?" were the last words on their lips (Acts 1:6) just before he left them at the Ascension.

One would have to reach beyond all credibility to make a case that the prophets' promised kingdom of peace and righteousness has come about in the years since the Ascension. Our own century has included two world wars, several hundred lesser wars, two atom bomb attacks, a holocaust, the Gulag Archipelago, and numerous mass killings by half-crazed dictators. Where is the time promised by Isaiah when swords will be beaten into plowshares and the lion will lie down by the calf?

Revelation adds a two-word message: Just wait. God is not finished with this planet. The Bible stakes God's own reputation on his ability to restore this planet to its original state of perfection. Only when that happens will history have run its course.

As the book opens, the apostle John has been banished on the island of Patmos, a hard-labor colony. In that bleak setting, he receives a vision remarkably similar in style to those reported by the prophets Ezekiel and Daniel. Many details of John's vision no one can claim to understand with confidence. But this first chapter establishes why the visions were given. John presents a new picture of Jesus.

Yes, Jesus is the babe in the manger, the Good Shepherd, the teacher of disciples, the model of humanity, and the Son of God who died on a cross. But he is something else as well: he is the blazing supernatural creature whose very presence knocked John to the ground. He is the Creator of this world who will someday return to *re-create*, and make new all that humankind has spoiled.　　　　　　　　　　　　　　　—PY

676

DAY 362

Revelation 2:1–29

TO THE CHURCHES IN EPHESUS, SMYRNA, PERGAMUM, AND THYATIRA

"To the angel of the church in Ephesus write:

These are the words of him who holds the seven stars in his right hand and walks among the seven golden lampstands: I know your deeds, your hard work and your perseverance. I know that you cannot tolerate wicked men, that you have tested those who claim to be apostles but are not, and have found them false. You have persevered and have endured hardships for my name, and have not grown weary.

Yet I hold this against you: You have forsaken your first love. Remember the height from which you have fallen! Repent and do the things you did at first. If you do not repent, I will come to you and remove your lampstand from its place. But you have this in your favor: You hate the practices of the Nicolaitans, which I also hate.

He who has an ear, let him hear what the Spirit says to the churches. To him who overcomes, I will give the right to eat from the tree of life, which is in the paradise of God.

"To the angel of the church in Smyrna write:

These are the words of him who is the First and the Last, who died and came to life again. I know your afflictions and your poverty—yet you are rich! I know the slander of those who say they are Jews and are not, but are a synagogue of Satan. Do not be afraid of what you are about to suffer. I tell you, the devil will put some of you in prison to test you, and you will suffer persecution for ten days. Be faithful, even to the point of death, and I will give you the crown of life.

He who has an ear, let him hear what the Spirit says to the churches. He who overcomes will not be hurt at all by the second death.

"To the angel of the church in Pergamum write:

These are the words of him who has the sharp, double-edged sword. I know where you live—where Satan has his throne. Yet you remain true to my name. You did not renounce your faith in me, even in the days of Antipas, my faithful witness, who was put to death in your city—where Satan lives.

Nevertheless, I have a few things against you: You have people there who hold to the teaching of Balaam, who taught Balak to entice the Israelites to sin by eating food sacrificed to idols and by committing sexual immorality. Likewise you also have those who hold to the teaching of the Nicolaitans. Repent therefore! Otherwise, I will soon come to you and will fight against them with the sword of my mouth.

He who has an ear, let him hear what the Spirit says to the churches. To him who overcomes, I will give some of the hidden manna. I will also give him a white stone with a new name written on it, known only to him who receives it.

"To the angel of the church in Thyatira write:

These are the words of the Son of God, whose eyes are like blazing fire and whose feet are like burnished bronze. I know your deeds, your love and faith, your service and perseverance, and that you are now doing more than you did at first.

Nevertheless, I have this against you: You tolerate that woman Jezebel, who calls herself a prophetess. By her teaching she misleads my servants into sexual immorality and the eating of food sacrificed to idols. I have given her time to repent of her immorality, but she is unwilling. So I will cast her on a bed of suffering, and I will make those who commit adultery with her suffer intensely, unless they repent of her ways. I will strike her children dead. Then all the churches will know that I am he who searches hearts and minds, and I will repay each of you according to your deeds. Now I say to the rest of you in Thyatira, to you who do not hold to her teaching and have not learned Satan's so-called deep secrets (I will not impose any other burden on you): Only hold on to what you have until I come.

To him who overcomes and does my will to the end, I will give authority over the nations—

'He will rule them with an iron scepter;
    he will dash them to pieces like pottery'—

just as I have received authority from my Father. I will also give him the morning star. He who has an ear, let him hear what the Spirit says to the churches."

The letters in this chapter and the next are the words of Christ to seven of the early churches. The letters appear in geographical order as one would travel the route from the seaport town of Ephesus heading north along the coast of the Aegean Sea and then circling south and east to the four remaining cities. Jesus speaks specifically to the churches of John's time and the characteristics they displayed, but his words apply to churches and individuals in future times as well. God's words in the epistles of the New Testament are meant as guidelines for Christians of all times.

Christ commends the members of the Ephesian church for their hard work, perseverance, and hatred of evil men. He warns, though, that they've forgotten the most important thing of all. Second-generation Christians in Ephesus are living outwardly like believers yet with hearts not deeply devoted to Christ. Jesus pleads with them to return to their first love—himself.

Christians in Smyrna (SMUHR-nuh) are experiencing severe persecution and poverty. Their suffering has kept them pure, and Jesus doesn't rebuke them. Rather, he encourages them to hold to the true riches they possess and stay faithful to the end.

Cults abound in Pergamum (PER-guh-mum), a wealthy city caught up in the worship of prominent Greek gods. Although sincere believers live in the city as well, some have compromised and taken on the morality of the city. They have begun imitating the lifestyle of the pagans and have allowed the world's thinking to influence their church doctrine. The church is growing corrupt and Jesus urges repentance.

Believers in Thyatira (THIE-uh-TIE-ruh) are facing similar problems. Although Christ commends their love, faith, service, and perseverance, he rebukes many for tolerating Jezebel, a prophetess who leads others into sexual immorality and the eating of food sacrificed to idols. This tolerance will carry a cost, Jesus says: intense suffering. To those believers who have not been drawn into Jezebel's web, Jesus encourages perseverance until he comes again.   —BQ

DAILY CONTEMPLATION

Which of Jesus' rebukes in this chapter hits closest to home with you? Which encouragement speaks to you?

DAY 363   Revelation 3:1–21

TO THE CHURCHES IN SARDIS, PHILADELPHIA, AND LAODICEA

"To the angel of the church in Sardis write:

These are the words of him who holds the seven spirits of God and the seven stars. I know your deeds; you have a reputation of being alive, but you are dead. Wake up! Strengthen what remains and is about to die, for I have not found your deeds complete in the sight of my God. Remember, therefore, what you have received and heard; obey it, and repent. But if you do not wake up, I will come like a thief, and you will not know at what time I will come to you.

Yet you have a few people in Sardis who have not soiled their clothes. They will walk with me, dressed in white, for they are worthy. He who overcomes will, like them, be dressed in white. I will never blot out his name from the book of life, but will acknowledge his name before my Father and his angels. He who has an ear, let him hear what the Spirit says to the churches.

"To the angel of the church in Philadelphia write:

These are the words of him who is holy and true, who holds the key of David. What he opens no one can shut, and what he shuts no one can open. I know your deeds. See, I have placed before you an open door that no one can shut. I know that you have little strength, yet you have kept my word and have not denied my name. I will make those who are of the synagogue of Satan, who claim to be Jews though they are not, but are liars—I will make them come and fall down at your feet and acknowledge that I have loved you. Since you have kept my command to endure patiently, I will also keep you from the hour of trial that is going to come upon the whole world to test those who live on the earth.

I am coming soon. Hold on to what you have, so that no one will take your crown. Him who overcomes I will make a pillar in the temple of my God. Never again will he leave it. I will write on him the name of my God and the name of the city of my God, the new Jerusalem, which is coming down out of heaven from my God; and I will also write on him my new name. He who has an ear, let him hear what the Spirit says to the churches.

"To the angel of the church in Laodicea write:

These are the words of the Amen, the faithful and true witness, the ruler of God's creation. I know your deeds, that you are neither cold nor hot. I wish you were either one or the other! So, because you are lukewarm—neither hot nor cold—I am about to spit you out of my mouth. You say, 'I am rich; I have acquired wealth and do not need a thing.' But you do not realize that you are wretched, pitiful, poor, blind and naked. I counsel you to buy from me gold refined in the fire, so you can become rich; and white clothes to wear, so you can cover your shameful nakedness; and salve to put on your eyes, so you can see.

Those whom I love I rebuke and discipline. So be earnest, and repent. Here I am! I stand at the door and knock. If anyone hears my voice and opens the door, I will come in and eat with him, and he with me.

To him who overcomes, I will give the right to sit with me on my throne, just as I overcame and sat down with my Father on his throne."

This chapter contains the last three of Christ's letters to seven early churches. To Sardis (SAR-dis), he gives the stern declaration that although they may appear alive, they are dead. Sardis in John's time is a wealthy city located on an important trade route. A center of pagan worship, it also contains a Christian church. Some scholars feel this letter applies to churches of today that are busy and display elaborate buildings but lack evidence of genuine life in Christ.

Jesus encourages faithful believers in Philadelphia to endure patiently. Jews who oppose their Christian beliefs are currently oppressing them, but Christ promises that one day the same people will fall down and acknowledge him and his love for his own.

To the church at Laodicea (LAY-uh-dih-SEE-uh) Jesus gives his harshest rebuke. Christians in this prospering city live content with their wealth and blind to their spiritual poverty. In light of a custom of the day to drink liquids either hot or cold, never lukewarm, Jesus gives a vivid message: they are lukewarm and unacceptable in his eyes. Laodicea's wealth stems from its wool industry. The city is famous for a black garment made out of black wool, but its people take pride in the wrong product. They need to be clothed instead in the white of right relationship with God.

Similarly, a Laodicean medical school offers a special salve for eye problems, yet what the people really need is spiritual sight.

All who are blind to the riches of God's kingdom need to open their eyes and repent. Out of love, Jesus rebukes Laodicea and believers of today. He wants us, his people, to walk in the fullness of relationship with himself, seeing through God's eyes rather than our own.

—BQ

DAILY CONTEMPLATION

When did you first become conscious of your own spiritual poverty? Where were your eyes focused before they caught sight of God?

DAY 364
Revelation 12:1–17

THE WOMAN AND THE DRAGON

A great and wondrous sign appeared in heaven: a woman clothed with the sun, with the moon under her feet and a crown of twelve stars on her head. She was pregnant and cried out in pain as she was about to give birth. Then another sign appeared in heaven: an enormous red dragon with seven heads and ten horns and seven crowns on his heads. His tail swept a third of the stars out of the sky and flung them to the earth. The dragon stood in front of the woman who was about to give birth, so that he might devour her child the moment it was born. She gave birth to a son, a male child, who will rule all the nations with an iron scepter. And her child was snatched up to God and to his throne. The woman fled into the desert to a place prepared for her by God, where she might be taken care of for 1,260 days.

And there was war in heaven. Michael and his angels fought against the dragon, and the dragon and his angels fought back. But he was not strong enough, and they lost their place in heaven. The great dragon was hurled down—that ancient serpent called the devil, or Satan, who leads the whole world astray. He was hurled to the earth, and his angels with him.

Then I heard a loud voice in heaven say:

"Now have come the salvation and the power and the kingdom of our God,
    and the authority of his Christ.
For the accuser of our brothers,
    who accuses them before our God day and night,
    has been hurled down.
They overcame him
    by the blood of the Lamb
    and by the word of their testimony;
they did not love their lives so much

as to shrink from death.
Therefore rejoice, you heavens
and you who dwell in them!
But woe to the earth and the sea,
because the devil has gone down to you!
He is filled with fury,
because he knows that his time is short."

When the dragon saw that he had been hurled to the earth, he pursued the woman who had given birth to the male child. The woman was given the two wings of a great eagle, so that she might fly to the place prepared for her in the desert, where she would be taken care of for a time, times and half a time, out of the serpent's reach. Then from his mouth the serpent spewed water like a river, to overtake the woman and sweep her away with the torrent. But the earth helped the woman by opening its mouth and swallowing the river that the dragon had spewed out of his mouth. Then the dragon was enraged at the woman and went off to make war against the rest of her offspring—those who obey God's commandments and hold to the testimony of Jesus.

In this passage from Revelation John uses bizarre, cosmic symbols: a pregnant woman clothed with the sun; a seven-headed red dragon so enormous that its tail sweeps a third of the stars from the sky; a flight into the desert; a war in heaven. Despite its many interpretations, almost all agree that this chapter has something to do with Jesus' birth and its effect on the universe. When a baby was born, the universe shuddered.

In a sense, Revelation 12 presents Christmas from a cosmic perspective, adding a new set of images to the familiar scenes of manger and shepherds and the Slaughter of the Innocents. What was visible on earth represented ripples on the surface; underneath, massive disruptions were shaking the foundations of the universe. Even as King Herod was trying to kill all male babies in Palestine, cosmic forces were at war behind the scenes. From God's viewpoint—and Satan's—Christmas was far more than the birth of a baby; it was an invasion, the decisive advance in the great struggle for the cosmos. Revelation depicts this struggle in terms of a murderous dragon opposing the forces of good.

Which is the "true" picture of Christmas: the account in Matthew and Luke or that in Revelation? They are the same picture, told from two different points of view. This view of Christ's birth in Revelation 12 typifies the pattern of the entire book, in which John fuses things seen with things normally not seen. In daily life, two parallel histories occur at the same time: one on earth and one in heaven. Revelation, by parting the curtain, allows us to view them together. It leaves the unmistakable impression that as we make everyday choices between good and evil, those choices are having an impact on the supernatural universe we cannot see.

Revelation portrays history through sharply contrasting images: good vs. evil, the Lamb vs. the Dragon, Jerusalem vs. Babylon, the bride vs. the prostitute. But it also insists that, no matter how it appears from our limited perspective, God maintains firm control over all history. Ultimately, even the despots will end up fulfilling the plan mapped out for them by God. Pontius Pilate and his Roman soldiers demonstrated that truth. They thought they were getting rid of Jesus by crucifying him. Instead, they made possible the salvation of the world. —PY

DAILY CONTEMPLATION

When have you ever felt part of a spiritual battle?

DAY 365

THE NEW JERUSALEM; THE RIVER OF LIFE

Then I saw a new heaven and a new earth, for the first heaven and the first earth had passed away, and there was no longer any sea. I saw the Holy City, the new Jerusalem, coming down out of heaven from God, prepared as a bride beautifully dressed for her husband. And I heard a loud voice from the throne saying, "Now the dwelling of God is with men, and he will live with them. They will be his people, and God himself will be with them and be their God. He will wipe every tear from their eyes. There will be no more death or mourning or crying or pain, for the old order of things has passed away."

He who was seated on the throne said, "I am making everything new!" Then he said, "Write this down, for these words are trustworthy and true."

He said to me: "It is done. I am the Alpha and the Omega, the Beginning and the End. To him who is thirsty I will give to drink without cost from the spring of the water of life. He who overcomes will inherit all this, and I will be his God and he will be my son. But the cowardly, the unbelieving, the vile, the murderers, the sexually immoral, those who practice magic arts, the idolaters and all liars—their place will be in the fiery lake of burning sulfur. This is the second death."

One of the seven angels who had the seven bowls full of the seven last plagues came and said to me, "Come, I will show you the bride, the wife of the Lamb." And he carried me away in the Spirit to a mountain great and high, and showed me the Holy City, Jerusalem, coming down out of heaven from God. It shone with the glory of God, and its brilliance was like that of a very precious jewel, like a jasper, clear as crystal. It had a great, high wall with twelve gates, and with twelve angels at the gates. On the gates were written the names of the twelve tribes of Israel. There were three gates on the east, three on the north, three on the south and three on the west. The wall of the city had twelve foundations, and on them were the names of the twelve apostles of the Lamb.

The angel who talked with me had a measuring rod of gold to measure the city, its gates and its walls. The city was laid out like a square, as long as it was wide. He measured the city with the rod and found it to be 12,000 stadia in length, and as wide and high as it is long. He measured its wall and it was 144 cubits thick, by man's measurement, which the angel was using. The wall was made of jasper, and the city of pure gold, as pure as glass. The foundations of the city walls were decorated with every kind of precious stone. The first foundation was jasper, the second sapphire, the third chalcedony, the fourth emerald, the fifth sardonyx, the sixth carnelian, the seventh chrysolite, the eighth beryl, the ninth topaz, the tenth chrysoprase, the eleventh jacinth, and the twelfth amethyst. The twelve gates were twelve pearls, each gate made of a single pearl. The great street of the city was of pure gold, like transparent glass.

I did not see a temple in the city, because the Lord God Almighty and the Lamb are its temple. The city does not need the sun or the moon to shine on it, for the glory of God gives it light, and the Lamb is its lamp. The nations will walk by its light, and the kings of the earth will bring their splendor into it. On no day will its gates ever be shut, for there will be no night there. The glory and honor of the nations will be brought into it. Nothing impure will ever enter it, nor will anyone who does what is shameful or deceitful, but only those whose names are written in the Lamb's book of life.

Then the angel showed me the river of the water of life, as clear as crystal, flowing from the throne of God and of the Lamb down the middle of the great street of the city. On each side of the river stood the tree of life, bearing twelve crops of fruit, yielding its fruit every month. And the leaves of the tree are for the healing of the nations. No longer will there be any curse. The throne of God and of the Lamb will be in the city, and his servants will serve him. They will see his face, and his name will be on their foreheads. There will be no more night. They will not need the light of a lamp or the light of the sun, for the Lord God will give them light. And they will reign for ever and ever.

In its "plot," the Bible ends up very much where it began. The broken relationship between God and human beings has healed over at last, and the curse of Genesis 3 is lifted. Borrowing images from Eden, Revelation pictures a river and a tree of life. But this time a great city replaces the garden setting—a city filled with worshipers of God. Nothing will pollute that city; no death or sadness will ever darken that scene. There will be no crying or pain. For the first time since Eden, *The World As It Is* will finally match *The World As God Wants It*.

John sees heaven as the fulfillment of every Jewish dream: Jerusalem restored, with walls of jasper and streets of gleaming gold. For someone else—say, a refugee in the Third World today—heaven may represent a family reunited, a home abundant with food and fresh drinking water. Heaven stands for the fulfillment of every true longing. As C. S. Lewis has said, all the beauty and joy on planet Earth represent "only the scent of a flower we have not found, the echo of a tune we have not heard, news from a country we have never yet visited."

Revelation promises that our longings are not mere fantasies. They will come true. When we awake in the new heaven and new earth, we will have at last whatever we have longed for. Somehow, from out of all the bad news in a book like Revelation, good news emerges—spectacular Good News. A promise of goodness without a catch in it somewhere. There is a happy ending after all.

In the Bible, heaven is not an afterthought or optional belief. It is the final justification of all creation. The Bible never belittles human tragedy and disappointment—is any book more painfully honest?—but it does add one key word: *temporary*. What we feel now, we will not always feel. The time for re-creation will come.

For people who feel trapped in pain or in a broken home, in economic misery or in fear—for all those people, for all of us, heaven promises a future time, far longer and more substantial than the time we spend on earth, a time of health and wholeness and pleasure and peace. The Bible began with that promise, in the book of Genesis. And the Bible ends with that same promise, a guarantee of future reality. The end will be a beginning.   —PY

DAILY CONTEMPLATION

What do you long for in the re-created earth?

DAY 366   Reflection

CONFIDENCE IN THE FUTURE

For many years as a Christian I avoided the book of Revelation. I didn't understand it, and worse, it scared me. I'd heard lots of interpretations of the book—everything from predictions of who the Antichrist might be and how Christians could soon expect to be tattooed with a number to the belief that the entire book is merely symbolic, describing events in the spiritual realm that will never be seen on earth. How was a person to know the truth about such a fantastical book?

I felt it better to concentrate on the rest of the Bible, doing my best to embrace God's straightforward teaching and invest my time in what I understood. Why flounder with what would remain mere speculation and would likely cause me to live in fear rather than passion for God?

When finally I did study Revelation as part of a writing project, my view changed unexpectedly. Questions remained, but a whole new vision of the future took hold in me. Not only is God wise and loving and compassionate; he is powerful in a sense I'd never grasped as clearly through any other book. Not only is Jesus the God who walked the earth and whose Spirit now lives in believers; he is the one who will reign forever with full strength and authority over every other power. The images of Revelation make that startlingly real. As a believer, this future lies ahead for me, and knowing it is coming impacts everything about my life here and now.

Theologian and scholar Dallas Willard, writing about heaven and eternity, says, "You are never going to cease existing, and there is nothing you can do about it."[69] If this is true and God indeed commands all that happens after this life on earth, our perspectives should radically shift. Life now is just a foretaste, a preparation for something inconceivable ahead.

The Bible supplies just a few scattered passages and a colorful vision of how eternity will come about. Our minds now can handle no more. Yet what lies ahead will become clear. "When we pass through what we call death," Willard says, "we do not lose the world. Indeed we see it for the first time as it really is. . . . We will not disappear into an eternal fog bank or dead storage, or exist in a state of isolation or suspended animation, as many seem to suppose. God has a much better use of us than that."[70] It will feel like waking up from a dream rather than falling asleep. Everything we've learned of God in this life will take on striking new dimension. It will appear as vivid as the images we find in Revelation, yet without confusion or unfamiliarity.

The book of Revelation is the flag God waves at the end of the Bible, motioning us to the exciting finish of his story. Don't miss this, he alerts us. This is what you've been waiting for, the goal of the Book, the culmination of all you've invested in the life you're living. Surely, Revelation is the one book of the Bible that we should feel compelled to read out of turn. It's the ending we can't resist discovering.

I don't know what lies ahead in my lifetime concerning the end of life on this earth. I don't know whether I'll be called to suffer, to see the unfolding of the events Revelation heralds. I may be seeing some of them now. They may await my children or several generations that follow. Yet I do know that the book of Revelation is for me. Without it I would be left hanging, left without a powerful word of assurance to ground me and guide me in all the decisions I make. This life is vital for me because it is the life I'll carry into eternity. God has prepared something fantastic and wondrous, and for those who know him the future is not a bit scary.   —BQ

DAILY CONTEMPLATION

How do you react to the book of Revelation? Do you fear the future? Consider spending more time in Revelation, praying as you read that God would give you his perspective on what lies ahead. You belong to him, and he has magnificent things in store for you.

NOTES

1*A phrase like "God learns" may seem strange because we normally think of learning as a mental process, moving in sequence from a state of not knowing to a state of knowing. God, of course, is not bound by time or ignorance. He "learns" in the sense of taking on new experiences, such as the creation of free human beings. Using the word in a similar sense, Hebrews says that Jesus "learned obedience from what he suffered."

1. Adapted from Philip Yancey, *Disappointment with God* (Grand Rapids: Zondervan, 1988), 63–65.

2. Adapted from Philip Yancey, *What's So Amazing About Grace?* (Grand Rapids: Zondervan, 1997), 96–106.

3. Gary Smalley and John Trent, *Love Is a Decision* (Dallas: Word, 1989), 8.

4. John Maxwell, *Developing the Leader within You* (Nashville: Nelson, 1993), 146.

5. Tom Wolfe, *The Right Stuff* (New York: Farrar, Straus, Giroux, 1979), 122.

6. Frederick Buechner, *Peculiar Treasures* (San Francisco: Harper & Row, 1979), 24.

7. Brother Lawrence, *The Practice of the Presence of God*, quoted in Richard J. Foster and James Bryan Smith, eds., *Devotional Classics* (San Francisco: HarperSanFrancisco, 1990), 82–83, Brother Lawrence's emphasis.

8. Hannah Whitall Smith, *The Christian's Secret of a Happy Life* (1870; reprint, Old Tappan, N.J.: Revell, 1942), 67.

9. Smith, *The Christian's Secret*, 68.

10. Smith, *The Christian's Secret*, 69.

11. Smith, *The Christian's Secret*, 73–74.

12. Jim Cymbala and Dean Merrill, *Fresh Wind, Fresh Fire* (Grand Rapids: Zondervan, 1997), 16–17.

13. Corrie ten Boom, *He Cares for You* (Grand Rapids: Revell, 1978), 189–93.

14. Richard Foster, *Celebration of Discipline* (London: Hodder & Stoughton, 1978), 122.

15. Eugene Peterson, *A Long Obedience in the Same Direction* (Downers Grove, Ill.: InterVarsity Press, 1980), 11–13.

16. Peterson, *A Long Obedience*, 11–13.

17. Richard J. Mouw, *Uncommon Decency* (Downers Grove, Ill.: InterVarsity Press, 1992), 41–42.

18. Mouw, *Uncommon Decency*, 11.

19. Brent Curtis and John Eldredge, *The Sacred Romance* (Nashville: Nelson, 1997), 145.

20. Curtis and Eldredge, *The Sacred Romance*, 147–48.

21. Curtis and Eldredge, *The Sacred Romance*, 196.

22. Ted W. Engstrom, *The Pursuit of Excellence* (Grand Rapids: Zondervan, 1982), 20.

23. Engstrom, *The Pursuit of Excellence*, 24.

24. Excerpted from Philip Yancey, *Where Is God When It Hurts?* (Grand Rapids: Zondervan, 1977, 1990), 81–84.

25. Tom Sine, *Wild Hope* (Dallas: Word, 1991), 212.

26. Sine, *Wild Hope*, 218.

27. Sine, *Wild Hope*, 213, 226.

28. Philip Yancey, *What's So Amazing About Grace?* (Grand Rapids: Zondervan, 1997), 45.

29. Adapted from Philip Yancey, *The Jesus I Never Knew* (Grand Rapids: Zondervan, 1995), 72–82.

30. Richard E. Eby, *Caught Up into Paradise* (Grand Rapids: Revell, 1978), 91–101.

31. Mother Teresa, *A Simple Path* (New York: Ballantine, 1995), 80–81.

32. Mother Teresa, *A Simple Path*, xxx–xxxi.

33. Catherine Marshall, *Meeting God at Every Turn* (New York: Bantam, 1980), 59–60.

34. Marshall, *Meeting God at Every Turn*, 71.

35. Marshall, *Meeting God at Every Turn*, 84.

36. Adapted from Philip Yancey, *The Jesus I Never Knew* (Grand Rapids: Zondervan, 1995), 105–44.

37. John Muir, *The Wilderness World of John Muir*, ed. Edwin Way Teale (1954; reprint, Boston: Houghton Mifflin, 1982), 103.

38. Muir, *The Wilderness World*, 70.

39. Muir, *The Wilderness World*, xvi.

40. Ravi Zacharias, *Can Man Live without God?* (Dallas: Word, 1994), 78.

41. Zacharias, *Can Man Live without God?* 79.

42. Zacharias, *Can Man Live without God?* 89.

43. Zacharias, *Can Man Live without God?* 91.

44. Macrina Wiederkehr, *Seasons of Your Heart: Prayers and Reflections*, Revised and Expanded (San Francisco: HarperSanFrancisco, 1991), 58.

45. Oswald Chambers, *My Utmost for His Highest* (New York: Dodd, Mead & Co., 1963), 39 (February 8).

46. J. I. Packer, *Keep in Step with the Spirit* (Old Tappan, N.J.: Revell, 1984), 9–49.

47. John Stott, *The Contemporary Christian* (Downers Grove, Ill.: InterVarsity Press, 1992), 329–30.

48. Catherine Marshall, *Something More* (Grand Rapids: Chosen, 1974), 276.

49. Marshall, *Something More*, 279.

50. Marshall, *Something More*, 281.

51. Marshall, *Something More*, 281.

52. J. B. Phillips, *Your God Is Too Small* (New York: Touchstone, Simon & Schuster, 1997), 30.

53. Phillips, *Your God Is Too Small*, 31–32.

54. Phillips, *Your God Is Too Small*, 32.55. Charles Colson, "Reaching the Pagan Mind," Christianity Today (November 9, 1992), 112.

55. Charles Colson, "Reaching the Pagan Mind," *Christianity Today* (November 9, 1992), 112.

56. Adapted from Philip Yancey, *Church: Why Bother?* (Grand Rapids: Zondervan, 1998), 45–47, 61–65.

57. Brennan Manning, *The Signature of Jesus* (Old Tappan, N.J.: Revell, 1988), 110.

58. Larry Crabb, *Inside Out* (Colorado Springs: NavPress, 1988), 86, 102.

59. Stephen R. Covey, *The Seven Habits of Highly Effective People* (New York: Simon & Schuster, 1989), 158.

60. Covey, *The Seven Habits,* 158.

61. Elisa Morgan and Carol Kuykendall, *What Every Child Needs* (Grand Rapids: Zondervan, 1997), 25–26.

62. Dietrich Bonhoeffer, *Life Together* (San Francisco: Harper & Row, 1954), 23–24.

63. C. S. Lewis, *Reflections on the Psalms* (San Diego: Harcourt Brace Jovanovich, 1958), 74.

64. Vernon Grounds, *Radical Commitment* (Portland, Ore.: Multnomah Press, 1984), 42–45.

65. Grounds, *Radical Commitment,* 44.

66. Excerpted from Philip Yancey and Brenda Quinn, *What's So Amazing About Grace* Study Guide (Grand Rapids: Zondervan, 1998), 119–21.

67. C. S. Lewis, *The Problem of Pain* (New York: Macmillan, 1962), 93.

68. Henri J. M. Nouwen, *Lifesigns* (New York: Doubleday, 1986), 36.

69. Dallas Willard, *The Divine Conspiracy* (San Francisco: HarperCollins, 1998), 391–92.

70. Willard, *The Divine Conspiracy,* 395.

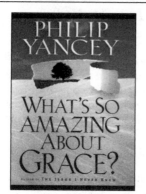

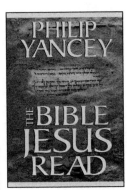

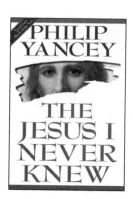

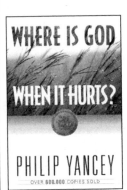

Philip Yancey and Paul Brand

Fearfully and Wonderfully Made

Mysterious, Intricate, Pulsing with Energy...

The human body is an endlessly fascinating repository of secrets. The miracle of the skin, the strength and structure of the bones, the dynamic balance of the muscles . . .your physical being is knit according to a pattern of incredible purpose. In *Fearfully and Wonderfully Made,* renowned surgeon Dr. Paul Brand and best-selling writer Philip Yancey explore the human body. Join them in a remarkable journey through inner space—a spellbinding world of cells, systems, and chemistry that bears the impress of a still deeper, unseen reality. This Gold Medallion Award-winning book uncovers eternal statements that God has made in the very structure of our bodies, presenting captivating insights into the Body of Christ.

Softcover 0-310-35451-X

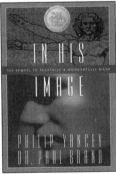

In His Image

The Voice of God Is a Heartbeat Away

In *Fearfully and Wonderfully Made,* Philip Yancey and Dr. Paul Brand revealed how God's voice is encoded in the very structure of our bodies. *In His Image* takes up where its predecessor left off, beckoning us once again inward and onward to fresh exploration and discovery.

Yancey and Brand show how accurately and intricately the human body portrays the Body of Christ. In five sections—Image, Blood, Head, Spirit, and Pain—the acclaimed surgeon and the award-winning writer unlock the remarkable, living lessons contained in our physical makeup. This Gold Medallion Award-winning book will open your eyes to the complex miracle of the human body, and the even more compelling spiritual truths that it reflects.

Softcover 0-310-35501-X

IN HIS IMAGE

The voice of God is a heartbeat away.

In *Fearfully and Wonderfully Made*, Dr. Paul Brand and Philip Yancey reveal how God's voice is encoded in the very structure of our bodies. *In His Image* takes up where its predecessor left off, beckoning us once again inward and onward to fresh exploration and discovery.

Brand and Yancey show how accurately and intricately the human body portrays the Body of Christ. In five sections—Image, Blood, Head, Spirit, and Pain—the acclaimed surgeon and the award/winning writer unlock the remarkable, living lessons contained in our physical makeup. This Gold Medallion Award-winning book will open your eyes to the complex miracle of the human body, and the even more compelling spiritual truths that it reflects.

Pick up a copy today at your local Christian bookstore!

Softcover 0-310-35501-X

We want to hear from you. Please send your comments about this
book to us in care of the address below. Thank you.

ZONDERVAN™

GRAND RAPIDS, MICHIGAN 49530
www.zondervan.com